Rev. Mark D. Lottis
Notre Dame
1992

Presence, Power, Praise

Edited by Kilian McDonnell

PRESENCE, POWER, PRAISE

Documents on the Charismatic Renewal

Volume I — Continental, National, and Regional
Documents

Numbers 1 to 37, 1960–1974

THE LITURGICAL PRESS

Collegeville, Minnesota

1980

Library of Congress Cataloging in Publication Data

Main entry under title:
Presence, power, praise.
  Includes index.
  CONTENTS: v. 1-2. National documents.—v. 3. Inter-
national documents.
  1. Pentecostalism—Addresses, essays, lectures.
I. McDonnell, Kilian.
BR1644.P73   269   79-26080
ISBN 0-8146-1126-5 (set)
0-8146-1066-8 (volume 1)

Design by Frank Kacmarcik

Printed by The North Central Publishing Company
St. Paul, Minnesota, U.S.A.

To Walter J. Hollenweger, who matches
classical Pentecostal scholarship of rare depth
and a knowledge of contemporary theology with
an understanding of non-literary cultures and
the Third World
and
To Arnold Bittlinger, who brings pastoral
sensitivity and theological insight to the task of
integrating the charismatic renewal into the
churches

CONTENTS

Contents

FOREWORD

Most of the documents in this ecumenical and international collection are from the churches as they relate to the charismatic renewal in their midst. Some are from within the renewal as it tries to define itself and its relationship to the churches. A few are interdenominational in character, and three come from classical Pentecostal churches. As the users will quickly discover, the documents are of unequal merit. Some are hurriedly prepared working or interim documents to meet a new situation. These tend to be impressionistic. They are important because they chronicle the theological and pastoral attitudes of the churches. Other than historical importance, many may have no lasting value. This is especially true of some of the earliest documents. But for understanding that history, they are essential.

A number of the documents are serious and multi-disciplinary in their approach, the products of deep theological and pastoral reflection. Most are not multi-disciplinary but are serious and critical evaluations.

A one-volume publication could have been possible if the editor chose to publish only those sections he thought important. From an historical-scientific point of view, this procedure is unsatisfactory for reasons which are obvious. Rather, the editor decided to print, whenever possible, whole documents. This principle was violated only when a document was excessively long or when a larger document was concerned with a number of disparate, essentially unrelated issues, of which the charismatic renewal was one. The latter is true of the statement which developed from the special meeting of the House of Bishops in the United States (Episcopal) in 1962 (1:3). Here only the section on "New Movements in the Church" is reproduced. Another case is that of certain paragraphs from the Puebla documents of the Third General Conference of the Latin American Episcopate (Roman Catholic) in 1979 (2:78). The charismatic renewal in South America would want to say that its perspective is as broad as the gospel and as wide as human experience. In that sense Latin American charismatics would not want it to be thought that only those paragraphs which refer to the Holy Spirit or to the charismatic renewal are of interest or pertain to them. However, again for obvious reasons, only those paragraphs are included here. Also, in a document from the Council of the Latin American Episcopate (CELAM), found in *Renovacion en el Espiritu: Movimiento Carismático en América Latina*, only the section of Archbishop Alfonso Lópes Trujillo's preface which immediately touches on the charismatic renewal is reproduced (2:66).

The Division of Theological Studies of the Union of Evangelical Churches in the German Democratic Republic issued a detailed and extensive report entitled *The Charismatic Movement in the German Democratic Republic: Report on the Phenomena and Activities of a Charismatic Nature in the Evangelical Churches in the German Democratic Republic.*[1] This Lutheran document from East Germany is not printed in its entirety. It is an extensive sociological description of various charismatic groups in that country and an elaboration of their theological bases. A document of ninety-four single-spaced legal-size pages, it was made available to the editor in mimeographed form. Because of its length (approximately a two-hundred-page book), it was feasible to reproduce only certain sections (2:72).

Most of the documents came from commissions and committees appointed to study this movement. In using the documents care should be taken to note the nature of the body issuing the statement. To take a Catholic example, the report of the study commission made to the United States Catholic Conference of Bishops in 1969 (1:15) is that of a relatively minor committee and is not the official document of the whole hierarchy. On the other hand, the document which issued from the Canadian Catholic Conference of Bishops (2:46) is not the report of a committee but is the statement adopted by the Canadian Catholic hierarchy addressed not just to those in the charismatic renewal but "to all Canadian Catholics." This is a statement of the whole hierarchy and therefore enjoys more authority than the report of a small committee of bishops.

In the first two volumes have been placed all local, regional, national, and continental documents. Except for the first documents on the renewal, which often tended to be diocesan, purely local and diocesan documents are not included in this collection. A second exception is a Baptist document (2:50) which is included because of Baptist polity.

The third volume contains documents which generally issue from international agencies of world church bodies, e.g., World Council of Churches (3:9, 3:11); Baptist World Alliance (3:6); Pope Paul VI's addresses (3:2, 3:4); the extensive document of Léon

Cardinal Suenens (3:7) and that of Kilian McDonnell (3:8) because of the broad international cooperation which produced this latter document. In the appendix are the documents issuing from the international Pentecostal-Catholic dialogue; they touch on many key issues with which the other documents are concerned. They have been relegated to an appendix because they do not directly address the issue of the charismatic renewal in the churches.

The arrangement in the three volumes is by years, which facilitates an historical study. Within each year the documents are arranged alphabetically by denomination. The year assigned to each document is determined not by the date of publication but by the date when the document was adopted or issued by the competent body or authority.

For purposes of cross reference, each document has been given a numerical designation. A reference such as 1:21, 32 refers to volume 1, document 21, page 32 of the continuous pagination of volume 1.

In order that the reader may avoid the necessity of reading the whole document to determine its general character, content, and tone, there follows a brief outline of the material and an indication of the theological perspective and direction. These introductions serve not to evaluate the merits of the document but to indicate the nature of its contents.

In presenting each document the actual title of the document or a generic title covering a series of related documents, e.g., "Six Documents on the Discipleship Controversy," is given first (2:51). This is followed by the editor's introduction. All of this introductory material appears in italics. Without repeating the title, the document begins immediately in ordinary type face.

The editor's introductions try to situate the documents historically and theologically. Sometimes there is an abundance of such historical information available; sometimes it is almost non-existent or is safely guarded, especially in those cases where the charismatic renewal was perceived as, or actually was, a disruptive force in the church. For these reasons the amount of historical background material varies from document to document.

In the introductions "charismatic renewal" is used to designate a spiritual movement in the churches, even though in some countries other terms are used. Large objection can be taken to the terms if they are interpreted to mean that the charisms are the unique focus of the movement or if there is an underlying supposition that the charisms belong to the movement in some proper and exclusive way, not true of the church at large. Almost all those involved in the charismatic renewal would reject those two interpretations. An example: the liturgical movement does not claim that the sacraments are the special preserve of those who identify with the movement. Rather, they are saying that the sacraments belong to the nature of the church and they are interested that they be celebrated in full awareness of their meaning and with the appropriate rites by the whole of the church's membership.

"Charismatic renewal," therefore, designates a movement as a spiritual force within the churches. Though it jars the theological sensitivities, there has sprung up, in some countries, a practice of referring to Lutheran charismatics, Baptist charismatics, etc. These refer to persons who have accepted the goals of the charismatic renewal but who remain active members of their respective churches.

"Classical Pentecostalism" and "classical Pentecostals" are terms which this editor coined in 1968 to refer to that group of religious persons who trace their spiritual origins, directly or indirectly, either to the events which took place in Topeka, Kansas, in 1901, under the leadership of Charles Parham, or to those of the Azusa Street Mission in Los Angeles in 1906.[2] Classical Pentecostals include persons belonging to denominations such as the Apostolic Faith Mission in South Africa, the Mülheim Association of Christian Fellowships in Germany, the Assemblies of God in the United States and Britain, and the Christians of Evangelical Faith in Russia. But it also includes independents who do not belong to any denominational organization or to a purely local one. "Classical Pentecostal" has been preferred to "denominational Pentecostal" because this latter term seems to exclude the very large number of independents.

In some places in the documents and even in the introductions, classical Pentecostalism is viewed as something the historic churches are reacting against, and therefore it appears pejorative. It should be remembered that classical Pentecostalism represents a major stream in the Christian West with its own areas of strength.

Some confusion might arise from the use of "interdenominational" and "ecumenical." The first identifies a controversy (discipleship) in which a number of people from various churches were involved without any specific questions of church unity being raised. The second refers to the character of meetings or documents in which unity was a specific preoccupation.

An introductory essay to the three volumes is printed at the beginning of volume 1. "Parameters, Patterns, and the Atypical" attempts to show some of the emerging patterns, the foci of polarization, the change in positions, and the developing understanding of the churches. Not a summary of all the documents contained but an exposition of some neuralgic themes, it gives an understanding of the main issues faced by the churches.

Those who wish to follow the development of an idea should consult the index at the end of each volume. Only at the end of the third volume are placed the geographical and denominational indices which list the contents of all three volumes.

There is considerable variety in the manner of indicating the original source of the document. In a number of cases the document has appeared in no printed volume of minutes or proceedings. Many were available only in mimeographed form. Where that is the case, there is no indication of a printed source.

Because this is a collection of documents and the editor wished to respect the integrity of each one, little endeavor was made to obtain uniformity in the manner of biblical or other citations. Therefore, where there is no uniformity of citation, punctuation, or capitalization within a given document, corrections have not been made. This accounts for the wide variety of styles and the want of consistency. However, obvious mistakes in the original typesetting of the documents have been corrected.

Some users of these volumes might wish to obtain copies of the individual documents. To facilitate this the publishers and their addresses are given at the end of the editor's introductions.

An attempt has been made to be as comprehensive as possible, yet recognizing that the collection is not exhaustive. Undoubtedly there are documents whose existence is unknown to this editor. Some documents were not included because they came to light after the presses were closed, permissions could not be obtained, etc. Among them are:

"Report on Prayer Groups and Sects," Presbyterian Church of Ghana, 1966.

"Supplementary Report of the Committee on Church Doctrine," 1972, and "The Neo-Pentecostal Movement and the Presbyterian Church in Canada," no date.

"Report to the 1974 Synod of the Moravian Church, Northern Province, on Glossolalia," United States.

"Charismatic Renewal in the United Reformed Church in England and Wales," 1975.

"The Charismatic Movement: Problem or Promise," United Church of Canada, 1975.

"Charismatic Renewal," Methodist Church of New Zealand, 1975.

"The life of the Spirit in the Life of the Church," Pastoral Letter of Ruben Sheares, Executive Director, Office for Church Life and Leadership, United Church of Christ, United States, 1975 (obtainable from Church Leadership Resources, Box 179, St. Louis, MO 63166).

"New Zealand Baptist Churches and the Charismatic Renewal," 1976.

"The Pentecostal Communities," United Evangelical Lutheran Churches, Germany, 1976.

"The Fullness of the Spirit," 1977, and "OJB Committee — Subcommittee on the Charismatic Movement: Fall 1977 Report on Spiritual Gifts," Reformed Church in America.

"The Holy Spirit, the Church, and the Charismatic Movement," Church of the Brethren, United States, 1977.

"Background on the Charismatic/Pentecostal Movement in Ghana," Christian Council of Ghana, 1979.

"The Church and Charismatic Renewal: Concerning the Opportunities and Problems of a Movement in Our Church," Section of Theological Studies of the Union of Evangelical Churches in the German Democratic Republic, 1979.[3]

"The Charismatic Renewal and the United Church," Papua, New Guinea, and the Solomon Islands, no date.

"The Holy Spirit and Christian Experience," United Methodist Church, United States, no date.

Two other collections of charismatic documents small in size might be useful. The first is *Obispos y Carismas* (*Coleccion Iglesia*, no. 2), Centro Carismático, El Minuto de Dios, Bogotá, Colombia, 1976. It is available from Centro Carismático, Calle 23, no. 4–61, in Bogotá. This collection contains documents from Roman Catholic hierarchies in Canada, Mexico, Panama, and the United States, as well as declarations or pastoral letters from twenty-six cardinals and bishops. Pastoral letters from individual bishops and cardinals (unless they are exercising an international responsibility) are not included here in *Presence, Power, Praise*. Something of an exception was made for three documents from the Episcopal Church, United States, because of their historic importance (1:1, 1:2, 1:7).

The second collection contains six Presbyterian documents from four national churches (Presbyterian Church in the United States, United Presbyterian Church, Presbyterian Church in Canada, and the Church of Scotland), as well as three presbytery reports from the Presbyterian Church in the United States (Hannover, Piedmont, and Southwest Georgia). The collection is entitled "Church Studies on the Holy Spirit," compiled by the Council on Theology and Culture, Presbyterian Church in the United States, undated. A companion piece, "Study Guide for Church Studies on the Holy Spirit," was prepared by Robert H. Bullock in 1979. Both of these are available from John Knox Press. The six Presbyterian documents, excluding the presbytery reports, are contained in *Presence, Power, Praise*.

A collection of international documents can only be made with the help of friends around the world. Even at the risk of omitting someone, the editor feels he should mention those on whose good graces he so often called: *Argentina*: Alberto Ibañez; *Australia*: James Glennon, Hamish Christie-Johnston, Winston O'Reilly, Michael Putney, Brian Smith; *Belgium*: Carlos Calvente, Thomas Forrest, Ralph Martin, Gary Seromik; *Brazil*: Bishop Robert McAlister; *Chile*: Carlos Aldunate; *Colombia*: Diego Jaramillo; *England*: Alan J. Davies, William R. Davies, Rex Davis, Michael Harper, Walter J. Hollenweger, Thomas Smail, Michael Walker; *Ethiopia*: John Bakke; *France*: Albert de Monleon; *Germany*: Heribert Mühlen; *Holland*: Piet Schoonenberg; *Mexico*: Salvador Carrillo Alday; *New Zealand*: Donald Glenny, James E. Worsfold; *Norway*: Tormod Engelsviken; *Peru*: Michael LaFay; *Puerto Rico*: Landelin Robling, Francisco Schulte; *South Africa*: Justus du Plessis; *Switzerland*: Arnold Bittlinger, David M. Gill, Bishop Franz Schäfer; *United States*: Knute Anderson, Don Basham, Roland Behrendt, Michael Brady, Eugene L. Brand, Larry Christenson, Steve Clark, Wayne K. Clymer, Engelbert Dufner, Pamela Eastlake, Gall Fell, Otto K. Finkbeiner, Robert Hawn, Peter Hocken, John Kulas, R. Herbert Minnich, Bob Mumford, Philip O'Mara, Donald Pfotenhauer, Derek Prince, Pat Robertson, Delbert Rossin, Thorpe Running, William G. Rusch, Theophane

Rush, Kelly Ryan, Julian Schmiesing, Eugene L. Stowe, Vinson Synan, Robert Tuttle, J. Rodman Williams; *Vatican City*: Basil Meeking.

To Frank Kacmarcik thanks are due for producing a sensitive typography of real artistic merit and for his willingness to give attention to the details of galleys and page proofs, though pressed by a heavy travel schedule. Mark Twomey, as an editor for The Liturgical Press, has labored for more than a year on this project. His patience under duress is only exceeded by his quiet competence. That such a diverse collection of documents could be brought into any kind of manageable unity is due to the skill with which he translated Frank Kacmarcik's design into a nuanced whole. To Sr. Dolores Schuh, CHM, many thanks for the seemingly unending typing and retyping of the manuscript, often after hours or on weekends, with gentle notes correcting my academese or my Germanized English. Finally, I owe gratitude to Fr. Cloud Meinberg, OSB, who heroically read galley after galley, surely a burden for an artist.

1. "Charismatische Bewegung in der DDR: Bericht über Phänomene und Aktivitäten charismatischer Prägung in den evangelischen Kirchen in der DDR," *Beiträge*, A, Gemeinde, August 3, 1978. This is obtainable from the Theologische Studienabteilung beim Bund der evangelischen Kirchen in der DDR, Auguststrasse 80, 104 Berlin, East Germany.

2. *See* Kilian McDonnell, "Holy Spirit and Pentecostalism," *Commonweal* 89, no. 6 (November 8, 1968), 198–204; McDonnell, "Catholic Pentecostalism: Problems in Evaluation," *Dialog* 9 (Winter 1970), 35–54.

3. "Kirche und charismatische Erneuerung: Über Chancen und Probleme einer Bewegung in unseren Kirchen," *Beiträge*, A, Gemeinde, August 4, 1979. This report is obtainable at the same address as given above.

KILIAN MCDONNELL

September 16, 1980

INTRODUCTION

This essay is not an attempt to summarize the 104 documents in this three-volume collection. Nor is it a critical evaluation of them. Rather, it indicates the parameters of the discussion, the emerging patterns, the atypical reflections, the foci of polarization, the shift in positions, and the developing understanding in them of the charismatic renewal. Therefore, some essential points in the documents will not be covered here. Though note will be made of the criticism leveled at the renewal, often fully justified and furthermore supported by those personally involved in the renewal, this essay does not present a refutation of such criticisms, nor does it attempt to give a fully balanced account of it, weighing negatives against positives. The earlier documents tend to be negative in their judgments while the later ones are more positive. To some extent this represents a maturing of the charismatic renewal and a better grasp on the part of the churches of the real issues involved. But problem areas remain also in the later documents.

Each document will not be given an equal hearing. Some of them are dependent on each other, so there is some repetition. Further, a preference is given to those documents which situate the renewal in a theological framework. Aside from that preference a wide sampling of the documents has been sought, including documents from the churches and from the renewal.

If this were a theological treatise, this editor would order the material differently than one finds it in the documents or in this essay. The documents are problem-oriented, which accounts for the manner in which the topics are treated here. For instance, one would hardly structure a viable theology around experience (understood in a rather restricted charismatic sense), which is the dominant note in these pages. Even a pronounced "charismatic theology" (if such a gross misnomer will be allowed here for purposes of argument) would be seriously vitiated from the beginning if experience in this sense were the organizing principle.

RENEWAL: A PROPHETIC PROTEST FROM WITHIN

The charismatic renewal is a prophetic renewal movement. To a large degree its prophetic protest and its renewal goals are directed to the churches. Directly or indirectly those in the movement are saying "the churches need renewal." How do the churches react to this implied criticism? What does the renewal offer which so many in the churches find compelling?

There is general admission on the part of the churches that many Christians are living "below their expected spiritual potential" and that persons who are drawn to the renewal "are not indifferent people but persons who are genuinely and sincerely seeking a deeper and more meaningful spiritual life."[1] The tendency to live below the expected spiritual potential is, in part, due to "a lack of a sense of reality in matters of faith, an absence of the awareness of the presence of Christ in worship and daily life, a lack of joy, of peace, and of hope. They spell an emptiness in the church's life, which imparts itself to the daily life of its members."[2] Ministers who lack nothing in education are wanting in warmth and conviction of personal dedication. Over and over again ministers preach the same message and no lives are changed. The hunger for God remains unsatisfied.[3]

Christians are aware of a void which accompanies materialism and secularism, a dissatisfaction which expresses itself in a desire to be fed substantial food and in a desire to reach out to God in prayer and praise.[4] Presence is a major category in the charismatic renewal. God is presence: here, now, real, a person, loving, acting. He is not the Great Absent One.[5] Nor is he the God of yesterday who was present in power to the early church "and yet leaves us . . . to simply grit our teeth and believe like mad that God is around some place."[6] One evidence that God is present and acting, say the churches, is the lives of those in the renewal which have been changed.[7] How can one receive the gospel and remain unchanged, asks the renewal in the various churches. Is not *metanoia* the first demand of the Good News?

Although many have been touched in a significant way, some say that there is evidence that this usually concerns those who were already committed Christians. There is less evidence of awakening "among nominal Christians and persons finding Christ for the first time."[8] Other churches are not so sure that its effectiveness is restricted to the already fully committed. "Apart from the great numbers who have, for the first time, met Christ in this way, who have previously only thought that they were Christians, there are literally thousands, who before had been lukewarm and carnal children of God, who have been freed from this situation to a life of joy and commitment. . . ."[9] The change seen in the lives of others is a major tool of recruitment.

Among Roman Catholics the charismatic renewal reaped the benefits of the unfulfilled promises of Vatican II. Many Catholics judge that these reforms were never realized because the post-Vatican II era saw them too exclusively in external terms: remodeling church structures, reformulating liturgical rites, updating and streamlining procedures. There was too little emphasis on change of heart and holiness of life, public and private prayer.[10] The renewal wanted to supplement this more exterior approach by interiorizing the promises of Vatican II; logically, renewal is first and reform second.

Many of the documents list the positive effects of the renewal. These effects constitute spiritual magnets which draw others into the renewal. Among these one could find the following: a release of spiritual gifts and power; a strong effective ministry of evangelism; great unity and love among the believers; new forms of community and local church life; winning the active support of many young people who would otherwise be lost to Christ and to the church; miracles of healing; the rediscovery of tongues; the gift of knowledge; a commitment to work within existing churches rather than to separate from them; a great love for Jesus Christ our Lord, and for his church as his body;[11] openness to the possibility of non-rational communication; giving experience a greater role;[12] the taste for deep prayer, personal and in groups; a return to contemplation and a reemphasizing of the praise of God; a great availability for the calls of the Holy Spirit; more assiduous reading of Scripture;[13] conquest of doubt and a deepened faith;[14] the development of lay ministries; spontaneity in prayer; a richer sense of community; ecumenical fellowship;[15] an experiential corrective to a too rational, credal, or barren Christianity;[16] a purification of the prayer experience through the growth in praise and thanksgiving;[17] the instrument of many sincere and profound conversions of persons who had abandoned the practices of the Christian life and fallen into serious sin and vice, such conversions resulting in a return to the sacraments, especially the Eucharist, to a life of personal prayer and dedication to the apostolate; an appreciation of Christian asceticism undertaken through an inner need to be more open to the Lord and his Spirit and to share the experience of privation with their poor and hungry brethren in the world.[18]

TOWARDS EXPERIENCE OF PRESENCE

Obviously the renewal has an experience orientation, but there is no claim that experience exhausts New Testament witness. To place the whole of the biblical testimony under the dominance of religious experience would be falsification. In the renewal it is recognized that one whose religious focus is dominated by religious experiences is a spiritual infant. But to excise religious experience from either the New Testament or from the Christian life is to impoverish them both. Both Old and New Testaments have recorded charismatic experiences.[19] Especially as regards the reception of the Spirit, it seems clear that in the New Testament this event or process "was something experienced, evidenced, and often immediately perceived, rather than merely inferred."[20] Experience is linked to enthusiasm "which is an essential feature of New Testament Christianity."[21] Beyond this New Testament witness there "has been a fairly continuous tradition of such experience, often disregarded by the 'main body' of Christendom, but insistently claiming a place."[22] Mention could be made of Wesley's doctrine of the witness of the Spirit to the believer's spirit, which is the direct and immediate sense that one is God's child, the creation and object of his love.[23] Pope Paul VI spoke of an intimate contact with God and fidelity to commitments undertaken in baptism, "and at the basis of everything, a personal conviction, which does not have its source solely in a teaching received by faith, but also in a certain lived experience."[24] This is not an experience sequestered for a few elect. Rather, "every Christian should have the experience of the presence of the Spirit."[25] The categories for expressing the content of this experience are most commonly presence,[26] power,[27] praise,[28] and of these presence is the most primary. The experience of presence is not something that can be standardized. "No epoch can inherit that presence of the Spirit but must experience that presence for itself."[29]

To understand the presence and words of the Spirit, the Scriptures are normative, but the whole of Christian experience, both contemporary and historical, should be consulted.[30] Obviously the experience of the Spirit and his coming to visibility in ministries and charisms has never been absent from the church.[31] "That in the charismatic renewal the renovation of Christian lives is manifested in exterior phenomena (baptism in the Holy Spirit, healing, imposition of hands, tongues) is due not only to the inherent charismatic nature of the church but in part to the eagerness with which contemporary culture disposes persons to seek a personal experience of reality."[32] The way in which much of contemporary life has been depersonalized prompts believers to search for the personal dimensions of ultimate reality.[33] Even classical Pentecostals, who have often been unjustly accused of substituting experience for doctrine, would urge the renewal in the historic churches to anchor experience in doctrine, thus avoiding the vagaries of a purely experience-oriented approach to religious reality.[34]

What must be recovered is the breadth of faith; the faith relationship is not exhausted by doctrinal statements.[35] Within that faith relationship is a total response: intellect, will, memory, emotions, body, soul. It would be impossible to imagine an experience devoid of all emotional content, and it would be dangerous to exclude the emotions from the global assent of faith.[36] The role assigned to the personal does not mean that what is experienced by many in the charismatic renewal is "meaningless emotionalism."[37] "It cannot be denied that there are many Christians in the Pentecostal Movement who have had a genuine experience of the grace of God."[38] Parallel to its openness to presence, power, and praise is the renewal's turn toward personal commitment, personal appropriation of what has been inherited. Catholics, with their practice of infant baptism, are told that "as an adult one cannot be Christian by proxy."[39] This return to the personal moment in faith is seen as a reevaluation not only of the biblical meaning of faith but of the scholastic teaching on *ex opere operantis*.

FEAR OF RELIGIOUS EXPERIENCE AND SUBJECTIVISM

Not without reason is there fear of religious experience. Sometimes it is simply fear of the unknown; sometimes experience is equated with emotionalism, which is, of course, vigorously rejected by the various expressions of the renewal. Even when it is not seen as excessively emotional, the churches detect a primacy given to feelings, a disordered "taste for the 'immediate' to which one gives priority over all concern for deep reflection that would reveal still hidden treasures."[40] The polarity which builds around intellect and emotions was recognized. There is a real danger of exalting intellect and understanding at the expense of emotions which triggers an anti-intellectualist emotional form of piety. What is offered to God in worship is the total person, including intellect and emotions.[41]

Suspicions persist in the churches, even granting they have neglected religious experience, that there is in the renewal an unhealthy craving for experience, which is a type of religious egoism.[42] History has been painful in its demonstration that fellowship based on experience can lead to divisions and schisms.[43] But there was a willingness in the churches to face the imperatives of such an argument when turned against the denominations. When religious experience does not lead to self-righteousness and divisions, it should be acknowledged as authentic.[44]

What later documents tended to call religious experience earlier documents called subjectivism. Bishop James Pike, who later came to regret his stigmatizing the charismatic renewal as "heresy in embryo,"[45] strenuously objected to the "heavily subjective emphasis upon a personal relationship with Jesus."[46] This subjectivism turned the believer inward in an unhealthy way, so that he becomes an enthusiast who "experiences his own conversion and the resultant spiritual glow rather than Jesus Christ and His Church. When he bears testimony, it is to speak of his new-found happiness, rather than to confess that Jesus Christ is Lord."[47] Because of the spiritist movements in South America, Archbishop Alfonso Lópes Trujillo linked subjectivism with the danger of illuminism.[48]

The obverse side of subjectivism is the neglect of the objective elements of the gospel. The Lutheran Church has in its history Martin Luther's fight against the *Schwärmer* (fanatics) out of which he developed his doctrine of the relation of the Spirit and the external word. What was seen as subjectivism was judged a desire to seek "divine comfort and strength through 'a personal experience' instead of in the objective word of the Gospel."[49] Such misguided subjectivism led either "to pride or to despair."[50] There are ample warnings in the Lutheran Confessions "against all forms of subjectivism which imply that the Holy Spirit deals directly with a person apart from Word and sacraments."[51] Particularly singled out is the Lutheran doctrine of baptism which the charismatic emphasis on the power of the Spirit seems to challenge.[52]

The search for certainty is related to the experience of presence, power, and praise. Certainty is based on God's faithfulness to his promises, while security is based on faith itself. The Lutheran Council in the United States (LCUSA) affirmed certainty in this sense but questioned the security claimed by those in the renewal.[53] Their certitude seems to be based not on the objective promises of the gospel but on wondrous signs.[54] Because those in the renewal have experienced an overwhelming joy and liberation, the Calvinists in Holland suggested, "problems of uncertainty simply are not raised."[55]

Also within the Calvinist tradition it was judged that the emphasis on the subjective and personal relationship was a devaluation of the objective structural elements of church life.[56] No appeal to the Reformation can be made for this highly individualistic conception.

PATTERNS OF EXPERIENCE

Even granting that one must reexamine the role of experience in the New Testament, there can be no insistence on uniformity of experience. Neither the evidence of the New Testament nor contemporary Christian experience will sustain rigid patterns of uniformity.[57] Experience and enthusiasm open the doors to a new spontaneity. When this happens in a broader popular movement where everyone is a participant with a passage of Scripture to read, a hymn to sing, a prophecy to proclaim, there are, warn the churches, dangers of emotionalism. In Ethiopia the renewal in the Lutheran Church (Mekane Yesus), where the youth predominated, some all-night prayer meetings were enthusiastic, and there were admonitions that worship had become disorderly.[58] In other places, such as Brazil, Argentina, and Puerto Rico, religious emotionalism was described as a potential threat.[59] Especially in the first years of the movement in East Germany, when the renewal took on spontaneous and uncontrolled forms, there was danger that it would develop into a sect, an eventuality which was avoided by the firm intention of the leaders to integrate the renewal into the Lutheran Church.[60] That the affective life plays a role in the encounter with God is granted, but in some prayer groups there is an undue stress on the emotional experience of God.[61] "It is not the irrational part of man that connects him with God."[62] In the context of "an emotionally charged environment . . . and trance," Léon Cardinal Suenens discussed "resting or slaying in the Spirit" as a parapsychological phenomenon. Since auto-suggestion and hypnosis can play a part in these manifestations, the cardinal asked leaders "not to induce these phenomena by the way they pray with people."[63]

The experience orientation of the renewal together with the

presence of certain gifts of the Spirit sometimes leads to the impression that one must belong to the movement or to a prayer group in order "to be a complete Christian."[64] No such necessity exists. To receive the gifts of the Spirit one need not belong to a charismatic group.[65]

EXPERIENCE AND SCIENTIFIC THEOLOGY

If one takes the experience of God as the point of departure, then one collides with the contemporary understanding of reality, which leaves no room for the experience of God. Without any real faith demand to support it, one may thus place oneself in the danger of uncritically accepting the biblical world view.[66] In contrast to the theological pluralism in the churches at large, some theologizing which goes on in the renewal is not favorably disposed to such diversity.[67] Beyond this there is, in some circles, a deep suspicion of modern theology in general, especially that of a scientific nature.[68] In East Germany theology students who are in the charismatic renewal face a conflict. They complain that their theological studies are too unrelated to faith, too little supported by the Holy Spirit, too one-sidedly directed to the scientific, and therefore they cannot serve the gospel. In a particular way these criticisms are leveled against the historical-critical method of exegesis, which, it is charged, "does not allow one to hear the Bible as the word of God."[69] A broader representation of Protestant churches in Germany working for charismatic renewal in local congregations had a wider vision and they desired "dialogue with all theological trends which contribute to the renewal of the church."[70] Roman Catholics involved in the renewal in Canada were urged by their bishops "to open the mind to scientific methods of interpretation" and to stimulate theological reflection.[71]

With some notable exceptions the churches wish to evaluate the experiential dimensions of the renewal positively, though no experience of God can claim to be final.[72] Greatly to be deplored is any attempt to discredit or ridicule another's experience or to bring it into disrepute by explaining it away.[73] To be avoided is a one-sided exaltation of either "pure doctrine" or "true experience."[74] Occasionally the churches find the theological categories in which experience is presented so alien to their tradition that they reject the experience as spurious and the theology as erroneous. How experience is given a theological substructure may vary, and there are different degrees of

Introduction

acceptability and unacceptability. To question the viability of that theological substructure and its relationship to the biblical witness does not necessarily imply the inauthenticity of the experience.[75] The reality and meaningfulness of the experience, however assailable the theological justification given, "is beyond question."[76]

ALL IS NOT EXPERIENCE

Having vigorously defended the role of the experiential in New Testament witness and therefore in the Christian life, there was recognition that the renewal did not assume that experience is all.[77] A conception of the Christian life which is seen as a progress from mountain-top experience to mountain-top experience is essentially a perversion of the gospel.[78] It would be difficult to find responsible representatives of the renewal who would hold to such a view of the Christian life. Critics of the Lutheran charismatic renewal fault it for building a whole spirituality around private religious experience. "Yet a cavalier spiritual individualism is challenged in the milieu of the charismatic renewal just as much as it is in the average Lutheran congregation. Charismatics see personal experience and behavior as subject to structures of authority."[79]

Where religious experience is an issue there needs to be not only vigilance on the part of the churches but also within the renewal itself. LCUSA, on examination of the literature emerging from within the Lutheran movement, found that there are "self-critical and evaluative forces at work" within the Lutheran renewal.[80] "Both the theology and practices taking place within the movement came in for searching evaluation."[81]

WHAT IS EXPERIENCED? CHRIST THROUGH THE SPIRIT

There was some concern that the charismatic renewal represented an overblown pneumatology, attributing an exaggerated role to the Spirit and a diminished one to the saving work effected by Jesus Christ.[82] These fears were especially apparent where the churches judged the renewal to have come under the influence of classical Pentecostalism,[83] sometimes attributing to classical Pentecostalism an unbalanced pneumatology not borne out by the facts.

Whatever may be the relationship of Christology to pneumatology in individual cases, the charismatic renewal was and is more in danger of slipping into a Jesus cult than into a

Spirit cult.[84] The experience and on-going life is wholly centered on Jesus Christ.[85] Charisms themselves all come from the glorified Christ who is at the right hand of the Father.[86] In relating the roles of Christ and the Spirit, there was a caveat given lest they be related in a disjunctive, parallel manner, as though there were two foci: Christ plus the Spirit, and Christ alone.[87] The mission of Christ and the Spirit do not represent two completely independent and unrelated missions. Rather, "the continuity of the work of the Spirit does not consist in his always doing the same thing but in always establishing the authority of the same person, Jesus Christ."[88] It is in the Spirit that faith in Jesus Christ is nourished and grows;[89] he leads one to proclaim the Lordship of Jesus. The Spirit, in fact, is a Christological reality.[90]

The attention in the renewal given to the Spirit is not based on an abstract desire to give symmetry to a theological system, to fill in the voids and gaps. Not only the biblical witness issues a pneumatological imperative, but the attention given to the Spirit also arises from below, "out of necessity to formulate a theological framework adequate to the experienced reality."[91] In some measure experience precedes theological reflection and informs though not necessarily determines it.[92] In the liturgical churches documents tend to give this experience a specific ecclesial accent. The movement within the Roman Catholic Church sees itself as "a renewal in the Spirit of the first Pentecost."[93] Pope Paul VI spoke of a "need that the miracle of Pentecost should continue in the history of the church and of the world," an extract from a speech which Roman Catholic bishops of the Committee for Pastoral Research and Practices in the United States appended to their 1975 report.[94] The bishops of Canada too placed the renewal within the context of the church where it serves "as a new witness proclaiming that Pentecost continues."[95] Later Pope Paul spoke of the celebration of Pentecost in Rome on the occasion of the 1975 International Charismatic Conference as a celebration of "the spiritual renewal of the world, of our society, and of our souls."[96] For the Mennonites and Lutherans, among others, it is not possible to speak of the church in its full reality apart from Pentecost.[97]

Beyond all of this the foundations are unambiguously Trinitarian.[98] In the theological suppositions to the renewal, one can "recognize the trinitarian structure of the Christian faith."[99] From within this trinitarian framework devotion to Mary finds its place in the Roman Catholic tradition.[100]

Even given these theological assurances, there were some doubts as to the balance within Christology and pneumatology. Granted the mutuality between Christology and pneumatology, it is still inadequate to the New Testament witness to view the Christian life only in terms of the resurrection and Pentecost.[101] Where is the centrality of the Cross?[102] This is a criticism which surfaces with some frequency. Understandably Lutheran churches voice the suspicion that the Cross of Jesus receives only truncated attention, and they insist that Christian experience is by necessity the experience also of the Cross. The grounding of the faith experience in the Christ event and in its sacramental expression in baptism assures that the accents on "Christ crucified for us" are also central to religious experience and the whole Christian life.[103]

HOW IS THE EXPERIENCE NAMED?

The documents issuing from within the churches give large place to their rejection of a two-level doctrine of sanctification, or, as it is sometimes called, to the doctrine of subsequence. In briefest terms this two-level doctrine holds that after the first conversion-water baptism there is a second level of sanctification, namely, baptism in the Holy Spirit. This subsequent experience is the second work of the Spirit. This doctrine (or its three-level counterpart: conversion, sanctification, baptism in the Holy Spirit) was borrowed from classical Pentecostalism, which in turn borrowed its two-level doctrine (minus tongues as the sign) from the Holiness movement. Many of the more liturgical churches, as well as the free churches, find this doctrine alien to their traditions and unacceptable on exegetical grounds. "The total absence of reference to baptism in the Spirit in the epistles, as a work of grace subsequent to regeneration" makes it difficult to support the two-level doctrine.[104] "The modern elaboration of a doctrine concerning a special event called 'baptism in the Holy Spirit,' different in kind from any other operation of the Holy Spirit, is a sectarian over-interpretation."[105] While John Wesley used the phrase "second blessing," there is some reluctance to identify the "witness of the Spirit," or "the assurance of personal salvation," or the experience of "entire sanctification," or the Aldersgate experience, with the baptism in the Holy Spirit.[106] When speaking of Wesley's mature doctrine of sanctification, "the Spirit-filled life is, rather, a sustained line of gifts, experiences, and divine support, beginning with conversion, constantly moving us toward that goal." [107] In contrast to this two-level doctrine, many churches proposed what might be called a one-level doctrine. The coming of the Spirit or baptism in the Holy Spirit, if you will, is understood in relationship to water baptism.[108] Or more broadly, the Holy Spirit and his gifts are bestowed on a person in baptism which presupposes *and* includes conversion. Both baptism and conversion in this conception are once-for-all events which need constant reinforcement by the power of the Spirit and personal acceptance.[109] Pointing to this double aspect of baptism in the Holy Spirit as event and process, the Methodists in England noted that in the New Testament the phrase is usually applied to Christian initiation and not to a later experience.[110] The Anglican Church in New Zealand stressed Christian initiation as a composite of repentance, faith, baptism, laying on of hands, and reception of the Spirit.[111] The sequence of these elements may vary. What happens in the experience is that the theological reality received in initiation breaks into conscious awareness,[112] and there is a new openness in the believer to the Spirit received at baptism.[113] For this reason some choose to call the experience "the release of the Spirit."[114]

The Baptists in England used Jesus' baptism as the moral model. That baptism is the baptism in the Holy Spirit indicating commitment to a life in the realm of the Spirit under the Lordship of Christ.[115] In the United States the Baptists looked to Pentecost as the event when the church was experientially baptized in the Holy Spirit, and therefore the church is by nature charismatic. Every believer partakes "through personal experience in that baptism of the Holy Spirit at the moment of new birth."[116]

However one relates the reality of baptism in the Holy Spirit to the Christian life, it is impossible to distinguish between Christians on the basis of having or not having the Spirit since the Spirit belongs to the very definition of a Christian.[117]

Lutherans have always placed emphasis on the outer sign, Word, and sacrament as the locus where the Spirit makes Christ present. The Spirit, though sovereign and free, has chosen only the outer sign.[118] When there appears in charismatic teaching to be a separation of baptism from the Spirit,[119] or the positing of two baptisms,[120] or when the sacrament of baptism is placed in a position subordinate to baptism in the Spirit,[121] the Lutheran reaction is strong.

The Lutheran doctrine of the relation of outer sign to the Spirit sometimes led to an extreme Lutheran doctrine of sequence, as though the outer sign had to come first in an all-embracing temporal sequence before the Spirit could act. A stance was taken against this distortion. To say that the Spirit works through Word and sacraments is a theological assertion, not a description of a given person's experience. In a particular experience the temporal sequence may seem disconnected or even inverted. That the Spirit works through Word and sacraments "should not be understood as implying an immediate cause — immediate effect sequence."[122] This less rigid insistence on temporal sequence would not seem acceptable to all Lutherans.[123]

There was a Presbyterian attempt to show that the doctrine of subsequence, or at least some variation of it, was not out of harmony with the Reformed confessional tradition, namely, what was conferred in baptism may become efficacious by the Spirit at a later time, or appropriated later.[124] There is, at minimum, the possibility of a separation in time between baptism with water and the baptism of the Holy Spirit.[125]

The dominantly Anglican, evangelical-charismatic consultation in England pointed out the problems encountered when in a two-level framework baptism in the Holy Spirit is the term used to describe an experience separated, often by a long period of time, from the person's initial conversion. "This usage suggests that what is subnormal in the New Testament should be regarded as normal today."[126] In New Testament times it would have been subnormal that a long interval should elapse between new birth and a conscious realization or reception of the Spirit's power. Solve this problem as one will, the Church of Scotland recognized that enough theological options are open to those in the charismatic renewal, so that they are not bound to a doctrine of subsequence in the sense of a two-level doctrine of sanctification.[127]

A number of pragmatic problems seemed to be associated with the two-level doctrine of sanctification: a community divided into the "haves" and the "have nots,"[128] elitism,[129] and the supposition that if one has not had certain experiences one is unconverted.[130] The two-level doctrine sometimes had serious implications when applied to those holding church offices. Since the gifts of the Spirit came only with the reception of the "second blessing," those pastors and church leaders who have not had this experience do not possess the necessary gifts to be acknowledged as church leaders. Either their programs and authority are rejected by those in the charismatic renewal or, at best, their leadership is tolerated. The two-class Christianity led to an *apartheid* within the Christian community.[131]

The Arminian influence in the charismatic renewal[132] led on occasion to a theology of conditions, where faith is transformed into the greatest of human works and then is seen as a prerequisite for God's action.[133] In Ethiopia this tendency was countered by recalling that for Paul, as for Luke in Acts, there are two basic conditions for the reception of the Spirit: the preaching of the gospel (hearing) and faith in the gospel.[134] Renewal in the Spirit is "not a human possibility" but a gift of God.[135] If any precondition exists, it is the admission of helplessness and emptiness. Therefore one expects everything from God.[136]

The appeal to Scripture to solve the dilemmas was recognized by the Methodists in Great Britain as a blind alley because various interpretations of the work of the Spirit exist in the New Testament alongside of each other, unharmonized. No attempt should be made to absolutize any one pattern as to how the Spirit is to be experienced.[137] Laws should not be made for the Holy Spirit.[138] One should not move from theological formulation to experience or from experience to theological formulation as though the two will always perfectly coincide. The Spirit is sovereign and free.

A distinction is made between the authenticity of the spiritual experience and the acceptability of the two-level doctrine of sanctification.[139] "We must neither cast doubt on the authenticity of 'baptism in the Holy Spirit' nor accept a Pentecostalist explanation of it."[140]

CHARISMS: WHICH CANON-WITHIN-THE-CANON?

In approaching the discussion of charisms, there was a caution expressed lest the Acts of the Apostles — a book dear to the renewal — be used in isolation from the rest of the New Testament.[141] What Paul said to a particular congregation, at a certain time, on a special occasion, should not be applied "literally and indiscriminately to congregations today."[142] What Scripture itself regards as descriptive, those in the renewal are in danger of making normative.[143]

There was some concern that the Acts of the Apostles and the descriptive writings of Paul be used as a canon-within-the-canon, giving this descriptive material preference over the clearly didactic sections of the New Testament.[144] There is no mention of certain charisms, tongues in particular, in Romans. "This letter, more than any other we have from St. Paul, is designed to set forth the whole counsel of God. It is actually a handbook on Christian doctrine, a miniature dogmatics, but there is no discussion of or instruction about speaking in tongues."[145] Romans is more properly a canon within a canon. But the basic hermeneutical norm is broader: Scripture interprets Scripture.[146]

DISPENSATIONALISM: MATURITY OR IMMATURITY?

These discussions raised the question of dispensationalism. Are the spiritual gifts for the church in her infancy or also for her on-going life? Here a variety of modified positions are found. The Anglicans in Australia thought it a misreading of the historical elements of the gospel if one understands them as a commission for spiritual healing in the church today.[147] Such healings form no part of a Christ-commanded assignment in the on-going church.[148] Especially as regards tongues, the church is not called upon to repeat first-century practices but to "obedience in contemporary life."[149] An early Episcopal statement regarded the phenomena which accompanied the first Pentecost to be abnormal. They are "scaffolding surrounding a new edifice," which became unnecessary and was discarded; they are marks of infancy and immaturity to which one does not return.[150] As the renewal grew in wisdom and as the churches looked more carefully at the theological sources, these views were set aside or at least modified. The Lutherans of the Missouri Synod opted for a modified dispensationalism. Out of hand one should not reject the possibility that God may endow some Christians with the same gifts he gave to the early church.[151] Such gifts may be found in the contemporary church; they are not necessarily found there.[152] A similar "relaxed dispensationalism" was adopted by the Baptist General Conference in the United States. The more extraordinary charisms (prophecy, tongues, healing, exorcism) are manifested in the church as she needs them. "They may or may not be evident at any given time."[153] But mostly dispensationalism was left unmentioned or rejected.[154]

NAME, RANK, AND NUMBER

The lists of charisms in Paul are not exhaustive lists but rather open-ended lists;[155] their number may vary according to the need and the situation.[156] If new needs arise, the Spirit can give totally new gifts not found in the New Testament lists.[157]

In the Würzburg theses, it is considered inconceivable that there is "any order of precedence among the charisms."[158]

Reformed churches in Holland and South Africa were not so sure. A certain gradation is perceivable based on how immediately and directly they minister to the common good and build up the church.[159]

When questions of rank are raised inevitably, the relation of charisms to charity arises. Charity belongs to a more basic, more primary order of religious reality than do the charisms.[160] The charity of which Paul speaks in 1 Corinthians 13 is the matrix and criterion of the charisms.[161] One must not contrast them as though they were alternatives and were free to choose between them. Paul is concerned to say that "no single gift can be of any value if it is practiced without love." [162] Neither should the church set up a theological situation where one is forced to choose between a charism and the fruits of the Spirit. "The church should also exercise care not to play off the fruit of the Spirit against the gifts of the Spirit as though only the fruit were important." [163] Thus a false opposition between charisms and fruits is avoided. An early Lutheran document did not posit an opposition between charisms and fruits but found charity more to be recommended because "it never confuses people. It is understood and appreciated by all people — irrespective of their language, race, age, or social class. Even the animals understand it." [164] The Roman Catholic bishops of the Antilles, whose document is remarkably supportive of the renewal, warned that charisms can be dangerous if exercised without the sanctifying gifts (wisdom, understanding, right judgment, courage, knowledge, reverence, and awe) received in Christian initiation.[165]

HUMAN EXPERIENCE AND RELIGIOUS MEANING

In general the documents, including those in which persons involved in the renewal helped write, tended to move away from what was judged to be an over-spiritualizing of the gifts.[166] The intent was to include social workers, doctors, nurses, musicians, therapists, and ploughmen as all exercising a gift of the Spirit.[167] This is a move away from what might be called the "Zap theory," where there is a sudden moment when the Spirit endows one with a totally new faculty of a completely different order, a capacity one never possessed before. Here the emphasis is on newness and on the difference between charisms and natural faculties elevated by grace.[168] In contrast to this theory, a more cosmological approach is offered in which the Holy Spirit renews creation and discloses new possibilities (already present in God's work of creation) of intercommunion and patterns of life. "Therefore speaking in tongues, prophecy, dance and vision are not infused, supernaturally imposed extras of the divine being. They are, on the contrary, disclosures of patterns of human life, 'in the presence of God,' disclosures brought about by God's own Spirit."[169] These disclosures bring persons into contact with the heritage of primal religions and other religious expressions. This openness frees one from both anxiety and self-centeredness and, more importantly, "from an ethno-centric misinterpretation of the Christian faith."[170] In a word, charisms are signs of the renewed creation, not supernatural happenings.

Others took a slightly different approach. Natural talents are charisms if they are in the service of the kingdom and infused with the power of the Spirit.[171] Indeed, phenomenologically they are not uniquely Christian. What makes them so is their function in the power of the Spirit to build up the church.[172] The Spirit takes possession of our own talents and "seals them as his own gifts of grace . . . the Spirit does not need to act outside of an already present talent."[173]

Though this more cosmological view typifies the dominant trend, there are some major qualifications. These natural faculties are rooted in pre-Christian human endowments which are caught up in the cleansing, energizing power of the Spirit. But the Mennonites in the United States did not want to exclude the possibility that in some cases "new abilities now appear for the first time."[174] In Scotland it was also considered appropriate to identify a charism as an inborn talent which is heightened, but the Presbyterians did not want to exclude "the possibility that the believer would then be able to do something he was unable to do before."[175] As evidence they suggested that "speaking in tongues is miraculous."[176] Most documents, as well as many persons involved in the renewal, would assert that speaking in tongues is a "graced event" but would generally deny its miraculous character. Others in the renewal would consider tongues, interpretation, healings, and prophecy to be "absolutely miraculous and supernatural."[177] Note the equation between miraculous and supernatural. Beyond this discussion what is decisive is not what kind of gifts are found in the church but how they are used.[178]

Those in the Lutheran charismatic renewal were concerned that this more cosmological approach not end up reducing the expression of God's love "to manifestations consistent with the limitations imposed by an autonomous humanity."[179]

THE UNUSUAL AND TRIVIALIZATION

A persistent and recurring complaint in the documents was the stress in the renewal on what are called the extraordinary gifts.[180] This leads to a species of spiritual impoverishment,[181] partly because there is a suspicion that the extraordinary is in some way more spiritual than the ordinary.[182] Even while calling on Paul to support their stance, the renewal gives the impression of standing nearer the position Paul was criticizing than to the one he was expounding.[183] In Paul it is clear that it is the ordinary which comes first and in its very ordinariness it is stamped with the grade "special."[184] To be precise, the whole distinction between ordinary and extraordinary is foreign to Paul.[185]

Lest all of this seem to be a criticism imposed on the renewal from the outside, the Canadian Roman Catholic bishops noted that the renewal itself indicts as false any seeking after exclusively extraordinary manifestations of the Spirit.[186] From those involved in the renewal also comes a warning concerning the trivialization of the gifts, which occurs when only the remarkable and spectacular is considered a gift.[187] Trivialization also occurs when it is forgotten that the experience of God's immediacy "remains a mediated immediacy."[188] The Spirit does not wish to work without or outside the given processes of nature and history. In no sense does the recognition of these mediations (cultural, historical, social, psychological, etc.) imply any diminution of the knowledge of God.

THE FULL SPECTRUM

Malines Document I introduced the concept of a spectrum of charisms from A to P, including what many would call ordinary charisms of teaching and other acts of mercy toward the sick and the poor. The other section of the spectrum extending from P to Z included such gifts as prophecy, healing, tongues, interpretation. This document suggested that not only the gifts in the A–P section but also those in the P–Z section were real possibilities for the life of the church. These latter also belong to the normal everyday life of the local church.[189]

Churches reacted differently to the concept of spectrum, One group asked hard questions about the role the gifts in the P–Z section should play in the life of the church. Were not the gifts in the A–P section "more significant for the renewal of the church than the gifts of P–Z?"[190] Has not the Holy Spirit renewed the church in many times and places without the P–Z charisms?

Further, the experience of the Corinthian church demonstrates that there is no direct correlation between the exercise of the P–Z gifts and spiritual maturation in commitment and life.

Quite different is the stance of the continental European Methodist document which asks the question: If the church is ineffective in giving witness, may this not be found in the church's satisfaction "with only a section of the reality of divine salvation," while closing her eyes to other possibilities, specifically the charisms of tongues and prophecy?[191] This Council of the Evangelical Methodist Central Conferences in Europe recalled that John Wesley, while restrained, remained open to the possibility of these particular spiritual gifts demonstrating the reality of the kingdom, insofar as they are functions of ministry, that is, they build up the community.[192] The Evangelical (Lutheran) churches in East Germany granted that while certain special charisms do not necessarily belong to authentic Christianity, their absence will be considered a deficiency both in the life of the individual and the community.[193] Other churches took a stronger stance, asking their membership to be open to the full spectrum of the gifts, recognizing all the gifts as having a place in the life of the church, excluding every *a priori* decision that certain gifts are no longer given by the church and thus have no place in her life.[194]

A CHURCH ENTIRELY MINISTERIAL

Quite apart from the discussion of the full spectrum, there was a growing recognition that the renewal restored the gifts of the Spirit to the realm of the ordinary, where they belong to the everyday functioning of the normal Christian community.[195] "A church that is fully alive undoubtedly possesses all the gifts of the Spirit."[196] They are signs that the community is truly alive.[197] Fundamentally they are not adjuncts to the life of the church; rather they belong to the basic structure of the church.[198] "If anything in history is to be rightly called 'the charismatic movement,' it is the church itself."[199] The church is a community in which each member has a charism and the body is therefore an ordered mutuality of ministries serving the whole.[200] Belonging to the inner structure of the church and serving the whole body, their function is not to call attention to themselves. "A gift-centered fellowship" is not an ideal.[201] Charisms focus attention on themselves when they are seen as things to be possessed, independent of the giver. "It is never a question of having (something new), but always a question of being (somebody new)."[202] Ultimately it is not a question of special gifts but of the charismatic life.[203]

Balance is difficult to obtain once a group of persons calls for the restoration to the church's life of an area which has been neglected. And except for the gifts relating to office, the church has neglected the charisms in question.[204] To situate the charisms at the center of the church's life is not necessarily to place the accent on a special charismatic experience, nor on a special movement, but it is simply to insist that they are constitutive of the normal life of the church and of the Christian life.[205]

THE TONGUES OF MEN AND ANGELS

Either because persons in the renewal focused attention on tongues in the first years of the movement's existence, or because church committees were puzzled by this socially unacceptable form of behavior, or because the gifts of tongues proved to be divisive — for whatever reason the early reports were dominated by the question of tongues. As the years went on, it became clear that tongues was not the issue and the reports from the churches reflected this broader vision.

The Dutch Reformed Church in South Africa asked that a judgment not be made on the charismatic renewal solely on the issue of tongues.[206] Further, those on the outside often are in error as to the role this gift plays in the actual lives of persons in the renewal.[207]

Many of the reports give extensive exegetical material which will not be reviewed here. There was an admission that because it is exegetically not possible to know exactly what glossolalia is in the New Testament, it is consequently not possible to declare the experiences of contemporary Christians to be either valid or invalid reproductions of New Testament glossolalia.[208] From the biblical narrative it is evident that tongues were neither specifically expected nor demanded by the apostles. "But when it occurred it was seen as an attestation of the authenticity of the Spirit's presence."[209]

Early in the confrontation between the Christian Missionary Alliance and classical Pentecostalism, tongues as the initial evidence that one had received the baptism in the Holy Spirit was rejected as one of the greatest errors of the new movement.[210] Those churches which comment on the doctrine of initial evidence tend to reject tongues as a sign of a special presence of the

Spirit.[211] Nor were tongues to be considered normative for the Christian life.[212] Although speaking in tongues should not be prevented, "we need not deplore the lack of this gift in our lives or the fact that it is not manifested in the church."[213] In a style of studied understatement, the committee of the American Lutheran Church reported that "the presence of this phenomenon has not been an unmitigated blessing" but rather "the cause of confusion . . . ."[214] Divisiveness seemed to characterize much of the Protestant reaction to tongues.[215]

That this seems not to have been typical of the Catholic experience is evidenced in the complete lack of any mention of tongues in the 1969 report of the committee of the Catholic bishops in the United States,[216] or any attribution of divisiveness in the more extensive report of 1975,[217] and the positive evaluation it received in the document which appeared under Cardinal Suenens' patronage.[218]

PSYCHOLOGICAL PROFILES: SUSPICION AND VINDICATION

The whole question of the psychological profile arose when it was a matter of persons who engage in socially unacceptable behavior such as healing, giving prophecies, or performing exorcisms. But for the most part psychological reflections were centered on tongues. The earliest reports from the early 1960s balance statements about its having biblical precedent,[219] about psychiatrists evaluating tongues positively as an irrational expression of the deepest sentiments,[220] with declarations that in its non-religious manifestations it appears among persons suffering from schizophrenia and hysteria.[221] While clearing persons who spoke in tongues of charges of being psychologically disturbed, there persisted a sub-clinical suspicion that such persons were pushing against the boundaries of normalcy even while not transgressing them.

Of great influence in clearing the atmosphere was the 1970 report of the United Presbyterian Church in the United States. First, professionals in the behavioral sciences called attention to the limited competence of psychology in the presence of religious experience: "It will be a dark and tragic day in the life of Christianity if psychological norms are to become the criteria by which the truth or the untruth of religious experience is judged . . . to ask it to assume the role of arbiter and judge in the sphere of religion is to ask it to do something which is an affront to psychology as a science and a scandal to religion."[222] No evidence of pathology was found in the movement, the data indicating that the participants in the renewal are emotionally and psychologically quite similar to the normal church population and to their occupational identity group, being essentially well-adjusted and productive members of society.[223] Other Presbyterians took an even stronger stand. "Regardless of the scientific conclusions which may be reached, the question of the theological significance of these phenomena will remain, and it may be answered only within the context of faith."[224] In a more guarded formulation the Dutch Reformed Church in South Africa granted that while the Spirit does not work outside our psyche or cultural life, what can be explained psychologically or in cultural terms is not necessarily unrelated to the Spirit of God.[225]

APPEAL TO TRADITION

Another methodological facet surfaced at this point. Among some of the churches which hold a *sola scriptura* principle, the emergence of tongues pushed them beyond the Scriptures to appeals to the tradition of the church as a means of effectively, if not literally, outlawing tongues. In 1970 the Church of the Nazarene invoked "the doctrine and practice of the church."[226] Against glossolalia and healing services the Dallas Baptist Association called on "historic Baptist practices,"[227] while in New Zealand those Baptists in the renewal were described as "differing from the main stream of doctrine and practice among Baptists."[228] At the international level the Baptist World Alliance reported that some dismiss the charismatic renewal as "untrue to Baptist tradition."[229] The United Methodists had a larger concern, namely, members of the church taking over classical Pentecostal views or adopting no theological position at all and becoming floaters, "no longer rooted in the traditions that could sustain them."[230]

PROPHECY: GOD'S LIGHT ON THE PRESENT

Though less preoccupied and seemingly less threatened by prophecy, the churches tended to take a defensive attitude toward it. Like some within the renewal, they were more than cautious when it came to predictive prophecy.[231] Directive prophecy, whether concerning the group or the individual, was seen by some as "dangerously subjective," prompting persons to change jobs and their whole life style.[232] Also a matter of consideration was the naive view of prophecy in which there is "an almost magical belief that one's life in every detail is infallibly guided by the Spirit."[233] Some thought that the use of prophecy in the renewal was too inward looking, too exclusively seen in individualistic and privatistic terms. In the renewal the ministry of the prophet was not understood as the great prophets of the Old Testament understood their ministry, including the social and political ills of Israel. The hope was expressed that the true voice of the prophet would be rediscovered, outward looking and relating to the world.[234] Abuses were clearly the focus of attention. Yet it was recognized that for many of the early Christians, though not for St. Paul, the supreme manifestation of the Spirit in the church was the gift of prophecy. Since the New Testament witnesses considered the Spirit to be a constitutive factor in the life of the church, they saw the prophets together with the apostles as the foundation of the church. Rather than marginal, the prophet was seen as integral to the church's corporate ministry and mission.[235]

Speaking in a summary way of tongues and prophecy, the Canadian bishops pointed to the biblical evidence. That there are differences of opinion concerning the significance of these gifts does not affect their authenticity. "It is arbitrary to treat them with doubt *a priori*."[236]

"BE THOU WHOLE"

The gift of healing mentioned in two of Paul's lists could be understood to be a continuation of Jesus' healing ministry and of his commission to the disciples to heal.[237] "Healing is not so much a proof of the truth of the gospel as part of the good news itself."[238] Or the ministry of healing is an accompaniment of the gospel and must be considered as an integral part of the coming of the kingdom. Here the accent is not on healing, as though it were an end in itself, but on healing as a faith response to Jesus Christ.[239] Some would say that healing as practiced in the church today is not the fulfillment of a particular specific command of Christ for the on-going life of the church. Rather it is part of the more general ministry of the church.[240] One cannot deduce from a New Testament commission that the charism of healing has to be present in the church everywhere and constantly.[241] The Dutch Reformed report from South Africa held that nowhere in the New Testament is healing particularly emphasized, and in any event no special prominence is given to it in the labors of the apostles.[242] Those claiming this gift are forced by publicity and "other factors" into "an impious life" insofar as they start to make claims which no longer accord with the truth.[243] Two Lutheran churches in the United States saw the healing ministry displacing ultimates with penultimates.[244] What is of ultimate significance is faith, forgiveness of sins, and the resurrected life. "If bodily healing becomes central, then all is lost."[245]

One cannot say that healings do not take place, but the great healing services do not harmonize with the healing practice of the early church.[246] The fanfare and publicity which accompanies the healing which takes place "outside the context of the Christian congregation" does not further the gospel.[247] To claim a healing which cannot be verified is not giving glory to God.[248]

Not acceptable is the supposition that all forms of sickness are contrary to God's will since Christ has redeemed us from all ills, physical and spiritual, when he gave his life for us on the cross.[249] Redemptive suffering is still part of the Christian life. Nor can one say that it is only the sick person's lack of faith which impedes the miraculous healing.[250] No limit is to be placed on God's power to heal but he has not promised to heal everyone who asks.[251] When miraculous cures are reported, "they seem to occur in inverse ratio to the observer's medical knowledge."[252] In speaking of abuses which persist, the Australian Roman Catholic consensus statement reported: "There are still cases of 'healing!'"[253]

The World Council of Churches (wcc) attempted to situate healing in a broad theological context, thus avoiding isolation from its larger biblical framework. The Holy Spirit renews creation and bestows fullness of life. The dawn of the renewed creation is not yet complete, but its first beginnings are already with us. Within the process of this renewal of creation, one can rightly expect healing of social relationships, healing in one's relations with one's own human self, and healing of bodily sickness.[254] Healing is not to be understood apart from the total work of the Spirit in a renewed creation.[255]

If validation is sought for a healing ministry, it can be found on three grounds: it is scriptural; it reflects the reality that personality is composed of an interrelatedness of mind, body, and spirit; it affirms the reality of the living God in human affairs.[256] Many who have participated with a new seriousness in an intercessory prayer group "and seen the results of their prayers in various forms of guidance, comfort, and actual healings, are brought to a new realization of God's living reality."[257]

Introduction

TESTING THE SPIRITS

Manifestations are, in the first instance, ambiguous, and that ambiguity is taken away by the process of discernment.[258] There are three possible explanations for manifestations: they are the product of the immediate supernatural action of the Holy Spirit; they are rare natural phenomena which the Spirit uses; they are demonic in origin.[259] One of the criteria is Christological. Any teaching or religious experience that does not shed light on Jesus or is not congruous with his life and ministry is not of the Spirit of God.[260] Other criteria are their appropriateness for upbuilding the church, their capacity to disclose faith, hope, and love as the matrix of the Christian life.[261]

The primary locus of this discerning process is the church.[262] The prophetic Spirit has fallen on the entire believing community which has a full right to test the spirits.[263] Within Roman Catholicism the local bishop has a special role to play in the discerning process.[264]

THE SPIRIT CONSTITUTES THE CHURCH

By its nature the church is charismatic.[265] The Spirit and his charisms are constitutive of the church and are not added to an already existing Body of Christ. The Spirit belongs to the first moment of the church's existence and is not merely a post-factum vivifier and animator, who comes into effective action in the second moment of the church's existence.[266] In the first instance charisms are given to the whole church and not primarily to each individual.[267] Therefore there can be no opposition between charism and institution.[268] "There must be no playing of charisms and institution against one another. In the Spirit the institutional is made charismatic and the charismatic is made institutional."[269]

This makes it problematic to have a distinct charismatic renewal in the church, which in turn can give the false impression that other Christians are not charismatic.[270] Those actively involved in the liturgical movement do not contend that the liturgy and the sacraments belong to them in any proper sense. On the contrary, they are saying that liturgy and sacraments belong to the nature of the church, and therefore all should take a more active part in their celebration. So also with the charisms and the charismatic renewal.

It is recognized that the renewal does not bring anything to the church which she does not already possess. Nonetheless there is a place within the church for a distinct renewal. The possibility of a renewal of the whole church will be all the greater if there is an identifiable charismatic renewal,[271] which is looked upon as part of the normal life of the church.[272] In relating to the renewal within the church, one should neither enthusiastically embrace it (thus freezing the development of the renewal), nor totally reject it as something that the church has already dealt with years ago (e.g., the "enthusiasts" at the time of Luther).[273] Integration is the goal of the renewal, and thus even now it does not want to see itself as a "special community" but prefers to understand itself as a renewal cell in the church.[274] When integration has taken place, unity and healing will be effected,[275] and a special charismatic movement will be rendered superfluous.[276] With these pronounced ecclesiological objectives, the church has fewer fears of the renewal taking on an alien theology, in effect sectarian in character, and thus remaining outside the authentic ecclesial tradition.[277]

ORDER OR FREEDOM

The Council of the Evangelical Methodist Central Conference in Europe asked: "Will the power of the Holy Spirit, manifest in these charismatic groups, be able to deliver our church from its torpidity?"[278] More particularly, what contribution can the renewal make to sacramental worship, with its innate proclivity for mechanistic ritualism and formalism? Some in the charismatic renewal react to the liturgical life of the church negatively. Roman Catholics who were sacramentalized without an accompanying evangelization sometimes feel deceived by the church when they have been led into an experience of God in a non-sacramental context. After all those years of Mass, Communion, confession, when, they now claim, "nothing happened," they have an experience of God in a charismatic group and are transformed. Evidently the church thought, they say, that the face of God was to be found in the liturgical life, in the sacraments. Their lives indicate she is wrong. They conclude that the face of God is to be found in religious experience, which is then set over against liturgical life.[279]

   In New Zealand those Anglican groups which had come under classical Pentecostal influence were more likely "to regard forms of church order, leadership and liturgy, as irrelevant."[280] All of this would indicate that the charismatic renewal would flourish in the freer atmosphere of the non-liturgical churches. But the contrary is true. It is the liturgical churches, with their more structured and disciplined worship traditions, which have had the fewest problems embracing the charismatic renewal and have been more successful in making place for charismatic expressions within their liturgical services (e.g., the Roman Catholic Eucharist and the Anglican Communion),[281] though this integration usually takes place at special services for charismatic groups at retreats and conferences.

In Ethiopia it was recognized that a reawakening of faith among Lutherans will bring new demands for change in the worship, and the recommendation was made that there be a possibility of having some worship services with more freedom and openness to the charisms of the Spirit.[282] In making this suggestion appeal was made to article 7 of the Augsburg Confession: "It is not necessary that human traditions or rites or ceremonies instituted by man should be alike everywhere." A similar stance was taken by lcusa when it considered liturgical worship and the charismatic renewal. "Any form of worship that is genuinely doxological and edifying should be acknowledged. In matters of polity and terminology, we are not tied inflexibly to particular forms; rather we expect that changing insights and circumstances will bring revision."[283] The liturgical and theological advisability of creating new forms or orders within the church's worship structure might obviate the necessity some involved in the charismatic renewal feel to have themselves re-baptized,[284] a practice which has appeared in several countries.[285]

But even before one is pressed to rethink old liturgies, one is forced to deal with what is "the most characteristic feature of the charismatic renewal," namely, "spontaneity of praise."[286] This gives rise to extemporaneous physical movements of all sorts (hand clapping, arm raising, dancing, embracing) which have given a greater sense of liveliness to the worship, but have also caused some bewilderment among outsiders.[287] The freedom in worship has expressed itself in a new musical literature of hymns and songs which encourage a broader range of corporate participation. Worship in charismatic groups is first and foremost the worship of the community, in which the leadership is shared by all, in contrast to the worship services in many churches which are the sole responsibility of the minister in charge.[288]

Lutherans in the charismatic renewal, when asked in the lcusa consultations to formulate what they had to say to the church as regards worship, maintained that "the form of charismatic worship is not as important as that which gives rise to it: a sense of *expectancy*."[289] This refers not to miraculous events but to the presence of the living God who still acts and changes lives. People gather to celebrate his presence among them, and they expect that presence to be effective.

Alongside the stream in the renewal, which, for a variety of reasons, reacts negatively to formal liturgical worship, is another stream which rediscovers the riches of the liturgy.[290] Precisely because the renewal is so praise-oriented, liturgical worship has retained a relatively large role in this stream.[291] Many recognize the mutuality of enrichment which exists between spontaneous prayer and liturgical life.[292] This enrichment is seen especially in the eucharistic celebrations, which is at the center of a charismatic form of worship.[293]

In some groups in East Germany, the Lord's Supper is celebrated daily. Within Lutheranism this evaluation of the Lord's Supper is important for understanding the difference between Pietism and the charismatic renewal. Spiritual experience should in some objective way be manifested in its ecclesiological form. The Lord's Supper is not only an objective factor of the profound relationship with Christ but also a stabilizing element in relationship to the communion of Christians with Christ.[294]

COMMUNITY AS COMMITTED RELATIONSHIPS

Out of the double mission of the Son and the Spirit arises the community which transmits to the world the new reality of salvation. "Every Christian who is reborn by faith and baptism lives in this charismatic reality, which is communitarian."[295] There is a new awareness of the church as community in which the charismatic reality is manifested in a people who love and care for one another and deeply share one another's life along a wide spectrum.[296] Besides participation in group prayer and liturgical worship, this includes recreation, housing, counseling situations, pastoring, and finances. Within the renewal there is a deep conviction that such caring communities have a specific function as regards evangelization; indeed community is the primary locus of evangelization. To restore persons' willingness to believe the gospel, there is need for committed communities whose witness, without explanation, carries its own conviction. Without communities to which one can point and say, "Come and see. I will show you what the gospel means," the church is inoperative and, in her evangelization, ineffective.[297] People feel that God is dead because there are no communities in which they can experience his presence.[298]

Sometimes this community sense is seen as elitism,[299] sometimes as signaling a withdrawal from fellowship with those who do not share a similar experience,[300] sometimes as a possible danger of developing into a church-within-the-church.[301]

When it is evaluated positively, it is looked upon as an opportunity to develop new forms of community and local church life,[302] with strong emphasis on the "personalizing of community life, where simplicity and spontaneous behavior replace the stereotyped forms of communication and exchange characterizing certain Christian communities."[303]

In the Antilles the Roman Catholic bishops spoke of the need to establish "Spirit-inspired basic communities" within the larger parish communities. They judged that the charismatic prayer group "is very effective in forming this needed type of basic community."[304] In the case of parents and guardians of infants to be baptized and those who live on the margin of the church, the bishops looked to the charismatic renewal to provide a warm, authentic community environment in which they could receive nurture.[305]

Those in the Lutheran renewal in the United States think they are doing more than just theorizing about the structure of Christian community. In the context of radically committed relationships, they are shaping their understanding of authority, submission, headship, responsibility, obedience, and freedom.[306] Committed relationships in community belong to Christian hermeneutics.

Of major significance is the emergence of covenant communities, groups of persons who have made a commitment to the Lord and to each other to share their lives. This development which appeared in Episcopal and Baptist groups is now to be found in Mennonite, nondenominational, and Roman Catholic churches. Within Roman Catholicism, these centers of charismatic renewal are so strong that they tend to dominate the renewal in countries such as the Philippines, Australia, India, Sri Lanka, France, Ireland, Belgium, and the United States. An international association of communities has developed, binding the groups, which are either Catholic, Catholic-ecumenical, or ecumenical, into a network of mutually supporting communities. Though many of them are involved in formation programs for prayer groups, the association tends to see itself as a movement distinct from the broad-based charismatic renewal. Its commitment to community building is understood in much more radical terms, and therefore its precise objectives make it a movement apart from but related to the broad-based charismatic renewal as expressed in most local prayer groups.

EVANGELIZATION AS IMPERATIVE

However the various groups structure themselves, they hold in common the conviction that out of community comes evangelization. To receive the Spirit is to change; to receive the Spirit is to be moved and to move others to the recognition that Jesus is Lord.[307] The handing on of the personal and community encounter is a self-understood imperative about which one need not discuss.[308] If such groups attract new adherents, it is not because unusual gifts are there displayed. Rather, it is the new freedom in fellowship with God and men and the new joy in witnessing to the Lordship of Jesus.[309] It is not sufficient to answer that all of this is implied and present in the message of the church. True, but people should not have to delve too deeply for answers which are implicit. "They need a message and a fellowship in which answers are explicit."[310]

So strongly is the accent on this aspect that in Ethiopia one could say that the renewal is really "a movement of evangelization."[311] In the concrete this is bound up with the substantial financial commitment individuals make, many of them tithing. Individual Christians in Ethiopia, often untrained, are being sent out to evangelize, supported by two or three friends who are working and pay part of their salaries for the support of the evangelist. Financial commitment of a similar magnitude is not unusual in any of the countries.

The evangelization imperative also flows from awareness that many Christians are so only nominally and "have never been truly converted to Christ."[312] In a church which practices infant baptism, there is still need for a structure which can bring persons to a mature faith and responsibility. These are baptized adults who have not yet heard the message of the mystery of Christ. Their conversion is based on the baptism they have already received. They must only unfold its power. To bring these unconverted Catholics to adult faith requires a program of evangelization, contact with a community of believers, and the participation in certain liturgical celebrations. In the Antilles the Catholic bishops pointed to the success the Catholic renewal has

Introduction

had in such adult catechetical-formation programs in which there are "many examples of conversion among baptized Catholics."[313] This success would indicate the need to set up structures which would do the same for the whole Catholic community.

The heavy involvement in programs of evangelization raises the question of competence. The Canadian Catholic bishops noted that formation is of unequal caliber and in some cases leaves much to be desired. "As a result some leaders are little prepared for their duties. Their knowledge of Scripture is superficial, their theological information very scant. These deficiencies render a disservice to the movement."[314] Not only the teaching of the church but also an understanding of the Scriptures is an essential element in the formation of leaders.[315] Pope Paul also pointed to the necessity of "an ever deeper biblical, spiritual and theological formation."[316]

ECUMENISM: A DECISION FOR THE CHURCH

No one can take Christ seriously if one does not take the church seriously,[317] or, in more evangelical terms, any decision for Christ is a decision for the church.[318] A deep seriousness about ecumenical questions is found in the renewal. People come together across denominational lines to witness to a common Lord and to share their lives. Long standing denominational hostilities disappear. "A common experience has accomplished rapidly what many years of patient discussion and explanation have failed to do."[319] Its ecumenical dimensions are not the result of any conscious decision, but the renewal was *de facto* ecumenical from its very beginnings.[320]

During the European Charismatic Leaders Conference in 1975, three theological principles operative in the ecumenical process were set forth: self-discovery, openness, and takeover. Every church has a particular spiritual tradition, and in no one church are all the gifts of grace fully realized. Consequently every church must ask itself what her inalienable vocation is in the light of her historical origins. This is self-discovery. Openness is the readiness not to absolutize her own gifts of grace and allow herself to be enriched by the gifts present in the other churches. Because gifts are granted for the common good, each church should press to the limit of what is possible the willingness to take over the gifts of the other churches.[321]

Two other extensive attempts were made to come to terms with the ecumenical opportunity which the renewal presents. Cardinal

Suenens, in his continuing role of relating the renewal in Roman Catholicism to the larger experience of the church, saw the renewal as a being called to an ecumenical vocation and fidelity to its Catholic identity.[322] The other ecumenical document, which was authored by Kilian McDonnell, saw the preservation of Catholic identity as of paramount importance but considered a purely preservationist attitude inadequate to the situation.[323] The ecumenical dimension is integral to one's Catholicity and flows from it.

ECUMENICAL AMBIVALENCE

Aside from these documents which for the most part come from those within the renewal, there is an ambivalence in other more institutional documents as the church relates to the ecumenical aspects of the renewal. In the United States the Catholics bishops saw the continual and exclusive participation of Roman Catholics in ecumenical groups as running the risk of diluting the sense of Catholic identity, while granting that occasional ecumenical sharing in prayer groups can be beneficial.[324] In the same year, 1975, the Canadian Catholic hierarchy perceived Catholic participation in ecumenical prayer groups as a laudable initiative which may bring Christians closer together. Yet they saw the danger of a false ecumenism in which differences were belittled so that no one emerges with a true identity.[325] Very little doctrinal agreement could be seen in the denominationally mixed groups which formed in South Africa. Theirs is a unity "which is not found in truth but in experience."[326] This leads to a relativizing of the Christian message with grotesque consequences.

A group of Anglican evangelicals and others involved in the Protestant charismatic renewal in England thought that "a unity based on experience at the expense of doctrine would be less than the unity envisaged in the New Testament and would be dangerous in the long run," especially where relations with the Roman Catholic Church were concerned.[327] Even when authentic personal and corporate renewal has taken place (here again the reference is to the Roman Catholic Church), this has not always meant "the dropping of all anti-biblical or sub-biblical traditions and practices."[328] This Anglican and Protestant group recalled that the Roman Catholic Church, "a massive international community," has only in recent years "begun to question its own historic stance."[329] The group counseled others to be realistic in their expectations and to allow time (how long was not for them

l

to say) for the forces of "reformation and renewal to operate widely enough for changes in official formulations and interpretations of doctrine to become possible, where they are necessary."[330]

Beyond these ecumenical accents there is, in some expressions of the renewal, a despair of institutional Christianity with a consequent move to vaporize the church. If one has Jesus and the Bible, does one really need the church?

Partly as a consequence of an anti-intellectual current in some sectors of the renewal, partly because of impatience with a church which is living below her expected potential and is therefore an obstacle to the gospel, the move is toward a churchless Christianity.[331] The teaching presented in some centers and seminars indicates that confessional matters are without importance.[332] In other cases confessional matters are important enough for some to propagate them in "supposedly 'ecumenical groups.'"[333] The Puerto Rican Catholic bishops did not hesitate to say that the competent diocesan committee "will publicly denounce, if it should be necessary, any groups or leaders who propagate Protestant or non-Catholic ideas."[334]

Under the pejorative title of "Unionism," the Missouri Synod Lutherans were reminded that agreement on the theology of the Holy Spirit or shared experience of baptism in the Holy Spirit is not sufficient basis for Christian fellowship. Such a basis exists only when there is "agreement in the doctrine of the gospel, in *all* its articles, and in the right use of the holy sacraments. . . ."[335]

In the past many classical Pentecostals belonged to that same theological stream which saw ecumenical activity as a man-made attempt at ecclesiastical mergers. The Executive Presbytery of the Assemblies of God in the United States reflected this tradition when it declared that unity does not have an organizational expression. Rather, the unity created in and by the Spirit transcends all now existing and all future organizational structures. What is to be promoted is fidelity to scriptural principles; what is to be avoided is a denominational narrowness which excludes true Christians.[336]

At the international level the Baptists had grave reservations about a form of Christian life which primarily follows para-church channels. Persons cross denominational lines and "tend to create quasi-denominations of their own, at least in embryo."[337] One result of this process is the diversion of energies and resources away from Baptist projects "in inverse ratio to the extent of involvement with the charismatic movement."[338] Baptists also recognize that denominations do not demand exclusive or absolute loyalty.

Both the Re-reformed in Holland and the Roman Catholics at the international level called attention to the flow of persons from these churches to classical Pentecostal churches and to charismatic nondenominational groups,[339] a flow which is not unrelated to the inability of some to find in their own churches the spiritual food and community they seek. In the case of Roman Catholics, this flow is not directly tied to the rise of the Catholic charismatic renewal. The flow predates the Catholic renewal. Making a pragmatic judgment rather than a strictly theological one, some Roman Catholics abandon the church in which they think, rightly or wrongly, they can find neither food nor community. The flow is not, however, a one-way street. Some classical Pentecostals and Protestants who are exposed in a Roman Catholic context to a vibrant, vital Christian life, communitarian in character, are drawn, without proselytism, to become Roman Catholics.[340]

DANGEROUS MEMORIES OF THE PAST

In assessing the ecumenical impact of the charismatic renewal, a WCC advisory committee expressed astonishment that an explicitly ecumenical organization such as the WCC took longer to recognize the necessity of studying the renewal than did the Vatican.[341] In dealing with the renewal, the churches and the ecumenical movement will be confronted with "dangerous memories of their past," namely, they come face to face with groups who do that which the churches have always talked about, bring Christians together in a real community.[342] Does this not, asked the advisory group, at least raise the question whether the church today is called to do what it has always said it should do?

Given the growth of prophetic independent churches in Africa and of classical Pentecostalism in South America, the charismatic renewal may well be the instrument for spreading the ecumenical movement to the Christian communities on those two continents which have so far kept aloof. Often misinformed and isolated by lack of significant contact, they have looked with suspicion and mistrust on such world bodies as the WCC. Perhaps the intercultural abyss can be spanned by the liturgies of the charismatic renewal,[343] whose unitive character has already been noted. The sense of presence and of the sacred, the spontaneity, the depth of praise, the vibrant music, and, most especially, the realized community are ecumenical points of contact between cultural and ecclesiological expressions which are vastly different.

SOCIAL ACTION: MAKING THE WORLD COME OF AGE OR FINDING GOD

The stance of those in the renewal on the socio-political implications of the gospel was in large part a reaction to what was perceived as an overemphasis on social involvement, as though social action were the whole of the gospel. In this dominantly socio-political view of the gospel, there is little time or importance given to prayer, worship, biblical preaching.[344] Conscious and unconscious attitudes in the renewal are formed by the rejection of such a view of the gospel message.

When the documents spoke on the social implications of the gospel, they almost unanimously faulted the charismatic renewal. Some groups are indifferent to the church's active involvement in the world,[345] in fact have lost the faith responsibility for the world.[346] In such circumstances openness to the Spirit "can easily degenerate into an unacknowledged desire to seek compensation for the disappointments of everyday life."[347] Where this dominant tendency to self-centeredness is present, prayer groups and communities become ghettos, closed circles providing a few hours of escape from reality.[348] Here witness means personal and communitarian housekeeping within a limited horizon, with emphasis on changing one's own personal life style. In prayers of petition global problems (war, hunger, oppression, etc.) are often taken as themes, but "the acute socio-ethical engagement of the church is mostly looked upon with skeptical eyes. One applauds the 'small steps,' one's own behavior, and helping the immediate situation with one's means."[349] A truncated vision of the gospel might account for the lack of interest in the poor by the charismatic renewal.[350]

In its own defense the charismatic community says that "it must be certain that the Spirit is leading them to deal with a specific situation."[351] Obviously one needs to discern whether the necessary gifts are present in the community to engage in programs of social development, but it is also true that the selective posture could easily become an excuse for non-involvement.[352] Dom Helder Camara, who saw the only thing necessary to revolutionize the world was for Christians to live and spread the gospel with real conviction, made it a matter of entreaty that those in the renewal "never use prayer as a pretext for neglecting social and apostolic action."[353]

SOCIAL INVOLVEMENT AS A DEMAND OF PERSONAL RENEWAL

In opposition to what is seen as the exaggerated engagement of the church in social affairs, many in the renewal concentrate on the renewal of the individual as a necessary presupposition to the renewal of society.[354] Taking the same point of departure, the Catholic bishops of the Antilles saw personal renewal as that which should move persons toward service of the community, in particular, toward "the liberation and development of all their brothers and sisters."[355] The Spirit does not lead us out of the world. Rather "he tightens the knots of the world on our hearts."[356] Charismatic groups should be springboards for plunging into the world.[357] While much concerned about prayer, the center of the renewal is action.[358] Though the imperative that such action be directed to social structures, and not just to individual cases, cannot be proof-texted from the New Testament,[359] the claim is undeniable. Any Christian movement of prophetic protest must take the social protest of the Old Testament prophets seriously.[360] A look at prophetic utterance in the renewal demonstrates that it lacks this dimension of Old Testament witness.[361] Unless the cry of a prophet is heard in the church, many, especially the young, will abandon her and turn to violence and radicalization.[362]

SOCIAL INVOLVEMENT AS CONSTITUTIVE OF EVANGELIZATION

No foreshortened view of evangelization should be entertained. Christianity must evangelize the whole of man's existence, including the political.[363] Social commitment is not simply an extra moral duty; it is integral to evangelization.[364] Temptations to postpone humanization until evangelization has taken place should be resisted as vigorously as that of postponing evangelization for the sake of humanization. The Christian engages in both simultaneously.[365]

If one speaks of authenticating a movement, one can point to social awareness as one of the norms of discernment.[366] It is with this truth that the church has to confront those in the renewal as something which they have all but ignored.[367] In their turn those in the renewal, by demonstrating the joy of the Spirit-life, are a sign to the church to keep this service of the world from degenerating into a grim duty ethic.[368]

Medellin, when interpreted in a genuinely ecclesial perspective, was seen in Latin America as a form of Pentecost.[369] From a new social experience of the church (including a new contact with creation and that which is primal in other religions) new patterns of human relations can emerge, "a new form of human fellowship."[370] Cardinal Suenens, borrowing from Pope Paul VI and Puebla, spoke of a wholly new anthropology and theology which embraces the concreteness of human life, personal and social.[371] These are the points of departure for the political and social tasks of Christians. The Medellin experience of Pentecost, the new forms of fellowship which arise from it, and the new anthropology which is inspired by it, demonstrate the spiritual dimension of a fellowship which is concrete and social.[372]

How immediately this fellowship will have universal applicability is still debatable. "But it is not debatable that the world needs to see in this fellowship an alternative to its own behavior — not a life of undisturbed harmony, but of conflicts shared with mutual respect."[373] Community and fellowship, which are normed by a plurality of experiences,[374] in which are synthesized the radically transcendent and the insistently immanent,[375] are what the charismatic renewal brings to the social task. Rather than being narrowly preoccupied with special religious experiences or with pure inwardness or interiority, it should see its task as the total transformation of human life and culture according to the demands of the gospel. The fourth meeting of the Conference of the Latin American Catholic Charismatic Renewal (ECCLA) studied the Puebla document and made its own the demands of the Latin American episcopate. In order to situate the renewal in the context of the social situation in Latin America, ECCLA drew up a list of priorities for evangelization. High on that list is the integral formation of conscientious servants of the social reality who identify with its pain. According to this charismatic group, human social development, denunciation of injustice, and the liberation of the whole person are proper goals of evangelization.[376]

RENEWAL UNDER JUDGMENT

Reports from church commissions usually gave some indication of the kind of judgment they would make upon the renewal. The earlier documents were carefully tentative in character, dealing as they were with a new movement. But even the 1978 LCUSA document, which issued from a series of theological studies of greater depth than was usual for most of the statements, was not seen as a "last word."[377] The earlier documents manifested a concerted effort to be fair and open in the face of something new, unusual, and not entirely proper when judged by the norms of social acceptability. Some are surprisingly positive and affirmative in their judgment. Yet most of these earlier documents tended to be either negative or to have a non-specific atmospheric negativity. With some notable exceptions, later documents are generally more positive and permissive, without neglecting to list the possible areas of abuse and excess.

For a variety of reasons the Baptists, both locally and internationally, as well as the Church of the Nazarene, appealed against the charismatic renewal to church doctrine, practice, and tradition.[378] A "seek not — forbid not" stance was taken by the Christian and Missionary Alliance.[379]

Though guarded and hesitant the Presbyterian and Reformed churches have generally arrived at positive conclusions. The report of the United Presbyterian Church in the United States in 1970 was essentially favorable in its evaluation, though it focused almost exclusively on baptism in the Holy Spirit and tongues. In Canada the Presbyterian Church concluded in 1976 that the charismatic renewal "is evidence that God is at work in His Church."[380] The Dutch Reformed Church in South Africa asked that the negative aspects of the renewal not blind anyone to the real elements of spirituality found there,[381] nor should the church move against those in the renewal from impure motives.[382] While remaining critical the restraint "must not mislead the church so that the presence of the Spirit himself can no longer be noticed."[383] The renewal presents questions which demand a new look at the Scriptures.[384] In its formal resolutions the Dutch Reformed Church urged its ministers "to present the full counsel of God with great faithfulness. ". . . Naturally, special attention should also be given to the Holy Spirit, his Person and Work."[385]

The Mennonites in the United States judged the over-all contribution of the renewal to be positive and, whatever its future course, one should recognize "the authentic hand of God in it."[386]

The history of the charismatic renewal is in some sense rooted in

Methodism. The renewal posed to European Methodists the question of the nature of the Christian life which within Methodism had given rise to a positive struggle between a life dominated by Christ and the observance of legalities. The Methodists "tried to abandon legalities and were faced by the risk of abandoning everything."[387] The renewal has brought Methodism back to questions of the nature of holiness. Australian Methodists granted that there is a place for the charismatic renewal in the Methodist Church. "The Church has nothing to fear from the charismatic movement, but rather has much to gain from it. . . ."[388]

Partly for historical reasons the Lutheran judgment has been more ambiguous. The Lutheran Church — Missouri Synod was highly critical of the renewal. With all of the qualifications and restrictions, her stance has been essentially a pragmatic denial of the insights which form the central witness of the renewal. The Lutheran Church in America also had serious criticism to level at the renewal but nonetheless contended that "there is no cause for Lutheran pastors or people to suggest either explicitly or implicitly that one cannot be charismatic and remain a Lutheran in good standing."[389] In Germany the Lutheran bishops recognized that through the renewal in the parishes "God is laying claim to the total man — his thought, his feelings, his activities."[390] To set aside this claim is to reject the central meaning of life. "Therefore we pray that God will pursue his work of renewing his church — also in and through the charismatic movement."[391] This more positive stance might be due to the greater stress among those in the Lutheran renewal in Germany on integration and theological reflection, so that the renewal is not over against the church.

The Ethiopian Mekane Yesus Church, which belongs to the Lutheran tradition, concluded that despite misunderstandings which arose between older and younger members of the church and the want of scripturally based teaching, the church had to be "open to it [the renewal], see it as a blessing and guide it according to the Word of God."[392]

The LCUSA document counseled openness to the new insights which the renewal brings to the churches, while recalling that openness without discrimination is irresponsible. The Lutheran charismatics do not hold that their message is the whole counsel of God. "Their goal is to see a separate 'movement' fade out as its message is integrated into the life of the church."[393] Prejudice and suspicion should not typify one's reaction to the new and unfamiliar. "Lutheran charismatics are friends, neighbors, fellow-members of the body of Christ. All Lutherans should relate to them in a positive, pastoral way. Rejection and hostility cannot be the way of wisdom and love."[394] Once again, the LCUSA document did not really represent either the last word or the consensus of those involved in the study. For instance, one person refused to identify with the document solely because of the inclusion of the sentence "The movement should be allowed to develop."[395]

An early (1963) report of the commission appointed by Episcopal Bishop James Pike of the diocese of California was concerned about the fundamentalism among lay participants in the renewal and noted that speaking in tongues is not *per se* a religious phenomenon. Moreover the same verbalization is found among those suffering from schizophrenia and hysteria. But the over-all judgment was positive. "As part of the initiatory process of entering the Christian community, as part of one's ongoing private devotional life, and as one aspect of public worship, albeit carefully limited, glossolalia has biblical precedent, even if there is no scriptural warrant for making it normative for all Christians, then or now."[396] The inclusion of tongues in Christian initiation is theologically significant. At this stage the judgment on the renewal was positive even though seen almost uniquely as a tongues' movement. Bishop Pike's pastoral letter which labeled the movement as "heresy in embryo" was among the more harsh judgments.[397] Beyond this, statements from Episcopalians in the United States and at the international level tended to be generic, taking cognizance of the renewal's existence, recalling that God moves in new ways and in new movements, pointing out that the renewal needs the balance and discipline which the total life of the church presents.[398]

A much more detailed examination was made in Australia. There the Anglican Church concluded that one of the reasons why those in the renewal have difficulty living within the context of the church is that the movement has brought with it the ethos of the classical Pentecostal churches, which is not essential to the beliefs and experiences of the charismatic movement within the major denominations. Where the distinctive elements of the renewal were considered essential, continued coexistence in the same church would be difficult, and the possibility that one would be best advised to leave the congregation and go elsewhere was envisaged.[399] The possibility of continued fellowship would flow from two things: the recognition that those in the charismatic renewal and those not identified with the movement are one in Christ and a readiness "not to make neo-Pentecostal distinctiveness the test of fellowship."[400]

Within Roman Catholicism the conclusions have been generally positive, but still a wide diversity persisted. The documents heaviest with controversy came from Latin America.[401] The 1972 statement of the Puerto Rican bishops was quite defensive, concentrating mostly on problem areas. They were reluctant to accept in its totality the 1969 report from a committee of bishops in the United States. Their considerations did not lead them at that time "to reprove the movement."[402] Though the 1977 report of the Puerto Rican bishops was far more positive and supportive, the bishops decided to neither approve nor disapprove of the renewal.[403] Even as late as 1977 the Argentinian bishops' statement was more regulatory than affirmative.[404] In Costa Rica there was a guarded acceptance. However, the bishops linked their statement with what they judged to be the aggressive proselytism by classical Pentecostal groups.[405] The common elements in Catholic charismatic groups and in classical Pentecostalism, as well as the ecumenical contacts, prompted this linkage in the bishops' statement. The survey of Brazilian bishops showed them puzzled, seeking more information, but on the whole, manifesting an attitude of support and encouragement.[406]

As general secretary of CELAM, Archbishop Trujillo expressed a wish that there be in the church a pluralism of experiences, including the charismatic. What exercised the Latin American church the past decades had been the conflicting views of the church's social and religious apostolate. The charismatic renewal presented a good occasion to demonstrate that a synthesis was possible between the transcendent and the immanent.[407] At Puebla, which was dominated by the tensions arising out of a lack of such a synthesis, the Latin American bishops recorded the satisfaction Pope Paul VI had shown in the renewal and its positive results; joyful prayer, intimate union with God, faithfulness to the Lord, and a profound communion of souls.[408] These remarks were made in the context of the life of the Spirit with its demands of love, sacrifice, and justice.[409]

The very first document to issue from any committee of Roman Catholic bishops appeared in 1969 in the United States. At that time the bishops concluded that the movement, theologically, had legitimate reasons for existing, that it should not be inhibited but be allowed to develop.[410] In 1975 a second statement seemed to be more reserved but closed with the sentence, "We encourage those who already belong and we support the positive and desirable directions of the renewal."[411] In the same year the Australian bishops called attention to the firm Catholic character of the renewal in the church and brought their reflections to an end with the observation that "at this point of time it appears to bear much fruit in the lives of many of our Catholic people."[412]

Three of the most positive Catholic statements came from the Canadian bishops, the Antilles Episcopal Conference, and the Belgian bishops. The Canadian bishops averted to the problem areas but concluded that "like every living organism, it [the charismatic renewal] has growing pains and this should not surprise us."[413] They were sure of the aptitude of those in the renewal to act as a leaven in their own communities, an aptitude of which the bishops had already received many proofs. The renewal was seen as "a hymn of whole-hearted trust in the all-powerful presence of the Spirit in the world. Its expansion across our country casts the light of hope on new horizons towards which the Spirit is irresistibly drawing the Church in Canada."[414]

The Antilles Episcopal Conference was convinced that the renewal was "very beneficial for those involved and for the Church."[415] Not unaware of the dangers to be avoided, the bishops nevertheless pronounced themselves "glad about these manifestations of the Spirit" and they encouraged their people "to be open to them and to participate as the Spirit leads them."[416] "We wish to give it [the charismatic renewal] public encouragement and assure it of our approval."[417]

There are no explicit recommendations of the renewal in the statement of the Belgian bishops, but the whole document, even while recognizing the problem areas, is very supportive of a movement which is significant, among other things, "because of the intensity of life to which it calls."[418]

These patterns manifest some of the ways in which the churches have reacted to the charismatic renewal. Varied in the extreme though they have been, there is a general development, with notable exceptions, toward more acceptance of the major ideals of the renewal as consistent with, and, according to some, even demanded by the normal Christian life. Prophetic, experiential, back-to-the-source movements challenge, call into question, demand, accuse, and occasionally give comfort. No one would say that they fit like a glove on ecclesiastical structures. The documents would indicate that the churches are somewhat at a loss as to what to do with "the pietistic euphoria," as the Belgian document calls it.[419] Even while wincing at the force of the judgments brought against them, while objecting to what is seen as the acned righteousness of the objectors, while pointing out what they judge as the excesses in the renewal, the churches have generally reacted with generosity and calm. Those documents which come from the renewal indicate that the charismatic movement is unrepentant about its bold witness, receives criticism with the air of being misunderstood, desires to attain some maturity in theological reflection, wants to remain in and of the churches, looks for acceptance but fears it, and refuses domestication. The struggle goes on.

KILIAN MCDONNELL

1. 2:70, 419 (*see also* 1:20, 286).
2. 2:43, 57.
3. 2:43, 58.
4. 2:48, 101.
5. 3:8, 267, 268.
6. 1:30, 504.
7. 1:30, 503, 504.
8. 2:56, 218 (*see also* 1:30, 508).
9. 2:70, 418, 419.
10. 3:8, 190.
11. 2:63, 339, 340.
12. 2:70, 420, 421.
13. 3:2, 12.
14. 1:30, 500.
15. 2:38, 10.
16. 3:6, 80.
17. 2:65, 352.
18. 2:58, 259.
19. 1:30, 499.
20. 2:61, 298.
21. 2:41, 28.
22. 1:30, 499, 500.
23. 2:54, 189.
24. 3:4, 72.
25. 1:36, 575.
26. 2:72, 464 (*see also* 1:16, 213; 1:28, 447; 2:58, 258).
27. 2:58, 258 (*see also* 1:16, 213; 1:30, 505, 506; 2:80, 530).
28. 3:3, 27 (*see also* 2:41, 35; 2:58, 258; 2:72, 465).
29. 2:41, 29.
30. 2:63, 344 (*see also* 2:57, 253).
31. 3:3, 63, 64.
32. 2:67, 369, 370.

33. 1:14, 153, 154 (*see also* 2:66, 362, 363).
34. 2:68, 378.
35. 3:3, 17 (*see also* 1:25, 372; 2:71, 452).
36. 3:8, 193, 194.
37. 2:70, 418.
38. *Ibid.*
39. 3:1, 8.
40. 2:46, 94.
41. 2:61, 298 (*see also* 2:59, 269).
42. 2:70, 423.
43. 2:70, 422, 423 (*see also* 1:28, 448).
44. 2:70, 421.
45. 1:8, 100.
46. *Ibid.* (*see also* 2:75, 498).
47. 1:1, 7 (*see also* 2:80, 529).
48. 2:66, 362 (*see also* 2:64, 347).
49. 2:62, 315.
50. 2:62, 313.
51. 2:62, 321.
52. 1:34, 554; 2:40, 17.
53. 2:71, 446.
54. 2:40, 17.
55. 1:14, 154.
56. 1:14, 177.
57. 2:63, 344 (*see also* 1:28, 448).
58. 2:53, 181.
59. 2:65, 353 (*see also* 1:24, 367; 2:64, 347).
60. 2:72, 470–474.
61. 2:46, 93, 94.
62. 1:25, 372 (*see also* 1:2, 13).
63. 3:7, 142.
64. 2:46, 93.
65. *Ibid.*
66. "Charismatische Bewegung in der DDR: Bericht über Phänomene und Aktivitäten charismatischer Prägung in den evangelischen Kirchen in der DDR," Theologische Studienabteilung beim Bund der Evangelischen Kirchen in der DDR, *Beiträge*, A, Gemeinde, August 3, 1978, 89.
67. *Ibid.*
68. *Ibid.*, 24.
69. 2:72, 473, 474 (*see also* 2:74, 488).
70. 2:52, 150.
71. 2:46, 94.
72. 2:55, 198.
73. 1:30, 502.
74. 1:25, 373.
75. 1:33, 545.
76. 2:63, 333.
77. 3:3, 35, 36 (*see also* 2:80, 529).
78. *Ibid.*
79. 2:71, 443.

80. 2:71, 442, 443.
81. 2:71, 443.
82. 1:23, 349.
83. 2:72, 481.
84. 1:35, 570.
85. 2:46, 87, 88.
86. 1:9, 105.
87. 2:70, 423, 424.
88. 3:9, 289.
89. 2:46, 87, 88.
90. 2:71, 432.
91. 1:35, 569.
92. 2:72, 469.
93. 1:15, 209.
94. 2:49, 113.
95. 2:46, 86.
96. 3:4, 76.
97. 2:63, 330 (*see also* 1:23, 335, 336).
98. 2:53, 153, 154 (*see also* 2:61, 295; 2:74, 488; 2:78, 514).
99. 2:46, 88.
100. *Ibid.*
101. 3:5, 78.
102. 2:71, 436; 3:3, 33.
103. 2:72, 468 (*see also* 2:80, 525).
104. 1:26, 392 (*see also* 1:23, 332–337; 1:33, 545; 2:40, 17; 2:53, 174; 2:70, 399; 3:6, 81).
105. 1:18, 270.
106. 1:29, 468, 469.
107. 2:60, 285.
108. 1:34, 553, 554; 2:52, 149.
109. 3:9, 288.
110. 1:31, 512; 1:35, 571; 2:55, 204; 2:61, 297.
111. 2:38, 8.
112. 3:3, 27, 28.
113. 2:46, 89.
114. 3:3, 41, 42 (*see also* 1:21, 311; 1:33, 529, 545).
115. 2:69, 388.
116. 1:32, 518.
117. 2:44, 79; 2:63, 330.
118. 2:62, 312.
119. 1:34, 554.
120. 1:25, 372.
121. 2:40, 17.
122. 1:34, 564.
123. 1:23, 351; 2:62, 312.
124. 1:21, 309.
125. 1:21, 311.
126. 2:61, 296, 297.
127. 1:33, 529.
128. 2:69, 383.

129. 1:31, 513, 514 (*see also* 2:58, 262; 3:6, 80).

130. 2:66, 363.

131. 2:44, 78; 2:66, 361.

132. 1:35, 569.

133. 1:34, 559 (*see also* 1:23, 351).

134. 2:53, 163.

135. 2:59, 268.

136. 2:52, 149 (*see also* 1:23, 351).

137. 1:35, 571.

138. 2:61, 296.

139. 1:33, 545 (*see also* 2:44, 70; 2:70, 403; Tormod Engelsviken, "Report on the Pentecostal Movement in Ethiopia and Its Relation to the Evangelical Church Mekane Yesus," 9.

140. 1:34, 554.

141. 1:21, 305.

142. 1:5, 61.

143. 1:26, 380, 389 (*see also* 2:71, 446, 447).

144. 2:71, 447.

145. 2:10, 111.

146. 2:71, 446.

147. 1:26, 431.

148. 1:4, 41.

149. 1:12, 137 (*see also* 1:7, 84).

150. 1:1, 8 (*see also* 1:14, 176).

151. 2:62, 311.

152. 1:23, 347.

153. 1:33, 519.

154. 1:9, 107 (*see also* 1:33, 532, 545; 2:46, 91; 2:57, 249; 2:61, 302).

155. 2:46, 91; 2:55, 206.

156. 2:70, 405.

157. 2:55, 208.

158. 2:52, 149 (*see also* 2:80, 529).

159. 1:14, 173 (*see also* 2:70, 408).

160. 2:46, 90.

161. 2:70, 408.

162. *Ibid.*

163. 2:70, 407–408.

164. 1:10, 110.

165. 2:58, 264.

166. 1:33, 542.

167. 1:30, 497.

168. 3:3, 55.

169. 3:9, 288.

170. *Ibid.*

171. 2:70, 408.

172. 2:54, 187.

173. 1:14, 176.

174. 2:63, 335.

175. 1:33, 540.

176. 1:33, 542.

177. 1:26, 394.
178. 2:70, 409.
179. 2:71, 444.
180. 1:13, 143 (*see also* 1:33, 541; 2:46, 93; 2:61, 305; 2:62, 313; 2:80, 527).
181. 2:61, 304, 305.
182. 1:33, 541.
183. 2:42, 43.
184. 1:14, 176.
185. 2:70, 407.
186. 2:46, 93.
187. 2:70, 404–409.
188. 3:9, 290.
189. 3:3, 28–30.
190. 2:71, 448.
191. 2:55, 208, 209.
192. 2:55, 208.
193. "Charismatische Bewegung in der DDR," 52.
194. 2:42, 36, 43 (*see also* 2:43, 67; 2:44, 80; 2:54, 197).
195. 1:35, 569 (*see also* 2:46, 91; 2:54, 185; 2:69, 384).
196. 2:58, 264 (*see also* 2:43, 67).
197. "Charismatische Bewegung in der DDR," 52.
198. 1:10, 108 (*see also* 2:46, 91).
199. 2:54, 194.
200. 2:55, 205, 206 (*see also* 2:80, 526).
201. 2:61, 303.
202. 3:9, 290.
203. "Charismatische Bewegung in der DDR," 52.
204. 2:70, 419.
205. 1:9, 107.
206. 2:70, 420.
207. 2:69, 384.
208. 1:12, 135.
209. 2:57, 239.
210. 1:6, 68.
211. 1:20, 286 (*see also* 2:58, 262; 2:61, 297; 2:63, 336; 2:70, 411; 2:80, 529; "Charismatische Bewegung in der DDR," 46).
212. 1:5, 58 (*see also* 1:7, 84; 2:54, 195).
213. 2:70, 411.
214. 1:10, 111.
215. 1:5, 58 (*see also* 3:6, 80).
216. 1:15, 207–210.
217. 2:49, 104–114.
218. 3:3, 56–58.
219. 1:7, 84.
220. 1:7, 85.
221. 1:7, 86.
222. 1:18, 237.
223. 1:18, 234.
224. 1:21, 316 (*see also* 1:31, 514).
225. 2:70, 421.

226. 1:17, 221.

227. 2:50, 116.

228. 1:16, 218.

229. 3:6, 80.

230. 2:60, 283 (cf. *also* 2:77, 508).

231. 1:26, 396.

232. 2:69, 385.

233. 1:34, 558.

234. 1:33, 541.

235. 1:3, 58.

236. 2:46, 91.

237. 2:63, 337.

238. *Ibid.*

239. 1:11, 122.

240. 1:11, 126.

241. 1:26, 431 (*see also* 2:62, 316).

242. 2:70, 415.

243. 2:70, 416, 417.

244. 1:4, 44, 45 (*see also* 1:11, 127).

245. 1:4, 48.

246. 2:70, 416.

247. 1:11, 128.

248. 1:12, 130.

249. 2:40, 17 (*see also* 1:14, 184).

250. 2:70, 416 (*see also* 1:26, 407).

251. 1:11, 129.

252. 1:26, 432.

253. 2:45, 83.

254. 3:9, 288.

255. 1:11, 120.

256. 1:18, 241.

257. *Ibid.*

258. 2:49, 106–108.

259. 2:67, 370.

260. 2:71, 433.

261. 3:9, 290.

262. *Ibid.*

263. 3:6, 81.

264. 2:49, 106 (*see also* 2:47, 100; 2:79, 519).

265. 1:25, 370 (*see also* 1:32, 518; 2:46, 91; 2:54, 194; 2:55, 202; 2:57, 248, 249; 2:67, 368; 2:71, 433, 434; 2:80, 523).

266. 3:1, 4.

267. 1:27, 443 (*see also* 2:63, 344).

268. 3:7, 112, 113.

269. 3:8, 223, 224.

270. 3:9, 285.

271. 3:9, 286.

272. 3:9, 285.

273. *Ibid.*

274. 2:72, 478.

275. 2:58, 267.
276. 2:52, 150 (*see also* 2:71, 452).
277. 2:72, 478.
278. 2:55, 202.
279. 3:8, 206, 207 (*see also* 2:38, 5; 2:67, 373, 374).
280. 2:38, 6.
281. 1:29, 485.
282. 2:53, 181.
283. 2:71, 451.
284. 2:44, 70.
285. 1:14, 191–198 (*see also* 2:58, 266; 2:70, 397; 2:72, 467).
286. 2:69, 385.
287. 2:69, 385, 386 (*see also* 2:58, 267; 2:64, 347, 348).
288. 2:69, 285, 286.
289. 2:71, 441.
290. 3:8, 204–206 (*see also* 2:58, 259).
291. "Charismatische Bewegung in der DDR," 59.
292. 3:5, 78.
293. 2:52, 149 (*see also* 2:49, 108).
294. "Charismatische Bewegung in der DDR," 76, 78.
295. 2:52, 149 (*see also* 2:71, 434).
296. 2:58, 259 (*see also* 2:65, 352; 2:79, 521; 3:3, 53, 54).
297. 3:8, 194–196.
298. 3:9, 287.
299. 1:26, 437.
300. 2:63, 340.
301. 2:58, 262.
302. 2:63, 339.
303. 2:46, 88 (*see also* 2:69, 383).
304. 2:58, 261.
305. 2:58, 266.
306. 2:71, 443, 444.
307. 3:3, 27.
308. "Charismatische Bewegung in der DDR," 71.
309. 2:54, 194.
310. 2:43, 58.
311. Tormod Engelsviken, "Report on the Pentecostal Movement in Ethiopia,"
3 (*see also* 2:79, 517).
312. 2:58, 265.
313. *Ibid.*
314. 2:46, 95 (*see also* 2:58, 261; 2:67, 375).
315. 2:49, 110.
316. 3:4, 73 (*see also* 2:76, 506).
317. 2:72, 471.
318. 3:8, 223.
319. 2:69, 389 (*see also* 2:74, 489; 2:76, 508).
320. 3:3, 54.
321. 2:39, 14.
322. 3:7, 84–86.
323. 3:8, 259.

324. 2:49, 110 (*see also* 2:64, 348).
325. 2:46, 96.
326. 2:70, 424.
327. 2:61, 301.
328. *Ibid.*
329. *Ibid.*
330. 2:61, 301, 302.
331. 3:8, 196–210.
332. 2:72, 475.
333. 2:67, 375, 376.
334. 2:67, 376 (*see also* 2:76, 505).
335. 1:23, 353.
336. 1:22, 320.
337. 3:6, 81.
338. *Ibid.*
339. 1:14, 151 (cf. *also* 2:76, 506; 3:8, 233–235).
340. 3:8, 235.
341. 3:9, 284.
342. 3:9, 285.
343. *Ibid.*
344. 1:34, 561.
345. 2:46, 94, 95.
346. 2:72, 478.
347. 2:46, 95.
348. *Ibid.* (*see also* 2:80, 530).
349. "Charismatische Bewegung in der DDR," 72.
350. 2:65, 351, 352.
351. 1:34, 561, 562.
352. *Ibid.*
353. 3:10, 329, 343.
354. 2:60, 286, 288 (*see also* 2:47, 99).
355. 2:58, 266 (*see also* 1:19, 283).
356. 1:14, 167 (*see also* 2:80, 528).
357. 2:46, 95.
358. 2:46, 96.
359. 1:34, 561.
360. 3:10, 323.
361. "Charismatische Bewegung in der DDR," 48.
362. 3:10, 328.
363. 3:10, 350.
364. 3:10, 312.
365. 3:10, 342.
366. 2:48, 102 (*see also* 2:67, 371).
367. 2:44, 80.
368. 1:34, 561.
369. 2:66, 360.
370. 3:9, 287.
371. 3:10, 350.
372. *Ibid.*
373. 3:9, 287.

Introduction

374. 2:66, 364.
375. Ibid.
376. 2:79, 520.
377. 2:71, 431.
378. 1:16, 218; 1:17, 221; 2:50, 116; 3:6, 80 (see also 1:8, 99).
379. 1:6, 67.
380. 2:57, 246.
381. 2:70, 420.
382. 2:70, 426.
383. 2:70, 420.
384. 2:70, 397.
385. 2:70, 427, 428.
386. 2:63, 341.
387. 2:55, 205.
388. 1:28, 448.
389. 1:34, 562.
390 2:59, 269.
391. Ibid.
392. 2:53, 178.
393. 2:71, 450.
394. 2:71, 449.
395. 2:71, 431, 449.
396. 1:7, 84. This report is interpreted too negatively in my book *Charismatic Renewal and the Churches* (Seabury, New York, 1976), 46–49.
397. 1:8, 100.
398. 1:3, 21; 3:5, 77, 78.
399. 1:26, 439.
400. 1:26, 440.
401. 1:24, 2:47; 2:64; 2:65; 2:67.
402. 1:24, 368.
403. 2:67, 373.
403. 2:64, 345–348.
405. 2:76, 506.
406. 2:65, 353.
407. 2:66, 364.
408. 2:78, 514.
409. 2:78, 513.
410. 1:15, 210.
411. 2:49, 111.
412. 2:45, 83.
413. 2:46, 96.
414. Ibid.
415. 2:58, 258.
416. Ibid.
417. 2:58, 260.
418. 2:75, 493.
419. 2:75, 501.

Presence, Power, Praise

THE SPEAKING IN TONGUES AND THE CHURCH

Though there were scattered instances of persons in the historic churches receiving the baptism in the Holy Spirit during the latter half of the 1960s, the beginnings of the charismatic renewal in these churches usually dates from the events which took place in St. Mark's Episcopal Church, Van Nuys, California, in 1959 and 1960. Through a vicar and lay persons in his parish, the rector of St. Mark's, Dennis Bennett, received the baptism in November 1959. By April 1960, seventy members of his parish had received the Pentecostal experience. During a Palm Sunday service Bennett explained these events to his parishioners. One of his curates resigned in public protest, another declared that the Episcopal Church could not tolerate such matters, and the church treasurer demanded his resignation. Two days later Bennett did resign and shortly after that Bishop Francis Bloy of the Los Angeles diocese banned any more speaking in tongues at functions held under church auspices.

In April 1960 a commission appointed by Bishop Bloy reported on the outbreak of tongues. The commission had studied the New Testament evidence, the attitudes of the historic church, and contemporary examples of glossolalia. Three basic approaches to glossolalia (Catholic, Protestant, and that of Enthusiasm) were described, an evaluation was given and the report closed with some remarks on discernment.

The report identified the tongue-speaker as an enthusiast who "experiences his own conversion and the resultant spiritual glow rather than Jesus Christ and His Church. When he bears his testimony, it is to speak of his new-found happiness rather than to confess that Jesus Christ is Lord." The commission had doubts regarding the normality, in psychological terms, of the phenomena as it is related in Acts 2. The miracle of Pentecost, whereby tongues are understood by those who would not otherwise understand them, "would be an interesting and helpful phenomenon for missionaries if it were a dependable and verifiable procedure. No historical evidence supports this possibility." The commission held to a theological dispensationalism which contends that tongues belong to the church in her beginnings but not to the church in her continuing history. Further, tongues belong to a stage of spiritual infancy which is left behind in the process of maturing: "The abnormal physical and psychological phenomena, which attracted so much attention on the day of Pentecost, tended to disappear within the Body of Christ, and at the last seemed to have died out. The Whitsunday phenomena could be compared to a scaffolding surrounding a new edifice.

Once the edifice (the Church) had been completed, the scaffolding became unnecessary and was discarded. . . . The glossolalia occurred in the infancy of the Church. With her growth and maturity the Church wisely discarded the marks of infancy."

INTRODUCTION

A great revival of concern for the person of the Holy Spirit and His function in the Church has been witnessed in the past twenty or thirty years. Popular interest has been practically attracted to the "gifts" of the Holy Spirit, manifestations of the working of the spirit that could be taken as "signs" of His presence. One particular aspect of this concern for visible, verifiable evidence of the Spirit in operation has been the "Gift of Tongues", technically known as "glossolalia".

1. *The Varieties of Glossolalia in the New Testament*

A. EVIDENCES

With the exception of a passing reference to the Tongues in the Appendix to St. Mark (16:17), they are mentioned only in Acts 2 and 1-Corinthians. The passages are as follows: Acts 2:4, 11; 10:46; 19:6; 1-Corinthians 12:10, 28, 30; 13:1; 14:2-5, 13, 18, 21f.; 14:26ff.; 14:39.

B. THE EXPERIENCE OF PENTECOST

Contemporary protagonists of the "gifts" of talking in tongues state that the experience at Pentecost and present-day glossolalia are one and the same.[1] The Pentecost experience, although not analyzed by the author of Acts, enabled persons of diverse linguistic backgrounds to hear the wonderful works of God in a language that they themselves could understand; but most remarkable is the fact that the Apostles were able to articulate the Gospel in a more dynamic and effective manner than before Pentecost, as evidenced by the fact that about three thousand were converted (Acts 2:41). There are a few examples in the history of the missionary expansion of Christianity where similar claims have been made, but in such cases the evidence is of a highly legendary nature.

However, to confirm attention to inquiries whether the gift of tongues constitutes a case of spiritual mass hysteria or a sudden access to miraculous linguistic power is to miss the essential

Speaking in Tongues and the Church

significance of the scene. Acts 2 represents the descent of the Spirit of the Living God upon the Christian community, thereby endowing it with supernatural powers, constituting it a divine extension of the incarnation. In other words, Whitsuntide signifies the birth-hour of the Church (Fr. Heiler). We might perhaps also agree with Bishop Gore who states that "the gift of tongues represents by anticipation the catholicism of the coming centuries."[2]

C. GLOSSOLALIA AFTER PENTECOST

The second or unintelligible variety of glossolalia is argued to be testified to in Acts 8:14-19, when Simon Magnus wants to buy the gift because he sees what has happened to the Samaritans. Similarly Acts 15:7-8 is used as evidence that when St. Peter spoke to Cornelius and his household, the Holy Spirit caused the hearers to speak with tongues, and the Apostles were obliged to baptize because of the Pentecostal evidence. In Ephesus, when St. Paul preached and laid his hands on the newly baptized disciples (Acts 19:1-7), "they spoke with tongues and prophesied". Finally, the well-known passages in the First Epistle to the Corinthians testify to the speaking in an unknown tongue, together with St. Paul's apparent disapproval in the Church.

Nine spiritual gifts of *charismata*, not directly common to all Christians, are enumerated in the 12th chapter of First Corinthians, and it is easy to discover in the list a certain order. The first two are endowments of the Christian teacher which are rarely found in the same individual: one is distinguished by his insight into Divine mysteries (sofia), another by the intellectual breadth or acuteness which creates a scientific theology (gnosis). The next three belong to the thaumaturgic side of early Christianity, the faith which could move mountains (12:9), the healing powers, the working of physical signs and wonders; lastly prophecy with its complementary power to distinguish the true prophet from the false prophet, and "glossolalia" or speaking in tongues, with its necessary accompaniment, the ability to interpret tongues for the benefit of the Church. St. Paul makes it clear that all cannot be apostles or prophets, nor can all speak in tongues, for this would destroy the completeness, the balance, and even the efficiency of the Body of Christ. At this point there comes the great statement of St. Paul's praise of love: "But earnestly desire the higher gifts. And I will show you a still more excellent way: If I speak in the tongues of men and of angels, but have not love, I am a noisy gong, or a clanging cymbal" (1-Cor 12:31–13:1, RSV).

2. *The Attitude of the Historic Church*

Isolated examples, particularly associated with heresy and schism, can be cited. But they are remarkably few. Msgr. Ronald A. Knox notes that "perhaps the most striking thing about the claim to speak in tongues is its infrequency. All enthusiastic movements are fair to revive, in a more or less degree, the experience of Pentecost; a new outpouring of the Holy Spirit has taken place, and a chosen body of witnesses is there to attest it. . . . Accordingly, if you consult the works of reference, you will find a long Litany, copied from one encyclopedia into another, purporting to show that all enthusiastic movements have in fact given rise to glossolaly . . . Authors who have studied the matter show more caution . . . I do not mean to deny the existence of glossolaly all through the period under dispute. To speak with tongues you have not learned was, and is, a symbol of alleged diabolical possession. What does not appear is that it was ever claimed, at least on a large scale, as a symptom of divine inspiration, until the end of the seventeenth century."[3]

Msgr. Knox does not embarrass his argument with examples of St. Vincent Ferrer (1350–1419), whose travels throughout Europe required the use of languages which he could not command, but who nevertheless was supposed to be understood, by the power of the Holy Spirit. St. Francis Xavier (1506–1552), whose missionary journeys to the Orient were always requiring different languages, had a similar experience. The evidence seems doubtful since his journal testifies constantly to the difficulties he has with each new language, although it appears that he was a most accomplished and natural linguist. Both of these cases, however, clearly refer to the Pentecost more than the Corinthian experience.[4] St. Thomas Aquinas (c. 1225–1274) would say that *the gifts of the Spirit contribute to man's freedom of choice rather than take it away*. For there would be a greater loss in merit if the Spirit determined the will and worked in it by violence rather than by breathing. For this reason the Apostle wrote that "the spirits of the prophets are under the control of the prophets" (1-Cor 14:32). This is interpreted by St. Thomas Aquinas to mean that, so far as the use of the power of announcing prophecies is concerned, the spirits are subject to the will of the prophet and are not like delirious ravings. For where the spirit of the Lord is, there is liberty (2-Cor 3:17).[5] Authenticated cases of glossolalia within orthodox Christianity seem to indicate that they are, on the whole, one phase, and an ephemeral one at that, of the mystics' private "ladder of ascent" to Heaven. The life story of St. Hildegard of Bingen (1098–1179), German abbess and mystic writer, is a case in point.[6] The same can be said of Eastern Orthodoxy where glossolalia often has its beginnings in the so-called "Jesus-Prayer." (Read Fedotoy's *Treasury of Russian Spirituality*. Within Reformation Christianity there are recorded instances of glossolalia among French Huguenots (a group known as the Cevenal Prophets), among Camisards, Quakers, Methodists, schismatic Zinzendorfian Moravians, etc.

3. *Modern Glossolalia*

The major modern manifestation of glossolalia was in the so-called Catholic and Apostolic Church of Edward Irving.[7] The outbreaking of tongue-talking was in Scotland but moved to London with Irving when he assumed the pastorate of the Caledonian Church, Hutton Garden. He began with the Pauline prohibition against tongue-talking in church, but soon was interrupted during his brilliant preaching by tongue-talkers (this seems to be a recurrent pattern). He took this as evidence of God's will that the glossolalia should be allowed in the context of worship.[8] There seemed to be no inducing of the phenomenon beyond the contagion of being present in the room when the spirit-filled person began speaking. A member of Parliament thus broke out with a prophetic utterance, being unable to talk with tongues, it must be assumed: "Ye have been warned. Ah, Sanballatt! Sanballat! Sanballat! The Horonite, the Moabite, the Ammonite! Ah confederate, confederate, confederate, with the Horrite! . . ."[9]

Pentecostals date the beginning of the present-day movement at 1900 at a Bible School in Topeka, Kansas. The sole text used with the forty pupils was the Bible, and the subject of "Baptism of the Holy Ghost" was taught. The evidence for the Baptism was the gift of "Speaking in other tongues as the Spirit gives utterance."[10] The original speakers were all convinced that the languages spoken were genuine and identifiable foreign languages. Testimonies of Jewish rabbis were certified as to the tongue sometimes being in Hebrew or Hebraic cognates. Other observers testify the irrelevance of the fragments which seem to correspond with some known languages.

The widely used monograph on the subject from the viewpoint of the Assemblies of God, *Tongues like as of Holy Fire* by Robert Chandler Dalton, states his thesis as follows:

1. That the speaking in tongues as it is found in the Pentecostal movement today is in its best form identical to that found in the New Testament and in the early Church.

2. That the ability to speak in tongues and prophesy today is contingent upon an experience beyond regeneration, which is identified with the experience of the disciples at Pentecost as recorded in Acts, chapters 2, 8, and 19.

3. That this spirit-filled life found among the Pentecostal people today in its best form is the *normal* Christian experience rather than an abnormal one.

4. That what is needed today to give the Christian Church power in this rational and materialistic age, is that each individual within its fold have this spirit-filled life. This will be the beginning of a real, genuine revival.[11]

4. *Theological Considerations of Glossolalia*

We venture to state that there are three basic theological approaches to glossolalia:

A. CATHOLIC, ANGLICAN, ORTHODOX

The Catholic view is succinctly expressed in the formula echoed at Lambeth: "The Holy Spirit is the Soul of the Church." The imminent principle of the Church is found in the gifts of the Spirit, but as it is the Spirit Who bestows these gifts and makes them operative in the Church, He may fittingly be described as the animating and unifying principle of the Church. Furthermore, without an adequate concept of Grace, there can be no adequate concept of Anglicanism. For in Anglican understanding the Church with its means exists primarily for the communication of Grace in the souls of men.

B. PROTESTANT

The Protestant point of view does not recognize the imminence of indwelling of the Spirit, which is the main feature of the New Testament, and it fails to recognize the Incarnation as "the real and actual gift of the Divine life to human nature." Fr. Congar writes, "as a form of religion and of relation to Christ and in Him

Speaking in Tongues and the Church

to the Blessed Trinity, Protestantism has stopped short with John the Baptist and still awaits the fulfillment of the baptism of water and of the Spirit, and the gifts of the Spirit, first fruits of our heritage. It forgets that since John the Baptist God is Incarnate." (*Divided Christendom*, p. 91)

C. ENTHUSIASM

A third view of the relation of the Holy Spirit and the Church current especially in Western and American Christendom is known by various names, such as: enthusiasm, Schwaermerei, Spiritualism, Pentecostalism, etc. It is the view represented in its extreme form by the Anabaptists of the Reformation period. Enthusiasm exalts the sovereign freedom of the Spirit over against the Church's teaching of the Spirit channelled through the Church's means of Grace. It virtually severs the connection between the mission of the Spirit and the historical Christ. The emphasis is laid upon the immediate, subjective, experience of the Spirit in the individual rather than on his participation in the extension of the incarnation.

The enthusiast, and this includes the "speaker in tongues", experiences his own conversion and the resultant spiritual glow rather than Jesus Christ and His Church. When he bears his testimony, it is to speak of his new-found happiness rather than to confess that Jesus Christ is Lord. Enthusiasm tends to issue in "varieties of religious experiences" rather than a saving knowledge of God in Christ experienced in the redemptive fellowship of the Church. This enthusiastic viewpoint ignores completely the other New Testament doctrine that the fruits of the Spirit are the real test of the presence of the Spirit.

5. Evaluation of Glossolalia

1. The Miracle of Pentecost whereby the tongues of men are understood by others who would not otherwise understand them, would be an interesting and helpful phenomenon for missionaries if it were a dependable and verifiable procedure. No historical evidence supports this possibility.

2. The Fathers of the Church have interpreted the Pentecost experience as a single and anomalous miracle testifying to the fact of man's redemption i.e. as in the Tower of Babel man's powers of communication with one another were lost, so in the Incarnate Life of Christ and the Gift of the Holy Spirit, man's statement is testified to by the restoration — if only for a moment — of the

universal language. "There are many languages of earth, but one heavenly."

3. St. Paul deprecates the public use of glossolalia, and even where he mentions it in passing, it is associated with other competences such as the management of church finances and the gifts of healing. It has been similarly condemned on the few occasions when it has arisen in Christian history as being irrelevant.

4. "In Church I would rather speak five words with my mind in order to instruct others, than ten thousand words in a tongue" (1-Cor 14:19 RSV).

6. Discerning the Gifts of the Spirit

It is obvious to the modern Christian that man's subconscious may be touched directly either by the demonic or the Divine. In commenting on the phenomenon of glossolalia which cropped up in the England of his day, Bishop Gore stated, "the gift of tongues in itself is not necessarily the evidence of the action of God. St. Paul implies that they occurred in heathen worship. The subliminal is not always sublime.

1. "The fruits of the Spirit are the real test of the presence of the Holy Spirit. If the result of spiritual gifts is greater harmony, greater love, and greater discernment, *within the whole parish or the whole Church, then these fruits may be ascribed to the Holy Spirit.*

2. "If, on the other hand, the result of the particular manifestation in a given congregation, can be spelled out in terms of strife, division, spiritual pride ('we are better than our fellow Christians because we have the gift of tongues and they have not'), and lack of charity and the bond of peace within the whole parish of the whole Church, then it would be blasphemous to ascribe such fruits to the Holy Spirit.

3. "Though I speak with the tongues of men and of angels, and have not charity, I am become a sounding brass, or a tinkling cymbal."

The abnormal physical and psychological phenomena, which attracted so much attention on the day of Pentecost, tended to disappear within the Body of Christ, and at the last seemed to have died out. The Whitsunday phenomena could be compared to a scaffolding surrounding a new edifice. Once the edifice (the Church) has been completed, the scaffolding became unnecessary and was discarded. "When I was a child, I spake as a child . . . but when I became a man, I put away childish things" (1-Cor

Speaking in Tongues and the Church

13:11). The glossolalia occurred in the infancy of the Church. With her growth and maturity the Church wisely discarded the marks of infancy.

The Rev. Canon Enrico S. Molnar, Th.D., The Rev. John S. Gill, The Rev. Evan R. Williams, Ph.D.

FOOTNOTES AND BIBLIOGRAPHY

1. Robert Chandler Dalton, *Tongues like as Fire* (Springfield, Mo.: The Gospel Publishing House, 1945), p. 13.

2. Charles Gore, ed., *A New Commentary on Holy Scripture* (New York: Macmillan Co., 1929), p. 389.

3. Ronald A. Knox, *Enthusiasm: A Chapter in the History of Religion* (Oxford: Clarendon Press, 1950), p. 549.

4. Schaff-Herzog, *Encyclopedia of Religious Knowledge*, vide "tongues."

5. John of St. Thomas, *The Gifts of the Holy Ghost* (London; Sheed and Ward, 1951), p. 28.

6. Hildegard Von Bingen, *Wisse die Wege: Scivias* (Salzburg: Otto Mueller, 1954), p. 386.

7. George B. Cutten, *Speaking with Tongues* (Yale University Press, 1927), p. 93.

8. *Ibid.*

9. *Ibid.*, p. 102–03, quoted from Mrs. Oliphant, *Life of Irving*, pp. 307–09.

10. Dalton, p. 31.

11. *Ibid.*, p. 53.

OTHER LITERATURE CONSULTED

Emile Dermeghen, *Muhammad and the Islamic Tradition* (New York: Harper and Brothers), 1953, Contains section of glossolalia in the Sufi tradition.

F. W. Dillistone, *The Holy Spirit in the Life of Today* (Philadelphia: Westminster Press), 1957.

Charles Gore, *The Holy Spirit and the Church* (New York: Scribner's), 1924.

George S. Hendry, *The Holy Spirit in Christian Theology* (London: S.C.M. Press), 1957.

Dr. A. M. Ramsey, *The Gospel and the Catholic Church* (London), 1931.

Henry Barclay Swete, *The Holy Spirit in the New Testament* (London: Macmillan Co.), 1931.

John of St. Thomas, *The Gifts of the Holy Ghost* (London: Sheed and Ward), 1951.

Henry P. Van Dusen, *Spirit, Son and Father* (New York: Charles Scribner's), 1958.

REPORT OF THE SPECIAL COMMISSION ON GLOSSOLALIA

In 1955 a Methodist layman by the name of Dunscombe received the baptism in the Holy Spirit under classical Pentecostal influence in a small town near Fort Wayne, Indiana. Dunscombe led a series of informal prayer meetings in Oak Park, Illinois, as a result of which Fr. Richard Winkler, rector of Trinity Episcopal Church in Wheaton, Illinois, received the baptism on April 26, 1956, possibly becoming the first Episcopal clergyman to receive the baptism in the Holy Spirit. Winkler's church in Wheaton became a center of charismatic influence. To deal with the issues which arose out of this series of events, a special commission reported to Gerald Francis Burrill, bishop of Chicago, on December 12, 1960. A short introductory section is followed by a series of broad pastoral counsels and another series of six more specific guidelines. Two appendices are attached, one with the observations of three members of the commission who witnessed the phenomenon of tongues, and the other a precis of New Testament data on the subject of tongues.

The report maintained that there is a real danger that glossolalia may be exaggerated, "especially when it is viewed in isolation and separation from the wholeness of God's inspiration." The church has a pastoral obligation to protect the faithful "from any possible incursion of the irrational or pathological forces which prey upon the depths of our nature." In dealing with an expression which wells up from the profound levels of human consciousness, "where in so many forms primal evil wrestles with the urgency of redemptive good, there is always a most serious danger of delusion, and even of diabolic deception." Sectarianism is to be avoided and all Christians should submit their experience to the church, which moves through history by steps of reason, law, and institutional authority. "Reason is supremely the voice of the Holy Ghost and . . . the Holy Ghost will speak to us in the vocables of rationality," the report urged. On the other hand, the report wishes to recognize that the experience of speaking in tongues can be "unquestionably genuine." St. Paul himself believed that speaking in unknown tongues could be authentically the utterance of the Holy Spirit.

Right Reverend and Dear Sir:

In response to your commission for a study of the recent instances of "spiritual speaking" among people associated with one of the parishes of this Diocese, we respectfully submit the following statement to which we have subscribed our signatures. In addition, we attach two appendices: one marked Appendix A, setting forth the observations of three members of the commission who witnessed the phenomenon of "tongues". Appendix B is an analysis of the New Testament evidences of the phenomenon and is the work of the Reverend Canon William Nes.

From age to age the Church, in her fulfillment of the mission committed to her by our Lord, must seek with fervent effort to follow the leading of the Holy Spirit. From the point of view of history in its totality, the Church must have made plain the wholeness and the fullness of God's truth and of God's love, and it is our faith that God will give his Church power to do this. And yet at any single moment or period of time, although the wholeness and fullness of the divine revelation must be the goal and purpose of the Church, there is always the possibility of incompleteness, distortion, or exaggeration. Human weakness and fallibility are always present, to say nothing of the ever-vigorous action of sin, with consequence of ignorance, misdirected zeal, or sloth. Frequently, throughout the history of Christendom, failure or forgetfulness in one area of the spiritual life has led to reaction and excess in another, as earnest men and women seek to compensate for previous failure.

To the Church's pastors, and particularly to her chief pastors, the Bishops, our Lord has entrusted the responsibility for guiding the Church through the perilous possibilities of excess and negation, of superstition and godlessness. The shepherds must protect the flock from error, and especially from error which may carry within it the possibility of hurt and damage to the community of Christians, and to the wholeness of the Gospel committed to the Church's care.

In recent months some devout and dedicated members of the Episcopal Church in this Diocese have felt within their lives and within praying groups living the full discipline of the Church's fellowship the touch of a spiritual inspiration strikingly different in character from the usual ordinary experience of the majority of the faithful. This has manifested itself in a kind of "spiritual speaking" (to be distinguished from the "speaking with tongues" described in the second chapter of the Book of the Acts of the Apostles, for that was an utterance which conveyed significance in known and identifiable languages) [see Appendix B] reminiscent of expressions of fervor which characterized the Church of Corinth in the time of St. Paul.

Contemporary Christendom yearns for renewal, for a revival of apostolic zeal which will free the Church from bonds of what sometimes appears to be apathy and institutional rigidity. And it is evident that the Holy Spirit is indeed working within the hearts of Christians of all persuasions and in all lands to stir up a new ardor and a fresh vigor in the approach to ancient problems. In manifold outpourings of human effort, in new forms of Christian art and literature, in the cry for Christian witness in social reform and experiment, in the foundation of new types of religious orders, in revolutionary techniques of evangelism, in an almost universal resurgence of Biblical studies, in a reawakening of the laity to their vocation in the corporate work and worship of the Church, in the tremendous upsurge of the ecumenical spirit: in countless ways the voice of Christian revival has cried out in the hearts of Christian people everywhere. The Holy Ghost is, always has been and continues to be at work in his Church. The new voices of prophecy and holiness which have been speaking in these many ways and in a variety of tongues may be indications of this work.

It is not surprising, then, that small groups of sincere Christian people, gathering for deep and attentive prayer, might find their souls stirred to depths of new utterance, and might feel that the Spirit of Renewal, which is everywhere at work in Christ's Church, has touched them too. The "spiritual speaking" which has occurred in some of our parishes may possibly be understood in these terms. It is, however, the duty of the Church in its teaching and pastoral office to point out that the experience of "spiritual speaking", although apparently unusual and perhaps spectacular, is not the only way in which the work of the Holy Spirit in a soul may be evidenced. St. Paul himself in his letters to the Church of Corinth [see Appendix B — Notes and General Conclusions, C] has made this quite clear. It would be wrong indeed, and destructive of all true spirituality, to allow the unusual nature of this manifestation to elevate it to some special eminence of spiritual importance, and to overlook the omnipresent action of the Holy Spirit throughout the history of the Church, and throughout Christendom at the present time.

There is a most real danger that the significance of "spiritual speaking" may be exaggerated, especially when it is viewed in isolation and separation from the wholeness of God's inspiration. The eagerness with which popular curiosity seizes upon stories of such happenings is a clear signal of warning. Furthermore, in

Report on Glossolalia

anything like "spiritual speaking" which wells up from the mysterious depths of our humanity, where in so many forms primal evil wrestles with the urgency of redemptive good, there is always a most serious danger of delusion, and even of diabolic deception [see Appendix B — Notes and General Conclusions, C]. It is the pastoral obligation of the Church to protect the faithful from any possible incursion of the irrational or pathological forces which prey upon the depths of our nature. "Beloved, believe not every spirit, but try the spirits whether they are of God . . ." (1 John 4:1). In view of these considerations, we believe it is our duty to suggest the following counsel:

1. *Separatism and the development of any kind of sectarian spirit is to be deplored.* Special and extraordinary spiritual experience of this type has often in the history of the Church shown an unfortunate schismatic tendency, and has generally not been a continuing experience within the Church at large. A spiritual "elite" has been produced and it arrogates to itself, perhaps unintentionally at first, a certain superiority of insight and qualification; this leads to the disruption of the total fellowship of Christians. A sure test of the genuine basis of such phenomena in spiritual reality, as distinct from emotional delusion, would be the willingness of those involved to submit to the direction and guidance of the duly constituted authorities of the Church, and to participate humbly with others in the regular work and worship of the Church.

2. *The danger of irrationality and emotional excess is to be acknowledged as a real danger and to be shunned.* Assessment of phenomena of the type of "spiritual speaking" cannot rule out the possibility that there is a pathological element in them, and also the possibility that they may have a pathological influence on certain types of personality.

3. *All Christians must be ready to submit special experiences of this type to the judgment and decision of their pastors.* The Church of Christ moves through history by steps of reason, law and institutional authority. The historic Church of which we are part is the voice of the Apostolic Order, and this order is in its origins the creation of our Lord Himself. The Church is built upon the conviction that God works through these regular procedures of everyday human experience through the ages, even as He works through the regular processes of nature. All human communication, all human knowledge, all human community and concord, the Holy Scriptures, theological science, and the sacramental Church, all rest upon the primacy of rationality. The

intrusion of the non-rational into these areas — although the possibility of authentically divine action expressing itself through such an intrusion should always be humbly *investigated* — must always, nevertheless, be regarded with charitable reserve. God has hallowed the reason of mankind, and we must always believe that reason is supremely the voice of the Holy Ghost and that the Holy Ghost will speak to us in the vocables of rationality.

4. *The contemporary fondness for the new and sometimes for the bizarre is a temptation, and must be avoided.* In a restless and impatient age we must be especially on guard against the frenzied search for novelty, particularly in the realm of the spirit. There is no substitute for the long-tested disciplines of spiritual growth and health. For most Christians, growth in holiness will be painstaking and slowly evolved. It would be tragic if the spiritual training of any of our people were interrupted or misdirected by the dangerous expectation that the quest for "spiritual speaking" is an approved way of seeking sanctity.

5. *Methods of instruction and prayer which are unquestionably grounded in the Holy Scriptures and proven through centuries of Christian practice are to be given priority over methods which rest on tentative if not dubious foundations.* To those earnest Christians seeking a revival of the Church, the Committee feels impelled to call attention to the fact that a great awakening has occurred in our Church as well as other Communions in America through increased emphasis on the Family Eucharist, adult Bible study, and lay participation in the whole parish program. Bible Study Classes and such similar enterprises have a tremendous advantage over groups meeting for spiritual speaking in that they have an objective record to study, in the first place, and, in the second place, a great and continuous tradition of commentary. They also have the clear teaching of all the great Christian Communions that through the Holy Scriptures God's word reaches the hearts and minds of men. This is why the Church can commend the study of the Scriptures in every parish, to believer and non-believer alike, as a great teaching and devotional aid. To those interested in discovering the truth about God and hearing what God has to say to our age, as well as to those who are interested in the proclamation of the Gospel to the unchurched, we can recommend unreservedly the study of the Scriptures while we cannot with the same assurance suggest a continuation of meetings held for the purpose of speaking in tongues.

6. *Our strongest Apostolic authority is St. Paul (in 1 Corinthians*

12-14). The principles which support his directions to the Church of Corinth in the matter of "spiritual speaking" are valid today. He acknowledges "spiritual speaking" as a gift of the Holy Spirit, among other gifts, but one which requires careful control and regulation. In Chapter 14 of 1 Corinthians his regulations for its control are quite clearly and emphatically set forth; for example, in verses 27 and 28: "If any man speak in an unknown tongue, let it be by two, or at the most three, and that by course; and let one interpret. But if there be no interpreter, let him keep silence in the Church; and let him speak to himself and to God." In this chapter, St. Paul stresses that the order and the well-being of the Christian community are of the first importance; for example, verse 19: "Yet in the church I had rather speak five words with my understanding, that by my voice I might teach others also, than ten thousand words in an unknown tongue"; verses 36-37, "What? came the word of God out from you? Or came it unto you only? If any man think himself to be a prophet, or spiritual, let him acknowledge that the things that I write unto you are the commandments of the Lord"; and verse 40, which concludes the chapter, "Let all things be done decently and in order." The order and well-being of the Christian community, to St. Paul, are clearly of the highest consideration, even as "charity" with relation to "the best gifts" is "a more excellent way" (1 Corinthians 12:31–13) [*see* Appendix B].

In conclusion, we concur in the admonition of St. Paul, "Let all things be done unto edifying" (1 Corinthians 14:26b). The building up of Christ's Church — both through a deepening of the true spirituality of the faithful and through her redemptive mission to the minds and souls of those who have yet to acknowledge the Lordship of the Holy Ghost — is the criterion by which we should both desire and value spiritual gifts.

In these terms, then, we recommend that provision be made: (a) that the exercise of "spiritual speaking" shall in no way intrude itself into the regular worship and work of the Church so as to disturb the order and peace thereof; (b) that those who engage in this activity avoid occasion for giving offence to the Church either by exalting themselves or by suggesting that others seek this gift as a mark of spiritual superiority; (c) that the exercise of this gift be guarded with vigilance so as to protect both the faithful and the weak from the dangers of irrationality and emotional excess; (d) that the persons who experience this gift consult regularly with their pastors; (e) that groups of people who exercise this gift under the auspices of any minister of this Church shall, through such minister, report regularly to the Bishop of their activities.

"If we live in the Spirit, let us also walk in the Spirit". In profound and ever-renewed humility we must submit our judgments in these high matters to God the Holy Ghost, who leads His Church into all truth, who sustains His Church by His love. Let us strive together in patience and in love to witness to His working in us by showing forth the fruit as well as the phenomena of His working. "But the fruit of the Spirit is love, joy, peace, long suffering, gentleness, goodness, faith, meekness, temperance: against such there is no law . . . If we live in the Spirit, let us also walk in the Spirit." (Galatians 5:22-23, 25).

Respectfully submitted, (Signed): William H. Baar, William F. Maxwell, Jr., Christopher Morley, Jr., G. F. Tittmann, William H. Nes, J. Ralph Deppen, Chairman

APPENDIX A

GLOSSOLALIA (OBSERVATIONS, OCTOBER 6, 1960)

1. This is a special kind of ecstatic activity. It can become routine and imitative, but it can also be unquestionably genuine. There can be no doubt whatever that it is a practice enjoyed by certain sincere people who attribute to it the clue to a complete and desirable change in their outlook and way of life.

2. Its participants are not theologically articulate or systematic. They are divided as to whether it is (a) a latent faculty in everyone (Christian or not), (b) a special gift only meant for some (Christian or otherwise). They seem to agree that it can be given, or awakened by the laying on of hands with prayer by a group — with the earnest desire of the recipient.

3. The practice consists of two phases: (1) a rapid, unintelligible series of utterances, eyes closed, voice quiet, body relaxed — sounding like true language in its inflections and pauses and intonations, seeming very close to various tongues which might be heard any day in the United Nations, and (2) an "interpretation" done in the same manner except in English, consisting of an introduction, "Thus saith the Lord", and an opening form of address which is always plural and affectionate in the Johannine manner "My little ones", "Little children", "My beloved ones", followed by various admonitions and general promises or warnings, some hackneyed, some sounding rather original, concluding with "Thus saith your Lord" — after which the group joins in "Amen".

4. It is said that it can all be private and silent; that interpretation can take place without the preliminary "tongues".

5. Upon questioning, the participants clearly distinguish between the activity of tongues with interpretation and the work of the Spirit: that is, their indebtedness is not to the practice itself but to the sense of the power and indwelling of the Spirit Himself to which the activity attests. As is to be expected, this distinction is

Report on Glossolalia

not likely to be firmly maintained in personal attitude and general feeling but only during the attempt at objective analysis.

6. There is no sign of disorder, overexcitement, etc. The activity can follow, almost immediately, light conversation and ordinary party-talk, and when all have had their turn, the resumption of casual chatter and objective observations of what has happened is instant and easy.

7. Without exception, all the participants testify that their having discovered this faculty and their regular sharing together of it have made the most profound and permanent change in their lives from top to bottom, all day all night; that it has launched each and every one of them into a moment-by-moment "practice of the presence of God" for which they are obviously grateful to the Lord beyond telling; that the daily routines in home and at work and play, as well as the regular practices of the Churchman's life have all taken on new meaning and new joy and quiet excitement; that they feel in their spirit and conversation and faces the marks of real and sustained conversion to lives of faithfulness and obedience to God.

APPENDIX B

GLOSSOLALIA IN THE NEW TESTAMENT

"Speaking with tongues" is not frequently referred to in the New Testament; and if it were not for the long discussion of it in I Corinthians we should know of it only through the following mentions:

1. St. Mark XVI, 17. (Among the signs that accompany them that believe) "they will speak in new tongues".

2. Acts of the Apostles:

a. Acts II, The Pentecostal narrative. In the Descent of the Holy Ghost, "there appeared to them tongues as of fire"; and when the Apostles spoke, the multitude were amazed because "each one heard them speaking in his own language." We should note that here the Apostles are said to have been speaking in "other tongues" whereas in St. Mark the prophecy is of speaking "in new tongues".

b. Acts X, 46. "For they heard them speaking in tongues and extolling God." This is the passage about the manifestation of the Holy Ghost in the house of St. Cornelius the Centurion. The event is treated as having very high significance, as a "pentecost of the Gentiles" both in the preparation of St. Peter for it and in its impression on those who accompanied him, for they were amazed "because the gift of the Holy Spirit had been poured out even on the Gentiles." This significance is heightened, as being that of a unique and *initiating* event, like Pentecost, in the reception of the Holy Spirit *before* they were baptized.

c. Acts XIX, 6. "And when Paul had laid his hands of them, the Holy Spirit came on them, and they spoke with tongues and prophesied." This is the account of the baptism *with Christian baptism* of twelve believers who had formerly had baptism from St. John Baptist.

It should be noted that in the case of the Samaritans whom St. Philip had baptized, the Holy Spirit came on them after the Apostles had laid their hands on them, as in the case of the twelve men at Ephesus; but they are not said to have spoken with tongues or to have prophesied. Clearly, then, there is no suggestion in the Acts that speaking with tongues or prophecy ordinarily accompanied the gift of the Holy Spirit at baptism and/or laying-on-of-hands. On the contrary, we are given to understand that there were particular manifestations of the Holy Spirit joining the first Pentecost to the coming of the Holy Spirit to the Gentiles and to Christian believers who had been followers of St. John Baptist.

3. I Corinthians XII–XIV. To this we must now turn our attention in some detail.

It is one of a number of passages dealing with matters with which St. Paul found it necessary to deal because of situations in Corinth involving error and disorder. In this case there was an error regarding charismata and a disorder arising from people who considered themselves to be "spiritual" (*pneumatikoi*). The particular disorder was the "speaking with tongues" which these people supposed to be an eminently distinguished operation of the Holy Spirit.

He lays down, therefore, at the very outset, the absolute criterion of spiritual utterance and of the discernment of spirits. All "spiritual" utterance is not from the Holy Spirit, for there are spirits who say *IESOUS ANATHEMA*: only by the Holy Spirit can a man say *KURIOS IESOUS*. Similarly St. John says (I John IV, 2) "every spirit that confesses that Jesus Christ has come in the flesh is of God, and every spirit that does not confess Jesus is not of God."

St. Paul, then, has begun his discussion of "spiritual" phenomena: all that is or may be "spiritual" is not so in the Christian sense; and with regard to *utterance* the test of authenticity is not one (as we may commonly suppose it to be) between an inspired utterance and a merely psychical one, *but rather* between *inspired* utterance from the Holy Spirit and inspired utterance of demons. The test of the utterance therefore is by *what it says*.

With verse 4 the Apostle proceeds to the gifts (charismata) of the Holy Spirit. He lists them, and uses the rest of the chapter to show that they are manifestations of the Holy Spirit *in the Church*, operations within the Body of Christ, "for the common good". This is indeed the ground on which he wishes to chasten the presumption of all who consider themselves to be "pneumatikoi" pre-eminently because they exercise what they suppose to be a pre-eminent gift.

In this same chapter he has *two* lists — the one, of charismata; the other, of the function of these gifts in relation to the persons who exercise them. In both lists the gift of tongues is mentioned last. Now it is important for us to compare here the list in Romans (XII, 6). This is similarly based on the doctrine of the Body of Christ, and since it is more particularly like the list (the second in the chapter) beginning I Corinthians XII, 28, it must be carefully noted that in Romans XII there is no mention of speaking with tongues.

Chapter XIII proceeds from the statements: "Desire earnestly the better gifts, and yet I show you a still more excellent way." Certainly the intention of this is evident. Here are people who seem to be or think they are *"the spiritual ones"*. They suppose that a particular charisma gives them eminence. To them St. Paul points out that all gifts are *in the Body*, they are exercised by particular persons severally, but only for the common good. If there is any question as to relative excellence of gifts, he has already placed prophecy above tongues, which he has put at the bottom of the list. But quite beyond any question of greater or lesser gifts, there is a supreme affusion of the Holy Spirit and it is "agape". In the economy of the Holy Spirit's operation in the Church there are various gifts. But the *greatest* gifts are for all and supremely to be desired, — namely faith, hope, and love. These are intrinsically self-authenticating. Tongues can be the tongues of devils; they can even curse Christ. But love is the work of the Holy Spirit who says "Kurios Iesous."

Chapter XIV continues and concludes the discussion. He says: "Aim at love, and be eager for the spiritual gifts (*pneumatika*), but especially that you may prophesy. He that speaks in an unknown tongue edifies only himself. He who

18

prophesies is greater than he who speaks in tongues, unless someone interprets so that the Church may be edified. If in a meeting you all speak in tongues you may very well appear to be mad. But prophecy is comprehensible. Even though prayer can be in an unknown tongue it would not engage the understanding of him who prays, and therefore one should pray with the spirit and the understanding. Especially is this true of "blessing" and "thanksgiving" (*eulogia* and *eucharistia*); it cannot be in a tongue because there must be Amen."

At the end of the discourse he comes to his specific directions both with regard to *pneumatika* (the spiritual manifestations) and the *pneumatikoi* (the spiritual persons). He orders that: (1) In the assembly speaking with tongues must be orderly — in course, one by one; by a few. (2) There must be an interpreter; otherwise let them be silent. (3) Let two or three prophets speak and let the others weigh what is said. (4) If a revelation is made to one sitting by, let the first speakers be silent. (5) You can all prophesy one by one so that all may learn and be encouraged.

"In Church all must be done decently and in order, for God is not a God of confusion but of peace. And if any one thinks he is a prophet or spiritual let him acknowledge that what I say to you is the commandment of the Lord."

NOTES AND GENERAL CONCLUSIONS

A. A clear distinction must be drawn between the meanings of pneumatica and charismata. The latter are the "grace gifts", through Jesus Christ, of the Holy Spirit. The former may indeed be "spiritual" but they are not necessarily — and very often they are not — the operations of the Holy Spirit that says *Kurios Iesous*.

B. In viewing the Corinthian discourse with the Pentecost narrative in Acts we will discern a sharp difference and one ambiguity.

At Pentecost the Apostles spoke in "other tongues as the Spirit gave them utterance" and the multitude, in the diversity of their dialects or languages, comprehended the utterance *directly and immediately*. In I Corinthians it is a speaking in *unknown tongues* which cannot be understood by the auditors and may indeed be incomprehensible to the speaker, and which therefore demands the exercise of *another* charisma, that of interpretation.

But, as to the ambiguity: In the Pentecost narrative there is also the remark that some who heard mockingly charged the Apostles with being drunk. This reminds us of St. Paul's observation that "they will think you are mad".

The Acts passage seems to emphasize Pentecost as a reversal of Babel: by man's pride and sin peoples cannot speak to each other and a world-communication is confused and inhibited; but by the coming of the Holy Spirit, a restoration is made through the preaching of the Gospel. The minor reference to drunkenness may be a remembrance of the Corinthian phenomenon in the retrospect of the Church when Acts was written.

C. St. Paul clearly believed that speaking in an unknown tongue could be authentically the utterance of the Holy Spirit, for he says he did it himself. Therefore he is not prepared at all to forbid it, if it is properly safeguarded by interpretation and by the good order of the Church. But — and this is never to be forgotten — speaking in a tongue is not self-authenticating, and indeed may be the work of demons.

D. St. Paul is concerned with the control and regulation of the practice. This requires the chastening of pride in "spiritual ones" and the obedience to his directions "as the commandments of the Lord."

But behind his effort to regulate and control, and clearly fundamental to his argument, is his effort to *divert the zeal for spiritual manifestations to other channels —* "pursue the better gifts, and above all that, pursue the far more excellent way of faith, and hope, and love," for these are the supreme charismata and the intrinsically and supremely Christian pneumatika.

Respectfully submitted, William H. Nes, D.D.

3 *Episcopal Church, USA, 1962*

NEW MOVEMENTS IN THE CHURCH

At the national level the Episcopal bishops sought to give some broad indications of attitudes which should be taken regarding the emerging charismatic renewal in the church. In 1962 the bishops issued a brief statement. "God's Spirit is ever moving in new ways," counseled the bishops, and "new movements have in history enriched the Body of Christ." The church should not be a sect, but should be spacious.
The bishops observed "that the danger of all new movements is self-righteousness, divisiveness, one-sidedness, and exaggeration." Therefore the charismatic renewal should relate itself to the "full, rich, balanced life of the historic church."
The bishops' statement was published in the "Journal of the General Convention, 1962," pp. 16–17.

Since, from time to time, new movements rise within the life of the Church, we, your Bishops, share two observations.

a. When a new movement rises, which may stress some aspect of the richness of Christ, it is the duty of the whole Church to view it with sympathy, to work to keep it within the great fellowship, and to discern what in the movement is of God that we all may learn from it. Our attitude must be generous, and charitably critical. If, for example, a movement rises concerned with the fact of the Holy Spirit, the proper response is for all of us to consider anew the divine promises and divine gifts, trying the spirits by their fruits. We must bear always in mind that souls differ, that God's Spirit is ever moving in new ways, and that new movements have in history enriched the Body of Christ. We observe further that we are a Church, and not a sect, and that our spiritual home is, and should be, spacious.

20   *New Movements in the Church*

b. Having said that to the whole Church, we observe that the danger of all new movements is self-righteousness, divisiveness, one-sidedness, and exaggeration. We call, therefore, upon all new movements to remain in the full, rich, balanced life of the historic Church, and thereby protect themselves against these dangers; and we remind all clergy of their solemn vow to conform to the doctrine, discipline, and worship of this Church. The Church, transcending in its life both the generations and the nations, is by its nature more comprehensive than any special groups within it; and the Church, therefore, is both enriched by and balances the insights of all particular movements.

4 Lutheran Church in America, USA, 1962

ANOINTING AND HEALING

Both the United Lutheran Church in America (which in the year this report was issued joined the Augustana Lutheran Church, the Suomi Synod, and the American Evangelical Lutheran Church to form the Lutheran Church in America) and the American Lutheran Church (1965) issued statements on the healing ministry. While not a policy statement of the Lutheran Church in America, it has been retained as a study document.

During World War II classical Pentecostals in the United States, after generations of clawing their way up the social ladder, became part of the fabric of middle-class America. War, the great social leveler which raises up the lowly and brings down the lordly, brought classical Pentecostals into contact with every level of society. Partly because of this social phenomenon, the soil was ripe for the emergence of the charismatic movement in the early 1960s.[1]

In the aftermath of the war, there was a revival in the small classical Pentecostal churches. This revival nurtured a generation of classical Pentecostal and independent evangelists. By the mid 1950s most of the classical Pentecostal denominations had withdrawn their endorsement of the traveling evangelists, which was a crushing blow to the smaller revivalists.[2] The stronger and more enterprising took stock of their methods, changed their procedures, and sought new audiences. To some extent the main-line Protestant churches provided resources to fill their tents.

"The great revival that launched the careers of the independent ministers lasted roughly from 1947 to 1958 and was preeminently a healing revival . . . theirs was a sign-gift-healing, a salvation-deliverance, a Holy Ghost revival. . . . The common heartbeat of every service was the miracle – the hypnotic moment when the Spirit moved to heal the sick."[3]

The healing ministry very likely is based on an interpretation of Christ in the gospel texts themselves as "the divine man," a concept taken over from a Hellenistic tradition because of the similarity with the miracles of Jesus. In the "divine man" the divine reality was present as a substance or power enabling him to enjoy ecstatic experiences, to utter prophecies, to work miracles, and to perform marvelous feats.[4]

Into the tents and auditoriums went a cross section of the American Protestantism (not only classical Pentecostals) where they prayed, clapped, sometimes shouted, and supported the healing evangelist as he urged the cripple to walk and the blind to see.

The manner in which the healing evangelists exercised their ministry was quite varied, as were their successes and failures. The plains of middle America are strewn with the bodies of those who broke under the pressure, and they were many. When what had begun in 1947 was over in 1958, the healing evangelists had had an impact on America's understanding of religious experience, prayer, prophecy, ecumenism, as well as of the relation between faith and health which is still with us under various guises.

The most decisive factors in the decline of the healing evangelists was the loss of financial support, the multiplication of miracles to the point of weariness, claims which strained the willing hearts of even the expectant, the plethora of prophets, the frauds and extremists who competed with the honest moderates.[5] The criticism within classical Pentecostalism of the excesses was as strong, if not stronger, than that which issued from the main-line Protestant churches.[6]

By 1962 the charismatic renewal had entered the Lutheran congregations in the United States. But the problem posed in this present document antedated the emergence of the Lutheran charismatic renewal. The presence of Lutherans in the charismatic renewal in small numbers (a very recent development) did not mitigate the problem but rather exacerbated it. To some extent this was due to the uncritical appropriation of classical Pentecostal exegesis, doctrine, and cultural baggage by Lutheran pastors newly involved in the charismatic renewal. This made it difficult, if not impossible, for them to operate effectively within a Lutheran context.[7] The appeal by many Lutherans to the Lutheran tradition in order to oppose the goals of the charismatic renewal seemed to indicate to Lutheran charismatics that the Reformation principle of sola scriptura would not be allowed them. Anyone but a Lutheran charismatic, so it seemed to them, could confront the church with the gospel.

At the height of the healing ministry in the United States, namely 1947–58, and also in the following years, many Lutherans were exposed to healing services in a religious and theological context which was alien to the Lutheran ethos. A considerable number of Lutherans who attended the services of various faith healers did not end up in the Lutheran charismatic renewal. Their interest did not extend that far. But some did involve themselves in the renewal.

That voices from within the healing ministry were raised against the patent abuses there present, not to say immoralities, is evidence that this was not a peculiarly Lutheran problem. In 1962, the very year G. H. Montgomery, himself a leader in the healing ministry, exposed the gross abuses in that ministry,[8] the United Lutheran Church in America adopted the present statement. It opened with introductory comments by individual committee members, definitions of terms, a statement of focus, and a brief historical survey to give context to the problem. The committee elaborated a broad theological background against which to situate the healing ministry. In the light of this theology, the committee deduced a stretegy and closed with some guidelines formulated as answers to specific questions.

The Committee on Anointing and Healing asserted that healing miracles in the New Testament were among the important signs that the kingdom of God was present. A major concern of the committee was that ultimates such as the central concerns of forgiveness, faith and a resurrected life, not be displaced by penultimates such as healing. "It is the gospel that comes first in importance for Christians. . . . It is wrong for Christians to try to use the gospel for any secondary purposes such as bodily healing." Frequently the healing ministry allows the penultimates of bodily healing to be treated as an ultimate and therefore warps and misuses the gospel. "If bodily healing becomes central, then all is lost." All of this does not exclude the possibility of bodily healing. On the contrary, the expectancy of Christian faith should include such a possibility being effected by God's saving act through faith.

One cannot find in Scripture any explicit command of Christ for the church today with regard to healing. "Christ's injunctions to his disciples to perform such authoritative miracles were specific commissions for that time and circumstance, when the apostolic age marked a unique turning point in the history of redemption. Healing miracles are not part of any specified, Christ-commanded assignment for the on-going church."

The committee wished to be open to a concern for healing which was part of a fellowship created by the gospel. They warned against participating in a healing ministry outside such a "face-to-face Christian fellowship." Faith healers were defined as those who, "claiming to possess or convey spiritual powers that heal the sick, distort the gospel by trying to direct the power of Christ into a miraculous act of bodily healing." Such persons endanger lives by creating a false sense of security and thus delay early diagnosis and treatment. In many instances they "directly contribute to an untimely death." In brief, Lutherans should refuse to participate in activities with faith healers.

The committee did not recommend the introduction in the parishes of public worship designated as healing services. They considered the use of oil in administering to the sick in Lutheran congregations to be unwise, to a degree because of the danger of a "magical value" being attached to it. Though somewhat ambivalent with regard to the laying on of hands, it was greatly to be preferred to the use of oil.

The report is available as a pamphlet from the Lutheran Church in America, 231 Madison Ave., New York City, 10016.

1. Kilian McDonnell, "Pentecostal Culture: Protestant and Catholic," One in Christ, vol. 7 (1971), 310–18.

2. David Edwin Harrell, All Things are Possible (Bloomington: Indiana University Press, 1975), pp. 4–5.

3. Ibid., 5–6.

4. Reginald H. Fuller, The Foundations of New Testament Christology (New York: Charles Scribner's Sons, 1965), pp. 97–98.

5. Harrell, 7.

6. Donald Gee, Trophimus I Left Sick (Springfield, Mo.: Gospel Publishing House, 1952; Walter Hollenweger, The Pentecostals (Minneapolis: Augsburg Publishing House, 1972), pp. 357–58. The Assemblies of God publication Pentecostal Evangel refused to print reports of healing evangelists. Leonhard Steiner, the Swiss classical Pentecostal, gave a lecture at the World Pentecostal Conference in Toronto in 1968 in which he alleged that the healing evangelists wanted to make God their servant. See Hollenweger, 357.

7. See Kilian McDonnell, "The Relationship of the Charismatic Renewal to the Established Denominations," Dialog, vol. 13 (Summer 1974), 223–29.

8. The exposé appeared in a series of articles printed in the International Healing Magazine managed by Juanita Coe. She was the widow of Jack Coe, who had a major national healing ministry from the early 1950s until his death in 1957. See Harrell, 138–49.

CONTENTS

INTRODUCTORY COMMENTS

I. by ROBERT WITMER

The challenge of human misery presents itself alike to the physician and the pastor. Day by day in their respective callings they deal with the issues of life and death. Both minister to people who are passing through deep crises. It is imperative therefore that they have some understanding of each other's role and of the goals they seek to achieve. The physicians on this committee have unanimously endorsed this document in both theology and practical recommendations, and are all deeply indebted to their brothers, the theologians on this committee, for their patience, tolerance and keen insights imparted through three years of tireless effort.

The physician who is a Christian has a great opportunity

through his constant daily contacts with his patients to instill courage, radiate hope, and inspire faith to the wavering soul. For in his daily tasks, the physician constantly sees God's hand as he does the best he can for his patient; even when he has done all for a patient that modern medical science has taught him and the treatment fails, he knows that he is but a channel open upwards to heaven by faith and outwards to his patient, his neighbor, through love. All that a Christian physician possesses has been received from God that he may pass it on. He has nothing of his own to give, for he is but an instrument through which redeeming love is further mediated. Thus the Christian physician is called to be a Christ to his neighbor. A physician's calling is therefore the normal context for the exercise of his Christian faith; his calling is the God-given means whereby he may serve and edify his neighbor in love.

Jesus was called a physician, and it is the physician whom people ask for first when they are looking for health. This is good, for as all generations knew, there is healing power in nature, and much healing is possible if this power is wisely used and skillfully aided. Those who despise this aid and rely on the power of their will ignore both the destructive might and the constructive friendliness of nature.

Sickness is not necessarily the result of a lack or a faltering of faith. God has given to every man a share in the care of his body and mind. If man refuses to accept his personal responsibility for himself, then he cannot expect God to be present with the miracle to do it all. Man's responsibility must include first a realistic faith that God is master of the whole situation and that his personal desire may not be God's will. This includes the entire range from complete healing, through adjustment to disability, to no healing. Secondly, man must conduct his life so as to avoid trauma to his physical or mental being. Thirdly, man must accept God's gifts of medical sciences and the healing arts and use them to the best of his ability.

The doctrine of creation and the practical application of Christian Stewardship require the Christian to view all good and constructive resources in the world as blessings from God to be used for his glory and for the welfare of his fellowmen. Therefore, whatever scientific or technical skills are required to facilitate healing and foster the well-being of any person are welcomed, and whatever person or group of persons are required to administer the various therapeutic agents and treatments will also

Anointing and Healing

be embraced as co-workers with the ministry of the church in God's work of healing the sick. It is for this reason that the committee strongly condemned "faith healers" in paragraph 62 of this report.

Just as man is made up of many "parts" or aspects, so specialized knowledge has developed about these various functions or segments. Unless there can be a unifying theme or co-ordinating principle, we may fail to minister to the "whole man." Here the church can be a real help if it can speak about man's nature and destiny in an informed way, not minimizing the contributions of a dozen specialties just because they are a bit narrow in themselves, but by providing that wholesome perspective which views man as body and soul with a moral and social context and with an eternal destiny. In this way, the church makes its specific witness and contribution as its part of the health team approach.

The physician and other members of the health team, therefore, should always work closely with the pastor, for their work is so closely related in helping sick people to become whole. The team approach to healing should be strengthened by a free interchange of knowledge between physician and pastor with consultations held as often as necessary for the good of the patient. Dedicated Christian physicians should enlighten and encourage their medical colleagues to consult with pastors more frequently when the situation calls for pastoral help. Failure for cooperation in the past lies not so much with the clergy but with the medical profession.

II. by the REV. DAVID BELGUM, Ph.D.

Theological and medical implications of this report are numerous and intricate. But in the practical parish situation, which has been the central focus of this committee, the layman asks his pastor a simple straight-forward question: "Is it all right for us to take Mother to Evangelist Blank's faith healing service or does our own church have anything to offer?" Hopefully the committee has stated what is, and ought to be, available in our own Lutheran Church.

The report has taken into account two emerging trends: first, an increasing appreciation of and co-operation with the healing ministry of modern medicine; secondly, a growing desire of the church to recapture its indigenous and unique function in the pastoral care of the sick. Just as some naïve misunderstanding or ignorance of science leads to repudiation of medicine, so some rejection of spiritual aspects of life and too quick acquiescence to a totally materialistic and closed-system view of the universe has weakened the church's ministry of healing which is so unmistakably a concern of the Lord of the Church.

The pastoral care of persons in crises such as illness and impending death is one of the great historic ministries of the Church. Renewal of spiritual life in the local congregation could well begin with the earnest study by pastor and laity alike of the mission of the Church and the expectancy of the individual believer concerning illness and healing. Perhaps if the study report of the committee has done nothing more than lay the ground-work for such local concern, it will have served a useful purpose. It would be dangerous for any congregation to launch out upon some enthusiastic ministry in this regard without full understanding of all the factors involved.

We must be aware of more than the impact of such ministry upon one local church. On the average, Americans move every five years. It is unsettling and confusing for parishioners to become accustomed to a particular resource or service in one parish only to discover that in the church in their new community this ministry is unknown, unavailable, or even looked down upon. This problem becomes more acute in a controversial sphere. That is why sensationalism must be avoided in study, discussion, or practice of various items in the report.

But it was neither the assignment nor intention of the committee to outline procedures, liturgies, or rubrics for the practical implementation of any ministry of healing. The findings of the committee are not conclusive enough to warrant such tangible suggestions; whether or not our contemporary Lutheran church were willing to implement such suggestions would require much more study and evaluation.

III. by Leopold W. Bernhard, Chrm.

If Lutherans express their evangelical freedom by holding differing viewpoints and convictions, this committee of physicians and clergymen proved to be Lutheran with a vengeance. The presentation of a unanimous report is nothing short of a miracle. The members of the committee gratefully and humbly acknowledge the working of the Holy Spirit in this their agreement.

To say this is not just to point to the unanimity of the report presented here, but, above all, it is to mention one of the factors which became decisive for the nature of the report itself. Both the composition of the committee and the subject assigned to it assured conversation between theology and science. For all too long a period of time such conversation had nearly ceased. During the period of almost complete silence, science developed in the most astounding manner and gained such stature and self-assurance that it no longer apologizes either for its findings, its hypotheses, or for its stance. It is therefore a most delicate, complicated, and laborious task to carry on this conversation, particularly because theology and science have great difficulties in communicating with each other at all.

Due to this fact, the report before you has certain limitations. That the subject under study had to be treated theologically hardly needs to be mentioned in a Lutheran assembly. Yet the state of the conversation between science and theology often made it necessary to use a theological approach which is not always traditional either in regard to emphasis or language. Furthermore, only immediately relevant, theological issues could be treated. May it be understood that theological issues not dealt with in the report even though they might be more distantly related to the subject, are not rejected here by implication.

Another peculiarity of the subject under study, necessarily reflected in the nature of the report, is the fact that the problem of faith and health is an emotionally loaded issue. In crisis situations, especially in illness and death, man's relationship to God is not so much a matter of religious reflection, even less one of theological deduction; it becomes in a very real sense a question of being, of existential experience. That is true for an afflicted church member as well as for his pastor who tries to serve him. When the church had asked for guidance in the matter of healing and anointing, it therefore called for the handling of a highly sensitive problem. That the committee would not come up with the kind of guidance which would even faintly resemble canon law goes nearly without saying among evangelical Christians. Actually the committee nowhere suggests very definite practices, some of which could be said to be more in harmony with evangelical teaching than others.

Basically, the report calls for a renewal of faith and for an intensification of the life of faith among the people of God. What expressions a ministry of healing assumes in the church depend chiefly, if not totally, on the kind of faith living in the hearts of

Christian people. The modes of such expressions can hardly be prescribed, nor can they readily be judged, if they may be judged at all. At best, possibilities can be suggested and pointed out, and perhaps helpful examples can be cited. It is only when such free expressions of the life of faith are pressed into norms that they may be weighed in the light of Scripture as to their usefulness as vehicles of the Holy Spirit and as channels of faith.

The committee recognizes in the wide-spread interest in healing, yes, in the very fact that the church ordered this study, signs which indicate that faith is searching for relevant expressions in crisis situations.

On the one hand the church must take care lest it stifle a legitimate movement of faith; while on the other hand the church must guard against the danger that such movements of living faith either miscarry in the direction of enthusiasm or degenerate into attempts at magic. The history of the church proves amply that enthusiastic distortion and attempts at magic are always the twin dangers which threaten movements attempting to express the renewal of faith. To meet these conditions requires of the church courage, imagination, faithfulness to the Biblical message, and prayerful commitment to the Lord of the Church, Who is the living God and not a doctrinal or liturgical principle.

You find therefore in this report not law but the appeal to serve with new zeal and devotion the expectancy of faith in crisis, if need be through methods and approaches which have not been customary in our church. You find a clear warning against possible aberrations which threaten to violate Biblical truth and to distort the true nature of faith. You find what we confidently believe to be a restatement of the evangelical approach to Scripture and its interpretation. You find an earnest attempt to show that certain customary practices of the church such as portions of the liturgy, the laying on of hands, and group prayers, somewhat reminiscent of the "consolation of the brethren" offer both the structure and the solid foundation through which and on which renewal of faith can find full, free, relevant, and yet Biblical expression.

Let it finally be noted that the report has clearly an air of being tentative, i.e. historical and practical. When it comes to the discussion of practices, the report speaks about possibilities which appear to be advisable or inadvisable "at the moment" in the light of the living tradition of our churches in *this* land rather than to set forth unchangeable principles. While this might give the impression that guidelines are drawn all too faintly, it will be recognized, we trust, that only thus could justice be done to the nature of living faith which is never static, but grows and bears fruit.

The committee is convinced that the Church has a healing ministry and must exercise this ministry with determination as well as with discretion. The committee feels that the expectancy of faith may not be denied or ignored, but must be served. The committee believes that a renewal of faith is essential to the life of the Church in our day of anxiety and crisis, and that this report points to possibilities which would relate Christian people in crisis vitally to the action of God. United in this belief, the committee presents this unanimous report.

IV. by Rev. Frederick K. Wentz, Ph.D.

Your committee has labored under a strong sense of the gravity of the subject assigned to it. Here are many and complex issues about which men feel strongly and differ sharply. Virtually the whole of theology has bearing upon the question of the relation of the Gospel to bodily healing. Many fields of knowledge impinge upon that problem. And who is not personally involved in the subject of human health?

There are many ways to try to grasp a nettle, none entirely satisfactory. Your committee has sought to skewer this one, driving sharply for the core of the issue and pushing on out to the practical implications. This does not lay the whole subject open. It leaves many prickly problems untouched and untamed. But as this report is laid before the convention the committee hopes that it will serve as an adequate handle providing a firm grasp, careful balance, and a shaft that pierces the marrow of the matter.

In the early paragraphs the report tries to pinpoint the problem underlying present-day ferment and confusion among Christians concerning the field of spiritual healing. Since contemporary thought currents are bringing a fresh realization of the degree to which "nature and spirit intermesh, the question takes on new urgency: For the Christian believer what expectancy concerning healing is to be included in his faith in Christ" (paragraph 14)? This question becomes the piercing-point for the report.

Then the report endeavors to penetrate the problem from that point of access with the instrument of God's revelation recorded in Scripture and interpreted in the Lutheran tradition.

The affliction connected with sickness cannot be attributed to

God, according to the report, but results from the rebellion of God's creatures. The New Testament centrally tells what God has done in Christ Jesus, who ushered in the Kingdom of God, chief sign of which was the appearance of the Christian fellowship. Among other important signs were healing miracles.

Since the Kingdom is still coming among us today, since Christ continues to make men new, and since saving faith involves the whole man, "the expectancy of Christian faith should include the possibility that healing may result from God's saving act through faith" (paragraph 29). However, the Kingdom is not now perfected upon this earth. Neither faith nor health is perfect in any Christian or in any man. Within every circumstance, and especially in sickness, Christ's victory must be realized afresh for this time and place and person. That is the crucial expectancy from the Christian standpoint. If that victory is won, then whatever follows may be for the believer a sign of that victory. If bodily healing follows, that may be such a sign. But the believer's gratitude for such a sign will quickly merge with his gratitude to God for all the other healing influences which minister to him and all the other signs which bespeak Christ's victory.

The report does draw from its theological perspectives considerable support for a positive concern with spiritual healing. Indeed, its recommendations urge that Lutheran congregations carefully nurture such concern. But the report balances this urging with warnings in two directions. One is that Christians must always seek to keep first things first. Of central concern is forgiveness, faith, and a resurrected life. Even the important matter of bodily healing is secondary to these central matters. It is wrong for Christians to try to use the Gospel for any secondary purpose such as bodily healing. We must remain open to the possibility that God may, in the mystery of his willing and acting, bring to pass such consequences, but only as we are primarily intent upon receiving Jesus Christ.

The second warning is in the area of discernment. When and how does the Christian see acts of spiritual healing? This takes the eyes of faith and is the gift of the Holy Spirit. One seeks the guidance of that Spirit within the Christian fellowship, where people are drawn together first of all around Jesus Christ himself, and only secondarily are drawn together for any other purpose such as bodily healing.

The quick sketch just made of Part One of the report cannot really sum up the report. I have merely made an effort to show its

Anointing and Healing

structure and thrust. This naked exposure of an already stripped-down exposition fails to point out one important truth. The committee has always realized, and the report reflects this realization, that the way in which God broods over his creation and acts in the giving or withholding of human life and health remain profound mysteries even in our day. Men must try strenuously to understand these matters, but, in the last analysis, the Christian, at least, does not hesitate to acknowledge his ignorance. Your committee in this report has simply tried to provide one true shaft of insight that will guide Christians in the matter of spiritual healing as they seek to act in obedience to their Lord.

REPORT OF SPECIAL COMMITTEE
ON ANOINTING AND HEALING

The special committee appointed in March 1959 to conduct the study of anointing and healing which was called for by the 1958 convention has finished its complicated and demanding task and is now laying the results of its research and reflection before this board in ample time for transmission to the adjourned meeting of the 1960 convention:

The Committee on Anointing and Healing met seven times in New York: on June 6 and November 12, 1959; March 12, June 10 and 11 and October 21 and 22, 1960; June 2 and 3 and on October 20 and 21, 1961. A medical-theological conference was held at Gettysburg, Pennsylvania, on January 16, 1960 and a theological conference also at Gettysburg on September 16 and 17, 1960. At its first meeting it elected the Rev. Leopold W. Bernhard, chairman, and Joseph J. Baker, M.D., secretary. The president of the church appointed the Rev. Harold W. Reisch, Director of Inner Missions of the Board of Social Missions, as staff support and recorder for the committee. The Rev. Herman G. Stuempfle, Jr., Associate Director of Social Action, assisted Pastor Reisch.

The committee expresses its gratitude to the Rev. Howard N. Bream, the Rev. Jacob W. Heikkinen and the Rev. Jacob M. Myers of the Gettysburg Seminary faculty for consulting with the medical-theological and the theological conferences held at Gettysburg and recalls thankfully the contribution made by the late Rev. Reginald W. Deitz to the medical-theological conference. The frequently sought and given advice of these professors and papers by Drs. Bream and Heikkinen were of decisive aid to the committee. A special word of appreciation is recorded to the Rev. Martin J. Heinecken of the Philadelphia Seminary faculty for a critical review of an earlier form of this report.

The manifold labors of Pastor Reisch in recording the proceedings and in furnishing copies of the numerous papers written by the members of the committee and of the several drafts of the report as well as his constructive suggestions are greatly appreciated. Pastor Stuempfle's assistance and especially his drafting of several critical paragraphs of the report are gratefully acknowledged.

The committee's work was greatly facilitated by papers written by the physicians serving on the committee, especially by Dr. Witmer's summation of these medical opinions and by Dr. Eckert's drafts of important paragraphs.

Special credit is due the Rev. Frederick K. Wentz who wrote several papers which became basic to the report and who performed the difficult task of drafting the report itself. He also served with Dr. Witmer and Pastor Bernhard on the editorial subcommittee.

The committee which consisted of a deaconess, four physicians, two seminary professors and three parish pastors was confronted by diverging, often diametrically opposed convictions and by the fact that basically different points of view were regarded as decisive. At times it appeared that a unified report would not be possible, but that a minority report would have to be presented. To the committee it appears therefore so much the more remarkable that the report submitted here was approved unanimously. The members of the committee are grateful for the opportunity which has been theirs to gain new insights and deeper understanding over the years.

The committee is aware of the fact that the question of faith and health is indeed of vital and wide-spread interest to the church. A questionnaire mailed through the *Pastor's Desk Book* not only brought an astonishingly large number of replies but elicited a great many differing comments reflecting deep and even passionate concern. Furthermore, members of the committee were repeatedly requested by pastoral associations, by synodical committees and many others to speak on the subject under study. Even other national church bodies invited us to present a "Lutheran" viewpoint on healing and faith to official assemblies. The committee declined all such invitations because it felt that only after completion of its work a unified view might possibly emerge and above all because the committee is aware of the fact that the report belongs to the Executive Board and that its disposition has to await Executive Board action. We mention this matter only to indicate that the committee not only worked with the consciousness of the general interest in the subject but also attempted so to structure its report that it might meet the expressed needs.

The report therefore does not elaborate all the implications of the assigned subject but confines itself to some of the crucial questions which have arisen. In Part One of the report, the committee presents as much of a theological basis as appeared necessary in the light of these questions. In Part Two, practical principles and guidelines based on the theological statements of Part One are offered insofar as they pertain to those same questions.

STATEMENT ON ANOINTING AND HEALING

Part One

I. THE FOCUS

1. *Questions*. The mandate of this committee is to study "the entire field of anointing and healing." The purpose of the study is to offer practical help for congregations and pastors. With this purpose in mind the committee has discovered in the course of its work that it should limit its report so as to focus attention upon the most crucial questions involved in the total topic.

2. Accordingly, in our report anointing is regarded as simply one important subsidiary topic under the main concern of healing. And it is evident that the committee is not asked to study the whole vast subject of healing *per se* but only to assess *the church's ministry of healing*.

3. Reasons given by the ULCA Convention (1958) for seeking this study are "widespread interest" and "many questions in the mind of the church."

4. This committee, in the course of considerable investigation in a number of areas, has indeed sensed widespread interest.[1] Several other denominations have been studying the church's ministry of healing. There is a vast contemporary literature. This interest and study reflect the increasing activity during recent decades aimed at providing bodily healing through religious agencies.

5. The committee's study has led it to the following questions as the most pressing for our church in this field of concern:

a. How are we to regard the work of the "faith healers" of our day? What should be the relationship of Lutheran people to such activities?

b. How are we to regard the healing ministries practiced by other Christian churches or by groups of Christians closely related to the traditional Christian churches? What should be the relationship of Lutheran people to such activities?

c. Should the Lutheran church and its congregations provide a healing ministry beyond their present general practice?

d. If so, how should the Lutheran church and its congregations provide a healing ministry beyond their present general practice?

e. Are healing services a wise practice for Lutheran people?

f. Is anointing with oil a wise practice for Lutheran congregations?

g. Is the laying on of hands in ministering to the sick a wise practice for Lutheran congregations?

h. What is the place of intercessory prayer in the healing ministry of the Lutheran church?

i. What is the role of the Christian physician in the healing ministry of the church?

6. *Definitions*. The term "healing" must be defined. The word "health" is a synonym for wholeness and salvation. Theologically, therefore, health means salvation and healing means saving. But the common sense meaning, used in this report, defines health as one's ability "to command his powers to serve his goals"[2] or the ability of the individual to adapt to his environment and to live usefully and comfortably within it. *Healing* then becomes the restoration to normality of deranged physical and mental functions.[3]

7. However, even with such a definition of healing, the church's ministry of healing is very broad. For example, individual members of the church have made important contributions to scientific knowledge, psychological insight, medical skill, and human love as these factors have helped to heal the sick. The questions listed above indicate that the focus of concern for this study lies in the *distinctive* contribution of the church to the healing process, namely, spiritual healing.

8. *Spiritual healing* may be defined as that restoration of mental and physical health which results from the impact or influence of

Anointing and Healing

supernatural, superhuman spirit. For Christian theology such spirit is the Holy Spirit.

9. *The Problem*. Behind the questions that have been raised and behind the increased interest in spiritual healing, one can readily discern a basic problem concerning the church's ministry of healing. It is necessary to ask why this is a problem at this particular time. A clue to one fundamental reason lies in the immediate historical background. Mention of several highlights of the relevant church history will point to this reason.

10. The New Testament shows that the early church had a natural though secondary concern for healing. Sickness was viewed as a significant part of the whole of human need. In Jesus Christ, it is clear, God was showing concern for the whole of human need. Miracles of healing by Christ and the early church were chiefly viewed as signs of the coming of the Kingdom of God among men as Christ was Himself ushering in that kingdom. As with all the mighty deeds in the New Testament, healing evidenced a power stemming from the authority of Christ and took place in the context of expectancy usually associated with a total faith in Christ.

11. Quite early in church history this power and this expectancy seem to have faded so that healing miracles were regarded as rare and surprising. In succeeding centuries such miracles continued, but Christian healing came to resemble healing miracles in the pagan world and was confused with or mingled with superstition and the practice of magic. Based largely on James 5, the practice of using oil in a ceremony with the sick evolved as the sacrament of unction. By the ninth century in the western church this sacrament had lost virtually all expectation of healing and had become preparation of the dying for death. In the Middle Ages men turned increasingly to the intercession of the saints for hope of healing. The impact of the Reformation meant a great reduction in the role of superstition and magic for the Christian community. On the positive side, the Reformers believed that the Sacrament of the Lord's Supper, bringing the assurance of forgiveness, was an important carrier of God's healing power.

12. In recent centuries the most spectacular gains in healing have largely by-passed the direct ministrations of the church. The rise of science has meant, on the one hand, great progress in technology in the healing arts, and, on the other hand, a dualistic

viewpoint which separates sharply the realm of spirit from the realm of nature. Nature was held to consist of discoverable and trustworthy laws. Increasingly men gained confidence that they could control nature with ever-growing completeness as they mastered these laws. The healing of the human body, and the human mind along with it, was given over to scientists as an activity in the natural world where spirit is largely irrelevant. Healing miracles in the New Testament sense were ruled out and the church's ministry to the sick was confined to other types of service. It was felt that only charlatans or the very naïve could claim such an impact of spirit upon nature.

13. Today, however, in the second half of the twentieth century, the sharp distinction between nature and spirit has faded both for medical theory and for the general philosophy of science. The increasing importance of psychosomatic medicine shows the close relationship, for medical thinking, among a man's mental, physical, and spiritual states. In the scientific thought-world man is again viewed as an indivisible whole. Spirit and nature merge at the deepest points of investigation. Modern man interprets "matter" as the foci of forces, and laws become statistical probability; and as the source of these forces and statistics one points either toward random motion or toward a mysterious expression of will. Hence the modern world is again open to the possibility that the New Testament is correct in picturing immediately behind the world of nature and human experience a reality of divine and demonic spirits (or wills) in conflict.

14. Thus, in a world where nature and spirit intermesh, the question takes on new urgency: for the Christian believer what expectancy concerning healing is to be included in his faith in Christ? This is the inner question that must be answered in order to fulfill the committee's stated purpose. Since the church's uniqueness lies in its headship in Jesus Christ, the uniqueness in the church's healing ministry lies in that same Jesus Christ and his contemporary activity through the Holy Spirit apprehended through the faith of Christians. This question, concerning the expectancy of Christian faith toward healing, must be answered primarily from the authority of Scripture.

II. THEOLOGICAL STATEMENTS

15. What follows is not a systematic exposition but rather constitutes such statements from Biblical theology as will focus

Anointing and Healing

upon the question of the preceding paragraph and will help to answer the practical questions listed earlier.

16. *God, Man, and Sickness.* God created man as an integral part of the created universe. Man has full participation in the flux and cycles of nature, in the curve of growth, deterioration, and decay, in the vicissitudes, wear and tear, accidental invasions, parasites and diseases, as well as the glow and beauty and energy of the whole round of natural life.

17. But man also transcends nature. God has made him a spirit, a free and responsible person, capable of decision and able to modify his environment and shape his course to an extent. He is made for fellowship with other persons and fits into a social context as part of the fulfillment of his being. Above all, man is created with a capacity for fellowship with God, his Creator, and man finds completion only within such fellowship. In all this he is one of God's creatures dependent upon God for his integrity and his life. A complete man, then, is one whose natural body and transcending spirit are a unity, harmoniously related to its environment of things and persons, and in free, perfectly dependent fellowship with God. This is man's wholeness (health in the theological sense).

18. This, however, is not the whole human condition. Man is a sinner, and sin, which is the inconsistent use of human freedom to rebel against God, brings spiritual death because it cuts the sinner off from God's fellowship and delivers him into the power of the evil one (the devil). The sinner in his defiant effort at independence from God finds himself at odds with his fellowmen and with all God's created world. Disease, sickness, and bodily death take on an evil meaning through sin. Man experiences them as affliction, thwarting his prideful self-sufficiency and his over-weening drive for unlimited mastery over nature.

19. For the whole human race, then, sickness as affliction is the result of the rebellion of the creature. Such a statement does not offer a key to the mystery of evil in the creation, nor does it resolve the problem of the causes of evil to the satisfaction of human logic. It does insist, however, that God is not the creator of affliction. Affliction is an intruder in God's world, due neither to any imperfection in creation nor to the existence of some co-eternal power. Even the evil one and the "spiritual hosts of wickedness" (Ephesians 6:12) are rebellious creatures. Sickness as affliction is the consequence of sin and creaturely rebellion.

20. But this does not imply a consistent causal connection

between the afflictions of a given individual and his sin. In some instances, to be sure, there is a direct relation to be seen between a particular sinful act and consequent affliction. But it is impossible to build a formula which can be applied to individual cases with final justice. The rebellion of the creature has brought disorder into the whole of creation. The consequences of sin have penetrated deeply into man's social and natural environment. Thus, some individuals experience man's common lot of disease and sickness in greater measure than others for no discernible reason. Similarly, though all men die, the death of some at an earlier stage of their potential life span defies rational explanation.

21. This does not mean that sickness, suffering, and bodily death are experienced only as afflictions. Even for sinners they have other and positive meanings — as part of the created structure of human existence and as raw material to be used for the shaping of character and life. Besides, in God's plan of redemption the sufferings of Christ play a positive, central role. Christians in order to share in Christ's glory must suffer with him and are called to participate in his redemptive work through their sufferings. It may readily be God's will, then, for a particular person in a particular circumstance, that he endure sickness and suffering. "For godly grief produces a repentance that leads to salvation and brings no regret." (II Corinthians 7:10)

22. *Christ and the Kingdom.* What, then, is the relation of faith in Christ to healing? We cannot approach Scripture in proof-text manner and put our weight on individual passages. Nor can we make a beach-head assault by asking about healing without an over-all view of the warfare. Scripture has a unity. There is a central truth from which all else within Scripture takes its ultimate meaning. Indeed, this central scriptural truth provides the ultimate reference for all else within the whole orbit of human existence.

23. Centrally, Scripture tells what God has done in Christ Jesus. The incarnate Son of God lived as a man, went through pain, suffering, crucifixion, and death, and was raised from the dead. He has thus won for all men the crucial victory over sin, death (and sickness), and the powers of evil, providing men the opportunity of resurrection and eternal life. Christ thus proclaimed and ushered in the Kingdom of God among men. Chief sign of the coming of this Kingdom, beyond Christ Himself, is the appearance of the koinonia (Christian fellowship). Where sinners are brought into a fellowship in which sins are forgiven,

the Holy Spirit is at work, faith in Christ is created, God's Word is proclaimed, the Sacraments are administered, prayers to Christ are raised, men are made new — there the kingdom is evidenced.

24. *Signs of the Kingdom.* Instances of spiritual healing are also important events described in the New Testament. Viewed from the central message of Scripture they are one kind of signs of the coming of the Kingdom of God. They are foretastes of our resurrection. They are patchwork indications within this mortal existence that death is conquered by Christ and that we shall rise again beyond the grave. They are free, unmerited, unpredictable, creative acts of the Christ, adapted to individual needs. In general they are to be associated with faith in Christ and with the expectancy that springs from such a relationship.

25. However, healing miracles were not the only signs. The nearness of the Kingdom, evidenced in Christ and in the expectancy and events of the apostolic church, was accompanied by many other striking signs. For example, the dead were raised, rocks were split, tombs were opened, demons and deadly snakes lost their power to harm (Matthew 11:4f; Matthew 27:51ff.; Matthew 10:5-8; Mark 6:7; Luke 10:17-20; Acts 9:38-43; Acts 28:1-6.) Miraculous healing and these other happenings had unmistakable eschatological implications. That is, they pointed to a fulfillment of God's purposes by opening a new age among men. They were works of power serving as signs pointing to the supreme miracle of the Incarnation.

26. But it can be asked: do we not have Christ's command to his disciples to heal, whereas we have no such command to split rocks and to open tombs? Scripture does not convey explicit commands of Christ for us; it conveys to us Christ himself as God's Word. Christ's injunctions to his disciples to perform such authoritative miracles were specific commissions for that time and circumstance, when the apostolic age marked a unique turning point in the history of redemption. Healing miracles are not part of any specified, Christ-commanded assignment for the on-going church. Both Christ Himself as God's Word and the church's universal commission for all time, a commission made explicit at several places in the New Testament (Matthew 28:19; Acts 1:8), are communicated to us through the witness and interpretation of the apostles and the whole early church. The relevant question is: how did the early church conceive its commission from Christ? The answer is simply the central message of the whole of Scripture (cf. paragraph 23 above) communicated by the church

through its kerygma (proclamation), koinonia (community), and diakonia (service). Healing miracles were not performed by that early church as fulfillment of Christ's explicit directive. At that time (cf. James 5:13-16) and in later centuries the church did continue its concern for healing as part of its general ministry (diakonia) to the sick, but not as a continuation of Christ's command to his disciples to perform miracles of healing. Healing miracles in the New Testament were primarily signs of the breaking-in of the Kingdom.

27. *Faith and Health.* However, this does not say that healing may not be a part of the distinctive ministry of today's church. Though we are not living in the time of Christ and the Apostles, nevertheless the Kingdom is still coming. The question remains: what are today's signs of the still-coming Kingdom? What shall be the expectancy of Christian faith in this matter?

28. Saving faith, which is both God's gift and the means by which a man receives God's gifts, so undercuts and then undergirds man's life as to provide a total re-orientation of his whole existence. Salvation means wholeness (or "health" in its theological meaning). Since salvation redirects the totality of a man, it is evident that a man is fundamentally a unified whole and only quite secondarily divisible into parts such as body and spirit. His nature is first of all a unity and his destiny awaits the whole man. What God has done in Christ and does through a man's faith in Christ reveals God's gracious concern for the whole man. Nothing human lies beyond the orbit of God's gracious intention.

29. In Christ, then, one becomes a new man. He has a new wholeness, unified with God and integrated anew into God's created universe. Where such newness includes healing of mind and body, the Christian should not be surprised. In other words, the expectancy of Christian faith should include the possibility that healing may result from God's saving act through faith.

30. However, so long as we live on this earth, saving faith in Christ will never bring a man to perfect health. The long-established effects of sin and evil remain. A man's immediate environment may continue to be unhealthy; he may still be lacking an arm or an eye. His mortality remains; he will die to this life. His new wholeness is not perfect wholeness but simply a wholeness of response to God in his particular earthly circumstance.

31. Furthermore, he remains a sinner. He is both a faith-filled Christian and a sinner at the same time. He is a new man but the old man remains with him, repeatedly rending his new-found wholeness. Thus there still rages within the Christian man, as within the whole universe, the conflict between God and his rebellious creature, the devil.

32. Christians know that Christ has won the crucial victory for all who will accept Him. To use the World War II illustration, His resurrection was the crucial D-Day re-invasion of this occupied territory of sin-marred creation. But V-Day and final victory are not yet won and we live between the times with the tyrants of evil still powerful over us. At every point we who live by faith in Christ's victory must yet struggle to realize the victory for this time and place and person. When we are failing — and we always are — we need the church's ministrations of Word and Sacraments and prayer to assure us that Christ is "for us" and will give us the victory.

33. Since sickness as an affliction is the lot of the human race as a whole because of sin (cf. paragraph 18 above), its appearance in an individual readily serves as a sign of the triumph of evil over mankind. In sickness, when Christian faith is threatened by this sign of evil, the church's ministry must help to proclaim and to win Christ's victory by helping faith hold firm. If that victory is won, then whatever happens will be for the believer a sign of that victory. Where sickness and death continue, that will be a "dying with Christ," a conforming to his crucifixion, a crucifying of the "Old Adam" or sinful self in order that the new Christian man may emerge. Where healing and health follow — with or without medical explanation — these become signs of Christ's victory and foretastes of our resurrection.

34. Where Christ's victory is made explicit through faith, the church must keep open the possibility that that victory may directly lead to or "cause" such healing of mind and body as may follow.

35. *Many Ways of Healing.* However, God's ways of working remain largely a mystery; He has many ways of healing only partially perceived by man. It cannot be assumed that, because of Christ's victory in their lives, Christians can expect healing effects not available to other people. Nor can the healing of Christians, in the main, be expected to serve as signs to unbelievers, drawing them effectively into the Kingdom of God. It is for the eyes of

Christian faith that these are signs. This also means that empirical evidence can never be accumulated to demonstrate that such an act of healing is supernatural.

36. In fact, he who is a new man in Christ and responds wholesomely to God will immediately find God (as well as the devil) at work in his particular circumstances. He will realize that the same God who comes to him in Christ through faith also comes to him constantly through every creative and health-giving influence that impinges upon him. His gratitude to God for Christian faith and for healing as evidence of Christ's victory will quickly merge into his gratitude to God for life itself, for the recuperative powers in nature, for scientific and medical knowledge, for laws and institutions and an ordered society, for the technical skill and personal concern of doctors and others who work with the sick. When saving faith contributes to healing it is never an isolated event but always takes place within the context of innumerable influences from God's creation.

37. The doctrine of creation and the practical application of Christian stewardship require the Christian to view all good and constructive resources in the world as blessings from God to be used for his glory and for the welfare of one's fellowmen. Therefore, whatever scientific or technical skills are required to facilitate healing and foster the well-being of any person are welcomed, and whatever person or group of persons is required to administer the various therapeutic agents and treatments will also be embraced as co-workers, consciously or unconsciously, with the ministry of the church in God's work of healing the sick.

38. *Primary and Secondary.* However, while that healing which comes through saving faith is inextricably bound up with that healing which comes through other means, it is important to distinguish between God's saving action through faith in Christ and the rest of God's action in his universe. God intends that men shall seek out to organize and to use for human welfare those forces which work in nature, in the social order, and in human effort. God does not intend that men shall seek out Jesus Christ, the Gospel, and faith in Christ in order to use these for some other purpose.

39. For Christians forgiveness of sins, faith in Christ, and a resurrected, eternal life are central concerns. These alone are ultimate. Pain, sickness, therapy, and healing are important but secondary matters. They are penultimates.

40. These penultimates may function as God's Law. Then they

hold great value within the Christian life. Sickness and therapy may serve to uphold human life and the structures of society so that men can continue to exist on this earth and to hear the Gospel. They may also bring men to a sense of their inability and futility before God so that they will be open to grace and faith in Christ. Thus these penultimates may be agencies which bring us to the ultimates and to Christ.

41. These penultimates may also function as expressions of the Christian life, among the fruits of faith in Christ, as the outflow of forgiveness of sins. When God's grace so operates in the preventing of sickness, in the healing of sickness, or in the courageous handling of sickness, these are to be taken as signs of Christ's unpredictable and unpatterned personal victory over the forces of evil at that time and place.

42. The distinction between penultimates and ultimates is the distinction between the Law and the Gospel and is of crucial importance. Theological bases from which to approach an understanding of healing must stress a wholeness of purview and must provide a balanced stance, but they must above all keep first things first. It is the Gospel that comes first in importance for Christians.

43. When people attempt to use faith in Christ to gain physical and mental health, they are making God's grace the means toward some other end and are thus misusing the Gospel. When people talk of discovering spiritual laws that enable one to tap Christ's supernatural powers for purposes of healing, they are misusing the Law in an attempt to coerce God. These are attempts at magic. If there are supernatural powers to be tapped, they are ultimately destructive even though they appear to heal. When people point to healing or good health as evidence of one's righteousness, this is a false reliance upon outward obedience to the Law as the way of entry into God's good gifts. Sin and sickness as affliction are common enemies of Christ, but the specific correlation between them remains in large part a mystery. In a word, any effort to pin down and control God's acts in Christ in order to command healing is attempting to live by the Law instead of by the Gospel.

44. The Christian Gospel, then, has a central message which must be kept clear. However, it has implications for the whole of human life and it is always addressed to whole persons. Thus healing is not central but it is important from the Christian perspective.

45. *Within Koinonia.* How does the Christian discern these matters aright as they touch his own experience and decision? How can he maintain the right quality of expectancy within his Christian faith? How will he know when to mark Christ's victory, when to discern God's creative power, when to find that a concern for healing is proper and when to condemn health seeking as misuse of the Gospel?

46. The Holy Spirit is the Christian's guide, for the Christian lives in the fellowship of that Spirit. And that Spirit is evidenced primarily within the koinonia, the fellowship of the Christian church. In healing, as in all matters, it is within the immediate context of the Christian church that one finds help in living the Christian life.

47. In sickness or in health the Christian meets Christ through involvement with his fellow Christians. The gift of saving faith is always accompanied by the gift of incorporation in the community of those who share the same faith and acknowledge the one Lord. For the Christian spiritual healing is found only within that community.

48. Since the church is marked first of all by the Word and the Sacraments and corporate worship, it is in the midst of these that faith finds strength, that the expectancy of faith finds guidance, that healing may flow through saving faith. The Reformers were right when they affirmed the therapeutic value that follows or accompanies the assurance of forgiveness as it is received in the Sacrament of the Lord's Supper.

49. Furthermore, the Christian fellowship finds equally vivid expression in all personal relationships of Christians. When the pastor works with individual members, when two believers are associated in any way, especially when small enabling and supporting groups of Christians take shape, there Christ is in the midst and Christian fellowship takes on specific face-to-face meaning. In the earliest church Christians both worshiped corporately and gathered in small groups (Acts 2:46).

50. Such Christian fellowship involves a sharing and love and mutual ministry which include a concern for the totality of each member's life, a mutual confession of sins and assurance of forgiveness, a compassionate intercession through prayer, a common edification and guidance, and a bearing of one another's burdens. The oft-quoted passage in the Epistle of James (5:13-18) shows how the first Christians sought to care for the sick and to encourage healing within the setting of a praying, confessing

Anointing and Healing

fellowship where there was a concern for the total person.

51. In such a context Christians find their greatest support in facing all life's difficulties. It is in this context that spiritual healing, and all other aspects of healing find their best opportunity. It is within this context that the Holy Spirit guides the Christian in the expectancy of his faith, enabling him to discern God at work in his world.

Part Two

III. FROM PERSPECTIVES TO PRACTICE

52. *Method of Procedure*. The foregoing theological statements provide perspectives within which the Christian can assess his situation and determine his strategy. But when he moves toward decision he must ask not only "What is God's truth?" but also "Where do we stand?" Since men always stand at the juncture of history and present circumstance, the theological perspectives must be applied to both these factors. For this report the present circumstances are implied in the sections on "Questions" and "The Problem."

53. For this report the role of history is carried by tradition (remembered history) and lives as a strong element in the church's present thought and practice. Obviously, tradition has also had a hand in guiding our effort to draw perspectives from Scripture.

54. Our method of procedure, therefore, is to start from the living tradition incorporated in present practice, assess it and the demands of present circumstances in the light of the theological perspectives, emerging with suggestions for an over-all strategy on the one hand, and guidelines in relation to specific questions on the other hand.

55. Most emphatically this report does not seek to formulate either ready answers or canon law in order to relieve individuals and congregations from making their own decisions in evangelical freedom when faced by difficult questions. Rather the effort is to lead toward a broad consensus that would provide a strategy and some general guidelines for the church as a whole.

56. *Analysis*. It is the judgment of the committee that the ministry of contemporary American Lutheranism should focus more adequately the power of the Gospel upon the modern world of sickness and healing. Christian believers are not, by and large, led into a right expectancy concerning healing through their faith in

Christ. One reason is the failure of our congregations to provide a fellowship that evidences concern for the totality of each believer's life.

57. It is the committee's equally strong conviction that much of the ferment in the area of spiritual healing, which takes place outside our congregational life and attracts the interest of our members, too easily engenders a false expectancy concerning healing through faith in Christ.

58. Our Lutheran concern for the ultimates (the Gospel) has allowed us to neglect some of the penultimates (bodily healing), failing to stress the total implications of that ultimate Gospel. In contrast, much modern activity in spiritual healing allows the penultimate of bodily health to be treated as an ultimate and therefore to warp or misuse the Gospel.

59. *Strategy.* The committee recommends, therefore, that Lutheran congregations provide increasing opportunities for their members to develop the expectation that through their faith in Christ God will touch their total existence, thus opening the possibility of bodily healing. That is to say, the committee recommends that there be a larger place in the normal, ongoing life of congregations for such concern about the totality of each believer's life that the burden of bodily sickness will be shared and will be met with concerned prayers, thus providing an open door for spiritual healing when and where God sees fit to heal through Christian faith.

60. The committee also recommends that Lutherans — and all who will heed this warning — be very careful about participating in efforts at spiritual healing that do not develop within the context of face-to-face Christian fellowship, a fellowship that is created first of all by the Gospel. That is to say, the committee warns that the expectancy of Christian faith for spiritual healing is always secondary to the expectancy of faith for receiving the Gospel. Always the central concern must be Christ's victory in the believer in the face of the threatening fact of sickness. If bodily healing becomes central, then all is lost.

IV. GUIDELINES IN RELATION TO QUESTIONS

61. *Question a. How are we to regard the work of the "faith healers" of our day? What should be the relationship of Lutheran people to such activities?*

62. We define "faith healers" as those who, claiming to possess or convey spiritual powers that heal the sick, distort the Gospel

by trying to direct the power of Christ into a miraculous act of bodily healing. They fail or refuse to distinguish between the primary and secondary (ultimate and penultimate) elements of Christian faith. "Faith healers" are often less concerned with the spiritual and physical well-being of people than with the demonstration of their personal power or the attainment of prestige and financial gain. This is religious quackery.

"Faith healers" do great harm through such abuses as the following:

1. They fail to recognize as God's gift to man proven scientific methods and recognized therapeutic procedures or to cooperate with those who practice them.

2. They mislead credulous people by offering physical cures which cannot honestly be promised by anyone.

3. They endanger the whole spiritual life of believers by so claiming that God is able and ready to heal, that they leave the implication that failure to be cured is due to lack of faith on the part of the afflicted.

4. They use mass meetings and mass communications to reach an unknown public and use faulty evidence and false hope to lead people to expect more than God has ordained for them.

5. They make a spectacle of human misery and exploit the hopes and fears, the frustrations and disappointments of the desperate, disturbed and credulous.

6. They oversimplify faith and healing and, both directly and by implication, distort the image of those dedicated to serving the spiritual and physical well-being of people.

7. They endanger human lives by misdirecting believers into a sense of false security with respect to sickness. In so doing they delay early diagnosis and treatment and in many instances directly contribute to an untimely death.

8. They use the power of suggestion and mass hypnosis to create an individual sense of well-being, confusing this with the work of the Holy Spirit.

63. It is the committee's conviction that Lutheran people should refuse to participate in the activities of such "faith healers." It is each Christian's responsibility when he faces a decision to discern to the best of his ability where God is clearly at work and where other forces may prevail.

64. *Question b. How are we to regard the healing ministries practiced by other Christian churches or by groups of Christians closely related to*

the traditional Christian churches? What should be the relationship of Lutheran people to such activities?

65. Here a word of caution is in order. Christian fellowship that centers in the Gospel is not to be confined within congregational and denominational boundaries. Nor is it to be discouraged when people of special interests gather about those interests in the name of Christ. Sickness and healing certainly represent an important interest, and spiritual healing should naturally be an open possibility when Christians gather in fellowship around a concern for the sick. So far so good.

66. But with the appearance of any of the signs of abuse described in paragraph 62 above, the whole undertaking becomes suspect. Many people who sincerely name the name of Christ do not evidence enough care, from the Lutheran standpoint, in distinguishing ultimates and penultimates. And the human tendency to try to misuse the power of the Gospel constantly resides in every one of us.

67. Furthermore one always has the responsibility to try to discern whether a given gathering or organization really evidences koinonia, i.e., genuine Christian fellowship. When there is held open the expectancy of Christian faith for spiritual healing, it should be within a fellowship which gives clear priority to an expectancy for receiving the Gospel and a central concern for Christ's victory through faith in a specific situation of sickness. Besides, the fellowship should also include a balanced concern for the total person of each believer. Such conditions are difficult to fulfill in an interdenominational, intercongregational fellowship or organization which stresses spiritual healing.

68. For these reasons the committee would advise Lutheran people to use caution and discretion in participating in healing ministries practiced by other Christian churches or by groups of Christians closely related to the traditional Christian churches.

69. *Question c. Should the Lutheran church and its congregations provide a healing ministry beyond their present general practice?*

70. Within the ministry and fellowship of Lutheran congregations there should be much greater concern for sickness and healing. Here our congregational life should be measured by the same plumb line used with the groups mentioned in questions a. and b. Does our fellowship both make central our need to receive the Gospel and give balanced concern to the implications of that Gospel for the total person of each believer? Does concern for sickness and healing find an important place in

Anointing and Healing

congregational life as one major facet of the Gospel's total implications? The fact that some of our members participate in spiritual healing activities outside our church may indicate a failure in our own church life.

71. *Question d. How should the Lutheran church and its congregations provide a healing ministry beyond their present general practice?*

72. The committee cannot answer this question either with authority or in detail. Here and there in our church, steps are being taken in this direction; answers may emerge from such ventures.

73. Certainly it will not do to provoke great excitement within our congregations about spiritual healing as though some new gospel has come upon us. Neither will it be wise to urge upon our congregations a new technique or program as though we could fulfill our healing ministry through added procedures.

74. In this matter, as in many others, we need a new receptivity to the Gospel and a fresh responsiveness to its total implications. Specifically, Lutherans need a greater awareness of the significance of sickness and healing for people, for Christian faith, and for the living of the Christian life. Lutherans need to be more aware of and open to the possibility of spiritual healing by God through Christian faith. Lutheran fellowship needs to provide among its members a more effective mutual ministry to minds and bodies in sickness and in health.

75. Realizing that this implies a shift in perspective in regard to healing within the whole life of the church, the committee confines its comments to providing guidelines in response to several specific questions.

76. *Question e. Are healing services a wise practice for Lutheran churches?*

77. Speaking for our own time and situation, the committee would not recommend the introduction of public services designated as healing services. The committee believes it would invite misuse and misunderstanding to hold public worship at stated times, open to all comers or even to the whole membership of the congregation, in which the implied purpose is the healing of sick minds and bodies.

78. Quite another matter would be the holding of public worship which is not designated as a healing service, in which there is special concern for sick people, and in which doors are held open to the possibility of spiritual healing. The validity of

such a service would depend on the circumstances (cf. the answer to question b. above).

79. *Question f. Is anointing with oil a wise practice for Lutheran congregations?*

80. The committee believes that the use of oil in ministering to the sick would be unwise for our Lutheran congregations today. Though such use of oil belongs to the living tradition of some other churches, it is not a part of the traditional practice of Lutherans. Though there is Biblical precedent (notably James 5:14), no direct application is possible because in Biblical times oil was thought to have medicinal value.

81. Furthermore, there is danger that magical value would be attached to oil thus used, or that it would be considered a new sacrament alongside Baptism and the Lord's Supper.

82. Since our day is one of confusion both about sacramental signs and about spiritual healing, the introduction of such an unfamiliar practice would run great risk of misunderstanding and misuse.

83. *Question g. Is the laying on of hands in ministering to the sick a wise practice for Lutheran congregations?*

84. This practice is to be encouraged where it will readily serve as a sign of concern and as a sign of a desired blessing upon the sick person on the part of the ministering person or on behalf of the wider Christian fellowship. It is to be discouraged where it readily suggests that through the hands are conveyed in a special way God's grace or God's healing power.

85. The committee believes this practice can be used by Lutherans as an aid to their ministry much more readily than the practice of anointing with oil. It belongs naturally in our tradition and society without adding a strange element and a new rite. Whether the setting be formal and liturgical, reminiscent of confirmation and ordination, or whether it be informal, reminiscent of a handshake and the encouraging touch of a physician or clergyman, the laying on of hands can serve as a valued symbol — tangible and personalized for the sick — of a healing ministry. The context for such laying on of hands should always be prayer and other evidences of concern and the seeking of God's help for the sick.

86. *Question h. What is the place of intercessory prayer in the healing ministry of the Lutheran church?*

87. Praying, including intercession, belongs to virtually every aspect of the church's life and ministry. Intercession has an

integral and significant place in The Service of our church, in the other corporate worship experiences, in Christian group life, in the ministrations in the sick room and hospital, and in family and private devotions. The committee urges each congregation and Christian to ask seriously whether intercession for the sick should not find larger place in every sphere of the church's life. In intercession for the sick, as throughout our prayer life, there is urgent need for greater wisdom, care, meaning, and effectiveness in our church's practice.

88. Included in any strengthening of our intercession is the responsibility to keep open the possibility and expectancy that God may heal through faith and prayer. Assured that God answers prayer, and cheerfully confident of God's blessing, Christians always pray "Thy will be done." But we must be careful not to imply any prejudgment, not to suggest fatalistically that God wills this sickness, nor to suggest presumptuously that God wishes to heal this person. Our only certainty in respect to God's will concerning a given sickness is that he wills Christ's victory in this situation. But we have the responsibility to be open to any signs of that victory which are given us, including bodily healing.

89. The committee further recommends that congregations give careful consideration to a strengthening of a healing ministry at two particular points. One is the Prayer of the Church in The Service (*Service Book and Hymnal*, p. 6; *Common Service Book*, p. 20). In this prayer many congregations could more pointedly and effectively hold up before God through the praying fellowship the special needs of those who are sick.

90. The second point is within the group life of the congregation. It is the committee's conviction that most congregations need to utilize small face-to-face "enabling groups" in which the fellowship of the congregation becomes personal and envelops the totality of the believer's life. Here prayer, concern, and service for the sick would form a natural part of the group life. Since most congregations will not have the whole membership in such groups, it would also be important to have groups or cells with a particular concern for the sick of the congregation and the community, so that their group life would center upon prayer, concern, and service for the sick.

91. Where the congregational fellowship is thus sensitive to the particular needs of its members and thus ready to serve the special needs of the sick, there spiritual healing and all other

aspects of healing will find their best opportunity (cf. paragraphs 46–51 above). Then we can urge our members with real hope to turn in their need to their Lutheran church rather than to "faith healers."

92. *Question i. What is the role of the Christian physician in the healing ministry of the church?*

93. As has been stated (paragraph 37 above), whatever person or group of persons is required to administer the various therapeutic agents and treatments will be embraced as co-workers, consciously or unconsciously, with the ministrations of the church in God's work of healing the sick. Because of the essential unity of man and because of God's loving concern for the whole man the development of a genuine team ministry of physician and pastor is essential. Pastors must be alert to physical concomitants of spiritual ills in order to enlist medical aid. Physicians must be aware of spiritual conflicts in connection with physical ailments in order to enlist pastoral aid. It is hoped that progress in recent years in this respect will continue until it becomes general rather than exceptional for pastors to work together with physicians as part of the health team. This approach to healing should be strengthened by a free interchange of knowledge and a readiness to refer patients between pastor and physician with consultations held as often as necessary for the good of the patient.

94. The church can make a worthwhile contribution to healing when it brings wholeness to the ministry to the sick, recognizing the contributions of many specialties, each narrow in itself, and providing a wholesome perspective which views the patient as a unity, with a moral and social context and with an eternal destiny.

95. Since a Christian is called to serve his neighbor for Christ's sake, and since a physician is a significant agent of healing, the Christian physician is an important expression of the healing ministry of the church. The physician who is a Christian has a great opportunity through his constant daily contacts with his patients to instill courage, radiate hope, and inspire faith within the wavering soul. In his daily tasks the physician constantly sees God's hand as he does the best he can for his patient. When he has done all for a patient that modern medical science has taught him, whether the treatment fails or succeeds, he knows that he remains a channel open upward to heaven by faith and outward to his patient, his neighbor, through love. It is important for the

church's total ministry of healing that all Christians recognize the significant contribution Christian physicians make to the church's healing work.

1. This was borne out by a survey conducted in August 1961, of attitudes and practices of parish pastors within our church with respect to spiritual healing.
2. "The Relation of Christian Faith to Health," report of the Committee on the Relation of Christian Faith to Health, Adopted by the 172nd General Assembly, May 1960, of the United Presbyterian Church in the United States of America (Witherspoon Bldg., Philadelphia), p. 10.
3. Cf. "The Church's Ministry of Healing," Report of the Archbishops' Commission (Westminster, England, 1958), p. 12.

5 American Lutheran Church, USA, 1963

A REPORT ON GLOSSOLALIA

A special committee of the Commission on Evangelism of the American Lutheran Church submitted "A Report on Glossolalia" in 1963. This report was preceded by two earlier ones. The first, the "Report of the Field Study Committee on Speaking in Tongues," issued from a study group, consisted of three members: a theologian, a psychologist, and a psychiatrist. Essentially, they reported on a field trip made to observe "several congregations in different states." In addition to extensive interviews with fifteen persons, there were group interviews and the committee attended prayer meetings. There were certain convictions common to those interviewed which the committee thought to be un-Lutheran. "It is erroneous to equate 'Spirit-filled' with 'speaking in tongues.'" Further, "there is no Scriptural reason for calling glossolalia the 'gateway to the gifts of the Spirit.'" Among the beneficial results the committee found there was a sense of fellowship, and they bore one another's burdens. Those interviewed testified to growth in the spiritual life, less irritability, more sensitivity to the feelings of others, better marital relationships. Several pastors who had experienced glossolalia reported of other tongue-speakers: "They are our best members." They mentioned especially more involvement in the organizational life of the church and more generosity in their financial support of the local church. In the opinion of the committee the speaking in tongues which they heard during their investigations "was not gibberish."

More negatively the committee noted the adverse effects of evening meetings which were prolonged past midnight, pressure being exerted on

persons to speak in tongues (including induced tongues) and the
exaggerated preoccupation of some pastors with the experience of speaking
in tongues. Thirteen of the fifteen persons given more extensive
interviews gave evidence of a "clearly defined anxiety crisis preceding
their speaking in tongues." The anxiety was related to intrapsychic
conflicts, depression, marital difficulties, financial concerns, and ill
health. The report concluded that the promotion of tongues "is very
disturbing in a congregation." "There has been enough talking about
glossolalia in our Church and . . . further publicity would fan the
flames and do more harm than good." This report was for "restricted
use" and is not reproduced here.

The second document is the "Report of the Committee on Spiritual
Gifts of the Commission on Evangelism," an interim report. The
committee called on the Lutherans to "recognize that the spiritual life of
Christians can be deepened by a variety of spiritual experiences." Those
not involved should be cautioned about suggesting that "speaking in
tongues is not Lutheran." Note was made of the difficulties arising from
the use of tongues in public meetings. Christian maturity is not
guaranteed to accompany the experience of glossolalia. Because of its
similarity to the final report it is not included in the documents here
published.

The Committee on Spiritual Gifts of the Commission on Evangelism
issued "A Report on Glossolalia," a final statement. From the procedural
point of view, the commission represented a change, namely, the
inclusion in the membership of one Lutheran pastor involved in the
charismatic renewal. In some initial way this is a recognition that the
phenomenon must be wholly judged from the outside. The Committee on
Spiritual Gifts made a series of introductory statements, recorded a
number of brief impressions, and concluded with some suggestions.

The gift of tongues, asserted the report, is not normative for salvation,
nor "for the Christian's growth in grace." Paul's injunction, "Earnestly
desire the spiritual gifts" cannot be directly applied, without
qualification, to glossolalia. Those who had received the gift of tongues
seemed to find it difficult to speak of it with reserve. A special appeal of
tolerance and understanding was made for those who had had the
experience of tongues but were no longer using the gift. A caution was
expressed concerning the length of meetings during which glossolalia was
exercised, and a plea was made that witnessing to one's experience not
deteriorate into "promotion and exploitation." Examples of such
promotional activities were preaching on tongues, prolonged laying on of
hands to encourage the experience of tongues, and escorting parishioners
to meetings where "speaking in tongues is being exalted and promoted."

In the American Lutheran Church "the integration of speaking in tongues into the life of a Lutheran congregation has proved very difficult for both pastor and people."

"A Report on Glossolalia" is published in Towards a Mutual Understanding of Neo-Pentecostalism, *eds. Walter Wietzke and Jack Hustad (Minneapolis: Augsburg Publishing House, 1973), pp. 7–11. Not included in* Towards a Mutual Understanding of Neo-Pentecostalism *are study papers used in the preparation of the final report: Lowell J. Satre, "Glossolalia in the New Testament"; Reider A. Daehlin, "Speaking in Tongues"; "A Study Document Produced by the Luther Seminary Theological Faculty and Used for the Purpose of Discussing this Phenomenon with Five Members of the Senior Class Who Have This Experience."*

Prepared by the Commission on Evangelism of The American Lutheran Church and Approved for Release by the Church Council

The Commission on Evangelism appointed the following people to serve on a Committee on Spiritual Gifts: Chairman, Bruno Schlachtenhaufen, Pastor, Decorah, Iowa; Secretary, James Hanson, Pastor, Glendive, Montana; Maurice M. Nesset, Ph.D., President, Board of Trustees of Lutheran General Hospital, Park Ridge, Illinois; Lowell J. Satre, Ph.D., Professor of New Testament, Luther Theological Seminary, St. Paul, Minnesota; Paul Qualben, B.Th., M.D., Psychiatrist, Lutheran Medical Center, Brooklyn, New York; Stanley Schneider, A.B., B.D., Professor of Homiletics, Evangelical Lutheran Theological Seminary, Columbus, Ohio; W. H. Weiblen, Th.D., Assistant Professor of Systematic Theology, Wartburg Theological Seminary, Dubuque, Iowa; Conrad Thompson, D.D., Director of Evangelism, Minneapolis, Minnesota; Advisor, Mars A. Dale, D.D., Assistant Director of Evangelism, Minneapolis, Minnesota.

The Committee on Spiritual Gifts was asked to make a study of glossolalia. A preliminary report was submitted by the Commission on Evangelism at the General Convention of The American Lutheran Church at Milwaukee, Wisconsin, October 24, 1962.

In preparing its final report the Committee on Spiritual Gifts asked two of its members (Drs. Qualben and Satre) to make a ten-day field study that included visitation in four congregations where speaking in tongues exists. A third man, Dr. John Kildahl of New York, a clinical psychologist, was coopted to serve with the field study committee. The three men are all on the clergy roster of The American Lutheran Church.

The report of the Committee on Spiritual Gifts follows:

I. INTRODUCTORY STATEMENTS

1. We recognize that God comes to man through the Word and the Sacraments and that where these are, there is the Church. It is further recognized that God uses the Means of Grace in various ways to call men to Him and renew the life of His people.

2. Speaking in tongues is one of several gifts of the Spirit described in Scripture (cf. I Cor 12-14, especially 12:4-11).

3. In previous documents it has been stressed that glossolalia is not normative for salvation. Neither is it normative for the Christian's growth in grace. The fruits of the Spirit do not necessarily accompany the gifts of the Spirit (cf. I Cor 13:1-3).

4 . The testimony of the Christians who have witnessed to blessings associated with their speaking in tongues has been respected as being valid for these individuals.

II. IMPRESSIONS

1. The integration of speaking in tongues into the life of a Lutheran congregation has proved very difficult, for both pastor and people. Divisions and tensions have been found in varying degrees in the congregations where glossolalia is known to exist.

2. It is the pastor's privilege and responsibility to serve *all* in his parish, both through his public proclamation of the Gospel and administration of the Sacraments, and through his private soul care. When the pastor and some members speak in tongues in a congregation, it happens frequently that the other members feel the pastor is showing partiality, *whether he is or not.*

3. If the pastor has often associated tongues and the Spirit, his sermons tend to be misunderstood, especially when he mentions the Holy Spirit.

4. Because of the ease with which a group speaking in tongues may indulge in various forms of excess, the pastor's immediate, judicious, strong leadership is indispensable.

5. The experience of glossolalia is no guarantee of Christian maturity and knowledge. Doctrinal instruction must be given promptly to those needing it, especially if they are to be received into church membership and accept positions of responsibility in the congregation.

Report on Glossolalia

6. The pastor who does not speak in tongues is just as responsible for the spiritual well-being of glossolalists in his flock as for the soul care of the members who are not.

7. It appears to be difficult for persons who speak in tongues to be reserved about it. For a variety of reasons it seems necessary to them to witness to the experience enthusiastically.

8. It is possible to have unity with diversity if Christ is Lord and His love reigns over all. The respect of members of one group for those of the other is occasionally expressed, but a statement such as "Speaking in tongues is not Lutheran", does not make for a better spirit in the congregation nor does the "If-you-don't-like-it-lump-it" attitude.

9. There are those who have had the experience of speaking in tongues but are no longer practicing it. They also need tolerance and understanding from the pastor and all other members of the congregation.

III. SUGGESTIONS

1. The Christian congregation should recognize that the spiritual life of Christians can be deepened by a variety of spiritual experiences.

2. Any group or person introducing a new element into a congregation has a grave responsibility for doing this in such a way that peace and unity are not destroyed. Responsibility for maintaining the integrity of the congregation is shared by all.

3. Self-righteousness tends to be accentuated in situations where diversity of opinions and practices exists. All members of a congregation, whether glossolalists or not, should be aware of this besetting sin.

4. The ministry of intercessory prayer is an integral part of the worship life of the Lutheran Church and finds expression both in various liturgical services and in many other forms of group and individual experience in the congregation.

a. The Committee sees the value of fellowship groups which serve as a "bridge" for those non-members who would not immediately feel at home at a Sunday morning service of worship.

b. If a particular Bible study or prayer group has become identified as one where there is, has been, or may be speaking in tongues, it may be advisable to start another group in which there would be no speaking in tongues whatsoever.

5. Those who speak in tongues must be encouraged to press on to a concern for "the whole counsel of God." There is a danger of overemphasis on glossolalia on the part of some, with an unbalanced, distorted Christian perspective as the outcome. By definition heresy is the selection of and concentration on a part, with a resultant distortion of the whole.

6. The total well-being of each individual must be respected. A meeting at which there may be glossolalia should be conducted according to the prevailing practice in the congregation just as any other meeting in the church. Particular caution must be exercised as to the length of such meetings.

7. It is recognized that a combination of factors may result in an intense desire to witness to the experience of speaking in tongues. It is also recognized, however, that in many places good judgment has not prevailed and the "witnessing" has deteriorated into promotion and exploitation. This is deplored and to be avoided. The following promotional activities have been observed in some congregations of the American Lutheran Church.

a. Escorting parishioners to meetings where speaking in tongues is being exalted and promoted, whether such meetings be in a Lutheran, Episcopalian, Pentecostal, or other church, or home.

b. Helping people uncover their feelings of need for more spiritual "power", "peace", "boldness", and then presenting glossolalia rather than or in addition to God Triune in His Gospel as the answer.

c. Praying for extended periods of time with the "unlearned" that they may speak in tongues.

d. Prolonging the meeting to the point of wearing down defenses, that the phenomenon may be experienced.

e. Preaching sermons to promote speaking in tongues.

f. Prolonged laying on of hands to encourage the experience of glossolalia.

g. Speaking in tongues in public assembly for the purpose of getting others to do so.

8. It is incorrect to apply Paul's injunction "Earnestly desire the spiritual gifts" directly to glossolalia without qualification. Attention is directed to the following facts:

a. Paul's exhortation in I Cor 14:1 is followed by the Greek words *mallon de*. An authoritative Greek lexicon says the following about the translation and meaning of these words: "'but rather', 'or rather,' or simply 'rather' introduces an expression or thought that supplements and thereby corrects what has preceded" (Arndt-Gingrich). In other words, Paul's command in 14:1 cannot be applied to tongues without qualification.

b. Similar is Paul's statement in I Cor 14:5: "Now I want you all to speak in tongues, but rather (*mallon de*) to prophesy."

c. I Cor 14:39 is a commentary on 14:1. Paul exhorts: "Earnestly desire to prophesy" and adds: "Do not forbid speaking in tongues." It is significant that in these concluding remarks Paul does *not* say: "Earnestly desire to speak in tongues."

d. In I Cor 12:31 Paul says, "But earnestly desire the higher gifts." In the light of the general context in I Cor 12–14, and especially of the verses cited above, glossolalia is not included in the higher gifts.

Paul, then, gives no unqualified exhortation to people to try to speak in tongues. He saw fit to permit, not promote.

9. Some alleged interpretation of tongues has been called prophecy; we can not but be skeptical of any saying which claims to be prophetic unless it is clearly a correct exposition and forthtelling of the message of the Scriptures. Furthermore, since we find no Biblical warrant for identifying the interpretation of tongues with prophecy, we caution against doing so.

10. The following suggestions are made regarding the public and private use of speaking in tongues in our congregations:

a. If glossolalia is practiced, its use should be in harmony with the spirit of Paul's words in I Cor 12–14. Point number 2 of the statement on speaking in tongues by the Faculty of Luther Seminary expresses a principle of Biblical interpretation which it is relevant to state here:

"It is a dangerous hermeneutical practice to take what Paul said to a particular congregation, in a specific place, at a certain time, on a special occasion and apply it literally and indiscriminately to congregations today. (Cf. I Cor 14:35b: 'For it is shameful for a woman to speak in church.' This statement is cited because it is within a section dealing primarily with 'tongues' and because it is not applied literally and indiscriminately in the Church today.) Nevertheless, Paul's way of dealing with this problem (one of the 'matters about which [they] wrote' — 7;1) in the congregation at Corinth gives clues for the way in which it might be dealt with today."

b. In a congregation where there is speaking in tongues but where it is not practiced publicly, the public practice should not be initiated.

c. In a congregation where there is a public meeting at which glossolalia is practiced, the question whether the public practice should be continued or not should be weighed by the pastor and the members practicing glossolalia in the light of the following considerations:

(1) Paul's very low estimate of the value of speaking or praying publicly in tongues as compared with speaking or praying intelligibly in public (I Cor 14:13–18).

(2) The counsel Paul gives in Romans 14 and I Cor 13. (The most subtle form of legalism may have overtaken him who insists: "I have a right. . . .")

(3) What such public practice is doing to the life of the congregation.

(4) What the public practice means to those engaging in it.

(5) The attitude of the church council of the congregation.

(6) The advice of the district president.

(7) The fact that in all such matters as this the congregation is sovereign.

d. Speaking in tongues in private for the individual's personal edification is not to be forbidden.

11. Through the ages the Church yearns for spiritual renewal, in some periods more than in others, at some times more consciously than at other times. The present scene is characterized by many expressions of "the thirst for the living God." Let the Church thank God for Jesus of Nazareth, the risen, ascended Lord Christ who made Pentecost possible (Acts 2:33), who is the One preached and present in Peter's Pentecost sermon. For the Christ who comes in Word and Sacrament to inhabit our faith and to be our righteousness, let the Church be unceasingly thankful. Let her continue to thank God for the Holy Spirit, given to him who is baptized into Christ by the Father through water and His Word of promise. Let the Church pray that more of its people be "faithful to their covenant of Baptism even unto the end." It is urged that the whole Christian Church "continue to pray regularly for the gifts of the Holy Spirit with the assurance that this prayer is being and will continue to be answered."

12. Our day presents a glorious challenge to the Church of "The Word Alone, Faith Alone, Grace Alone." Even as "all the

parables of Jesus compel his hearers to come to a decision about his person and mission," so let every hearer in our congregations today be confronted with the living Jesus who in His Gospel compels men, now and to the end of this age, to come to a decision about Him. Let us pray for, work for, anticipate, thank God for awakening, renewal, revival, conversion, growth, deepening in our congregations. It should be the concern of *every pastor* and *parishioner* to try to minister effectively to each member of the community, whether he be spiritually dead, alive, or revived, and regardless of the phenomenon or phenomena which may or may not accompany his experience with God.

6 Christian and Missionary Alliance, USA, 1963

"SEEK NOT—FORBID NOT!"

Early in this century the classical Pentecostal movement and the Holiness movement, out of which Pentecostalism emerged, parted ways. Though the two were clearly of one mind on a broad range of doctrinal and scriptural issues, they were just as clearly divided on the matter of tongues as the initial evidence that a person had been baptized in the Spirit, a position which came to be identified with classical Pentecostalism, even though segments of that movement did not subscribe to the doctrine. After the outbreak of tongues at the Azusa Street mission in Los Angeles in 1906, the position of the Christian Missionary Alliance was formulated in 1907 by A. B. Simpson, its founder. When the charismatic renewal emerged in the historic churches in the early 1960s, the Alliance issued an official position and statement entitled "Seek Not — Forbid Not," which title rather accurately sums up its doctrinal stance. The 1907 statement of A. B. Simpson was repeated verbatim, augmented by some supplementary remarks and issued in 1963.

Simpson recognized the possibility that both the baptism in the Spirit and tongues could be authentic, noting the marked deepening of the spiritual life, an increase in missionary zeal, and liberality in those who claimed to have had these experiences. He labeled the doctrine of initial evidence to be one of the "greatest errors" of the new movement, "as though none had received the Spirit of Pentecost but those who had the power to speak in tongues. . . ." A tendency to be shunned was the pursuit of "signs and wonders and special manifestations" rather than focusing on "the great trust which God had given to us in the salvation of sinners and the sanctification of believers."

The Board of Managers of the Alliance in 1963 reaffirmed Simpson's 1907 statement "as the unchanged position of the Christian and Missionary Alliance." The doctrine of initial evidence was again rejected, as was the supposition that tongues is a gift all Christians should possess, though as one of the gifts of the Spirit "it may be present in the normal Christian assembly. . . ." In a word, "Seek not, forbid not!"

The "Official Position and Statement of the Christian and Missionary Alliance" is reprinted in The Alliance Witness *(May 1, 1963). Copies may be obtained from the Alliance office: 260 W. 44th St., New York City, 10036.*

Early in this century, when The Christian and Missionary Alliance was small and struggling, a religious movement began in California and moved eastward. It was to some degree a carryover from the great revival in Wales, but it soon took on characteristics which were alien to those of the Welsh revival. Among these was a strong emphasis on the gifts of the Spirit, especially the gift of tongues. This gift, indeed, soon became the test of spiritual excellence, and in spite of the efforts of some of the more balanced leaders, speaking in tongues finally came to be regarded as the one true evidence of the Spirit's baptism.

A "TONGUES" MOVEMENT

The movement became known as the "tongues" or "pentecostal" movement, though it was also sometimes called "Azusa" from the name of the street on which the church stood where the manifestations were first noticed.

This movement had an independent origin and was not, as some erroneously suppose, a split from The Christian and Missionary Alliance. But the Alliance soon felt its influence. Certain Alliance people accepted the extreme position of the "Azusa" movement and left the Society to throw in their lot with it. Others remained, but were badly confused by the tongues teaching and needed sound instruction and sane leadership. These Dr. Simpson was able to give them; so the crisis passed and the Society was preserved.

"Seek Not–Forbid Not!"

A WIDESPREAD MANIFESTATION

After an extended period of relative quiescence the peculiar manifestations of the tongues movement are appearing again among certain Christians; and oddly enough they are appearing among some of the old, historic denominations. These manifestations are sufficiently widespread as to disturb some of our people who are unfamiliar with our spiritual history and inexperienced in the deeper workings of the Holy Spirit.

The restored movement is on a much higher plane intellectually and culturally than the original tongues movement of old Azusa days. It even has a new and more euphonious name, "the charismatic movement," charismatic here being a learned word referring to spiritual gifts, especially the gift of tongues.

The Christian and Missionary Alliance is completely familiar with the teaching and phenomena of this movement no matter what they are called or where they occur. The Society went through all this half a century ago and knows well both the strengths and weaknesses of the men and the movement. What may appear new to some groups is not new to the Alliance. We still have scars to show for our battle for truth from the days when we stood against some who denied the gifts of the Spirit and others who insisted that tongues was the evidence of the baptism of the Spirit.

DR. SIMPSON'S ANALYSIS

In 1907 when the tongues movement was at its peak Dr. A. B. Simpson made a study of it and reported his findings to the General Council. He analyzed the movement, admitted its virtues and marked its errors, and then gave some sound advice. This was adopted by the Council and became the official position of the Society.

This report is again relevant, almost as much so as if it had been written in 1963. Though not all the characteristics of which Dr. Simpson writes in his report of 1907 are present today, and though The Christian and Missionary Alliance is to this point blessedly free from any abuses or excesses or division having to do with the charismatic movement, it is felt nevertheless that the position of the Society on this matter should be made known to the Christian public.

At a meeting of the Board of Managers held in New York City April 2–4, 1963, it was unanimously voted that we reaffirm our beliefs concerning the work of the Holy Spirit and readopt the following report as the unchanged position of The Christian and Missionary Alliance on this subject:

"These grave and distressing results have usually been averted in connection with our Alliance work where wise leaders have firmly held the work on scriptural lines, giving perfect liberty for the working of the Holy Ghost in His sovereign will in the hearts and assemblies of His people, whether with or without these special manifestations, but at the same time holding the work and workers steadily to the directions of the Word, repressing all disorder, confusion, fanaticism and false teaching, keeping out unwise and untried leaders, and pursuing steadfastly the special work which God has committed to our hands, namely the salvation of souls, the building up of believers and the evangelization of the world.

"In this way, under the most critical conditions, our largest conventions and our strongest branches have been held in unity, order and spiritual power and blessing." (*End of Dr. Simpson's Report*)

FULL CHARITY AND UNDERSTANDING

The present revival of interest in spiritual gifts is such that it cannot be ignored. We must deal with it as becomes dedicated Christians, in full charity and with cordial understanding. Certainly some persons of impeccable Christian character are associated with the present charismatic movement. But the gift of tongues belongs in the category of things easily imitated and by the very nature of it is capable of abuses and wild excesses.

An example of this was given by Dr. Simpson in his report: "Another result of the influence of which we have been speaking has been the sending forth of bodies of inexperienced and self-appointed missionaries to foreign lands under the honest impression on their part that God had given them the tongue of the people to whom they were to minister the gospel. Without preparation, without proper leadership and without any reasonable support, several of these parties have gone out to heathen lands only to find themselves stranded upon some foreign shore without the ability to speak any intelligible tongue, without the means of support or even of returning home. These unhappy victims of some honest but misleading impression have been thrown upon the charity of strangers, and after the greatest

"Seek Not—Forbid Not!"

sufferings have, in most cases with much difficulty, been compelled to return to their homes, disappointed, perplexed and heartbroken. In some cases our Alliance branches have been seriously disrupted by such outgoing parties, and a strain created which it will take years to heal. The temptation has come to new missionaries to abandon the study of the native language and wait vainly for some supernatural gift of tongues."

OUR ATTENTION ON CHRIST

We urge our people to keep the Person of Christ in full focus in every consideration of the gifts of the Spirit. We should make the Lord Jesus Christ, not gifts, and surely not the least of all the gifts, the object of our constant attention.

The Word of God and Christian history agree to teach that the church is safe only as long as she follows Christ Himself, and that she is in serious danger when she allows lesser things to hide His face from her.

THE SCRIPTURAL TEACHING

We believe the scriptural teaching to be that the gift of tongues is one of the gifts of the Spirit, and that it may be present in the normal Christian assembly as a sovereign bestowal of the Holy Spirit upon such as He wills. We do not believe that there is any scriptural evidence for teaching that speaking in tongues is the sign of having been filled with the Holy Spirit, nor do we believe that it is the plan of God that all Christians should possess the gift of tongues. This gift is one of many gifts and and is given to some for the benefit of all.

The attitude toward the gift of tongues held by pastor and people should be "Seek not, forbid not." This we hold to be the part of wisdom for this hour.

Unanimously adopted by the Board of Managers, The Christian and Missionary Alliance, April 4, 1963, for distribution to the Alliance constituency and friends.

SPECIAL REVIVAL MOVEMENTS

Annual Report of the President and General Superintendent of The Christian and Missionary Alliance for the year 1907–08 (*Pages 9–12, paragraph 5*):

"A year ago reference was made in our annual report to the special outpouring of the Spirit in many places, accompanied by speaking in tongues.

"At that time attention was called to the great need of our maintaining the spirit at once of candor and caution — openness on the one hand to all that God had to give us, and watchfulness on the other hand against counterfeits, extravagances and false teachings. During the year this movement has developed on lines which more and more emphasize the need for both these attitudes. We believe there can be no doubt that in many cases remarkable outpourings of the Holy Spirit have been accompanied with genuine instances of the gift of tongues and many extraordinary manifestations. This has occurred both in our own land and in some of our foreign missions.

"Many of these experiences appear not only to be genuine but accompanied by a spirit of deep humility, earnestness and soberness, and free from extravagance and error. And it is admitted that in many of the branches and states where this movement has been strongly developed and wisely directed, there has been a marked deepening of the spiritual life of our members and an encouraging increase in their missionary zeal and liberality. It would, therefore, be a very serious matter for any candid Christian to pass a wholesale criticism or condemnation upon such movements or presume to 'limit the Holy One of Israel.'"

GUARD GOD'S TRUTH AND WORK

"But at the same time and with increasing intensity there are other developments which make it very plain that those who have been made shepherds of the flocks of God and stewards of the mysteries of Christ have need to guard with firm and fearless hand God's truth and work, seeking from Him the spirit of 'discernment concerning things that differ' and carefully guarding the little flock from seducing spirits and false teachers.

"One of these greatest errors is a disposition to make special manifestations an evidence of the baptism of the Holy Ghost, giving to them the name of Pentecost, as though none had received the Spirit of Pentecost but those who had the power to speak in tongues, thus leading many sincere Christians to cast away their confidence, plunging them in perplexity and darkness or causing them to seek after special manifestations of other than God Himself. Another grave tendency is the disposition to turn

"Seek Not–Forbid Not!"

aside from the great trust which God has given to us in the salvation of sinners and the sanctification of believers, and seek rather for signs and wonders and special manifestations.

"When we seek anything less than God we are sure to miss His highest blessing and likely to fall into side issues and serious errors.

"Another evil is the spirit of separation and controversy and the turning away of many of our people from the work to which God called them, to follow some novel teaching or some new leader, perhaps little known or tried. In several cases our Alliance work has been almost broken up by these diversions and distractions, and many have forgotten their pledges for the work of evangelization and become involved in separation and often in bitterness and strife. Surely the Spirit of Pentecost is the Spirit of peace and love and holy unity, and when we fully receive His baptism we shall be like them of old, of one accord and one soul.

SOME WANT PROPHETIC AUTHORITY

"One of the most alarming tendencies of this movement has recently developed in several places in the form of a sort of prophetic authority which certain persons are claiming over the consciences of others, and men and women are seeking counsel and guidance from them in the practical matters of private duty, instead of looking directly to the anointing which they have received of Him and obeying God rather than men. It is said that in some instances Christian men and women go to these new prophets almost as the world goes to the clairvoyant and fortuneteller, and follow their advice with a slavish superstition that may easily run into all the dangers of the Romish confessional or the delusions of spiritualism.

STUDY COMMISSION ON GLOSSOLALIA

The charismatic renewal came to national attention through the stories in Newsweek *(July 4, 1960) and* Time *(August 15, 1960) of the outbreak of tongues at St. Mark's parish in Van Nuys, California, and the personal involvement of the pastor, Dennis Bennett. Previous to this Bishop Francis Bloy banned speaking in tongues in events sponsored by the church. Bishop Pike appointed a Study Commission on Glossolalia of nine members, including a priest involved in charismatic renewal, a director of the diocesan department of education, two professors (Scripture and systematics), two psychiatrists, and an expert in parapsychology.*

The report had in common with other early investigations concentration on tongues. A description of the larger framework in which glossolalia was practiced is followed by an exegetical section, an analysis of the psychological aspects, and a series of conclusions and recommendations.

The cultural baggage of classical Pentecostalism was often taken over when Episcopalians spoke of their religious experience. There was also a lack of theological understanding of glossolalia and other gifts. Biblical fundamentalism did not seem to be a necessary undergirding for the movement, but it was found to be widespread. But the attention charismatics give to Scripture constituted a rebuke for "the great number of Episcopal congregations where serious Bible study is totally ignored by both clergy and laity."

The experiential aspects "can lead to an unhealthy subjectivism in religion," but Episcopalians tend "to over-formalize and over-objectify the workings of God." However helpful some Christians find praying in tongues, "it must not be taken as necessary to Christian commitment and life in the Spirit, nor necessary as a sign of spiritual progress or status."

Commenting on the biblical evidence in Acts, the report remarked that nowhere is "tongues suggested as part of the ongoing life of the Christian." The biblical data gave the commission grounds to conclude: "As a part of the initiatory process of entering the Christian community, as part of one's ongoing private devotional life, and as one aspect of public worship, albeit carefully limited, glossolalia has biblical precedent, even if there is no scriptural warrant for making it normative for all Christians then or now."

In studying the psychological dimensions, the psychiatrists on the team concluded that they would evaluate positively tongues as an

irrational expression (many students now prefer the term non-rational),
pointing out that "our deepest feelings and convictions with their roots
in the subconscious, seldom can be adequately articulated by the
conscious," and therefore the psychological propriety of a prayer
language which transcends the rational. But from a purely psychological
point of view "glossolalia is not necessarily healthy or wholesome. . . .
Its 'goodness' or 'badness' for an individual depends upon his ability to
harmonize it with his other experience." Glossolalia is not of itself a
religious phenomenon. In its non-religious manifestations, it appears
among persons suffering from schizophrenia and hysteria. The
commission hastened to add that it did not wish to suggest that
Christians "who speak in tongues therefore must be mentally
disordered." Tongues can also exercise a creative influence freeing one to
grasp new insights and "to change a way of life for the better."
 The commission concluded that use in tongues should not be denied in
private devotions. As regards the public use this was left to the discretion
of the bishop.

INTRODUCTION

Submitted to the Bishop May 2, 1963, Released May 14, 1963

A. Composition of the Division

As constituted by the Bishop, the Committee is composed of the
following members: The Rev. John Ashey, The Rev. Thomas
Bogard, The Rev. David Forbes (Ch.), The Rev. Trevor Hoy, the
Rev. Charles Whiston, John W. Perry, M.D., Richard M.
Sutherland, M.D., Mrs. John Buenz, The Rev. Edward Hobbs.

 Of the present constituency, Canon Forbes is chairman; Fr.
Ashey is a parish priest who speaks "in tongues" and maintains a
ministry to others who do so in his parish; Fr. Bogard is a parish
priest not thus involved and who has undertaken graduate study
in the behavioral sciences; Canon Hoy is Director of the
Department of Education and actively involved in conferences
and institutes where the group process gives some insight into
human behaviour and motivations stripped of some of their usual
defenses; Drs. Hobbs and Whiston are professors at the Church
Divinity School of the Pacific specializing in Biblical Studies and
Systematic Theology respectively; Drs. Perry and Sutherland are
practicing psychiatrists, the latter, Consultant to the Diocese; and
Mrs. Buenz is a layman who has completed doctoral work in the
field of parapsychology.

It has been recommended that others might be co-opted for the Commission, so the membership as now constituted may well be added to in the future.

B. Plan

The Commission files this as a preliminary report and proposes to continue its work in what clearly is a subject requiring careful study in depth.

C. Nature of the Report

The report will cover the following subject areas: I. Statement of the Task, II. Review of Present Situation, III. Review of Existing Resource Material, A. Literature of those in the Movement, B. Studies by other groups and individuals, IV. Description of Glossolalia, V. Review of Biblical Background, A. Use of Scripture in the Movement, B. The Scripture References, C. Comment on these References, VI. Psychological Aspects of Glossolalia, VII. Conclusions and Recommendations.

I. STATEMENT OF THE TASK

Bishop Pike constituted this Commission as a study group to report to him on the nature and present status in the Church of glossolalia, and to make recommendations to assist him in setting diocesan policy on the subject.

This assignment has proven general indeed, for we have spent considerable time simply in defining and clarifying what we are to study and report on. We have felt hesitant to come to many conclusions. In the first place, the core of the problem lies in the relationship of the Holy Spirit to the ability to speak "in tongues", and here we can state no decision as finally authoritative. The most we can do is to suggest outer limits beyond which churchmen should move with great caution or not at all. In the second place, we do not pretend to have undertaken a scientific study of glossolalia even as a human phenomenon and realize that conclusions would require this. In the third place, those who speak in tongues are agreed that this action in itself is far less important than what they assert it signifies; namely, the conscious reception of the Holy Spirit and His continued activity in a person's life. A study which does not emphasize the larger question of the nature of all the gifts of the Spirit and their place in Christian life can only be preliminary and, we hope, clarifying.

Study Commission on Glossolalia

At the start, therefore, the Commission wishes to emphasize, first, that it recognizes how large is the scope of its assignment thus understood, and, second, that this report is indeed preliminary. We shall appreciate comment and correction.

II. REVIEW OF THE PRESENT SITUATION

A. Background

Glossolalia, of course, has been a well-accepted element in the practice of the Pentecostal sects since late in the 19th Century. It is a phenomenon new, however, to the Episcopal Church and the other "main-line" denominations in the United States, although individual churchmen are reported to have been involved for many years.

Apparently its Episcopalian beginnings were in 1958 at the Church of the Holy Spirit, Monterey Park, California, and at Trinity Church, Wheaton, Illinois. In both instances it began among laymen and soon involved the clergy. It first received major publicity at St. Mark's Church, Van Nuys, California, where the rector and a number of laymen in the parish became involved. Controversy developed leading several months later to his resignation. Since that time, glossolalia has appeared in a number of dioceses scattered across the country.

In this diocese, the phenomenon has spread rapidly in the last two years to the point where now it is estimated that at least 12 clergy and more than 200 laity are actively involved.

B. Its Practice in this Diocese

The manner in which two parishes in this diocese have used this ministry may illustrate some of the variety to be found throughout the Church in the use of glossolalia.

1. PARISH "A"

Here a program has developed over a period of about a year where initially some lay people and the rector met once weekly in the Rectory for prayer, study, and fellowship. A variety of the gifts of the Holy Spirit are reported as having been experienced from time to time, including, of course, glossolalia. Most of those involved used tongues as part of their devotional life day by day. An active healing ministry featured this group's activity as well as prayers and hymns of praise and adoration both liturgical and non-liturgical. No-one was allowed to speak in tongues (except inaudibly) unless another felt moved to speak in interpretation.

Recently, the group's size and the feeling that the parish as a whole might resent "private" meetings of this sort led to the establishment of weekly programs in the parish church. These programs feature instruction on some aspect of the Christian life followed by a social period over coffee. A service follows of an informal nature with hymn singing, psalm reading, testimony by individuals as they feel moved as to the meaning of Christ in their life, and extemporary prayer shared by all as they feel moved. At the conclusion of the service, those who wish to remain form small prayer groups for both study and prayer with the manifestation of such gifts of the Spirit as tongues. At the conclusion of the evening individuals as they wish return to the Church for Unction, or for prayer for the "quickening" of the power of the Spirit, or for a Blessing.

2. PARISH "B"

In this parish there is a continuing ministry through small groups called together from time to time by the Rector, but here, too, the focus of the parish program is in a weekly public service of healing and intercession at which he is the officiant. Anyone in or out of his parish is encouraged to attend and all are encouraged to pray for the reception of the Holy Spirit into their life as this is represented by the experience of glossolalia. These services are attended by people of different denominational backgrounds who in many cases come from a considerable distance.

The services are emphasized as non-liturgical. The rector, for example, wears no special vestments, but simply his street garb with clerical collar. The service typically includes most or all of the following: familiar hymns; a Scripture reading with lay interpretation as well as clerical; psalm recitation; intercessions in litany form both for the ill and distressed and for the diocese and the church at large; informal testimonies of witness by members of the congregation as they feel moved; "praising the Lord, each in his own way" (some in tongues); a ceremony of healing at the altar rail where priest and laymen (who previously have "commissioned" one another by laying on of hands accompanied sometimes by glossolalia) lay hands on those who desire it; the bringing of a message in tongues with interpretation; and prayer with laying on of hands for the reception of the Holy Spirit with glossolalia.

In November 1962 this parish sponsored a "Christian Advance" mission in cooperation with clergy and congregations of other denominations. It was given publicity in principal San Francisco newspapers. Its stated point is to bring people to a "baptism in the Holy Spirit", phraseology typical of the movement which we are studying. It might be noted that in the publicity the movement was described as "the greatest revival in the Church since the Reformation".

III. SOURCES IN LITERATURE

A. The Commission has on file a Bibliography, largely Pentecostal in origin, on the subject of glossolalia and baptism in the Spirit. We shall be glad to share it with anyone desiring to make use of it. Episcopalian literature on the subject is scarce. *The Blessed Trinity Society*, Box 2422, Van Nuys, California, issues a handsome quarterly, *The Logos*, carrying a variety of articles on all phases of what is usually termed the "Pentecostal Experience". The Society also prints pamphlets available at nominal cost.

Also a periodical issued monthly is the *Full Gospel Men's Voice*, published by the *Full Gospel Business Men's Fellowship International*, 836 South Figueroa, Los Angeles 17, California. Persons of all denominations write for its pages.

B. The Diocese of Chicago on December 12, 1960, issued the Report of a special Commission appointed by Bishop Burrill to study this movement. It has been very helpful in preparing this Report.

A brief statement entitled "New Movements in the Church", and dealing with problems raised by the so-called "Pentecostal" movement in the Episcopal Church was issued by the House of Bishops in November 1962. Articles have appeared during the last 2 years in both secular and church periodicals.

C. Episcopalians within the movement have expressed their regret that little serious study has yet been made of the movement by churchmen involved in it. It is the lack of such study and of scholarly leadership that perhaps has forced Episcopalians involved back to understandings and vocabulary developed by the Pentecostal sects in a quite different theological and devotional milieu.

IV. DESCRIPTION OF GLOSSOLALIA WITHIN THE EPISCOPAL CHURCH

A considerable variety of experience is reported. It is agreed that there has been no systematic treatment of glossolalia within the

Episcopal Church thus far, and that this is very much needed since without it people involved are turning to Pentecostal vocabulary and literature for help.

The remainder of this section should be understood to be a reporting of what the Commission has read and heard to be typical of the experience among Episcopalians. The phenomenon takes different forms among us, often different from that reported as typical of the Pentecostal groups whose activities are beyond the scope of our Report.

In any case, the issue of tongues is centered in its asserted relationship to the Holy Spirit and His reception and continued activity in a person's life. A distinction is usually drawn between the "sign-tongue", tongues as part of one's private prayer life, and the "gift of tongues".

Certain language is commonly used; it is said to be an experience of "surrender"; it is a "release" from anxiety and tension; it transmits the "power" of the Holy Spirit; it "transforms" all life including prayer, sacraments and personal relationships; it gives one a "warm full" feeling; its fruit is a "spirit-filled" life; it gives a sense of "joy" and "happiness".

It is claimed by those involved to be a transforming experience which gives new life and a new meaning to Christian faith and practice. Many speak of how they have been enabled to save marriages and redeem family and business relationships because of the awareness of the Holy Spirit in their life. Others have given up smoking and drinking as mechanisms of release no longer needed. Some emphasize that it has given new meaning and depth to their worship life through the sacraments. All feel that their life before the experience by comparison was shallow and largely conventional in the degree of their commitment to God. In Episcopalian literature a distinction is commonly drawn between two baptisms; that is, "in water" and "in the Holy Spirit". Such terminology, of course, is drawn from Pentecostal sources, but some of our writers, at least, make it plain that while Confirmation is not necessarily equivalent to Baptism in the Holy Spirit, the latter ideally should be part and parcel of the former.

The three kinds of tongues can be described briefly in the terminology of the Movement within our Church as follows:

The sign-tongue is a normal part of baptism "in the Holy Spirit". As part of his surrender to the Holy Spirit, a person "gives" his tongue and voice as well as his heart and mind to Him. Speaking in tongues at this time, therefore, becomes, on the one hand, a sign that a person has made such a surrender, and, on the other hand, a sign that God has "filled" him. To quote a Trinity Movement pamphlet (#B102, p. 14), "It is undoubtedly possible that God could fill somebody with His Holy Spirit without this supernatural sign of the new language, but it is God's wisdom that there should be an objective sign".

The continuing use of tongues as a type of private prayer has as its key the distinction drawn between prayer with "the mind" and prayer in tongues where the mind must surrender its domination of the person. The former is usually called prayer "with the understanding" and the latter, "prayer in the Spirit". This latter is a prayer of praise and, as such, a fruit of the experience of union between God and the believer. Obviously no interpretation is needed for what here is essentially a facet of one's private prayer life intended for God alone. If practiced in public it would rarely be audible unless one were placed very close to the person involved. It might but need not involve a display of emotion, and, at least among some, can be begun and stopped more or less at will.

The "gift of tongues" involves speaking in tongues in public in order, according to some, to convey a message from God, and according to others, to speak to God. One may be moved to speak one night and not the next. One may, after so speaking, be moved to give an interpretation or, more commonly, another present may receive that gift for the occasion. It is suggested by the literature that, using St. Paul's categories, this sort of tongues plus interpretation can fulfill the same function as "prophecy", if the tongues involved is meant to convey a message from God to man.

According to a priest who was involved in the Movement in another diocese, in his experience more than 75% of those who receive the sign-tongue continue afterwards to use the gift of tongues.

What does tongues sound like? Again, two kinds must be distinguished. Most common is a "lalling" in a tongue without human counterpart. It usually has a more or less developed phonic structure as might be expected. According to those who use tongues, as one becomes practiced in its use, the "language" becomes more fluent. It stresses open vowels and a general lack of harsh gutterals, somewhat in the manner of Hawaiian or a southern Romance language. The other kind is far more rare, but that which receives the greater publicity; namely, the use by a person of a human language which he has not studied and could not "possibly" have learned. The literature abounds with examples where this is reported to have taken place. Obviously a special problem is raised by such cases and we have not undertaken sufficient study to deal with it in this Report.

One aspect of tongues is the question of "spirit possession". Does one become merely a mouthpiece for the Holy Spirit, or does one remain "in control?" Some claim to be able to choose when and whether to speak in tongues. All agree, however, that a measure of control is given up for what is said is not pre-determinable by the individual nor is he able to duplicate what he has said once he has finished. The Commission has no answer at this point to the question, but will comment further when speaking of its psychological aspects.

V. SCRIPTURAL BACKGROUND

A. Introduction

It will be obvious to all, of course, that Holy Scripture is subject to many interpretations. In the hands of a Pentecostalist a given passage may well be given far different treatment than at the hands of an Episcopalian who is trained to view it with a more critical eye. The problem of Literalism is a relevant one in our case because most lay persons involved in the use of tongues tend to treat the Bible in Literalist fashion. In a recent article, a prominent member of the Trinity Society exclaims with approval, "The Lord appears to be making a lot of Episcopalian Fundamentalists in these end time days". While Fundamentalism (meaning, here, Literalism) according to some is not necessary to the Biblical undergirding of the Movement, nevertheless it seems to be the most common approach to Scripture used.

In discussing the Biblical background of tongues with lay members of the Movement, therefore, one may expect to meet with this basic difficulty; namely, that the interpretation of the texts in question will be widely divergent simply because there may be underlying disagreement as to the authenticity of the text or its admissibility as evidence in the first place. A good example is St. Mark 16:17 which is widely quoted by those involved in tongues as being an approving reference by our Lord Himself to glossolalia. The text seems quite clear on the subject and on the face of it allows for little discussion. One versed in and believing in the use of Biblical criticism however, will hasten to point out that all available evidence points to the fact that this passage is not part of the original Gospel at all, nor even a part of the New Testament as originally canonized; hence this passage has scant claim either in dominical or canonical authority.

The members of the Commission point this out simply to give some perspective to the use of Scripture in relation to tongues. While not all Episcopalians would accept the results of Biblical Criticism, even if they were aware of its fruits, most scholarship in the Church does albeit in somewhat varying degree, and the Commission feels bound to follow their lead.

B. The Scripture References

We need to concern ourselves with parts of four books of the New Testament, these being St. Mark, the Acts of the Apostles, Romans, and I Corinthians. We shall review the texts involved, summarizing them before adding some comments as to their relevance and validity as justification for the contemporary use of tongues.

In St. Mark, the text involved is 16:17, where Jesus mentions speaking "with new tongues" as one of the signs which "shall follow them that believe". This text, therefore, is taken to furnish dominical basis for the "sign-tongue", that which accompanies baptism in the Holy Spirit.

Of the several references in Acts to tongues, Acts 2:1-4, 8:14ff., 10:44-48, and 19:6, are taken as fulfillment of our Lord's promise of St. Mark 16:17. Acts 2:1-4, of course, is the story of Pentecost; and Acts 19, the story of baptism "in the Lord Jesus" at Ephesus Acts 10:44-48, the story of the reception of the Holy Spirit by Gentiles at Caesaria; [Acts 8:14 ff, the story of a reception of the Holy Spirit at Samaria which caused Simon to offer money for the power to act as did Peter and John]. In Acts 2:4 we read, "And they were all filled with the Holy Ghost and began to speak with other tongues as the Spirit gave them utterance." In Acts 10:46 we read, "For they heard them speak with tongues, and magnify God". Acts 8 contains no mention of tongues, but it is assumed by those referring to it that only an observable and impressive sign of the reception of the Holy Spirit would have induced Simon to offer money for the power to "confer" Him! That sign, in the light of Acts 2 and 10 is taken to be speaking with tongues, Acts 19:1-6 recounts Paul's time at Ephesus when he talks with disciples there about their baptisms. When they say that they have been baptized only "unto John's baptism", he proceeds to baptize them "in the name of the Lord Jesus" after which (19:6) "they spake with tongues and prophesied".

In Romans, the passage to which reference is made is Chapter 8 which deals with the Holy Spirit in Christian life. In the 26th verse we read, "Likewise the Spirit also helpeth us with our infirmities; for we know not what we should pray for as we might: but the Spirit itself maketh intercession for us with groanings which cannot be uttered'" ("sighs too deep for words" in the Revised Standard Version). This is taken to refer to the language of the Spirit, or tongues, as over against normal speaking in our normal language. It is used particularly to refer to the use of tongues as a prayer of praise in one's private devotions.

The most extensive reference to tongues, and the only Biblical attempt to discuss it or evaluate it, is found in I Corinthians 12, 13, and 14. Here it appears as one of the gifts of the Holy Spirit to the Church. Chapter 12 lists the gifts of the Spirit, emphasizing, first, that all come of the one same Spirit in whom alone, one may say "Jesus is Lord". In the list, the last two are "divers kinds of tongues" and "the interpretation of tongues". Verse 28 lists some of the ministries which God has appointed in His Church, and, again, the last is "diversities of tongues". Verse 30 reads, "Have all the gifts of healing? do all speak in tongues? do all interpret?" Then we are exhorted to seek the "higher gifts" and then follows the famous "Ode to Love" in Chapter 13. Chapter 14 discusses tongues at length. Paul points out in verse 2 that in tongues one "is talking with God not with men" and, though "no doubt inspired . . . speaks mysteries". This is contrasted with prophesy in which, Paul points out one's words, being understood, "have power to build". Then in verse 5 he commends speaking in tongues and, even more, prophecy, since the latter edifies the Church and the former only one's self. In verses 11 through 13 he suggests that he who speaks in tongues "pray also that he may interpret" since otherwise tongues will be "gibberish" (new English translation) to the hearer. Again the point is made that one should "aspire above all to excel in those (gifts) which build up the Church". In verse 15 Paul says he will pray and sing "in the spirit" (meaning "in tongues") and "with the understanding also".

After saying in verse 18 that he speaks with tongues "more than ye all", he adds at verse 17 that "in the Church" he would rather speak "five words with my understanding" than "10,000 words in an unknown tongue". In verses 23, 24, and 25 he points

Study Commission on Glossolalia

out that an unbeliever, entering a service where "all speak with tongues" will think them "mad", but, hearing prophecy in the same circumstance will be "convinced" and "worship God". Then, in verses 26ff, he sets the discipline that no more than "two", or at the most . . . three" speak in tongues "in turn", followed by interpretation. If no interpreter is present, then no tongues should be spoken except by one "to himself and to God"; i.e., silently. Then he concludes the Chapter in verses 39 and 40 by saying, "Wherefore, brethren, covet to prophecy, and forbid not to speak with tongues. Let all things be done decently and in order".

As a whole, then, Chapter 14 is clear; first, that all must be done so as to edify or build up the Church; second, that while Paul himself thanks God for the gift of tongues, he subordinates it to that speaking with understanding which will benefit others; third, "in the Church", that is, in public assembly, public use of tongues is destructive unless accompanied by interpretation; but, fourth, that tongues is not to be forbidden when used as he allows. No stricture whatsoever is placed on private use of tongues, and it is placed alongside "prayer with the understanding", the two complementing each other.

In Chapter 12, tongues clearly is given a place in the Church as a gift of the Holy Spirit. Chapter 13, situated, of course, between 12 and 14, serves with regard to the former to make clear that the greatest gift of the Spirit and "the higher way" is Love, and with regard to the latter that if love is to be advanced then discipline of the gift of tongues is essential to its continued use in public assembly.

To refer by title to the different uses of tongues distinguished by those in the movement, the "sign-tongue" is referred back to St. Mark 16:17 and to Acts 2, 8, 10, 19; tongues in private prayer, Romans 8:26 and I Corinthians 14: 3, 15, and 28; and "the gift of tongues" in public worship, I Corinthians 12 and the appropriate verses of 14 not mentioned above.

C. Comment on Biblical References

1. ST. MARK 16:17

With regard to St. Mark 16:17, it already has been noted that modern scholarship is agreed that it is neither part of the original Gospel according to St. Mark, nor was it part of that Gospel as later given canonical status. St. Jerome himself attacked it as spurious. Hence it can hardly have dominical status and its standing within the Canon is tenuous at best. It will be admitted that it may reflect the practice of tongues present at Corinth and elsewhere, but that is to assign to it no more than importance as historical information of questionable import and not as authoritative basis for the so-called "sign-tongue".

2. ACTS

References to tongues in Acts all mention it as part of the initiatory process for Christians. In Acts 2 alone are the tongues stated as being understandable to others although the idiom in Acts 10:46 may also indicate this. In any case, all are related to the receiving of the Holy Spirit. A word is in order as to how the book is to be approached in the first place. Scholarship is agreed that Acts is written in the same vein as the Gospels. Its author is not so much concerned to report day-to-day actions of the Apostles as to weave a well-integrated and dramatic story in which the showing forth of the Good News comes first, and all materials are made subservient to this aim. Such a view cannot be taken to rule out the possibility that some or all of the events portrayed in the book happened just as stated, but it is to say that to the author, historicity of this sort is not necessary to his purpose which is kerygmatic.

Speaking in tongues appears in the first great preaching of the Gospel and receiving of the Holy Spirit at Jerusalem (Acts 2); in the receiving of the Holy Spirit in Samaria (assuming Acts 8 does reflect glossolalia); in the much-emphasized story of the baptism of the God-fearing Gentiles at Caesaria (Acts 10); and in the story at Ephesus where the vital distinction is drawn between John the Baptist's baptism and Christian baptism.

It has been pointed out that these four events constitute key episodes in the ever-widening influence of the Gospel, from the Jewish community at Jerusalem to the Samaritans, to God-fearing Gentiles (that is, Gentiles closely associated with the Jewish religion), and, finally, to Gentiles in a Gentile city, Ephesus. It is a good example of how the author has used historical method to drive home the significance of Pentecost where in the power of the Holy Spirit nations of men are drawn together by Him. Whereas at Babel men lost their ability to communicate with one another, at Pentecost, in the faith of Christ and the power of His Holy Spirit, they regained that ability. Glossolalia becomes, therefore, a sign of the reconciliation between men made possible by the death and resurrection of Jesus Christ. It should be noted that nowhere in Acts is tongues suggested as part of the ongoing life of the Christian. Also, tongues-speaking requires no interpretation since in Acts 2 and 8 it apparently is understood, while in the others, its presence in itself is what is important.

Finally it should be noted that the receiving of the Holy Spirit is never a private matter. It takes place in community and has as its fruit the widening of that community. The Holy Spirit is not akin to a pagan spirit conceived as an ethereal individual in search of a person vulnerable to possession. He is the Christian "esprit de corps", the Spirit indwelling the whole Body, in whom as we live together we participate in His communion.

3. ROMANS 8:26

Romans 8:26 cannot be taken as a trustworthy basis for tongues of any kind. The Greek words used in this verse, "stenagmois alaletois", mean unverbalized sighs or groans. While tongues usually are not in a human tongue they are verbal patterns because they consist of words and languages. In fact it will be noted that the root of the verb-form in this phrase, "lal" is the same as in glossolalia, while the prefix "a" is a negative. Hence it is highly unlikely that reference to any tongue is here meant. Unspoken or wordless prayer, on the other hand, provides a rich part of every committed Christian's devotional life, and it is to this that the passage has immediate and appropriate reference.

4. I CORINTHIANS

In I Corinthians, Paul speaks to a church which has been characterized as "one of the most erratic and troublesome" of his missions. In the letter he speaks out against a number of pagan practices from which he seeks to wean them insofar as they militate against life in Christ.

Chapters 12 to 14 constitute a discussion of the Holy Spirit and his gifts to the Church and their use in it. Quite apart from his discussion on tongues *per se*, Paul makes these central points: first, those who confess "Jesus is the Lord", do so in the power of the Holy Spirit; second, there is a variety of ways in which the power of the Spirit is manifested in the Church, but all of them issue from the same Spirit; third, all are exhorted to seek out the "best" gifts and above all to follow the more excellent way at the heart of which is love. Paul is not suggesting that there need be a fundamental conflict between the gifts of Chapter 12 and the way of faith, hope, and love. But he is insisting that the exercise of any ministry of the Spirit in the Church must take place in such a way as to advance love ("though I speak with the tongues of men and of angels, and have not charity, I am become as sounding brass and tinkling cymbal"). Chapter 14 spells out the meaning of this, everywhere equating "edifying" or "building up" the Church with acting in the spirit of love. Part of the "more excellent way" is to build up the Church.

Evidently he considers vital the distinction between public and private use of tongues. He who speaks privately in tongues, "speaketh unto God" and "edifieth himself", and so is not to be condemned. But when tongues is to be spoken in public, then the way of love demands that this ministry of the Spirit be carefully channeled and disciplined. All speaking in assembly should edify hence he would "rather that ye prophesied", or, in any case, have interpretation when tongues is spoken.

His conclusion of the matter, "covet to prophesy and forbid not to speak with tongues", clearly provides for the latter and yet can hardly be considered an enthusiastic or unqualified endorsement of it. In public, at least, it is prophecy which is to be sought after and coveted, not tongues.

5. CONCLUSION

This section has dealt with the Biblical references to glossolalia. In casting doubt on the use of the Marcan and Acts of references as "proof-texts" for contemporary tongues-speaking, we do not thereby cast doubt upon the reality and the meaningfulness of what obviously is a transforming experience for a number of our Christian brethren.

As a part of the initiatory process of entering the Christian community, as part of one's ongoing private devotional life, and as one aspect of public worship, albeit carefully limited, glossolalia has biblical precedent, even if there is no scriptural warrant for making it normative for all Christians then or now.

At least some Episcopalians involved in the Movement feel the need to free themselves from a Literalist approach to the Bible and we encourage them in leading their brethren in that direction. As long as the approach to Scripture does not "stretch" the valid use of texts and recognizes the complexity of Biblical exegesis and interpretation, then we can appreciate the need and desire of Christians to return time and again to its pages feeling confident that thereby they will be led in the Spirit to insights helpful to their present experience.

Study Commission on Glossolalia

VI. PSYCHOLOGICAL ASPECTS OF GLOSSOLALIA

A. Introduction

The Committee has spent much of its time discussing this aspect of the subject. The presence of two psychiatrists and an expert in parapsychology has provided a resource which both encourages scientific study and suggests healthy caution in it! At this point, however, we emphasize again that this Report indeed is preliminary and tentative in its conclusions. We realize that this aspect of the Study cannot produce in itself a theological value judgment. On the other hand, whether the Pentecostalist movement within our Church be of God or not, it definitely is of Man and hence susceptible to study and analysis which can clarify ambiguities, relate the phenomenon to other types of human behavior, and dispel unfounded suspicions and opinions.

B. Glossolalia as Psychological Phenomenon

Glossolalia is not *per se* a religious phenomenon. That is to say, glossolalic phenomena in their sound and psychological effect identical to the Christian experience can appear in a non-religious context. Our psychiatrists point out that the term "surrender" used so often by Pentecostalists in connection with tongues-speaking, is a familiar one to them. The Christian speaks of surrender to God the Holy Spirit; the psychiatrist speaks of the surrender of the rational and conscious to the "irrational" or "transrational" and unconscious. Of course, the former speaks of surrender to the person of God and the latter to part of his inner-life but there need be no contradiction between the two concepts and, indeed, they might well be quite in harmony. The action of surrender may bring, psychologically speaking, a true sense of release and freedom. All that Christian tongues-speakers say of their experience strikes a familiar note to the psychiatrist. He can well understand how transforming an experience glossolalia might be, and how helpful it could be as an act of release periodically practiced. Both of our psychiatrists point out that much of our religious life as Episcopalians is so externalized and formalized that all too easily we become spiritually strait-jacketed. The phrase, "God's frozen people" apparently has serious emotional overtone as well as evangelistic! Without judging whether glossolalia be of God or not, our psychiatrists sense that it could be for some a healthy outlet, freeing and enlarging religious life.

Lest this be taken as blanket support for glossolalia, however, serious qualification must be made. In its non-religious manifestations it appears among adults who are suffering from mental disorders such as schizophrenia and hysteria. Here it serves as a release necessary due to the tensions of the illness. We do not suggest that Christians who speak in tongues therefore must be mentally disordered! We do point out, however, that glossolalia is not necessarily healthy or wholesome in a given person's life. Its "goodness" or "badness" for an individual depends upon his ability to harmonize it with his other experience; that is, to be integrated as part of him as he lives in society. They also point out that there is a significant difference between the person who can "decide" to indulge in glossolalia and then withdraw from it at will, and the one whose conscious is overwhelmed by his unconscious until sufficient release has taken place. The latter hardly could be considered as in emotional good health. As indicated elsewhere the degree of self-control really open to those who use glossolalia as part of their religious life has not received close scrutiny, although some of those involved testify that they are able so to control it.

Canon Hoy points out, incidentally, that the freedom which comes "when people are freed to be themselves" is from the Church's point of view enriching, illuminating, and a fertile field for the operation of the Holy Spirit. He makes the further point that in thus freeing people glossolalia may have in part as an end result the same sort of effect as some of the deep interpersonal encounters which the Church has provided in her Leadership Skills Institutes, Group Life Laboratories and Parish Life Conferences where unguarded encounter in small groups provides the basis for all that goes on. Anyone familiar with these workshops recognizes, of course, that the key to their success is the sort of encounter which allows a participant to relax his defenses and share his deeper feelings more openly than he could in normal situations. But the purpose of such experiences is to increase the depth of community and communication between persons. "Training" in human relations, however, by no means claims to control behavior — or "condition" response. Rather it takes seriously the wide variety of learnings which may occur in any group where the guidance of the Holy Spirit is primary and sub-conscious as well as conscious influences are recognized. In drawing this parallel, however, Canon Hoy goes on to remind us that the reason for such freeing of a person in the case of these institutes and laboratories is to gain helpful insights, and to work a freely chosen transformation of life in the participant.

In this connection, those familiar with the group dynamics process in and out of the Church are all too well aware that not all persons benefit from involvement in it. They customarily exercise as much control as possible to prevent such persons' enrollment in their conferences and institutes.

To return then to glossolalia, psychologically speaking, we are faced with a phenomenon which may be either an unhealthy element within personality or a creative influence freeing one to grasp new insights and to change a way of life for the better. Certainly, scientific study might produce needed guidance on the subject in this regard.

C. Suggestibility

The question of suggestion and especially auto-suggestion as part of the glossolalia experience has been raised. Tongues-speaking frequently is induced or at least is prefaced by repetition of some key phrase such as "Jesus, Jesus, Jesus". Moreover, prayer for baptism of the Holy Spirit with the sign-tongue usually comes at the end of a time of testimony and prayer together and therefore, after considerable emotional involvement, if not display. Might this act as suggestion or as a type of hypnosis? When used by the individual in private prayer can such repetition act as sort of an auto-suggestion? Further study of this aspect of glossolalia might clarify the means by which it is or can be induced. It might thereby indicate that certain types of personality are more apt to speak in tongues than others.

D. Spirit Possession

Earlier in the Report (IV) the question of demonic possession was raised. Is one "possessed" who speaks in tongues? With quite different reasons, the tongues-speaker and the scientist could answer "Yes." To the former, glossolalia indeed is a sign that one is "possessed" by the Holy Spirit — has received Him and been indwellt by Him. One cannot speak in tongues, he would say, without God's action — it is the Holy Spirit who "utters prayers through us in His own way" (B. T. Socy. pamphlet B 102, p. 13). Such possession as this is, however, something to which the person willingly and eagerly surrenders, according to their testimony. Possession is involved in tongues-speaking according to the scientist, too. It may be a loose use of the term, but we who are unversed in psychiatric terminology might say that the person becomes "possessed" by his unconscious, which temporarily takes control of the voice and tongue from the conscious and rational. Obviously possession by the Holy Spirit is quite different from incursion of the conscious by unconscious processes, if only because in the former case, there is, so to speak, an encounter with an outside "person", God, while in the latter, there is a "civil war" with the personality with the tide of battle going first one way and then the other.

As a religious phenomenon, glossolalia, of course, is not Christian in origin. It was widespread in the mystery religions; it is referred to by Plato, Virgil, Plutarch, and early Egyptian writers. In all cases it is a sign that one has been possessed by one God or another. Dr. Nes in the Chicago Report attributes the reference in I Corinthians 12 to the contradictory assertions, "Jesus is anathema" and "Jesus is the Lord" to Paul's belief that other spirits than God may possess a person. "Possession" in one way or another, therefore, is closely involved in glossolalia according to those involved and those who observe it. In further studies we may be able to clarify its role and nature if not form conclusions about it.

E. Glossolalia as the Language of the Irrational

One last aspect of this phenomenon needs comment. Although critical investigation casts doubt on the use of Romans 8:26 as a proof text for a tongue provided by the Holy Spirit, it does reflect what many Christians know; namely, how we all feel the inadequacy of our verbalized prayers in praising and adoring God. I Corinthians 14:15 is taken by some to show that Paul believed in two kinds of prayer, "with the understanding" and "in the spirit". Such an interpretation, if true, again would reflect a felt need for language of prayer transcending the rational and expressing more adequately what our psychiatrists term the "Irrational."

A writer for the Pentecostalist Movement within the Episcopal Church says, "Because our own language is simply inadequate for the praise and adoration of God, He gives us a new language which is adequate" (op cit). Our psychiatrists' reaction to this in general is affirmative, for they point out that our deepest feelings and convictions with their roots in the subconscious, seldom can be adequately articulated by the conscious.

Referring again to the group dynamic process, those familiar with the sort of learning which goes on within it know how hard it is for the participant to articulate satisfactorily what he has learned. The more life-changing the insight gained, the more the person treasures this insight for others, and yet, the more frustrating becomes the problem of communication. We all know how poetry by its ability to communicate through emotional or dramatic tone goes beyond verbalization for its power. The language of music is yet another means by which emotions can more fully be expressed than through verbalization.

Again the scientist's research cannot determine whether it is the Holy Spirit Who provides the language of the glossolalist or not, but he can affirm that the need for expression beyond normal verbalization is a wholesome part of a normal person's life. To satisfy it is to enrich life so long as the means itself is not self-destructive.

VII. CONCLUSIONS AND RECOMMENDATIONS

This Report has been largely descriptive as befits a preliminary one, and has been based upon available literature, first and second-hand observation of glossolalia, and the testimony of clergy and laymen involved. We stress that the reaction of others to the Report as well as further study may well correct what is here said either by correction, addition, or omission.

The presence of glossolalia as an aspect of a growing movement within the Episcopal Church is obvious. Those involved claim that it is "of God" and potentially the most transforming movement of the Holy Spirit since the Reformation. All agree that tongues-speaking is of significance only as a sign of or gift from the Holy Spirit. In a sense, therefore, it is the life of the Spirit within the Church which really is at issue. The need for the Church to consider anew the nature of His workings among us is undoubted and acknowledged on all sides. Nevertheless glossolalia, claimed as one aspect of those workings, is for the Episcopal Church, at least, so "different" and so liable to bring controversy that we are forced to give it in particular more attention than some of its users might feel it merits.

We have noted three types of glossolalia as its proponents distinguish them. Their use of Scripture to justify these types we have not accepted entirely because we have difficulty accepting in all cases their conclusions about the texts involved. Nevertheless the categories are as follows: the Sign-tongue, the tongue of praise in private prayer, and the "gift of tongues" for use with the gift of Interpretation in assembly. All glossolalia has in common as its prerequisite a surrender of the "understanding" and a giving over of the voice and tongue to God, the Holy Spirit. The fruit of such surrender may be a growing sense of freedom accompanied by a feeling of deep joy and a direct communion with God. The further fruit may be a transformed life freed of old anxieties and insecurities and newly committed to God.

The presence among us of the Movement under study poses several potential dangers and raises issues which need to be faced both by those within the Movement and those in the Church at large. We list these below discussing each one from these two viewpoints, pair by pair:

A. Vocabulary and Theology

1. One important limitation within the Movement is the lack of theological approach to glossolalia and the other gifts of the Spirit growing out of this Church's understanding of Christian faith and practice. As a result the interpretation of the experience of the Holy Spirit is couched in a vocabulary almost wholly borrowed from the Pentecostal sects. Without judging the suitability of that vocabulary for them, it has theological consequences for us in that it does not take into account the emphasis on God's action through the sacraments and the ordered liturgical life which we share with the historic churches of Christendom. If the Movement is to continue peaceably within the Episcopal Church it needs to come to terms with our ethos, not only in vocabulary but also in theology.

2. On the other hand, the foreign nature of the vocabulary and spirit of this Movement itself has dramatized how narrow and formalized many Episcopalians' approach to God is. At times we seem to have Him so "captured" by our sacramental rites that His ability to speak and act as He wishes is ignored or forgotten. We need surely to face afresh the working of the Holy Spirit and to give our people better opportunity to meet Him and receive Him in power in whatever way He chooses.

B. View and Use of Scripture

1. Closely allied to "A.1.", but of special importance is the Literalist approach to Scripture which is so dominant among the laity in the Movement. In a day when informed people are only just re-acquiring a respect for the Revelation of God in and through Scripture as understood in the light of biblical criticism any large-scale return to Literalism may well impede rather than aid the operation of the Holy Spirit. Leadership is needed which

Study Commission on Glossolalia

accepts the fruits of biblical scholarship while yet seeking to be instructed by God through the record of Scripture.

2. On the other hand, the Church needs to be reminded that biblical criticism is justified only in making the Bible more clearly a channel of Grace for God the Holy Spirit. In their wholehearted if naive acceptance of the biblical record as verbally inspired, Literalists at least affirm that the Bible is primarily a means of grace through which the Word of God is mediated to the faithful reader. By their attention to Scripture they also rebuke the great number of Episcopal congregations where serious Bible study is totally ignored by both clergy and laity!

Further it is at least possible that the Literalism of Episcopalian laity which surely is far more widespread than in just our own Pentecostalist Movement, is due in large measure to the failure of our clergy to share the outlook and fruits of Biblical Criticism with them in our use of Scripture be it in sermon or bible class.

C. Subjectivism

1. Again, due perhaps to its birth in the Pentecostal sects, the Movement in the Episcopal Church can lead to an unhealthy subjectivism in religion. It is always a mistake to confuse a feeling of God's presence with His presence; a *feeling* of being saved with being saved. God's presence and His salvation are far surer than our feelings about it. In particular, the distinction between the conferring of the Holy Spirit in Confirmation and "the baptism of the Holy Spirit" with its *feeling* of His power is theologically dubious and all-too-easily destructive of one's faith in the reality of God's action in the sacrament. From the psychological point of view, an overly subjective orientation to religion, especially when related to emotionalism, is unhealthy in that it hinders the development of a personality well-balanced in its view of itself and its relationship to the objective realities of life.

2. The other side of the coin is that the Episcopal Church only too obviously tends to over-formalize and over-objectify the workings of God. Our over reliance on the externals of worship life does indeed "freeze" the faith and hinders a whole-hearted commitment to God as Lord and Saviour of *my* life as well as my brethren's. In this regard we need to hear and perceive what the Holy Spirit may be saying to us through this Movement's stressing of the need for the individual's conscious sharing in His indwelling Presence within the Church.

D. Self-righteousness

1. A clear danger in this and any minority movement within the Church is the rise of self-righteousness or a sense of spiritual superiority. It seems apparent that the Corinthian Church was thus divided. St. Paul's emphasis on the Holy Spirit as equally the source for any and all ministries within the Church and his insistence that in all things love be the *sine qua non* of all Christian living surely are intended to condemn self-righteousness as destructive to the one Body of Christ. Leonard Hodgson, in a recent unpublished letter, reminds us, "For the question of spiritual status and progress what one has to look to is whether one is growing in a humble and contrite heart and love towards God and neighbor". With this sentiment responsible leadership in the Pentecostalist Movement will agree, of course, but the danger remains and needs to be clearly stated where speaking in tongues as a sign of the presence of the Holy Spirit is stressed. As helpful as it may be for some, it must not be taken as necessary to Christian commitment and life in the Spirit, nor necessary as a sign of spiritual progress or status. Again it is Leonard Hodgson who reminds us that we cannot "dictate to the Holy Spirit"!

2. As obvious as the danger is, it is no more likely to be present than an ignorant out-of-hand condemnation by churchmen of glossolalia and, in fact, of all religious experience out of the ordinary and conventional. There is present among us a contempt too commonly held whose ingredients are a protective concern for externalized religion, a fear of overt emotional expression, and a very real snobbery towards anything smacking of the Pentecostal sects. Love is no more present in such attitudes and in the resulting persecution of tongues-speakers (which indeed can be documented) than in any suspected self-righteousness on the latter's part. We *all* need to look to the growth of love toward God and neighbor as the only sure sign of spiritual progress. In particular, the Church at large in its approach to those who speak in tongues is as bound by the way of love as are the latter.

E. Participation in the Common Prayer of the Church

1. One further danger comes to mind and that is the temptation born of the joy and sense of fulfillment in the experience of tongues to find in this rather than in the ordered liturgical life of the whole Church the central expression of one's worship. For all its formality and frequent lack of spirit, it is the Prayer Book round of weekly eucharist and daily choir offices in which we are

called to participate and to symbolize and perfect our unity in the Holy Spirit. There is ample testimony from the Movement that many have found "baptism in the Holy Spirit" with its attendant experience a gate through which to enter the sacramental life of the Church more fully and meaningfully than ever before. Yet we think it will be necessary to stress continually the centrality of the sacraments as sure and sufficient means of grace for any who enter into them with faith in Jesus as Lord. In particular, the problem of the relationship of Confirmation to "Baptism in the Holy Spirit" is already present. Reports coming to us are that some within the Movement give little weight to the former unless it is immediately and observably connected with the latter. It should be added that at least some Episcopalians in the Movement agree that we need to work for the situation where people will understand "Confirmation as the time when the 'Baptism in the Holy Spirit' is to be received" (B.T. Pamphlet B 102 p. 6). In other words, it is being said that the administration of the sacrament of Confirmation needs again to be the time for our people when in faith in the Lord Jesus Christ they truly accept the Holy Spirit in all His proffered strength into their life. With such a hope there can be no disagreement, so long as a particular manifestation of His Presence such as glossolalia is not taken as normative. It certainly should not lead to a denial of the real and dynamic action of the Holy Spirit in Confirmation.

2. All that has been noted in "C.2." above, applies here, of course. No-one suggests that what is offered by God through the sacrament redounds to one's spiritual growth or benefit without at least the germ of Christian faith. The sacramental life for too many Episcopalians is either ignored or treated with polite and uncommitted lip-service. For such churchmen we must find a way to bring them to an inner awareness of their need for God's strength and an attendant reliance upon the life of faith, sacraments included, as the means to receive that strength. Certainly the occasions of Holy Baptism and Confirmation could be far more effectively used as means to this end by most of us.

F. Conclusions

Several conclusions are embodied in the section above; namely, leaders in the Movement within our Church need to develop an acceptable vocabulary and theology for it; they need to face the biblical background with full awareness and acknowledgment of biblical criticism of the texts involved; they must be warned against an undue emphasis upon a subjectivism which equates being saved with the feeling of being saved; all churchmen need to be warned against a breach of that rule of love which is to govern all our dealings one with another, whether that breach be caused by self-righteousness or ignorant condemnation; all need to be reminded that, as in centuries past, Christians in faith are to find the focus of their worship life in the ordered sacramental life of the Church; finally, they all need to be recalled to the centrality of that personal relationship to Jesus Christ in the community of the Holy Spirit which alone gives basis to all that we pray and do.

In addition we are agreed that where it is practiced in love and faith by churchmen who retain their loyalty to the doctrine and discipline of their church, their use of tongues in private devotions can hardly be denied. At this stage in our inquiry we would add that it *should* not be denied, since at least some testimony indicates that it has meaning and brings progress in Christian faith and practice.

It is more difficult to recommend policy regarding public use of glossolalia. The Episcopal Church states its policy regarding Public Worship on page vii of the Book of Common Prayer. It lists the Orders for Holy Communion, Morning Prayer, Evening Prayer, and the Litany "as set forth in this Book" as the "regular Services appointed for Public Worship". It makes two further provisions as follows: first, in addition to the above services, other devotions taken from the Prayer Book or from Holy Scripture, or "set forth by lawful authority within this Church" may be used at the Minister's discretion "subject to the direction of the Ordinary"; second, such devotions may be used "in place of" Morning Prayer or Evening Prayer "in Mission Churches or Chapels, and also, when explicitly authorized by the Ordinary, in Cathedrals or Parish Churches or other places . . . when the edification of the Congregation so requires".

Whatever meaning these provisions have, it is clear that the Ordinary has authority and responsibility to determine the nature and content of non-Prayer Book services. In their conduct and use, the Minister is required to seek the direction of the Bishop. The Episcopal Church characteristically enforces this provision with considerable latitude and in differing degree from diocese to diocese. Where the use of a particular non-Prayer Book service is apt to cause controversy, however, the Bishop well may feel duty-bound to assume sufficient direction over it to satisfy himself that it is expressive of the Gospel as received and taught by this branch of Christ's Church as well as conducive to its upbuilding. With this in mind, therefore, we recommend to the Bishop that he assume such direction of public services involving glossolalia, as the Prayer Book expects of him, both for the sake of the Church at large and those directly involved in the Movement.

The Pentecostalist Movement is in such flux within the Episcopal Church at this time that we think considerable flexibility needs to be maintained in settling policy for these public services. On the other hand, because they are public, they need to be subject to discipline now as in St. Paul's day. His concern that all public worship "build up" or "edify" is as essential today as then. Our Church provides freedom but not license in worship, and any congregation has a responsibility to all their brethren as well as to God not to offend charity or conscience. Where they do not show such responsibility our Church expects that the Bishops will guide them or require them to do so.

We trust that our clergy will be aware of the great responsibility that is theirs in leading the congregations "committed to their charge" in this matter. If charity is to rule the life of the Church, surely the clergy will be instrumental in advancing its reign. If they react to the Pentecostalist Movement, and glossolalia in particular, only in suspicion and unthinking rejection, laymen generally will be quick to follow their lead. If clergy involved in the Movement teach that glossolalia is the essential sign of God's presence and that those lacking it are in any sense second-rate citizens in His Kingdom, then their laity, again, will be only too quick to express the same belief in their relationship to the brethren. We hope the Bishop will commend this matter to his clergy with emphasis.

We conclude by stating again that we welcome comment, correction, and all constructive criticism. We wish to study the Movement further as the Bishop directs, hoping thereby to achieve greater understanding, and consequently, further conclusions regarding its place, and that of glossolalia in particular, in the life of the Episcopal Church.

PASTORAL LETTER

Bishop Pike's pastoral letter is dated May 2, 1963, the same date on which the Study Commission issued its report (see preceding document). The bishop called the findings of that commission to constitute "the most thorough objective report on this subject yet issued in the Anglican Communion." The bishop's pastoral letter is decidedly more negative in tone.

The task of a bishop is to be open to manifestations of the power of the Holy Spirit in "an incalculable and unpredictable variety of ways" and at the same time to safeguard the peace and unity of the church. Confronted with the considerable growth of the phenomenon of glossolalia among clergy and laity, he felt compelled to remind his flock that the normal vehicles for the Holy Spirit are the reading and preaching of the Word and the administration of the sacraments, a position which does not necessarily deny that the Holy Spirit may come to expression in glossolalia. Bishop Pike quoted a statement of the House of Bishops in 1962 which recalled for Episcopalians that "God's Spirit is ever moving in new ways" and then went on to enumerate the dangers present in all movements: self-righteousness, divisiveness, one-sidedness, and exaggeration. In spite of the good intentions of the persons in the movement, "every one of the dangers pointed out by St. Paul and by the House of Bishops' statement have by now already become evident here" (Italics as in the original). The bishop doubted whether religious categories and practices borrowed from classical Pentecostalism could be harmonized with the sacramental and priestly tradition of the Episcopal church. In particular he objected to the "heavily subjective emphasis upon a personal relationship with Jesus," induced tongues, the indiscriminate use of laying on of hands, the practice of speaking in tongues at public services. In the light of these convictions the bishop urged his clergy not to take part in the movement. A point had been reached where the movement was "dangerous to the peace and unity of the Church and a threat to sound doctrine and polity. . . ." In the mind of Bishop Pike the movement represented "heresy in embryo," a position he is later reported to have changed.[1]

The letter is reprinted in Pastoral Psychology *15, no. 144 (May 1964), 56–61.*

1. See *Kilian McDonnell,* Charismatic Renewal and the Churches *(New York: Seabury Press Inc., 1976), p. 46.*

Pastoral Letter

Pursuant to Canon 43, § 3, required by the Ordinary to be read in all Churches of the Diocese at all morning services on the Third Sunday after Easter, 1963

To the Faithful in Christ Jesus in the Diocese of California:

Grace be unto you, and peace, from God our Father, and from the Lord Jesus Christ.

With regard to new movements of thought, devotional life and action in the Holy Catholic Church from apostolic times to the present, the Bishops of the Church have always been confronted with special responsibilities of a two-fold character: (1) They are called upon as consecrated by the Holy Spirit operating through the consent and action of the visible Church, to be open to manifestations of His revelation and power in an incalculable and unpredictable variety of ways; and (2) to safeguard the peace and unity of the Church, and to maintain its doctrine, discipline and worship against the threats of party spirit, sectarianism, and a distorted focus upon any particular type of phenomenon attributed to the Holy Spirit by movements within the Church.

Your Bishops in the Diocese are now confronted with the necessity of exercising this dual responsibility. It is no longer a secret that there has been a considerable growth here of the phenomenon known as glossolalia, or "speaking in tongues". In this experience the subject regards the Holy Spirit as speaking through him words of praise and prayer as he utters expressions in an unknown tongue or in a known language which the subject has not learned. And it is claimed that there are such beneficial results as physical cures, personal integration, marital reconciliation, the elimination of alcoholic addiction and greater devotion of the work of Christ in the world. By now a number of our clergy and hundreds of our laity have personally experienced this phenomenon and hundreds of others have vicariously done so. There is a similar spread in other Dioceses and in other principal Christian Churches of this phenomenon which has until recently been associated only with the pentecostal denominations.

Soon after the initiation of the practice here, the Diocesan Council, on my proposal, referred to the Division of Pastoral Services of the Department of Ministry the task of study, evaluation and recommendation. The study was made by a Commission of the Division consisting of a theologian, a New Testament scholar, two psychiatrists, a priest-anthropologist, one who has completed doctoral work in the field of parapsychology, two parish priests (one of whom speaks in tongues) and a

Canon-to-the-Ordinary and a Canon Residentiary of the Cathedral Church. This group gave careful study to a report of the Commission appointed by the Diocese of Chicago and other literature on the subject as well as the actual manifestations here and in other Dioceses and has completed what to my knowledge is the most thorough objective report on this subject yet to be issued in the Anglican Communion. It will be ready for distribution to all of our clergy shortly and copies will be supplied at cost to inquirers. Your Bishops have been much aided by this report in their consideration of this matter.

From this report, from consultations with clergy of this Church, and other Churches, from a review of the New Testament references to speaking with tongues and the statements of recognized Biblical scholars on these passages, from reliable reports of services and meetings in which tongue-speaking has been involved, and with the unanimous concurrence of the Standing Committee acting as the Council of Advice, after much prayerful thought, we have come to the following conclusions:

1. At least, glossolalia is a psychological phenomenon which has been known over many, many centuries quite apart from any particular religious orientation; in more extreme forms it is associated with schizophrenia. But within the Christian dispensation it has appeared from time to time as identified with the work of the Holy Spirit. Its existence among some in the very early Church is attested by accounts in the Book of Acts and by the expression of pastoral concern as to its effects in the Epistles of St. Paul. The latter regarded it as one of the many gifts of the Holy Spirit, but took pains to keep it in perspective, namely, as only one possible aspect of a "variety of gifts and diversity of administrations", involving some people, but in no wise essential — and in any case subordinate to the gift of love and to the unity of Christ's Body, the Church. The Apostle also carefully delineated the dangers involved in the practice.

2. Proponents of this movement are indubitably right that our Church is in need of a greater sense of the activity of the Holy Spirit in the here and now and a greater resultant zeal for the Mission of the Church, for a change in lives and for personal testimony to Christ.

3. Under our doctrine, liturgy and polity, the normative vehicles for the Holy Spirit in the Church are the reading and preaching of the Word, and the administration of the Sacraments. We affirm that through all of these means the Holy Spirit works

and abides, as is made evident by the words of the Book of Common Prayer. That His objective work in the Church may be received, appropriated and shared by our people is a principal aim of the ongoing life and work of our parishes, the Diocese and the national Church. This reference to the Word and Sacraments and the program of the Church is not meant to deny that the Holy Spirit may express Himself in other ways in the life of Churchmen, including glossolalia.

Therefore, your Bishops affirm again at this time the relevant statement of the House of Bishops issued in 1962, and, at my direction, read at Divine Service in the Churches of the Diocese. Its text follows:

"Since, from time to time, new movements rise within the life of the Church, we your Bishops, share two observations.

"a. When a new movement rises, which may stress some aspect of the richness of Christ, it is the duty of the whole Church to view it with some sympathy, to work to keep it within the great fellowship, and to discern what in the movement is of God that we all may learn from it. Our attitude must be generous, and charitably critical. If, for example, a movement rises concerned with the fact of the Holy Spirit, the proper response is for all of us to consider anew the divine promises and divine gifts, trying the spirits by their fruits. We must bear always in mind that souls differ, that God's Spirit is ever moving in new ways, and that new movements have in history enriched the Body of Christ. We observe further that we are a Church, and not a sect, and that our spiritual home is, and should be, spacious.

"b. Having said that to the whole Church, we observe that the danger of all new movements is self-righteousness, divisiveness, one-sidedness, and exaggeration. We call, therefore, upon all new movements to remain in the full, rich, balanced life of the historic Church, and thereby protect themselves against these dangers; and we remind all clergy of their solemn vow to conform to the doctrine, discipline and worship of this Church. The Church, transcending in its life both the generations and the nations is by its nature more comprehensive than any special groups within it; and the Church, therefore, is both enriched by and balances the insights of all particular movements."

In line with the spirit of this statement we have indeed remained open as this movement has developed, seeking to learn all we could and to evaluate aright. *However, every one of the dangers pointed out by St. Paul and by the House of Bishops' statement have by now already become evident here.* And this in spite of the patent sincerity and the good intentions of the priests who have been active in this movement. While no one of the latter, I am certain, has in any respect intended to other than conform to the doctrine, discipline and worship of this Church, the religious categories and practices borrowed from pentecostal denominations raise serious questions as to their consistency with the sacramental theology of the Holy Catholic Church and with the role of the three-fold ministry, and the imbalances and overemphasis of this other system of thought and practice presents the Church with heresy in embryo. For example:

1. The emphasis upon the crucial character of the experience of "Spirit baptism" seems to minimize or neglect the Church's conviction, as expressed through the Book of Common Prayer, as to the real action of the Holy Spirit in Baptism, Confirmation and the Eucharist.

2. The heavily subjective emphasis upon a private personal relationship with "Jesus" (sometimes repetitively used almost as an incantation, apparently overlooking our Lord's injunction against "vain repetitions", which injunction would seem to apply to the use of His own holy Name), while it presents part of the truth, tends to the neglect of the full Christology of the Catholic Faith: the assertion in objective terms of Jesus Christ as God and man, crucified for our justification, risen and reigning over the Kingdom of God.

3. And the strong emphasis on the indwelling of the Holy Spirit in a highly individualized way in a given moment of time, while reminding us of the importance of personal appropriation of the gifts of the Holy Spirit, would seem to minimize the underlying premise of our sacramental theology, namely, that the individual is once for all grafted in the Body of Christ, the Church, which is already indwelt by the Holy Spirit.

4. The laying on of hands by presbyters and/or laymen, in connection with this experience or with the inducing of speaking with tongues, raises questions as to what ministers of Christ (also including the lay ministry) are authorized under our polity to confer the Holy Spirit in various sacraments and rites.

5. The use of tongues in public services would seem to run counter to the Anglican tradition in favor of the use of the vernacular in worship, as expressed in the XXIVth Article of Religion, which is entitled "Of Speaking in the Congregation in such a Tongue as the people understandeth". And it is in

connection with glossolalia that St. Paul asks, how can people say "Amen" to what they don't understand? (1 Cor 14:16).

Further, insufficient is known about the psychological processes — individual and group — involved in glossolalia or in what is known as "exorcism of demons" for us to feel secure about the effects of such ministrations and expressions without the benefit of psychiatric oversight.

Therefore, as to the laity: as your Chief Pastor acting with the concurrence of the Suffragan Bishop, I urge caution in connection with the exercise of this gift; as St. Paul says, "test all spirits", whether they be of God. At the same time, we have neither the authority nor the desire to quench the Spirit in any respect, or, in particular, to discourage the individual exercise of the gift of tongues by anyone in his private devotional life. Any of you who have experienced this gift, or do so in the future, and who feel the need of counsel and guidance in its exercise, are commended to your own pastor, who may, of course, in appropriate cases seek the counsel of one of the Bishops.

With concern for the peace and unity of the Church and for the maintenance of its doctrine, worship, and discipline, as Ordinary of the Diocese, and with the concurrence of my episcopal colleague and of the Standing Committee of the Diocese, I am issuing to the clergy considered words of advice, along with four directives. I share these with the faithful of the whole Diocese because of the number of our people involved in this movement and because of the number of our priests and laymen who have expressed concern to us about it.

ADVICE

1. While there is no inhibition whatsoever as to devotional use of speaking with tongues, I urge that there be no services or meetings in our Churches or in homes or elsewhere for which the expression or promotion of this activity is the purpose or of which it is a part. Nor do I believe that our clergy should lead or take part in such gatherings under whatever auspices. However there is a place, in the discretion of the clergy, for informal services which include instruction, testimony and extemporary prayer on the part of clergy and laity. However, in connection with such less disciplined gatherings the clergy are asked to heed the words of the holy Apostle, "I thank my God, I speak with tongues more than ye all: Yet in the church I had rather speak five words with my understanding, that by my voice I might teach others also,

than ten thousand words in an unknown tongue." (I Cor 14:18-19)

2. I urge our clergy not to take part in the movement to nurture and spread the practice of speaking with tongues and not to invite visiting preachers or speakers who have this purpose. While I did license one such visitor (for whom, incidentally, I have high personal esteem) I can no longer be prepared to license clergy of other Dioceses to come here to preach and speak in propagation of this movement.

3. In preaching and teaching, emphasis should not be placed on this particular gift in distinction from the other gifts and fruits of the Holy Spirit; nor should the word "baptism" be used in connection with non-sacramental spiritual and/or psychological experiences.

4. Those clergy who practice speaking in tongues are asked to undertake the special vocation of examining the underlying theological premises and the terminology of this movement toward its correlation with, and conformity to, the Church's doctrine, worship, and discipline.

DIRECTIVES (as godly admonitions)

1. The clergy shall exert no pressure in any form upon any person to induce the use of glossolalia.

2. Laying on of hands shall not be administered by a layman, nor by a priest or deacon except in connection with the Prayer Book Office of the Unction of the Sick. (In connection with the blessing of children who, at the Holy Eucharist, come to the altar rail with their parents, while laying on of hands may not be used, a blessing in the form of the sign of the cross or outstretched hand may continue to be given).

3. Exorcism of those presumed to be possessed may be performed or attempted by the clergy or laity only with the explicit authorization of the Ordinary, which permission shall only be granted when the Bishop, aided by professional advisors in this field, has determined that there is adequate psychiatric collaboration in the process.

4. The clergy shall not speak in tongues as the Bishop lays on hands in Confirmation. Nor shall communicants be presented for "reaffirmation of confirmation vows", with which such tongue speaking has also been associated. (This prohibition does not bar the fairly infrequent practice of "receiving back" into our Church a person who had left it to enter another religious body.)

Now a more personal word. It is after considerable wrestling of the spirit that we have prepared this Pastoral Letter and issued the above directives. In one sense it goes against the grain for us to do so. Each of your Bishops has been very grateful for the breadth in Anglicanism and the permissive variety within it. But the fact that this particular phenomenon has reached a point where it is dangerous to the peace and unity of the Church and a threat to sound doctrine and polity compels us to act.

Since your Bishops are firm in their sense of responsibility in this matter we have taken into account in advance what we know will be criticism and perhaps even personal hostility. Our Lord told us to "count the cost". We have.

Some of you who have not been acquainted with the extent of this movement will regard our action as a "tempest in a teapot"; some would prefer that I remain silent on this matter, when in fact my silence and openness so far already has been misunderstood in some quarters as support for the movement; some conventional Episcopalians, horrified at the very thought of pentecostal practices among Churchmen, will feel that the position we have taken is too open and lax, just as others will feel that it is too rigorous and authoritarian. We have weighed all of these things as we have sought the guidance of the Holy Spirit; and thus, while we realize that we are not infallible and thus will respect any differences of opinion as to the wisdom of the step we have taken, we beseech continued loyalty to your Bishops and to the Church for which they are seeking to act in purity of heart and with courage, wisdom and prudence. To the extent that we have failed in any of these respects, we rely through faith on the justifying grace of God in Christ.

Before closing, your Bishops would point out that the very rise of this movement within major Churches in this country is a sign of a real need and hunger for a more vital, Spirit-filled Christian experience in life. For their concern and intentions, we commend those priests and laymen who have sensed this need and at the risk of scorn and misunderstanding have sought to be avenues for the filling of the Church with the Holy Spirit. The above instructions, issued under our pastoral responsibility for the furtherance of what the statement of the House of Bishops calls "the full, rich balanced life of the historic Church" are meant to be no damper on zeal for the renewal of the life of the Church in the prosecution of its mission in this Diocese and in the world. We call upon all our people to be generous and open-minded as to the forms in which this renewal may express itself in the lives of particular fellow Churchmen, whether clergy or lay. In all this, we pray in the words of Percy Dearmer:

"O God, our Shepherd, give to thy Church a new vision and a new charity, a new wisdom and a fresh understanding, the revival of her brightness and the renewal of her unity; that the eternal message of thy Son, freed from the taint of man-made traditions, may be hailed as the good news of our day; through Him who can make all things new, the same Jesus Christ our Lord."

Issued from the Cathedral Close in our See City, on the Feast of St. Athanasius, the second day of May, A.D. 1963, and in the fifth year of our Consecration.

Faithfully your Bishop and Chief Pastor, James A. Pike, Bishop of California

9 Lutheran Churches, Germany, 1963

MÜHLHEIM THESES ON COMMUNITY AND CHARISM

The Regional Offices for Male Employees, the Social-Ethics Committee, and the Office for Lay Missionaries of the Lutheran churches in the Rhineland and Westphalia met in Mühlheim on the Ruhr, December 3–6, 1963, to discuss the calling of the lay person. One of the groups took the theme of the charisms. The results of this discussion came to be known as the "Mühlheim Theses." Though they have no official character, Dr. Arnold Bittlinger, who was at that time the head of the Office of Lay Mission of the Lutheran Church of Rhineland — Palatia (Pfälzische Landeskirche), attempted to have them regarded as representing the position of the three united churches of Germany.

The intent of the Mühlheim Theses of 1963, as of the Würzburg Theses of 1976, was to situate the charisms in the center of the church's life. The accent was not on a special charismatic experience, nor on a special movement, but on the charism as constitutive of the normal life of the church and the Christian life. ". . . we Christians do not wait for a special act of sealing or for a special baptism of the Spirit." Nevertheless, members of the community should be exhorted to strive after the gifts. Those in positions of spiritual authority should lay hands on each Chris-

Mühlheim Theses

tian with the assurance that the Holy Spirit confers his gifts on every member. When all the members of the community are exercising their proper gifts, the local church will no longer depend exclusively on the efforts of one person, the pastor. All of the gifts of the Spirit come from the glorified Christ who is at the right hand of the Father. The text closed with a quote from Ernst Käsemann to the effect that the function of the community of Christ is to make ever newly available the grace which renders itself concrete in service. Concern for the continuity of the church should be left to him who alone can make grace a continual reality.

The Mühlheim Theses were reprinted in Arnold Bittlinger's "Der frühchristliche Gottesdienst," Oekumenische Texte und Studien, *vol. 30 (Marburg an der Lahn: Oekumenischer Verlag Dr. R. F. Edel, 1966), pp. 29–32.*

I. THE GIFTS OF GRACE IN THE NEW TESTAMENT

Charisms are gifts of grace bestowed on us by Jesus Christ (Rom 5, 15). The Holy Spirit who dwells in every Christian manifests himself through the charisms for the benefit of the community (1 Cor 12, 7). Under the term χάρισμα in the New Testament, the following gifts are mentioned:

1. *Prophecy* (προφητεία Rom 12, 6). Prophecy is the direction given to community and members by the glorified Christ for concrete situations where similar events in the past might throw light on the future.

2. *Deaconship* (διακονία Rom 12, 7; ἀντίλημψις 1 Cor 12, 28). Deaconship is the ministry of the glorified Christ to the bodily needs of community and members.

3. *Teaching* (διδασκαλία Rom 12, 7, and διδαχή 1 Cor 14, 26). Teaching is a gift from the glorified Christ guiding man's mind to understand that salvation and christian living belong together.

4. *Care of souls* (παράκλησις Rom 12, 8). This is ministry of the glorified Christ consoling and exhorting community and members.

5. *Sharing one's possessions* (μετάδοσις Rom 12, 8, and 1 Cor 13, 3a). This is the sharing of earthly goods, through the glorified Christ for the benefit of community and members.

6. *Leadership* (προϊστάμενος Rom 12, 8, and κυβέρνησις 1 Cor 12, 18). This is the guidance of community and members through the glorified Christ.

7. *Mercy* (ἔλεος Rom 12, 8). Mercy is heartfelt compassion of the glorified Christ shown to members who need sympathy.

8. *The word of wisdom* (λόγος σοφίας 1 Cor 12, 8). In special cases the glorified Christ shares his divine wisdom with members and community.

9. *The word of knowledge* (λόγος γνώσεως 1 Cor 12, 8). By the word of knowledge the glorified Christ opens the minds of community and members to understand that the various teachings of salvation of the glorified Christ are one coherent theological message.

10. *Faith* (πίστις 1 Cor 12, 9). Faith is the boundless trust in the heavenly Father which the glorified Christ bestows on the community and her members.

11. *Healing* (χαρίσματα ἰαμάτων 1 Cor 12, 9). By this gift the glorified Christ bestows on community a share in his power of healing.

12. *Effective Power* (ἐνεργήματα δυνάμεων 1 Cor 12, 10). With this gift the glorified Christ extends to community and members his power to overcome difficulties.

13. *Distinguishing of spirits* (διάκρισις πνευμάτων 1 Cor 12, 10). With this gift the glorified Christ gives to community and members the power to distinguish divine, human and evil spirits.

14. *The Gift of Tongues* (γένη γλωσσῶν 1 Cor 12, 10). With this gift from the glorified Christ, community, and members are enabled to speak the unspeakable.

15. *Interpretation* (ἑρμηνεία γλωσσῶν 1 Cor 12, 10). This is the gift from the glorified Christ to community and members to understand the meaning of what is spoken in tongues.

16. *Martyrdom* (παράδοσις τοῦ σώματος 1 Cor 13, 3b). Martyrdom is the bestowing of strength by the glorified Christ on community and members to give up body and life.

17. *Song* (ψαλμός 1 Cor 14, 16 and 26; and ὕμνος and ᾠδή Eph 5, 19; and Col 3:16). The glorified Christ gives the new song to community and members.

18. *Revelation* (ἀποκάλυψις 1 Cor 14,26). By revelation the glorified Christ gives to community and members an insight into the mysteries of God's world.

19. *Marriage and single state* (1 Cor 7, 7). The glorified Christ bestows on members and community marriage or the single state as a gift and as a mandate.

20. *Eternal Life* (ζωὴ αἰώνιος Rom 6, 23). The charism which comprises all other charisms is eternal life in Christ Jesus our Lord.

II. THE GIFTS OF GRACE TODAY

In his Pentecost message 1963, the president of the Ecumenical Council had this to say: "All Christians agree on one point, namely, to be a Christian means to have received the Spirit of God. Since the first Pentecost, church means to be filled with the Holy Spirit." Hence we Christians do not wait for a special act of sealing or for a special baptism of the Spirit. For we know that the Holy Spirit dwells in every Christian, and that he can and wants to become visible. He does become visible in the charisma.

The community of today too may expect the gifts of grace referred to above and mentioned in the New Testament.

1. What can we do to stir up the gifts of grace? (2 Tim 1, 6)

a. The message of the Holy Spirit and the gifts of grace should be proclaimed more and given more consideration by the church.

b. Pastors and official co-workers should keep more in the background in order to allow the creative work of the Holy Spirit to come to the fore in the members of the community (1 Thess 5, 19; 1 Cor 14, 39; Eph 4, 30). They should make use of their respective gifts in their own work.

c. Community and members should be exhorted to strive after the gifts of the Spirit (1 Cor 12, 31; 14, 1) by preparing themselves spiritually, by prayer and then lay hold of their gifts with confidence.

d. Let those in charge encourage and lay their hands on each Christian with the assurance that on him too the Holy Spirit confers the gifts of grace (1 Tim 4, 14; 2 Tim 1, b).

e. By being obedient to the mandate of the glorified Christ the gifts are recognized and made effective (Acts 5, 32).

f. In a changed world it is indeed possible that God might grant new gifts in addition to those mentioned in the New Testament.

2. How are the gifts of grace rightly put to use in the community?

a. They should be used only in a community united with Christ as their glorified Lord (1 Cor 12, 3; Rom 14, 7-9).

b. Normally, any of the gifts might be used during the celebration of the agape (that means divine love; 1 Cor 13).

c. The gifts of grace are for the building up of the community and members (1 Cor 14, 26c; see also Karl Barth, *Church Dogmatics*, IV, 2, p. 614ff.).

d. With the fullness of the gifts the community serves the world (Matt 5, 13-16).

e. Community and members should guard against a disheartened underestimation and against a proud overestimation of the gifts they have received (Rom 12, 3 and 12, 10b; Phil 2, 3; 1 Cor 12, 15-21).

f. Charisms should not be valued as ecstatic manifestations; they are essential constituents of the church of Christ.

g. With the fullness of gifts the one-man-system vanishes and the mature community, which lacks no spiritual gift, emerges (1 Cor 1, 7).

h. The gifts of grace are signs of the presence of the Lord who will come again. They will cease when he does come again (1 Cor 13, 8 ff.).

"The church as the community of Christ is never other than this: it is grace seizing us ever anew in order to serve in ever new ways. The solicitude for the continuity of the church must be left to him who alone can make grace endure." (Ernst Käsemann. *Exegetische Versuche und Besinnungen*, Vol. I.)

10 American Lutheran Church, USA, 1964

A STATEMENT WITH REGARD TO SPEAKING IN TONGUES

After "A Report on Glossolalia" was issued in 1963 requests were received asking for more specific guidance. The present statement in large part was based upon the 1963 report. Some pastors had given the impression that the fulness in the Spirit is attested to especially by speaking in tongues. "This tends to confuse glossolalia with fulness of the Spirit and to give it the status of a permanent possession." In the New Testament fulness of the Spirit is an expression of dependence on the Holy Spirit, a dependence which must be renewed from time to time, just as forgiveness is to be daily sought.

Many who profess to have the gift of speaking in tongues report great blessings have derived from it, permitting them to enter a worship where the conscious mind is somewhat suspended for the moment. "Any posture where the conscious mind is not in full control is more readily open to the influence of evil spirits as well as the Holy Spirit, and therein lies the danger."

More to be recommended is love, the fruit of the Spirit, which never

*confuses people. "It is understood and appreciated by all people —
irrespective of their language, race, age or social class. Even the
animals understand it."*

*A scriptural balance is to be cultivated. While Paul devotes
three chapters to tongues in 1 Corinthians, no mention is made of
tongues in Romans. "This letter more than any other we have
from St. Paul, is designed to set forth the whole counsel of God.
It is actually a handbook on Christian doctrine; a miniature
dogmatics."*

*In recalling the marginal attention tongues received in Scripture and
in recording that "the presence of this phenomenon has not been an
unmitigated blessing," but rather caused confusion and other results out
of harmony with the fruit and gifts of the Holy Spirit, the American
Lutheran Church asked that there be "neither promotion nor practice of
speaking in tongues at meetings of the congregation," that there be no
instruction in the technique of speaking in tongues, and that the gift be
restricted to the private sphere.*

*The statement was reprinted in "Reports and Actions" of the Second
General Convention of the American Lutheran Church, 1964, Exhibit J,
pp. 162–64. It was also published in* Towards a Mutual
Understanding of Neo-Pentecostalism, *eds. Walter Wietzke and Jack
Hustad (Minneapolis: Augsburg Publishing House, 1973), pp. 12–13.*

In September, 1963, the Church Council approved a statement
prepared by the Commission on Evangelism regarding Speaking
in Tongues. The statement provides a summary of field
observations in congregations where glossolalia is a known
experience and some suggestions based on these observations,
together with an exegetical study on 1 Corinthians 12-14.

Requests have come in from the field asking for more specific
guidance than the present Church Council statements provide.
These requests come out of the bewilderment and confusion that
results when some testify to personal blessings derived from
speaking in tongues and others report dissension and conduct
that reflects more pride than love.

It cannot be emphasized too much that we live in the era of the
Holy Spirit. This period in time began on the day of Pentecost,
the day when the disciples were empowered by the gift of the
Spirit as promised by Christ.

The Lutheran Church believes and teaches that the Holy Spirit
is given in baptism. It also teaches that when there is expectant
waiting on God, the fruit of the Spirit is made manifest in the

believer's life and the gifts of the Spirit are distributed as the Lord of the Church wills.

Recently some pastors in their teaching regarding the fullness of the Spirit have given the impression that this is attested to especially by speaking in tongues. This tends to confuse glossolalia with the fullness of the Spirit and to give it the status of a permanent possession.

The New Testament makes it clear that fullness of the Spirit is an expression for dependence on the Holy Spirit, a dependence that must be renewed from time to time. Just as forgiveness is to be sought daily, so also renewal of dependence on the enabling power of the Holy Spirit is to be sought for each task to which we put our hands.

Many who profess to have the gift of speaking in tongues report that great blessings have been derived. These blessings are said to be found in the ease with which they can give themselves to worship in adoration, thanksgiving and prayer. It is worship in a posture where the activities on the conscious mind seem to be somewhat suspended for the moment. Any posture where the conscious mind is not in full control is more readily open to the influence of evil spirits as well as the Holy Spirit, and therein lies a danger. In the presence of potential blessing there is also potential danger and the possibility of much confusion.

It is important to note that Paul's long discourse on speaking in tongues (1 Cor 12-14) was provoked by a question, a question in regard to spiritual gifts. In his answer, Paul first emphasizes that a confession of Jesus as Lord is unmistakable evidence of the work of the Holy Spirit. He then discusses spiritual gifts, including their rank, and points out that the gift of tongues is a lesser gift.

Paul makes it crystal clear that the most excellent way is the practice of love. At no time is there greater manifestation of the presence and the power of the Holy Spirit than when God's love lives in us and flows through us. This fruit of the Spirit never confuses people — it is understood and appreciated by all people — irrespective of their language, race, age or social classification. Even the animals understand it.

In the 14th chapter of 1 Corinthians, Paul speaks more directly to the question of speaking in tongues. He announces that he is more expert in this gift than any of them. "Nevertheless, in church I would rather speak five words with my mind, in order to instruct others, than ten thousand words in a tongue."

Statement on Speaking in Tongues

It must be noted that while Paul devoted three chapters to tongues in answer to a question in writing to the Corinthians, there is no mention of this gift in the Epistle to the Romans. This letter, more than any other we have from St. Paul, is designed to set forth the whole counsel of God. It is actually a handbook on Christian doctrine, a miniature dogmatics; but there is no discussion of or instruction about speaking in tongues.

The perspective provided by the whole New Testament must not be set aside. While tongues get marginal attention in the Scriptures, the gift of love is everywhere acknowledged as the greatest of all that with which the Holy Spirit may endow the believer. In the extended list of the fruits of the Spirit in the letter to the Galatians, it is love that is given first place: "But the fruit of the Spirit is love, joy, peace, patience, kindness, goodness, faithfulness, gentleness, self-control; against such there is no law" (Gal 5:22-23).

The American Lutheran Church does not forbid speaking in tongues. But it believes the glossolalia receives only a muted recognition in the Scriptures. And it knows from its own experience that the presence of this phenomenon has not been an unmitigated blessing. It has caused confusion and has produced results not in harmony with the fruit and the gifts of the Holy Spirit.

Therefore The American Lutheran Church asks of its pastors and congregations: (1) that there be neither promotion nor practice of speaking in tongues at meetings in the congregation or at meetings where congregations are acting together; (2) that there be no instruction in the technique or the practice of speaking in tongues; (3) that those who profess to have the gift reserve its use for their devotional life.

CHRISTIAN FAITH AND THE MINISTRY OF HEALING

Though the healing ministry eventually came into open opposition with the classical Pentecostal denominations, it was chiefly from classical Pentecostals, if not from their denominations, that the healing ministers drew their adherents during the eleven years when the healing evangelists were at their height, namely 1947–58. At the very time when the healing revival was obviously faltering, the charismatic renewal emerged in the historic churches in the late 50s and early 60s. The causes of the decline were multiple: disaffection of the classical Pentecostal denominations, failure of financial support, the cheapening of miracles, popularity of frauds and extremists. The attack came not only from those outside the classical Pentecostal ranks but also from those who identified completely with the healing revival. Gordon Lindsay, himself a healing evangelist with a national ministry and the publisher of the magazine The Voice of Healing, *contended that many healing ministries withered "largely because of a lack of humility and because of a tendency to self-exaltation."* [1] *In 1962 G. H. Montgomery, one of the most prominent leaders of the healing revival, exposed the abuses, excesses, and dishonesty in a series of articles in the* International Healing Magazine *entitled "Enemies of the Cross." He did not indict all healing evangelists. Montgomery was as critical of classical Pentecostal denominations as of the revivalists, which, because of jealousy and short-sightedness, excluded and isolated the revivalists and thus contributed to their worst excesses: incredible wealth gained by outright fraud, gimmick tactics, fake miracles, and other assorted immoralities.* [2] *From across the Atlantic Ocean, the highly respected classical Pentecostal Donald Gee also raised his voice in protest.* [3] *Both Montgomery and Gee were believers in the ministry of healing and wanted only to purge and protect it.*

The healing revival survived the Montgomery articles and through the efforts of persons such as Gordon Lindsay the healing ministry entered the charismatic renewal in the historic churches. The Full Gospel Business Men's Fellowship International (FGBMFI), a nondenominational association of charismatic businessmen who were unhappy with the restrictions of old-line Pentecostalism and the lack of zeal on the part of ministers, grew from its first meeting of twenty-one persons in 1951 to over three hundred chapters by the mid-1960s. During the mid-1960s this lay association (clergymen were welcomed to the meetings but could not become members) formed an unspoken alliance with the independent healing revivalists who now had a new platform and a more educated, wealthier constituency. The style was still revivalist and the theology was not over-refined but the climate was different. The conversion of Oral Roberts to Methodism in 1968 and the conventions of the FGBMFI held in the Hilton hotels of the nation were two signs among many others that the healing ministry was being exercised in a new social context, with a different kind of sophistication. Derek Prince called the period of 1956–66 the "testimony revival." Christians from the historic churches who had never been in a revival tent witnessed to the miraculous conversions, healings, and other spiritual wonders. This new movement was the beginnings of a "Third Great Awakening."

In this context the American Lutheran Church issued its report, which was prepared by eight theologians from four theological faculties. It recognized that Jesus claimed for himself the authority both to forgive sins and to heal the sick, that healing was an integral part of his ministry as well as that of the disciples. But primarily he came to seek and save sinners that they might have eternal life. "The ministry of healing is an accompaniment of the preaching of the Gospel. . . ." Jesus wished to touch persons in their wholeness, physical, mental, and spiritual. Healing ministry therefore must be understood as an integral part of the coming of the kingdom. The accent is not on the healing itself as though it were an end in itself but on healing as a faith response to Jesus Christ.

When confronting the question of the relation of bodily healing to Christian mission today, "it must be said that healing miracles are not part of any specific Christ-commanded assignment for the ongoing church of Jesus Christ. Healing miracles were not performed by the early church as fulfillment of an explicit directive from Christ." In the early church healing was seen as part of the general ministry of the church rather than as a continuation of Christ's command to his disciples to perform miracles of healing.

This is not to say that miracles of healing are inherently impossible or absurd. "Healing may be a real experience in the life of many Christians. . . . Faith healing, in the sense in which we now use the words, may be part of the distinctive ministry of today's church as it was in the early church." This is to say healing is part of a general ministry, not a specific fulfillment of a particular command of Christ.

The report criticized the healing which was going on "outside of the ongoing life of the congregation" because it engenders a false expectancy concerning healing through faith. The fanfare and publicity which accompanies healing which takes place "outside of the context of the Christian congregation" does not further the gospel. Rather it dislocates *what is of ultimate significance, namely, forgiveness of sins, faith in Christ, eternal life. Pain, sickness, therapy, and healing are important but secondary. And there must be some place in the Christian life for suffering borne with faith and fortitude.*

Faith healing must permit faith to remain faith: "There can be no dictation to God in the matter of healing, only supplication. . . . There is no limit to God's power to heal, but he has not promised to heal everyone who asks." Care must be taken not to call into question the faith of those who are not healed.

The report was printed as a pamphlet and is available from the American Lutheran Church, 422 S. 5th St., Minneapolis, 55415.

1. "Statement of the Scriptural Basis of Fellowship in the Body of Christ," The Voice of Healing (July 1962), 4–5.

2. David Edwin Harrell, Jr., All Things Are Possible (Bloomington: Indiana University Press, 1975), pp. 140–44.

3. "The Value of the Supernatural," Pentecost, no. 62 (December 1962–February 1963), 17.

A statement prepared for the Church Council and approved for circulation to congregations of The American Lutheran Church*

The question before us concerns especially what is often called *faith healing*. It is prompted by the rising interest in the healing of the sick by prayer, accompanied by the laying on of hands and/or the anointing with oil. Since brief labels are likely to be misleading, we must define more accurately the real nature and scope of the question pressing for an answer. Then we must look at the witness of Scripture concerning healing, as well as at the Theology of Healing. When this has been done we will consider faith healing in terms of the ministry of the Christian church, and more specifically of The American Lutheran Church, in today's world.

TERMINOLOGY

We have chosen to formulate our thinking under the theme *Christian Faith and the Ministry of Healing*. There is a definite reason and a deliberate purpose in so doing.

---

*The statement was prepared under the auspices of the Theological Council which is composed of eight theological faculty members as follows: two from the Evangelical Lutheran Theological Seminary, Columbus; three from Luther Theological Seminary, St. Paul; one from Luther Theological Seminary, Saskatoon; two from Wartburg Theological Seminary, Dubuque.

Faith and the Healing Ministry

We prefer not to use the term *faith healing* as a thematic label, because it may suggest that faith is operative only in a particular mode of healing. It is misleading also because it stresses human faith rather than the divine act, without which no healing can take place.

We also prefer not to use the term *spiritual healing*, for this may imply a healing only for man's sin-sick soul, such as is experienced through forgiveness; whereas we are thinking also of physical healing in a spiritual context.

We prefer not to use the term *divine healing* as a label, for it may give the erroneous impression that God never uses human means in healing but always acts in a supernatural way.

The term *healing* is in itself too indefinite to pinpoint the question before us. To speak simply of *the Ministry of Healing* is more definite; but it too may be misleading if we associate it only with the medical arts as practiced by the physician, the surgeon, the nurse, etc.

We have chosen rather to speak broadly of *Christian Faith and the Ministry of Healing*, and to present what is pertinent in each of the other terms under this broader heading. The basic question then is: what relation has Christian faith to the ministry of healing, in the broad as well as in the narrow sense of that term?

DEFINITION OF HEALTH AND HEALING

The term "healing" must be defined. The word "health" means the state of being hale, sound, or whole, in body, mind, and/or soul. It is, therefore, a comprehensive term for the well-being of the whole man, physically, mentally, and spiritually. In the broadest sense healing means the restoration to normality in any or in all of these respects; it is therefore incorrect to speak of a person as being completely healed unless he is restored to spiritual as well as physical or mental health.

The term spiritual healing may be used in two ways. It may be defined as the healing ministry of the Holy Spirit in bringing to the sinner through the Gospel the assurance of the forgiveness of sins. Such a ministry is of primary significance for the total well-being of man. Only trust in the gracious forgiveness of sins through Jesus Christ our Lord can give to man the inner peace and joy which marks a spiritually whole personality. But spiritual healing may also be defined as that restoration of mental and physical health which results from the impact or influence of supernatural, superhuman, power in a human life; and this power of healing Christian faith also ascribes to the Holy Spirit.

Spiritual healing is therefore necessarily divine healing; for whether it concerns sickness or sin the power to heal is of God. It can also be called *faith healing* because faith wrought by the Spirit of God is the prerequisite for the experience of true spiritual health. The question which confronts us is whether Christian faith is also a prerequisite to, or at least a significant factor in, the experience of physical and mental health. If the answer is Yes, another question follows: how does Christian faith function in relation to the ministry of healing to the whole man?

THE WITNESS OF SCRIPTURE

Before we attempt to answer the question as to the function of Christian faith in healing, and therefore also the question as to the place of faith healing within the total ministry of the Christian church, we must consider what the Holy Scriptures say about healing. It is not sufficient to select a single so-called "proof" passage for faith healing, such as James 5:14-16, and to begin and end the matter there. We must consider the significance of healing in the larger perspective of the total witness of the Scriptures, as well as of the saving acts of God as their central theme.

There are many references to healing in the Old Testament which provide a significant background for a New Testament teaching about healing.

In Exodus 15:26 we read, "For I am the Lord, your healer." What kind of a healer did the faith of Israel conceive the Lord their God to be?

There are references to physical healing. Moses prayed for the healing of Miriam from leprosy (Num 12:13). Hezekiah, sick and at the point of death, also prayed and was promised and given healing (2 Kings 20:1-5). In this case the prophet Isaiah directed that a cake of figs be laid as a healing poultice on the boil with which the king was afflicted. In Isaiah 1:5-6 the imagery of the prophet seems to be borrowed from current medical practices. Among other things the use of oil for medicinal purposes is indicated. Medical care is also indicated by the law in Exodus 21:18-19, which required that a man who injured another in a quarrel so that he became bed-ridden "shall pay for his loss of time, and shall have him thoroughly healed." Nevertheless the

Faith and the Healing Ministry

primary emphasis in the Old Testament is on physical healing as an act of God. The psalmist summarized this faith of Israel when he urged his soul to bless the Lord "who heals all your diseases" (Ps 103:2-3). The healing power, even when human means were employed, was recognized as coming from God alone. God was a healer. God was *the* healer. God alone.

There are more references in the Old Testament, however, to spiritual healing. These are found primarily in the psalms and in the prophets. The false prophets are condemned because "they have healed the wound of my people lightly, saying, 'Peace, peace,' when there is no peace." (Jer 6:14). The true prophet proclaims that God will heal the covenant faithlessness of his people (Hos 14:4; Jer 3:22). This spiritual healing of the people is still in the future. Before there can be healing there must come the discipline of judgment because of their faithlessness. The prophets speak of grievous wounds which are the result of their rebellion against their God (Isa 1:5-6; Jer 30:12; Ezek 30:21).

> "There is none to uphold your cause,
>   no medicine for your wound,
>   no healing for you" (Jer 30:13).

Yet, salvation and healing will come for Israel "in the day when the Lord binds up the hurt of his people, and heals the wounds inflicted by his blow" (Isa 30:26).

There are some references to healing in a more personal and individual sense. This is true especially in the psalms, where individuals pray for and are assured of healing.

> "Be gracious to me, O Lord, for I am languishing;
>   O Lord, heal me, for my bones are troubled.
> My soul also is sorely troubled.
>   But thou, O Lord — how long?" (Ps 6:2-3).

> "Oh Lord, my God, I cried to thee for help,
>   and thou hast healed me" (Ps 30:2).

> "As for me, I said, O Lord, be gracious to me;
>   heal me, for I have sinned against thee!" (Ps 41:4).

> "Bless the Lord, O my soul,
>   and forget not all his benefits,
>   who forgives all your iniquity,
>   who heals all your diseases" (Ps 103:2-3).

"He heals the brokenhearted,
and binds up their wounds" (Ps 147:3).

The context of these prayers will show how closely the spiritual and the physical aspect of healing were related in the experience of the devout Israelite. The anguished cry of Jeremiah may even suggest the mental aspect of suffering such as he endured as a part of his vocation as a prophet.

"Why is my pain unceasing,
my wound incurable,
refusing to be healed?" (Jer 15:18).

Whatever the nature of the illness, or of the evil, whether sin, sickness, sorrow, or suffering, the cure, the source of healing, was in God alone.

"Heal me, O Lord, and I shall be healed;
save me, and I shall be saved;
for thou art my praise" (Jer 17:14).

Malachi 4:2, a prophetic passage with Messianic significance, supplies the transition from the Old Testament concept of healing to that of the New Testament: "But for you who fear my name the sun of righteousness shall rise, with healing in its wings."

THE MINISTRY OF JESUS

Matthew 4:23-24 describes Jesus' ministry in terms of preaching, teaching, and healing: "And he went about all Galilee, teaching in their synagogues and preaching the gospel of the kingdom and healing every disease and every infirmity among the people. So his fame spread throughout all Syria, and they brought him all the sick, those afflicted with various diseases and pains, demoniacs, epileptics, and paralytics, and he healed them."

It is clear from the Gospels that healing was an integral part of Jesus' mission to men. The cases of individual healing reported are numerous. There are also other summary statements, such as in Mark 1:34, "He healed many who were sick." When the crowds sought him in Bethsaida, "he welcomed them and spoke to them of the kingdom of God, and cured those who had need of healing" (Luke 9:11). According to Matthew, when he saw the throng "he had compassion on them, and healed their sick" (Matt 14:14). John introduces his record of the same event, the feeding of the five thousand, by saying that "a multitude followed him, because they saw the signs which he did on those who were diseased" (John 6:2). Both in preaching and in healing Jesus acted

Faith and the Healing Ministry

with authority (Matt 7:28-29; Luke 4:36); and he claimed for himself the authority both to forgive a man his sins and also to heal him of paralysis (Matt 9:1-8). Healing was an integral part of his ministry.

When Jesus sent forth the Twelve he gave them the same twofold mission: to preach the kingdom of God and to heal (Luke 9:1-2; Matt 10:7-8). Mark summarizes their mission under preaching and healing: "So they went out and preached that men should repent. And they cast out many demons, and anointed with oil many that were sick and healed them" (Mark 6:13). When Jesus appointed seventy others and sent them ahead of him as "he set his face to go to Jerusalem" (Luke 9:51; 10:1), the instructions were the same as to the Twelve: to heal the sick, and to say that "The kingdom of God has come near to you" (Luke 10:8-9).

Healing was an integral part of the ministry of the disciples as well as of Jesus. This was during his lifetime, while he was still with them as their Master; but according to Acts 5:16 it continued to be so after his death and resurrection. Healing as well as preaching characterized the ministry of the early Christian church. The witness of Scripture is unequivocal at this point. We have noted that in dealing with the paralytic Jesus claimed to have authority to forgive sins and also to heal the body. The evangelist records the effect of this double "miracle" in these words: "When the crowds saw it, they were afraid, and they glorified God, who had given such authority to men" (Matt 9:8). The healing of physical and mental illnesses was a part of our Lord's work in the days of his flesh. The New Testament seems to say that it is intended to be a part of his disciples' work as well.

THE THEOLOGY OF HEALING

It is necessary at this point to consider some of the theological implications of healing as set forth in the Scriptures. It is not intended to be a complete and definitive theology of healing, which would be far more comprehensive than the compass of this statement of position; but it is intended rather to point out and to stress a few significant theological factors involved in the biblical concept of healing.

1. Healing is an expression of God's saving love for man. For the most part the Gospels do not indicate our Lord's purpose in healing. When they do indicate it, it is his *compassion* for the physical and spiritual needs of the people which is mentioned.

Compassion is born of love. The ministry of healing as recorded in the Scriptures is one facet of "the love of God in Christ Jesus our Lord." According to the witness of the Gospels, Christ healed out of mercy towards a sinful and suffering humanity, in the sure knowledge that it is God's will to deliver men from all kinds of evil. God acts in love.

2. However, healing is not the only, nor even the primary, facet of this compassionate love of God. The New Testament defines the primary purpose of Christ's ministry as salvation. That from which man needs most of all to be saved is his sin, by which he is estranged from God. Jesus Christ came into the world to seek and to save the lost (Luke 19:10); to save sinners (1 Tim 1:15); to destroy the works of the devil (1 John 3:8); to give his life a ransom for many (Matt 20:28); that whoever believes in him may have eternal life (John 3:16); that the world might be saved through him (John 3:17). There is no comparable passage which says that he came to heal. The ministry of healing is an *accompaniment* of the preaching of the Gospel, which is "the power of God for salvation" (Rom 1:16). There can be no salvation without forgiveness of sin and restoration by faith to the fellowship with God broken by sin.

3. Nevertheless, in speaking of salvation it is necessary to keep clearly in mind the Biblical concept of the wholeness of man. Man does not live in two separate and unrelated compartments, body and soul; he is a living being, a person (Gen 2:7). This definition of man has two corollaries. The first is that spiritual ill health may affect man's physical well-being; or, conversely, that physical illness may affect his spiritual condition. The *whole* man needs to be healed, or saved, if he is to be healed indeed. The second corollary is that God's loving concern is for man as a person, in the totality of his being, and in every aspect of his need. Christian faith rightly looks for ultimate deliverance from all manner of evil, whether it affects the body or the soul, including the last enemy, death. Such a deliverance is experienced only in part in this life on earth. Man may experience the forgiveness of sin, but he is still a sinner. Man may experience bodily healing, but he is still mortal. Any maladjustment in man's relation to God, to himself, or to the social context of his life is an evil and is a hindrance to achieving that perfect wholeness or health as a person which the Creator intended for him. Therefore the ministry of healing as it relates to man's body must consider many factors besides the

Faith and the Healing Ministry

restoration of bodily health. The cure of a specific bodily ailment, such as paralysis, cannot be equated with health, though it may be a part of health; nor may such healing of the body be made an end in itself. The ministry of healing must be concerned with the total need of man.

4. With reference now to physical and mental healing it must be remembered that the power to heal is from God alone. This fact is implicit in the Biblical doctrine of creation. It is made explicit in the case of Jesus by the statement in Luke 5:17, "And the power of the Lord was with him to heal." Jesus himself acknowledged this power when he said, "But if it is by the finger of God that I cast out demons, then the kingdom of God has come upon you" (Luke 11:20). The manner in which Jesus performed his acts of healing followed no set pattern: with a spoken word, or with an accompanying touch of the hand, or with the use of some earthly symbol or means (John 9:6-7). Regardless of the method, the authority and power was of God. The man born blind intuitively recognized this truth: "If this man were not from God, he could do nothing" (John 9:33). Jesus himself said of all his ministry, including healing, "I can do nothing on my own authority" (John 5:19, 30; 8:28). To his disciples he said, "Apart from me you can do nothing" (John 15:5). When Peter healed the lame man in the temple he did so "in the name of Jesus Christ of Nazareth" (Acts 3:6; 4:7-10), acknowledging thereby that the power was not his own. When James says that "the prayer of faith will save the sick man," he adds immediately, "and the Lord will raise him up" (James 5:15). The power to heal is from God alone; our Creator is also our healer (Ex. 15:26).

5. The ministry of healing must be understood as an integral part of the coming of the kingdom of God through the total ministry of Jesus Christ. In Jesus' ministry healing and preaching were closely associated. The central theme of his preaching was the Gospel of the kingdom. He began preaching, after the arrest of John the Baptist, by saying: "The time is fulfilled, and the kingdom of God is at hand; repent, and believe in the gospel" (Mark 1:15). Jesus Christ proclaimed and ushered in the kingdom of God among men. The chief sign of this kingdom, beyond Christ himself is *the koinonia*, or the Christian fellowship of believers. Where sinners are brought into a fellowship in which sins are forgiven, the Holy Spirit is at work, faith in Christ is

created, God's Word is proclaimed, the Sacraments are administered, prayers to Christ are raised, men are made new: there the kingdom is evidenced.

But among the signs of the coming of the kingdom of God are the healing miracles of Christ, and of the disciples in the name of Christ. They are signs of the victory of Jesus as Lord and Savior over all the forces of evil which would hinder the coming of the kingdom with power and blessing for all. They are foretastes of our resurrection, which is the final victory. They are signs of hope within our mortal existence that death has been conquered by Christ, and that we shall see the day when "death shall be no more, neither shall there be mourning nor crying nor pain any more, for the former things have passed away" (Rev 21:4). The healing miracles and other miracles performed by Christ had unmistakable eschatological implications, at the same time as they were evidence of his compassion for those in need. There is a "now" and "not yet" aspect to the coming of the kingdom which applies also to the ministry of healing. The kingdom is here. At the same time we pray, "Thy kingdom come." There is healing that is experientially real now. At the same time we look forward in hope to the day when suffering and death shall be no more.

6. The experience of healing is closely associated with faith. It is true that the healing miracles of the New Testament were free, unmerited, unpredictable, creative acts of Christ, adapted to individual needs as evaluated by him. The power by which they were wrought was not the faith of the one healed, but the word of Christ. Nevertheless they were generally associated with faith in Christ. Jesus frequently commended the faith of those who sought his help. The statement in Matthew 13:58 indicative of the normal procedure of Jesus in relation to the performance of miracles: "And he did not do many mighty works there, because of their unbelief." This does not imply that he could not have performed miracles of bodily healing in spite of unbelief. It rather indicates that healing as well as preaching was aimed at creating and strengthening faith in himself as the Christ, the Son of God, so that by believing they might have life in his name (John 20:31). Healing was not an end in itself. It was a part of Christ's ministry to the whole man, which sought first the restoration of a right relation with God through faith in Jesus Christ as Lord and Savior. Faith was not the creative power that brought healing to the sick. It was response to Jesus Christ, which he acknowledged

and used as a means to an end in his sovereign creative ministry of healing.

7. The spiritual or faith healing of the sick by our Lord and by his disciples to which the New Testament bears witness does not in any way disparage nor supplant the healing ministry as practiced by physicians, surgeons, nurses, and others who care for the physically and mentally ill. Rightly understood, by stressing and stimulating the spirit of compassion, it rather encourages *every* effort to help, and, if possible, to heal the sick. It recognizes realistically that there are limitations to such a medical ministry, as indeed there are also to spiritual healing (Mark 5:26; Luke 8:43). There is an implied recognition of the medical profession in Jesus' statement, "Those who are well have no need of a physician, but those who are sick" (Luke 5:31). In Colossians Paul refers to Luke, his friend and companion, as "the beloved physician." There is reason for believing that the anointing of the sick with oil (James 5:14; see also Mark 6:13) is indicative of a *medical* practice, as in Isaiah 1:6. The use of medicine need not minimize the importance of faith, and certainly not the power of God, in the healing process. When we speak of faith healing in the sense of a direct divine miracle of healing in response to the prayer of faith, we must not discredit the presence and the power of faith in the experience of the Christian who is healed by the same power of God working through and with the medical practitioner, using the gifts and the skills that God has given.

THE CHRISTIAN MINISTRY

In the light of the witness of the Scriptures and of the theology of healing based on that witness, we confront now the question of the relation of bodily healing to the Christian mission today.

It must be said that healing miracles are not part of any specific Christ-commanded assignment for the on-going church of Jesus Christ. Healing miracles were not performed by the early church as fulfillment of an explicit directive from Christ. The church did continue its concern for healing as part of its general ministry to the sick, but not as a continuation of Christ's command to his disciples to perform miracles of healing. Healing miracles in the New Testament were primarily signs of the breaking-in of the kingdom among men through the presence and activity of Christ in their midst.

It must also be remembered that the "great" commission given to the early church was to proclaim what God has done in Jesus Christ for the salvation of the world. The church was charged in the first instance with the preaching of the Gospel to the whole creation. It was commanded to go and make disciples, with the Word and the Sacraments as the means to this end (Matthew 28:18-20). The command of the risen Christ to the men who formed the nucleus of the church that he promised to build was this: "You shall be my witnesses . . . to the end of the earth" (Acts 1:8).

The Christian church today has the same divine commission to preach the gospel of God's redeeming love in Christ to all men. It has as its primary responsibility the salvation of sinners through faith in Jesus Christ. Its primary ministry is to sin-sick souls. In the exercise and performance of this ministry, it seeks to bring men into the healing experience of forgiveness through faith in Christ. It seeks to create in men a living hope, whereby they are filled "with all joy and peace in believing" (Rom 15:13). It seeks to help men to "fear, love, and trust in God above all things" and in every circumstance of life. It says to men that they can have "a peace which passes all understanding," a peace which will keep their hearts and minds in Christ Jesus (Phil 4:7). The primary mission of the church is to enable men to be restored to and kept in trusting fellowship with God; for he has made us for himself, and our heart is restless until it rests in him (Augustine). The Gospel must be kept central in the ministry of the church at all times. "Seek first his kingdom and his righteousness" is Jesus' word still to his church and to those to whom this church is called to minister.

The ministry of the church, however, like that of Christ her Lord, is rooted in compassion for the whole man. It is therefore not unconcerned with sickness in the life of man. It shares the compassion of Christ for every human need; compassion for the poor and needy, for the anxious and fearful, for the lonely and discouraged, for the scorned and rejected, for the forgotten and neglected, for the sick and the dying. It has this compassion in so far as it shares the mind of Christ (Phil 2:5-8). Therefore the question of physical and mental healing is not beyond its concern nor outside its distinctive ministry. It lives and serves in the conviction that nothing human lies beyond the orbit of God's gracious intention with man. It asks one simple question: What can we do to help?

Faith and the Healing Ministry

The compassion and concern of the Christian church in the area of healing finds expression in a number of ways.

It finds expression in a spiritual ministry to the sick. This ministry is not the function of the pastor only but of the whole Christian community. Where faithfully performed it means that the sick person is embraced in the fellowship of Christian love and of fervent prayer. It means that he is encouraged and strengthened through the Word and prayer to have faith in God even in the midst of suffering. He is comforted in the Christian hope which looks expectantly for healing now, if it be God's will, but which also looks beyond suffering, and even death, to that day when God will make all things new (Rev 21:5). He is reassured through the Word and prayer of God's forgiving grace *now*; he is strengthened to say with Paul that nothing can separate him from the love of God in Jesus Christ our Lord.

Through such a spiritual ministry a Christian on the bed of pain is enabled to lay hold on the Lord's word to Paul, "My grace is sufficient for you, for my power is made perfect in weakness" (2 Cor 12:9). We pray for healing; but as we do so, we are reminded of God's gracious will that we learn to trust him in sickness as well as in health. To be healed of sickness is a great gift of God for which we should not fail to give thanks when the gift is given; but to be made strong and patient in faith so as to endure sickness without complaining, and to bear witness to the sustaining grace and love of God even in suffering, is no less a gift of God, to be received with thanksgiving. Such is the spiritual ministry of the pastor and of every Christian to those who are ill, whether they experience bodily healing or not.

The compassion and concern of the Christian church find expression also in the use of all God-given human means for the healing of those that are physically or mentally ill. The doctrine of creation and the practical application of Christian stewardship require the Christian to view all good and constructive resources in the world as blessings from God, to be used for his glory and for the welfare of our fellow men. Therefore whatever scientific or technical skills are required to facilitate healing and to foster the well being of any person with whatever need are welcomed; and whatever person or group of persons is required to administer the various therapeutic agents and treatments are seen as co-workers, consciously or unconsciously, with the ministry of the church in God's total work of healing the sick.

As an expression of its compassion the church builds hospitals and other institutions for the care and healing of the sick. It thankfully acknowledges the healing ministry performed by doctors, nurses, and others who share in the medical care and treatment of the bodily ills which are a part of human existence. It rejoices over Christian men and women who are willing and able to serve their Lord and their neighbor in such a capacity. It thanks God for the "near miracle" of healing daily performed by dedicated men and women to whom God has given the skill of a physician or a surgeon. But it believes that the spiritual ministry of the Christian church, of which we have spoken earlier, can even here contribute significantly to the patient's physical well-being, through that inner peace and calm which are the fruit of the Spirit in the heart of one who puts his trust wholly in the love of God in Christ Jesus our Lord. It therefore believes that where physician and pastor cooperate with mutual understanding of what each has to offer in the care of the sick, the ministry of healing has greater promise of achieving its purpose with the one who is sick. The power to heal is from God; but he can and does make use of both physical and spiritual gifts entrusted to men.

The third way in which the compassion and concern of the Christian church for the sick may find expression will be indicated in the next and concluding section of this statement on *Christian Faith and the Ministry of Healing*.

FAITH HEALING

For we return now to the question with which we began: what does the Christian church say about *spiritual healing*, or *faith healing*, or *healing miracles*, where God acts directly in answer to prayer and heals without the use of therapeutic agents and treatments? What should be the position taken by the congregations of The American Lutheran Church with respect to faith healing, in answer to prayer, whether with or without the laying on of hands or the anointing with oil?

A few positive statements may be made.

1. It should be acknowledged that such healing may be a real experience in the life of many Christians, whether in answer to private prayer or to the prayers of the church. God has power to heal in whatever way and at whatever time he wills to do so. Miracles of healing are not inherently impossible or absurd.

2. It should be acknowledged that it is right to pray for healing,

Faith and the Healing Ministry

for oneself or for others within the Christian community. The Christian's prayer privilege is great, because God's love is great. His word to us is still the same: "Have no anxiety about anything, but in everything by prayer and supplication with thanksgiving let your requests be made known to God" (Phil 4:6). Paul prayed three times for healing from the "thorn in the flesh"; this was his privilege, and it is also ours: but Paul was willing to accept a greater gift than healing, the word of God to him, "My grace is sufficient for you, for my power is made perfect in weakness" (2 Cor 12:8-9).

3. It should be acknowledged that faith healing, in the sense in which we now use the words, may be a part of the distinctive ministry of today's church as it was in the early church. The church must not become lukewarm in compassion for the sick, nor weak in faith that God can heal. It should focus the power of the Gospel upon the modern world of sickness and healing and attempt to lead Christians into a right expectancy concerning healing which it may be God's will to grant to them through prayer and through their faith in Christ.

4. It should also be acknowledged, however, that much of the ferment today in the area of faith healing which takes place outside of the on-going life of the congregation often engenders a false expectancy concerning healing through faith. Such false expectancy arises when bodily health is treated as an ultimate, to the neglect of the central implications of the Gospel.

5. It should be acknowledged that for the Christian forgiveness of sin, faith in Christ, and a resurrected, eternal life are central concerns. These alone are ultimate in their significance. Pain, sickness, therapy, and healing are important, but secondary, matters. The central concern of the church must therefore always be Christ's victory in the believer in the face of the threatening fact of sickness. There can be a victorious faith in Christ where there is no bodily healing. There can be a glorious witness to the grace of God in the midst of suffering. There can be joy in the Lord and in his saving power even when the body wastes away in incurable sickness. Where these truths are kept clear and central, the Christian's expectation, that through faith in Christ, God will in some way touch his total existence, may be encouraged in the congregation by providing an open door for spiritual or faith healing when and where God sees fit to heal through Christian faith in answer to prayer.

A few comments may also be made urging caution if "healing" services be held. There are certain dangers to be avoided, certain precautions to be taken.

1. The healing service should be held as a part of the on-going life of the Christian congregation, within the context of Christian faith in the Gospel. The Holy Spirit is the Christian's guide in all things, for the Christian lives in the fellowship of the Spirit; and the work of the Spirit is evidenced primarily within the koinonia, the fellowship of the Christian church. It is within the immediate context of the Christian church that one finds needed help in living the Christian life, whether in sickness or in health. It is within the context of the Christian congregation, where the Word is rightly preached and the Sacraments are rightly administered, that Christian faith is enabled to put first things first: to hold on to the centrality of the Gospel in the whole Christian experience, and in praying for healing, to seek above all to know and to accept the will of God as good and gracious whatever he wills to send us. The fanfare of publicity which so often accompanies the claim to healing powers by those who hold their healing services outside of the context of the Christian congregation does not further the cause of the Gospel of the kingdom. The gift of healing, as with every spiritual gift, is given to the church, within which the Holy Spirit ministers every spiritual blessing in Christ.

2. The healing service should therefore be held within the context of true Christian faith in Jesus Christ as the One sent by God to save sinners. Faith to be healed is not to be equated with faith unto salvation, but is always a blessing from God (Matt 5:43-45).

3. The healing service must not minimize in any way the state of man in this life as fallen man. Sin and sickness are continuing evils in human existence. The kingdom of God has indeed broken in among us through the life and ministry of Jesus Christ, but it has not yet won the final victory over evil in the world. The New Testament does not promise perfect freedom from either sin or sickness in this present life. Consider the Christian believer and sin: when we put our trust in Christ who was crucified for us and raised from the dead for our salvation, sin is completely forgiven; but we still continue to sin by thought, word, and deed. *Simul justus et peccator* is the Lutheran way of describing the forgiven sinner: he is at the same time one who has been justified by faith in Christ and yet one who is still a sinner.

So also sickness is a continuing experience of men since the

Fall. Even though God may glorify himself by individual acts of healing in response to the prayer of faith, sickness continues as a part of human existence and of universal human experience. When healing is granted for a season, there will come a terminal sickness which ends in death. Christian faith must not lose sight of the full scope of human sickness as illustrated by deformities at birth, by physically handicapped and mentally retarded children, by crippling accidents which befall both Christians and non-Christians, by organic as well as psychic disorders, by the infirmities of old age, by the hopelessly ill and about to die; but in our awareness of these things we also remember and rejoice that our faith and hope do not depend on miracles of healing, however real and wonderful they may sometimes be, but on the fulness of the Gospel of Christ which bears witness to us of God's eternal and all-sufficient love, a love which transcends the few years of our life on this earth.

4. The healing service must carefully avoid every impression that the power of God to heal can be manipulated and controlled, even by Christian faith and prayer. The Bible speaks much of the covenant faithfulness of God to his people; but the uniqueness of the Hebrew covenant, as seen in both the Old and the New Testaments, lay in that God is never regarded as automatically obligated upon request to help his people. His will is sovereign, and often mysterious, and is perceived only by the eye of faith. He moves in a mysterious way his wonders to perform. This is true of his providence, but it is also true of the wonderful, mysterious work of the Holy Spirit which can sustain the Christian's courage and enable him to trust the Lord for his grace in whatever circumstance of life. Faith healing must never claim magical powers to move God to action; it must permit faith to remain faith, which has confidence in God to act according to his own good and gracious will. There can be no dictation to God in the matter of healing, only supplication.

5. The healing service must be so conducted as not to impugn the faith of such as are not healed. It cannot be taken for granted that it is the will of God to heal all who have faith to be healed, and that therefore the only reason why there is no healing is lack of faith in him who is sick. It may be that the Lord wills that we shall witness to his sustaining grace in the midst of sickness and suffering. Such was the experience of Paul. He prayed three times to have the thorn in his flesh removed, which implies a prayer for healing from some form of illness, but God said No: he had

something better in store for Paul, a deeper experience of his all-sufficient grace made perfect in weakness.

The Scriptures tell us that the Lord disciplines him whom he loves (Heb 12). Discipline is not the same as punishment. Its purpose is gracious rather than punitive. "For the moment all discipline seems painful rather than pleasant; later it yields the peaceful fruit of righteousness to those who have been trained by it" (Heb 12:11). Such may be the purpose and effect of illness in the life of a Christian. His prayer for healing should be accompanied by the prayer that *all* things, including sickness and pain, may work together for good to him who loves God (Rom 8:28).

6. The healing service must never resort to false claims that healing actually has taken place. It must be careful not to arouse false hopes by extravagant claims. Christian faith *may* be the channel through which healing is given to some. For this God alone deserves and should receive the glory and praise. Unless he does receive the glory that is his due, the healing by itself will bring no real blessing. We may be sure that God is never glorified if divine healing is claimed where it cannot be verified. There is no limit to God's power to heal, but he has not promised to heal everyone who asks. What is important is that we seek to know, and in faith to accept, the will of God for us, whether it be to glorify him in sickness or in health. As we pray for healing we naturally hope for it; but it must not be permitted to become a false hope which insists on healing, or which rests on padded statistics as to the experience of healing. The Christian's faith and hope is in God alone (1 Peter 1:21).

7. Finally, the healing service must not ignore the *eschatological* character of the final victory over all evil, whether it be sickness or sin, or death itself. The future as well as the present hope of deliverance "from all manner of evil", as Luther says in the Catechism, must be clearly stressed. The words of John summarized the whole Christian experience from this twofold point of view of what we are and what we shall be; for the words are relevant to the physical as well as to the spiritual aspect of our existence: "Beloved, we are God's children now; it does not yet appear what we shall be, but we know that when he (Jesus) appears we shall be like him, for we shall see him as he is" (1 John 3:2).

For further information relative to Christian faith and the ministry of healing the following study-reports are recommended:

(1) Report on Anointing and Healing, adopted by The United Lutheran Church in America as its final convention in Detroit, Michigan, June 25–27, 1962; (2) Report on The Relation of Christian Faith to Health, adopted by the 172nd General Assembly of The Presbyterian Church in the United States of America, May 1960.

12 Presbyterian Church in the United States, 1965

GLOSSOLALIA

The committee appointed in 1964 by the General Assembly of the Presbyterian Church in the United States was asked to focus on three questions: Is glossolalia a valid experience for today? If so, under what circumstances is it proper, efficacious, and expedient for tongues to be exercised? If not valid, is it a heresy or an abuse? To the first question the commission replied that even if it were possible to establish an unequivocal definition of glossolalia in the New Testament church, one would not thereby have a standard of validity for today. "The church . . . is called upon not for reiteration of first century practices, but for obedience in contemporary life." Glossolalia is an experience which can "never be proved or disproved." Therefore the committee cannot declare the experiences of contemporary Christians "to be either valid or invalid reproductions of New Testament glossolalia." Excessive concentration on spiritual phenomena "is a false spirituality." "The urgent need of the church today is not for glossolalia . . . but for a relevant language in which it can communicate with the world." There is no reason to suppose that the phenomenon of tongues cannot be simulated by persons variously motivated.

The report on glossolalia was published in the "Minutes of the 105th General Assembly of the Presbyterian Church in the United States," Anderson Auditorium, Montreat, North Carolina, April 21–26, 1965, pp. 174–78.

This committee, appointed by the 1964 General Assembly in response to Overture 46 from the Presbytery of Central Texas, was instructed "to study the matter of glossolalia . . . taking such time in its deliberations and prayerful considerations as may be necessary to answer at least these three minimal questions:
a. Is Glossolalia valid in contemporary Christian experience?

b. If Glossolalia is valid now, what manifestations of it does the Church deem proper, efficacious, expedient, and wise, and under what circumstances?

c. If Glossolalia is not valid now, does the Church deem it heresy of such nature as to demand excommunication for those who persist in practice of it; or is it to be considered an abuse of Christian freedom, demanding one of the lesser censures?"

The committee has met three times: on October 12–13, 1964; January 17–18, 1965; and March 14–15, 1965. We have had full attendance with the exception of one member who missed the January meeting.

There was available to the committee a considerable amount of material: extensive Biblical studies, theological reports, papers by church commissions and scientific bodies, personal interviews, and direct information about the modern phenomenon under discussion. We have not lacked, therefore, a basis for a report.

The committee has made every effort that limited time has allowed to study the experience of glossolalia in our own denomination. A request was published in each of the Church papers, asking for "reports at this time from any members of The Presbyterian Church in the United States who would like to share their experiences in this matter . . . those who have found the experience of 'speaking with tongues' helpful in their spiritual life, and those who feel that it has had negative or harmful effects in the Church." Direct reports came from eight ministers and indirect reports from two. (Two have left our denomination since having this experience). Personal testimonies were also received from twenty laymen and women from Virginia, West Virginia, North Carolina, South Carolina, Florida, Alabama, Missouri, and Texas. Two of these may not have been members of The Presbyterian Church, U.S., but all the rest were. Members of the committee attended two group meetings of ten or more persons, and were granted permission to use a tape recorder. Other tapes have been made available by interested persons. It is obviously impossible for the committee to judge how widespread this movement may actually be in the total life of the denomination.

If it is possible to make generalizations from such a wide variety of experiences, it should be noted that in almost every case these testimonies came from individuals who are active (and apparently constructive) members of their local churches. They practice "speaking with tongues" in their private devotions, or in small group meetings, but not in the public worship of the congregation. They feel it is an aid to prayer, a means of expressing emotions that cannot adequately be phrased in words.

Our report is divided into three parts:

Part 1: The reply of the 1964 General Assembly to Overture 46 from the Presbytery of Central Texas.

Part 2: Our answer to Question "a."

Part 3: A statement of principles regarding the work of the Holy Spirit which relate to Questions "b" and "c."

PART 1

It is the judgment of this committee that the 1964 General Assembly, in its reply to Overture 46 from the Presbytery of Central Texas regarding "Glossolalia," used inexact theological language which may be misleading to our people.

(1) a. "The normative covenant relationship between God and His people is initiated, confirmed, and maintained through proper preaching and hearing of the word of God and the celebration of the Sacraments as these were instituted by Christ, namely Baptism and the Lord's Supper . . ." This might convey the impression that the covenant can be initiated from the human side by preaching and sacramental observance, and that its maintenance depends on the proper character of our preaching or liturgical action. In contrast, the Westminster Standards clearly make *God* the initiator of the covenant; the decisive action is not man's preaching or sacramental observance, but God's offer of life and salvation to fallen man in the Mediator, Jesus Christ. The standards very carefully refer to the Word and Sacraments as the ordinances in which the covenant is *dispensed* or *administered* (Confession of Faith VII, Larger Catechism QQ. 30–35).

(1) a. (Cont.) ". . . and the Word and Sacraments in themselves are, by the Grace of God, more than sufficient to convey to the people of God the full power and fruits of the Spirit, under the authority of Scripture, of the Confession of Faith and Catechisms and of the experience of the people of God in history." The last phrase, beginning with "under" is unclear. Surely the Word and Sacraments do not draw their authority from the Confession or from experience. What then is meant?

The crucial phrase, however, is that "the Word and Sacraments in themselves are, by the Grace of God, more than sufficient to convey to the people of God the full power and fruits of the Spirit." This reverses the historic position of our church as to the relative authority of the Spirit and the means of grace. It is not, as this statement would indicate, the means of grace which conveys the power of the Spirit; it is the power of the Spirit which makes the means of grace efficacious.

Thus our standards declare that "the Spirit of God maketh the reading, but especially the preaching of the word, an effectual means . . ." (Shorter Catechism Q. 89, Larger Catechism Q. 155). Again, "the sacraments become effectual means of salvation, not from any virtue in them, or in him that doth administer them; but only by the blessing of Christ, and the working of his Spirit in them that by faith receive them" (Shorter Catechism Q. 91; cf. Confession XXIX, 2; Larger Catechism Q. 161). Nowhere in our standards is it stated or intimated that Word or Sacraments "convey" the power and fruits of the Spirit. The Spirit, being the third person in the Trinity, is quite capable of conveying his own power and fruits "when, and where, and how he pleaseth" (Confession of Faith XII:3). He does indeed condescend to *use* the Word and Sacraments, but in so doing he remains free and sovereign.

(1) b. is a quotation from the Confession of Faith, XXIII, 3 to the effect that prayer, if vocal, should be made in a known tongue. The implication seems to be that the Confession here explicitly condemns glossolalia. It is the common opinion of historians and commentators that vocal prayer here refers to public prayer in the public worship of the church, and that this injunction was directed against the practice of the Roman Church, where prayers were offered in Latin, a language that was unintelligible to the congregation. It is true that the Westminster Divines, when asked by Parliament to supply Scripture texts, appended I Corinthians 14:14: "for if I pray in a tongue, my spirit prays but my mind is unfruitful." The Westminster Divines were concerned that the mind be involved in the worship of God. This would rule out *any* vocal (public) prayer that the congregation cannot understand, whether in Latin, in glossolalia, or in outmoded, pietistic terminology that is now meaningless.

(1) c. "The Sacrament of Baptism as treated in Chapter XXX of the Confession of Faith with its explications is the only baptism known to the people of God . . ." This statement does not take into account the fact that Jesus could speak of his death as a baptism (Mark 10:38; Luke 12:50); nor the fact that Scripture in several cases clearly distinguishes between a baptism with water and a baptism with the Holy Spirit (Matt 3:11; Mark 1:8; Luke 3:16; Acts 1:5). We would agree that, since Pentecost, baptism and

receiving the Spirit belong together in a single experience (Acts 2:38). But both Scripture and the Confession face the possibility that there may be a lapse of time between the two (Acts 8, 10, 19; Confession XXX:3).

For the above reasons we recommend that the 1965 General Assembly rescind the action of the 1964 Assembly adopting Part (1) of the reply to Overture 46 from the Presbytery of Central Texas and adopt this report as a substitute therefor.

PART 2

In regard to question (a) "Is Glossolalia valid in contemporary Christian experience?" we reply that the question posed cannot or should not be answered with a direct "yes" or a direct "no." Either a positive or a negative answer would be in error, and we believe that neither committee or court can pronounce in such fashion without involving itself in error. We would like to make it plain that we are not implying a negative answer to the question, nor do we suggest an evasion of responsibility to reach a reasoned opinion. The conclusion we have reached is perhaps best understood in the light of the various presuppositions in the question itself and the implications that must necessarily be drawn from either a positive or a negative answer.

To speak, as the question speaks, of "glossolalia" is to imply an answer or to give an *a priori* validity to the experience. To name the phenomenon by the New Testament name at the very least presupposes a clear understanding of the modern phenomenon and a precise definition. More seriously, the implication of the name is that the modern phenomenon is the same as the New Testament phenomenon or is somehow directly connected with it. Thus to name a particular experience "Glossolalia" is already either to answer the question or to urge a particular answer.

We do not believe that it is possible so simply to identify and define a phenomenon which is complex and multiform. In the range of phenomena under study there are experiences that run all the way from utter simplicity of private devotional practice through public and corporate manifestation to more esoteric experiences usually associated with so-called "psychic-phenomena," or extra-sensory perception, and even "drug-mysticism." We recognize that vast differences separate the varieties of experience, but it is difficult, if not impossible, adequately to isolate a particular set of phenomena to which the name "glossolalia" may be given and which by definition differ from similar phenomena. It is certainly not possible to move from such a definition to a description of the circumstances under which the experience is deemed proper and recognizable.

A concomitant matter is the complex and often apparently contradictory character of the New Testament evidence itself. There is agreement that there was a phenomenon which can be named "glossolalia" in the early church, notably mentioned in connection with the account of the happenings at Pentecost and as a factor in the Corinthian life and worship. The *fact* of the experience is clear; the *nature* of the experience cannot be determined with any precision or certainty. In Acts, at least in the Pentecost narrative, although by terminology an ecstatic type of utterance is implied, the author uses the experience as a symbol of the reestablishment of communication between men in the new Age of the Spirit, a reversal of Babel. At other places in the New Testament it is relatively clear that the experience involves the use of a nonrecognizable tongue, as for example, the "tongues of angels." It is probable that at times we are meant to understand a kind of combination of intelligible and non-intelligible utterances. A factor of great importance, although it is often overlooked in contemporary studies of the phenomenon, is the scarcity of references to the phenomenon in the other New Testament writings and especially the relative disinterest in the phenomenon in the early Christian literature. Once again, to recognize these facts is not a hint at a negative answer, but to indicate the difficulty of identifying a modern-day phenomenon with the New Testament experience.

To speak of a phenomenon in the life of the individual Christian or in the total experience of the church as "valid" presupposes that there can be applied some standard of measurement. It is obvious that for the Protestant Church the New Testament itself provides the standard. But to make the New Testament the standard of validity does not mean simply that any practice that occurred in the first century church may or must occur in the twentieth century church. Many first century practices are no longer current among us, such as baptism for the dead, the kiss of peace, the obligatory covering of the heads of women, foot washing, and so on. On the other hand, practices never envisioned by the first century church are integral to the life of the church in our day. The Holy Spirit continues to lead and guide the church beyond the letter of the New Testament though not contrary to its deep and abiding principles. Thus, even if we

Glossolalia

could establish an unequivocal definition of glossolalia in the New Testament church, we would not thereby have a standard of validity for today. The church under the authority of the Word of God is called upon not for reiteration of first century practices, but for obedience in contemporary life.

We have before us the kind of experience that can never be proved or disproved precisely because it is "immune to proof." The difficulty is more intense because we are dealing with a phenomenon that seems to be itself "proof," or that is often taken as confirmatory evidence and that can be measured and recorded by human instruments. "The Spirit blows where it wills . . . we do not know." To speak of "validity" in this instance would be to say that we *do* know, can identify, and even chart the movements of the Spirit. Thus to standardize and categorize the work of the Spirit would certainly involve us in heresy.

PART 3

Although this committee cannot declare the experiences of contemporary Christians to be either valid or invalid reproductions of New Testament glossolalia, we can set forth the following principles regarding the work of the Holy Spirit:

1. *The Holy Spirit is Lord* (II Cor 3:17-18). The sovereign freedom of the Holy Spirit to act where and by whatever means He will must be recognized and respected. Such a recognition eliminates the possibility of manipulating or coercing the Spirit by audible and physical means to act or speak in a particular fashion.

2. *The Holy Spirit bears witness to Christ* (John 15:26). In the New Testament the activity of the Spirit never becomes an end in itself but always a means to the confession, both in public worship and in life, that Jesus is Lord (I Cor 12:3). Any genuine manifestation of the Spirit, therefore, will lead to a Christological concern and witness. An excessive concentration on spiritual phenomena to the neglect of the centrality of the once-for-all revelation of God in Jesus Christ is a false spirituality.

3. *The Holy Spirit convinces the world* (John 16:8-11). In an era in which the Christian church finds the search for a proper language to express its faith a difficult one, a preoccupation with ecstatic speaking in which the intelligibility of the gospel is obscured can be an escape. The urgent need of the church today is not for glossolalia in which the church talks only to itself or to God, but for a relevant language in which it can communicate with the world. An inner spirituality which neglects the "worldliness" of

the gospel, which is not concerned for righteousness in the world, and which does not prompt an involvement in the church's mission of service and love in and for the world, is a false spirituality.

4. *The Holy Spirit is the bond of the church's unity* (Eph 4:3). Those who claim to speak in tongues should not regard themselves as the only Christians who have an authentic gift from the Spirit. It is clear that Christians who do not speak in tongues have also been baptized by the Holy Spirit and given gifts by him (I Cor 12:4-13). They should not set themselves up as a spiritual elite, somehow superior to those who have different gifts (I Cor 12:14-21). They should not cultivate a closer fellowship with others who claim to speak in tongues than with those who do not (I Cor 12:22-26). They should not disturb the order and decency of the public worship of God. (I Cor 14:14).

5. *The Holy Spirit bestows his varied gifts for the common good* (I Cor 12:7). No one should insist that all Christians should have the gift of glossolalia (I Cor 12:30). There is no indication that Christians should be eager to receive this particular gift (I Cor 12:31; 14:1). Rather, we are urged to seek the higher gifts. Those gifts which are to be exercised in public should be those which edify the church (I Cor 14:4, 12) and equip the saints for the work of ministry, for building up the body of Christ (Eph 4:12). Above all, all Christians should seek love, without which tongues are a noisy gong or a clanging cymbal (I Cor 13:1).

6. *The gifts of the Spirit can be counterfeited or sought for the wrong motive* (I John 4:1). There is no reason to suppose that forms of utterance voiced at the prompting of the Spirit cannot be imitated or cultivated by men and women variously motivated. While there may be among us some who "speak in tongues" as the Spirit gives them utterance, there may also be present among us those who, succeeding in the effort to "speak in tongues," unwarrantedly assume their utterance to be an evidence of the spirit of Christ. The gift may be sought and its counterfeit achieved from wrong motives.

This is a time when the church, rather than concentrating upon some one apparent manifestation of the Spirit, should be in prayer for all His gifts and the fullness of His power, in order that the church may be renewed. In this broad sense it is not difficult to say, on the basis of clear and unequivocal New Testament evidence, what the work of the Spirit is and what are his gifts and fruit in Christian life. The prayer of the church has always been

Veni, Creator Spiritus, seeking these gifts and fruit and praising their Giver for them; and that must be our prayer and praise still.

Respectfully submitted: Mary Boney, Robert H. Bullock, Charles B. Lousar, Stuart D. Currie, Balmer H. Kelley, Albert C. Winn, and J. Sherrard Rice, chairman

13 Presbyterian Church, New Zealand, 1967

PENTECOSTALISM

This 1967 report made to the Presbyterian General Assembly in New Zealand began with a series of questions to be answered, an assessment of the impact of charismatic renewal on the Presbyterian Church, some account of what was claimed to have happened, together with the claimed results, and an appraisal. A brief look at the biblical evidence was followed by a list of dangers and a conclusion.

At the time this report was published the charismatic renewal did not involve many Presbyterians and was generally confined to the northern part of New Zealand. The committee confessed itself to be at a disadvantage, saying, "We cannot speak from inside information or experience." The claims as to what has happened and the results were presented in essentially positive terms, though the committee noted that prophecy, healings, and tongues were emphasized almost to the exclusion of other perhaps more important gifts such as wisdom, knowledge, and faith. Many of the positive effects of the baptism in the Holy Spirit have been experienced by others not in the charismatic renewal without the charismatic experience. To some extent what charismatics describe as particularly typical of their approach to God "should be the normal experience of every Christian who receives Christ into his life." There is scriptural evidence in Acts that a filling with the Holy Spirit "in some additive way is a valid experience. . . ." But baptism in the Holy Spirit cannot be presented as a panacea for the world's ills nor as a substitute for personal discipline. Nor does this central charismatic experience always result in growth in even the more important fruits. It may divide the church into the "haves" and the "have nots," with the "haves isolating themselves from the mainstream of the church's life." Excessive time spent in prayer and Bible study may result not only in the withdrawal from life but the neglect of both work and personal relationships. Or the experience itself can be thought of as of first importance, while Christ, the Source of the Experience, must be glorified. Sometimes there results an exaggerated doctrine of the Holy Spirit, throwing the trinitarian basis of the Christian life out of balance. A "naïve sentimentalism" was observed. Some suggested that "only odd and emotional people go in for this sort of thing. This may be a legitimate observation of many."

The committee concluded that those in the church "involved in this experience are probably mostly in the early stages of it. They may need to come through it more to see it in the whole context of believing in Christ and working in His world for Him."

The report was published in the 1967 "Proceedings of the Presbyterian General Assembly." It was also reprinted in James E. Worsfold's A History of the Charismatic Movements in New Zealand, *privately published by the Julian Literature Trust, 1974, pp. 331–36.*

This report is "sent down to Presbyteries and Sessions and commended for study." Reprints of this are also available for those interested and may be obtained from the Junior Clerk. It is suggested that Session members read the report before their meeting and that questions such as the following be made the basis for discussion. Presbytery's Life and Work Committees could either obtain replies on these questions from Sessions and carry them further, or have papers prepared on the second set of questions and discuss them.

There has been some misunderstanding of what the Report was referring to by the word Pentecostalism. There are at least three "Brands."

a. The teaching of the N.Z. Pentecostal Fellowship, which includes The Apostolic Church, The Assemblies of God, and the Elim Four Square Gospel Alliance.

b. The teaching of groups which stem from some individual leader and remain independent.

c. The teaching of those who "have a Pentecostal experience" but remain within their original denomination.

There is of course considerable variation and overlap, but the report was concerned chiefly with c.

SESSION

1. What is the extent of this phenomenon in your area? What cases have you come across, what has been claimed and what have you observed of consequences? What good features do you recognise?

2. (See the section, Appraisal.) What features of the so-called Pentecostal experience are parts of normal Christian experience? In working towards the Renewal of the Church, how important do you feel this Pentecostal experience to be?

3. Is it true that our worship is too planned and does not allow room for the leading of the Holy Spirit? How would you alter it?

4. Have you any special problems in this respect, affecting the life and work of your people? Have you any criticisms of the Report? Are there any questions you would like the Committee to pursue?

PRESBYTERY

1. What is included under the word "prophecy" in the New Testament? What is the "word of wisdom" and the "word of Knowledge" in Cor 12:8?

2. What were the positive values and relative importance in N.T. times of the gifts of the Spirit (e.g. 1 Cor 12 ff.) and the fruit of the Spirit (Gal 5:22)? What are their values and relative importance today?

3. What is the significance of the fact that the Pentecostal arm of the Church is the fastest growing?

4. Any matter raised under the Session questions.

An illustration of how the constructive sharing of disagreements can lead to growth comes from the work of the fourth sub-committee which was following up the question whether modern Pentecostalism has something to teach us. The Committee endeavoured to be open to the truth as it came from the varied reading of new books, interviews with those involved, letters and tapes. They found that this repeated meeting modified their thinking and feel that such encounters (on a wider scale and with groups who differ on other subjects than the pentecostal emphasis) can allow an activity of the Holy Spirit such as took place at the Jerusalem Council (Acts 15), and could lead to the reduction of other tensions and to the discovery of a contemporary authority.

The report which follows is intended to help the ordinary Presbyterian to come to terms with Pentecostalism as a growing factor in many main line denominations today, with individuals who claim a pentecostal experience and with the yearning of many for some fuller spiritual life.

The term "Pentecostal" may have misleading connotations, but it is a popular description of certain activities penetrating the orthodox denominations. The interest in, and experience of "Charismatic Renewal" or "Baptism of the Holy Spirit" was for long regarded as the sole prerogative of the Pentecostal sects; today we find it affecting some of our own Church people. Many have looked askance at such developments. Some have been actively opposed to the accompanying phenomenon of "speaking with tongues."

Although these developments have not yet penetrated to the south, this has been of advantage and disadvantage. A disadvantage has been that we cannot speak from inside information or experience. Even so, many personal contacts have been made. An advantage has been that an objective view has been possible with, we hope, a sympathetic appraisal and constructive criticism despite our warnings.

The extent of the movement within our Church, or involving our people is not great as yet. We understand it is limited to small groups in Auckland, Hamilton, Palmerston North, Wellington and Christchurch. It is, however, a growing influence, so that this is the stage to look at it carefully.

CLAIMS OF WHAT HAS HAPPENED

Those involved say that their lives are transformed, that they have a new enthusiasm and love for Christ, for prayer, Bible study, and witnessing. This has come about through the experience described as "Baptism of the Holy Spirit." They have been dissatisfied with living their spiritual life at a low ebb, or they have felt a great need through some problem or other. They have sought God's Spirit to come into them, and to operate through them, by the "Baptism of the Holy Spirit."

Certain steps are taken, usually amidst the moral and spiritual support of a group that has already "received." The first step is private confession of every known sin, and acceptance of Christ's forgiveness. The sense of need is then made known to someone else, and there is usually laying on of hands. The person must abandon all reservations, and yield himself utterly to Christ. Prayer for the filling of the Holy Spirit is accompanied by believing that God does pour out, in fact has poured out, His Spirit.

Results — Then may follow, immediately or subsequently, an experience in which they say they know something has really happened. There is relief through conscious forgiveness of sins, sometimes accompanied by release of tensions, maybe even quite forcefully. With the filling of the Spirit, they say there comes new love for Christ, and a deep need for maintaining close relationship with Him through prayer and Bible study. There is also the ability to witness naturally and freely.

At the same time or later there may be one or more "manifestations of the Spirit" within, as listed by St. Paul in 1 Corinthians 12:7-11 (wisdom, knowledge, faith; prophecy and discernment; healing and working of miracles; speaking in tongues and their interpretation) — gifts, which as Paul says, are for the common good and for the building up of the Church (14:12). (The Committee observes that prophecy, healings, and tongue-speaking are emphasised almost to the exclusion of the other perhaps more important ones, such as wisdom, knowledge and faith.)

Appraisal — What are we to make of this? Many of the steps and processes involved are part and parcel of the Christian life. Many of us find that when we confess our sins and ask and believe that God's Spirit comes into us indeed, and works in us WITHOUT the experience described here as the "Baptism of the Holy Spirit." God's Spirit can and does work increasingly in us, producing some of the gifts Paul mentions, WITHOUT the "Baptism of the Holy Spirit." God does not limit His strengthening and working only to those who have "received" in this sense. Helpful as this experience may be to some, it is not the only means of the Spirit's operation. The counter-argument is that God's working would be even greater if all "were filled with the Holy Spirit." This may well be. But it is "by their fruits that you shall know them," and it has been observed by someone that those who claim this experience are not necessarily any more effective than others.

To some extent, the particular processes described above should be the normal experience of every Christian who receives Christ into his life. This normal experience may be heightened for some in terms of "Baptism of the Holy Spirit" but every Christian should be increasingly aware of the working of the Holy Spirit within him.

Scriptural Material — That a filling of the Holy Spirit in some additive way is a valid experience for Christians is supported by the Acts of the Apostles; at Pentecost (Chap. 2), in Samaria

(Chap. 8), among the Gentiles (Chap. 10:44f), and at Ephesus (Chap. 19:1-7). The sub-committee found the most helpful study in 1 Corinthians, Chaps. 12-14. Looking particularly at the phenomenon of Speaking with Tongues:

In Paul's list of manifestations of the Spirit, this appears as one of the last. It has been described by du Plessis in "The Spirit Bade me Go" as the least of the gifts, yet because of this, the one to begin with and keep up! It is this particular phenomenon that has occasioned from others towards those involved, the most suspicion, fear and opposition. It is a strange gift truly. Those with it say it is a great means of prayer and praising God amidst more "normal" devotions. The sounds uttered are unidentifiable to the speaker, but, according to Sherril in "They Speak in Other Tongues" language experts who have studied tapes, describe them as having authentic language structure and including obscure dialects. Only on rare occasions are the languages identified by someone present. Usually the gift is for prayer and praise when the mind and ordinary language proves inadequate. It is intriguing that this "ability" in some people can be virtually switched on and off at will. Paul warns against the exercise of the gift without love (1 Cor 13:1). In Chapter 14 he says it edifies only the speaker unless someone is present to interpret. Thus it must be controlled, otherwise it will not build up the Body of Christ.

It is a gift apportioned to whom the Spirit wills (12:11). Obviously then it is for some, but not for all. Paul himself spoke in tongues (14:18) and he says to those without it "Do not forbid it" (14:39), but he advises those with it to go on, earnestly desiring higher and more important gifts (12:31). To all he says "make love your aim, and earnestly desire the higher gifts" (14:1). But "do all decently and in order" (14:10) for confusion is not of the nature of God. Thus being a gift only apportioned to some, its use cannot be essential to the working of the Holy Spirit. Those who have not the gift can still pray as effectively in silence. Kelsey in "Speaking with Tongues" advises that this gift be not specifically sought, though neither must it be forbidden in others. It can be of great help to them but it is of no use if it is just for self-satisfaction, and an occasion for boasting or display in public.

Dangers — Preoccupation with such "Baptism of the Holy Spirit" can result in a number of observable dangers which must be carefully watched.

i. It is not the panacea for the world's ills. The experience is not an easy way out of problems or a substitute for personal

Pentecostalism

discipline. It apparently sharpens up the personality, in both good points and weaknesses. The person continues very much in need of the continuing redeeming activity of Christ through the power of the Cross. Some have made the observation that only odd and emotional people go in for this sort of thing. This may be a legitimate observation of many. It has been countered by saying that these are the people who most deeply realise their need. It is important to distinguish however, between need and the sense of need. Simon the Magician (Acts 8) thought he needed the gift, but Peter bluntly explained his real need.

ii. The experience claimed as a "Baptism of the Holy Spirit" may in some individuals not be associated with the even more important FRUITS of the Spirit: love, joy, peace, patience, goodness, faithfulness, humility and self-control (Gal 5:22; 23). (See also 1 Cor 13:1-10).

iii. It may produce division between the "haves" and "have-nots." This should not take place where there is an eagerness to "maintain the unity of the Spirit in the bond of peace" (Eph 4:3). Those who "have" naturally seek fellowship among like-minded folk. Such fellowship must, however, be designed not only to build up personal faith, but to strengthen one to seek and work and witness as servants of Christ IN the mainstream of the Church. The "haves" must remember that God's Spirit does indeed work in other ways, and in other people of humble, simple faith and Christian character.

iv. An unbalanced Christian life can result, with almost total withdrawal from life and excessive time spent in prayer and Bible study to the neglect of work and personal relationships. We note that our Lord's stay in the wilderness was not escapism but a limited occasion to which He was driven by the Spirit immediately after His Spirit-filling baptism and before he commenced His ministry. Afterward withdrawal for prayer and active ministry went hand-in-hand.

v. An unbalanced Christian Doctrine can develop, where there is an over-emphasis on the Holy Spirit out of all proportion to the other persons of the Trinity.

vi. Teaching can be overlooked in relation to experience. Growth in knowledge of all aspects of the faith must continue or we will remain children at a kindergarten stage.

vii. The experience itself can be thought of as of first importance. But it is Christ, and Christ alone, the Source of the experience, Who must be glorified. Further, those who have had the experience may feel they have arrived at the top of the spiritual ladder. In fact we are all only on the lower rungs and there is a long way to climb toward Christian maturity.

viii. The experience produces in some a naive sentimentalism and literalism which puts others off, and does not lead them to Christ. Others are put off by tactless words, and rash actions.

CONCLUSION

The Committee considers that those in our Church involved in this experience are probably mostly in the early stages of it. They may need to come through it more to see it in the whole context of believing in Christ and working in His world for Him. There is much need for patience both toward them and from them. God works in mysterious ways beyond our expectations and we must all allow Him to move beyond any patterns we may like to set.

In Christian love, we must all accept each other and try to understand and help each other.

While SOME may really feel the need to seek a "baptism of the Holy Spirit" and OTHERS must not forbid them, ALL OF US must yield ourselves to Christ to equip and empower us as He wills. We all need to cultivate the gifts He chooses to give, AND the fruits of the Spirit He wants to produce in us all.

Other books also worth looking at: Wilkerson, "The Cross and the Switchblade." Frost, "Aglow with the Spirit." Newbigin, "The Household of God" (Chap. 3).[1]

1. Some thirty members were on the committee convened by the Revd. J. D. S. Moore, M.Sc., B.D. The Moderator of the General Assembly was the Right Revd. E. G. Jensen, M.A. There has never been any suggestion to this date that the subject should be handled by the Doctrine Committee. The Very Revd. S. C. Read, LL.B., B.D. to Author.

In the intervening seven years the winds of change have brought about a greater theological openness. Cf. report of Doctrinal Committee to the 1973 General Assembly, *"The Holy Spirit and the Charismatic Renewal of the Church."* Convener, The Revd. S. J. D. McCay, M.A., together with the Life and Work Committee report, *"The Church and Pentecostalism"*; convener, the Revd. R. H. Lane, M.A., B.D. Both reports were referred to presbyteries and sessions for consideration. The Revd. W. A. Best, General Assembly Executive Officer to Author.

Pentecostalism

THE WORK OF THE HOLY SPIRIT
IN THE COMMUNITY

In Holland there are two major Reformed ecclesiastical traditions. Since the period of King Wilhelm I (1806), the then existing Reformed Church took a new form and was called in Dutch Nederlandse Hervormde Kerk (NHK). In 1834 and again after 1860, a number of parishes separated themselves from the NHK because of what they considered the liberal theological ideas which dominated church life. In 1892 these and other Reformed dissident groups formed what in Dutch was called the Gereformeerde Kerken (GK), which would be translated "The Re-reformed Churches." The great leader of the GK was the theologian and statesman Abraham Kuyper.

If one speaks of a major document coming from the historic churches, this document of the GK was the first. This was no accident. In Holland the classical Pentecostal movement and the historic churches had been in dialogue for some years. Many of the early classical Pentecostals had grown up in one of the two major Reformed Churches and, in spite of their rejecting the Reformed tradition, maintained a living relationship with the churches. Relatively easily they entered into dialogue with the tradition which had nurtured them.[1] In 1958 the American healing evangelist T. L. Osborn came to Holland and held a ten-day rally in The Hague, which on a single day was often attended by one hundred thousand people. Of the literally hundreds of American healing evangelists, T. L. Osborn has been one of the most successful — and most enduring — with a highly organized, disciplined, varied, and well-financed outreach.[2] It was clearly classical Pentecostal in style and doctrine. Later he ministered in Groningen in northern Holland.[3]

Because large numbers of those attending these rallies were from the historic churches, more specifically from the Reformed and Roman Catholic Churches, Osborn's rallies were the occasion for the Pentecostal movement to enter these churches. More affected were the Reformed Churches. They faced the immediate pastoral problem of what to do about the thousands of their faithful who felt drawn to the Pentecostal movement (at this time the Protestant charismatic movement within the historic churches did not exist or was just emerging). Osborn's visit, and to a lesser degree that of the German Pentecostal evangelist Hermann Zaiss, were the occasion of an unorganized but nonetheless continuous dialogue with the churches of the Reform. The most decisive factor was The Church and the Pentecostal Groups: Pastoral Letter of the General Synod of the Reformed Church (NHK), *published in 1960,* two years after Osborn's huge rallies in The Hague. [4] This official letter to the classical Pentecostal churches also gives some attention to the NHK members who felt attracted to the Pentecostal movement. Though sharply critical of classical Pentecostal theological positions, the NHK showed itself open and capable of self-criticism: "The first thing which the church has to say concerning Pentecostal doctrine should not be a word of rebuke or criticism, but a word expressing the shamed recognition that such a movement as the Pentecostal groups can even exist because there is too little 'evidence of the Spirit's power' (1 Cor 2:4) in the church. . . ." [5]

An answer was given by the classical Pentecostals in The Pentecostal Community and the Church. [6] They were grateful that their Reformed brethren did not point an accusing finger at them but extended a friendly hand. Even though the Reformed publication was critical of their doctrine and exegesis, the classical Pentecostals rejoiced at how the Pastoral Letter entered into the dialogue. It was judged "a great help" (een belangrijk middel). [7] In particular, the classical Pentecostals pointed to the Acts of the Apostles as normative for Christians today. [8]

The impulses of this exchange prompted books by the Reformed pastors D. F. Molenaar [9] and by H. J. Zweers. [10] Of special importance among intellectuals was Karel Hoekendijk, the son of a pastor from Indonesia. Finally, both the Dutch counterpart of the Full Gospel Business Men's Fellowship International (Volle Evangeliezakenlieden) and the magazine Fire (Vuur) promoted the dialogue between the Reformed tradition and the now emerging Protestant charismatic renewal in the NHK and the GK.

Vuur was specifically attempting to interpret the Pentecostal insight for those who were remaining in the historic churches. It also tried to bring the Pentecostal message into the Reformed churches, emphasizing the integral role that sacrament, sermon, and charism play in official worship. [11] For years the editorial board was drawn exclusively from the NHK and the GK. It is against the background of this extensive contact which the present document from the GK, The Work of the Holy Spirit in the Community (Het werk van de Heilige Geest in de Gemeente), is to be seen.

The document's introduction discussed elements in the charismatic renewal which members of the GK find attractive: the personal element, certitude, the spectacular. It also considered the image of the church. Then followed an extensive section on the general work of the Spirit in the community (whether all Christians are baptized in the Spirit, the role of experience and spiritual growth, the relationship to one's secular vocation). The document then entered into more specific consideration of

The Holy Spirit in the Community

the gifts, their variety and purpose, ordinary and extraordinary gifts, the role they play in a maturing community, and the relation of office and charism. Three gifts were singled out for special attention: tongues, prophecy, healing. A whole chapter was devoted to infant baptism and re-baptism. The document concluded with a short history of classical Pentecostalism and its introduction into Holland. The final pages contained some decrees of the Synod of Assen (1957–58) and that of Groningen (1963–64) which relate to the charismatic renewal.

The immediate reason for preparing the document was the pastoral problem stated in the foreword: "Various members of our churches joined Pentecostal groups or expressed their sympathy for the Pentecostal movement." Frantic development of technology and communications has depersonalized life. Thus the charismatic renewal with its emphasis on the personal element in faith is attractive to many. Those who have been exposed to this Pentecostal piety seem also to have satisfied their desire for certitude in an overwhelming experience of joy and liberation. Here problems of uncertainty simply are not raised. In the enthusiasm of charismatic meetings, the spectacular elements are visible demonstrations that God is not the great Absent One. Nonetheless, straining after the spectacular often leads to disillusionment. "Although history itself has taught that these extra-ecclesial revival movements lose their influence after a while anyway, without having contributed essentially to the reformation of the church, they still keep returning under a new guise."

The two-level doctrine of conversion and baptism in the Holy Spirit, the latter demonstrated by the gift of tongues, was rejected. To what does the entire work of Christ direct us? God who makes all things new in Christ and the Spirit makes of us new men, a new creation, and gives us life in the Spirit. With sobriety the Scripture paints a picture not of "spiritual supermen" but of "new men." The Spirit does not lead us out of the world. Rather, he "tightens the knots of the world on our hearts." The fruits of the Spirit are of greater importance in bringing the gospel to that world than are the spectacular gifts.

Great variety of gifts in the body is a manifestation of the many-sided character of community life, but charisms are means, not ends. The higher gifts are not those which attract the most attention but those which more directly serve the common good. It is to maturity that the Spirit leads. In the Pentecostal movement, however, "people put lesser value on the maturing of the community through the Holy Spirit." They want "to return to those gifts which more properly belong to an immature community." An indication of this move back to immaturity is the willingness to put more confidence in "an authorization from above" than in patient research and argument. There is a longing for a special and "clearly apparent" self-revelation of the Spirit. In Paul it is clear, on the contrary, that it is the "ordinary" which comes first and, strange to say, is stamped with the grade of "special."

No opposition exists between the natural and supernatural. Our talents are taken into possession by the Spirit who "seals them as his own gifts of grace." In fact "the Spirit does not need to act outside of an already present talent."

Admittedly there are those in the GK for whom the offices in the church are "the one and only thing." An opposite extreme among charismatics is the undervaluation of the church as an institution. Here the accent is on the personal relationship to God. No appeal to the Reformation can be made for this highly individualistic conception. "A church member by himself is an amputated member." The New Testament gives no distinction between office and charism.

Tongues were evaluated as an "ecstatic phenomenon" in which the ego-awareness disappears. In principle, misuse does not exclude good use. Recognition was given to tongues as an authentic gift of the Spirit, when a person is so overwhelmed by the power of the Spirit that speech overflows the limits of language. Even though this behavior is widely prevalent in other cultures "which the Evil One made use of (and still makes use of), nevertheless the Holy Spirit wanted to confiscate it. He imparts a certain content to it."

The document gave extensive space to the charism of healing, a result of T. L. Osborn's campaigns. Until Osborn's appearance, healing was not an important factor in classical Pentecostalism in Holland.

The document contended that in the gospels Jesus commissioned a definite group of followers to go about healing, but it is not clear that the charism of healing has to be present in the church everywhere and constantly. Much less is it clear that every baptized person has the gift of healing. Nor is it evident that "a believer does not need to be sick." One would want to grant that healing gifts are given to definite persons in very limited situations. "When this is true it will be unmistakably evident." So the question is not whether such healings are possible. Rather, there is a much more fundamental question: Why do people long for signs? "Yet we may not resist the gifts, even the extraordinary ones, out of fear of derailment, when the Spirit grants these gifts to the community."

In the matter of rebaptism the authors of the document saw it as a devaluation of infant baptism and said that the church "will make absolutely no compromise" on this issue, which leads those involved in charismatic-Pentecostal groups to break with the church. In spite of this firm stand the authors recalled that the Synod of Assen in 1957–58

The Holy Spirit in the Community

concluded that "rebaptism" of itself was not sufficient reason for declaring that concerned members have withdrawn from the church.

The Dutch original was published in booklet form: Het Werk van de Heilige Geest in de Gemeente; *Voorlichtend Geschrift over de Pinkstergroepen, Uitgegeven in Opdracht van de Generale Synode van de Gereformeerde Kerken,* (Kampen: J. H. Kok N.V. 1968).

1. Walter Hollenweger, Handbuch der Pfingstbewegung, *II Haupteil (duplicated),* *(Geneva, 1965/1967), 05.20.007.*

2. David Edwin Harrell, Jr., All Things Are Possible *(Bloomington: Indiana University Press, 1975), pp. 169–72.*

3. *Hollenweger.*

4. De Kerk en de Pinkstergroepen, *Herderlijk Schrijven van de Generale Synode der Nederlandse Hervormde Kerk,* ('S-Gravenhage: Boekencentrum N.V., 1960).

5. Ibid., 34.

6. De Pinkstergemeente en de Kerk, *de Broederschap van Pinkstergemeenten Geeft Antwoord op het Herderlijk Schrijven dan de Generale Synode der Nederlandse Hervormde Kerk, Stichting Volle Evangelie Lectuur, (Rotterdam and Groningen, 1962).*

7. Ibid., 7.

8. Ibid., 10.

9. De doop met de Heilige Geest *(Kampen: J. H. Kok, 1963).*

10. Het volle Evangelie. See also *Zweers,* Osborn en de Bijbel: Gods nodiging tot gebed om genezing, *no date given.*

11. *Hollenweger, 05.20.016.*

FOREWORD

The 1963–64 General Synod of Groningen of the Reformed Churches in the Netherlands decided to appoint several delegates to compose a directive document concerning the Pentecostal movement. Need for this document evidently existed because various members of our churches joined Pentecostal groups or expressed their sympathy for the Pentecostal movement.

The text of this document on the Pentecostal movement, which was composed by Rev. H. C. Endedijk, Rev. A. G. Kornet, Doctoral Candidate G. Y. Vellenga, and their advisor Professor Doctor H. N. Ridderbos, was presented to the General Synod of Amsterdam in 1967.

The Synod expressed its appreciation to the document's authors and, after some alterations had been made in the text, decided to approve its publication with a word of introduction by the synodal board.

The synodal board hopes that church councils and community members can obtain a correct viewpoint concerning the nature and background of the Pentecostal movement with the help of the Biblical guidance which this booklet offers.

INTRODUCTION

Purpose

The phenomenon of the Pentecostal movement and everything related to it remains on the agenda in the Church and outside of it. In the Dutch Reformed churches, too, once again members feel attracted to this movement or wrestle with the questions which it presents to the churches. Even the statistics seem to prove that at least in some regions of our country the thought patterns of the Pentecostal movement have received special attention from members of the Reformed Churches.

For these reasons the General Synod of these churches urged that this matter should continue to receive attention. It also gave the impetus to publish the present document.

Indeed, various works concerning this spiritual movement have already appeared and have even been published by the church. It is not our purpose to repeat in this document what others have already done in a way that was often outstanding. Consequently, this is not a new and exhaustive treatment of the entire phenomenon of the Pentecostal movement. Rather, to answer questions put to the community, we intend to go somewhat deeper into the practical experience of the spiritual life and into what Scripture teaches about the work of the Holy Spirit in the community.

In this we hope to contribute towards a positive exchange of thought with supporters of the Pentecostal movement itself. We also want to offer some assistance to those in the community who need it or who, for instance, by virtue of their office give spiritual direction.

Why Did It Happen?

Almost self-evidently the question arises: "Why is it that a spiritual current like that of the Pentecostal movement, in itself in no way new, but all through history a satellite of the church, again in our times has so much attraction for so many members of the church?"

Of course, although an answer to this question, satisfactory in

The Holy Spirit in the Community

every respect, cannot be given, several important points are to be noted. We want here to mention three elements.

1. THE PERSONAL ELEMENT

Many people say that what they miss all too much in preaching, visiting homes, and the fellowship of the faithful, is the personal element. To be sure, at one time this personal element was more apparent than it is at present, including that in the Reformed churches. That this is no longer true can be seen as a reaction to the attention directed too exclusively to the individual in a way which was not always healthy and fruitful.

It has indeed always been the aim — and the power — of Reformed preaching to draw men out of themselves and to point to Christ as the sole Security and Savior. In our age the appearance of what is in many respects massive and impersonal, coming to the fore at the expense of the particular and the individual, is also to be reckoned with.

By their very nature the frantic development of mankind's capacity, the removal of all sorts of barriers, and world-wide communication bring about this accent on the massive and the impersonal. The church also, much more than in the past, is today involved with the general problems of the times, problems which affect the fellowship of the entire people, and truly of the whole world.

Even though on the one hand there is a clear relationship to what Scripture teaches concerning the world-wide dimensions of the Kingdom of God (a relationship also to the character of the Reformed faith in which the Biblical verse "The Lord's is the earth and its fulness" always echoed), on the other hand the danger is not imaginary that in this development the *personal* emphasis, the *personal* requirement of faith and conversion, the *personal* bond to Christ and the work of the Holy Spirit do not always receive the attention they deserve.

Although one can easily generalize in this matter, nonetheless the *general* aspects of church life, the struggle to keep up with the times in organization and theology, and the struggle to satisfy those demands which have been made on the church body, readily lead to a certain neglect of the pastoral care of souls, conversation concerning one's personal life, leisure for prayer, and attention to the future.

It is therefore not surprising that some persons who particularly cherish this personal element would show their discontent and feel drawn to certain spiritual groups within or without the church and thus quickly come upon the Pentecostal movement. And precisely in the Pentecostal movement all the emphasis is put on what the individual believer personally experiences. No longer does he experience, first, as a member of the church who is on a pilgrimage, as the church teaches. Above all, it is a very individual experience which takes him out of what he had been experiencing as a routine and out of the experience of the massiveness of church life. It stands him on his own spiritual feet, as it were.

2. THE ELEMENT OF CERTITUDE

Closely related to this is the question of the personal certitude of faith. In the Reformed religion, particularly in Dutch religious life, problems relating to certitude have always played a major role.

For many Christians, especially those with a definitely pietistic upbringing, the spiritual life consists in a search for certitude. Whenever these persons fail to receive attention or find a solution in the church as they understand it, it is not surprising that the Pentecostal movement constitutes a certain temptation for them.

Although this movement, with its Methodist background, springs from a different root than the piety colored by Pietism of the Reformed stamp, nevertheless, it appears to many who struggle with the personal certitude of faith to offer a way out of all sorts of spiritual doubts and worries. And that comes about in a very radical way.

Here there is no longer uncertainty and anxiety, but rather great resolution. Here one does not hear the constant repetition of "Oh, if only I could have that certitude once again!" Instead, there is [in the Pentecostal movement] jubilant certitude that it *is* there, that it exists, and that it is there with all its surpassing power for the taking, offered to anyone who only dares to believe. This is because *here* in fact, to the new and, unfortunately for many "churchy" Christians, veiled certitude is being preached, namely, that God follows up the *first* work of faith and conversion with another *second* blessing, a greater work which consists in the sealing by the Spirit in an overwhelming experience of joy, of liberation, sometimes of ecstasy, in which problems of uncertainty simply are not raised. The reason is that gifts of the Spirit descend upon the believer as a number of audible and visible signs of being God's children and having new life.

3. THE SPECTACULAR ELEMENT

The preceding already touched on another element. What binds many to the Pentecostal movement, and appears to be a proof of authenticity, is the spectacular. In the spectacular, they sense a balance and a refutation of the assertion which is often heard, namely, that God is the great Absent One who no longer reveals himself or intervenes in affairs of this world. And although the church perseveres in the profession of God's presence and providence, she herself offers no clear proof of it. Church gatherings are not characterized by sensational happenings. In the life of ordinary Christians, too little seems to be "happening." The Pentecostal movement, on the contrary, is precisely full of sensational matters and consciously relates itself to the miracles and signs of the Bible.

The Pentecostal movement can point to many sensational and spectacular phenomena: the mysterious phenomenon of speaking in tongues, spiritual enthusiasm accompanying baptism in water (baptism in the Spirit, rebaptism), healings (faith healing), prophecy, "receiving" the Spirit at certain moments in a way that can be proven.

All of these phenomena are a proof for many that the Spirit is present there, and even though not present exclusively, nevertheless present in a much more convincing way.

And does not this relate to the earliest Christianity and to the texts which are preached about so little in church and which are so often just read through? But did not the Spirit come down upon the baptized in Samaria and in Ephesus (Ac 8 and 19)? Did not Jesus promise his disciples that they would work signs and miracles (Mk 16)? Is not healing of the sick community member promised to the earnest prayer of the elder (Jm 5)? Does not Paul speak at length in his letters about spiritual gifts, speaking in tongues, prophecy, faith as a supernatural power, the gift of healing and similar things (1 Co 12:14)?

Now, we do not intend to assert that the Pentecostal movement consists of these spectacular and spiritually sensational phenomena. But the emphasis which is put on the extraordinary is nonetheless one of the reasons why so many people who have vainly waited in the church for the "movement of the water" turn to the movement. But we will have to qualify this at once by saying that due to spiritual *over*-exertion and strained protestations of belief and the disillusion resulting from it, many persons turned away from the Pentecostal movement after a shorter or longer period and then often fell into a kind of spiritual drifting.

The Importance of the Matter

From the preceding it is now evident to what extent the church in our days is right in concerning herself thoroughly and continuously with the phenomenon noted here. Although history itself has taught that these extra-ecclesial revival movements lose their influence after a while without having contributed essentially to the reformation of the church, they still keep returning under a new disguise.

The reasons for this are often to be found in the very life of the church. Extra-ecclesial spirituality frequently blooms in periods of dead orthodoxy, churchly traditionalism and moral laxity. And without being able to call (too readily and too automatically) the present Pentecostal movement an unpaid bill of the contemporary church, there is still reason for each church which sees its members yearning for or going to the full "meal" of the Pentecostal movement from the "meagerness" of the church, to ask itself whether the obvious reasons for this are not to be found in contemporary church life.

In forming a judgment about all of this we surely must not take as a starting point the spiritual preference of certain people. Still less can our point of reference be what is thrilling and impressive at first sight. But as has already been stated, we want to search for our point of departure in what the *Scriptures* teach us about the work of the Spirit in the community and in the life of the faithful. Full attention is devoted to this in the following parts of this document. But it must still always be kept in mind that it is not only a matter of explanation and insight, but also the question of whether what has been thus explained and understood actually *inspires* and rules the life of the community.

Let it be said at the outset that the writers of this booklet are of the opinion that the Pentecostal movement and its supporters have a very one-sided, and therefore wrong notion of the way in which the Holy Spirit works and of the nature of the spiritual life. They intend to render an account of that judgment in the following parts of this document. But as members of the

The Holy Spirit in the Community

Reformed Churches they are not of the opinion that after all of this has been stated and explained, they can simply go on to the day's business.

Not only criticism by human beings but in particular the continuing and deeper investigation of the Scriptures will have to bring the Church, including the Reformed Church, to a re-examination and reflection of herself as to whether the image which the Scripture paints of new life through the Spirit is recognizable in her. Then we will have to ask ourselves in each instance what the special factors and dangers are which threaten to make this image invisible and unclear in the contemporary shape of the church.

The Image of Our Churches

If we ask which dangers threaten our churches at the moment, we will, as much as possible, have to guard against commonplaces and generalizations in answering that question. In this matter we are furthermore asked to judge with spiritual discernment. Thus in our judgment, as concerns the Reformed Churches, these dangers must not presently be sought in a rigid traditionalism or in the immobility or inactivity of the church.

Concerning the first, an increasing fear of traditionalism is much more to be observed in the church's midst, a new reflection on the traditional confession and a marked relativizing of all sorts of forms and mores that had long been preserved. In this respect one certainly cannot speak of deadness and rigidness, even though any criticism of what has been transmitted does not yet mean a return to the living sources from which the church must live.

Still less can the church in which we live be denied readiness to undertake something and to make financial sacrifices for it. There is the organization of various new tasks, interest in what is happening elsewhere, and awareness of the length and breadth of the Kingdom of Christ in this world.

The shortcoming of the church in our days, we think, has to be sought then in other dimensions rather than in the breadth of interest and the effort of the church accompanying it. We mean by that, that (due to various causes easy to point out and in part already noted) the *many* does sometimes threaten to supplant the *One.*

Relationship to Christ becomes more impersonal because

people more easily "walk past themselves." Preaching does gain breadth but not depth, and so its prophetic power declines. Our working puts our praying in the shade. Belief in the progress of God's work and the expectation of the Lord's coming is embarrassed at seeing what human beings accomplish in the scientific and technical field. The contemporary world, with all its power and limitations, with all its challenging questions and unsolved problems, enters our houses in the literal sense, confiscates our attention, often fills our horizon, and threatens the simplicity of our belief in God the Creator and the Completer of all things.

In fact, it has always been a characteristic mark of Reformed life (and we have already alluded to it), that it does not shut itself off from the world. And it belongs to the "maturity" of faith of which Scripture speaks (Ep 4:14, 15; Col 2:6, 7) that it is aware that not only the interior life of man, but *all* things in heaven and on earth have been taken up into the redeeming work of Christ.

Therefore, Christian life which lives by the *full* Gospel will never be able to content itself with a spirituality or a piety directed exclusively inwardly and which looks for the proof of authenticity in various phenomena, which would be isolated and intelligible only to initiates.

On the other hand, no demonstration is needed to show that dangers, large as life, threaten the church precisely in these times of increasing communication. So does not resistance of the faith have to be equally strong to find that spiritual resistance and that spiritual answer to the challenge of the forces and questions of the world surrounding her in which her confession that Christ is the Lord of the world is not an empty echo but a living witness?

If the church is going to be able to answer that, it will have to search for this power before everything else in its foundation and in its source of life, namely, in the living and conscious faith of its members, in fellowship, and in the animating action of the Holy Spirit. Many, rightly or wrongly, complain that precisely as regards the preaching of the church and the mutual association of the faithful, they have lost hold on their plank of safety, lost their personal relationship to Christ and sealing with the Holy Spirit. All this makes it apparent how profoundly the questions put here must concern the church.

In response to the criticism which the church meets from Pentecostal groups in this respect, she must not settle back self-contentedly, or as if crippled. Rather, she must, for her own sake and for the sake of so many serious and devout Christians who wrestle with these problems, ask herself whether and to what extent she is lacking this true life which comes from Christ and which the Spirit wants to work in her. But the measuring rule to be employed in doing this cannot be any other than that which has been given to us in the Scriptures.

Therefore, in the following pages we want to try to enter more closely into the nature of the work of God's Spirit just as the Bible speaks of it. Our document is directed not only negatively and defensively against what, for instance, we see as the one-sidedness of the Pentecostal movement; it is also intended, above all, positively, specifically to search for a way in which the church and all believers must go so as not to lose the track of the Spirit and to be recognizable and fruitful as the community of Christ in the contemporary world situation.

I. THE GENERAL WORK OF THE HOLY SPIRIT IN THE COMMUNITY

General and Particular

To gain a good insight into the work of the Holy Spirit in the community, we must observe that Scripture speaks about this from two points of view:

a. The gift of the Spirit is a grace of Christ which the whole community and all believers without exception share. This might be called the general character of the work of the Spirit. It consists in the bond which unites Christ with all those who are His.

b. Besides this general gift of the Spirit, there are also various special gifts, workings, powers which the Spirit wants to bestow in the midst of the community. Scripture speaks of this with a great variety of expression and teaches clearly that not every believer has the same gift. No, the Spirit distributes these gifts like a sovereign to whom he wills, although the faithful are also admonished to seek these gifts in faith and to use them for the advantage of the whole community and for the glory of God.

In this chapter we intend to direct our attention to the general work of the Holy Spirit, whereas in Chapter II the matter mentioned under point (b) will be treated.

All Baptized in the Holy Spirit

Every believer united to Christ by faith shares also the gift of the Holy Spirit. This is one of the most important and fundamental things stated in the Scripture concerning the New Testament community. Where Christ, the Head and the Lord of the community is, there also is the Spirit (2 Co 3:17), and whoever belongs to Christ, has also in him access to and a share in the Spirit.

Scripture witnesses to this in varying ways. For example, Paul certainly puts it very plainly in Rm 8:9, "You — that is, the community of Christ — on the contrary are not in the flesh, but in the Spirit (the meaning is: you no longer live under the lordship of the flesh, but under that of the Spirit). In fact, the Spirit lives in you. But on the other hand, if anyone does not have the Spirit of Christ, that person does not belong to Him."

It could not be stated more emphatically than this that the gift of Christ is a grace for the *entire* community and all its members. If one would not have that Spirit, neither would one belong to Christ and be united to Him. Further, this thought is in fact expressed in such a way that the community is the *body* of Christ. And since the Spirit of Christ totally fills his body, the members of this body likewise share the Spirit.

This is related to baptism and to the Last Supper in particular. For baptism incorporates us into the body of Christ and so brings us into the communion of all the gifts and powers with which Christ as Head wishes to fill his body. Therefore, one may say of baptism that it is a baptism in or with the Holy Spirit, "for by one Spirit we were all baptized into one body" (1 Co 12:13). This signifies that by our all having been initiated and incorporated through baptism into the communion of one and the same body, we have also all been made sharers ("baptized") in the one and same Holy Spirit.

This is also true of the sacred banquet in which the faithful practice the communion of the one body of Christ, "for by one Spirit were all baptized" (1 Co 12:13). Here too, being gifted ("baptized") with the one Spirit is thus closely related to the community as the body of Christ. And with another image one may also say that the community is the *house* of God in which the Holy Spirit dwells. It may also be called the *temple*, the *dwelling place* of the Holy Spirit (1 Co 3:16; 2 Co 6:16; Ep 2:22).

So two things come to the fore in Paul's instruction about the Holy Spirit:

a. Receiving the Holy Spirit is not, in the first place, a private matter or a private experience. One receives the gift of the Holy Spirit as a member of the body of Christ which is his community.

The Holy Spirit in the Community

Not diversity but unity, not individuality but community in receiving and possessing the Spirit are primary.

b. Receiving the Holy Spirit is closely connected to the means of grace instituted by Christ, God's Word, baptism and the eucharist. That is so, not as if these would have a kind of magical or instrumental effect, but simply because especially baptism and the eucharist put us in communion with the body of Christ, and so too, with the Spirit of Christ. For where the Lord is, there his Spirit is; where the Lord dwells, there the Spirit is working. That is why, for the reception of the gift of the Spirit, we are directed to the preaching of the Gospel and to the means of grace which open for us the entrance (baptism) to that communion, and encourage the preservation of that communion (the eucharist).

Is It Not Much Too "Easy"?

All of this, although it has been taught us by Scripture in a way that is not unclear, appears to many as a concept that is much too automatic and much too "easy." There is no objection to saying that we belong to Christ through faith. But does this actually include the gift of the Spirit also? Is not this latter something more, a plus, a second degree? Is not the gift of the Spirit something which reveals itself in a special way as a breakthrough, an enlightening which one cannot ascribe to every believer with qualification? And it is felt particularly objectionable to fasten the Spirit "just like that" to the church, baptism and the eucharist.

One can speak of "baptism in the Spirit" according to popular opinion only if this is accompanied by the outpouring of special gifts and powers, as indeed we sometimes read in the New Testament.

Many reject baptism of infants too, because this is not useful for that, and it is urged that those who did receive baptism with water but not "baptism in the Spirit," understood as stated, have themselves "re-baptized" so as to receive at last the fullness of the Spirit by means of baptism. As regards the eucharist, it is likewise denied that those who take part in it are baptized in the Spirit as long as this gift of the Spirit does not reveal itself in a clearly observable way with extraordinary gifts and powers.

Because all of this is fundamental to the matter occupying us, we have to enter into these conceptions and objections in somewhat more detail. What leads to a dead end in this train of thought is that too much of a separation is made between sharing in Christ and in the gift of the Spirit. As is apparent from the

Scripture passages cited above, we must not sunder what God has joined together here either. For just as it is the Spirit who makes us take refuge in Christ and produces faith in our hearts, so, too, is Christ an inexhaustible fountain of spiritual gifts for all who belong to him.

Anyone who imagines that a person does not share the fullness of Christ until he or she has received assurance of it in special gifts and powers is like the son who will not stay in his father's house unless he is immediately paid the entire amount he thinks he has coming as an heir.

Growth and Increase in Grace

Sharing the gift of the Spirit promised us as members of the body of Christ, and assured and given us through baptism and the eucharist, does not mean that we should receive all the gifts of the Spirit at once and without distinction.

Scripture speaks clearly of *growing up* in grace and in the knowledge of Christ. Or to use another image, it speaks of the spiritual *upbuilding* of the community upon Christ, the foundation, and that through the power of the Holy Spirit. Baptism as the *deed of incorporation* brings us into this communion of life and opens for us the way to all the gifts and treasures of Christ. But it is an error to think that baptism, to be capable of being called not only baptism by water but also baptism in the Spirit, must immediately be a peak of spiritual *experience* which has to be accompanied by a special awareness and various signs.

Besides, that is not at all the meaning of those passages in the Acts of the Apostles in which it is said that the Holy Spirit "fell" upon certain persons who had themselves baptized. What happened there had to be *the proof* and *the sign* of the kingdom of Christ. The kingdom was intended not only for Christians from among the Jews, but also for those from among the Samaritans (Ac 8:14-17) and the Gentiles (Ac 10:44-47; 11:15-18). Similarly, the fact that John baptized with water whereas the disciples of Christ were baptized with the Holy Spirit (Ac 11:16; 19:4-6) constituted a proof of the Lord's word.

But anyone who would want to deduce from this that a person does not share the fullness of Christ until he or she has received these special experiences, and that baptism also would not be baptism in the Spirit until he makes us share these special experiences, is in conflict with Scripture. He misunderstands the character of baptism as a sacrament of initiation and takes a

The Holy Spirit in the Community

position with regard to the giving of the Spirit's gifts which is an interpretation peculiar to himself.

First, does it not often happen in the New Testament that people come to faith and are baptized without these special manifestations and signs of the Spirit? Let us just think of the conversion and baptism of the court official, of Paul, of the proconsular governor at Paphos, and of the jailer at Philippi. Would anyone want to say that all of these "first born" in Christ did *not* receive full baptism, and did *not* receive baptism in the Spirit when they were baptized? Yet we do not read anything in their accounts about special manifestations of the Spirit during or after their baptism.

So who would *dare* to say, after he has once been incorporated into Christ through baptism — and in that way has the entrance opened for him to the fullness, to Christ and to the gifts of the Spirit — that that baptism had not been a baptism with the Holy Spirit unless he has simultaneously also received the gift of tongues, or of prophecy, or of some other special experience? Who would think that he could test the Lord and his Spirit, and dare to lay down the law in that way?

That is why the church considers this "re-baptism" not simply superfluous, but even unpermitted. For God did not institute baptism to be an exhibition of everything the Spirit can do in his almighty power, but as a sign and seal of our belonging to Christ and of our sharing in the grace of his Spirit. And this hallmark of his grace upon us is so clear and plain, that it does not need to be approved each time by special and spectacular manifestations of his Spirit.

If this baptism is not sufficient for us, we ought not think we need a better, more complete baptism. No, rather we have to live henceforth by faith in the power of God's promise which had been given us in our first and only baptism. For we would risk the danger of looking for the cause of our poverty in the Lord and in the insufficiency of his means of grace, instead of with ourselves and in the imperfection of our faith.

The Purpose of the Spirit

Moreover, it is a matter of great importance to know the *purpose* of the Spirit and the *nature* of his work, of which incorporation into Christ by faith and baptism makes us participants. For it could happen that we have a mistaken notion of this purpose and for that reason look for ways and means of satisfying our poverty and attaining the certitude of faith other than those which are indicated and offered us in Scripture.

If we ask ourselves to what the entire work of Christ is directed and towards which all ways and gifts of the Spirit lead, we can express that in a scriptural way in a single sentence: God makes all things new in Christ and through the Spirit and so he wants to make us *new men* too.

Whatever further amazing gifts are mentioned in the Bible, like speaking in tongues, prophecy, healing prayer, etc., let us not forget that the greatest and mightiest work of the Spirit is that he makes us new men. Then, too, all other gifts have been subordinated to that and they should all serve that purpose. They ought to shape the new life from God in the community as a whole and in every believer in particular. Prophecies will pass away; tongues will cease; knowledge will pass away. But love never ends. And love is the core and summation of the new life.

The Bible speaks about it in various ways: rebirth, new creation, new man, resurrection. The Spirit reveals himself in these ways to all who belong to Christ. It is called a "life in (i.e., under the lordship of) the Spirit" and no longer "in the flesh" (sin). It consists in being led and in allowing ourselves to be led by the Spirit in such a way that we are no longer subject and bound to the service of sin, but are available to God in Christ.

By what do we recognize this new man? In Gal 5 Paul names these signs of recognition, this fruit of the Spirit: love, joy, peace, gentleness, kindness, goodness, faithfulness, and self-control. Whoever keeps in mind this purpose of the Spirit and this nature of the work of the Spirit can be kept from any kind of error.

On the one hand, he will not let himself be taken in by every spiritual outburst, yearning for special experiences, discoveries and whatever else. He will remain safe with the sobriety of Scripture which paints for us the picture of God's children, not as that of spiritual supermen but as of spiritually *new* men. The Lord God created us to bear that image.

On the other hand, every thought has to be rejected that all of this might become our lot "of itself" and "automatically," whenever we just go along with the church's practice of a certain ruling or custom. For being led by the Spirit also means *letting* oneself be led by the Spirit and that is the way, the battle, the exercise of *faith*!

God *bestows* us his Spirit so that we may be new persons, new fathers and mothers for our children, new persons in all relationships of life. But he also *calls* us to that. Being a child of God is a conscious, struggling, praying, and always a believing, life. That involves our whole existence, our heart and our body, our interior and our exterior person. Love, joy, and peace are *gifts* of the Spirit, but they are received on the route of the militia of Christ, in the military service of our Lord. The devil fights with us over them. They lie in the balance of human life with all its difficulty and conflict. They seem unreachable, and they are indeed, unless we are guided as God's children, and allow ourselves to be led by his Spirit.

So too, it is only in such a way that the *church* is viewed correctly. It is the household of God. Thus being a member of the church is not something automatic. It consists in our being living members of the body of Christ, eager for the living Word, searching for communion with all engaged with us in the same battle and the same wrestling match for the same victory. For to be new men, we have to belong to the new *humanity*. Moreover, we will only display the fruits of the new man (love, joy, peace . . .) by being living branches of the vine Christ, which also means, by belonging to the new Israel, the vine which God planted.

What Can We Expect of the Spirit?

It is an error to think that in this life there is something still higher and better to be expected of the Spirit than that we may be new men and living members of Christ's community.

Yet there are people who do think that. They too regard this "general" thing as important and grant that this fruit of the Spirit is of great significance for ordinary living. But they still seek more. Thus they also claim that a person has only then come to the "fulness" of Christ when, besides these ordinary and general gifts, he has also received the special and extraordinary ones. They also think that only in the "extraordinary" way does the full light and steadfast certitude of our being children of God, sealed by his Spirit, break through.

Now it cannot be our purpose to hold these special gifts cheaply. In the following we are going to speak again extensively about them. Here, however, this question is in order: "Is there really something that can be thought of which is more extraordinary and more spectacular than that a person, instead of being ruled by hatred and resentment, is moved by love? That instead of being sad, he is joyful? That instead of unrest he shows peace; instead of irritableness, gentleness, kindness and self-control?"

Should God, who once and for all created us to be *human beings* and not supermen, angels or miracle-workers, ask more of us and intend to do more with us than being reborn according to his image, the image of Christ? To be able to know him as our Father, to be reconciled with him in Christ, a holy life to his glory? Do not all the admonitions of apostles and prophets come down to this, that the Lord asks nothing else of us than that we should do what is right, that we should love each other, and should walk humbly with the Lord our God?

So too, the *certitude of faith* is effected and confirmed in us by being led along *this* way and in letting oneself be led by the Spirit? For all who let themselves be led by the Spirit are children of God. This new life is not only a new morality in which we would have to test and exercise our own moral power. It is a struggle of faith for the face of God and communion with Christ. It finds its support in prayer. It consists of returning again each time to Christ, of pleading for his promise, of seeking his companionship, of receiving his power.

For faith, conversion, and rebirth are not simply once-and-for-all affairs. They are new matters each time. They are choices, but they are also a continuing, a persevering. They see the door opening, but each time they keep knocking on it. Paul calls this being renewed in the inner man day by day (2 Co 4:16). And in that struggle faith is strengthened and the certitude that we are God's children is confirmed in us. For in that struggle not only are we seeking the Lord, but the Lord is seeking us.

Yes, he first seeks us, so that we would seek him. He draws us so that we would run after him. He accompanies our entire life with his word, his promise, his invitation. While he teaches us to abandon the crippling condition of being a slave, he brings us to freedom in our struggle and he bears witness through his Spirit with our spirit that we are children of God.

The Relationship to Our Secular Vocation

We never want to forget that this struggle of faith does not take place apart from our *daily life*, but precisely in close relationship with our secular vocation. The Spirit does not simply ask for our hearts. The struggle of faith is not simply a struggle of the soul.

166   *The Holy Spirit in the Community*

New life consists precisely in this, that we should present "our bodies" (thus our whole existence as humans) to become a living sacrifice, pleasing to God.

What puts faith to the test and what repeatedly makes us seek the help and guidance of the Spirit is not what takes place outside of ordinary life, but rather what occurs within it. This is the full life that so much needs the full Gospel. To the extent that we actually see this full life, with all its testings and results, with all its problems, heights and depths, as more than the place in which God asks of us the living sacrifice, we will also discover the ordinary to be less ordinary, at least less self-evident. We will stretch out our hands more towards him, yearn more for the help and guidance of his Spirit, find more of our hidden power in him.

As a matter of fact, Scripture has nothing else in mind when it urges us to seek the things that are above. It bears witness to us that our life is hidden with Christ in God (Col 3:1-3). Thereby it does not put earth at a distance from heaven. Scripture teaches us not to strive after the strange and distant, but really wants to tell us that to fulfill our task on earth we have to receive power and help from heaven.

The more we are thus led by the Spirit and grow in the knowledge of Christ, the more we will come to realize better that he is not only the Lord of *our* life, but also Lord of all things. For the Spirit teaches us to look for the coming of the *Kingdom* and the return of Christ. He also teaches us to see the relationship between the Kingdom of Christ and life on earth with all its involvements and relationships. He brings us into the communion of his church and also points out for us our place and our calling there. He opens our eyes and our hearts for the advancement of the Gospel in the world, and suggests to us new ways and new undertakings. He does not place us outside the world but tightens the knots of the world on our hearts.

For God, by sending his Son, loved the *world*. So the hallmark and fruit of the Spirit is not that we station ourselves outside the current of the times out of fear for the new, and out of diffidence towards what we have not previously had. No, it is rather that we go *into* it, because the Lord of the Kingdom is also the Lord of the times. And all of this is to be seen in communion with all who have been called by the same Lord and moved by the same Spirit. For he does not call us one by one, but together with all the saints in the communion of the body which is the community.

Self-examination

The image which Scripture gives us of the new life and of the goal of the Spirit in the life of the faithful and of the whole church is grand and beautiful.

There is in fact good reason to ask ourselves time and again whether our own lives and that of the church correspond to that image. There is also reason, as we noted earlier, for fearing that in our times, with its tremendous development of power, affluence and science, our attention becomes so distracted and captivated that the many displace the one thing necessary. While the branches of church life keep extending themselves further out, there may be a skimpiness at the root.

In case this is the malady, what is the remedy? Could it possibly consist of searching for the extraordinary whenever ordinary life loses its force? Or that whenever the preaching of the Gospel no longer touches us and "does not do anything any more", we turn to speaking in tongues and to ecstatic prophecy so that we look for the certitude of our faith in signs and miracles which could possibly happen to us or through us?

Can this truly be the remedy? Would not it be escaping our first calling and bypassing what has to happen first? Could we, if our daily bread no longer tasted good to us, find any advantage in what seems more pleasing and attractive to our spiritual senses? Is there another place and another means of finding security and peace other than in the preaching of the living Word of God and in the food and drink given us by God at his table of eternal life? Yet how could we reach maturity in any other way than by sending down our roots always deeper into Christ and his completed work?

In this we do have a means of testing ourselves. And *this* is the question we may put to the church and the measuring rod we may apply to her. Does she lead us to the fountains of salvation? Does she know us in our true spiritual need? Does she direct us along the length and breadth of the Kingdom of God? Every other remedy is vain; in fact, it is often worse than the illness!

We cannot research Scripture and we cannot hear the Word of God without discovering that there is many a fault in the church and in the life of believers. An awakening is ever and again needed, in our days too, a rising from the dead, a waking up from sleep, a deepening of what is superficial — in a word, a return to the true service of God. In that regard we have to examine ourselves and the church in which we live. For that reason we have to look ahead to a new spring, to the visible appearance of new fruits in the great harvest of the Lord.

We fail to recognize that fruit if there is no more hunger for the living Word of God and if people can be brought to go to church only with difficulty and for one time. We fail to recognize it, too, if preaching seeks its power just in what is known and traditional, or in what suits best the spiritual fashion of the day.

We miss that fruit whenever prayer becomes lax and love grows cold, whenever the church no longer has a message for the world or whenever she has so accommodated herself to the world that membership in the church, choosing faith, and the difficulty of conversion, no longer seem worth it.

Still less do we recognize the fruit of the Spirit in those who do not expect the awakening of the spiritual life any more in the preaching of Christ crucified, but in a higher knowledge or in the power of signs and miracles.

But we recognize this fruit when the Word is preached with the full authority of Christ, deriving from the wealth of the Scriptures. We recognize this fruit if it brings us to the Cross and to Jesus' feet. We recognize it if people eagerly come to that preaching, if youth lend their ears, if the Lord's table is full, and if we eat and drink from his hand his body and blood given up for us.

Fruits of the Spirit are disclosed whenever the power of our love converts us from our powerlessness and its sovereignty makes us free, whenever in our families spiritual discernment of what is important and unimportant in God's service is present, whenever someone in the community thinks of the other as superior to himself. Further, these fruits are disclosed if in conflicts, self-control shows forth, if a resolute missionary impulse can be observed, if a genuine desire for the unity of the churches in submission to God's Word is alive, if the honor of Christ is sought in all relationships of society's life.

These are the fruits God expects of us and with them we receive the seal of the Holy Spirit.

We could ask, "But is this in fact the most important?" Yes, indeed. For thus the Spirit restores life, by union with Christ. Thus will the Kingdom come. And everything extraordinary, of which we must still speak, has no other purpose than to serve this which is "ordinary". For the Spirit is the Spirit of re-creation.

He brings what God made back to him again by sanctifying natural life in his service, so that we may bear the image of him who is the Head of the community, his body.

II. THE SPECIAL WORK OF THE HOLY SPIRIT IN THE COMMUNITY

The Charisms ("Gifts")

Alongside the general character of the work of the Spirit, of which we spoke in the preceding pages, there are also the special gifts of the Spirit to be mentioned now. They are occasionally designated in the New Testament by the Greek word *charismata*. Because Pentecostal groups put great emphasis on these special gifts or charismata, we intend, in this document, to investigate them more thoroughly. What are these gifts? What do they consist of? And what place do they hold in the scope of the entire re-creative work of the Spirit? In this study we would like to begin with the enumerations of these charisms as we find them in the letters of Paul in Rm 12:6-8; 1 Co 12:4-11; and 28; Ep 4:11.

We find in these passages a great variation. In Rm 12:6-8 mention is made of the gift of *prophecy* (we will return to this in greater detail later), of *diakonia* or offering service, which might be called the art of helping; next come the gifts of *exhorting, giving alms, ruling, performing works of mercy*, various special abilities and capacities which are distributed by the Spirit to the members of the community according to measure. But all these must serve to build up the whole, the body, and provide it with the necessary instrumentation.

The enumeration in 1 Co 12 is somewhat different from that of Rm 12. This is definitely related to the fact that the community in Corinth showed a strong bent towards the ecstatic and the immediate command and action of the Spirit. The spiritual gifts which Paul observes and enumerates among the Corinthians are thus also more concerned with direction and channeling than was the case with the Romans who were definitely more sedate. He names the gifts of *wisdom* and of *knowledge* (gnosis). That means the deeper insight whereby a person knows that he is no longer bound by various primitive notions and anxieties (as met with among the "weak" in faith). He next notes the gift of *faith* and of *healings*. That refers to the ability to effect sensational deeds of faith (1 Co 13:2b) and is also actually called the working of *powers* (1 Co 12:10, 28). Still other sensational gifts of the Spirit follow. In them emphasis is put on speech, namely, *prophecy, discernment of spirits*, speaking in *various kinds of tongues* and interpretation of them. These are the spectacular gifts, purposely mentioned in the letter to Corinth, which have continually attracted special attention and so deserve a still closer review.

Elsewhere, specifically in 1 Co 7:7, the apostle even speaks of the charism of *continence*, by which is not meant that someone would be less suited for marriage. No, moved by God he receives power to abstain from marriage in view of a special service to the Kingdom of God. About that see also Mt 19:11-12. And to mention still another important list of gifts, in Ep 4:11 Paul speaks of apostles, prophets, evangelists, pastors and teachers as gifts of the ascended Christ to his community. So here too it is obvious that the *office* belongs with the charisms. For that matter, we find the same thing also in 1 Co 12:28, where apostles, prophets, teachers, powers, healings, gifts of helping and administrating, and tongues are enumerated in a single list in which the apostles, prophets and teachers assume first place in the enumeration.

If Rm 12 is compared to 1 Co 12, and Ep 4, it is clear that no distinction is made between the gifts of the Spirit and the gifts of Christ. Further, no opposition exists between the offices and the rest of the gifts. In 1 Co 12:28, they are put in the same category. The border line between office and gift of the Spirit has not yet been sharply drawn.

The office is more continuous. It presupposes a more or less fixed and defined assignment. The gifts of the Spirit are characterized as grace gifts, ministries, and works. On that see 1 Co 12:4-6. So they are not the products of human exertion, but gifts on the part of God, which, as services (literally, "deaconries") are directed towards the upbuilding of the community. The expression, "workings," indicates that specific gifts are not continuously present, but that the Holy Spirit in his own time bestows them in and for the community where and through whomever he wills.

The Variety of the Gifts

When we investigate the entire matter, before all else the variety of these special gifts or charisms becomes glaringly apparent. That is also why Paul enumerates these gifts at such length. His purpose is not to give a complete list; yet it is indeed to give the community an impression of the wealth of the gifts of the Spirit.

But at the same time he wants to teach them that in that variety of gifts the *many-sided character of community life* also reveals itself. That means, on the one hand, that a living community ensouled by the Spirit, has many more possibilities than one might in fact superficially think. On the other hand, that implies (and the apostle puts his whole emphasis on it) that everyone has received his own gift from the Spirit. He must recognize himself therein and be acknowledged by the other.

The dissimilarity in the community implied by this should not thus become a cause of rivalry, nor should it become the occasion of wanting to be more than one has been called and destined to be by virtue of the freedom of the Spirit. For that reason Paul constantly applies the image of the body.

The community members are as varying as the members of the same body, which all have their own function. This is not to the harm of the body, but the necessary presupposition for it. Unity is opposed to uniformity. "If all were a single organ, where would the body be?" (1 Co 12:19) Yes, those members which seem to be weakest are indispensable and precisely those members of the body which we think less honorable we invest with the greater honor (vv. 22-24). Each person has to recognize the gift which he has received. He must not envy or despise another because that person received a different gift. Are all apostles? No, there were only twelve. Are all prophets? Are all teachers? Do all work miracles? Do all possess gifts of healing? Do all speak in tongues? No, Paul says. So how can one assert that one should desire everyone who has been baptized with the Holy Spirit receive all the gifts? A person should be contented with his own gift.

Paul says this especially in Rm 12:3, "I bid every one among you not to think of himself more highly than he ought to think, but to think with sober judgment, each according to the measure of faith which God has assigned him." And then once again he speaks from the viewpoint of that one body in Christ in which the members individually have their function in relationship to one another, "having gifts *that differ* according to the grace given to us" (v. 6). Everyone can develop the gift which he received. The point is that each one know his place in the community of Christ, which is his Body. The eye cannot say to the hand, "I have no need of you" (1 Co 12:21).

Whoever would think that those who can "only" speak the word of knowledge or of wisdom and cannot prophesy, or that someone who "simply and solely" has the gift of serving or of mercy, and does not possess the gift of healing, for that reason has not yet attained the proper or full life of the Spirit, or knows

The Holy Spirit in the Community

the Bible only in part. And whoever seeks proof of baptism in the
Spirit by speaking in tongues and not by simply rendering service
contradicts the apostle. Every form of pride is from the evil one.
And impatience, whereby one strives for definite, mostly
spectacular gifts, can be a sign of pride.

In such cases what can only be a means is seen as a goal. Thus
community members are in danger of being derailed and of
coming to an unspiritual vaingloriousness. So here too the
question arises, "What is the purpose of the gifts?"

The Purpose of the Gifts

It is a matter of our making the right use of the gifts and correctly
understanding the purpose they serve. Paul gives plain directions
about this. In the first place, no one can say, "Jesus is Lord,"
except by the Holy Spirit (1 Co 12:3). The utterances of the Spirit
have to be tested by that standard. They must be serviceable for the
revelation of the Lordship of Jesus Christ. Otherwise they are not
from the Spirit, but serve the self-glorification of the devout
person.

It becomes still more concrete when we hear that "to each is
given the manifestation of the Spirit for the common good" (1 Co
12:7). They are not bestowed so that the faithful could parade
them. No, their purpose is that others may profit from them. The
more gifted members must honor the rest by putting their own
gifts in the service of these less gifted people. Everything we have
is subordinate to the purpose "that there may be no discord in the
body, but that the members may have the same care for one
another" (vv. 22–25). The gifts form a tool set for the upbuilding
of the community and for its task in the world.

Consequently, as means towards a goal they may never become
an end in themselves. Indeed, we ought to strive for "the higher
gifts" (v. 31), but the apostle first explained well what has to be
understood by "higher," namely, what advances the "common
good."

That is why Paul shifts at once to the love in which the gifts
must be rooted. Love is the basic motive. "Higher" does not
mean that for which men have the most respect and whereby
they can attract the most attention. On the contrary, they would
then sow discord. The Lord cannot use them then for the
progress of his work, if the community is not being built up by
them. They become parasitic plants in the vineyard of Christ.

Likewise, fear of derailment may not prevent the community of Christ from being eager for the gifts. Paul says, "Are you not after all one body?" And it has to build *itself* up in love.

The community may not leave that to some who are very gifted or to the officeholders. The Spirit wants to supply the entire community with the equipment whereby all can become his co-workers in the church and in the world. The Spirit wants to employ everyone. All the faithful are involved in this. Truly they have a calling, not to parade their gifts but to be of service to another so as to advance the work of Christ in this world.

The New Testament idea of community as the mature people of God has to be taken more seriously. Then each one will have to discover the possibilities which are bestowed on him to offer "diakonia," to be able to serve the others lovingly.

If we keep that purpose present to us, we will not want to neglect the gifts of the Spirit, but we will, rather, rekindle them (*see* 1 Tm 4:14; 2 Tm 1:6). Only by the power which "each member exercises in his own way" does the growth of the body come about in such a manner as to upbuild itself in love (Ep 4:16).

Ordinary and Extraordinary

Closer consideration of the variety of the "gifts" (charisms) teaches us that among them one meets both unsurprising and "ordinary," as well as more out of the ordinary and spectacular gifts. There are gifts which appear more simple at the first glance, as, for instance, the gifts of serving, teaching, contributing charitable aid. There are also gifts which immediately attract attention through their extraordinary and unexplainable character, such as the gifts of speaking in tongues, prophecy, and healing.

It is especially to these latter gifts which special value is attached by the Pentecostal groups and which they often consider a kind of measure of the value of someone's spiritual life. In doing so they appeal to what Luke in the Acts of the Apostles repeatedly reports about the outpouring and the "falling" of the Spirit upon groups of people who converted to Christianity, among whom baptism was accompanied by similar special workings of the Spirit. But Paul, too, speaks of that. *See* 1 Co 12:7-11 concerning it.

One certainly needs to reflect about how Scripture speaks of these things in order to reach a correct concept of them. In the Book of Acts Luke describes the surprising progress of the gospel.

Each time we see great breakthroughs occurring: first on Pentecost day itself, after that in Samaria, among the proselytes in the country of the Jews, among the Gentiles outside of Palestine, until at last Rome is reached. These breakthroughs are accompanied by definite explosions of the gifts of the Spirit, signs and miracles, which mark the road, as it were, along which the gospel makes its triumphal march in the world. They are the proof and the sign of the wealth of Christ, and, unlike the case of John the Baptizer, that His disciples baptized with the Spirit.

Later, specifically in Paul and the other epistles, one sees *consolidation*, confirmation of the breakthrough of the gospel. That does not mean that the special would then cease. Particularly amid the community in Corinth this special dynamism of the Spirit is still visible later also and Paul also acknowledges it as such. At the same time, however, we notice that the apostle warns the Corinthians who attached special value to these gifts against onesidedness. He refers them to something other than the sensational and spectacular for the upbuilding of the community.

In the letters to the Romans and to the Ephesians one sees the same development. Paul appeals there too (*see* Rm 15:18 and 19) to the signs and miracles of his apostleship, and to the power of the Spirit with which God accompanied his preaching among the Gentiles. But when he speaks about the progress of community life and the gifts of the Spirit in the community needed for that, he no longer mentions these special and extraordinary gifts.

All of that gives us a clear indication of the correct concept of the gifts of the Spirit in the upbuilding of the community. In this undoubtedly everything depends upon the working and the grace of the Spirit. But the Spirit does not create an opposition between nature and grace and does not make use only of the perfume and radiance which the supernatural brings with itself.

The Maturity of the Community

In Pentecostal circles it is often forgotten that the Spirit makes the New Testament community "mature." Urim and Thummim, lots and extensive Old Testament prescriptions, now make place for independent decisions made by the light of God's Spirit.

A very plain example of this is the employing of lots for selecting officeholders. After Acts 1 we never again hear of lots. On the contrary, whenever officeholders or delegates have to be chosen, it happens by raising hands, that is, by vote;

occasionally, too, by the simple appointment of the candidate by an apostle or his helper. But in any case choices are made by people judging personally the gifts and capacities of the one concerned. Here the *mature* community is at work. The Spirit teaches us to judge things and persons ourselves, and he makes us decide in the light of Scripture.

Without this working of the Spirit the New Testament community would never have been capable of developing among so many different peoples and in so many different periods of history. We now see, in the Pentecostal movement, however, that people put lesser value on the maturing of the community through the Holy Spirit, but just want to return to those gifts which more properly belong to an *im*mature community.

People put more confidence in "an authorization from above," than in research or argument. They recognize the hand of God more in miraculous healings than in medical practice. A flashing insight is more readily viewed as the work of the Spirit than the outcome of diligent study of a portion of the Bible.

There is a longing for a special and "clearly apparent" self-revelation of the Spirit, whereas he just wants to sanctify all the natural gifts of man. When he renews man, he does indeed oppose what is sinful in our nature, but not what he himself has made. He confiscates the faculties of the believer and makes them holy. In Rm 12 it is clearly evident that the charisms are linked to the "natural" gifts, now used in the service of the Lord and one's neighbor.

The Bible does not speak of the opposition between natural and supernatural. It speaks in other terms, such as "extraordinary" (Ac 19:11). The Holy Spirit knows the mystery of each one's individuality. He takes possession of our various capabilities and seals them as his own gifts of grace. One gets a gift different from the other. Thus Paul continually emphasizes the variety of the gifts wherein the "ordinary" and the "extraordinary" are mentioned indiscriminately. In fact, the "ordinary" often comes first. It is the Holy Spirit who, as it were, stamps all these gifts with the grade of special.

All of this is as equally valid for helping and serving as it is for prophesying and speaking in tongues. The Holy Spirit apportions his gifts as he wills, but in doing so, he does not need to operate outside an already present talent. On the contrary, even with the "extraordinary" gifts like speaking in tongues and healing, a certain aptitude can often be pointed out.

The Holy Spirit in the Community

A gift of the Spirit does not become more unspiritual by the fact that this talent is simultaneously being made to serve the coming of the Kingdom. That is no less a miracle than that the Spirit would bestow his gifts independently of any aptitude. We may respect and use various endowments, keen insight, talent for organization, and so much more, as "charisma" as soon as the Spirit takes them in his holy hands and enrolls them in the service of Christ.

Individual or Community

In the Pentecostal community an underevaluation of the church as an institution is to be noted. This often leads to a neglect of what the church has to offer in preaching and in the administration of the sacraments. There is no clear concept of the relationship between the Spirit and the church. This is limited to the relationship between the Spirit and the individual. Then the church is nothing more than a human fellowship, at most a gathering of believers who come together on their own initiative.

Although there are groups which admit the seven offices of apostles, prophets, evangelists, pastors, teachers (Ep 4:11), elders and deacons, *all* are opposed to the institutional concept of office as the churches accept them. Only a calling and an authority received personally from Christ is recognized. Only those who received a certain charism and who distinguish themselves by a service flowing from it are accepted as successors.

Unless one can prove having received the baptism in the Spirit, people do not listen, or listen hardly at all, to the church officeholders who appeal to Christ for their authorization.

This religious individualism is, quite the contrary of that conception, current in some circles where the office is the one and only thing. There we meet the other extreme. In it the individual shares the Spirit to the extent that he shares the official ordained actions of the church. Then the church is a sort of warehouse of the Spirit who disappears in and behind the totality of churchly functions. In it the Spirit is hidden from the believer. The relationship between the Spirit and the believer becomes chiefly indirect.

In fact the Reformation undoubtedly did strongly accent the *personal* relationship between God and the believer. But that does not negate the Reformers' continual conviction that the church is "the mother of the devout, who gives us birth, nurses us, and finally takes us under her protection and guidance" (Calvin, *Institutes* IV, 1, 4).

The Bible does not speak in an individualistic fashion about these matters. The community is the body of Christ. It is not a product of human endeavor; it is rather God's work. The Spirit is poured out upon the community (Ac 2). And the epistles emphasize that individuals are used as living stones for the construction of a spiritual house. Time and again it is a question of the upbuilding of the body. A church member by himself is an amputated member.

Only in the community does the individual member have a meaningful existence. In the community the Spirit of God dwells as in a temple.

Office and Charism

The Savior himself called and educated the disciples for their office. For that he gives them the Holy Spirit. Paul says to the elders of Ephesus, "Take heed to yourselves and to all the flock, in which the Holy Spirit has made you guardians" (Ac 20:28).

How close the connection between the Holy Spirit and the office is, becomes clear from Ac 15:28, "For it has seemed good to the Holy Spirit and to us. . . ." And when the apostle speaks about the offices as gifts, charisms, he refers to the body which as a harmonious structure is held together by the service of all the joints (Ep 4:16). Thus in the community the offices must function like the joints, tendons and nerves in the body (*see* Col 2:19). When they do not function well, the whole body suffers from it. In the official ministry the Savior wants to "equip" the community "for rendering services." For the matter concerns the community and its upbuilding. That community is the mature people of God.

At the beginning, the border line between the rather incidental charism and the office as the more continuing and circumscribed assignment, was still fluid. One hears of the gift of *knowledge*, but also of that of *teacher*, of the gift of *prophecy* and of the *prophets*.

Although in the Acts of the Apostles mention is made several times of "elders" (e.g., 14:23; 15:4; 20:17), the apostle Paul usually seems to be speaking about unofficial charisms. That is why appeal is often made to Paul for the "free" work of the Spirit, and against the "regulated" work of the Spirit in the community.

Nevertheless, one must indeed be very cautious in making this

The Holy Spirit in the Community

appeal. When a kind of hierarchy of gifts is mentioned in 1 Co 12:28, "apostles, prophets, and teachers" come first (see also Ep 4:11). Both in the case of "apostles" and of "teachers and pastors," one most likely needs to think not of incidental gifts, but of "fixed" powers in the community, which are referred to it and recognized as such (see also Ga 6:6). In Ph 1:1, "overseers" and "deacons" are expressly mentioned in the address to the community. In the later epistles to Timothy and Titus various requirements and demands are noted which have to be kept in view in the appointment of elders and deacons.

Indeed it is possible that in the earliest period more spontaneous gifts and actions came to the fore, whereas later the institutional and official were developed more. But nowhere in the New Testament is opposition made to them. Nor is the more regulated order in the community seen as a regression. It is rather evident that the community constantly acquired a greater need of the latter, both by the disappearance of the apostles and through the appearance of various heretical currents. Therefore it is a *fiction* to think that only the "free" gifts of the Spirit would restore original Christianity. Instead, people are trying to imitate the situation in Corinth (to which Paul had serious objections) or to realize anew and repeat the unrepeatable event of Pentecost. But that is an incorrect appeal to the earliest Christian community.

The criticism of the offices by the Pentecostal groups had the consequence of raising the incidental gifts to the throne at the cost of the offices. Among them the Spirit-bearers form the true community, so that one gets there two categories of believers: the born again and those who have been filled with the Spirit.

In spite of that, the New Testament simply knows believers who profess, "It is no longer I who live, but Christ who lives in me." And just as the officeholders in the community cannot comprise a separate spiritual class, still less may there be a separate class of the baptized in the Spirit, the "initiated" (see Col 2:18). Just as the distinction between clergymen and laymen was denied by the churches of the Reformation, so likewise we ought to oppose any doctrine which proposes a two-stage membership in the community, faithful and Spirit-filled, as the Pentecostal movement teaches.

Both attack the essence of the New Testament community. There, both offices and charisms are put in the same category. They are, without distinction, gifts of the Holy Spirit for the upbuilding of the community. Office, too, is a gift of the Spirit. The community has persons who themselves have a charism (Ac 7) and who are therefore called to an office.

The Danger of Over-officing

In this connection reference has to be made to the danger of the church's "over-officing," so that the gifts entirely disappear in the office. In such circumstances the special gifts do not sufficiently have their role. A consequence of this is that community members rely too much upon the officeholders with the result that the latter become overburdened.

In this way the gifts of many community members remain insufficiently utilized. All of the branches must bear as many fruits as possible. It has to become clearer to the community that the offices are only part of what is needed for equipping the community. Just because office presupposes certain gifts, it is not true that all the gifts lead to an office.

Officeholders have to search out the gifts present in the community, and in this way "equip" the community "for rendering services." "We need to ask ourselves whether our gaze is actually keen enough to detect the special gifts of each of the members, and whether we are actually continually striving to encourage these gifts and to offer them the opportunity to develop themselves" (Report on the Status of the Spiritual Life, Utrecht, 1959).

In our community life we have to begin with the belief that every one of the faithful has from Christ a special contribution to make towards the coming of his kingdom.

Gifts of simple rendering of service in apparently small details are just as direly needed as gifts of governing, knowledge and instructing. How many people there are in the community who have not been called to be an elder or a deacon, but who nonetheless are indispensable for the upbuilding of the community. These community members must be shown their calling so that they also employ their gifts for the advancement of God's work in the world. There is a calling not only for the missions and for evangelization, but to every area of life.

Not in education nor child care, social work nor social care; not in industry, business nor politics; nowhere may the gifts be neglected. They must be used for the benefit of society. And to end with a quotation from the report cited above, "For that we

The Holy Spirit in the Community

need nothing less than an awakening by the Holy Spirit, a new distribution of his gifts and powers, and as a consequence a renewal of heart and life, of family and church."

Some Spectacular Gifts

1. THE GIFT OF TONGUES

Among Pentecostal groups *speaking in tongues* is highly esteemed. There are even groups which consider this phenomenon necessary as a proof that a person has received baptism in the Holy Spirit. But really, what is speaking in tongues or glossolalia?

A person expresses himself in strange sounds, which another person sometimes does understand and at other times does not. Speaking in tongues occurs in all sorts of religions and is an ecstatic phenomenon. In ecstasy ego-awareness disappears. This is accompanied by an intense feeling of happiness. Paul recalls that the mind remains unfruitful (1 Co 14:14). Because this phenomenon was widespread among the Gentiles in his day too, he is probably alluding to that ecstatic condition in 1 Co 12:2, "When you were heathen, you were led astray to dumb idols, however you may have been moved."

He recalls that ecstasy as such is not a sign of the Spirit, because people in such a condition can even say, "Jesus be cursed!" (1 Co 12:3). He hesitates to allow in the community signs of ecstasy in which spirit and mind no longer go together (1 Co 14:14-16). So although it was a broadly prevailing phenomenon which the Evil One made use of (and still does make use of), nevertheless the Holy Spirit wanted to confiscate it. He imparts a certain content to it.

On the feast of Pentecost people were lifted above themselves. They spoke in other tongues, as the Spirit gave them utterance (Ac 2:4). The wonderful thing is that the bystanders were able to understand it. That never happened again.

Later it had to be explained, either by him who spoke in tongues or by another who received the *"gift of interpretation."* If that explanation is lacking, the community is not edified thereby (1 Co 14:17). This was the norm by which Paul judged the gifts. The community had to become better through them. That is why he would rather speak five words with his mind in order to instruct others than ten thousand words in a tongue (1 Co 14:19).

As in many Pentecostal groups, where propaganda is made for

these gifts, so in Corinth, too, tongue-speaking was strenuously advanced as if it were a very important charism, if not actually the highest gift. Paul plainly took an opposing position. Twice in an enumeration he put it last (1 Co 12:10 and 28). What is desired as the greatest is evidently the least!

We quote here from the pastoral document of the General Synod of the Dutch Reformed Church ("The Church and the Pentecostal Groups"), "We cannot escape the impression that among the Pentecostal groups the (human) need of a strong life-experience has been the standard rather than an accurate listening to the *whole* Bible, and that in this way people came to overload certain passages. Here too, in our judgment one may speak of a wrong use of the Bible."

In fact, tongue-speaking has continually disappeared from the meetings of Pentecostal groups, and has been transferred to the inner room. There it is a means of expressing praise and prayer. The question may be raised with Dr. J. H. Bavinck (in his publication entitled *I Believe in the Holy Spirit*) why the Spirit gives such gifts, if they are not useful for others. He argues that tongue-speaking of itself in the inner room can be a rich blessing and a gift from God. A person is so overwhelmed by the power of the Holy Spirit in his approach to God and in his speaking to God that speaking in tongues, as it were, overflows the limits of language and takes the form of "sighs too deep for words" (Rm 8:26).

Paul also received this gift (1 Co 14:18), but he does not want to foster it for use in the community. The gift which is so wonderful and fruitful in hidden fellowship with God then becomes an ostentatious event, which so readily leads to misuse and can develop into an expression of unspiritual vaingloriousness. To quote Dr. Bavinck once again: "In that way man becomes too important; the drive towards the sensational, the newsmaking, which drive is always too active, begins to assert itself tremendously" (p. 84).

Even though the apostle puts tongue-speaking after the less "sensational" gifts of helping, administrating, and teaching, he does not intend to exclude this gift. Misuse does not exclude good use. For that reason 1 Co 14:39 says, "So, my brethren, earnestly desire to prophesy, and do not forbid speaking in tongues."

2. THE GIFT OF PROPHECY

If speaking in tongues is thus a rather private affair, it is different with the gift of prophecy. He who speaks in a tongue edifies himself, but he who prophesies edifies the community.

Now, what is prophesying?

Prophesy is the gift of understanding and expressing what the will of God is in a given situation (Ac 11:28; 13:1-2; 15:32; 21:10-11; 1 Tm 1:18; 4:14). The prophet does not speak out of his mind. His spirit is subordinate to the control of his mind and will. Just as for tongue-speaking there had to be the gift of interpretation of tongues, so alongside this gift of prophecy there had to be that other one, namely, the gift of *discernment of spirits* (1 Co 12:10). The reason is that a distinction has to be made between true and false prophecy.

Visions and revelations are received which go beyond sacred Scripture or even directly oppose it, as if the Spirit would contradict himself. The light of God's Word is frequently snuffed out with an appeal to the "inner light." God's Word is sufficient to be of itself a rule of faith which may not be added to or taken away from (Rv 22:18-19; Art. 7 Ned. G.B.). Among Pentecostal groups where people gladly listen to "prophecies," besides touching instances of genuine enlightenment by God's Word, all sorts of excesses have made their appearance.

The most marvelous predictions led to the greatest disturbances. There can be such a passionate longing for new revelations that people start "prophesying from their own heart," with the result that false prophecy arises. Time and again in the history of the Church false prophets and prophetesses arose, whose prophecy ultimately proved to be false.

We may not view prophecy as an individualistic gift; the church as a whole must test it. For this the other gift of the "discernment of spirits" is necessary. In preaching, the prophetic element comes to the fore when the speaking is done with *authority*, "Thus says the Lord!" Dr. Bavinck says: "It is thus a matter of x-raying the situation in which we are engaged in such a way that everything is set in the searching light of God, and in that way the lines along which the event is developing become immediately clear. Consequently, from there a light can be thrown on the future towards which these lines point."

Does not the community have to pray much for this gift in these times of chaotic confusion, so that it will be told plainly how to act in various situations, in every area of life? The failure of a prophetic witness is frequently felt to be a great lack. Did false prophecy bring true prophecy into such discredit that not only in church life, but also in the social and political area the authoritative word of the prophet or prophetess is heard far too little?

It is possible that prophets are present, but that we consider their insights and warnings as nothing more than the umpteenth personal opinion. We have to test the spirits to see whether they are of God. "Do not quench the Spirit, do not despise prophesying, but test everything; hold fast what is good" (1 Th 5:19-21). Paul encourages the community to strive for the gift of prophecy!

3. THE GIFT OF HEALING

We encounter this gift originally in the gospels; for the first time at the mission of the disciples. Jesus sent them out "and gave them authority over unclean spirits, to cast them out, and to heal every disease and every infirmity" (Mt 10:1). After this we come into contact with this gift in Ac 5:12.

From none of these texts may far-reaching conclusions be drawn. In the mission of the disciples we see clearly an assignment and a promise of the Lord to a definite group of his followers, whereas from the other passages it is not at all clear that the charism of healing has to be present in the church everywhere and constantly. Still less have we been promised that all the sick will always be cured.

In the dialogue with the Pentecostal movement it is especially 1 Co 12:9 and 28 that come in for discussion. Among the gifts of the one Spirit "gifts of healing" are also mentioned there. On the basis of these texts the reproach is often directed to the church that she does not use the gifts bestowed on her. Specifically, the opinion gains currency that all charisms, consequently also that of healing, have been bestowed in all periods of the church's existence, and so they must also be used. Some even think that all the gifts of the Spirit are available to everyone who has been baptized in the Holy Spirit. Thus everyone would also have to use the gift of healing. And to that is related the notion that a believer does not need to be sick. Just as everyone who has received baptism in the Spirit may use the charism to effect the cure, so may every sick believer make use of the gift bestowed on others to be freed of his sickness.

It is true that among the various gifts of 1 Co 12:28-31, that of healing also appears after those of apostles, prophets and teachers. It was, as is clear from the gospels, one of the greatest charisms of Christ himself, and was also promised by him to the apostles. Thus Paul too speaks of "signs of his apostleship" (2 Co 12:12; see also Rm 15:19), especially with regard to this gift, and the question is whether one may extend this gift, without qualification, as something given at all times and to all the faithful. This latter is certainly not the case. It is clearly contradicted in 1 Co 12:28.

Far be it from us to deny that it would lie in the sovereign authority of Christ and in the power of his Spirit to *continue* to grant this gift of healing to those, for instance, who have been called to give visible shape to the ultimate victory of the gospel in the struggles with paganism and the belief in the power of the evil spirits. Such healings are known in the history of the missions and we would not want to diminish anything of their reality. However, we are of the opinion that where Christ still wants to give a gift of that kind to very definite persons and in very limited situations, this will be unmistakably evident. We need not be afraid that where Christ wishes to work in such a way, this would find no admittance.

Our fear is rather directed against every sort of arbitrariness and incompetence in this area which harm the work of Christ, occasionally have the character of tempting God, and cause great confusion and damage in the life of many simple believers.

We are particularly sensitive to this objection whenever a kind of technique is made of healing prayer, and whenever it is linked with a definite spiritualistic doctrine of sickness and healing, as in the campaigns of Zaiss and Osborn, mentioned below.

Healing prayer — Since the campaigns of the German H. Zaiss and the American T. L. Osborn, whose work has been continued in our country by John Massbach, among others, questions concerning healing prayer (also called faith healing) have been current. It is not as if the church had paid no attention to intercessory prayer for the sick. On the contrary, every Sunday prayers were and are offered for them. But now the reproach resounds, especially from the Pentecostal groups, that the church has not taken into account the promises of the Bible.

The reasoning goes as follows: a Christian is a redeemed person. When he is baptized in the Spirit, that redemption will have to be radical and total, because Christ does not do things by halves. After all, he took our sicknesses upon himself and he is the same yesterday and today — and forever. God does not intend for us to be sick. That is the work of the devil. And Christ came to annul Satan's work.

One who really prays with faith does not need to be sick. Appeal is made to texts like Mt 10:1; Mk 16:17-18; Ac 3:6-8 and 5:12. Above all, reference is made to Jm 5:14 to make it clear to us that we do not take God's promises for the sick person earnestly enough. Here we want to devote some attention to this latter text.

James 5:14 — This passage reads as follows: "Is any among you sick? Let him call for the elders of the church, and let them pray over him, anointing him with oil in the name of the Lord."

Now do all the "elders" have to possess the gift of healing, so that the sick person, according to James, has to call for them? In our viewpoint the matter of concern here is something else. In antiquity the priest was likewise the doctor. The faithful who lived in a pagan environment entered into a grave conflict of conscience in case of illness. For such a priest-doctor ascribed the power of the cure to his idol. And in fact James puts the emphasis on the "prayer of faith" which the elders must utter.

In prayer we put matters in God's hand, in the believing trust that he will do his part for our salvation. Thus healing is ascribed to the Lord and not to the idols. We may see the anointing with oil as an indication of the use of medicine. Oil was highly regarded for such use. Just think of the parable of the Good Samaritan who poured oil in the wounds. So prayer does not exclude remedies.

Thus in Jm 5 the discussion concerns a special situation. The Lord too takes special measures to protect his community.

Then is every sick person cured? The prayer of a righteous man has great power in its effects — but not in all of them. Did not Paul have to leave his co-worker Trophimus ill at Miletus (2 Tm 4:20)? Was not he himself harassed by a frightful ailment, a "thorn in the flesh," from which he was not released, despite his prayer (2 Co 12:7-9)? Christ considered it better, even for the advancement of his missionary work, that he should keep this hindrance.

"Thy will be done" holds true also in prayer by and for the sick person. If the Bible would indeed mean that the faithful would not be obliged to remain sick, then it may rightly be asked, "How, then, can they still die?" After all, if one posits, "Christ took upon himself our sicknesses and bore our pains. He does not act by

The Holy Spirit in the Community

halves, so the faithful need not be sick," then it may rightly be asked, "because he overcame death too for us." Yet the believer too has to die!

Sin and Sickness — James speaks also about the relationship of sin and sickness in 5:15, 16. Confession of sin and prayer are both mentioned as conditions for the cure. Indeed it is possible that a certain sin had existed among these believers for which the Lord punished them with illness. Reference can be made to 1 Co 11:29-30.

Sometimes a direct relationship between sickness and sin can be pointed out. Just think of the affairs of Herod (Ac 12:20-23) and Elymas (Ac 13:6-12). That relationship is far from being always present. We refer to the case of Job and above all to the healing of the man born blind (Jn 9:1-3) where the Savior emphatically opposes a doctrine of immediate retribution. There is indeed a connection between a person's being sick and his belonging to the sinful world.

There is a general disturbance in the relationship with God resulting from sin, which manifests itself also in sickness. To quote Dr. G. Brillenburg Wurth (*Christelijke zielszorg in het licht der moderne psychologie*, p. 268), "From the biblical point of view, sickness and sin should be brought together under a single common denominator, namely, isolation." The believer experiences this in being sick, although he knows too that the punishment has been borne by Christ. In this connection reference needs to be made too to the "chastisement" (Heb 12:5-6), which evokes not only God's wrath but also his love. For thus he keeps "every son whom he receives" on the path of holiness.

In certain circles it is pointed out that Christ's redemption is complete. He it is "who forgives all your iniquities and heals all your diseases" (Ps 103:3). Thus a believer may no longer be sick. In this framework there is a perfectionistic anticipation of the times in which death shall be no more, neither shall there be mourning nor crying nor pain, i.e., sickness (Rv 21:4). And when Psalm 103 is cited, that has to be done in full. For the fourth verse continues, "who redeems your life from the pit." What then is that "redemption from the grave?" That is only complete with resurrection from the dead.

Some forget that we are still living between the paradises, and that the "in part" and the "not yet" still hold true here. Here we still have to fight against sin. Here we are still groaning inwardly as we wait for adoption as sons, the redemption of our bodies (Rm 8:23).

Sickness and the Devil — When Paul writes about his ailment, he also mentions an "angel of Satan." We hear of a "spirit of infirmity" and of possession (Lk 13:10-17). In the Bible, sickness and the work of Satan are clearly brought into relationship.

The Blumhardts, above all, pointed that out. The "role of the demonic," including being sick, was clearly brought up again for discussion by Dr. G. Brillenburg Wurth in one of his last publications. On biblical grounds he argues, more than has heretofore been customary, the necessity of taking into account the influence of the powers of darkness in the background of our whole life as an individual, and in all aspects of society. That role is "the disintegration, putting asunder what God has joined together, severing the Creator and his creature, and as a consequence of that, or at least in connection with that, various forms of physical and spiritual disintegration as well" (page 107). He points out that medical science does not replace the miraculous power of Christ in the days of the New Testament, but that it does have a place in its continuation. Medical science may apply Christ's saving power to the advantage of the sick and disturbed.

But in this matter there are two things that we may not forget. The first is that Christ is capable of working miracles when those who belong to him pray, if he wishes, even apart from medical means. Also he is able "to cast out evil spirits," even where from the medical viewpoint there is no hope of a cure.

Still more important is that even when we accept medical aid with great thankfulness, that does not for a moment cancel Jesus' word to his disciples after the healing of the epileptic lad, "This kind is never expelled except by prayer and fasting" (Mt 17:21). In other words, the background of all of our health care will have to remain "a community, which, with loving solidarity and priestly intercession, carries on the struggle with and for all the unfortunate against the powers of darkness, who beset our human lives with so much misery" (page 113).

Christ conquers the powers! He came to destroy the works of the devil.

Indeed, a warning does have to be given against spiritualistic prayer healers and occult practices. There is a form of "banishing the devil" which, though sailing under the Christian flag,

The Holy Spirit in the Community

destroys souls. It is reminiscent of sorcery; a sinful appeal is made to God's power.

In the Pentecostal movement people are frequently distrustful of the "ordinary" means, as if a healing without medications or medical intervention would be more to the glory of God than when a doctor and a nurse energetically devote themselves to combatting illnesses. After all, God created the means of healing too, with his creation, and he brought about their discovery. "For beneath the tree the molds were growing which today supply penicillin; around the tree digitalis was growing which today cures the heart patient. Therefore divine healing decidedly does not mean that something should happen without the application of means or men."

Opposing a doctor or refusing medicine can mean that one is tempting God, that one wants to compel him to intervene immediately, although he himself made the remedy. It is in conflict with the sixth commandment, indeed, with the commandment of love "which does no wrong to a neighbor" (Rm 13:10). The remedies too are his. Faith sees that. It knows that the healing is from the Lord who has mercy.

4. HEALING AS A SIGN OF THE KINGDOM

The Bible deals with the coming and the future of God's Kingdom. The revelation of the Kingdom is Jesus Christ. The miracles of healing are also signs of it. They are more than the disclosure of facts; they are preaching. Jesus has nothing about him of the ancient wonder-worker. He heals the sick (although not all of them), but he does not advertise himself at all. There is no question of a healing campaign. His proper goal is something else. He effects the revelation of the Kingdom of God. The healings are signals of heaven, they are signs that the reign is now here. They speak of a having come, and of a still to come.

Faith sees through them like a crack into God's Kingdom and understands the meaning that "here is the fulfillment of God's promises in Jesus Christ. Those signs are not just times past. Christ is the present Lord who, with his community, is making the way of the cross through a broken world subject 'to the Evil One.'

"Since the powers of the world to come have moved into action, it is no wonder now that cripples become well. It is rather surprising that healthy people can still become crippled. Now the raising of Lazarus does not seem strange to us, but just the reverse, that Lazarus dies again!" (Dr. J. L. Koole, *De boodschap der genezing*, p. 125). No matter what questions we may have regarding faith healing and healing prayer, the question of whether it is "possible" is not allowed to faith. The question does have to be posed as to why people long for signs. Is it because one has been so taken by the message of the Kingdom?

Or is a devaluation of Word and sacrament and a weakening of the power of faith playing in the background? There is an unbelieving attitude which is not satisfied with God's promises and thinks that the promises really only get a grip on them if they are accompanied by miracles (*see* Jn 6:26). Then "blessed are those who have not seen and yet believe."

Calvin speaks a word of wisdom in his explanation of the synoptic gospels about the signs which will accompany those who believe: "The miracles will not be common to all ages without distinction." There can be periods in which there is a more urgent need for other signs than precisely for miraculous healings now. That is why it is incorrect to want to call down miracles, by force as it were, as if a living faith could not blossom without a miracle. The promises of God are not therefore the less. In Acts 3 Peter did not "ask" for the miracle. So the community does not force the signs — but signs will "follow" the one who believes (Mk 16:17).

"Thus we must humbly leave signs in God's hand. Every monopoly, all methods, every deformed 'faith,' are objectionable, by which human hearts are aroused to want to work miracles or to want to see them happen. Christ is 'Lord' over signs and he remains that."

We quote here, with hearty approval, from the report of the Reformed Synod, "Questions about Healing Prayer" (p. 131). True faith is not a psychic power, a means alongside other medical aids. Rather, it is a relationship of trust and obedience whereby everything God revealed to us in his Word is held as true. Faith is not directed towards the healing of illnesses, but to Christ, the Savior.

The Highest Gifts

The apostle urges us to strive for the highest gifts (1 Co 12:31). So we need not tarry concerning a specific situation. There are "higher" and "highest" gifts for which we must strive. What standard of measure are we to apply?

The apostle clearly showed that the gifts have to be rooted in

The Holy Spirit in the Community

love. The basic motive behind that word, "highest," lies the power of love. Gifts must serve the common good. The "higher" gifts are thus not those which would be still more sensational, but they are those gifts with which we can serve our neighbors in love to the glory of Christ, to the utmost and in the very best way.

All the gifts of the Spirit are directed to loving service. Those gifts whereby we can best serve the Lord and our neighbor, from our own place in the church and in the world, in our situation, with our own nature, are the highest. We may strive after them and foster them. When we misuse or neglect them because we are seeking ourselves and because we put them at the service of our own interest, we derail them, and they cease to be gifts of grace.

Yet we may not resist the gifts, even the extraordinary or spectacular ones, out of fear of derailment, when the Spirit grants these gifts to the community.

It is true that dealing with these extraordinary gifts requires, to a special degree, purified humble hearts which "keep company with the holy in a holy way." Persistent evidence has surfaced that mistaken propaganda for certain spectacular gifts, as often happens among Pentecostal groups, does not advance the upbuilding of the community. Alertness is needed so that people do not try to force such gifts, attempting to receive them through special efforts and with great impatience, or even trying to induce them by means of suggestion. Because paganism with its spiritualism and occultism displays parallel phenomena, the community has the duty of testing the spirits, following the scriptural norms (1 Jn 4:1), so that demonic activities do not make their appearance instead of the spiritual gifts.

III. BAPTISM OF INFANTS

A Very Important Matter

We want to say something in particular about the right to administer infant baptism which is called into question or sharply contested by many adherents of the Pentecostal movement. Among the consequences is that people are not content with their having been baptized as children and have themselves rebaptized by the biblical baptism, by immersion, as it is called. And because the church regards this "rebaptism" as a devaluation of churchly baptism and will make absolutely no compromise, this position of the Pentecostal groups frequently leads to a break with the church.

So in the dialogue with the Pentecostal movement baptism of infants is always a stumbling block. Also among others who incline to this opinion, but want to avoid a break with the church, there is frequently lack of clarity on this issue.

In this connection we want to refer to the pronouncements of the Synod of Assen in 1957–58 (Acta, art. 481). There the synod noted that allowing oneself to be "rebaptized" always implies an underevaluation of the richness of the sacrament administered in the community. "Rebaptism" is often accompanied by a neglect of the baptism already received.

Furthermore the synod came to the conclusion that "rebaptism" of itself is not sufficient reason for declaring that the concerned members have withdrawn from the Reformed churches. But at the same time the synod decided that in each case they have to be admonished seriously and patiently. It will depend upon the manner in which these members conduct themselves (each case to be judged individually) whether they must also be subjected to church discipline for having given scandal to the community. Scandal will certainly be present in case of complete contempt for the baptism they received as infants.

All of this is reason enough for our wanting to make particular, although brief, reference to the main points under discussion here.

Why Do People Have Themselves Rebaptized?

What is the real reason why church members, often loyal and active, join a Pentecostal group and have themselves rebaptized? To answer this question we would like to refer to the introduction of our document. Some factors are mentioned there, indicating why the drawing power of the Pentecostal movement is so great for certain church members. We can mention these factors here also.

Rejecting infant baptism and having recourse to biblical baptism by immersion (as it is called) is closely related to the question of the certitude of faith. In our church life, it is said, one misses entirely too much reference to and talk about this certitude. Nor does infant baptism confer certitude. But opposed to this is the baptism of believers, the baptism of adults. In that baptism a separate revelation of the Holy Spirit is experienced and a person knows that he has been addressed by him as a son of the Lord.

Frequently a spiritual enthusiasm accompanies this baptism with water. That says much to some people. Is that not the proof

The Holy Spirit in the Community

of the correctness of their opinion, coming straight down from heaven, as it were? And, they say, beside this the church cuts a very wretched figure indeed. Infant baptism is not supported by these signs and heaven is silent. All of which is reason enough to take an extremely critical stand against "sprinkling sucklings."

However that may be, opposition to infant baptism depends, in any case, upon the special concept of baptism found in the Pentecostal movement. In its opinion, the Spirit should reveal himself in a special way at baptism. And because a child of a very tender age is incapable of [receiving] that, it should be apparent, from that above all, that infant baptism is basically an impossibility.

Now, we have already demonstrated above that such a concept of baptism is not in agreement with holy Scripture. In fact, in New Testament times baptism was accompanied by an outpouring of the Spirit's gifts in some cases. But that is certainly not the rule. Baptism does not mark the peak of Christian life, but its beginning. Thus, too, it is always called *incorporation* into the body of Christ. It represents the transition from the power of darkness to the Kingdom of God's beloved Son (*see* Col 1:13 and Ga 1:4). Now the question is whether this holds true solely of adult believers and whether their little children are outside Christ's redemption as long as they themselves are incapable of choice and of the act of faith.

The Fundamental Reason for Infant Baptism

Our great and all-encompassing objection to the exclusion of children from baptism is that both the Old and the New Testaments nowhere put the children of believers (as long as they still lack the gift of discretion) outside the graced communion between the Lord and his people. The contrary is very clearly the case. One may even positively assert that the whole thinking of Scripture opposes it. The child belongs with its parents, is included with them in every respect, both for good and for evil.

This holds good not only of the relationship of parents and children in general, but this is the way they are talked about in their *relationship to God* also. Time and again the Lord includes children in the word he speaks to parents, both when he promises and when he threatens, both in his blessing and in his cursing. For that reason young children of the male sex were circumcised in Israel. That was a sign of Israel's covenant, and a seal of the rightness of faith wherewith they and their parents had been gifted by the Lord. This incorporation of little children into the covenant with God may certainly not bring about a diminishing of that faith and conversion which is required of them as soon as they can understand. This is clearly apparent from the Old and New Testaments. But it can in no way diminish the incontrovertible fact that in the Bible little children from the outset are taken into this bond of grace between the Lord and his people.

God does not set them outside His grace when they can still not embrace that grace themselves. He does not let them stay that long under the dominion of darkness; rather, in the believing parents he surrounds the children too with his grace. In the mother he sees the child also, her flesh and blood which cannot exist without her. And in the father he sees the child who depends upon his protection.

He does not destroy that intimate relationship which he himself established between parents and children when he offers the parents his friendship. On the contrary, the bond of love between the child and its father and between the infant and its mother is rather the image by which he makes his own love for his people intelligible, and affirms it. So how could he himself forget what they, the father and the mother, do not forget: the children upon whom they take pity!

Other Objections Against Infant Baptism

In opposition to this undeniable and powerful fundamental reason of the Scriptures the objections which are constantly adduced against infant baptism are of secondary importance. We are not thereby denying that infant baptism poses certain difficulties from the *theological* viewpoint about which the last word (and that on both sides) will not readily be spoken. However, what we emphatically deny is that the theological objections which are advanced would give us the freedom to deviate even just a little bit from this biblical foundation. And in so deviating we would exclude the children of the faithful from the fellowship of grace between God and his people as long as they are small and immature by refusing them baptism.

If we summarize the objections against infant baptism, they always seem to come down to these:

(a) nowhere in the New Testament do we find a command of Christ or the apostles to baptize infants; (b) in infant baptism there is no evidence of rebirth or faith; (c) infant baptism easily leads to a notion of "cheap grace" and deprives the requirement of faith and conversion of its force.

In no way do we want to trifle with these objections which, since the days of the Anabaptists, were and are adduced over and over. But we still think that they cannot deprive the basic already mentioned reason of its force.

We will investigate these objections one by one.

Is Infant Baptism Commanded Us in the Bible?

If we begin our considerations with this first objection (that nowhere in the Bible do we find an express command of infant baptism), we have to concede that we nowhere meet such an order. But may not this unmistakable fact be more correctly adduced for defending than for opposing baptism? In the entire Scripture, after all, the bond between parents and children is drawn very tightly, including their relationship to God. But then it will be permissible to see the lack of a separate command of infant baptism as a proof that infant baptism in the New Testament was presupposed as a matter of course rather than being considered something forbidden. In other words, not baptizing children and excluding them from the community would mean such a deviation from everything Scripture teaches us concerning the companionship between the Lord and his people, that without an express command against infant baptism, the Christian community would never even have thought of that.

Then, too, there are in the New Testament clear indications that in this matter the first Christian community judged, and also acted, differently than the contemporary opponents of infant baptism. That is, in fact, especially evident from the "household passages," as they are called. Each time, in the New Testament, mention is made of the baptism of believers "together with all their household" (Ac 11:14; 16:15; 16:33; 18:8; 1 Co 1:16). One can object that proof is missing that little children, minors, belonged to the "household." But then one is overlooking the unmistakable expression "with all his (her) household," which is not a sheer fabrication, but also has a clearly qualified content, as is evident from its repeated use.

In it there is a referral back to the Jewish and Old Testament linguistic usage, the meaning of which is clear. For that we only need to look at Gn 17. There the Lord speaks with Abraham about everyone who has been born in his house, so it is clearly evident to what extent Abraham's "house" includes his children too. Then elsewhere children are expressly mentioned as being correspondingly encompassed in God's command and in his promise. Let us think of the Sabbath command, of the blessing upon Abraham's house, even of the curse and the ban against the disobedient Israelites in the desert and at the triumphal entrance into Canaan.

So when the New Testament, continuing that tradition, repeatedly speaks of "you (he, she) and your (his, her) house" and does this especially when mention is made of baptism, the intent is unmistakable. Whether in this or that instance little children were or were not present diminishes it in no way and contributes nothing to it. In principle the house comprises the children, too. And so in this, too, the New Testament, in reference to baptism, preserves what can be demonstrated to be the continuing theme of Scripture.

Baptism and Faith

It is undoubtedly true that in the baptism of a child who is a minor, unlike the case of an adult, there can be no question of a demonstrable faith. Nevertheless, in the New Testament, baptism (of adults) always takes place with the profession of faith. In Mk 16:16 one finds the teaching that "he who believes and is baptized will be saved." Indeed, there is no denying that infant baptism confronts us with complexities in *theological* interpretation, which would not be there, if it were only necessary to speak about adult baptism. But even so, it is not a matter of how we can arrive at an explanation and theological reflection which is as simple and uncomplicated as possible. If such were the case, one would really do better if he could leave infant baptism out of consideration. But the question is how we can best allow the means of grace, which is baptism, regain its rightful place, also as regards children.

When we try to satisfy this requirement, it becomes evident that not only the baptism of adults, but also that of children has a rich content.

First of all, in infant baptism, even more than in the baptism of adults, is revealed how much the grace of God goes *before* our faith and how much our knowing and loving God rests in our first being known by him and *his* having loved us first. Undoubtedly the latter holds true of all who, by God's grace in Christ, have learned to believe. But God affirms this prevenient grace towards the children of believers *likewise* in this, that he not only had them born of believing parents. No, from their mother's womb he wanted to bring them into the communion of his covenant, to incorporate them into the community, and to bring them under the lordship of his Spirit and Word. In that way the bond arises by which God wanted to bind himself and the children of the faithful, not later at their conversion, when they answer the voice of his call. That bond encompasses their lives from the very beginning, and their baptism is the visible sign and proof of that bond.

But, so it will be said, it is in fact written, "He who believes and is baptized . . ." (Mk 16:16). Is not the foundation beneath infant baptism undermined in this text?

Concerning this Scripture passage certain things should definitely be said. Let it suffice to note at this point that these words of our Savior comprise part of the missionary command. In fact, in missionary territories the gospel will be brought first to adults. They come to faith and afterwards receive baptism. But for the rest, this passage is silent about infant baptism. This is asserted without even taking into consideration the fact that one may not derive from the sequence of these words ("believes . . . baptized") that only those who consciously come to faith may receive this sacrament.

Naturally, all of this does not mean that the bond between faith and baptism is broken. The question is simply whether faith must always precede baptism, if baptism is truly to remain baptism. But baptism is not a proof of our faith which is a gift from God. By baptism God inserts us into the communion of the body of Christ. By baptism we were buried with Christ into death, so that we too might walk with him in newness of life (Rm 6:4). By baptism God makes us share in the gifts of his Spirit.

This is true both of adults and of children. Only it is true of both, each in its proper way. What is at once conscious for adults, is for children at first unconscious. Still he incorporates them too into the body of Christ. In this way he brings them under the dominion of his Spirit. The small shoot which has been grafted into the tree will later become more of a unity with the tree. Surely this is not automatic. No, it occurs by means of the care and prayer of the parents, of the child's learning to pray, of the pasturing of the lambs by the Good Shepherd, by means of hymns and of preaching, and in that way too, of faith and conversion.

The image of the vine is not out of place here. For Christ is the true vine and he bears the branches. Indeed, only he who is incorporated into him *by real faith* can bear fruit. Whoever does not bear fruit is like a dead branch which is pruned. Very definitely, without faith and conversion one cannot belong to Christ.

This does not alter the fact that the way in which God makes us branches on the vine consists partly in being born into a Christian family and in being brought into the community from childhood. And that is what finds its expression at the baptism of infants in an incomparable manner.

This is why rejection of infant baptism signifies for us not only a violation of an ancient and venerable tradition, but much more. It is a disregard for the fullness of the gospel and the promise of the covenant of grace for the faithful and their children.

The Danger of Cheap Grace

Whoever thinks that he has to speak of cheap grace in this matter rejects something he does not understand. Specifically, infant baptism remains in force all our life long. Not only is the doctrine of infant baptism a powerful incentive to ready ourselves to receive the grace of God as we walk the path of faith and conversion. Not only is infant baptism a profound consolation for us if we fall into sin. But infant baptism also puts into clear light the guilt of those who, although baptized, do not bother themselves about this grace. For they do not perish as if they had never been sanctified in Christ and were strangers to the covenants of promise (*see* Ep 2:12). No, they perish like dead branches on the vine, like branches broken off the olive tree into which they were grafted (*see* Jn 15:6 and Rm 11:17 and 21).

Therefore one may not say either that infant baptism leads to rashness because the requirement of faith and conversion would be weakened. Precisely God's grace, proclaimed to us in our youth, will lead to a life of faith and conversion. Therefore, we will take that requirement of faith and conversion seriously. The parents, therefore, will be able to realize time and again that they themselves can live from the wealth of the covenant of grace. Therefore too, the church will have to keep watch over the riches and blessings of baptism administered to our children.

The Holy Spirit in the Community

The Pentecostal Movement in Earlier Times

At various periods in the history of the church we meet ideas and phenomena which make us think of the current Pentecostal groups, even though we cannot always indicate a direct connection.

Thus we can point to the Labadists, followers of Jean de Labadie who was the preacher of the Walloon church in Middelburg from 1666 to 1668, and to the followers of the Methodist preachers Wesley and Whitefield, who were active about 1750. It is true that John Wesley (1703–91) cannot be called a direct forerunner of the Pentecostal movement, but as the founder of Methodism he did have an influence on its beginnings.

One of the things which Wesley repeatedly emphasized in his preaching and writings was the possibility of becoming completely freed of sin already in this earthly life. We encounter this *perfectionism* at various times in the history of the Pentecostal movement. (For a correct understanding we have to say at once, in this regard, that certainly not everyone in these groups is an adherent of this teaching of perfectionism).

Wesley's doctrine of perfectionism had a great influence on Charles Grandison Finney, who was connected with the seminary at Oberlin, Ohio. In collaboration with two colleagues, Asa Mahan and Upham, Finney developed his teaching concerning baptism with the Holy Spirit. In his book, *The Baptism of the Holy Ghost*, he developed themes which we constantly encounter in the history of the Pentecostal movement. These doctrines are presently subscribed to by practically everyone in the Pentecostal groups. He made a clear distinction between the work of the Holy Spirit in conversion and rebirth, and the work at the baptism in the Spirit. Baptism in the Holy Spirit was, in his way of viewing the matter, a "plus," something bestowed on the believer "beyond that." The logical consequence of this doctrine was that he posited the existence of two groups of believers, those baptized in the Holy Spirit and those not baptized in the Spirit.

The thinking of Finney led to the rise of the so-called Holiness movement in the United States. In this connection Dwight Lyman Moody also has to be mentioned. This evangelist, who conducted many crusades in collaboration with the singer Ira D. Sankey, labored with many blessings and had a great deal of influence.

14 *Re-reformed Church, Holland, 1967*   199

To the Continent of Europe.

The "doctrine" of Wesley and Finney was brought to the continent of Europe by Doctor R. A. Torrey. He spoke on the subject at Blankenburg (in Thüringia) in 1905. Partly through his work a revival movement arose there.

The ideas which Torrey brought to Blankenburg were not wholly new. Specifically, the Gemeinschaftsbewegung (Community movement) had arisen in Germany. It had adherents especially in pietistic circles. Failing to find any satisfaction in the preaching in the churches, people gathered in small groups to strengthen each other in the faith. The influence of Methodism was clearly noticeable.

Most of these people never had the intention of establishing a group or community alongside of the existing church. People simply wanted to bring about an improvement in church life and to further a more scriptural preaching. Among other initiatives, annual conferences were held since 1800 at Gnadau near Madgeburg where efforts were made to that end. In 1897 was established Der Deutsche Verband für evangelische Gemeinschaftspflege und Evangelisation (The German Association Concerned with Evangelical Communities and Evangelization).

Not all of those inspired by the idea of revival remained faithful to the church. Groups and small communities arose. The men of the Community movement also tried to maintain the link with those who had left the church. One of the means was the Blankenburg Conference, held annually beginning in 1886.

One of the most important figures in the period *before* the rise of the Pentecostal movement was Doctoral Candidate Jonathan Paul. He elaborated his ideas about the various "degrees" in the spiritual life. There should be believers who were baptized in the Spirit and others who were not (yet). To this degree his "doctrine" coincides with that of the Pentecostal movement. However, distinctive was his deviation from the current opinion on an important point. In opposition to nearly all the others in the Pentecostal movement, he held the opinion that baptism in the Spirit is, in principle, not distinct from rebirth.

At a later stage of his career as an evangelist, perfectionistic tendencies entered into his preaching more and more. He propagated these notions very plainly in a report to the conference of Gnadau in 1904. There was, however, much criticism of this speech. Although Paul, in every respect, did not

The Holy Spirit in the Community

have the same conceptions which would later be found rather generally in Pentecostal groups, they nevertheless do coincide in their main lines. So it is not surprising that he joined the Pentecostal movement some years later and rose to a position of leadership.

The Pentecostal Movement in Our Times

For the real beginnings of the Pentecostal movement in the twentieth century we have to return to America.

As we have already seen, even before 1900 subjects were then coming up for discussion, which we discover later again in the Pentecostal movement. To a greater or lesser degree they were accepted.

In 1901 something new happened. Students at the Bible school in Topeka, Kansas, had made a study of baptism in the Spirit under the guidance of one of their teachers. They came to the conclusion that tongue-speaking was the proof indicated in Scripture for baptism in the Spirit. When this conclusion had once been drawn, people prayed continually to be able to receive this gift. That happened, and thereby attention was fixed on glossolalia. Since then the Pentecostal movement and tongue-speaking cannot be thought of apart from each other.

Glossolalia did not remain limited to Topeka. In Los Angeles also these phenomena made their appearance. The name of Los Angeles is important for the Pentecostal movement in Europe. In 1906, a Norwegian Methodist preacher, Thomas Ball Barratt, who was making a collection tour for his church, was a witness of the marvelous things which were happening there. He had already been influenced by the writings of Finney. When he heard what was going on in Los Angeles, he naturally went there as soon as possible. In one of the meetings he too was baptized in the Holy Spirit and began speaking in tongues. He wrote about it and tells us that he preached successively in various languages foreign to him and finally sang a splendid baritone solo.

Doctoral Candidate Barratt told his experiences in Norway. There a Pentecostal movement arose which spread over Western Europe. In Oslo Doctoral Candidate Paul, who was previously mentioned, came into contact with this movement, as did an evangelist from Hamburg, Emil Meyer.

The Pentecostal Movement in Germany

Two girls who spoke in tongues were introduced by Meyer at meetings in Germany. As a rule these meetings proceeded in a very disturbing way. In various cases people had reason to speak of excesses. Especially in Kassel all sorts of strange things happened. Of course the Pentecostal movement, as it revealed itself in Germany, had proponents and opponents. There was also a sort of "middle group" which sympathized with the Pentecostal movement, but decidedly disapproved its excesses.

The proponents of glossolalia held a conference in Hamburg in 1908. We may call it the beginning of the Pentecostal movement in Germany. Besides this we may say that by then the paths of the Pentecostal movement and of the Community movement had parted. The men of the Community movement could not agree with various points. In September 1909, they published the so-called Berlin Declaration in which the Pentecostal movement was completely condemned. In this declaration it was stated, for instance, that the Pentecostal movement is not "from above" but "from below," and that demons are at work in it. Led by Satan, they mingle lies with truth and deceive God's children. For a correct understanding of this declaration we may not lose sight of the fact that it was drawn up shortly after various excesses occurred, which later on were also rejected by persons in the Pentecostal movement itself. A negative standpoint was also taken at the Conference of Gnadau in 1910 against certain tendencies in the Pentecostal movement.

The Gnadauer Gemeinschaftsverband took a similar standpoint in 1960. This occurred in collaboration with Die Deutsche Evangelische Allianz (a union, not of churches and communities, but of individual believers) and Der Christliche Gemeinschaftsverband (on the part of the Pentecostal movement).

In their common declaration the following was laid down:

1. Rebirth and baptism in the Spirit are, according to the New Testament, one and the same, brought about as a marvel of God's grace.

2. The teaching of perfectionism, that a state of sinlessness is possible for the faithful while on earth, must be disapproved.

3. Tongue-speaking can certainly be a work of the Holy Spirit, but no overestimation of certain gifts of the Spirit may take place.

4. The fruits of the Spirit take precedence over the gifts of the Spirit.

5. Modern prophets of salvation and their mass meetings for the purpose of healing must be disapproved.

6. People are of one mind in a great longing to be equipped by

the Holy Spirit with his gifts in the sense of 1 Co 12-14; Rm 12:6ff; Ep 4:11-12.

The Pentecostal Movement in Holland

The Pentecostal movement came to Holland by way of Germany. The first Dutch Pentecostal community was established by Gerrit Roelof Polman who had first served as an officer in the Salvation Army, but had been discharged from it, because he held opinions on certain points (among them, concerning prayers for healing) which deviated from what was customarily heard in the Salvation Army. Because of these ideas he came into conflict with the Army leadership.

In the beginning the Pentecostal movement had a rather tenuous existence. Here and there small groups were formed and little communities established, but it did not obtain a hearing among the larger masses of people. Not much growth was evident.

The real growth came only with the appearance of foreign evangelists. We can call Hermann Zaiss and Thomas L. Osborn the best known of them. Since then, alongside of special gifts like speaking in tongues, the gift of healing and healing prayers are the subjects upon which much emphasis is placed in the Pentecostal movement.

Unity and Variety in the Pentecostal Movement

We turn now to Pentecostal groups. There are actually many communities and groups under various names: Pentecostal Community, Full Gospel Community, Philadelphia Community, Community of God, Bethel Pentecostal Church, etc.

In *Kracht van Omhoog* or *Power from on High* (vol. 29, nos. 3–4), Peter Bronsveld published two articles about the formation of communities in the Pentecostal movement. He demonstrated how absolutely necessary the formation of community is. As a rule a community is established by an evangelist, who at the time of the foundation, is active as an apostle. As soon as it is in any way possible, the "founder" must nevertheless withdraw, and turn the work over to the elders, whom he himself must appoint. Of course he will choose those persons who, in virtue of their faith and gifts, are most suitable.

The various groups and communities enjoy a high degree of independence. From the article of Bronsveld it is evident that members are unwilling to have anything to do with church meetings because "the idea of the uniform church" is rejected. Bronsveld expresses himself very pointedly in this regard. "The contemporary striving after uniformity is satanic." He puts the matter this way: divisions arose by striving for a uniformity which God did not intend. "The Gospel is a personal matter, requires personal faith and personal action."

In 1943, the Brotherhood of the Full Gospel Communities in the Netherlands was founded whereby the possibility emerged of forming a national community. However, this Brotherhood is not to be seen as a sort of synod. Actually, not all communities joined it and the bond between those who have joined is rather loose. The intent is to form a unity wherein each community may enjoy to the full its own character.

In a newspaper report of April 1965, mention was made of a meeting of eight Pentecostal groups in Amsterdam. The organizers stressed that this meeting was not called in the first place, for purposes of evangelization, but as a manifestation of the unity of the Pentecostal groups, which is occasionally called into question in church circles.

In other ways, too, it was intended to show that unity in fact existed. Thus, for instance, several times a huge convention was organized by the Union of Full Gospel Businessmen which met in the center of Holland. Not only businessmen gathered there, but persons from every possible group, while the speakers too, were from various domestic and foreign groups. In this way it was made clear that, despite many differences, Pentecostal brothers and sisters nonetheless want to form a unity. They know that they are united to each other.

We need to mention separately the movement called Stromen van Kracht (Streams of Power). The central figure in it is Karel andHoekendijk. There is a difference of opinion between Hoekendijk and the Pentecostal movement generally regarding tongue-speaking. In the periodical *Stromen van Kracht*, he published an important series of articles about glossolalia. In them it becomes clear that he wants to guard against the onset of hysteria and ecstasy. In opposition to others who have written about that topic, he asserts that faith and being justified by faith are central in tongue-speaking.

Whenever someone speaks in tongues, it is not the Holy Spirit who is speaking, but the believer himself. The believer is inspired by the Spirit, of course, but he can regulate the use of this gift himself. Thus in certain instances he can keep silent (*see* 1 Co 14).

At first people in church circles did not react negatively to this movement. Hoekendijk also wanted his work to be beneficial to the church. He himself wrote: "We are evangelizing in such a way as to help the church and hope that each person comes to an intense spiritual life in his or her own situation. So we want to cooperate in the spiritual awakening in all the churches." Unfortunately, in this movement people went ahead with the celebration of the Last Supper in their own circle, and with the administration of baptism, and so little or nothing came of "working to the benefit of the church."

Still Some Other Groups

As a reaction to this, different persons, who at first sympathized with this movement and lent it their support, withdrew. Thereupon another publication *"Vuur"* (*Fire*) appeared, which wanted to bring the good that was in the Pentecostal movement into the church. Preachers and members of different churches worked together on this paper.

On the list of periodicals the publication *Kracht van Omhoog* must also be named. It is described as "dedicated to fulfillment in the Holy Spirit and to the expectation of the coming of Christ." Although we find in it many articles which unmistakably propagate the ideas of the Pentecostal movement, nevertheless we cannot call it a specifically "Pentecostal publication." Sometimes we also find articles in it which deviate on certain points from the general Pentecostal opinion. The editor once wrote that any scribbler could publish his opinion in the paper, even though the editorial staff might sometimes not agree with it.

The paper *"Nieuw Leven"* (*New Life*) is published by the foundation Volle Evangelie Zending (Full Gospel Mission), which was "established to spread the Full Gospel over the whole world in the Name of Jesus Christ." It is under the editorship of the evangelist Johan Maasbach. Early in 1967 the former Capitol Theater in The Hague, after being completely restored, was put into use as "Capitol Centrum." From there the Foundation for the Full Gospel Mission reaches out. Also Maasbach has been functioning as a radio speaker in recent years. He speaks over the Luxemburg radio every Sunday evening for the Full Gospel Mission on "Een kwartier Goed Nieuws" (Fifteen Minutes of Good News).

We have mentioned earlier the Union of Full Gospel Businessmen. The first aim of this union is the encouragement of the spiritual interests of the business people. It is pointed out to believing businessmen that they can render their colleagues no greater service than to bring them into contact with the Full Gospel.

Lastly, we want to mention the name of Beukenstein. This is a country estate in Driebergen, where regular get-togethers and weekends are held. There is a permanent staff to receive guests, to give counsel and to plan courses of action. However, there are also frequently guest speakers. Considered in itself, it is a very good thing that there is an opportunity to meet with others, and discuss one's life and spiritual problems, and this outside the familiar circle in which one ordinarily moves. An objection to Beukenstein however is that it does not stop there. Baptismal services are regularly organized by the staff. To these are invited not only those who, partly through the work of Beukenstein, have accepted Jesus Christ as their Savior, but also church members whose request to be baptized as adults (thus the so-called rebaptism) was refused by their church boards.

APPENDIX II. SOME SYNODAL PRONOUNCEMENTS
Assen, 1957–58, acta, article 481
The General Synod declares:

1. that the church members in question must be admonished seriously and patiently in each case. In this matter it will depend upon the manner in which these members conduct themselves, each case to be judged individually, whether, by reason of giving scandal, they will have to be subjected to church discipline. Such will be the case whenever there is complete disdain for the baptism which was originally received;

2. that for officeholders active participation in the "Hoekendijk circle" is incompatible with the investiture in office.

Groningen, 1963–64, acta, article 471
The General Synod declares:

1. that church boards have to observe the pronouncement of the General Synod of Assen, 1957–58 (acta, article 481) regarding the pastoral and ecclesial treatment of members of the church who have had themselves rebaptized in a Pentecostal group;

2. that it is in conflict with the communal life of the church when a church board admits to the celebration of the Supper members of another reformed church who have been excluded from the sacred Supper;

The Holy Spirit in the Community

3. that in connection with what is noted under 2, church boards, in extending the right of hospitality for the celebration of the sacred Supper, have to make sure, as a safety measure, that the parties in question enjoy the right of celebrating the sacred Supper in their own church;

4. that it is incompatible with their investiture in office for officeholders to enter into such a relationship with the Pentecostal movement where they are co-responsible for propagating teachings which are in conflict with the church's profession of faith;

5. that church boards in caring for the community have to devote full attention to questions relating to the Pentecostal movement and when necessary ought to issue admonitions; and the general synod herewith decides: to appoint some delegates (*see* article 296, under J, 4) to compile a document giving information about the Pentecostal movement and to assign them the task of presenting this document to the next General Synod.

Translated by Knute Anderson

15 *Roman Catholic Church, USA, 1969*

REPORT OF THE COMMITTEE ON DOCTRINE

An episcopal Committee on Doctrine headed by Bishop Alexander M. Zaleski made its report to the meeting of the Roman Catholic bishops in November 1969. This report represents a turning point in the way the historic churches react to and reflect upon the charismatic renewal in their membership. One notes that many of the reports of church commissions up to this point go to great lengths to be fair, objective, and unprejudiced, sometimes in the face of forces which are considered by many in their churches to be sectarian, divisive, and judgmental. In a number of churches the charismatic renewal was experienced as a major source of friction and discord. Though the accommodation of the renewal within the Roman Church was not without its own problems, it was never the source of internal dissension that it was in the historic Protestant churches. One reason for this is that the Catholic movement tended to be more Catholic than were the Episcopal, Lutheran, and Presbyterian movements real representatives of their respective traditions. From the beginning of the Catholic movement, there were theologians involved who were reflecting on the theological meaning of the renewal and its place in the total Catholic experience and tradition. Generally this was not true of the charismatic renewal in the historic Protestant churches. To be remembered is that the movement in the Protestant churches was older and had no previous experience from which to learn. To some extent the Catholic charismatic renewal drew on the strengths of the older Protestant movement and learned from their mistakes.

Until this 1969 report of Bishop Zaleski's committee, the study of church commissions had focused on tongues, baptism in the Holy Spirit, and on their psychological meaning. This narrow focus, sometimes elicited because of the one-sided emphasis of those who were involved in the charismatic renewal, made an objective evaluation difficult. Broader acquaintance with the renewal movement in the churches showed that the issue is not tongues. The church commissions, beginning with the report to the American Roman Catholic bishops, expanded their perspective of the issues, and for this reason, among others, the results were more positive.

When the Roman Catholic report is read in the historical sequence of the conclusions of the church commissions which preceded it, the Catholic report appears to be a bold, positive evaluation of the renewal. Such was not the intention of the Committee on Doctrine. As a whole the American bishops were, to say the least, astonished at the appearance of the charismatic renewal in their parishes. With some persuasion they were willing to go along with a Gamaliel (Acts 5:38-39) document, which was noncommittal, open, cautious, and waiting. A report which was intended to be neutral appeared, because of the reports which preceded it, to be more positive than had been intended.

Though only about 650 words, it acknowledged that persons tend to react at the emotional level when faced with the charismatic renewal, due to a number of factors, among them fear of unusual religious experience and aversion to socially unacceptable behavior. Prayer groups do attract some emotionally unstable persons, whom the leaders try to discourage from further attendance, sometimes with and sometimes without success. Care was taken to distinguish it from classical Pentecostalism. The difference was to be found in theology and in religious style. "The Catholic prayer groups tend to be quiet and somewhat reserved."

"Theologically the movement has legitimate reasons for existence. It has a strong biblical basis." The committee then recalled the similar manifestations which were so abundantly evident in the early church.

Attention was given to the fruits of the renewal. "There are many indications that this participation in prayer groups leads to a better understanding of the role the Christian plays in the Church. Many have

*experienced progress in their spiritual life. They are attracted to the
reading of the Scriptures and a deeper understanding of their faith." The
report makes the final recommendation: "It is the conclusion of the
Committee on Doctrine that the movement should at this point not be
inhibited but allowed to develop."*

The report is reprinted in Edward D. O'Connor's The Pentecostal
Movement in the Catholic Church *(Notre Dame, Ind.: Ave Maria
Press, 1971), pp. 291–93.*

Beginning in 1967, the so-called Pentecostal movement has spread
among our Catholic faithful. It has attracted especially college
students. This report will restrict itself to the phenomenon among
Catholics. It does not intend to treat classic Pentecostalism as it
appears in certain Protestant ecclesial communities.

In the Catholic Church the reaction to this movement seems to
be one of caution and somewhat unhappy. Judgments are often
based on superficial knowledge. It seems to be too soon to draw
definitive conclusions regarding the phenomenon and more
scholarly research is needed. For one reason or another the
understanding of this movement is colored by emotionalism. For
this there is some historical justification and we live with a
suspicion of unusual religious experience. We are also face to face
with socially somewhat unacceptable norms of religious behavior.
It should be kept in mind that this phenomenon is not a
movement in the full sense of the word. It has no national
structure and each individual prayer meeting may differ from
another.

Many would prefer to speak of it as a charismatic renewal. In
calling it a Pentecostal movement we must be careful to
disassociate it from classic Pentecostalism as it appears in
Protestant denominations, such as the Assemblies of God, the
United Pentecostal Church, and others. The Pentecostal
movement in the Catholic Church is not the acceptance of the
ideology or practices of any denomination, but likes to consider
itself a renewal in the spirit of the first Pentecost. It would be an
error to suppose that the emotional, demonstrative style of prayer
characteristic of the Protestant denominations has been adopted
by Catholic Pentecostals. The Catholic prayer groups tend to be
quiet and somewhat reserved. It is true that in some cases it has
attracted emotionally unstable people. Those who come with such
a disposition usually do not continue. Participants in these prayer

meetings can also exclude them. In this they are not always successful.

It must be admitted that theologically the movement has legitimate reasons for existence. It has a strong biblical basis. It would be difficult to inhibit the work of the Spirit which manifested itself so abundantly in the early Church. The participants in the Catholic Pentecostal movement claim that they receive certain charismatic gifts. Admittedly, there have been abuses, but the cure is not a denial of their existence but their proper use. We still need further research on the matter of charismatic gifts. Certainly, the recent Vatican Council presumes that the Spirit is active continuously in the Church.

Perhaps our most prudent way to judge the validity of the claims of the Pentecostal movement is to observe the effects on those who participate in the prayer meetings. There are many indications that this participation leads to a better understanding of the role the Christian plays in the Church. Many have experienced progress in their spiritual life. They are attracted to the reading of the scriptures and a deeper understanding of their faith. They seem to grow in their attachment to certain established devotional patterns such as devotion to the real presence and the rosary.

It is the conclusion of the Committee on Doctrine that the movement should at this point not be inhibited but allowed to develop. Certain cautions, however, must be expressed. Proper supervision can be effectively exercised only if the bishops keep in mind their pastoral responsibility to oversee and guide this movement in the Church. We must be on guard that they avoid the mistakes of classic Pentecostalism. It must be recognized that in our culture there is a tendency to substitute religious experience for religious doctrine. In practice we recommend that bishops involve prudent priests to be associated with this movement. Such involvement and guidance would be welcomed by the Catholic Pentecostals.

THE EFFECTS OF NEO-PENTECOSTALISM
ON NEW ZEALAND BAPTIST CHURCHES

*Like many in the Free Church tradition, the various Baptist Churches
have had great difficulty accommodating the charismatic renewal in its
midst. This was for various reasons, such as differing views of
sanctification, involvement in the fundamentalist controversies of the
1920s (in which fundamentalists rejected Pentecostals along with
Darwinists and "modernists"), and dispensationalism (gifts are limited
to the church's beginning). In varying degrees this report from New
Zealand reflected this history.*

*The report opened by describing the contemporary scene, the conditions
in which the charismatic renewal develops, the positive and negative
effects and their duration, a few biblical reflections, and finally some
broad guidelines.*

*In recounting the positive effects mention was made of the claim of "a
deeper experience of the presence and power of the Holy Spirit in daily
life," together with a more fervent witnessing. Negatively the report
referred to misleading teaching, induced tongues, divisiveness, and
"psychological damage caused by preoccupation with evil spirits."*

*Exegetically the report held a position which identifies baptism in the
Holy Spirit with the initial act of God in regeneration, namely,
conversion. This is a rejection of the classical Pentecostal teaching that
there is at least one sanctification experience subsequent to conversion.
The filling of the Spirit is not to be identified with baptism in the Holy
Spirit, contended the report. The former, according to Scripture, is an
experience which may be repeated several times for the same person, so
that after conversion there may be a series of crisis experiences.*

*No specific command in Scripture would indicate that the individual
believer is to seek any one particular gift. Granted that at the theoretical
level one may exercise the gift of tongues in public as long as one fulfills
the stringent conditions laid down by Paul, these are of such a nature
that they "will in most cases cause, indirectly, a total prohibition of any
exercise of the gift in public."*

*Private exercise of the gifts is a private matter between the believer and
the Lord. But persons in pastoral leadership must not exercise a doctrinal
or behavioral influence which is at variance with the main stream of
Baptist doctrine and practice. The person who is convinced that he ought
to be free to teach others his own convictions and thus cause division has
probably only one honorable course: "He must seek a fellowship of*

Christians of like mind to himself." Yet the attitude of Baptists should not be one of censorious judgment but an expression of loving concern that the fruits of the Spirit will be seen in all believers.

"Report to the Baptist Union of New Zealand by the Special Committee Set Up to Investigate the Effects of Neo-Pentecostalism on New Zealand Baptist Churches" was published by the Baptist Union, Wellington, 1970. It was reprinted as appendix III in James E. Worsfold's A History of the Charismatic Movements in New Zealand, *privately published by the Julian Literature Trust, 1974, pp. 337–43.*

SECTION I — THE CONTEMPORARY SCENE

I. Concern

The need to investigate the Neo-Pentecostal Movement within New Zealand arose because in some cases its emphasis has been harmful, and has had confusing effects upon members of our Churches. Some have become unsettled in the faith and restless in the Church fellowship. At times Christian has been set at variance with Christian, and in some cases family unity has been divided. The Neo-Pentecostal emphasis has not always resulted in love and unity. The general desire in the community for excitement and spectacle seems related to the rise of interest in Neo-Pentecostal teaching in recent years.

Surveying this concern among the Churches, we feel the following observations should be noted:

a. In some of the Churches there have been, and are, individual members and adherents who are personally interested in the movement, but whose association with it is in relation to groups outside their own Churches.

b. In a few of our Churches there are small groups of Neo-Pentecostal adherents meeting privately without official recognition. In some cases the unobtrusiveness of such meetings results in little difficulty being created. In others, such meetings create a division in the fellowship which is a matter for concern.

c. A small minority of Churches have been seriously affected.

II. Neo-Pentecostalism Seems to Develop

a. Where the fellowship of a Church includes a number of new people, especially new converts, who are not established in the faith.

b. Where spiritual vitality and warmth seem to be lacking in the Church fellowship.

c. Paradoxically there are some cases where God's blessing was already evident.

d. Where an attractive personality has given a lead and won a following.

e. Where the Minister or other Church leader has been sympathetic and has himself in some degree become involved.

III. The Effect on our Churches

a. Some effects seem beneficial:

1. A renewed interest in and study of the person and work of the Holy Spirit. Some have claimed a deeper experience of the presence and power of the Holy Spirit in daily life.

2. A challenge to warmth and vitality in individual Christian experience and in the life of the Church.

3. A call to more fervent praying and more zealous witnessing.

b. But other effects can be harmful:

1. Misleading teaching with false emphasis, leading to confusion and uncertainty, and in some cases to a reaction against all teaching about the Holy Spirit.

2. The manipulation of people through recommended techniques to induce speaking in tongues.

3. The creation of division within the fellowship of the Church.

4. The encouraging of spiritual pride, especially among some young people, with a resultant disparagement of others.

5. A spiritual reaction on the part of some who, caught up in the movement for a time, forsook it and, with it, the Church. Often individual Church members claim to receive blessings, but these are not always beneficial to the whole Church.

6. Psychological damage caused by pre-occupation with evil spirits.

IV. Duration of Effect

a. In many of the Churches in which the Neo-Pentecostal influence has been felt, the effects have been evidenced among only a small percentage of the membership or for only a relatively brief period. There appears to be no resultant cause for concern.

b. In certain cases there are members who continue to practise speaking in tongues in their personal devotions, but who treat this as an individual experience and never to be obtruded in the life of the Church.

c. In some Churches the Neo-Pentecostal movement continues

with disturbing effects, due either to mistaken handling at some stage or to persistent influences. Where influential people in the Church are involved, the position is a particularly difficult one.

V. Further Observations Re Contemporary Scene

We feel that it is important to remember that where there is the genuine there may also be the counterfeit, and it is at this point we warn of the dangers that do disservice to the cause of Christ. 1 John 4:1 warns, "Believe not every Spirit, but try the Spirits whether they are of God."

There is a grave danger when an emotional attitude is worked up towards the manifestations of the Spirit, demanding that speaking in tongues is:

a. essential to the fullness of the Spirit, or

b. that it is the primary evidence of the fullness.

This we believe is against the authority of Scripture and where this gift has not been received leads to spiritual frustration and despair. Furthermore the insistence upon "healing within the Atonement" leads to grave dangers and often harmful spiritual and physical reactions. This last consideration has been confirmed to us by some pastors, and Christian doctors, who have to deal with people emotionally and spiritually disturbed because of these things. . . .

SECTION II — HISTORICAL AND BIBLICAL INVESTIGATION

An Examination of the Biblical Position

1. THE BAPTISM OF THE SPIRIT

a. The promise of John the Baptist, taken up by the Lord in Acts 1:5 anticipated a historic fulfilment, as shown by the phrase, "Not many days hence." It was thus fulfilled on the day of Pentecost.

b. The only other place in Acts where the phrase "baptise with the Holy Spirit" is used is 11:16, but even here it is not certain whether Peter is applying the phrase directly to the experience of Cornelius, or to his own experience at Pentecost, following which he says God gave the same gift to Cornelius, i.e. God gave the Holy Spirit as a gift to Cornelius and his household just as He gave Him to the apostles earlier, when He fulfilled His promise of the baptism of the Holy Spirit on the day of Pentecost.

c. In connection with each example quoted by Neo-Pentecostals as an illustration of the baptism of the Spirit in

Effects of Neo-Pentecostalism

Acts the phrase, "received the Holy Spirit" is used (Acts 8:17, 10:47, 19:2). This seems to place beyond dispute the fact that each of these cases referred to an initial experience of the Holy Spirit. It is sometimes argued in the case of the apostles themselves that their initial reception of the Holy Spirit took place in the Upper Room when Jesus breathed upon them and said, "Receive the Holy Spirit" (John 20:22), and thus their "baptism in the Holy Spirit" on the day of Pentecost was a second experience. However, we are not told in John 20 that the Lord's words were immediately fulfilled. Rather he performed a symbolic act in anticipation (as with the bread and wine in the Upper Room), so that they would know that the gift they were soon to receive would communicate to them His own continued presence. His words in Acts 1:8 make clear that the Holy Spirit had not up till then come upon them.

d. Speaking in tongues was on occasions given as a special sign of an initial experience of the indwelling Holy Spirit, but there is no record of this taking place on other occasions (Acts 8:17, 9:17). Nor is there any command or exhortation anywhere in Scripture that we should speak in tongues as a sign of our reception of the Holy Spirit.

e. The only other place where the phrase occurs in the New Testament is 1 Cor 12:13. This verse indicates that it is the baptism by the Spirit which incorporates us into the body of Christ. Again this would indicate an initial experience of the Spirit at the time of belief in Christ. It is the regeneration, or being born of the Spirit which incorporates us into His body. If we have not had the initial experience of the Spirit, i.e. if the Spirit does not dwell in us, we do not belong to Christ at all (Rom 8:9). It is noteworthy that all the Christian believers in Corinth, including the factious, the worldly, and the wicked addressed in earlier chapters, had been baptised by the Spirit so as to form the body of Christ. It was not the exclusive possession of some who had experienced a "second blessing."

f. From the scriptural evidence therefore we conclude that the phrase "baptism of the Spirit" should be applied today only to the initial act of God in regeneration. When God grants the gift of His Spirit to indwell the believer in response to repentance and faith, then he enters into the heritage of the historic "baptism of the Spirit" which occurred at Pentecost, for from that point on the gift of God (the Holy Spirit) was made available to everyone whom the Lord God calls to Himself (Acts 2:38, 39).

g. The filling with the Spirit is not to be identified with the baptism of the Spirit. Though men may be filled with the Spirit at the time of the baptism (Acts 2:4), the filling is an experience which may be repeated several times for the same person (Acts 4:8, 4:31, 9:19, 13:9).

h. In Acts some people received a sudden experience of being "filled with the Spirit," others are described as living in a continued state, "full of the Holy Spirit" (6:3, 5, 11:24).

i. The only reference in the Epistles is in Eph. 5:18. In regard to this vital verse, it should be noted:

1. As it is addressed to believers who are already indwelt by the Spirit, the filling comes from within, not from without. The believer is thus commanded to yield his life to the total control of the indwelling Spirit.

2. The tense of the verb "be filled" cannot be applied to a single once-for-all experience. It means "keep on being filled," and refers either to a repetitive or continuous response of allowing the Holy Spirit to fill and control one's life.

j. We conclude that there may be many fillings, as crisis experiences of the believer after conversion; but the command of Paul enjoins upon us a continuous daily yielding of our lives to the Spirit; and without this there cannot be a full obedience to Paul's injunction.

2. THE GIFTS OF THE SPIRIT

The portions of Scripture which speak most clearly of "gifts" in relation to the Church are Romans 12:3-8, 1 Cor 12:14, Eph 4:1-16, 1 Peter 4:10, 11.

It is noteworthy that in all these passages, the key theme is the unity of the body of Christ. The purpose of God's gifts to His people is always and only the building up of the Church, not personal spiritual edification . . .

Every believer has received some gift from God (Rom 12:3, 1 Cor 12:7, Eph 4:7, 1 Pet 4:10). These are given not in accordance with individual choice, but with God's sovereign appointment (Rom 12:6, 1 Cor 12:11, 18, 28). The words "earnestly desire the higher gifts" (1 Cor 12:31, likewise 14:1) are in the plural, not the singular. Paul is not saying that each individual should hanker for particular gifts, but that the Church should desire that its life be marked by the higher gifts, especially prophecy (i.e. the proclamation of God's message), rather than the lower. There is no specific command in Scripture to the individual believer to

Effects of Neo-Pentecostalism

seek any particular gift, but there is a specific command to use the gift which God has given him for the benefit of others (1 Peter 4:10).

There is great variety in the gifts of God. Nine are mentioned in 1 Cor 12:8-10. Nine are mentioned again in 1 Cor 12:28-30, but five of these are different. Rom 12:6-8 lists seven gifts of which at least three are different again, and Eph 4:11 adds yet two more. Thus, all told, some nineteen "gifts" are listed, but clearly no list is meant to be exhaustive. Any endowment which God gives to a person for the purpose of building up His Church is a "gift". It is quite misleading to talk of some gifts only as "charismatic." The Greek word charisma means a gift given by free sovereign grace, and applied equally to all types of gifts which God bestows. Particular "gifts" emphasised in Neo-Pentecostal teaching:

"Speaking in Tongues" . . .

The Corinthian Church was enthusiastic about "tongues". Paul writing to them discounts the gift. He discounts it in individual use in prayer unless the user can interpret, for the mind should accompany the spirit in prayer (1 Cor 14:14-15). He gives permission for speaking in tongues in church gatherings, but only on three most stringent conditions (1 Cor 14:27, 28):

i. Not more than two, or at most three, thus to speak in any meeting.

ii. They are to speak one after the other, not simultaneously.

iii. Before they speak at all, they must ascertain that there is one person present able to interpret for them all.

If these conditions cannot be met, the tongues-speaker must keep silent in Church, and exercise his gift privately.

We would conclude that, while speaking in tongues is not to be forbidden if it occurs as a genuine manifestation of the Spirit of God, people should be taught to recognise that it is a gift of little worth unless accompanied by the gift of interpretation so that the meaning of words given is known by the speaker. It can only be allowed expression in public under strict observance of the rules, enumerated by Paul. These difficult rules will in most cases cause, indirectly, a total prohibition of any exercise of the gift in public. . . .

SECTION III — PRACTICAL ADVICE TO CHURCHES

1. Our answer to some of the irregularities occurring through Neo-Pentecostal teaching must not be one of censorious

judgment, but an expression of loving concern that the fruits of the Spirit will be seen in all believers, and that our behavior patterns should testify of Christ.

This we believe can be done by strong and positive teaching on: (a) the Lordship of Christ, (b) the Person and Work of the Holy Spirit, (c) the Sovereignty of God, (d) sound Christian behaviour and moral integrity.

2. It is realised that no rigid rule of action can be laid down. However, pastors, elders and deacons have a responsibility to graciously but firmly request any member, adherent, or group, who holds convictions differing from the main stream of doctrine and practice amongst Baptists, to refrain from any form of active propagation or influence of others, who are under the care and influence of that Church. On the other hand, church leaders need to be careful not to attempt to restrict any person's private devotional life. The private exercising of gifts which an individual Christian sincerely believes to be genuine gifts of the Holy Spirit is a matter between him and his Lord. Within the Church and its sphere of influence, the Pauline injunction is "endeavouring to keep the unity of the Spirit in the bond of peace."

3. If, however, an individual feels that he ought to be free to teach others his own convictions on this or any matter that would be divisive, there is probably only one honourable course for that person to take. He must seek a fellowship of Christians of like mind to himself, and thus safeguard Paul's injunction. Apart from a clear directive to "mark those that cause division" there is no scriptural ground for the Church to excommunicate a member for reasons other than heresy or unrepented sin that would become a public scandal. The Apostle did not cut off the Corinthian Church for the childish misuse of the gifts of the Spirit. He did, however, insist on firm disciplinary action against one who blatantly persisted in immoral conduct.

4. Pastors and Ministers would be well advised to avoid any action that would produce a "persecution complex" in the minds of those who hold Neo-Pentecostal views, and preachers are urged to refrain from negative sermons designed to openly condemn.

5. It is no accident that the portion of Scripture which deals most fully with teaching and instruction for the operation of the so called charismatic gifts also contains a large section on the greatest Christian virtue, LOVE. "Love which suffereth long . . . and is kind . . . beareth all things . . . endureth all things."

Effects of Neo-Pentecostalism

Surely the Holy Spirit intended this to be THE GUIDING
PRINCIPLE in an area which would otherwise become a sphere of
misunderstanding, difficulty and division.

FINAL COMMENT

Past experiences in dealing with Neo-Pentecostalism has
emphasised the importance of adequate teaching concerning the
Holy Spirit. It has also proved that this in itself is not enough.
Knowledge must be translated into experience. We rejoice in the
revival of interest in the ministry of the Holy Spirit and recognise
that in many places the winds of God's Spirit are blowing and
bringing renewal to many believers. This is the great need of
Christendom today, and we must be eager to share in whatever
God has for His people. Without doubt all our Churches must be,
and must be seen to be, alive with the Holy Spirit.

Compiled by a committee of five which included two Baptist Theologians, the
Secretary being Revd. B. J. Denholm. Published by the Baptist Union, Wgtn.,
1970, pp. 1–10.

17 Church of the Nazarene, USA, 1970

RESOLUTION OF THE BOARD
OF GENERAL SUPERINTENDENTS

*The Church of the Nazarene emerged at the end of the nineteenth century
from the Holiness movement. The product of the merger of three
independent Holiness groups, which resulted in the largest of the
Holiness Churches, its doctrinal position stands in the Wesleyan
tradition, focusing on sanctification as a second definite work of grace
subsequent to regeneration. This crisis experience was called "Baptism
with the Holy Spirit," or "the blessing." During the latter part of the
nineteenth century and the early part of the twentieth century, the
Holiness movement used a "Pentecostal vocabulary." There were
Pentecostal meetings, Pentecostal churches, Pentecostal schools and
colleges, and an Association of Pentecostal Churches of America (one of
the parent bodies of the Church of the Nazarene). The Pentecost event
was very much a part of the Holiness religious culture. Until 1919 the
national denomination was called "The Pentecostal Church of the
Nazarene."*

There had long been unease in the church's association with persons in the Holiness-Pentecostal movement who gave some emphasis to second coming, healing, and finally tongues. A partial explanation could possibly be found in the geographical proximity of Phineas F. Bresee's Church of the Nazarene to the Azusa Street Church. Bresee's church, founded in Los Angeles in 1895, became a major factor in the formation of the national denomination. The Azusa Street Church in the same city became the center of a national Pentecostal revival starting in 1906 and eventually came to be recognized as the place from which the international Pentecostal movement took its origin.

However, Bresee and his co-worker Dr. J. P. Widney tended to be undogmatic and tolerant of divergent doctrinal views, except in the matter of Christian perfection and entire sanctification. Dr. Bresee, who became a general superintendent, fought against any narrowness, personal or denominational, which considered the Pentecostal Church of the Nazarene "the only way." To the end of his days his policy was "liberality in all matters not in his view absolutely essential to salvation." [1]

After Bresee's death in 1915, the Pentecostal Church of the Nazarene, at its 1919 General Assembly, felt compelled to drop the word "Pentecostal" from the denomination's name. This was to avoid identification with the Pentecostal movement which in its earliest form taught "a third blessing" beyond the sanctification crisis experience, of which the initial evidence was speaking in tongues. In so doing the Nazarenes agreed that they did not thereby relinquish their claim to the Pentecost event and its role in the life of the church. This decision of the largest of the Holiness Churches had the effect of isolating the nascent Pentecostal movement. Following the lead of the Nazarenes the Wesleyan Methodist Church, the Salvation Army, the Pilgrim Holiness Church, and the Free Methodist Church also dissociated themselves completely from the Pentecostal movement.

The sense of the 1919 action was restated in 1970 in a resolution adopted by the Board of General Superintendents. Though holding to a belief in the plenary inspiration of the Scriptures as containing all truth necessary to Christian faith and living, the appeal in the 1970 statement was to "the doctrine and practice of the church."

The resolution was reprinted in "The Journal of the Nineteenth General Assembly of the Church of the Nazarene," p. 240.

1. Timothy L. Smith, Called Unto Holiness (Kansas City: Nazarene Publishing House, 1962), p. 118.

Resolution of the General Superintendents

It is the judgment and ruling of the Board of General Superintendents of the Church of the Nazarene that any practice and/or propagation of speaking in tongues either as the evidence of the baptism with the Holy Spirit or as an ecstatic neo-pentecostal prayer language is interpreted as inveighing against the doctrines and practices of the church.

18 United Presbyterian Church, USA, 1970

THE WORK OF THE HOLY SPIRIT

In response to four requests, the 1968 General Assembly of the United Presbyterian Church established a commission in which a number of its members were involved in the charismatic renewal. In the 1969 preliminary report, the commission observed that involvement in the charismatic movement "has sometimes led to dissension within our church," and occasionally where pastors have been associated with the renewal "the pastoral relationship has been terminated." The introduction of beliefs and practices into a congregation concerning which the Book of Confessions (which are "subservient to the Holy Scripture") is silent cannot be prohibited as long as they "are not destructive to the external peace and order. . . ." The commission reminded "ministers, sessions, and presbyteries of their respective pastoral responsibilities toward those whose spiritual experience may differ from their own." When the final report was printed, this preliminary report was placed at the beginning.

In 1970 the Special Committee on the Work of the Spirit made its final report to the General Assembly. Like the Catholic report of 1969, it too evaluated the phenomenon of tongues but in a much broader perspective. It was also the most ambitious and the most pastoral of the reports made so far. After an exegetical and systematic summary of its findings, the psychological dimensions are treated in some detail. There is a section devoted to pastoral guidelines for ministers and laity who are personally involved in the renewal, another section for those who are not, and a final section for presbyteries. The report concluded with two appendices, one a biblical study and the other a review of the psychological literature.

While stressing the essentially private nature of tongues the report concluded "that the practice of glossolalia should be neither despised nor forbidden; on the other hand it should not be emphasized nor made normative for the Christian experience."

A subcommittee whose membership included persons competent in the behavioral sciences "found no evidence of pathology in the movement. . . . Varied educational backgrounds and personality patterns are present and the socio-economic status ranges from the uneducated through those in high executive positions carrying great responsibility. . . ." This subcommittee called attention to the limits of the behavioral sciences when dealing with religious experience: ". . . it will be a dark and tragic day in the life of Christianity if psychological norms are to become the criteria by which the truth or the untruth of religious experience is judged. Psychological insight has enriched, deepened, and humbled our knowledge of ourselves beyond measure; but, when it is asked for a decisive answer to the question of whether a man has or has not experienced the living Christ it is an aborted and inappropriate use of the science."

In its exegetical section, the committee reported that they found no warrant in the New Testament for two Spirit-baptisms as normal for the Christian life. Those who speak of one baptism which makes persons new creatures and another by which the Holy Spirit comes to dwell are constructing a division which is not found in the New Testament. In the New Testament baptism with water, which is related to the reception of the Spirit, may come before, at the same time, or after one has been baptized in the Holy Spirit. "The modern elaboration of a doctrine concerning a special event called 'baptism in the Holy Spirit,' different in kind from any other operation of the Holy Spirit, is a sectarian over-interpretation."

The report is found in the "Minutes of the 182nd General Assembly of the United Presbyterian Church in the United States of America," Office of the General Assembly, Philadelphia, 1970, pp. 145–98. It is reprinted in a 56-page pamphlet entitled The Work of the Holy Spirit, *which is available from the United Presbyterian Church Office of the General Assembly, Room 1021, 475 Riverside Dr., New York City, 10027. This pamphlet includes the 1969 preliminary report.*

The committee was appointed by the 180th General Assembly (1968) with instructions to study *Overtures 14, 15, 16,* and *17,* and to report to the 181st General Assembly (1969). These overtures requested study of the work of the Holy Spirit with special reference to glossolalia and other charismatic gifts within the fellowship of the United Presbyterian Church.

The committee made a preliminary report in 1969 and recommended that it be continued with a view to completing its mandate and reporting to the 182nd General Assembly (1970).

REPORT TO THE 181ST GENERAL ASSEMBLY (1969)

Your committee has been impressed by the fact that of all branches of Christianity that of Pentecostalism is one branch currently experiencing rapid growth in membership. This is especially true in that part of the Church to be found in Latin America and in Africa. We note, also, the fact that within the mainstream of Christianity in the United States, both Protestant and Roman Catholic, there is a small but growing movement of what has been called the "charismatic renewal" or "Neo-Pentecostalism." The real impetus of this development began about a decade ago and continues to this day. This is the second period of rapid growth by Pentecostalism within less than one hundred years.

The committee is grateful to observe the rapid breaking down of barriers that have separated Protestant denominations from our brethren in the Roman Catholic and Greek Orthodox Churches. Similarly, we are glad to note the beginning of a breakdown of the barriers that have deprived us of fellowship with Pentecostal denominations. Believing that both of these are the result of the work of the Holy Spirit, we call on United Presbyterians to be sensitive and responsive to the insights and experiences of fellow Christians within all traditions. And the end is not yet, ". . . no eye has seen, nor ear heard, nor the heart of man conceived, what God has prepared for those who love him, . . ." (1 Cor 2:9 RSV)

In the United Presbyterian Church the number of clergy and laity involved in charismatic experiences is comparatively small, although your committee finds that in some areas these numbers are growing significantly. This involvement in such experiences has sometimes led to dissension within our Church. Occasionally where pastors have been involved, the pastoral relationship has been terminated. As a result, many have found it necessary to seek an "independent ministry-evangelism," and some to demit the ministry of the United Presbyterian Church.

There is also something of a pattern in connection with the laity. When laymen have become involved in charismatic experiences, they have often felt alienated from both their pastors and fellow church members. As a result, they have sought other fellowship. Pastors have sometimes failed to show understanding of the laymen's experience and have been unable to counsel adequately with them. On the other hand, some laymen have not always been receptive to the pastor's guidance.

In a future report your committee hopes to make specific recommendations by which the Church may more adequately minister in these situations. Until then, guided by the Westminster Confession of Faith, Chapter XX, we plead for that tolerance, good will, and Christ-centered love which is at the heart of the thirteenth chapter of First Corinthians. We remind ministers, sessions, and presbyteries of their respective pastoral responsibilities toward those whose spiritual experience may differ from their own. We believe that these situations provide immediate opportunity for the application of the theme of reconciliation which is paramount in the Confession of 1967. Therefore, we say to the whole Church in the words of the Apostle Paul: "So, my brethren, earnestly desire to prophesy, and do not forbid speaking in tongues: but all things should be done decently and in order." (1 Cor 14:39-40 RSV)

Overture 14, On The Freedom of the Ministry and Other Matters, from the Presbytery of Phoenix was referred to this committee by the 180th General Assembly (1968). The committee requested the counsel of the Stated Clerk among others in arriving at the following statement.

The committee would refer you to the Westminster Confession of Faith, Chapter XX, "Of Christian Liberty and Liberty of Conscience" in its entirety. It is evident to your committee that the silence of the Book of Confessions on any matters of faith or practice does not prohibit the introduction of such beliefs and practices into the life of a congregation so long as such beliefs and practices are not destructive to the external peace and order which Christ has established in the Church. When a member of a local congregation is concerned, the local session is charged with making a determination as to whether or not censures are necessary; when a congregation or its pastor are concerned, then the presbytery is charged with making a determination; when a presbytery, the synod; and when the synod, the General Assembly.

We would remind you that all of the confessions of the Church are subservient to the Holy Scripture.

Members of the committee are: Rev. John H. Strock, *Chairman*; Rev. Joseph Bishop; Rev. Jack M. Chisholm; Mr. James D. Copeland; Rev. David E. Dilworth; Dr. Thomas Foster; Mr. Phil W. Jordan; Dr. Charles H. Meisgeier; Rev. Bruce M. Metzger; Chaplain T. David Parham; and Rev. David H. C. Read.

Since the last General Assembly the committee has met for extended study and discussion on October 2 and 3, December 11 and 12, February 12 and 13, at St. Louis, Mo., and has considered the reports of its sub-committees on exegesis, theology, psychology, and healing, as well as ecumenical correspondence. On two occasions there has been close contact with the permanent sub-committee on theology of The Presbyterian Church in the United States. We have also followed the practice of hearing personally from those with both positive and negative experience of charismatic phenomena both within and outside the United Presbyterian Church. Our discussions were marked by openness and vigor, and a wide diversity of view and experience has been disclosed within the charismatic dimensions of love, joy, and peace. We are convinced that "the work of the Holy Spirit" is not only a vaster topic than can be addressed by one committee of the Church, but points to a neglected area in our thinking and practice. It is very possible that the Holy Spirit is preparing a renewal of the Church in our time that may come in surprising ways and through unexpected channels. We are therefore conscious that, in addressing ourselves to the question of glossolalia and other unusual manifestations, we are dealing with only one small segment of a vast theme that has enormous potential for the Church.

VOCABULARY

In this report with its supporting documents we shall be using certain words and phrases that require preliminary definition.

By PENTECOSTALISM we refer to the movement, dating from the turn of the century, which arose out of various "holiness" sects that were expressing a reaction against rationalism and secularism in the institutional churches. Pentecostal churches emerged, laying stress on an experience called "the baptism in the Spirit" as a second stage (after conversion) in the life of holiness. This experience was believed to be attested by the gift of "tongues," although this was seen as only one manifestation of the fullness of life in the Spirit. In recent years Pentecostalism has been represented by denominations and groupings of churches that go by many different names, of which the "Assemblies of God" is now probably the best known and most structurally developed. The Pentecostal churches can no longer be viewed as minor sects on the fringe of organized Christianity. The movement is now worldwide and is recognized by ecumenical authorities to be one of the most dynamic and fastest-growing sectors of the church in the modern world.

By NEO-PENTECOSTALISM we mean the phenomenon of "Pentecostal" experiences within the traditional Churches. It is now fairly well-known that clergy and laymen within the Roman Catholic Church and all of the main Protestant denominations have claimed to have received a "baptism in the Spirit" with attendant manifestations, such as speaking in tongues, powers of healing, exorcism, and other practices not normally associated with our style of congregational life. "Neo-Pentecostalism" is thus a movement *within* the established churches, and its exponents would regard it as a legitimate instrument of revival with strong scriptural justification. It is notable that "Neo-Pentecostalism" has come now to stress the extraordinary gifts of the Spirit more than some of the historic Pentecostal churches.

By GLOSSOLALIA (a word which is not used in the New Testament) we mean the utterance in prayer and worship of sounds that give the impression of being either ecstatic or a language hitherto unknown to the speaker. The scriptural references to this phenomenon in the early church are to be found exclusively in the Book of Acts and Paul's First Epistle to the Corinthians (if we except the concluding section of the Gospel of Mark which is of disputed authenticity). The word has been recently accepted in popular speech and writing as the description of a psychological phenomenon without prejudice as to its religious validity.

CHARISMATIC GIFTS is a phrase properly used to describe *all* the endowments with which the Holy Spirit enriches the Church, but has come to refer especially to those that modern man regards as abnormal — such as tongues, healings, discernment, and exorcism. Since "charisma" is another theological word that has infiltrated our popular speech "charismatic gifts" will be readily understood to refer to unusual and non-rational facets of human personality.

PROPHESYING in the early church was not so much the

Work of the Holy Spirit

predicting of future events (though this sometimes occurred, e.g., Agabus in Acts 11:27), but was chiefly the gift of understanding and expressing through teaching or preaching what the will of God was for a given situation, resulting in "upbuilding and encouragement and consolation" (1 Cor 14:3).

The committee has used the word "ecstasy" in relation to glossolalia rarely and with hesitation because it may convey a wrong impression about the experience. In this report "ecstasy" implies only that one may feel emotionally lifted, inspired by God's Spirit, not that one behaves in an irrational or trance-like manner.

EXEGESIS

The committee felt it essential to examine the scriptural references to the Holy Spirit in general and the passages on the "gifts of the Spirit" in some detail. (See the supporting document in the Appendix prepared by a sub-committee).

The Old Testament speaks of the Spirit as the source of physical, intellectual, and moral life, and refers on occasion to exceptional gifts of the Spirit bestowed on individuals for special service. It points forward to a Messianic Age in which God will "pour out his Spirit on all flesh."

In the New Testament the doctrine is greatly developed. The synoptic Gospels emphasize the work of the Spirit in the conception, baptism, mission, and message of Jesus, and speak of his gift of the Spirit to the disciples. In the Fourth Gospel much is said of the future work of the Spirit as the one who will lead and empower the followers of Christ. The Book of the Acts sees again the work of the Spirit in the birth, empowering, mission, and message of the Church. We find in its pages continual reference to the prompting and power of the Spirit in specific situations.

It was the Apostle Paul who developed the doctrine of the Spirit as the sustaining power of the Christian life. Using a variety of titles Paul sets forth the possession of the Spirit as the means of overcoming the power of sin and as a pledge of complete redemption to come. It is Paul who elaborates the thought of special manifestations and gifts of the Spirit and certain passages in his epistles — particularly Chapters 12, 13 and 14 of 1 Corinthians — have formed the main exegetical basis of the committee's work.

A study of the lists Paul gives of spiritual gifts (Romans 12:6-8; 1 Corinthians 12:8-10; 12:28-31; Ephesians 4:11) shows rather considerable differences in the terms used and the types of gifts mentioned. It is only in the letter to Corinth that the more miraculous functions such as healing, miracles, and glossolalia are mentioned. Moreover, the apostle's estimate of the relative value of glossolalia is made clear by (1) the fact that, whenever speaking with tongues is listed it comes at the end; and (2) by his express statement he would rather "speak five words with my mind, in order to instruct others, than ten thousand words in a tongue." (1 Corinthians 14:18, 19.)

The charismatic gifts as a whole are defined as endowments necessary for the edification and service of the church, bestowed by the Spirit on its members whereby they are enabled to employ their natural faculties in a heightened degree, or to be endowed with new abilities and powers for this purpose.

The very limited reference in the New Testament to the gift of speaking with tongues we feel to be significant in view of the current stress laid on this phenomenon in Neo-Pentecostal circles.

The chief exegetical difficulty we find in the relevant passages is to determine whether the "tongues" were actual foreign languages or dialects not previously known by the speaker, or were a kind of rhapsody of sounds, unintelligible to others as well as to the speaker. Our conclusion, based on a study of the language and analogies used by Paul, is that in 1 Corinthians he is speaking of a peculiar kind of utterance attained in prayer in which praise and adoration overflow in ways that transcend ordinary speech.

The Book of Acts offers three passages referring to glossolalia: Peter's experience with the Roman centurion at Caesarea, where Gentiles were heard, after receiving the gift of the Spirit, "speaking in tongues and extolling God" (Acts 10:46); Paul's experience at Ephesus where the Holy Spirit came on a group after they had received baptism in the name of Christ, and "they spoke with tongues and prophesied;" and the description of the day of Pentecost. In the former two references there is no hint of a need to speak in foreign languages, so that most commentators have seen here an utterance of unknown sounds in ecstatic speech.

The Pentecost passage has given rise to the most diverse interpretations. Many see the plain meaning of the passage to be that the Holy Spirit miraculously enabled the believers to speak in various foreign tongues so as to be understood by the different nationalities present. Others claim that the narrative suggests that this was primarily an ecstatic act of worship, and point out that there was no need for a miracle of languages since all present would know either Aramaic or Greek. It is also noted that the accusation of drunkenness suggests "strange noises" much more than actual languages. Again it is pointed out that the writer of Acts does not affirm that the disciples actually *spoke* foreign languages, but only that the hearers so interpreted their utterances. Thus the miracle would be one of hearing rather than of speaking. We find it impossible to be dogmatic in our interpretation of this passage. It appears that either Luke was using two different accounts of the event, or else he himself introduced into an original account of ecstatic tongues certain features suggesting the use of actual languages in order to interpret to the reader the significance of the coming of the Spirit as the answer to the confusion of tongues at Babel.

Our conclusions from the exegetical study may be summarized thus:

1. The Church, according to the New Testament, is a supernatural fellowship in which the talents and services of the members are a continuation of the life and work of Christ himself, mediated by the Spirit.

2. Of all the spiritual gifts, that of speaking in tongues was open to certain dangers and abuses. But Paul did not forbid the exercise of this gift in private; he nevertheless restricted its exercise in public, demanding that the tongues be always interpreted.

3. For the apostle speaking in tongues is good, but prophesying is better, and love for God and men is best of all.

4. From the silence of the gospels and of the great majority of the epistles on the subject of the gift of speaking in tongues we conclude that it occupied a subordinate place in the life of Christians in the apostolic age.

5. In the light of current claims that glossolalia is a proof of having received the so-called "baptism of the Spirit," it is necessary to note that, while the verb "to baptize" is used by Scripture in connection with the Spirit, the noun "baptize" is never used in the form "baptism of the Spirit." The elaboration of the doctrine concerning this "baptism of the Spirit" seems to be a sectarian over-interpretation, and to contrast it to baptism with water is contrary to the apostolic teaching that there is but one baptism. Since "by one Spirit we were all baptized into one body" it is unwarranted to teach that speaking in tongues is an indispensable sign of having received the Spirit.

6. We believe that the correct method of ascertaining the revelation of the purpose of God in Scripture is to give *primary* attention to its didactic, rather than its historical parts. Hence we should look for guidance in such matters to the teaching of Jesus and the sermons and epistles of his apostles, rather than to the narratives of the Book of Acts. We must, however, keep in mind that the pattern of empowering by the Spirit revealed in these narratives is both a stimulus for the church today and a help in the understanding of Neo-Pentecostal experience among us.

7. We cannot, however, follow the view of some theologians that the purely supernatural gifts ceased with the death of the apostles. There seems no exegetical warrant for this assumption. Rather are we to "test the spirits to see whether they are of God," since each one of the charismatic gifts had its counterfeits and frauds.

8. We therefore conclude, on the basis of Scripture, that the practice of glossolalia should be neither despised nor forbidden; on the other hand it should not be emphasized nor made normative for the Christian experience. Generally the experience should be private, and those who have experienced a genuine renewal of their faith in this way should be on their guard against divisiveness within the congregation. At the same time those who have received no unusual experiences of the Holy Spirit should be alert to the possibility of a deeper understanding of the gospel and a fuller participation in the gifts of the Spirit — of which love is the greatest. (For further implications of these principles, see section entitled "Guidelines.")

SOME THEOLOGICAL CONSIDERATIONS

A survey of the theological field from the Fathers to the present day reveals that the doctrine of the Holy Spirit has received less attention than one would expect from the emphasis of Scripture. There is not much guidance, for instance, in the writings of Calvin and other Reformed theologians in the matters we have under consideration, and the confessions have little to say about the gifts of the Spirit.

Positive statements concerning the Spirit's relation to Christ, the Church, the forgiveness of sin, the Scriptures, reconciliation, sacraments are set forth, but there is no elaboration on the manifestations of the Spirit in the believer's life.

We find that today few theologians seem to have as yet reflected systematically on the data of recent experience in the

Work of the Holy Spirit

churches. Dr. Hendrikus Berkhof affirmed that "the many new insights in the field of Biblical theology with regard to the Holy Spirit have not yet found their way to systematic theology, let alone to the pulpit and life of the Church. The efforts of many theologians are needed to fill what is more or less a vacuum in the dogmatics of the contemporary churches." He suggests that one reason for this may be that the Spirit is self-effacing (John 14:26), and "hides himself in Christ, in the operations of the Church, and the lives of individuals." [1]

We note too that the Church has always been confronted with "enthusiasts" who have claimed the guidance of the Spirit for all kinds of excesses. Theologians of the traditional Churches have, therefore, been sensitive to any loosening of the ties between the Spirit and the historical Christ or between the Spirit and institutional church life. In modern times a certain kind of theological liberalism has been rejected because it seemed a mere extension of the human spirit and lacked a Christocentric foundation.

Three theologians of our times have drawn attention to the need for greater openness to the potential of the Holy Spirit in the life of the Church.

Dr. Karl Barth warns the contemporary Church against identifying the Holy Spirit with the Church. "As a foolish Church presupposes His presence and action in its own existence, in its offices and sacraments, ordinations, consecrations, and absolutions, so a foolish theology presupposes the Holy Spirit . . . Only where the Spirit is sighed, cried, and prayed for does he become present and newly active." [2] Dr. Barth also alerted the Church to the need for its being a creative community of the Spirit. "The Christian community can and must be the scene of many human activities which are new and supremely astonishing to many of its own members as well as to the world around because they rest on an endowment with extraordinary capacities." The outpouring of the Spirit bestows upon Christians "gifts and lights and powers." Dr. Barth continues: "Where these are lacking, there is reason to ask whether in pride or sloth the community as such has perhaps evaded this endowment, thus falsifying its relationship to its Lord, making it a dead relationship because a nominal and not a real relationship." [3]

Dr. Emil Brunner has written that "the operation of the Holy Spirit is not confined to bearing witness to us of Christ. Rather is He borne witness to by the Apostles as creative power, that produces new life, new will, new feelings, new spiritual, psychological, and even physical power."[4] He also states that "we ought to face the New Testament witness with sufficient candour to admit that in this pneuma which the Ecclesia was conscious of possessing, there lie forces of an extra-rational kind mostly lacking among us Christians today." He adds that theology is ill-equipped to deal with this realm of the dynamic and supralogical, for "theology has to do with the logos and therefore is only qualified to deal with matters that are in some way logical, not with the dynamic in its a-logical characteristics. Therefore, the Holy Ghost has always been more or less the stepchild of theology and the dynamism of the Spirit a bug-bear for theologians; on the other hand, theology through its unconscious intellectualism has often proved a significant restrictive influence, stifling the operations of the Holy Ghost, or at least their full creative manifestations."[5] Dr. Brunner concludes that "The miracle of Pentecost, and all that is included under the concept of the charismata — the gift of the Spirit — must not be soft-pedaled from motives of a theological Puritanism."[6]

We believe that the Holy Spirit is witnessing to the Church that it should be "praying and sighing" for his ministry and manifestations, but too often the charismatic dimension is being reduced to the level of psychological dynamics and dismissed as an emotional aberration.

Dr. Paul Tillich, reflecting on the "Spirit-movement" says that "Spirit-movements find it difficult to defend themselves against this alliance of ecclesiastical and psychological critics." He goes on: "This whole part of the present system is a defense of the ecstatic manifestations of the Spiritual Presence against its ecclesiastical critics; in this defense, the whole New Testament is the most powerful weapon. Yet, this weapon can be used legitimately only if the other partner in the alliance — the psychological critics — is also rejected or at least put into proper perspective."[7] Dr. Tillich is calling for an openness on the part of the Church to let God speak anew, but he also has a warning for those who overindulge in such activities. "At the same time, Paul resists any tendency that would permit ecstasy to disrupt structure. The classical expression of this is given in the first letter to the Corinthians where Paul speaks of the gifts of the Spirit and rejects ecstatic speaking in tongues if it produces chaos and disrupts the community, the emphasis on personal ecstatic experiences if they produce *hubris* (pride), and the other

Work of the Holy Spirit

charismata (gifts of the Spirit) if they are not subjected to *agape* (love)."[8]

From theological comments such as these we learn that historically the Church has been in danger of swinging to one of two extremes when it finds itself baffled by contemporary problems. Some who are conscious of the lack of spiritual power will seek a kind of ecstasy through the excitement of charismatic experience, through experiments with psychic research, and through various counterfeit "spiritual" movements, even as others are seeking an instant mysticism through drugs. On the other hand some become less and less tolerant of any spiritual reality and place increasing emphasis on the secular which absorbs all their gifts and energies. We are aware of these tendencies in the life of the Church today.

The committee would, therefore, call on the Church to undertake a new and creative theological exploration concerning the person and work of the Holy Spirit.

PSYCHOLOGICAL DIMENSIONS

In view of the particular relevance of psychology to the phenomena under consideration the committee offers the report of the Sub-committee on the Psychological Dimensions with editorial abridgement.

To avoid unnecessary footnotes bibliographical references are printed immediately following "A More Detailed Study of Relevant Psychological Literature" in the Appendix.

A Summary

The task of making a critical examination and evaluation of the charismatic movement in the Presbyterian Church is bewildering, for psychological and sociological theories are in conflict as to its origin, the reasons people participate, and the nature and origin of the charismatic gifts themselves.

Most of the so-called scientific studies and evaluations are based upon psychological models which either (a) assume at the outset that such states are pathological, or (b) have been prepared subjectively without following normally accepted controls; so as to make them almost meaningless from a research standpoint. For this reason, only theories supported or refuted by research data have been considered in this report. One of the more comprehensive studies reviewed by the subcommittee was conducted by Gerlach and Hine (1967, 1968). In a well-designed and controlled study they found that there is no empirical evidence to support theories that such a movement occurs because of the (a) social disorganization, (b) economic deprivation, or (c) psychological maladjustments or personality characteristics that predispose an individual to join a movement. Older psychological explanations of glossolalia as a concomitant of schizophrenia or hysteria have been found to be no longer defensible or acceptable in the light of recent socio-cultural and psychological data.

Many opinions and judgments have been rendered about the charismatic experience by persons with only superficial knowledge of the phenomena.

From its investigation of the psychological character and dimensions of the charismatic movement, the subcommittee has reached conclusions that are similar to those of many other observers and scholars who have engaged in first-hand evaluation. The first conclusion affirms that Pentecostals generally, whether they are from the classic Pentecostal denominations or the historic mainline Protestant denominations, are essentially well-adjusted and productive members of society. There is a paucity of empirical research relative to the charismatic gifts as they relate to the movement, however, the most current evidence available indicates no justification for making a sweeping generalization that participants in the movement are maladjusted individuals, emotionally unstable, or emotionally deprived.

The assumption has been made that suggestibility plays an important role in the practice of glossolalia. A popular opinion, reiterated by several individuals giving testimony before the committee, is that group hypnosis plays an important role in the movement and that those who are involved tend to be submissive and suggestible. Exactly the contrary has been documented by Gerlach and Hine (1967) who report that twenty-three percent of the participants in their study experienced the infilling of the Holy Spirit and spoke with tongues for the first time when they were alone. Individual committee members heard the testimony of several persons who had the experience of infilling with speaking in tongues long before they had contacted a charismatic group, attended a Pentecostal meeting, or associated with participants in the movement. Further contradictory evidence has been developed by Vivier (1960) a South African psychiatrist who has completed one of the most extensive studies of Pentecostal Glossolalia to date.

The opinion of some that participants in the movement exhibit a higher level of neuroticism, unadaptive anxiety reactions, a higher degree of susceptibility to suggestion or hysteria, or that charismatic meetings foster such behavior, has not been documented.[9] The data indicate that participants in the movement are emotionally and psychologically quite similar to the normal church population and to their occupational identity group.

One of the most noteworthy aspects of the charismatic movement is the keen interest directed toward its psychological dimensions, particularly from nonparticipants. It might even be said in this regard that since the charismatic dimension is considered by some to be no longer of theological or religious import, it may be discussed only as a psychological phenomenon.

Cognitive and Affective Relationships

Longtime conflicts have existed between the domains of cognitive and affective religious experience. An interesting history and documentation of this conflict as it relates to the Pentecostal movement is to be found in the writings of Father Kilian McDonnell, O.S.B.[10]

McDonnell, after years of direct observation and study, has concluded, "It should be stated unambiguously that the essential Pentecostal reality has nothing to do with emotional elevation." (McDonnell, 1970, p. 39.)

Father Edward O'Connor, a trained theologian with extensive experience among Catholic Pentecostals, has stated that, "The experience is not produced by emotion, it does not consist in emotion, and its chief and characteristic effects are not emotional." (McDonnell, 1970, p. 39.)

The committee has found, as have other such investigative groups in many other denominations, that it is extremely difficult to evaluate objectively the movement because of the negative public image of Pentecostalism. This negative image is projected through clergy and laymen alike and from those of the behavioral professions as well. Commenting on this problem in the Roman Catholic Church, Father McDonnell has stated, ". . . there are vast areas of the Pentecostal world where the public image is not reflective of the Pentecostal realities . . . for vast areas of the Pentecostal world there is a basic falsity about the public image. . . ." (McDonnell, 1970, p. 37.) However, for the general American public such behavior as speaking in tongues, prophesying, and interpretation are socially unacceptable ways of behaving, regardless of how authentic the manifestations might be.

The Fear of Religious Experience

The fear of religious experience further clouds the evaluation of the movement. "The majority of Christians in the main-line churches feel threatened by the kind of religious experience typified by Pentecostalism. And to judge while under the stress of fear is to almost preclude an objective judgment." (McDonnell, 1970, p. 37.)

Commenting that a healthy skepticism of religious experience is in order, Father McDonnell goes on to say, "But a deep fear of religious experience, with the consequent complete rejection of religious experience as hysteria, can lead to another kind of religious superficiality. And the alternative to an experience-oriented faith need not be its complete rejection, but an integration of the experiential into the total religious approach, with the experiential taking a subordinate role. But as long as an exaggerated fear of religious experience typifies one's outlook an objective evaluation of Pentecostalism is not possible." (McDonnell, 1970, p. 38.)

A Major Misconception

The Committee has noted the attention and preoccupation with "speaking in tongues." Tongues obviously play an important role in the movement. However, it appears from the committee's study that this preoccupation is a gross misconception of the real issue. Indeed, the main issue may not be the matter of certain charismatic gifts or experiences but the experience of God's power and presence in the life of the individual through the *gift* of the Spirit. McDonnell clarifies the issue in his statement, "Catholic and Protestant neo-Pentecostals do not come together specifically to pray in tongues. They are disturbed by neither the presence nor absence of tongues in a given prayer meeting. The issue in Pentecostalism is not tongues, but fullness of life in the Holy Spirit, openness to the power of the Spirit, and the exercise of all gifts of the Spirit." (McDonnell, 1970, p. 39.)

Kevin Ranaghan, instructor in theology of the faculty of St.

Mary's College, has articulated the experience in another way: "As each of us learned of what the other was doing, we rejoiced to see that in each case our testimony was not about tongues; not even primarily about the Holy Spirit. But wherever we went our talk was about Jesus Christ and the Power of his saving love to transform men and men's world." (McDonnell, 1970, p. 44.)

McDonnell identifies a major issue in his statement that:

"The very nature of the gifts of the Spirit, whether tongues, prophecy, interpretation or discernment of spirits, makes it difficult to arrive at an objective judgment. One can study the gifts of the Spirit from a psychological, sociological, economic point of view. All these approaches will tell one something about the gifts and the person who exercises them. However, the ultimate spiritual reality eludes all of these avenues of investigation. The gifts are spiritual gifts and, in their ultimate significance, they can only be understood spiritually. St. Paul said quite clearly that the things of the Spirit would not be understood, and because they would not be understood, would not be received. 'The unspiritual man does not receive the things of the Spirit of God, for they are folly to him and he is not able to understand them because they are spiritually discerned' (1 Cor 2:14). The unspiritual man who does not receive the things of the Spirit is not, in Paul's mind, the pagan. St. Paul is talking about the believer, who judges according to the flesh. So there will be good men, men of conscience, who will oppose the things of the Spirit and not receive them because they judge them according to the flesh. This makes it difficult to arrive at any kind of public consensus on Pentecostalism which is both objective and capable of sustaining a theological scrutiny." (McDonnell, 1970, p. 40.)

The sub-committee warns that it will be a dark and tragic day in the life of Christianity if psychological norms are to become the criteria by which the truth or the untruth of religious experience is judged. Psychological insight has enriched, deepened, and humbled our knowledge of ourselves beyond measure; but, when it is asked for a decisive answer to the question of whether a man has or has not experienced the living Christ it is an aborted and inappropriate use of the science. To ask it for its own dimension of understanding is valid; to use it as one instrument, among others, to lighten the darkness is appropriate; but to ask it to assume the role of arbiter and judge in the sphere of religion is to ask it to do something which is an affront to psychology as a science and a scandal to religion.

Mental Health and the Holy Spirit

The Holy Spirit is the dimension in the life of the believer that makes the concepts of traditional Christian theology operational. It is difficult for the psychological precepts in the Scripture to be personally activated without the Holy Spirit in the life of the individual. It is commonly assumed that the Christian experience is an integrating experience; however, the process of regeneration does not necessarily eliminate any personality difficulty an individual has. A disoriented life is not magically brought into focus when a man becomes a Christian. Nor does the infilling of the Holy Spirit necessarily bring such change. Such experience does not necessarily change a disoriented neurotic into a well-integrated extrovert. It seems that important data are being ignored if persons are being told that after either becoming a Christian or being filled with the Holy Spirit they now have a foolproof technique to pull themselves together.

There are many Christians in every congregation who are scarcely models of a healthy personality. This is likewise true of those who have had a dynamic infilling of the Holy Spirit. A major step has been accomplished however with the so-called empowering of the individual through the infilling of the Holy Spirit. Whether or not the potential power available through the Holy Spirit is actualized depends upon several human factors. Cooperation is necessary. After a profound experience with the Holy Spirit, a new life does not unfold automatically or spontaneously. It is a life that must be cultivated by teaching, by fellowship, by discipline, and this is what fosters good mental health. A Christian has the mental health resources not available to the non-believer. In summary, the potential for psychic integration is provided by regeneration and infilling of the Holy Spirit, but that potential must be utilized by the individual himself or no significant personality change is likely to occur.

It must be recognized that individuals with neurotic personalities are frequently drawn to the more dramatic religious movements. In a charismatic prayer meeting one may observe a disturbed individual and may note bizarre manifestations or statements coming from such an individual. Disturbed individuals also participate in the regular organized activities of the Church. Therefore, it is suggested that the group and the movement not be evaluated on the basis of the problems of a few of its members who come seeking help and advice. This would be akin to

Work of the Holy Spirit

criticizing the hospital or the psychiatrist for the problem brought by the patient. Although disturbed individuals occasionally may be attracted to the charismatic movement, there is no evidence that they exist in greater proportion in the movement under question than in the organized church. If a psychologically sick individual experiences a charismatic gift, it neither validates nor invalidates the gift. A person may be emotionally disturbed: this however does not prove his religious experience to be imaginary. If one sought to determine the validity of religious insight negatively or positively on the basis of a neurotic grasp of the situation, the task would be a hopeless one. It is better by far to admit freely that unbalanced persons are often among us in religious quests and to learn to live with them humbly and as lovingly as possible, recognizing that in all of us there are layers of unhealth which were perhaps prevented from becoming burdens to us through no merits of our own, but because of some good fortune in our genes or in the environment into which we were born.

Overview of Psychological Findings
The committee reviewed and examined data from various sources. Many of the findings and conclusions were subsequently found to be most ably summarized by McDonnell, who stated:
"Some scholars take a dim view of the psychological make-up of glossolalics. The standard treatise on tongue-speaking is by George Cutten who contended (in 1927) that glossolalia is related to schizophrenia and hysteria. Lapsley and Simpson (in 1964), while denying that glossolalics can be considered mentally ill in any clinical sense, still consider them 'uncommonly disturbed.' In their judgment, tongues fill the psychic function of reducing conflict brought on by a "developmental 'fixation' at an early age in their relationship with parental figures" and is a 'dissociative expression of truncated personality development.' William W. Wood (in 1965) came to the conclusion that 'Pentecostalism attracts uncertain, threatened, inadequately organized persons with strong motivation to reach a state of satisfactory interpersonal relatedness and personal integrity.' In an unpublished paper, Andrew D. Lester noted that glossolalic groups he studied manifested childish megalomania, had weak egos, confused identities, high levels of anxiety, and were generally unstable personalities. In a survey of the pertinent

literature (in 1968) George J. Jennings came to the conclusion that 'most scholars and observers maintain that glossolalists are usually characterized with some personality deficiency.'"

"Many researchers would not only reject these negative judgments, but also would reject the assertion that any such consensus as Jennings postulates exists. Taking up the conclusions of Cutten that glossolalia tends to be related to schizophrenia and hysteria, Alexander Alland (in 1961) countered that the socio-cultural data no longer support such a view. The members of the Negro Pentecostal church that Alland studied were well adjusted to their social environment and, by the norms of socially acceptable behavior, normal in every respect except for speaking in tongues. In 1939 Anton Boisen wrote that: 'the rapid growth of eccentric religious cults in recent years may be regarded as a direct result of the shared strain due to the economic depression,' but he found no mental illness among the people he studied. Indeed he found several disturbed individuals who found the Pentecostal experience psychologically beneficial. E. Mansell Pattison (in 1964) rejected the position that economic deprivation is a necessary factor in explaining growth. Pattison also found that glossolalics are neither contentious nor emotionally maladjusted. In an early study Lincoln Vivier (in 1960) showed that Pentecostals scale lower on suggestibility than non-Pentecostals; in a later study (1968) he asserted that 'glossolalia, as practiced in its religious context, is manifested in normal, non-neurotic persons.' Vivier found that glossolalia brings a change in the ego complex which 'tends toward the more mature and tends, furthermore, to add quality and enrichment of feeling and depth of meaningfulness.' Speaking of Pentecostals within the historic churches, A. W. Sadler (in 1964) contended that the psychic force of glossolalics may not be neurotic but rather the unconscious expressing itself positively in a creative way."

"Anxiety and tension, Vivier says, are obliquely associated with glossolalia, that is, not with the practice but with the frequency of tongues. One of the most interesting studies is that of the Jewish sociologist, Nathan Gerrard (1966, 1968), who observed a snake-handling Pentecostal church, using a conventional denomination as a control group. He concluded that there is very little difference between the two groups with regard to mental health, 'but whatever differences there are seem to indicate the serpent-handlers are a little more 'normal' than members of the conventional denomination.' The list of studies finding good the psychological health among Pentecostals could be extended. These studies and yet unpublished material show that to argue the dubious character of the Pentecostal experience or persons on the basis of psychological data is to argue from very shaky premises." (McDonnell, 1968, p. 201–202.)

HEALING, EXORCISM, AND OCCULT PRACTICES

Healing

A ministry of healing is validated on three grounds: it is scriptural; it reflects the reality that personality is composed of an inter-relatedness of mind, body, and spirit; it affirms the reality of the Living God in human affairs.

Even a casual review of the gospels brings undeniable evidence of the central importance of healing in the life of the Savior. Few images of Jesus are as poignant and unforgettable as that one in which he stands before Peter's house in the dusk, welcoming all manner of sickness to his healing touch. "That evening, at sundown, they brought to him all who were sick or possessed with demons. . . . And he healed many who were sick with various diseases, and cast out many demons." (Mark 1:32, 34) The apostles later went forth to heal the sick.

In our age of psychological awareness, we have rediscovered the delicate balance between body and spirit. We now know that man must be seen as a totality, not as though he consists of separate compartments. The best practice of medicine today no longer treats our bodies as though they were mechanical entities unrelated to what we feel or believe or dream. Most thoughtful people among us now fully recognize the profound interconnections which exist between illness and one's total life experience. This inter-dependence of the varying dimensions of life is at the base of our newly-found appreciation of the power of the spirit to effect positively the physical and emotional aspects of our experience.

The active presence of God in Christ is clearly apparent to those who have found that by prayer they are healed. Many who have participated with a new seriousness in an intercessory prayer group and seen the results of their prayers in various forms of guidance, comfort, and actual healings, are brought to a new realization of God's living reality; for they know that it is only he who heals and guides.

As we have recovered our confidence in the relevance of the spiritual life to our sickness, it is natural that we should find among us individuals from the laity, as well as the clergy, who feel themselves called to a special ministry of healing. Sometimes these persons pray for others with the laying on of hands and the anointing of oil, as did the apostles and elders of the first century, and sometimes they do not. Invariably, however, they are people who find by experience that remarkable influences of healing flow through them toward the sick. The rate of recovery is accelerated. The efficacy of medicine is increased. The disappearance of symptoms is observed; and most importantly, the faith of all who are involved in this process of healing intercession is strengthened.

Many questions are raised. Why does God endow some persons with this healing power more richly than others? Is there not a danger of an elitism of the spirit, promoting a divisive self-righteousness? Does not the practice of the laying on of hands engender a certain magical expectation that it is the intercessor who heals? What about the prayers for healing which are seemingly answered in the negative?

There are always dangers of misuse and misrepresentation in the gifts of the Spirit. Fraud in such matters is an ever present possibility. Where it is evident, however, that in fact by prayer and faith an individual has been undeniably assisted toward health and wholeness of life, one can only conclude that there is a valid basis for the healing ministry which has blessed that person. If one keeps the focus of prayer on the Healing Christ and offers oneself to his spirit for the blessing of others in whatever way he chooses to do, the likelihood of misuse is surely minimized.

In these matters there are always questions we cannot answer and mysteries we cannot fathom. Our task as Christians is not to know but to obey.

We would wish to make it perfectly clear that in commending an active ministry of intercession to the Church, welcoming God's gift of healing to whomsoever he gives it in love and humility, we are not suggesting the healing ministry as a substitute for medicine.

Medical science represents one of God's greatest gifts to mankind. It is an evidence of his providential care for us that we have been led by dedicated men and women in medicine to alleviate the burden of pain and misery so dramatically in this century of appalling violence, and we would affirm God's healing power in all the channels of his grace, including that abundant vessel we call medicine.

Exorcism

Another dimension in the discussion of the work of the Holy Spirit in the Church today is found in the phenomenon known as exorcism, that ancient rite by which satanic forces called demons, including Satan himself on occasion, are called forth from their possessive clutch upon an individual life.

There are three accounts of special significance in the life of Jesus when he encounters this demonic force. The accounts are particularly memorable because the Gospels record them in some detail.

One is the dreadful experience of testing which Jesus underwent in the Judean wilderness. He must have told the experience to his followers in vivid terms because they remembered it so well. They had no other way in which they could have learned of it because he was alone. There was no one else present to witness the occasion. Jesus clearly thought of it as a crucial turning point in his time of trials, for the nature of his testing reflects a basic questioning of his destiny, his vocation, and his identity.

The other two occasions which are especially noteworthy are the times when Jesus meets an epileptic boy brought to him by the father of the child, and the unforgettably vivid encounter between Jesus and the madman from the tombs of the Gadarene country.

The Gospels tell us about "unclean spirits," the disciples are sent forth to "cast out demons," among other commissions given to them. John's Gospel tells us that the devil is "the Father of Lies," and that he entered into Judas.

How are we to interpret these evidences in the life of Jesus of his recognition of demonic spirits? Shall we dismiss the problem by saying it is only a question of terminology? Or, shall we allegorize the occasions of demonic possession? Or, shall we conclude that the accounts represent a cultural limitation, reflecting the limited knowledge of the period? Or, shall we say flatly that what the New Testament calls demon possession we would probably call neuroses or psychotic states of being? And in the wilderness, shall we say that the adversary whom Jesus met in the story is a personification of evil?

Each of these conclusions is possible, and each represents a facet of the many-sided problem of demon possession; but what no amount of demythologizing can do is to discount the possibility that Jesus saw a dark reality which we often miss in our devotion to rationality, important as reason clearly is for any mature understanding of the Christian faith.

Is it not conceivable that beyond the testing of his nature and the uses of his powers, Jesus saw something more? Can we not assume that beneath the outward appearance of illness and psychoses, Jesus sometimes perceived a malignant force at work whose purpose was ever to bring sickness where there was health, division where there was wholeness, and death where there was life? Does it not seem likely that the one in whom truth and life were united in an unprecedented singleness of will should be extraordinarily perceptive about that which is the enemy of truth and life? Might it not be true that Jesus saw illness as clearly and accurately as we see it, both emotional and physical, but that he saw something else in some instances, a shadow behind the divisiveness, an adversary, an anti-Christ?

If the implication of these questions be true, it is of great importance that we observe the calm, unquestioned authority with which Jesus meets that malignant presence. There is never any sign of struggle in which there is a doubt about who the victor will be. With assurance, Jesus commands, "Get thee behind me, Satan," and with utter simplicity, he restores the Gadarene man to his rightful mind, and heals the demonic boy. It is never a question of dualistic division between the forces of darkness and the legions of light. Jesus is the Lord and wherever he meets that which is contrary to his love and Truth, he quietly overcomes it, as do his disciples. "Lord," they said on their return, "even the demons were subject to us." And since that time, there have been others among us who, by the power of the Holy Spirit, have also claimed to have the power of the Holy Spirit to cast out demons.

However, there are grave dangers in such practices. The history of the church is filled with those who have used Satan as a convenient escape from responsibility. To attribute angry and hostile feelings to the devil is to be freed from having to face the truth within oneself about where those feelings come from and what one must do to overcome them. To blame the adversary for the blight and burden of poverty, militarism, and racism is to cut the nerve of reformation and progress.

Moreover, to be looking for the devil in every situation of life is to commit oneself to an unhealthy quagmire of blame and

Work of the Holy Spirit

judgment in personal relationships which presently alienates one from the human family, with the result that the devil has only served the devil, "and the last state is worse that the first."

These dangers are so real and prevalent that there appears to be little usefulness served in encouraging any practice which would excuse human faults by blaming a personal devil. The belief, though representative of a reality in the experience of contemporary man, as well as the men of the New Testament, is so subject to distortion and misuse that wisdom would seem to encourage the most careful approach. There is ample explanation in the complexities and conflicts in all of us for the evil we do. Yet no man who has looked long and hard at the intractable, abysmal depth of human iniquity can deny that there is at least a shadow of an evil reality beyond human life.

Perhaps the only practical criterion we can follow is that of hard and constant day-labor against evil in all its multiplicity, personal and social, leaving the matter of its origin and nature to the mind of God.

Occult Practices

There are many phenomena of the occult today in which our people are engaged with varying degrees of commitment, among them being spiritualism, psychic communication between the living and the dead, astrology, horoscopes, and the like. It is not fair to lump all these phenomena under one heading. Psychic research is often a creditable, dignified pursuit, conducted by persons of integrity and responsibility. However, our purpose is simply to mention these areas as illustrative of the quest among us today for the reality of the spiritual order, and to observe that it can frequently become misdirected and possessive.

The only foundation on which we can judge such matters is on a practical basis of what fruits appear to issue from the activities involved, and what ground is in Scripture for the Christian's interest or participation in them.

Finally, it needs to be observed that the very fact of the rise of increasing interest in the occult today is a revelation of a spiritual vacuum in the Church which has given rise to occultist practices.

GUIDELINES

We believe the Church needs to pray for a sensitivity to see the manifestations of the Holy Spirit in our world today. We are not unmindful that the problems of discrimination between the true and the fraudulent are considerable, but we must not allow the problems to paralyze our awareness to his presence, nor should we permit our fear of the unknown and the unfamiliar to close our minds against being surprised by grace. We know the misuse of mystical experience is an ever-present possibility, but that is no reason to preclude its appropriate use. We believe that those who are newly endowed with gifts and perceptions of the Spirit have an enthusiasm and joy to give and we also believe that those who rejoice in our traditions of having all things done in "decency and order" have a sobering depth to give. We therefore plead for a mutuality of respect and affection.

In facing the issues raised by Neo-Pentecostal experiences, we plead for a spirit of openness and love. We commend to the attention of the Church the disciplines of 1 Corinthians 13, as well as the 20th Chapter of The Westminster Confession on Christian Liberty and Liberty of Conscience. The emphasis of The Confession of 1967 on Reconciliation is central to the attitude we seek for all parties to these problems in the Church. Without an active, calm, objective and loving understanding of our brother's religious experience, however different from one's own, reconciliation is impossible. Therefore we urge the reading of The Confession of 1967 on the theme of Reconciliation.

The criteria by which we judge the validity of another's religious experience must ever be its compatibility with the mind and spirit of our Lord Jesus Christ, as we know them in the New Testament. If the consequence and quality of a reported encounter of the Holy Spirit be manifestly conducive to division, self-righteousness, hostility, exaggerated claims of knowledge and power, then the experience is subject to serious question. However, when the experience clearly results in new dimensions of faith, joy, and blessings to others, we must conclude that this is "what the Lord hath done" and offer him our praise.

Guidelines for All

1. Be tolerant and accepting of those whose Christian experiences differ from your own.

2. Continually undergird and envelop all discussions, conferences, meetings, and persons in prayer.

3. Be open to new ways in which God by his Spirit may be speaking to the Church.

4. Recognize that even though spiritual gifts may be abused, this does not mean that they should be prohibited.

5. Remember that like other new movements in church history, Neo-Pentecostalism may have a valid contribution to make to the ecumenical Church.

For Ministers Who Have Had Neo-Pentecostal Experiences

1. Combine with your Neo-Pentecostalism a thorough knowledge of, and adherence to, United Presbyterian polity and tradition. Remember your charismatic influence will, in large part, be earned by your loving and disciplined use of the charismatic, and by your conduct as a pastor to *all* your congregation, as well as by your participation as a responsible presbyter.

2. Seek a deepening and continued friendship with your clergy colleagues within and without the Neo-Pentecostal experience.

3. Remember your ordination vows, particularly the vow to "approve the government and discipline of the United Presbyterian Church" and your promise to be "A friend among your comrades in ministry, working with them, subject to the ordering of God's word and Spirit." [11]

4. Avoid the temptation to force your personal views and experiences on your brethren. Seek to understand those whose spiritual experiences differ from your own.

5. Seek to grow in your skills as a Biblical exegete, a systematic theologian, and as a preacher in *all* the fullness of the gospel.

For Ministers Who Have Not Had Neo-Pentecostal Experiences

1. Remember the lessons of church history when God's people re-discover old truths; that the process is often disquieting, that it usually involves upheaval, change, and a degree of suffering, misunderstanding, and sometimes even persecution.

2. Seek first-hand knowledge of what Neo-Pentecostalism means to those who have experienced it. Avoid a judgment until this first-hand knowledge is obtained (i.e., by attending and evaluating their prayer meetings, etc.). Then evaluate the observations as a Christian, a United Presbyterian minister, and as a sympathetic, conscientious pastor. Keep an openness to Scriptural teaching regarding the charismatic gifts.

3. When speaking in tongues occurs, seek to know what it means to the speaker in his private devotional life, what it means when used for intercessory prayer, especially in group worship.

We should be aware that speaking in tongues is a minor "gift of the Spirit" for many of those who have had Neo-Pentecostal experiences.

4. Seek to know the meaning of the other "gifts of the Spirit" in the Neo-Pentecostal experience, such as the utterance of wisdom, of knowledge; the gift of faith, of healing, of working of miracles, of prophesying.

5. Keep in mind that Neo-Pentecostals may be prone to neglect formal exegesis, systematic theology, and adherence to tradition and polity of our denomination. They may, at times, tend toward a new form of legalism, and may consequently be in need of loving guidance from their peers, or from their pastor, or from their session. Like many of the laity within our fellowship, they too frequently need to understand the place and authority of their session. They may also, at times, tend to be over-enthusiastic concerning their experiences, to believe that their experiences should be duplicated by every sincere Christian, to limit their fellowship in the church to those who have had similar experiences so that pastoral guidance is sometimes needed to bring their prayer meetings under the authority of the session and open to all interested members of their congregation.

For Laity Who Have Had Neo-Pentecostal Experiences

1. Remember to combine with your Neo-Pentecostal enthusiasm a thorough knowledge of and adherence to the United Presbyterian form of church government. Neo-Pentecostalism is new in our tradition. Consult with your minister (or ministers) and if he (they) has not also had your experience, help him to know what it is, what it means to you, what it does for you. Urge him to attend your group meetings.

2. Pray that the Spirit brings understanding, and that he may help you to maintain empathy with your colleagues and all your fellow United Presbyterians. Remember that all members of any United Presbyterian congregation are under the authority of the session, welcome any opportunity granted you to interpret your experience to the elders, or to the session itself.

3. Strive for a scholarly knowledge of Scriptural content in combination with your spiritual experiences. Strive to integrate your experiences with the theological traditions of our Church.

4. Avoid undisciplined and undiplomatic enthusiasm in your eagerness to share your experiences with others. Resist the temptation to pose as an authority on spiritual experiences.

Work of the Holy Spirit

Failure in this area often causes your fellow United Presbyterians to accuse you of spiritual pride.

5. Strive to keep your prayer meetings, etc., open to all members of your congregation. When non-Neo-Pentecostals do attend, discuss with them the content of the meeting with an interpretation of the significance of the content to Neo-Pentecostals.

6. Seek attendance at your meetings by your ministers and members of your session.

7. Remember that there are many types of Christian experiences, which lead to spiritual growth. Neo-Pentecostal experience is only *one* of these.

8. Accept every valid opportunity to become personally involved in the work and mission of your own congregation. Let the results of Neo-Pentecostal experience be seen in the outstanding quality of your church membership. Be an obvious and enthusiastic supporter of your congregation, its pastor and session; of your Presbytery, your synod, the General Assembly, and the mission of each. This may well be the most effective witness you can offer to the validity and vitality of your Neo-Pentecostal experience. Strive to integrate your experience with the theological traditions of our Church.

9. It is not necessary to carry all the Pentecostal baggage.

10. Keep your Neo-Pentecostal experience in perspective. No doubt it has caused you to feel that you are a better Christian. Remember that this does not mean that you are better than other Christians, but that you are, perhaps, a better Christian than you were before.

For Laity Who Have Not Had Neo-Pentecostal Experiences

1. In our Reformed tradition, we believe God is constantly seeking to reform and renew his Church, including the United Presbyterian Church. The advent of Neo-Pentecostalism into our denomination may be one aspect of reformation and renewal. In any case, pray that God may make known to you your own place in the process of reformation and renewal.

2. Should some fellow members of your congregation be brought into Neo-Pentecostalism, accept this development matter-of-factly. Should it happen to edify, thank God.

3. Be aware of the tendency to condemn the Pentecostals and Neo-Pentecostalism. If such is your reaction, restrain the tendency and seek to observe personally the Neo-Pentecostals in

their prayer meetings, in your congregation, and in the mission of your church. Examine scriptural teaching about this. Pray about it. Discuss your concern with your minister. Remember that all members of any United Presbyterian congregation are under the authority of the session.

4. Do not be disturbed if this experience has not been given to you. This does *not* mean that you are an inferior Christian. Your function in the work and mission of your congregation may call for other gifts. Each Christian is a unique member of the body of Christ.

5. Should your minister be a Neo-Pentecostal, accept the fact calmly and affectionately. Discuss the matter with him. Help him to be mindful of the spiritual needs of *all* his congregation, to be a pastor and teacher to all, and encourage him in his preaching to present the fullness of all aspects of the gospel. Remember that your minister is the moderator of your session and that it is the elders on the session who have the responsibility to consult formally with your minister but that he is a member of, and under the authority of, the presbytery.

For Presbyteries

1. Refer prayerfully and thoughtfully to the other sections of these Guidelines.

2. Remember the pastoral responsibilities of the presbytery toward ministers, sessions, and congregations within the presbytery, particularly toward those whose spiritual experience may involve Neo-Pentecostalism.

3. While the General Assembly, in accepting the report of this Committee, takes the position of "openness" regarding the Neo-Pentecostal movement within our denomination, the presbytery must decide whether any given instance involving a minister or a congregation is for the edification and the purity of its area of the Church.

4. If there is divisiveness involved in a particular Neo-Pentecostal situation, make as careful an evaluation as possible, remembering that there are other kinds of issues which also divide our fellowships. Sometimes tensions and conflicts may result in the edification and greater purity of the Church, and need therefore to be wisely handled by the judicatories of the United Presbyterian Church.

5. When a Presbytery must assume its responsibility with regard to Neo-Pentecostalism, and deal with it administratively,

Work of the Holy Spirit

we urge Presbyteries so involved to gather not only factual but *interpretative* data. This should include first-hand evidence about Neo-Pentecostalism; its meaning for those involved in it; and its significance for the mission of the particular congregation.

6. Where a minister is following some Neo-Pentecostal practices, he should be counseled, if need be, to preach the fullness of the gospel (not only his Neo-Pentecostal interpretation of it), to minister to the needs of all his congregation, and as a presbyter to grow in understanding of our polity in the mission of the particular presbytery. Often ministers in difficulties, growing out of the Neo-Pentecostal experience, are newly ordained and are therefore in special need of the guidance and friendship of older presbyters.

7. Presbyteries may also be faced with a situation where there is a Neo-Pentecostal group within a congregation whose minister, or whose session, or both, may be hostile to or ignorant of Neo-Pentecostalism. Here we believe the presbytery has a pastoral responsibility to teach, mediate, and to guide in reconciliation.

8. Pray continuously for sensitivity to the will of, and the leading of, the Spirit.

For Sessions

1. Remember that in the United Presbyterian Church, the session is "charged with maintaining the spiritual government of the congregation, for which purpose it has power to inquire into the knowledge and Christian conduct of the members of the church. . . . to concert the best measures for promoting the spiritual interests of the congregation" (Form of Government, Chapter XI, Section 6 (41.06)). Thus it is the session which must decide whether or not Neo-Pentecostal practices are appropriate for the particular congregation. It is important that the session members be knowledgeable concerning Neo-Pentecostalism in regard to both its dangers and its potential contributions for the congregation's spiritual life and mission. The fact that Neo-Pentecostalism may be new and different is not in itself adequate reason for repression.

2. When members of a particular congregation are involved in Neo-Pentecostal experiences, the session of such congregation needs to gain, on the part of the elders belonging to that session, a first-hand understanding of the meaning of the experience not only to those involved in it but also for members of the

congregation outside Pentecostal experiences. This may be an excellent opportunity again to implement the spirit of reconciliation emphasized in our Confession of 1967.

3. If the minister is a Neo-Pentecostal, the elders should seek full understanding of what the experience means to him, their pastor. The elders should counsel with the pastor to maintain a balanced ministry to all members of the congregation.

4. Session members are reminded of the responsibility to maintain oversight of all groups within their own congregation.

RECOMMENDATIONS

1. That the report and appendices, which have received the unanimous approval of the committee, be received, that the guidelines be adopted, and that the entire report and appendices be printed in pamphlet form for distribution to local congregations, ministerial relations committees of judicatories, stated clerks, and judicatory executives.

2. That since the questions in the overtures have been given full consideration by the committee, the committee requests that it be discharged.

NOTES

1. *The Doctrine of the Holy Spirit*, p. 10.
2. *Evangelical Theology: An Introduction*, p. 58.
3. *Church Dogmatics*, Vol. IV, Part 2, p. 828.
4. *Dogmatics*, Vol. III, p. 15.
5. *The Misunderstanding of the Church*, pp. 48, 49.
6. *Dogmatics*, Vol. III, p. 16.
7. *Systematic Theology*, p. 118.
8. *Ibid.*, p. 117.
9. *See* Appendix "A Summary of Relevant Psychological Literature."
10. Father Kilian McDonnell is Director of the Institute for Ecumenical and Cultural Research, Collegeville, Minnesota. He was a member of a team of anthropologists who conducted a comprehensive in-depth study of the Pentecostal movement as a researcher and theologian. He has not received what classical Pentecostals call baptism in the Holy Spirit and does not speak in tongues. Quotations used by permission of Father McDonnell.
11. From *Overture F* (1969) amending ordination questions.

APPENDIX A. THE HOLY SPIRIT IN THE NEW TESTAMENT

The general topic assigned to this committee by the General Assembly is "The Work of the Holy Spirit." Our sub-committee was given the assignment to prepare an exegetical paper relating to the work of the Holy Spirit in the New Testament. Since this subject is very extensive (the Holy Spirit is mentioned — sometimes many times — in every book of the New Testament except 2 and 3 John), we have thought it best to concentrate our attention upon the following three themes: "The So-Called Baptism with the Holy Spirit," "Gifts of the Spirit," and "Speaking in Tongues."

We begin the paper with a brief overview, summarizing the role of the Holy Spirit in the Old and New Testaments. Then we present analyses of passages, chiefly from the Gospels and Acts, relating to the Holy Spirit in the life and ministry of Christ, with special attention being given to the prediction of John the Baptist that the Messiah would baptize with the Holy Spirit. This section is followed by a discussion of the teaching of Paul and the descriptive accounts in the Acts of the Apostles concerning the "Gifts of the Spirit," and "Speaking in Tongues." A concluding summary sets forth some of the main teachings related to our subject which we believe are most significant.

David E. Dilworth, Bruce M. Metzger

1. *The Holy Spirit in the Old Testament*

Both the Old and the New Testaments speak of the reality and activity of God's Spirit. In the Old Testament, the Spirit is described as the source of physical, intellectual, and moral life (Gen 1:2; Job 32:8; 33:4; 34:14f.; Ps. 104:30; 139:7). Besides passages that describe special gifts of the Spirit that were bestowed upon individuals — such as manual skill (Ex 31:3), wisdom (Num 27:18), strength (Judg 3:10; 1 Sam 11:6; 1 Chron 12:18) and prophetic frenzy (Num 11:24-29; 1 Sam 10:10; 19:23-24) — it is foretold that in the Messianic age God would pour out his Spirit upon his people (Isa 44:3; Ezek 36:27). In fact, the promise is given that God would pour out his Spirit on all flesh (Joel 2:28f.).

2. *The Holy Spirit in the New Testament*

In the New Testament the doctrine of the Spirit is greatly developed, particularly in connection with the person and work of Jesus. Besides referring to the miraculous conception of Jesus by the Holy Spirit (Matt 1:18-20) and the descent of the Spirit upon him at his baptism (Matt 3:16; Mk 1:10; Jn 1:32), the Gospel writers imply that Jesus' work is the work of the Spirit (Matt

12:28; Mk 3-29) and that Isaiah's prophecy (61:1) concerning the empowering of the Spirit finds its fulfillment in the mission and message of Jesus (Lk 4:18). In his teaching, Jesus promises the Spirit to his disciples when they are persecuted (Matt 10:20; Mk 13:11; Lk 12:12). According to the Fourth Gospel, the Holy Spirit, as Counselor or Advocate, is to be sent by the Father to teach and to guide Jesus' followers (Jn 14:26; 15:13).

Particularly in the Acts of the Apostles is frequent reference made to the Spirit — so much so that more than one expositor has suggested that a more appropriate title for the book might well be "The Acts of the Holy Spirit." The author stresses that the Church had its origin in the outpouring of the Spirit at Pentecost, in fulfillment of the oracle in the book of Joel (Acts 2:1-13; Joel 2:28f.). Those who carry on Jesus' work of preaching and healing are described as being "filled with the Spirit" (Acts 6:3, 5; 8; 7:55; 11:24). By the prompting of the Spirit, new areas of evangelistic work are opened; thus Philip (8:29, 39), Peter (10:19-20), Barnabas and Paul (13:2), and Paul and his companions (16:6-10) are guided by the Spirit to new areas of more extended service.

Whereas the book of Acts describes a variety of situations in which members of the early church felt and responded to the leading of the Spirit, it was the Apostle Paul who developed the doctrine of the Spirit. His special contribution is the recognition of the Spirit as the *characteristic sustaining, permanent power of the Christian life*. Paul uses a variety of expressions, referring interchangeably to the Spirit, the Spirit of Christ, the Spirit of the Lord, the Spirit of Jesus, and the Spirit of him who raised Jesus; also of being in Christ, being in the Spirit, having Christ in you, and having the Spirit. For Paul the possession of the Spirit is both the means of overcoming the power of sin in the flesh (Rom 8:1-5, 10-13) and a pledge or guarantee of complete redemption hereafter (2 Cor 1:22; 5:5).

THE SO-CALLED BAPTISM WITH THE HOLY SPIRIT

It should be observed that the expression, "baptism with the Holy Spirit," does not occur in the New Testament. The noun "baptism" is never so used. A few times the verb "baptize" is used in this connection with the Greek preposition *en*, which is translated in the R.S.V. "with" (Matt 3:11; Mark 1:8; Luke 3:16; Acts 1:5; 11:16). All of these refer to the same saying attributed to John the Baptist that the coming Messiah would "baptize with the Holy Spirit." The one other occurrence of the phrase is in 1 Cor

12:13, where it is stated that "by (Greek *en,*) one spirit we were all baptized into one body" (that is, the church).

In order to set in proper perspective the popular yet non-Biblical expression "baptism with (or, in) the Holy Spirit," it is necessary to examine passages in the New Testament that relate to the work of the Holy Spirit. We begin with the Synoptic Gospels.

A. The Synoptic Gospels

The majority of references to the Holy Spirit in the Synoptic Gospels relate the Spirit to the life and ministry of Jesus Christ. These include:

1. His conception in Mary by the Holy Spirit (Mt 1:18, 20; Luke 1:35).

2. His being blessed in the temple by Simeon who is inspired by the Holy Spirit.

3. The promise by John the Baptizer that Jesus would baptize with the Holy Spirit (Matt 3:11; Mark 1:8; Luke 3:16). The emphasis is on the superiority of Jesus' Spirit-baptism to the water-baptism of John. In Matthew and Luke the phrase "and with fire" is added; the probable reference is to the judgment-character of Jesus' ministry (cf. Luke 3:9, 17).

4. His Baptism and Temptation. The Spirit comes upon Jesus (Matt 3:16; Mark 1:10; Luke 3:22), drives (Mark 1:12) or leads (Matt 4:1, Luke 4:1) him into the wilderness. Following the temptation experience he returns "full of the Holy Spirit" (Luke 4:14).

5. His Ministry. Jesus ministered in the power of the Holy Spirit, particularly in casting out demons. He warned those who attribute the power to any other force (Luke 4:14, Matt 12:28-32, Mark 3:29, Luke 12:10).

6. His role as the Suffering Servant, anointed with the Spirit (Matt 12:18 — quoting Isaiah 42:1, 4).

7. There are two promises made by Jesus Christ to the disciples related to the Holy Spirit: (a) in the time of testing the Holy Spirit will guide them as to what to say (Matt 10:20, Mark 13:11, Luke 12:11-12); and (b) the Heavenly Father gives the Holy Spirit to the disciples more readily than an earthly father gives gifts to his children (Luke 11:13).

8. The few remaining references to the Holy Spirit in the Synoptic Gospels are: (a) the inspiration given David in the Psalms (Mark 12:36); (b) the Holy Spirit's relationship to John the Baptizer and his parents — (1) it is predicted by the angel to

Zechariah that John will be "filled with the Holy Spirit even from his mother's womb" (Luke 1:15), (2) Elizabeth is filled with the Spirit (Luke 1:41), (3) Zechariah is filled with the Spirit (Luke 1:67); (c) Jesus' final commission to his disciples: to "make disciples" and baptize in the name of the Trinity (probably the Evangelist's formulation) (Matt 28:19).

COMMENTS

1. It is quite amazing that the gospels, written from thirty to sixty years after the death and resurrection of Christ, should have so few sayings relating the Holy Spirit to *the disciples*. There is no mention of the gifts of the Spirit to them, of "tongues" as a sign of the Spirit, or of their seeking the fullness of the Spirit as something beyond their obedient faith in Jesus Christ. (One passage, Luke 24:49, does use "power" as a probable synonym for Holy Spirit, but the reception of the Spirit does not depend upon the disciples' seeking the Spirit, but upon God's promise, fulfilled at Pentecost.)

2. The Synoptic Evangelists explain the person and ministry of Jesus Christ primarily by reference to the Holy Spirit. It is by the Spirit that he is conceived, given power at baptism, and is able to perform miracles. His greatest gift to his followers is the Holy Spirit. It is not difficult to see how natural it was, therefore, for Luke in the Acts and Paul in his letters to develop the theme that the same Holy Spirit creates, guides, and empowers the Church, the body of Christ.

3. In each of the Synoptic Gospels it is stated (Matt 3:11; Mark 1:8; Luke 3:16) that the Messiah will baptize with the Holy Spirit. The implied effect of this baptism is an abiding transformation for which John's baptism to repentance was only a dim temporary preparation. There is no hint that this would be an experience for only a privileged few of the disciples.

B. *John's Gospel and Epistles*

INTRODUCTION: There are frequent references to the Holy Spirit in the Gospel of John, many more than in the Synoptics, particularly in the accounts of the Last Supper. The fact that John, in all probability, was written later than the Synoptics, provides a basis for seeing in it the later understanding and experience of the Christian Church. When considering the Johannine teaching concerning the Holy Spirit, the following passages are important:

Work of the Holy Spirit

1. JOHN 1:29-34:
"The next day he saw Jesus coming toward him, and said, 'Behold, the Lamb of God, who takes away the sin of the world! This is he of whom I said, "After me comes a man who ranks before me, for he was before me." I myself did not know him; but for this I came baptizing with water, that he might be revealed to Israel.' And John bore witness, 'I saw the Spirit descend as a dove from heaven, and it remained on him. I myself did not know him; but he who sent me to baptize with water said to me, "He on whom you see the Spirit descend and remain, this is he who baptizes with the Holy Spirit." And I have seen and have borne witness that this is the Son of God.'"

a. The baptism of Jesus is not described in John's Gospel.

b. However, Jesus' baptism is alluded to in the Baptizer's words, "I saw the Spirit descend as a dove from heaven, and it remained on him." (Note the emphasis on the *abiding* experience of the Spirit for Jesus.)

c. Jesus is designated as the one who "baptizes with the Holy Spirit," in contrast to John's baptizing with water.

2. JOHN 3:5:
"Truly, truly I say to you, unless one is born of water and the Spirit, he cannot enter the Kingdom of God."

Three points are significant:

a. Water is linked with Spirit as both being necessary for entrance into God's kingdom. There are several possible interpretations: (1) "Water" refers to John's baptism and "the Spirit" to Jesus' baptism, cf. John 1:31, 33 (C. H. Dodd). (2) Water refers to ritual baptism and Spirit to inner regeneration. (3) "Water" and "Spirit" are used metaphorically, representing baptism and Pentecost. (*The Interpreter's Bible*, Vol. 8, p. 439.)

b. Both water and Spirit are associated with the idea of birth. In John's Gospel one enters the family of God by divine birth (John 1:13). Water and Spirit are therefore designated as the agents by which this birth occurs.

c. When one is *born* of God he then "enters the Kingdom of God."

3. JOHN 3:34:
In this passage it is noted that: "God gives the Spirit without reserve," probably meaning to the Son (cf. Jerusalem Bible, John, p. 152–153).

4. JOHN 7:39:

"Now this he said about the Spirit, which those who believed in him were to receive; for as yet the Spirit had not been given, because Jesus was not yet glorified." In this passage, the following should be noted:

a. The Holy Spirit was not "given" to others than Christ until after his death and resurrection.

b. The Spirit is associated with water in two aspects: (1) it will satisfy inner thirst; and (2) it will be in the believer's life the spring out of which blessing will flow to others.

c. Believing in Jesus Christ results in the reception of the Spirit.

5. JOHN CHAPTERS 13–17:

The references to the Holy Spirit in these chapters describe the Spirit as being given by Christ (16:7), by the Father in Christ's name (14:26), and in response to the prayers of Christ (14:16). Also the activities of the Spirit, both in believers and in the world, are described (16:7-14, et al.).

6. JOHN 20:21-23:

a. In this passage the Holy Spirit is "breathed" on the disciples in what is apparently John's interpretation of the Pentecost experience.

b. Associated with the giving of the Spirit is the Christ-like mission, "as the Father has sent me, even so I send you" (20:21), and the authority to pronounce the forgiveness of sins.

7. THE LETTERS OF JOHN

In these letters, the references to the Spirit reinforce the Upper Room discussions, stressing the abiding of Christ in his people through the agency of the Spirit which "he has given" to them (1 John 3:24). An important summary is given in 1 John 5:6-8:

"This is he who came by water and blood, Jesus Christ, not with the water only but with the water and the blood. (7) And the Spirit is the witness, because the Spirit is the truth. (8) There are three witnesses, the Spirit, the water, and the blood; and these three agree."

a. Jesus Christ coming "by water and blood" is probably symbolic of his baptism by John and his crucifixion (his "baptism" of suffering). "With water and blood" means providing the benefits of baptism (the gift of the Spirit) and the benefits of the Lord's Supper.

Work of the Holy Spirit

b. The three witnesses signify: (1) *The Spirit:* Pentecost, the living presence of Christ in the disciples; (2) *The Water:* the baptism and its benefits; and (3) *The blood:* the death of Christ as represented in the Communion meal.

COMMENTS:

John's Gospel and Epistles contain the following teaching regarding the Baptism with the Spirit:

1. The primary meaning of Jesus' baptism was the receiving of the Spirit in full and permanent measure.

2. Jesus Christ bestows the Spirit on his disciples, committing them to the same mission which he has followed.

3. "New birth," "participation in the Spirit," "reception of the Holy Spirit," are all descriptions of essentially the same experience.

4. John's writings make no mention of "tongues-speaking" or "gifts of the Spirit," though there are many references to the Spirit and his ministry in the disciples.

C. *The Acts of the Apostles*

As was mentioned earlier, the book of Acts makes such frequent reference to the Holy Spirit that it has often been suggested that a more appropriate title of the book might well be "The Acts of the Holy Spirit." After the initial pouring out of the Spirit on the day of Pentecost, the quality of life of the early church at Jerusalem is described in terms of boldness in witnessing, accompanied by joy and gladness in the common life (Acts 2:42-47). The recurring expressions in the following account are "full of the Holy Spirit" and "filled with the Holy Spirit" (Acts 4:8; 6:3, 5, 8; 7:55; 9:17; 11:24; 13:9).

Not only are the lives of individual believers described as being strengthened and empowered by the Holy Spirit, but Luke is also concerned to show how the Spirit was the guiding and controlling factor in the early Christian mission. By the inspiration of the Spirit, Philip is instructed to speak to the Ethiopian treasurer (Acts 8:29, 39), and when his task is completed, Philip is removed to other spheres of activity by the same Spirit (ver. 39). Likewise Peter is directed by the Spirit to go to the home of the Gentile Cornelius, a centurion at Caesarea (10:19; 11:12). Later the Spirit directs the Church at Antioch to send out Barnabas and Saul as missionaries to Asia Minor (13:2-4). Subsequently Paul and his companions are guided by the Spirit into new areas of more extended service (16:6-10).

Luke does not tell us how this guidance was mediated; but we should probably infer that it was through prophetic insight, in the manner in which the Hebrew prophets had discerned the divine command to go to particular places and to carry out particular tasks. In this connection we should not overlook the presence in the early church of a special group who are called prophets. Mentioned along side of apostles and teachers, this group of prophetically sensitive persons (Acts 13:1; compare 1 Cor 12:28-29; Eph 2:20; 4:11) probably exercised a double function of proclamation and prediction. By the Holy Spirit a prophet named Agabus foresaw an impending famine and issued spiritual guidance to the church (Acts 11:27-29). On another occasion the Holy Spirit prompted Agabus to predict the persecutions that lay in store for the apostle Paul (21:10-11).

Throughout all these references in the book of Acts to different aspects of the work and activity of the Holy Spirit, it is significant that speaking in tongues is mentioned on only three occasions; namely, at Pentecost (though the account is susceptible of different interpretations), at the conversion of Cornelius, and at the establishment of the church at Ephesus. A fuller discussion of these passages is reserved for the following section; it will be enough here to draw attention (a) to the paucity of such incidents of speaking in tongues recorded in Acts, and (b) to the obscurity that attaches to the question of how Luke conceived of the Spirit to have been received by the ordinary members of the Christian society.

Concerning the latter problem, it has often been observed that, on the one hand, Luke reports that at Pentecost Peter proclaimed that the gift of the Spirit is now available to all who repent and are baptized in the name of Jesus Christ (Acts 2:38) — a teaching that is in harmony with explicit statements in Paul's Epistles and with the general implications of the New Testament as a whole. On the other hand, in the case of Cornelius and his household the Spirit "fell on" the converts immediately, prior to their being baptized (10:44-48). There is also the case of the Samaritan converts who were baptized by Philip but whose reception of the Spirit was delayed until Peter and John had come from Jerusalem and had laid their hands on the new believers (8:12-17). In these two cases the distinctive features of the narratives may be due to the special circumstances that were involved, namely, in each case Luke's account has reached a turning point in the church's mission, as it moves first from Judea into Samaria, and later into what can be called Gentile territory.

Somewhat similar to the last mentioned incident is the status of certain disciples whom Paul met at Ephesus (Acts 19:2-6) and who had been baptized with only "John's baptism." They accordingly had not received the Holy Spirit when they had believed (i.e., had been converted; the rendering of the King James version, "since ye believed," is erroneous). These persons were then baptized by Paul "in the name of the Lord Jesus," and "when Paul had laid his hands upon them, the Holy Spirit came upon them; and they spoke with tongues and prophesied" (19:6).

COMMENTS

1. The predominant testimony of the book of Acts concerning the Holy Spirit concentrates on the outpouring, the gift, the reception, the falling of the Holy Spirit upon Christian believers. The prediction made earlier by John the Baptist that Jesus the Messiah would baptize his followers with the Holy Spirit is mentioned twice (1:5 and 11:16), but nowhere is reference made to "the baptism in (or, with) the Spirit."

2. The notorious difficulty of ascertaining any single, consistent pattern in Acts of the sequence of conversion, reception of the Holy Spirit, and water-baptism, suggests that the correct hermeneutic in ascertaining God's will for the Church is to give primary attention to the *didactic* rather than the *historical* parts of the Scripture. As John R. W. Stott puts it: "We should look for it [i.e., the revelation of the purpose of God] in the teaching of Jesus, and in the sermons and writings of the apostles, and not in the purely narrative portions of the Acts. What is *described* in Scripture as having happened to others is not necessarily intended for us, whereas what is *promised* to us we are to appropriate, and what is *commanded* us we are to obey" (*The Baptism and the Fullness of the Holy Spirit*, Chicago, 1964, p. 4).

THE GIFTS OF THE SPIRIT

"Spiritual gifts" is a comprehensive designation for all those extraordinary and sometimes directly miraculous powers which were possessed by many Christians in the Apostolic age. These gifts, or *charismata*, had their origin in the gracious (Greek *charis*, "grace") operation of the Holy Spirit, and were bestowed in order "to equip God's people for work in his service" (Eph 4:12 New English Bible).

The primary section in the New Testament that deals with spiritual gifts is chapters 12, 13, and 14 of 1 Corinthians. Here the apostle provides three lists of such gifts (12:8-10, 28, and 29-30). It is instructive to compare the lists, beginning with verse 28 where Paul enumerates the first three gifts in a definite sequence ("first . . . second . . . third"). 1 Cor 12:28: (1) apostles, (2) prophets, (3) teachers, (4) workers of miracles, (5) healers, (6) helpers, (7) administrators, and (8) speakers in various kinds of tongues.

Somewhat similar is the sequence of gifts in the statements found in 1 Cor 12:8-10 and 29-30. (In the following lists the gifts are enumerated in the order in which they stand in the Scripture text, while the numerals in parentheses correspond to the numerals in the list cited above.) 1 Cor 12:8-10: (1) a word of wisdom, (3) a word of knowledge, (5) gifts of healing, (4) working of miracles, (2) prophecy, ability to distinguish between spirits, (8) various kinds of tongues, and (9) interpretation of tongues.

1 Cor 12:29-30: (1) apostles, (2) prophets, (3) teachers, (4) miracles, (5) gifts of healing, (8) speaking with tongues, and (9) interpreting (tongues).

Elsewhere in the New Testament other lists of spiritual gifts include the following:

Rom 12:6-8: (2) prophecy, service, (3) teaching, exhortation, contributing, giving aid, and doing acts of mercy.

Eph 4:11: (1) apostles, (2) prophets, evangelists, pastors, and (3) teachers.

One or two other lists occur, but these differ somewhat from the specific charismata enumerated above. Thus, in Gal 5:22-23 the apostle enumerates the ninefold fruit of the Spirit characteristic of the full Christian life, and in 1 Pet 4:10-11 the writer restricts himself to two typical Christian charismata, namely speaking the oracles of God (i.e. teaching) and rendering service.

Before making a comparison of items among the several lists of gifts of the Spirit, it will be useful to define several of the less familiar terms used in the lists. In 1 Cor 12:8-10, "a word of wisdom" and "a word of knowledge" appear to refer to discourses or briefer utterances that either expound Christian truths and their relations to one another, or that set forth ethical instruction and practical exhortation. "Faith" in this list cannot mean the saving faith possessed by every sincere Christian believer, but must refer to some exceptional kind or degree of potent faith that can work miracles (cf. 1 Cor 13:2). "Prophecy" in the early Church was not so much the predicting of future events (though this sometimes occurred; e.g. Agabus in Acts 11:27), but was chiefly the gift of understanding and expressing through teaching or preaching what the will of God was for a given situation, resulting in "upbuilding and encouragement and consolation" (1 Cor 14:3). The "ability to distinguish between spirits" refers to a deep and intuitive power that enabled its possessor to discriminate between true and false prophets and to judge whether what they taught came from God or was an illusion (cf 1 Jn 4:1). Except for the nature of the gift of "speaking in tongues" (which will be discussed later), the characteristics of the other gifts in the lists are no doubt sufficiently clear and do not require further comment.

A comparison of the four primary lists reveals certain instructive features. Each of the lists contains two or more gifts that are not mentioned in the other lists. It must not be assumed, however, that in all cases the difference in name means a difference of gift or function; for example, "service" in one list (Rom 12:6) and "helpers" in another list (1 Cor 12:28) are probably to be identified. In any case, it is clear that in general the gifts may be divided into the apparently miraculous and the non-miraculous. Included among the former are workers of miracles and healers, whereas among the latter are certain gifts of character and mental and spiritual endowments, such as exhortation, contributing, giving aid, and administrating. That is, the items in the latter group appear to be what are commonly called natural powers or talents which have been raised to a pitch that is not attainable apart from a special endowment of the Spirit. Paul's estimate of the relative value in public worship of the several gifts of the Spirit is made unmistakably clear by (1) the fact that whenever he mentions in a list of spiritual gifts the speaking in tongues, with the interpretation of tongues, he does so at the end of the list; and (2) his express statement, "I thank God that I speak in tongues more than you all; nevertheless, in church I would rather speak five words with my mind, in order to instruct others, than ten thousand words in a tongue" (1 Cor 14:18-19 — the proportion being one to two thousand!).

By way of summary, charismata may be defined as endowments and capacities necessary for the edification and service of the Church, bestowed by the Holy Spirit upon its members, in virtue of which they are enabled to employ their natural faculties in the service of the Church, or are endowed with new abilities and powers for this purpose.

SPEAKING IN TONGUES

Explicit references in the New Testament to the gift of speaking in tongues are confined to three books, namely Mark, Acts, and 1 Corinthians. The terminology used in these books to describe speaking in tongues varies slightly. The predominant text of the concluding section of Mark, a section of disputed authenticity (see below for further discussion of this matter), refers to speaking in *new tongues* (16:17); in Acts 2:4 reference is made to *other tongues*; and mention is made in 1 Cor 12:28 of *various kinds of tongues*. Usually, however, Acts and 1 Corinthians refer simply to *tongues* or (singular) *tongue*. The verb "to speak" is commonly used with both the singular and the plural noun (Acts 2:4; 10:46; 19:6; 1 Cor 14:2, 4, 13, 14, 19, 27); once Paul uses the phrase to "pray in a tongue" as distinct from praying with the mind (1 Cor 14:14-15). The following sections contain a more or less detailed examination of these passages, beginning with those in 1 Corinthians, which is the earliest written account in the New Testament that mentions speaking in tongues.

A. 1 Corinthians

The meaning of the word "tongue" (Greek *glossa*) in 1 Cor 12-14 has been differently explained. The primary use of the word in Greek is to designate the physical organ that lies on the floor of the mouth. This, however, is obviously not the meaning here, because in that primary sense everyone speaks with his tongue and because the plural "tongues" is used of a single individual (1 Cor 14:5, 18). Some scholars have thought that the charismatic gift in the church at Corinth was the miraculous speaking of existing foreign languages and dialects not previously learnt by the speakers. In support of this interpretation it has been urged that the seven occurrences in 1 Cor 12 and 14 of the verb *hermeneuein* must mean to interpret or translate a foreign language. This argument, however, is not water-tight, for the verb can also be used in the giving of an explanation of a statement or a passage of Scripture (Lk 24:32).

Furthermore, the opinion that it was foreign languages which the Corinthians spoke seems to be inconsistent with two comments that Paul makes in the context. For one thing, speaking in foreign languages, even though they were unknown to the hearer, would scarcely lead him to judge that the speakers were out of their mind (1 Cor 14:23). Likewise, Paul uses the analogy of musical instruments (1 Cor 14:7-8) and says that if they "do not give distinct notes, how will anyone know what is played?" It is altogether unlikely that the apostle is identifying speaking in tongues with speaking in foreign languages because in that case he would not have suggested that there was no distinction between the sounds — for in every language there must be such a distinction.

Apparently therefore the expression "tongues" in 1 Corinthians has the sense of a peculiar kind of speech which a person may attain in prayer, pouring forth his glowing spiritual experience in a rhapsody of sounds, unintelligible to others as well as to himself. In this connection the apostle directs that "he who speaks in a tongue should pray for the power to interpret" (1 Cor 14:13). If, however, there is no one present to interpret, the speaker shall "keep silence in church and speak to himself and to God" (1 Cor 14:28).

In light of the special usage of the Greek word for "tongue" it would be useful to have in English a corresponding special term to designate the gift of speaking in tongues. In older as well as in several more recent translations of the Bible (but not the Revised Standard Version, which gives a strictly literal translation of the expression), various paraphrastic renderings have been utilized in the interest of greater clarity. The Geneva Bible of 1560 used throughout 1 Corinthians, Chapter 14 the expression "strange tongues," and the King James or so-called Authorized Version of 1611 used the expression "unknown tongues." In both cases the qualifying word was printed in italics to indicate that it is an interpretative addition. In more modern times the New English Bible (1961–1970) employs the renderings "ecstatic speech," "the language of ecstasy," "the tongues of ecstasy," and "ecstatic utterance"; and the Today's English Version issued by the American Bible Society (1966) translates with the phrase "speaks with strange sounds." It may also be mentioned that during the past century the technical term *glossolalia* (a term that does not occur in the Bible) has often been used in referring to the Corinthian experience.

B. The Book of Acts

In the book of Acts three passages refer to the speaking in tongues. Perhaps it will be best to deal first with the two passages about which there is little or no dispute concerning their meaning. In the account of the conversion of Cornelius, the Roman centurion at Caesarea, we are told that while Peter was preaching the gospel to him and his kinsmen and close friends who had gathered together in his home, "the Holy Spirit fell on all who heard the word. And the believers from among the circumcized [i.e. the Jewish Christians] who came with Peter were amazed, because the gift of the Holy Spirit had been poured out even on the Gentiles [i.e. on Cornelius and those with him]. For they heard them speaking in tongues and extolling God" (Acts 10:44-46).

In another account in Acts (19:1ff.) reference is made to certain disciples at Ephesus who had previously been baptized in accordance with John the Baptist's teaching concerning the need of repentance, and who had not yet received the Holy Spirit. After Paul had given them further instruction, they received Christian baptism and, when he "had laid his hands upon them, the Holy Spirit came on them; and they spoke with tongues and prophesied" (Acts 19:6).

In the context of neither of these two passages is there any hint of the need of speaking in foreign languages. Accordingly almost all commentators regard the reference to "tongues" to be similar to the experience of believers at Corinth, namely the utterance of unknown words or sounds as a consequence of the exuberance of a newly acquired faith in Jesus Christ.

The remaining reference in Acts to speaking in tongues (2:4) involves a number of problems of interpretation, concerning which there is no general agreement among scholars. On the one hand, some commentators urge that the *prima facie* meaning of the account in Acts 2 is that the Holy Spirit enabled the one hundred twenty believers, who had been assembled in the upper room at Jerusalem, to speak in various foreign languages (Acts 2:6 and 8), which were understood by people of many nationalities (fifteen lands are mentioned in the list of hearers in 2:9-11).

On the other hand, a number of features in the narrative seem to other scholars to suggest that the speaking in "other tongues" (verse 4) was not the use of existing foreign languages but was essentially the same as the Corinthian tongues-speaking, namely an act of worship involving the giving of thanksgiving and praise

Work of the Holy Spirit

for "the mighty works of God" (Acts 2:11). In support of this interpretation, these scholars point to the following facts. First, the Pentecostal speaking in other tongues began before the spectators had arrived (compare verses 4 and 6), and was followed by the missionary discourse of Peter in plain, ordinary language. Secondly, a miracle of speaking in so many foreign languages to the multitude at Pentecost would have been superfluous, for Jews born abroad normally spoke a dialect of Aramaic, or the common Greek, or sometimes both. There was, therefore, no need for the apostles and their companions to speak in a wide variety of foreign languages. Thirdly, some of the multitude ridiculed the speakers as "filled with new wine" (2:13). Such is not the reaction of bystanders who hear others speak in real languages; it agrees, however, with the impression that outsiders received of speakers in tongues at Corinth ("When the whole church assembles and all speak in tongues, and outsiders or unbelievers enter, will they not say that you are mad?" 1 Cor 14:23). Fourthly, on another occasion Peter compared what happened to Cornelius and his companions with what had happened at Pentecost (Acts 11:15). Since the tongues in which Cornelius spoke were in all probability an act of worship, not of teaching (in existing foreign languages), Peter's comparison implies that the same kind of speaking took place at Pentecost. Fifthly, strict attention given to the account in Acts 2 discloses that, whereas the utterances of the apostles and their companions sounded in the ears of the excited crowd as the words of their mother tongues (2:6ff.), the writer of Acts himself does not really affirm that the speakers spoke the foreign languages of the several nationalities which made up the group, but only that the hearers so interpreted their utterances ("each one hears ...... we hear"). Thus the miracle would have been one of hearing rather than one of speaking. According to this interpretation of the account in Acts 2, the phenomenon at Pentecost involved a kind of spiritual intoxication, a rhapsodic telling of "the mighty works of God" (Acts 2:11). The import of the "tongues" was interpreted and applied by the Holy Spirit himself to those hearers who believed and were converted, to each in his own vernacular dialect. The difference between the experience at Pentecost and that at Corinth was that in the former case the "tongues" were immediately understood by some of the multitude, while at Corinth a special gift of interpretation was necessary.

The upshot of this rather lengthy discussion of the meaning of

Acts 2 may be expressed more briefly as follows. It appears that either (a) Luke (who, so far as we know, had not himself been present in Jerusalem at Pentecost) had found two reports of the event, one of which told of speaking in foreign languages and the other of which told of a charismatic speaking in unknown tongues, and he combined in Acts 2 features of both reports; or (b) Luke himself introduced into the original report of ecstatic tongues certain features suggesting the speaking of foreign languages in order to interpret to the reader of Acts the profound significance of the coming of the Holy Spirit, whose gracious work of illumination transcended all national boundaries and linguistic barriers.

C. The Gospel of Mark

The remaining explicit reference in the New Testament to speaking in tongues is found in the appendix to the Gospel according to Mark (16:17). Since the last twelve verses (9 to 20) of the Second Gospel are absent from the earliest and best manuscripts of the New Testament, and since the style and vocabulary of these verses differ from the rest of Mark's Gospel, it is almost universally held by scholars that, after the original ending of the Gospel had been accidentally torn off and lost at a very early date, the verses now widely current were added early in the second century by someone who wished thereby to provide a more satisfactory ending than the very abrupt close of the Gospel at 16:8, "for they [the women] were afraid."

Among the manuscripts that contain Mark 16:17, most read "they will speak in new tongues"; the adjective "new," however, is absent from several early manuscripts. It is difficult to decide whether the word "new" was accidentally omitted by early scribes, or whether it was added in order to differentiate the sign promised to believers from the gift of speaking in tongues. In either case, it is altogether probable that the addition of the last twelve verses was made at a time prior to the canonization of the Gospel of Mark; that is, when the Second Gospel came to be acknowledged as authoritative Scripture, the traditional ending was already attached.

SUMMARY OF NEW TESTAMENT EVIDENCE

This section will serve to pull together the different strands of New Testament teaching which have been indicated in the analyses given above.

Work of the Holy Spirit

1. Any study of the so-called "baptism with the Holy Spirit" must begin with John's baptism which was of "repentance for the forgiveness of sins" (Luke 3:3). It was a preparatory experience designed to make the hearts of people ready for the "Coming One." John's testimony concerning the coming Messiah was that the latter was so far greater than the Baptist that John was not worthy to be even his slave. The primary mark of the "Coming One" was that he would baptize with the Holy Spirit. (The experience of Apollos and the disciples at Ephesus, Acts 18:24–19:7, reinforces the idea of the superiority of Jesus' baptism compared with that which John administered. It should be noted that though both Apollos and the unnamed disciples "knew only the baptism of John," the former was not rebaptized, but was only taught "the way of God" more accurately, while the latter "were baptized in the name of the Lord Jesus.")

2. All of the Gospels see the coming of the Holy Spirit upon Jesus as the central feature of his experience of baptism at the hands of John (cf. Luke 3:22 and parallels; Acts 10:38).

3. The reception of the Spirit by the first disciples and later believers is regarded as the fulfillment of the promise that Jesus would baptize with the Holy Spirit (Acts 11:16; Acts 1:5; John 20:21-22).

4. Baptism with the Spirit means incorporation into the body of Christ, the Church (Acts 2:37-42; Acts 10:44-48; Rom 6:1ff.; 1 Cor 12:13; Col 2:12). The only condition for receiving this baptism is repentance and faith toward Jesus Christ (Acts 2:38; Acts 10:44-45; Gal 2:26-27; Rom 8:9-11; etc.?

5. Regarding visible evidences of reception in the Spirit, the following may be noted: Some speak in tongues (Acts 2:4, 10-44, 19:6); others give no visible sign (Acts 2:41; 4:4, 8:17). In 1 Cor 12:13 Paul says that *all* were baptized by the Spirit, but only some have the gift of "various kinds of tongues" (1 Cor 12:10); others have other gifts.

6. The phrase, "baptism in or with the Holy Spirit," is central in pentecostal theology. One writer summarizes thus:

"The basic dogma of pentecostalism, the one that distinguishes it from other branches of Christianity, is the dogma of 'the Baptism in the Holy Spirit.' Sometimes it is called 'the Baptism *of* the Holy Spirit.' Whatever preposition is used, this term refers to a decisive, usually for the Christian, a second encounter with God. This encounter empowers the Christian for service to the Lord, it is claimed, and in a way that nothing else can. Without this a Christian is 'only saved.' With it, he is an effective servant of Christ" (Peter Doyle, *The Theology of Episcopalian Pentecostalism*, p. 2).

We do not, however, find warrant in the New Testament for a doctrine of *two* Spirit-baptisms as normal for the Christian life. Those who speak of one baptism to "make us new creatures, spiritually," and another baptism by which "the Holy Spirit comes to dwell in us" (*The ministries of the Holy Spirit in the Church*, Blessed Trinity Society, 1962, p. 6), are making a division which is not found in the New Testament. In the New Testament, baptism with water, when practised or taught, is a ritual related to the reception of the Spirit, and may come before (Acts 19:5-6), at the same time (Acts 2:38), or after (Acts 2:38) one has been baptized with the Holy Spirit.

Furthermore, it should be noted that though several biblical writers use the verb "to baptize" in connection with the Spirit (Matt 3:11; Mk 1:8; Luke 3:16; John 1:33; Acts 1:5; 11:16); nowhere do the Scriptures use the noun "baptism" in the expression "the baptism of the Spirit." The modern elaboration of a doctrine concerning a special event called "the baptism of the Spirit," different in kind from any other operation of the Holy Spirit, is a sectarian over-interpretation. Furthermore, not only have certain persons today invented a non-scriptural phrase, but they contrast this so-called baptism of the Spirit with baptism with water, contrary to the apostolic teaching that there is but *one* baptism (Eph 4:5).

7. Of all the spiritual gifts, that of speaking in tongues was open to certain dangers and abuses, which at Corinth had led to loveless pride and chaotic confusion. Notwithstanding its liability to misuse, however, Paul did not forbid the exercise of this gift in private, which he recognized as an operation of the Spirit (1 Cor 14:39). But he restricted its exercise within the assembled congregation and demanded that it be interpreted (1 Cor 14:27f.). Whenever Paul makes a list of spiritual gifts, he always ranks speaking in tongues and their interpretation last in such lists (1 Cor 12:10, 28, 30).

8. The general impression made by Paul's discussion in 1 Corinthians, chapters 12, 13, and 14, is that speaking in tongues can be good, but prophesying in intelligible speech for the edification of the congregation is better (1 Cor 14:5), and love for God and men is best of all (1 Cor 12:31; 13:13). According to Paul, without love the greatest tongue-speaker imaginable is a mere

Work of the Holy Spirit

noise-maker ("If I speak in the tongues of men and of angels, but have not love, I am a noisy gong or a clanging cymbal," 1 Cor 13:1).

9. Although Paul has much to teach in his major Epistles about the Holy Spirit and about the Spirit's gifts to the Church, it is only in one Epistle (1 Corinthians) that he discusses (and regulates) the speaking in tongues. Tongues are not mentioned in the General Epistles or in the book of Revelation. And although the Acts of the Apostles makes a great many references to the activity of the Holy Spirit in the early Church, it is only on three separate occasions that explicit reference is made to speaking in tongues (2:4; 10:46; 19:6). Even though some have found allusions to tongues in a few other passages in the New Testament (e.g., in Acts 8:17; Rom 8:15; Gal 4:6; and 1 Thess 5:19), it is plain that this gift occupied a subordinate place in the life of Christian believers in the apostolic age.

10. There is not the slightest hint in the Gospels that Jesus Christ, to whom the Father gave the Spirit without measure (John 3:34), ever spoke in tongues. Nor do we find in his teaching concerning the coming of the Spirit as Counselor or Advocate any word of a miraculous gift of tongues. In fact, there is, as has been pointed out above, only one reference to "new tongues" in the four Gospels, and that is not in connection with the Spirit but as one of the five signs which should accompany those who believe, a reference to saving faith in general (Mark 16:17-18).

11. To insist that speaking in tongues is a necessary proof that one has been baptized by the Spirit is to overlook the clear statement of the apostle in 1 Cor 12:13, "For by one Spirit we were all baptized into one body [the Church]." Since only some of the Corinthian believers spoke in tongues (1 Cor 12:8-10), yet all of them (as Paul here specifically declares) had been baptized by one Spirit, it is unwarranted to teach that speaking in tongues is an indispensable sign of having received the Spirit.

12. Of all the many individuals and groups mentioned in the Acts who received the Spirit, in only three instances is speaking in tongues mentioned. There are many other references in the same book to the fullness of the Spirit or to receiving the Spirit in context where there is no allusion to speaking in tongues (Acts 1:5, 8; 4:8, 31; 5:32; 6:3, 5; 8:15, 17-19; 9:17; 11:15-16, 24; 13:9, 52; 15:8). In the face of such evidence it is entirely arbitrary to assert, as some do, that speaking in tongues always follows the reception of the Spirit. The authentic apostolic teaching, instead of referring

to the baptism of the Spirit, exhorts believers to be filled with the Spirit (Eph 5:18). The New Testament makes it clear that fullness of the Spirit is an expression referring to the Christian's dependence on the Holy Spirit, a dependence that must be renewed from time to time. Just as forgiveness is to be sought daily, so also a renewed sense of dependence on the enabling power of the Holy Spirit is to be sought for each task to which we put our hands.

13. With reference to modern instances of the bestowal of spiritual gifts similar to those at Corinth, Calvin confesses that "it is difficult to make up one's mind about gifts. . . . , of which the Church has been deprived for so long, except for mere traces or shades of them, which are still to be found" (*Commentary* on 1 Cor 12:28-31). Although some theologians have held that the purely supernaturalistic gifts ceased with the death of the apostles and their companions, it is difficult to validate this view either exegetically or historically. In accord with the apostolic exhortation to "test the spirits to see whether they are of God" (1 John 4:1), it appears that each of the authentic gifts of the Spirit has had its counterfeits and frauds. There are also instances, even within the circle of orthodox Christendom, when "divine healing" has been shamefully exploited. Such cases cannot but bring reproach to the cause of Christ and his Church.

14. By way of conclusion, the practice of speaking in tongues, when inspired by the Holy Spirit, should neither be despised nor forbidden. At the same time, tongues should not be overemphasized; normally they belong to private worship. Christians who have experienced, through speaking in tongues, a revitalizing of their faith should be on guard against forming divisive cliques within the congregation. On the other hand, those who have received no unusual experiences of the Holy Spirit should be alert to the possibilities of a deeper understanding of the gospel of Christ and a fuller participation in the gifts and fruit of the Spirit — of which love is the greatest (1 Cor 13:13).

APPENDIX B. A MORE DETAILED SUMMARY OF RELEVANT PSYCHOLOGICAL LITERATURE

1. *Objectivity.* There are several major obstacles to an objective evaluation of the charismatic type religious experience. According to McDonnell (1968, 1970) it is difficult for Pentecostals to receive a fair hearing because of: (a) negative public images relating to

emotionalism, fanaticism, illiteracy, credulity, etc.; (b) fear of religious experience as opposed to more abstract, cognitive, theological, and other considerations; (c) norms of socially accepted behavior such as manifestations of speaking in tongues, prophesying, giving interpretations, are generally thought in American society to be unacceptable ways of behaving however authentic they might be; and (d) a fear on the part of the organized church dealing with a dimension that knows no jurisdictional boundaries which cannot be regulated by decree or preprogrammed.

Although the church generally encourages effective religious experience, there seems to be a natural fear of religious experience and when it assumes or approaches amazing proportions, the church becomes uneasy and watchful.

Charismatic experiences in general are usually thought to involve an altered mental state. In Western culture and society such states are viewed with a great deal of suspicion and managed with a good deal of confusion. Pentecostal glossolalia appears to have fallen heir to both the confusion and the suspicion. (Gerlach and Hine, 1967.)

Analysis of altered mental states is frequently based upon psychological models which assume at the outset that the state is pathological or abnormal.

Altered mental states are usually treated as a loss of reality-orientation, interruption of normal associations or direction of behavior, unconnected with consciousness. (Gerlach and Hine, 1967.)

2. Alexander Alland (1961) studied a Negro Pentecostal Church and found that members who spoke in tongues were well-adjusted to their social environment and behaved in a normally accepted manner. According to Alland, earlier psychological explanations relating to glossolalia and schizophrenia are no longer acceptable.

NOTE: The committee after study and review of much relevant psychological data discovered a similar comprehensive review by Dr. Luther P. Gerlach and Virginia Hine. The committee is indebted to Dr. Gerlach for his generosity in making available this comprehensive summary of relevant psychological literature. This section of the committee's report contains extensive quotes from this review by Dr. Gerlach, Virginia Hine, and the team that was involved in their project. For a more comprehensive treatment of this subject the reader is referred to a forthcoming book by Dr. Luther P. Gerlach and Virginia Hine entitled *People, Power, Change*, Bobbs Merrill, tentative publication date: June 1970.

3. The testimony of spokesmen of the charismatic movement emphasizes that charismatic experiences, including speaking in tongues are not related in any way to ecstatic or trance states. With few exceptions participants are totally aware of the environment around them and exercise the "gift" of tongues at will.

4. Gerlach and Hine (1967, 1968) described three basic models used by social scientists to study religious phenomenon in related movements. They indicate that such movements can occur (a) if there is social disorganization, (b) among the economically or socially deprived classes or (c) when individuals involved are defective in some way, a theory that assumes psychological maladjustments or personality characteristics that predispose an individual to join a movement. According to these authors, there is no empirical evidence to support these theories as applicable to the modern charismatic movement.

5. George B. Cutten's *Speaking in Tongues*, written in 1927, illustrates an often quoted but inaccurate analysis of the movement. The account describes more dramatic instances of tongue speaking, and Cutten makes extravagant statements about tongues being received only by non-verbal individuals of low mental ability. Quoted and requoted through the years, his impressions "have taken on an aura of fact among laymen and churchmen cirtical of the movement. His assumptions that glossolalia is related to schizophrenia and hysteria have not been supported by any conclusive empirical studies." (Gerlach and Hine, 1967.)

6. *Suggestibility.* Joiners of the charismatic movement have been labeled highly-suggestible by laymen and professionals from many disciplines. Empirical studies do not support this opinion. For example, Gerlach and Hine (1967) reported that twenty-three percent of respondents in their study spoke in tongues for the first time when they were alone. Many others have reported spontaneous experiences after considerable prayer and searching, unrelated to any religious meetings or involvement of other individuals. Several individuals have reported a lapse of many months before they came in contact with those in the movement and determined that the phenomenon they were experiencing was "speaking in tongues." Vivier (1960) found further evidence of this kind and reported that those who spoke in tongues were no different from his control groups with respect to suggestibility.

7. In seven studies conducted by psychologists or psychiatrists

(reported by Gerlach and Hine, 1967) Pentecostal glossolalia could not be related to mental illness. Speaking in tongues was not considered an indicator of neurosis or psychosis. Data indicates that although disturbed individuals may be attracted to the movement there is no evidence that they exist in greater proportion within this movement than within the organized church. It is quite possible that the disturbed may be attracted because of their great need for help. They may do or say bizarre things as a manifestation of their illness — not as a result of the dynamics of the movement.

8. Anton Boisen (1939) having studied members of a "holy roller" church and certain types of mental patients, found no evidence of illness in the cases he studied in the church. He found in several cases of mentally disordered individuals that the experience of the "baptism of the Holy Spirit" and tongues within the church context played for the most part a constructive role.

9. Dr. Stanley Plog, using the California Psychological Inventory with a group of Neo-Pentecostals of California, reported that "those who entered into the tongues experience were very responsible and normally well-controlled individuals." (Gerlach and Hine, 1967.)

Mansell Pattison (1968), Department of Psychiatry, University of Washington, rejects the theory that glossolalics are malcontent, socio-economically deprived, or emotionally disturbed. Pattison advances the thesis that glossolalia is a psychological accompaniment of an intense and meaningful spiritual experience for normal devoutly religious people but that it must be seen as incidental to the attainment of spiritual goals and that it can be achieved as an end itself. His emphasis is on the natural speech mechanism which produces glossolalia, which he defines as a stereotyped pattern of unconsciously controlled vocal behavior. He feels that such an experience is available to any normal person under the right conditions, such as group-setting, appropriate motivation, and example.

10. Gerlach and Hine (1967) concluded from their interviews and interaction with members of the movement that Pentecostals are generally normally adjusted and productive members of society, and indicated that the notion that such persons were maladjusted, emotionally unstable, or emotionally deprived is contradicted by their field data.

11. L. N. Van Eetvelt Vivier (1960), a South African psychiatrist, has conducted one of the most comprehensive

studies of pentecostals. He reports empirical findings that tongue speakers scored *low* on three factors of the Cattell Personality test associated with conversion hysteria." Vivier reported no significant differences between the test and control groups on the Willoughby test for general level of neuroticism. Vivier found "no more evidence of persistent unadaptive anxiety reactions in tongue speakers or Pentecostals who have not yet spoken in tongues than in non-Pentecostals except for factors of desurgence and shrewdness naiveté on the Cattell inventory. On the desurgence factor Vivier reported that the glossolalics "although not far from the median appeared to be more 'long-circuiting' and renunciative in their habits than the control groups." They were "less realistic and practical, more concerned with feelings and thought actions and more human in their interests." (Gerlach and Hine, 1967.)

Vivier found that his test group scored lower than the control group on suggestibility and challenged the popular notion that tongue speakers are highly susceptible to suggestion. He characterized tongue speakers as "generally more sensitive, less bound by traditional orthodox thought processes, less depressed, having less generalized fear but more need for emotional catharsis." Vivier found no substantiation of "theories of dissociation as a result of an inherent weakness in neural organization, Freudian repression, or of suggestibility." For an explanation Vivier referred to Jungian concepts of the collective unconscious and what he called a "dynamic system acting on the organism." (Gerlach and Hine, 1967; McDonnell, 1970.)

"Even the most critical analysts of the movement who espouse the defective individual theory are forced to admit that glossolalics cannot be regarded as mentally ill." (McDonnell, 1970.)

Lapsely and Simpson (1964a, 1964b) have suggested that speaking in tongues resembles clinical hysteria and that the psychodynamics involved were similar to those in a person with hysterical symptoms. They point out however that this does not mean that all or even most who speak in tongues could be called hysterical in a clinical setting. "Like most writers who quote Vivier, they include Vivier's findings that most of the glossolalics in his test group had poor beginnings in life and that therefore one should expect disturbed ego development, difficulty in emotional control and disturbed interpersonal relationships. Most of these writers . . . do not include Vivier's companion statement that the glossolalics he tested showed marital adjustments similar to that of the control group, that is, non-tongue speaking Pentecostals and non-Pentecostals, and that their capacity for marital adjustment did not reflect higher childhood insecurity as might have been expected." (Gerlach and Hine, 1967.)

12. Nathan Gerrard (1966) of the Department of Sociology of Morris-Harvey University has conducted one of the more conclusive and interesting sociological-anthropological studies. Members of a serpent handlers cult in West Virginia, although independent of the Pentecostal movement as it is generally described, practiced glossolalia. Although not related to the present charismatic movement, from the psychological point of view this group was on the fringe, readily identifiable and constituted an excellent group for psychological study and testing.

Gerrard compared the church cult group with other church groups in the community and developed the hypothesis that the snake handlers were not psychologically disturbed individuals. He tested this hypothesis by administering the Minnesota Multi-Phasic Personality Inventory to the group and to members of the conventional church of a major protestant denomination in the same area. The 96 Minnesota Multi-Phasic Personality Inventories were analyzed in the Department of Psychology at the University of Minnesota. Dr. Gerrard found that both groups were essentially within the "normal limits" established by wide use of the Minnesota Multi-Phasic Personality Inventory.

He found no evidence of systematic differences between the two groups with respect to dimension of thought disorder (psychoticism). He found with respect to neuroticism an insignificantly higher incidence within the conventional denomination than among the snake handlers. One of the psychologists who analyzed the data, Dr. Auke Tellegan, indicated that the conventional denomination presented a "somewhat more repressive and dysphoric picture." He also found them "more likely to present more symptoms of distress than were the snake handlers." What differences existed were in the direction of the serpent handlers being more normal than the conventional denomination." (Gerrard and Gerrard, 1966.)

Three separate clinicians were given the Minnesota Multi-Phasic Personality Inventory profiles and were told that one of the groups were snake handlers. "They were asked to categorize the profiles diagnostically and then to sort out the profiles they thought belonged to the snake handlers." The clinicians' degree of bias was remarkably revealed in the results reported by Dr. Gerrard. The most abnormal profiles were assigned by the clinicians to the serpent handlers and the most normal profiles to the conventional denomination. The actual distribution indicated that the reverse was true.

"Dr. Gerrard concluded that while clinical psychologists are aware that standards of normalcy vary cross-culturally, they are less sensitive to sub-cultural differences and they are also subject to stereotyped pre-judgments concerning the pathology of sub-cultures that are defined as deviant by the larger society." (Gerrard and Gerrard, 1966; Gerlach and Hine, 1967; McDonnell, 1970.)

13. Psychiatrists Jerome Frank (1951) and William Sargent (1949) analyzed the function of dissociation from the point of view of psychological changes of an individual. Lapsely and Simpson (1964) and Nouwen (1967) indicated that glossolalic dissociation produces only temporary conflict reduction and therefore no lasting change. "In comparing the nature of revivalistic religious experience with the process of psychotherapy, Frank disagreed and reported that conversion of experience of the Baptism of the Holy Spirit was a mechanism through which attitudes toward God, the self, and those in significant relationships shift in such a way as to lead to permanent attitudes and behavior changes. According to Frank these stem from the reorganization of the assumptive system or world view that is possible during such experience. Similar results can be obtained through the process of successful psychotherapy. Sargent offers the thesis that experiences such as revivalistic conversions, snake handling, glossolalia can produce an effect similar to that of electro-shock therapy. Temporary cortical inhibition breaks up previous mental and emotional patterns and frees the individual to form new ones."

Both Sargent and Frank stress the fact that the dynamics of revivalism and conversion involving dissociational experiences are such that predisposing personality characteristics or emotional maladjustments are not required as an explanation of participation. They feel that the common denominator in processes of religious conversion, some methods of psychotherapy, thought reform, and brainwashing is not a psychological state but a physiological state which can be brought about in any individual." (Gerlach and Hine, 1967.)

Sargent's emphasis on the physiological mechanisms of

cognitive reorganization is based on his observations of the most extreme forms of these phenomenon. Gerlach and Hine point out the difficulty in finding any evidence for physiological breakdown of the type which Sargent has observed in brainwashing and war neurosis. (Gerlach and Hine, 1967)

14. William Wood (1965) used the Rorschach technique in an attempt ". . . to test the hypothesis that personality types participating in highly emotional religions will vary in some regular way from types participating in more sedate religions. . . . Unfortunately, the only significant differences between the Pentecostal and non-Pentecostal Rorschach results were in the area of shading which is the 'chief area of dispute' among Rorschach authorities concerning scoring the responses. . . . There are apparent inconsistencies in his conclusions. . . . Until we have more data on this aspect, all evidence concerning psychological characteristics that predispose individuals to glossolalia or to participation in the movement must be considered inconclusive." (Gerlach and Hine, 1967)

15. Gerlach and Hine (1968) found five factors which they felt were responsible for the growth of the movement. They reported these as: (1) reticulate organization, (2) fervent and convincing recruitment, (3) commitment after experience, (4) change oriented and action motivated ideology, and (5) the perception of real or imagined opposition.

16. A section of a report of the Diocese of California Episcopal Church study commission on glossolalia, May 2, 1963, is relevant to this investigation. The report indicated that the psychiatrists on the committee generally reacted in the affirmative to the concept that speaking in tongues provided a new language which helped to overcome inadequacy. They pointed out that "our deepest feelings and convictions with the roots in the sub-conscious seldom can be adequately articulated by the conscious." The report stated "without judging whether glossolalia be of God or not, our psychiatrists sense that it could be for some, a healthy outlet freeing and enlarging religious life. Again, the scientists' research cannot determine whether it is the Holy Spirit that provides the language of the glossolalists or not, but it can affirm that the need for expression beyond normal verbalization is a wholesome part of a normal person's life. To satisfy it is to enrich life, so long as the means itself is not self-destructive." (Diocese of California, 1963.)

17. Pattison (1968) has indicated that "many adherents of the

glossolalia movement assert that the experience has made a change in their lives, has improved their style and quality of personality and life. Clinicians have been hesitant to accept such testimonials. Yet a careful study of non-pathological mystical experiences, such as the work of Deckman, Underhill, Sedman, and Salzman have illustrated that mystical experience, often in a religious context can be an integrative emotional experience that results in an altered life style with subsequent improvement in life adaptation."

18. *A Definition*. Charisma can be defined as "a spiritual gift or talent regarded as divinely granted to a person as a token of grace or favor and exemplified in early Christianity by the power of healing, gift of tongues, or prophesying." This then is a proper label, but the term is not reserved only to the religious but has other references and many times is used in non-religious contexts. By further definition, charisma is "supernatural power or virtue attributed especially to person or office, regarded as set apart from the ordinary by reason of a special relationship or, that which is considered value and is endowed with the capacity of eliciting enthusiastic popular support and leadership, symbolic unification, or direction of human affairs."

Subcommittee Procedures

In reviewing the psychological dimensions of the charismatic movement, the subcommittee listened to the testimony of clergy, both in support of the movement and against the movement. The committee met with biblical scholars, theologians, and seminarians of this and other denominations. An exhaustive review was conducted of the relevant literature, including reports of other denominations, pamphlets, journals, articles, research reports, tapes, books, etc.

Members of the subcommittee visited numerous kinds and varieties of charismatic meetings, and the entire subcommittee visited a large Episcopalian church in one of the major cities of this country to meet with the members of the church, official boards, and the minister. Approximately 80 percent of this congregation were involved participants in the charismatic dimension of the Christian experience. Members of the subcommittee interviewed approximately forty members of the congregation in groups and individually, including children, teenagers, representatives of official boards, persons from all walks of life, educational backgrounds and social classes, those

Work of the Holy Spirit

who participated and were involved in the movement who had the charismatic infilling of the Holy Spirit and those who did not. Extensive interviews were held with the rector. Observations were made of a regular Friday evening charismatic meeting attended by approximately 250 persons. Individually, members of the subcommittee discussed the movement extensively with representatives of the various scientific disciplines and clergy from many denominations including the Roman Catholic Church.

The subcommittee found no evidence of pathology in the movement. The movement was found to be dynamic, growing, and involving persons from practically every denomination, walk and station in life. Varied educational backgrounds and personality patterns are present and the socio-economic status ranges from the uneducated through those in high executive positions carrying great responsibility in major corporations, in federal government and in the space effort. Physicians, psychologists, psychiatrists, scientists, professors of every description, clergy of every denomination including the hierarchy, and professors of religion and philosophy are to be found in the movement.

This portion of the report prepared by Thomas Foster, M.D., and Charles H. Meisgeier, Ed.D.

REFERENCES

Adorno, T. W., E. Frenkel-Brunswik, D. Levinson, R. M. Sanford. 1950 *The Authoritarian Personality*. Harper, New York.

Alland, Alexander. 1961 Possession in a Revivalist Negro Church. *Jnl. for the Scientific Study of Relig.* Vol. 1., No. 2.

Boisen, Anton. 1939 Economic Distress and Religious Experience: A Study of the Holy Rollers. *Psychiatry* 2: 185–194.

Cutten, G. B. 1927 *Speaking With Tongues*. Yale Univ. Press, New Haven.

Frank, Jerome C. 1961 *Persuasion and Healing: A Comparative Study of Psychotherapy*. John Hopkins Press, Baltimore.

Gerlach, L. P. and V. H. Hine. 1967 *Non-Pathological Pentecostal Glossolalia: A Summary of Relevant Psychological Literature, A Report Prepared for Director of the Pentecostal Movement Research Committee.*

Gerlach, L. P. and V. H. Hine. 1968 Five Factors Crucial to the Growth and Spread of a Modern Religious Movement. *Jnl. for the Sci. Study of Relig.* VII: 23–40.

Gerrard, Nathan L. and Louise B. 1966 *Scrabble Creek Folk: Mental Health Part II.* Unpublished Report, Dept. of Sociology, Morris Harvey College, Charleston, West Virginia.

Lapsley, J. N. and J. M. Simpson.

1964 a Speaking in Tongues: Token of Group Acceptance and Divine Approval. *Pastoral Psychology*. May: 48–55.

1964 b Speaking in Tongues: Infantile Babble or Song of the Self. *Pastoral*

Psychology. Sept.: 16–24.

McDonnell, Kilian.

1968 Holy Spirit and Pentecostalism. *Commonweal*. Vol. 89, No. 6. November 1968.

1970 Catholic Pentecostalism: Problems in Evaluation. *Dialog*. Winter 1970.

Pattison, E. M.

1964 Speaking in Tongues and About Tongues. *Christian Standard*, Feb. 15, Cincinnati, Ohio.

1965 The Effects of a Religious Culture's Values on Personality Psychodynamics. Read to Section H, Anthropology, Amer. Assn. for the Advancement of Science. December 1965.

1968 Behavioral Science Research on the Nature of Glossolalia. *Jnl. of the American Scientific Affiliation*. September 1968.

Sargant, William.

1949 Some Cultural Group Abbrective Techniques and Their Relation to Modern Treatments. *Pro. Royal Sco. of Medicine*. 42: 367ff.

1957 *Battle for the Mind*. New York.

Vivier, Lincoln M. V. E. 1960 *Glossolalia*. Unpublished thesis, University of Witwatersrand Dept. of Psychiatry. Microfilm available University of Chicago Union Theological Seminary.

Wood, William W. 1965 *Culture and Personality Aspects of the Pentecostal Holiness Religion*. Mouton, Paris.

Diocese of California, The Episcopal Church, Division of Pastoral Services, *Preliminary Report, Study Commission on Glossolalia*. May, 1963.

19 Episcopal Church, USA, 1971

1971 PASTORAL LETTER FROM THE HOUSE OF BISHOPS

The earlier documents of the Episcopal Bishops Pike, Burrill, and Bloy are not official documents of the Episcopal Church but are diocesan documents issued by the competent local bishop in dealing pastorally with the presence of the charismatic renewal in the parishes of his jurisdiction. The three sentences in the 1971 pastoral letter from the House of Bishops is the closest expression of an official position. The bishops recognized the presence of the Spirit's transforming power in the charismatic renewal, which finds expression in gifts of prayer, praise, and healing, but also in the liturgical life of the church. A frequent criticism of all the denominational expressions of the charismatic renewal is their lack of social awareness and involvement. The bishops call attention to the necessity of religious faith manifesting itself concretely in external works which further "justice and brotherhood."

The pastoral letter was reprinted in "Special Meeting of the House of Bishops, which was held at the Pocono Manor Inn, Pocono Manor, Pennsylvania, on October 24–29, 1971. See pp. 37–38.

To Our Brothers and Sisters of The Episcopal Church, Greetings.

We speak to you as fellow members of the Body of Christ. We also speak to you as Chief Pastors of Christ's Church. One of the privileges of our coming together as Bishops is that our meeting is one in which every single parish and mission in the Episcopal Church is known. Out of that closeness to all of you have come certain common observations and assurances which we want to share with you.

We affirm that our message is Jesus Christ.

Through His death and resurrection God has reconciled the world to Himself. Through Him God offers unity to all mankind. He has brought us into the new life lived in the power of the risen Christ. We witness to a common faith and a common life of love and service.

We affirm that our Lord has triumphed.

Therefore we live in sure hope and certain faith, even in the midst of the fears, troubles, and perplexities of the present day. His Spirit works through these also. God has shown us His mighty works in history. We stand expectantly at the beginning of a great period of the Church's history — a more glory-filled day than has gone before.

We see all around us evidences of the movement of the Holy Spirit . . . in the lives of individuals and in the life of the Church.

There is a new hunger for certainties of the spiritual life outside of the Church as well as within it. We see a search for a deeper and more truly human life. We observe a newly awakened understanding of the sacredness of God's creation.

We see a growing awareness of the pentecostal power of the Holy Spirit to transform men and women.

He is working in the devotional lives of His people, and in their experience of His charismatic gifts of prayer, praise, and healing, and in their joy in the sacramental life. We praise Him for showing us again that faith without works is dead, and that there can be no divorce between religious faith and active concern for justice and brotherhood.

We see in our Church a new openness in which differences can be accepted: a new willingness to face the future and to grapple with the problems of relating the Gospel to the realities of racism, war, and poverty.

We believe the Church is ready to pay the price for witnessing to the difference that Christian discipleship should make to attitudes toward society, and its unexamined assumptions.

We rejoice that He has called us to share in Christ's ministry of reconciliation.

We accept this ministry as one that is shared with all the people of God. We find true hope for the unity and mission of the Church in the growing ecumenical relations of all Christian bodies. We rejoice especially in the Christian fellowship across denominational and racial divisions which has been encouraged by the Consultation on Church Union and the Second Vatican Council of the Roman Catholic Church.

God has given us an abundance of vocations to the ordained ministry, but we are concerned by the Church's present inability to use this gift. We are aware of the suffering which this continues to cause. When we understand fully the mission of the Church, we find it impossible to think that God has provided more vocations than we need. There are new forms of mission and ministry emerging which may heal these wounds. However, this is only a beginning. A vast amount of work lies ahead of us, and we intend to keep moving.

Another evidence of the leading of the spirit in which we rejoice is the growing independence of the Churches overseas.

They are proud to be a part of their own cultures, and are determined not to be seen as dependents of a foreign institution. They have given us a new and refreshing concept of the meaning of the world-wide mission of the Church.

We are thankful for the steadfastness of so many of our people who have been faithful to Christ and His Church in times of confusion and controversy, at great cost to their own peace of mind and comfort.

Some of them have been leaders in change. Others have been loyal to the actions of the Church even when they did not understand or accept the changes that were being urged upon them. For this kind of costly discipleship we give thanks to God.

We ask all of you to join us in giving thanks to God for the privilege of serving Him in this time of unparalleled opportunity.

House of Bishops' Pastoral Letter

Christ has died! Christ is risen! Christ will come again!

Thanks be to God who has given us the victory in our Lord Jesus Christ. To Him be the glory forever!

20 Mennonite Church, USA, 1971

THE HOLY SPIRIT

The Lancaster Conference is one of the largest regional groups of the Mennonite Church and was for years considered one of the most conservative. It is noteworthy that a conference with a conservative tradition would take an open position on the charismatic renewal as early as 1971.

The brief statement explained the role of the Spirit as God's gift, his person, the charisms of the Spirit, and how the Christian community should react to the experience of the Spirit.

The gift of the Spirit effects a new birth, but this "does not assure the wonderful experience of being continuously filled with the Spirit." At the same time it is evident that many Christians are living below their expected spiritual potential. While the Spirit comes into the heart with fullness, he cannot make that fullness functional until there is a total surrender of heart and life. The gifts of the Spirit are for service. Neither the presence nor absence of certain gifts can be considered as the evidence that one is filled or not filled with the Spirit. Though the exercise of the gifts needs discernment "let us not attempt to control, criticize, explain away, or deny his workings. . . . Within a congregation's program there should be opportunity for unhindered manifestation of the Spirit's presence through the vibrant expression of praise and the fearless spreading of the Good News of the mighty works of God taking place in our time."

This brief statement was adopted by the Lancaster Conference on September 16, 1971. When the first Mennonite Church charismatic renewal conference was held in May 1974 in Lancaster, Pennsylvania, the moderator of the Lancaster Conference, Bishop Raymond Charles, read from this statement during his welcoming address.

The statement was reprinted in the "Report to the Lancaster Mennonite Conference," September 16, 1971, pp. 2–3.

THE GIFT OF THE HOLY SPIRIT

The Holy Spirit is God's gift to mankind under the New Covenant. The receiving of this gift brings about the new birth. (Joel 2:28-32; John 7:37-39; 14:20; Acts 2:1-4, 14-21, 38). The Holy Spirit brings the fulness of the Godhead into His sons (John 1:12; Colossians 2:9, 10). The new birth does not assure the wonderful experience of being continuously filled with the Spirit. (Ephesians 5:18). It is evident that many Christians are living on a low spiritual plane.

THE PERSON OF THE HOLY SPIRIT

The Holy Spirit comes into the heart with all the fulness of God. But He cannot make that fulness functional until there is a total surrender to Him in heart and life (Romans 8:2). Such surrender is never easy. Often it is made after defeat and dissatisfaction with one's experience. Only when that full surrender is maintained in daily life, can the indwelling Holy Spirit fill the heart to overflowing. (Romans 6:13) (Galatians 5:22).

THE GIFTS OF THE SPIRIT

The Holy Spirit gives gifts to each member of the church severally as He wills. These gifts are for service and for the unifying of the Body. We recognize the gifts of the Spirit that are in keeping with New Testament example and experience. (1 Corinthians 12:4-11, 25-27). No one has all the gifts. No one can claim superiority for himself nor judge another's gifts. Nor can the presence or absence of certain gifts be considered as the evidence of being filled or not filled with the Spirit. (1 Corinthians 12:29-31). We may discern true spiritual experience by its compatibility with the Spirit of Jesus Christ. He obeyed His Father, who has promised to give the Holy Spirit also to them who obey Him (Acts 5:32). If the experience produces self-righteousness, hostility, exaggerated claims of knowledge and power, it should be questioned. If, however, the experience produces new dimensions of love, joy, peace, and faith and blessing to others, we must conclude it is of the Lord.

THE SPIRIT'S WORKING AMONG US

The Holy Spirit is bringing new life and fulness into the lives of many Christians today. We should praise God for every work of the Holy Spirit even though our experiences and gifts differ. Let

The Holy Spirit

us not attempt to control, criticize, explain away, or deny His workings. Not everything that is new comes from the Holy Spirit. We need to try the spirits and let God and time reveal their true source. May God give us discernment as we try the spirits to see whether they be of God. (1 John 4:1, 2). Within a congregation's program there should be opportunity for unhindered manifestation of the Spirit's presence through the vibrant expression of praise and the fearless spreading of the Good News of the mighty works of God taking place in our time. Let us ask God by His Holy Spirit to bring new life in all its fulness to every Christian.

21 Presbyterian Church in the United States, 1971

THE PERSON AND WORK OF THE HOLY SPIRIT, WITH SPECIAL REFERENCE TO "THE BAPTISM IN THE HOLY SPIRIT"

A more ambitious study project than the 1964 report was initiated at the 1967 General Assembly of the Presbyterian Church in the United States which requested the Permanent Theological Committee to make a further study. Unlike the 1964 report, the larger and more extensive 1971 study is made within a broader theological context and does not concentrate on the phenomenon of tongues, as is indicated in its title. It has a more pronounced exegetical basis than the earlier report. Like the commission of the United Presbyterians, this commission also had in its membership persons who had associated themselves with the charismatic renewal. Some attention was given to the modes of contemporary experience of the Spirit, which was followed by an exegetical study of the Spirit in the Old and New Testaments. A section was devoted to the Spirit in the confessional writings and the report concluded with some theological and pastoral observations.

A matter of preoccupation for this report is the relationship of the bestowal of the Spirit to water baptism. "Though baptism is a channel of God's grace, this grace is not automatically efficacious. Accordingly, there may be special need in the Reformed tradition to lay stress on later occasions . . . on which God's grace may also be appropriated. . . . We need to be open-minded toward those today" who claim an intervening period of time between baptism in water and receiving the Spirit. Looking at the Westminster Confession of Faith and Catechisms, the report asserted that "what is conferred in baptism may become efficacious by the Spirit at a later time." A caution was expressed lest the Acts of the Apostles be read in isolation from the rest of the New Testament. In particular, "It would be concluding too much to say the writer of Acts assumes any particular spiritual manifestations accompany the reception of the Holy Spirit. On the other hand, it seems clear that the writer of Acts does view speaking in tongues as undeniable evidence that the Holy Spirit has been given."

Though little attention is paid to the psychological aspects, there was a caution with regard to the limits of behavioral sciences in validating religious experience: "An experience of the Spirit can neither be validated as such, nor evaluated with respect to its theological significance, by any scientific (i.e., psychological, sociological, etc.) means. . . . Regardless of the scientific conclusions which may be reached, the question of the theological significance of these phenomena will remain, and it may be answered only within the context of the Christian faith." At the same time the report is careful not to assert that the extraordinary or unusual nature of an experience is a standard by which to judge its significance for faith. In the first instance religious experience is an ambiguous event and needs discernment. "Not every dramatic event, experience, or ecstasy is necessarily a work of the Spirit."

The report is found in the "Minutes of the 111th General Assembly of the Presbyterian Church in the United States," Massanetta Springs, Virginia, June 13–18, 1971, pp. 104–17. An offprint is available entitled "The Person and Work of the Holy Spirit" from the church headquarters at 341 Ponce de Leon Ave. N.E., Atlanta, GA 30308.

INTRODUCTION

The following study on the Holy Spirit comes to the General Assembly in response to the Assembly's action on a resolution introduced at the 1967 Assembly (G.A. Min., p. 103) by the Reverend Andrew A. Jumper. Specifically, the 1967 Assembly referred the resolution to the Permanent Theological Committee "for a study of the doctrine of the person and work of the Holy Spirit."

As the remit to the committee is worded, it may be construed as a request for a dissertation of book length. Such a study, if possible for a committee at all, would be of staggering cost in time, effort, and money, and could not be expected to appear in print for a number of years. (Moreover, the committee calls attention to the selected bibliography appended to this report on which several rather thorough-going and comprehensive works on the Holy Spirit are listed.) In view of this situation, the committee has decided to offer a paper which does not claim to be comprehensive, but intends to speak directly to the specific situations and events which gave rise to the resolution. Fortunately, Mr. Jumper has provided a clear presentation of the background for his resolution in a printed pamphlet entitled "The Baptism of the Holy Spirit and the Renewal of the Church."

Examination of the background pamphlet and of the text of the resolution indicates that the central issue is the concept of the "baptism of the Holy Spirit" or "infilling" of the Spirit, together with the various "spiritual gifts" or manifestations of the Spirit which may follow that event. It is clear, furthermore, that the event of Spirit baptism is conceived as something which is not merely to be identified with, and may be removed in time from, one's conversion and/or baptism with water. An understanding of the Spirit's work becomes the more urgent when it is recognized that the entire ministry and mission of the church, present and future, is dependent upon his life and power in our midst. It is with special reference to these observations that the following discussion is presented.

The committee is also aware that this resolution and pamphlet stem from a situation that is fairly widespread today. Hence the reply which follows will seek first to give some outline of the contemporary scene before proceeding to Biblical and theological reflection.

I. CERTAIN CONTEMPORARY EXPERIENCES OF THE SPIRIT

A. There are a number of people in historic Protestant churches — and most recently in the Roman Catholic Church — who have had an experience which they call "the baptism of (with, in) the Holy Spirit," or sometimes "the filling of (with) the Holy Spirit." This experience has been so meaningful and vivid to those who have gone through it that they have difficulty putting it into words: "a new relationship, a deeper encounter, a closer walk." Many speak of it primarily as an extraordinary sense of God's reality and presence, and lay claim to a praise and adoration of God hitherto unknown to them. At the same time they often testify to a new bond of community with those who have had the same experience, and a heightened desire and capacity to bear witness to the gospel. In all aspects of life they claim a deeper love, joy, and peace. Frequently they testify to a multiplicity of "charismata," such as "speaking in tongues," prophecy, healing and so on. Many claim that "speaking in tongues" was the primary manifestation of their "filling" or "baptism," for it has been either an immediate accompaniment of their experience or has followed some time later. They usually disclaim an interest in the spectacular as such; rather, their testimony is to the reality of God, a deeper awareness of his presence, and the wonder that the Holy Spirit has filled their being.

As these people seek to understand what has happened to them, they generally speak of it as an occurrence within their Christian life. Usually they think of themselves as having been believers for a long time; hence, they do not interpret this experience as entrance into faith but as something beyond. Sometimes they speak of salvation *and* being "filled with the Spirit". They claim that both could (and sometimes do) occur at the same moment, but for most of them there has been a separation in time. Frequently this "baptism with the Spirit" has occurred after the laying on of hands; but this is not true in all cases. For most of these people the testimony is that — with or without the laying on of hands — the experience occurred after extended prayer and seeking. Some speak of this event as a transition within their Christian experience, from the state of Christ's (or the Spirit's) being *with* them to his being *in* them. Others say that the transition is rather to be understood as a fuller realization of what was already within them. In any case, these people feel sure that they have entered into a new and exciting life in the Spirit.

B. The events which we have enumerated have raised some critical problems for our Church, and especially for those congregations in which the events have occurred. In the first place, we have tended to stress the work of the Spirit in the life of the believer as uniting the believer to Christ and thereby bringing to him God's grace in salvation. Justification has been viewed as the initial work of the Spirit in applying to man the benefits of Christ's work, and sanctification as the ongoing work of the Spirit in completing the divine purpose by transforming a human life more and more into the likeness of Jesus Christ. But in this contemporary experience of the Spirit there seems to be testimony to an additional working of the Spirit that goes beyond the initiation of Christian life (justification) and its progress

The Person and Work of the Holy Spirit

(sanctification) — a "baptism" or "filling" with the Holy Spirit. The critical question here is how, in the light of the Biblical witness and the Reformed tradition, this understanding is to be adjudged.

In the second place, problems of another kind also arise from the situation to which we have referred. When some members of a congregation claim special pneumatic experiences, or claim extraordinary gifts — e.g., healing, speaking in tongues — the peace, unity, and fellowship of the Church may be seriously jeopardized. Differing views of the Spirit and his work may give rise to a schism between those who claim a Spirit baptism and those who do not, or between those who recognize the validity of such claims and those who do not. Obviously our Church ought to provide some guidance in these matters where strong differences of opinion may result in contention and the disruption of the Church's work.

Manifestly, any valid guidance that can be given on this, or on any other subject, must be derived from the teachings of Scripture, and must be evaluated in the light of the Standards of our church. We shall therefore attempt to sketch what the Old and the New Testaments have to say with regard to the Spirit, and then to examine the teachings of the Confession of Faith and the Catechisms, before proceeding to draw conclusions.

II. CONCERNING THE SPIRIT IN THE OLD TESTAMENT

The Old Testament offers no teaching regarding the Holy Spirit as a distinct person of the Godhead alongside the Father and the Son. On the few occasions when the term "holy Spirit" occurs (only Isa 63:10f, and Ps 51:11 [H. 13]), it is virtually a synonym for the person and presence of the holy God himself. But "the Spirit of God/Yahweh (the LORD)" is mentioned with great frequency throughout the Old Testament and clearly represents an important aspect of its understanding of God and his actions.

A. "Spirit" in General

The Hebrew word for "spirit," *ruach*, occurs approximately 375 times in the Old Testament. Although we are concerned here with the word only as it is applied to God, a few remarks regarding its usage in general would be helpful by way of background.

1. The basic force of *ruach* is physical; wind, breeze, air, breath.

The word frequently has this sense in the Old Testament, e.g., Num 11:31; Jer 14:6; Gen 3:8. From this physical force there develops quite naturally the metaphorical one: what is empty, vacuous, without substance, "windy." This meaning is likewise attested in the Old Testament (Isa 41:29; Jer 5:13; etc.).

2. Still with the physical sense of "wind, breath," *ruach* is used of the breath which is in man, which keeps him in life (e.g., Isa 42:5; Ps 104:29). It thus can denote the vital principle in man and beast (e.g., Gen 6:17; 7:15, 22; Ecc 3:19) and even on occasion, life itself (e.g., Job 12:10; Ps 31:5 [H. 6], "Into thy hand I commit my *ruach*"). Note, however, that although men die when their *ruach* is taken away (Ps 104:29), *ruach* is never used in the Old Testament to denote an apparition, a ghost, as "spirit" often is in English.

3. Most often, however, when "spirit" is used of man it denotes a dominant disposition, an impulse, a mood, feeling or temper (as in Gen 41:8; 1 Kings 21:5; Num 5:14; Hos 4:12; Prv 25:28; etc.). In this connection the Old Testament often depicts God as acting upon the dispositions of individuals or groups — for good or for ill — in order to accomplish his purpose. Thus he sent "an evil spirit" (i.e., bad blood) between the men of Shechem and Abimelech in order to prepare for the latter's downfall (Jds 9:23); or he sent "an evil spirit" (a demonic mood, a diabolical disposition) on Saul (1 Sam 16:14-23; 18:10; 19:9); or placed a "lying spirit" in the mouth of the prophets to entice Ahab to his ruin (1 Kings 22:22f); or poured out "a spirit of deep sleep" (i.e., of stultification) on his own people (Isa 29:10). On the other hand, he "put a spirit" (i.e., an anxiety) in the Assyrian king to turn him from Jerusalem (Isa 37:7; II Kings 19:7); he "stirred up" the spirit of the Medes against Babylon (Jer. 51:11), and that of Cyrus to decree the restoration of the Jewish community (Ezra 1:1); he likewise "stirred up the spirit" of Zerubbabel, Joshua, and the people to undertake the rebuilding of the temple (Hag 1:14). We see, thus, that God not only confers his Spirit upon men (below), but moves upon their spirits for the accomplishment of his purpose.

B. *The Spirit of God/Yahweh*

1. The word *ruach* when applied to God may have as wide a range of meanings as does *ruach* in general. Although some of these are not directly germane to our discussion, we shall briefly mention them.

a. Even when used of God, *ruach* may retain its primary sense and denote the wind, as when God piled up the waters of the Red Sea by the "blast" (*ruach*) of his nostrils (Exod 15:8). Frequently, however, "wind" (or "the breath of Yahweh" or "the blast/breath of his nostrils/anger," etc.) is used as a metaphor for God's wrath as he comes to judge (e.g., Isa 11:15, 40:7; Jer 4:12f.; Hos 13:15; Job 4:9).

b. Again, God's *ruach* may denote the "breath" which God infuses in man (cf. Gen 2:7), giving him life and sustaining him in it (e.g. Job 27:3; Ps 104:29f.). In such passages man's breath is spoken of as "the spirit of God" which is the source of his life, but which is finally withdrawn so that he dies (Job 34:14f.; Gen 6:3). Sometimes, indeed, the "breath" of Yahweh is extended to denote God's creative power in general, and is made synonymous with his "word" whereby he brought all things into being (Ps 33:6).

c. Most frequently, however, the term *ruach* (Spirit) of God/Yahweh" is used to denote a mysterious divine energy, or charisma, which from time to time came upon men and possessed them, enabling them for the performance of certain specific tasks. This usage of the term is, of course, central to our interest here. The Spirit is always depicted as manifesting itself in unusual powers, gifts, and abilities of various kinds. Sometimes this might be exceptional artistic and technical skill, as when Bezalel was filled "with the Spirit of God, with ability, with intelligence, with knowledge, and with all craftmanship" in order to undertake the preparation of the tabernacle and its furnishings (Exod 31:3; 35:31). Or it might be an extraordinary understanding and wisdom such as that which enabled Joseph (Gen 41:33f.) or Daniel (Dan 5:14) to interpret dreams and other divine revelations. Indeed, wisdom and understanding generally can be spoken of as a gift of the Spirit (Job 32:7f.). But although the gifts of the Spirit were considered exceedingly diverse, and not confined to any single class of people, in the overwhelming majority of its occurrences "the Spirit of God" is associated with the charismatic leaders of Israel's early period, and with prophetic inspiration.

2. The Spirit and Israel's Leaders. Israel's leaders prior to the establishment of the monarchy were said to be men who were filled with the Spirit. This is true of Moses (Num 11:25) and Joshua (Num 27:18). In the case of Moses this involved the gift of prophecy, for when "some of the spirit that was upon him" was placed upon the 70 elders, they prophesied. But the Spirit also conveyed the gifts of leadership, for when Moses laid his hand on

Joshua to appoint him as his successor we are told that Joshua "was full of the spirit of wisdom," so that the people obeyed him (Deut 34:9).

But the possession of the Spirit is associated especially with the Judges. Here the Spirit is conceived as an invading divine power, a charismatic fury, which seized the Judge and inspired him to rally the people and lead them to victory over their foes, and in some cases enabled him to perform feats of superhuman strength. Thus the Spirit of Yahweh "came upon" Othniel (Jds 3:10) and Jephthah (Jds 11:29), and "took possession" of Gideon (Jds 6:34; lit. "clothed itself" with him), enabling each to win mighty victories for Israel. Samson's career began when "the Spirit of Yahweh began to stir him" (Jds 13:25), and when the Spirit "came mightily upon him" he was able to kill a lion with his bare hands (Jds 14:6) and perform other feats of valor and prodigious strength (Jds 14:19; 15:14). Saul also stood in the line of the charismatic Judges, for we read (I Sam 11:6) that, when danger threatened Israel, "the Spirit of God came mightily upon him" and inspired him to rally the clans to battle. In none of these cases are we to think of the Spirit as a permanent possession of the Judge, but rather as a power from God which came to him in moments of emergency; it was not something that was with him always, still less could he pass it on to a successor, as Moses did to Joshua. In the case of Saul we are specifically told that because of his disobedience the Spirit was taken from him, and an "evil spirit" from God sent in to its place (above).

Although David is spoken of as a man of the Spirit (I Sam 16:13), it is with him that the line of charismatic leaders ends; thereafter king followed king by dynastic succession, and no other ruler in Israel is said to have possessed the Spirit of God (though in Zech 4:6 it is promised that Zerubbabel will be enabled to complete the temple by God's Spirit). But the ideal of the Spirit-endowed ruler was treasured as a promise for the future. The time will come (Isa 28:6) when God himself will be "a spirit of justice — and strength" to Israel's rulers. There will come an ideal king, "a shoot from the stump of Jesse," upon whom "the Spirit of Yahweh shall rest" (Isa 11:1-2); and this Spirit is characterized as "the spirit of wisdom and understanding, the spirit of counsel and might, the spirit of knowledge and the fear of Yahweh" (i.e., the presence of God's Spirit will endow the coming king with all these graces). Likewise, God's Servant, whose task it is to bring

The Person and Work of the Holy Spirit

God's salvation to the nations, will have God's spirit upon him (Isa 42:1; cf. also 61:1).

3. Prophecy and the Spirit. The Spirit also manifested itself in prophetic inspiration. As we have seen, when some of the Spirit that was on Moses was transferred to the 70 elders, they prophesied, as did Eldad and Medad (Num 11:25, 29). Balaam likewise gave his oracles under the influence of the Spirit (Num 24:2). When Saul met a band of prophets who were prophesying to the sound of music, the Spirit of God "came mightily upon him," and he too prophesied (1 Sam 10:5f., 10). The ecstatic nature of such experiences is evident from 1 Samuel 19:23f., where we read that Saul stripped off his clothes and lay naked on the ground all day and all night "prophesying." Elisha was gripped by God's "hand" (RSV "power") while a minstrel played and, in that condition, uttered an oracle (2 Kgs 3:15). Sometimes the Spirit is considered a quasi-physical force which carried the prophet from one place to another, like a great wind blowing the leaves (1 Kgs 18:12; 2 Kgs 2:16; Ezek 3:14; 8:3; 11:1; 43:5). So closely, indeed, were Spirit possession and prophetic utterance connected that it was possible to speak of the prophet as "the man of the spirit" (Hos 9:7): it was God's Spirit that spoke through the prophet's mouth (2 Sam 23:2; 1 Kgs 22:24). Spirit possession was primarily associated with ecstatic prophecy, and (outside Ezekiel) is seldom mentioned in the books of the classical prophets; but even Micah could say, "I am filled with power, with the Spirit of Yahweh, and with justice and might, to declare to Jacob his transgression and to Israel his sin" (Mic 3:8).

4. The Spirit and All Israel. Although it is occasionally stated that God's Spirit was with Israel in the wilderness days (Isa 63:11; Neh 9:20), the Spirit is never depicted as being bestowed on the people as a whole, but only on certain exceptional individuals. But the hope is expressed that the time will come when all Israel will receive the Spirit. Moses expressed the wish that all God's people might be prophets (Num 11:29); and Joel announced the time when the Spirit would be poured out on all flesh, and all would in fact prophesy (Joel 2:28 f.[H. 3:1f]). But the outpouring of the Spirit will bring not merely the gift of prophecy; it will bring to Israel a new spirit of obedience (Ezek 36:26f.; cf. 37:14; 39:29), and a new loyalty and devotion to God (Isa 44:3-5), a spirit of "compassion and supplication" (Zech 12:10). Indeed the gift of the Spirit is the sign and pledge of the fulfillment of his covenant

promises (Isa 59:21) and of the new future that God has prepared for his people (Isa 32:15).

5. In the Old Testament, then, the spirit is not distinct from God, but represents God himself in one aspect of his activity toward his creation. God is in his nature "spirit" and not "flesh" (Isa 31:3). The Spirit of God is indistinguishable from God in his work as creator (Isa 40:13), and the presence of the Spirit with God's people is equivalent to the presence of God himself (Hag 2:5). As the Psalmist said, "Cast me not away from thy presence, and take not thy holy Spirit from me" (Ps 51:11 [H. 13]); and again, "Whither shall I go from thy Spirit? Or whither shall I flee from thy presence?" (Ps 139:7). To have the gift of the Spirit is to be in the presence of God.

III. CONCERNING THE SPIRIT IN THE NEW TESTAMENT

A. "Spirit" in General

The New Testament word for spirit, *pneuma*, has many of the same general associations as the Old Testament word *ruach*. Its basic sense is that of a movement of air, a wind, a breath. By reason of its use to designate the breath of a living being, it accrued to itself the meaning of the vital principle of life or animation. It is then used generically to denote a simple essence which is without material substance, and thus may mean a human soul (in this sense often an equivalent of *psyche*), an angel, or a demon. Sometimes it carries the general idea of a disposition or influence, an affection, emotion, or desire.

B. The Spirit of God

As the term is applied in the New Testament to God, however, it takes on a special meaning. Much of this special meaning is determined by the fact that the writers of the New Testament, as the early Christians generally, were thoroughly schooled in and influenced by the Old Testament Scriptures. It is only natural, therefore, that "the Spirit of the Lord" or "the Spirit of God" (sometimes simply "the Spirit") occupies a special place in New Testament thought. By virtue of the prominence it has in the New Testament, the particular expression "Holy Spirit" was adopted by the post-apostolic church, the concept developed doctrinally and used in creeds through the centuries, and is the term most popularly used today by Christians (as evidenced by our own *Confession of Faith*, especially Chapter IX).

The Person and Work of the Holy Spirit

1. From the New Testament standpoint, the most significant divergence from the Old Testament usage and meaning appears in the fact that the Holy Spirit is now inseparably connected with Jesus Christ. The nature of this connection is stated in various ways. Among the most prominent are the following:

a. The Gospels of Matthew and Luke state that the Spirit was uniquely active in the conception of Jesus (Matt 1:20; Luke 1:35).

b. The Spirit descended upon Jesus in a special way at the time of his baptism (Mark 1:10 and parallels).

c. After his baptism Jesus was led (driven) by the Spirit into the wilderness to be tempted (Mark 1:12 and parallels).

d. The deeds and words of Jesus are due to the Spirit's presence with him (Luke 4:18), and according to Matthew (12:28) his exorcisms are explicitly by the power of God's Spirit.

e. The Gospel of John, in which the Spirit figures most prominently, presents Jesus as the one who will send the Spirit upon his disciples (1:33; 16:7), and the giving of the Spirit by the risen Lord is reported among the resurrection stories (20:22).

f. The Apostle Paul states outright: "The Lord [i.e., Christ] is the Spirit" (2 Cor 3:17).

g. The first epistle of Peter identifies the Spirit of the Old Testament as "the Spirit of Christ" (1:11).

h. There are numerous New Testament passages in which the "Spirit of Christ" is used as a synonym for, or interchangeably with the "Spirit of God" or the "Holy Spirit" (for example: Acts 16:6, 7; 2 Cor 3:17, 18; Romans 8:9; Galatians 4:6; Philippians 1:19; 1 Peter 1:11).

2. Moreover, the unique place occupied by the Holy Spirit in the New Testament is further determined by the faith of the disciples that in the events of the life, death, and resurrection of Jesus the new age had dawned. It was noted above that the messianic king for whom Israel looked was to be one on whom the "Spirit of God shall rest" (Isaiah 11:1-2), and the faith that Jesus was the Messiah is the basis for the New Testament's close association of the Spirit with Jesus. Also, when the Spirit is said to have descended upon the followers of Jesus on the Day of Pentecost (Acts 2), it is clear that this event is portrayed as a fulfillment of the eschatological hope of the Jews. Peter's speech (Acts 2:14-36) cites the words of Joel 2 to the effect that the "last days" have now come, and God is now pouring out his Spirit upon his servants, enabling them to prophesy (see especially Acts 2:16-18). These two aspects of the New Testament concept of the

Spirit are merely two of the most basic out of a multitude of ideas which point up the fact that the Spirit is to be understood as an eschatological reality. His presence is not only the fulfillment of Old Testament expectations, but, as we shall also mention again below, the guarantee of the completion of God's purpose in the future.

3. Since the Spirit is an eschatological reality, and because the church is to be seen as the eschatological people of God, the New Testament also teaches that there is a special connection between the Holy Spirit and the church. Although possession of the Spirit is sometimes said to characterize individual Christians and to work through them in a sense not common to the whole body (see below), the most common concept of the Holy Spirit in the New Testament is that he is present in and among *all* believers. It is not so much, therefore, a matter of an individual's special relation to God which is expressed by the concept of the Spirit, but the relation between God and his church ("church" being understood here as the body of believers, and not simply the earthly institution). The Spirit is present in *every* believer and sanctifies them *all* (Romans 8:9-11; 1 Cor 6:19; 1 Peter 1:2). He is the bond of unity, the power which makes the wholeness of the body a reality (1 Cor 12:4-11; Eph 4:1-16). Moreover, the Spirit equips church members with gifts, gifts which may seem on occasion to set apart the possessor of the gifts from other believers; but these gifts of the Spirit are always seen in the New Testament as special talents and abilities provided for the purpose of carrying out the church's mission (as in Acts 2:1ff. and throughout Acts), or for the purpose of edifying the whole body of believers (1 Cor 12:14; Eph 4:1-16). Never are they to be understood as a ground for boasting or personal glorification. The giver from whom they come is the same Spirit who dwells in all (emphatically in 1 Cor 12:4ff.). Nowhere in the New Testament is there a basis for considering these gifts as a mark of special "spirituality" or a greater degree of piety. Although Paul, for example, may speak of the Corinthian Christians as "spiritual men" (*pneumatikoi*), he makes it clear that their spirituality is not to be understood as an achievement on their part, something of which they may be proud and boastful (see 1 Cor 2:14–3:4, and 4:6-7). According to John's Gospel, "It is not by measure that he gives the Spirit" (3:34).

4. The work of the Holy Spirit is also quite variously expressed in the New Testament. The Christian life arises out of the fact that

The Person and Work of the Holy Spirit

Christians are "born of the Spirit" (John 3:5-8), or from the fact that the Spirit "falls upon" people (as in Acts 10:44, reiterated in 11:15). The Spirit convicts of sin, and it is through the power of the Spirit that men are enabled to turn in repentance and faith to Jesus Christ (Acts 2:1-38). By the Spirit men have access to God the Father and are built into a dwelling place of God in the Spirit (Eph 2:19-22). Paul repeatedly characterizes the whole manner of the believers' life as life "according to the Spirit," or by using a similar phrase (e.g., Romans 8:4, 5, 6, 10, 14, 16; Galatians 5:16, 25; etc.); and for him the life of faith is nothing other than life "in the Spirit" or led "by the Spirit" (e.g., Romans 8:9, 13, 14; 9:1; Galatians 5:16, 18, 25; etc.). According to John, the Spirit testifies to Christ and his words in the hearts of believers (John 14:26; 16:14); or, to put it another way, he testifies to "the truth" (14:17; 15:26; 16:13), but "the truth" is none other than Christ himself (14:6). The active presence of the Spirit bears concrete results in the believers' lives: love, joy, peace, patience, kindness, goodness, faithfulness, gentleness, self-control (Galatians 5:22f.). The Spirit acts as the believers' advocate before God (John 14:16; 15:26; 16:7), interceding for them also in prayer (Romans 8:26f.). He attests that the believers are indeed God's children and heirs of his grace (Romans 8:14-17), and serves as the guarantee of all that God will bestow upon them in the future (Romans 8:23; 2 Cor 1:22, 5:5; Eph 1:14). The Spirit is also active in the work of sanctification. By the Spirit all believers are sanctified (1 Peter 1:2), and the sanctifying Spirit enables believers to be changed into the likeness of Christ "from one degree of glory to another" (2 Cor 3:18). The Spirit at work among all believers is constantly summoning them to growth in Christ and obedience to his will.

5. There are in the Book of Acts five references to the coming of the Holy Spirit which demand special note. These are particularly important because of the problems of interpretation which they raise, and because many of those who claim or recognize a phenomenon of the present day as "baptism of the Holy Spirit" also lay special emphasis on these passages. The texts to which we refer are as follows: (1) Acts 2:1-42, The Pentecost account; (2) Acts 8:4-25, Samaritan converts receive the Spirit; (3) Acts 9:1-18, Saul of Tarsus is "filled with the Spirit"; (4) Acts 10:1-48, and 11:1-18, The Spirit falls on Cornelius and his household; (5) Acts 19:1-7, The Spirit comes upon those at Ephesus who had previously known only the baptism of John.

In the Pentecost narrative it is clear that we are to understand the disciples' being "filled with the Spirit" as the fulfillment of the promise of Jesus in Acts 1:5 ("before many days you shall be baptized with the Holy Spirit"), and also the word of John the Baptist in Luke 3:16 ("he will baptize you with the Holy Spirit and with fire"). Here the disciples are empowered by the Spirit to be the witnesses Jesus had commanded them to be (Acts 1:8), and the church is thus launched upon its mission. So much is clear. The problem with which we are faced is whether we should view the disciples as having received the Spirit some time after their initial coming to faith in Jesus as the Christ. Though the writer seems not to have been concerned with that question, it is still a legitimate one for us to ask.

In one way the answer points in the direction of a wide separation between coming to belief and receiving the Holy Spirit. The disciples had believed in Jesus for a long time. Many of them had followed him throughout his earthly ministry, and at least some of them had recognized him as the Messiah. So viewed, we have to say that coming to belief and the gift of the Spirit were widely separated in time.

But it is possible to look at the matter in another way. The passage reaches back ultimately (via Acts 1:3-5) to Luke 3:16 (and parallels), where John the Baptist promises that Christ "will baptize you with the Holy Spirit." Though all the Gospels record this saying (the Synoptics verbatim), none of them thereafter says any more of baptism with the Spirit. It is only in Acts 1:3-5, after the crucifixion and resurrection, that the theme is resumed. Jesus appears to the disciples, strengthens their faith (vs. 3), and promises that within a few days they will be "baptized with the Holy Spirit." The crucifixion had been a shattering experience to the disciples; it left them confused, discouraged, not knowing *what* to believe (e.g., Luke 24:21: "We had hoped that he was the one to redeem Israel . . ."; or vs. 38: "Why are you troubled, and why do questionings arise in your hearts?"). Moreover, it was only after the crucifixion and resurrection that they could really believe in Christ as the risen Lord, and could fully understand the gospel they were to proclaim. And within a few days of their coming to full understanding and belief — and after several days of prayer — the Holy Spirit is bestowed upon them.

Whichever way the story is understood, it seems clear that this particular event of the disciples' being "filled with the Spirit" is viewed as subsequent to their coming to faith in Jesus Christ. The filling with the Spirit came to those who already believed in

The Person and Work of the Holy Spirit

Christ. There is suggested a kind of movement from initial to a more complete faith as background for the coming of the Holy Spirit. But the precise nature of the relation between this event and the disciples' faith is not made explicit by the Biblical writer.

Acts 8:4ff. envisions a rather different set of circumstances. Philip the Evangelist has proclaimed the gospel to the Samaritans; they believe and are baptized. However, these converts do not receive the Holy Spirit until later when Peter and John come down from Jerusalem, pray, and lay hands upon them. Here the coming of the Holy Spirit is clearly removed in time, and thus differentiated, from their conversion. The emphasis in the narrative, however, falls upon the fact that God, through the outpouring of his Spirit, thereby confirms the new turn of events in which people other than Jews are being brought into the community of believers and so become involved in the mission of Jesus Christ. To Samaritan believers God also sends the Holy Spirit.

The narrative of Saul's conversion in Acts 9:1ff. (cf. 22:6-16; 26:4-18) is likewise significant in that there is a period of some three days between the crisis experience on the road to Damascus and his being "filled with the Holy Spirit." The difference here, however, is that there is no prior baptism followed sometime later by the reception of the Spirit. Rather, after his encounter with the Lord and three days of blindness, prayer and fasting, Saul is visited by Ananias who lays hands on him to receive the Holy Spirit and, following this, baptizes Saul. Although there is a separation in time between the crisis experience and reception of the Holy Spirit, once again the precise relationship between the crisis experience and coming to faith is not made explicit. Saul's being "filled" with the Holy Spirit is clearly for the purpose of his becoming a "chosen instrument" to carry the gospel to men and nations.

In Acts 10:1–11:18 where the Holy Spirit is described as falling on Cornelius and his household, this is represented as occurring at the time of their conversion. While the gospel is still being proclaimed by Peter, the Spirit is poured out upon these Gentiles, and baptism is administered thereafter. It may be noted that Cornelius before this event was said to be a "devout man" who "with all his household . . . prayed constantly to God." Following the outpouring of the Spirit, Peter finds himself unable to refuse baptism, since he recognizes that the same thing has happened to the Gentiles that occurred at Pentecost. The Gentiles also, through the reception of the Holy Spirit, have become a part of God's witnessing community.

In Acts 19:1ff. a group of people — apparently converts of Apollos — who know only the baptism of John, are baptized by Paul in the name of Jesus, and receive the Holy Spirit with the laying on of Paul's hands. The writer clearly sees the case of these "disciples" (notice the word used in 19:1) as differing from others: they had "believed," yet their belief and instruction was imperfect and incomplete; they had never even heard of the Holy Spirit. Thus Paul baptizes them — this time in the name of Jesus — and the Spirit comes. We may say, therefore, that in this instance the people involved occupied a sort of middle ground between unbelief and mature faith. What is important for our concern is that the reception of the Spirit is at some distance from their early conversion, and though it occurs in conjunction with their baptism in the name of Jesus, it is described as following thereupon.

This brief survey has dealt with various situations in Acts which treat of faith (baptism, conversion) and the coming of the Holy Spirit. Several of these passages have suggested a view that would allow for a separation in time, and thus a clear differentiation, between an initial act of faith or conversion and the reception of the Spirit. One passage has demonstrated a coincidence between the two. But it should be reiterated that even the initial act of faith itself is a work of the Spirit. What seems to be said in most of these passages is that additional manifestations of the Spirit, while presupposing faith and conversion, are bestowed for specific ministries.

Also it is to be noted that, though faith in Jesus Christ is invariably depicted in Acts as the context for the gift of the Spirit, other matters such as prayer and the laying on of hands are regarded as important preparation for the Spirit's coming. In some instances, as noted, there is also a kind of maturation in faith before the Spirit is received. Obedience is mentioned in one instance (Acts 5:32) as needed for the gift of the Holy Spirit. The total picture suggests that the Holy Spirit is given in the situation of believing openness, growth in faith and obedience and concern for other persons.

6. The expression "baptism of (with, in) the Holy Spirit" calls for further elaboration. Except for Mark 1:8 (see parallels in Mathew 3:11; Luke 3:16; John 1:33) the expression is peculiar to Acts. The Gospel passages report the words of John the Baptist

thus: "I have baptized you with water; but he will baptize you with the Holy Spirit." Yet Jesus is nowhere represented as "baptizing with the Holy Spirit" during his earthly ministry. The theme is taken up again in Acts 1:4-5, where the risen Christ, after making reference to the words attributed by the Gospels to the Baptist, promises his disciples that they would be baptized with the Holy Spirit within a few days. One further use of the expression is found in Acts 11:15-16, where Peter, referring to the event of the Spirit's falling on Cornelius and his household, says, "As I began to speak, the Holy Spirit fell on them just as on us at the beginning. And I remembered the word of the Lord, how he said, 'John baptized with water, but you shall be baptized with the Holy Spirit.'"

It is evident that "baptism with the Holy Spirit" is viewed as occurring in the coming of the Spirit upon the disciples at Pentecost and later upon Cornelius and his household. When these events take place, it is said that the Spirit was "poured out" (2:33 and 10:45), or the Spirit "fell on" certain persons (10:44; 11:15); and those "baptized with the Holy Spirit" are said to be "filled with the Holy Spirit" (2:4) and to have "received the Holy Spirit" (10:47). It would seem clear, by implication, that the other narratives in Acts about the Samaritans, Saul of Tarsus, and Ephesians, where the language is that of the Spirit's "falling" or "coming," and their "receiving" or being "filled" with the Spirit (8:16, 17; 9:17; 19:2, 6), likewise refer to fulfillments of the promise of "baptism with the Holy Spirit."

It is also to be noted that "baptism with the Holy Spirit" is not to be equated with baptism with water. Baptism with water is associated from the outset with repentance, forgiveness of sins, and therefore conversion. For example, according to Mark 1:4-5, John the Baptist comes "preaching a baptism of repentance [*metanoia* — "turning about," conversion] for the forgiveness of sins," and people are "baptized in the Jordan river, confessing their sins." The same association of water baptism with conversion and forgiveness is found in words of Peter on the day of Pentecost: "Repent, and be baptized every one of you in the name of Jesus Christ for the forgiveness of your sins . . ." (Acts 2:38). But, as earlier noted, John the Baptist says, in the words of Mark 1:6, "I have baptized you with water; but he will baptize you with the Holy Spirit"; and the promise is echoed in the words that conclude Acts 2:38 — "— and you shall receive the gift of the Holy Spirit."

"Baptism with the Holy Spirit" is associated with such symbols as fire and wind (e.g., note Mathew 3:11, ". . . he will baptize you with the Holy Spirit and with fire" and the imagery of Acts 2:2-3), and points particularly to the investment of power. Basic to all that occurs in Acts thereafter in reference to "baptism with the Holy Spirit" (or the "outpouring," "falling," "coming," etc. of the Spirit) are the words of 1:8 — "But you shall receive *power* when the Holy Spirit has come upon you. . . ." Here it is emphasized that, as a result, the disciples will be able to bear witness to Christ (". . . and you shall be my witnesses . . ."). In the various accounts of the coming of the Spirit in Acts immediate signs, particularly tongues and prophecy, often occur (Acts 2:4, 17; 10:46; 19:6). These all would seem to represent the coming of the Spirit for empowerment: to bring forth a mighty testimony to God's great deeds.

To conclude, in the Book of Acts the expression "baptism with the Holy Spirit" (and similar terms) points not to the forgiveness of sins (symbolized in baptism with water) but to the endowment of power. It is not necessarily identified with conversion. Only those who turn in faith and repentance to Christ may receive the baptism of the Holy Spirit — His power, gifts, etc. — but the actual turning is not necessarily the only point at which this baptism may occur (although it must be insisted that faith and repentance are themselves the work of the Spirit). But in Acts, this baptism of the Spirit invariably assumes faith, repentance, conversion, and the like. The Spirit is given, according to Acts, not only to convert but to empower. However, the concern of Acts seems clearly to be that of showing how one community after another is empowered by the Holy Spirit in the widening outreach of the gospel. Whoever receives this special endowment is enabled thereby to extol God mightily, to witness with great force, and to give to the world extraordinary demonstration of God's presence and activity. It must be repeated, however, that the teaching of Acts with regard to the Holy Spirit is not to be read in isolation from the teaching of the rest of the New Testament. For example, a similar expression to "baptism of (with, in) the Holy Spirit" is used by Paul in 1 Cor 12:13: "For by (or "in") one Spirit we were all baptized into one body — Jews or Greeks, slaves or free — and all were made to drink of one Spirit." Here the baptism of the Spirit brings about the unity of all believers in Christ.

7. Statement was made in the Introduction of this report that

The Person and Work of the Holy Spirit

the central issue is not only "baptism of the Holy Spirit" but also the various "spiritual gifts" or manifestations which may follow this event. Accordingly we now move on to the New Testament witness in this regard, and, in so doing, deal again primarily with the Book of Acts wherein occurrences of this "baptism" or reception of the Spirit are narrated. In the five accounts earlier discussed we may now note that three of these specifically record spiritual manifestations: Acts 2, 10, and 19. According to Acts 2:4, immediately after the disciples at Pentecost were "filled with the Holy Spirit" they "began to speak in other tongues." In the story of Cornelius and his household, Peter and those with him recognized that the Holy Spirit had been poured out upon the Gentiles: "For they heard them speaking in tongues and extolling God" (Acts 10:46). Following Christian baptism and the laying on of Paul's hands, the Holy Spirit came upon the Ephesians, and "they spoke with tongues and prophesied" (Acts 19:6). There is no direct reference to any spiritual gift or manifestation in the account of the Samaritans in Acts 8 or Saul of Tarsus in Acts 9. It is evident that the one sign appearing in all the other narratives (Acts 2, 10, and 19), that of tongues, represents a kind of ecstatic utterance (so New English Bible in reference to Acts 10 and 19 translates "tongues of ecstasy"). Even in Acts 2, where the record might suggest that the tongues spoken were foreign languages, the ecstatic element also appears (thus the accusation, "They are filled with new wine," verse 13). This ecstatic speech is depicted also in close connection with praise (10:46; cf. 2:11) and prophecy (19:6). Since there is no reference to tongues, praise, or prophecy in Acts 8 and 9, it would be concluding too much to say that the writer of Acts assumes any particular spiritual manifestations invariably to accompany the reception of the Holy Spirit. On the other hand, it seems clear that the writer of Acts does view speaking in tongues as undeniable evidence that the Holy Spirit has been given.[1]

The writings of Paul express a viewpoint which is concerned with another aspect of the Spirit's activity. Thus the spiritual gifts of which he speaks are not connected with such events as Acts reports, but are regarded as manifestations of the Spirit's continuing life and work within the church (see, for example, Rom 12:6-8; 1 Cor 7:7; 12-14; cf. Gal 5:16-26). The same understanding is found also in Ephesians 4:1-16 and 1 Peter 4:10-11. Moreover, in the discourses of Jesus in John 14-16, which are replete with promises concerning the coming of the Spirit and his future work among Jesus' followers, no mention is made of the kind of events we have seen in Acts; rather, the view of the Spirit and his work to be found here is much more closely akin to the thought of Paul.

8. This leads to the recognition that the New Testament also bears witness to the outpouring of the Spirit at various points in the lives of believers. It may occur at the initiation of the life of faith and/or at later times. According to Acts, the Christian community, already having received the Holy Spirit at Pentecost, and now coming under persecution, prays earnestly for courage to witness, and, as a result, are again "filled with the Holy Spirit" (4:23ff.). The same thing occasionally is said to happen to individuals. Peter, standing to testify before the rulers of the Jews, is "filled with the Holy Spirit" (Acts 4:8), and Paul is likewise so "filled" as he proceeds to denounce Elymas the magician (Acts 13:9ff.). Each of these men, according to Acts, had before been filled with the Spirit, Peter at Pentecost and Paul in Damascus.

It is also to be noted that certain persons are described in Acts as "full" of the Holy Spirit. The "Seven" who were chosen to serve the early church, as well as Paul's companion Barnabas, are singled out as men who were "full of the Holy Spirit" (see 6:3, 5; 7:55; 11:24). This statement, not made of all the Christians, would seem to emphasize the importance of spiritual endowment for leadership of the early community.

Alongside these references in Acts must be placed other New Testament references to such things as the fruits of the Spirit, the gifts of the Spirit, walking by the Spirit, life in the Spirit. The writer of Ephesians admonishes, "And do not get drunk with wine . . . but be filled with the Spirit, addressing one another in psalms and hymns and spiritual songs . . ." (5:18, 19). Thus here is a challenge to the church to be filled with the Spirit, whereby there is continuing enhancement of life in Christ. The Corinthians are encouraged by Paul to "earnestly desire the spiritual gifts" (1 Cor 14:1), and the Colossians are prayed for that they "may be filled with the knowledge of his [God's] will in all spiritual wisdom and understanding" (1:9). Such statements as these suggest that within the Christian community there is the continuing possibility of, and need for, growth in life in the Spirit.

In light of these statements it is evident that the New Testament witnesses both to the importance of being "filled" with the Spirit and the possibility of further bestowal of the Spirit. In the former

The Person and Work of the Holy Spirit

case there is both the challenge to such filling ("be filled . . .") and the depiction of certain Christians as "full of the Spirit." In the latter instance there is represented additional "filling" wherein is renewal of boldness to witness, the power to discern evil, and the like. There is, all in all, in the New Testament, the continuing challenge to live in the fullness of the Spirit.

9. Finally, the New Testament does not make its claims of honor for the Holy Spirit on the basis of the Spirit's "supernatural" character. Other spirits, evil in disposition and activity, are not only admitted as existing, but are set in opposition to the Holy Spirit and his purposes (e.g., 1 Tim 4:1; Rev 16:13f; Eph 2:2; 1 John 2:22; 4:1-6; 5:7f.). The Holy Spirit is to be honored and trusted, to be regarded as the Spirit of God who alone is the object of faith, not simply because he is *spirit*, but because of his unique identity as the Spirit of *God* or of *Christ*. In the same way, Paul teaches that the value of spiritual gifts is not to be judged by how "supernatural" or extraordinary they are. 1 Corinthians 12-14 makes it clear that those gifts are most to be desired which are most efficacious in the edification of others. The unusual quality of a gift does not make it a "higher" gift or its possessor a more spiritually mature Christian; rather, the more excellent gift is the one which excels in loving service. Among the long list of spiritual gifts the Apostle mentions several activities which are in no way extraordinary — *viz.*, teaching, helping, administration (1 Cor 12:28) — but which are nonetheless important for the mission of the church.

IV. CONCERNING THE SPIRIT IN THE STANDARDS OF OUR CHURCH

The teaching about the Holy Spirit in the Westminster Confession of Faith and Catechisms is found in a number of places and also gathered together in one chapter of the Confession entitled "Of the Holy Spirit" (Chap. IX). We shall briefly summarize, making use of the pattern of Chapter IX.

A. The nature of the Holy Spirit. The Holy Spirit is fully God, and therefore "to be believed in, loved, obeyed, and worshipped throughout all ages." At the same time as One who proceeds from the Father and the Son, He is a "third person," and accordingly has His own distinct personal reality and work. (See also Chap. II, 3.)

B. The activity of the Holy Spirit in relation to the world, revelation, and the proclamation of the gospel. The Holy Spirit is "the Lord and Giver of life," active in the work of creation (see also Chap. IV), and is to be recognized as the source of goodness, purity, and holiness wherever found among men. It is the Holy Spirit who moved the prophets to speak God's Word and the writers of Scripture to record it infallibly (see also Chap. I). This same Spirit continues particularly to act in the proclamation of the gospel, accompanying it with "persuasive power."

C. The work of the Holy Spirit in redemption. The Holy Spirit brings about conviction of sin, repentance, and faith in Jesus Christ (see also Chap. XII). Accordingly, the Holy Spirit "unites all believers to Christ" and "dwells in them," whereby they receive "the Spirit of Adoption and Prayer" (see also Chap. XIV). The Holy Spirit as the "Sanctifier" works in the lives of believers, performing various functions, until the day of final redemption (see also Chap. XV).

D. The relation of the Holy Spirit to the Church. The Holy Spirit who dwells in all believers and thus unites them to Christ also unites them to one another in the church (see also Chap. XXVIII). The Holy Spirit "anoints" ministers, "qualifies" officers, and "imparts various gifts and graces" to church members. He also gives efficacy to the "ordinances" of the Church (word, sacraments, worship — see also Chaps. XXIII and XXIX-XXXI). Finally, the Holy Spirit preserves, increases and purifies the church until it is at last "made perfectly holy in the presence of God."

Since the central question of this report has to do with "the baptism of the Holy Spirit," its relation to conversion and/or baptism with water, we may now note in more detail the teaching of the Standards in these areas. The crucial matter concerns whether it is proper to view a possible separation in time between conversion and/or baptism with water and a "baptism" or reception of the Holy Spirit. In order to deal with these matters, we shall consider, in order, baptism with water, conversion, and baptism with the Spirit. Thereafter we shall note the teaching of the Standards on "spiritual gifts" and further bestowal of the Holy Spirit.

1. Baptism with water is to be done in the name of the Father, and of the Son, and of the Holy Ghost (Chap. XXX, 2). Baptism, as a sacrament, is both sign and seal of the grace of God (ingrafting into Christ, remission of sins, regeneration, adoption, resurrection) so that "by the right use of this ordinance the grace

promised is not only offered but really exhibited and conferred by the Holy Ghost" (Chap. XXX, 6). Baptism with water accordingly is more than a representation and confirming of God's grace: It is also the means or channel of that grace to be conferred by the Holy Spirit. But note that the Confession says that grace is conferred only "by the right use" of this ordinance.

Two other points are also relevant: First, the Confession teaches that the efficacy of baptism is "not tied to that moment of time wherein it is administered" (Chap. XXX, 6), that is to say, the grace conferred may yet be in the future or it may, alternatively, already have been conferred before baptism. This statement would seem to be related particularly to infant baptism (which is mentioned in the same section), and provides for the efficacy of such baptism to be appropriated at a later date. Second, the Confession denies baptismal regeneration in two ways: Persons may be regenerated without baptism, and not all persons baptized are regenerated — "grace and salvation are not so inseparably annexed unto it [baptism] as that no person can be regenerated or saved without it, or that all who are baptized are undoubtedly regenerated" (Chap. XXX, 5). It may be observed that among the proof-texts cited in the Confession for this double statement are Acts 10:45-47 and Acts 8:13, 23, the former having to do with Cornelius and his household who receive the Spirit before baptism, and the latter relating to Simon the magician who despite his baptism remains "in the gall of bitterness and in the bond of iniquity."

It is evident that, according to the Confession, the grace of God — bringing about remission of sins and regeneration — while closely identified with baptism is not bound to it. What is conferred in baptism may become efficacious by the Spirit at a later time; without baptism there may be salvation; and not all baptized are also regenerated.

2. The word "conversion" is not frequently used in the Standards. It is to be found, as such, in the Confession of Faith only in Chapter XI on "Free Will." Here it is said that in regard to salvation man is "not able by his own strength to convert himself"; rather it is "God [who] converteth a sinner." In Chapter XII on "Effectual Calling," though the word "conversion" is not used, what the word signifies in terms of a "turning" is found in such a statement as that wherein God is said to call men "by his word and Spirit . . . enlightening their minds . . . taking away their heart of stone . . . renewing their wills . . . so as they come

most freely . . ." (Chap. XII, 1) . All of this occurs through "saving faith" (the title of Chap. XVI), which is described as "the grace of faith, whereby the elect are enabled to believe to the saving of their souls" by "the work of the Spirit of Christ in their hearts"; and through "repentance unto life" (the title of Chap. XVII), whereby a person through the conviction of the Holy Spirit "so grieves for, and hates his sins, as to turn from them all to God." When the word "conversion" appears in the two catechisms, it is used in connection with reading the Scriptures and preaching. The Larger Catechism, Question 4, speaks of the Scriptures as having the power "to convince and convert sinners;" and in Question 159 it directs those who preach God's word to his people to do so "aiming at his glory, and their conversion, edification, and salvation."

The concern of the Standards thus is for a total change of man — mind, heart, will, a faith that saves, and repentance that is unto life. It is through the Holy Spirit, in conjunction with the word, that this transformation comes about.

3. "Baptism by the Spirit," as such, is referred to only in the Larger Catechism, Question 167. This question deals with "the needful but much neglected duty of improving our baptism." According to the Catechism this "is to be performed by us all our life long." Illustrations of this are given such as "being humbled for our sinful defilement, our falling short of, and walking contrary to, the grace of baptism . . . by growing up to assurance of pardon of sin, and of all other blessings sealed to us in this sacrament; by drawing strength from the death and resurrection of Christ, into whom we are baptized . . . and to walk in brotherly love, as being baptized by the same Spirit into one body." This statement makes clear that baptism by the Spirit is to be understood in close connection with baptism by water; indeed, that it is not actually by water itself but by the Spirit that we are baptized into the body of Christ.

Accordingly, we may note that the Catechism lays stress on baptism by the Spirit as referring not so much to pardon of sin, and like blessings, but to the uniting power of the Spirit whereby we become one body with others. It may be added that there is some suggestion here that the effectuality of this baptism is not limited to the moment when the sacrament is received. Thus even as we are to "grow up" to assurance of pardon, so, through walking in brotherly love, are we to come to express our baptism by the Spirit into the one body.

4. It is evident that the Standards envision the possibility of separation in time between baptism with water and the baptism of the Holy Spirit. Whether this is understood in terms of a baptism with water that only becomes efficacious at a later time by the Holy Spirit, or as an aspect of that into which one may grow, there may be many years between. The Standards do not, however, seem to consider a possible separation in time between conversion and the reception of the Spirit, since the critical question, emerging especially from the practice of infant baptism, is the relationship of such baptism to its future efficacy, whether thought of as appropriation of grace, conversion of the whole man, or baptism into the one body. What is important for our consideration in this report, however, is that the Standards recognize a differentiation, and the possibility or chronological separation, between baptism with water and baptism with the Holy Spirit. The latter may precede the former, or may follow it.

5. "Spiritual gifts" have little mention in the Standards. We have already noted the statement in the Confession's chapter on the Holy Spirit (IX) to the effect that the Holy Spirit "imparts various gifts and graces" to the members of Christ's body. Outside of this reference in Chapter IX (a chapter not in the original Confession), there is nothing to be found about spiritual gifts in the Standards. The Larger Catechism also makes reference to "gifts and graces," however the giver there is described as the exalted Christ who "furnisheth his ministers and people with gifts and graces" (Q. 54). The Shorter Catechism is silent about spiritual gifts and graces.

6. Finally, the matter of further bestowal of the Spirit or of gifts of the Holy Spirit is not directly mentioned. The closest approximation would seem to be that of the Larger Catechism, Question 182, where the Spirit is described as helping in prayer by "quickening in our hearts (although not in all persons, nor at all times in the same measure) those apprehensions, affections, and graces, which are requisite for the right performance. . . ." There is also reference in the Larger Catechism, Question 75, to the "powerful operation" of the Holy Spirit in sanctification whereby God's chosen are in time "renewed in their whole man after the image of God" by various "saving graces" within being "stirred up, increased, and strengthened as that they more and more die unto sin, and rise into newness of life." Hence, there is some picture of further operations of the Holy Spirit in the direction of quickening and renewal.

V. CONCLUDING OBSERVATIONS

An evaluation of contemporary events involving a "baptism of the Holy Spirit" must begin, as the structure of the report implies, with the guidance furnished us by the Scriptures. At the same time we are called upon to give serious heed to the doctrinal Standards of our denomination. Likewise it is imperative that we seek to understand what is deeply involved, and at stake for those who claim to have had such a "baptism" within their Christian experience, and particular "charismatic" manifestations. The Scriptures remain our primary source; yet our understanding of Scripture depends upon the illumination provided by the Spirit himself.

Our study of the Old and New Testaments, however, has revealed no single consistent doctrine of the Spirit which is now immediately applicable to the contemporary situation; nor has it furnished us with a simple straight line of doctrinal development of this regard. Moreover, we must avoid the temptation to improve on the concept of the Spirit through any speculative theory drawn from other sources. Hence, our point of departure in this task can be no other than the New Testament's close identification of the Spirit with Jesus Christ. As Christians we must be guided first of all by God's self-revelation in Christ, testing our understanding by the Scripture's testimony to him who is our Lord.

A. As we seek to give an expression of our faith in the Holy Spirit that will be an aid in comprehending the experiences which have prompted the present study, there are several basic principles which we must bear in mind. First, as the Scriptures repeatedly affirm, the Holy Spirit is the Spirit of the holy God, the God of the Bible. All our speech about the Holy Spirit is therefore speech about God. We shall make no attempt to define the concept of "spirit" in general and then move to an understanding of the Holy Spirit based on our ideas about the essential properties or characteristics of "spirit." Rather, our task is to discern the meaning of God's action, in the person of his Spirit, in the lives of his people.

Second, as the New Testament makes clear, and as Calvin aptly reminds us (*Inst.*, III, i, 4), there is no understanding of the Spirit apart from faith. This means that all our statements about the Holy Spirit are in essence affirmations of faith. They are not "factual" statements in the sense that they purport to give

The Person and Work of the Holy Spirit

objective data or information which may then be tested for accuracy by scientific means. In speaking of the Holy Spirit we speak *from* faith *to* faith.

Third, since the Holy Spirit is the spirit of the God whom we know only through Jesus Christ, we are compelled, in regard to the contemporary spiritual phenomena, to "test the spirits to see whether they are of God" by the measure of their confession of Jesus Christ (I John 4:1-3). Nothing that contradicts what we see in Christ can rightly be regarded as the activity of the Spirit; on the other hand, whatever bears witness to Christ and his work of the redemption of mankind exhibits the incontrovertible evidence of the Spirit's presence.

B. With the foregoing principles in mind, and with constant reference to the Biblical teachings, the Standards of our Church, and the contemporary situation, the Permanent Theological Committee offers the following statement for the guidance of the Assembly.

1. The greatest emphasis in the Bible, and the most prominent aspect of our Reformed tradition, is to be found in the work of the Spirit in bestowing upon man all the benefits of God which come to him in Jesus Christ. Faith in Jesus Christ is the way whereby all benefits are received, such as justification, sanctification, and eternal life (1 Cor 6:11; John 3:16; Confession of Faith, XVI, 2), and through the Holy Spirit this salvation is a reality.

2. The Holy Spirit accordingly dwells in all who thus believe. If anyone does not have the Spirit of Christ, he does not belong to him (Rom 8:9). Thus it is impossible to speak of a transition within Christian existence from the state of Spirit's being *with* to being *in*. The Spirit indwells all Christians.

3. Baptism with water is a means of grace whereby the grace of salvation is not only offered but conferred by the Holy Spirit (Confession, XXX, 6). However, according to the Confession, the significance of baptism is not tied to the moment of administration, for, though God's saving grace is conferred thereby, such grace may become efficacious at a later time, or it may have become efficacious earlier. For example, there are those who do not come to an appropriation of this grace (especially if baptized in infancy) until a later date. Calvin speaks (particularly regarding infants) of being "baptized into future repentance and faith" (*Institutes* IV, 20), and urges that this should fire us with greater zeal for renewal in later years. From this perspective it is possible to say that baptism with water may very well be

separated from salvation, or at least from full entrance upon it. Though baptism is a channel of God's grace, this grace is not automatically efficacious. Accordingly, there may be special need in the Reformed tradition to lay stress on later occasions (such as entrance into communicant membership) on which God's grace may also be appropriated. Reformed teaching about baptism must be held in creative tension with all that is also said about the importance of conversion and regeneration, and the practice of our church should be in harmony therewith.

4. "Baptism with the Holy Spirit," as the Book of Acts portrays it, is a phrase which refers most often to the empowering of those who believe to share in the mission of Jesus Christ. The significance of "baptism with the Spirit" is also represented in terms such as "outpouring," "falling upon," "filling," and "receiving," being for the most part attempts to depict that action of God whereby believers are enabled to give expression to the gospel through extraordinary praise, powerful witness, and boldness of action. Accordingly, those who speak of such a "baptism with the Spirit," and who give evidence of this special empowering work of the Spirit, can claim Scriptural support. Further, since "baptism with the Spirit" may not be at the same time as baptism with water and/or conversion, we need to be open-minded toward those today who claim an intervening period of time.[2] If this experience signifies in some sense a deepening of faith and awareness of God's presence and power, we may be thankful.

5. We are called upon to recognize a work of the Spirit which involves the application of special gifts and benefits to the members of Christ's church. The Confession of Faith suggests this in Chapter IX, 4 where, following the paragraph on the Spirit's work in redemption, the words, in part, read, "He calls and anoints ministers for their holy office, qualifies all other officers in the church for their special work, and imparts various gifts and graces to its members." Here is a special work of the Holy Spirit of calling and anointing that is peculiarly related to the life of the believing community. We would add that it is important for the church constantly to bear this work of the Holy Spirit in mind so that there will be a continuing readiness for, and recognition of the calling, the qualifying, and the imparting of the gifts and graces of the Holy Spirit to the community of faith. Both a fresh confrontation with the biblical record and contemporary spiritual

The Person and Work of the Holy Spirit

experience, we believe, are bringing us into a fuller understanding of the work of the Holy Spirit.

6. The "baptism of the Holy Spirit" may be signified by certain pneumatic phenomena, such as speaking in tongues and prophecy (Acts 2:4; 10:46; 19:6). In the Old Testament, as we have noted, the Spirit is understood at times as an invading power, a charismatic fury; also it is frequently associated with ecstatic prophecy. However since the Spirit came only to certain exceptional persons, this was quite limited. With the New Testament dispensation the Spirit is now available to all who believe in Jesus Christ. Hence such signs of this invading power as ecstatic language and prophecy could occur with anyone who has experienced this visitation. Clearly it would be a mistake to say that all upon whom the Spirit comes *must* manifest specific pneumatic phenomena. The Spirit usually manifests himself in other ways. However, that such extraordinary manifestations *may* occur — and in so doing give evidence of the Spirit's working — is quite in accord with the witness of the New Testament.

7. There may be further bestowal of the Holy Spirit. "Baptism with the Spirit" signifies the initial outpouring of God's Spirit wherein the community and/or person is filled with the presence and power of God. But also there may be later bestowal in such fashion as to signify implementation of the original event, whether or not accompanied by pneumatic phenomena (cf. Acts 2:4 with 4:31). This renewed activity of the Spirit ought not to be designated "baptism" (at least, the New Testament never uses this term for it), but as "filling," wherein the empowering Spirit moves to renew the believer and believing community.

8. The bestowal and reception of the Spirit, or the gifts of the Spirit, does not signify a higher level of spirituality nor ought it to suggest that some Christians have more of the Holy Spirit than others. Such expressions as "baptism," "filling," and the like point rather to the Spirit's implementing activity: endowment for the witness to the gospel. The Spirit is active in all believers, and they may be "filled" with the Spirit in various ways for the mission of the Church. It should be added that such expressions as "having" or "filled with" the Spirit are not to be construed as obviating the possibility and actuality of growth in grace and knowledge.

9. Both the coming of the Spirit himself and the various abilities or charismata which he may bestow upon men are, above

all, to be received as the benefits of God's free grace. Neither the Spirit, then, nor his gifts may be considered "possessions" of the believer; he does not own them, nor can he presume that they are, or will be, at all times (or at any given time) available. Each occasion on which the Spirit's presence is known or his gifts made manifest is to be an occasion for new thanksgiving and praise to God. Hence, there should be no jeopardizing of the peace, unity, and fellowship of the church because of special experiences of the Holy Spirit, but a rejoicing together in all those ways whereby God leads His people into fuller apprehension of the riches of His grace.[3]

10. An experience of the Spirit can neither be validated as such, nor evaluated with respect to its theological significance, by any scientific (i.e., psychological, sociological, etc.) means. It is to be acknowledged that such events, just as any other human events, may become the legitimate objects of scientific inquiry without prejudging the results of such inquiry. But regardless of the scientific conclusions which may be reached, the question of the theological significance of these phenomena will remain, and it may be answered only within the context of the Christian faith. The Corinthians' ability to speak in tongues, for example, may have a perfectly good psychological explanation; but whether the Spirit of Jesus Christ was active in that phenomenon is a question which neither psychology nor any other science can answer. But this conclusion leads also to the observation that the extraordinary or unusual nature of an experience (and the same would apply to gifts) is no criterion by which to judge its significance for faith. Ecstasy is not in itself an unambiguous occurrence. Not every dramatic event, experience, or ecstasy is necessarily a work of the Spirit.[4]

11. It is clear that there is Biblical and Reformed witness concerning baptism of the Holy Spirit and special endowments of the Holy Spirit in the believing community. Of course, it is impossible to make any general pronouncement concerning the validity of particular claims made, since multiple factors may be at work. But where there is divisiveness, judgment (expressed or implied) on the lives of others, an attitude of pride or boasting, etc., the Spirit of God is not at work. However, where such an experience gives evidence of an empowering and renewing work of Christ in the life of the individual and the church, it may be acknowledged with gratitude. This means above all that Christ should be glorified, his own Spirit made manifest in human lives,

The Person and Work of the Holy Spirit

and the Church edified. For such evidences of the presence of the Holy Spirit the Church may rejoice.

1. So Alan Richardson in his An Introduction to the *Theology of the New Testament*: "St. Luke regards 'speaking with tongues' (glossolalia) as an unmistakable sign of the gift of the Spirit . . ." (p. 119).

2. We here call attention to the 1965 General Assembly declaration on Glossolalia which includes this statement: "Scripture in several cases clearly distinguishes between a baptism with water and a baptism with the Holy Spirit (Matt. 3:11; Mark 1-8; Luke 3:16; Acts 1:5). We would agree that, since Pentecost, baptism and receiving the Spirit belong together in a single experience (Acts 2:38). But both Scripture and Confession face the possibility that there may be a lapse of time between the two (Acts 8, 10, 19; Confession XXX, 5)."

3. The UPUSA Church 1970 declaration, "The Work of the Holy Spirit," in the section entitled "Guidelines," begins thus: "We believe the Church needs to pray for a sensitivity to see the manifestations of the Holy Spirit in our world today. . . . We believe that those who are newly endowed with gifts and perceptions of the Spirit have an enthusiasm and joy to give, and we also believe that those who rejoice in our traditions of having all things done in 'decency and order' have a sobering depth to give. We therefore plead for a mutuality of respect and affection."

4. Compare this statement from the 1965 General Assembly declaration on "Glossolalia": *"The Gifts of the Spirit can be counterfeited or sought for the wrong motive* (I John 4:1). There is no reason to suppose that forms of utterance voiced at the prompting of the Spirit cannot be initiated or cultivated by men and women variously motivated. While there may be among us some who 'speak in tongues' as the Spirit gives them utterance, there may also be present among us those who, succeeding in the effort to 'speak in tongues,' unwarrantedly assume their utterance to be an evidence of the Spirit of Christ. The gift may be sought and its counterfeit achieved from wrong motives."

CHARISMATIC STUDY REPORT

Though the early history of classical Pentecostalism was interdenominational (rather than strictly ecumenical, that is, concerned with restoring the unity of the church), it lost much of this character and became incarnated in various classical Pentecostal denominations. Their denominational consciousness was and is as strong as in any of the historic churches. The study report represents an attempt of a classical Pentecostal denomination to come to terms with the charismatic movement in the Protestant and Catholic churches and in the nondenominational groups.

The charismatic renewal could easily have been seen as a threat to the Assemblies of God. Rather than being a threat the Assemblies of God has profited by the renewal. Though the flow has not been entirely one way, there have been a number of persons in the charismatic renewal in various historic churches who have become members of classical Pentecostal churches. To speak only on the Catholic charismatic renewal, this flow is not a major factor, but it is a significant minor one. [1] *Not only is it noticeable from the side of the renewal in a number of historic churches but the Assemblies of God reported "it is experiencing a surge of membership largely due to increasing numbers of 'new charismatics' . . . . Some regional reports indicate that many Assemblies of God churches are 'bursting at the seams'. . . . Many new charismatics are coming to older pentecostal denominations such as the Assemblies of God for mature support."* [2] *Such a development would be an added motive for evaluating the renewal in the historic churches in positive terms.*

Especially noteworthy is the way in which doctrinal purity and behavioral correctness was related to the moving of the Spirit. Reflecting on their own sometimes painful experience in the past, they realized that the Spirit is not above manifesting himself in groups which are still struggling with problems of doctrine and conduct. Gone is the stiff dogmatism of doctrinal fundamentalism.

The Executive Presbytery of the Assemblies of God, which issued the statement at the Council on Spiritual Life (Minneapolis, August 14, 1972), recognized the authenticity of the Spirit's move "outside the normally recognized Pentecostal body" by pointing out the marks of a genuine movement of the Spirit. It remarked on the strong ecumenical character of the charismatic renewal and took the occasion to reassert its own position on the nature of unity. Drawing from rather well-known evangelical and classical Pentecostal thought on this topic, the Executive Presbytery declared that unity does not have an organizational expression, which it identified with man-made mergers. The unity created in and by the Spirit transcends existing and future organizational structures. The ecumenical vision is strong, wishing to be faithful to scriptural principles but avoiding a denominational narrowness which excludes true Christians.

This action had a prehistory in an action of the General Council which met in 1963. The General Council recognized that a number of persons in many of the historic denominations had expressed "an experimental interest in the baptism in the Holy Spirit," and recorded that "at least one denomination has already held conferences with the Executive Presbytery on the Pentecostal experience." ³ A formal resolution was passed in which the General Council expressed "its desire to meet with, pray with and in any other way assist any denominational minister in reaching an understanding of the Pentecostal experience." ⁴

In 1977 the Pentecostal Holiness Church issued a statement on the charismatic renewal in the historic churches which is almost a verbatim duplicate of the 1972 statement of the Assemblies of God. ⁵

The 1972 statement was reprinted in Live in the Spirit *(Springfield, Mo.: Gospel Publishing House, 1972), pp. 335–36.*

1. *Kilian McDonnell,* The Charismatic Renewal and Ecumenism *(New York: Paulist Press, 1978), pp. 67–70.*
2. *"Charismatics Swell A/G Ranks,"* Charisma, *vol. 4 (June 1979), 14.*
3. *"Minutes of the Thirtieth General Council of the Assemblies of God," Memphis, Tennessee, August 21–26, p. 41.*
4. *Ibid.*
5. *Reprinted in the "Minutes of the Eighteenth General Conference of the Pentecostal Holiness Church," Oklahoma City, Oklahoma, August 3–10, 1977, p. 68.*

There is thrilling evidence that God is moving mightily by His Spirit throughout all the earth. The winds of the Spirit are blowing freely outside the normally recognized Pentecostal body. This is the time of the greater fulfillment of Joel's prophecy. Thousands of people have prayed for years that this would come to pass. The coming of the Holy Spirit upon so many and in such a broad sweep of the church world is God's way of counteracting the liberalism, secularism, humanism and occultism that plagues our present day society.

Marks of the genuine moving of the Holy Spirit include the following: (1) emphasis on worship in spirit and in truth of almighty God; (2) recognition of the person of Christ — His deity, His incarnation and His redemptive work; (3) recognition of the authority of and the hunger for the Word of God; (4) emphasis of the person and work of the Holy Spirit; (5) emphasis of the Second

Coming of Christ; (6) emphasis on prayer for the sick; (7) emphasis on sharing Christ in witnessing and evangelism.

The Assemblies of God wishes to identify with what God is doing in the world today. We recognize that no existing organization fully represents the body of Christ. Neither do we believe that for all true Christians — whether Pentecostal in doctrine and practice or not — to align themselves with an existing organization or a new one, will bring the unity of the Spirit. We do believe in the institution of the church. We trust the Holy Spirit to bring the members of Christ's body into a true unity of the Spirit. If there is yet a truth to be revealed to the church, it is the essential unity of the body of Christ, which transcends but does not destroy existing organizational bounds.

The Assemblies of God does not place approval on that which is manifestly not scriptural in doctrine or conduct. But neither do we categorically condemn everything that does not totally or immediately conform to our standards. No genuine spiritual movement in church history has been completely free of problems or above criticism. The Pentecostal movement of this century has experienced its problems relating both to doctrine and conduct. Spiritual maturity leads to a balanced life which will bear the fruit of the Spirit while displaying the gifts of the Spirit.

We place our trust in God to bring His plan about as He pleases in His sovereign will. It is important that we find our way in a sound scriptural path, avoiding the extremes of an ecumenism that compromises scriptural principles and an exclusivism that excludes true Christians.

THE CHARISMATIC MOVEMENT
AND LUTHERAN THEOLOGY

In 1968 the Lutheran Church — Missouri Synod asked its Commission on Theology and Church Relations to study the charismatic renewal with special reference to the baptism in the Holy Spirit. The charismatic renewal began to appear in that church some twenty years before the 1972 report was issued, though the greatest influx was in the middle 1960s. By April 1968 forty-four pastors in the synod claimed to have received the baptism in the Holy Spirit and by May 1971 the number had risen to over two hundred pastors.

Given the very strong doctrinal and confessional stance of this church, the 1972 statement "The Charismatic Movement and Lutheran Theology" represents a balanced, calm, though essentially negative evaluation of the charismatic renewal. No sweeping statements were made as to the belief systems of persons involved in the renewal. "The commission has proceeded on the supposition that Lutherans involved in the charismatic movement do not share all the views of neo-Pentecostalism in general."

After some historical, sociological, and psychological reflections, the commission stated the theological views of Lutheran charismatics without engaging in caricature. An analysis of the biblical data was given and then the commission took issue with the stance of Lutheran charismatics. The commission did not think that Scripture teaches that there is a second encounter with the Spirit, separate and distinct from conversion and baptism in the name of Jesus. Nor did it agree that an encounter with God through faith should be thought of as an experience which the Christian can have only if he or she meets certain preconditions. It also rejected the doctrine which would single out the gift of tongues for special significance in the believer's experience of the Spirit. The commission proposed a modified dispensationalism: "While we Christians rejoice in this gracious promise (that the Spirit is for all generations of Christians), we should recognize that this gift of the Spirit does not necessarily include the promise of all extraordinary spiritual gifts that were once given to the apostolic church, such as speaking in tongues, miracles of healing, or prophecy." Such gifts may be found in the contemporary church; they are not necessarily found there.

Lutherans are deeply concerned lest attributing an exaggerated role to the Spirit diminish the saving work effected by Jesus Christ. The charismatic emphasis seems to construct supplementary means of grace alongside of the Word and sacraments, whereas both Scripture and the Lutheran Confessions teach that they "are the only means of grace" and that the Holy Spirit always accompanies their use. Through them the Spirit bestows on the church "all the blessings that are ours in Christ" as well as all the gifts needed to carry out the mission of the church. Therefore power and renewal is to be sought in the Word and sacraments, "not in special signs and miracles."

Under the title of "Unionism" the commission reminded Missouri Synod Lutherans that sufficient basis for fellowship exists only when there is "agreement in the doctrine of the Gospel, in all its articles and in the right use of the sacraments. . . . All biblical doctrine is taught by the Holy Spirit." Caution is needed in charismatic groups lest they come to depend more on charismatic speech than on the biblical word.

The rapid and widespread growth of the charismatic renewal may be an indication that the church needs to give greater attention to the doctrine of the Holy Spirit and to the Spirit's role in the life of the church.

The report is obtainable in pamphlet form from the Lutheran Church — Missouri Synod, Lutheran Building, 210 N. Broadway, St. Louis, MO 63102.

PREFACE

One of the significant developments in American church life during the past decade has been the rapid spread of the neo-Pentecostal or charismatic movement within the mainline churches. In the early sixties, experiences and practices usually associated only with Pentecostal denominations began to appear with increasing frequency also in such churches as the Roman Catholic, Episcopalian, and Lutheran. By the mid-nineteen-sixties, it was apparent that this movement had also spread to some pastors and congregations of The Lutheran Church — Missouri Synod. In certain areas of the Synod, tensions and even divisions had arisen over such neo-Pentecostal practices as speaking in tongues, miraculous healings, prophecy, and the claimed possession of a special "baptism in the Holy Spirit." At the request of the president of the Synod, the Commission on Theology and Church Relations in 1968 began a study of the charismatic movement with special reference to the baptism in the Holy Spirit.

The 1969 synodical convention specifically directed the commission to "make a comprehensive study of the charismatic movement with special emphasis on its exegetical aspects and theological implications." It was further suggested that "the

Commission on Theology and Church Relations be encouraged to involve in its study brethren who claim to have received the baptism of the Spirit and related gifts." (Resolution 2-23, 1969 *Proceedings*, p. 90)

Since that time, the commission has sought in every practical way to acquaint itself with the theology of the charismatic movement. The commission has proceeded on the supposition that Lutherans involved in the charismatic movement do not share all the views of neo-Pentecostalism in general. Accordingly, the commission has particularly endeavored to learn the views of representative Lutheran charismatics and to address primarily those aspects of the charismatic movement that are a matter of interest or concern within our Synod. Members of the commission have on a number of occasions consulted privately with Lutheran pastors who are involved in this movement; they have studied documents, position papers, and booklets produced by Lutheran brethren who claim to have been baptized in the Spirit; they have examined carefully official reports and study documents prepared by Lutheran and non-Lutheran church bodies on this subject.[1] Representatives of the commission have attended portions of two conferences conducted by Lutheran charismatics. Furthermore, preliminary drafts of this document were examined and criticized by a number of Lutheran charismatic pastors. The commission herewith expresses its deep appreciation to those pastors for their cooperation and assistance.

In this document, we are presenting materials that deal primarily with baptism in the Holy Spirit, speaking in tongues, and, to a lesser degree, miraculous healing, as these phenomena are occurring in The Lutheran Church — Missouri Synod. The first part presents general background information on the history of the movement, its sociological and psychological dimensions, and characteristic theological views of Lutheran charismatics. The second part of this document presents an analysis of relevant Biblical data, with particular reference to baptism in the Holy Spirit and the nature and purpose of spiritual gifts. In the final part, the commission offers its evaluation and recommendations from the perspective of Lutheran theology. The commission hopes this document will be helpful in encouraging further study and a proper evaluation of this increasingly significant movement.

1. BACKGROUND INFORMATION

A. Brief History

About a decade ago the Christian world became aware of a religious movement that suddenly sprang up within many of the major American denominations. Perhaps the most characteristic mark of this new movement was its emphasis on an experience called the "baptism of the Holy Spirit." Because some of its basic beliefs resembled those of the Pentecostal churches, it became known among the traditional Christian denominations as neo-Pentecostalism. However, the movement gradually and increasingly came to assume the name "charismatic." In this word the neo-Pentecostal Christians found a term that is both Biblical and popular without bearing the stigma that has often in the past attached itself to the emotionalism and excesses of some Pentecostals.

At first the new movement appeared to have arisen somewhat spontaneously, but on closer investigation it became quite evident that traditional Pentecostalism was having a strong influence on the charismatic movement.

The origin of neo-Pentecostalism is difficult to trace. It first attracted public attention in 1960 when Rev. Dennis Bennett, rector of St. Mark's Episcopal Church in Van Nuys, Calif., resigned his office rather than see his congregation divided over the practice of speaking in tongues by himself and some members of his congregation. But this action, instead of easing tension, seems rather to have signaled the public debut of a movement that had been going on in private since the middle fifties. Reports of similar experiences in other non-Pentecostal churches suddenly were made known, reports that previously had been suppressed perhaps for reasons of uncertainty about the legitimacy of the experience or for fear of denominational censure.

Since 1960 this modern "charismatic renewal," as its leaders like to call it, has spread far beyond the Pentecostal churches. It is found within such denominations as the Episcopalian, Presbyterian, Methodist, Baptist, Lutheran, and more recently, also the Roman Catholic and Eastern Orthodox. With the support of the Full Gospel Business Men's Fellowship International (FGBMFI), the Blessed Trinity Society, and individuals who are anxious to share their experiences with others, it has touched nearly every Protestant denomination in our own country as well as in many foreign countries. In spite of warnings by denominational leaders and even the removal of pastors from their charges, the movement seems to increase in influence. Periodicals published by the F G B M F I and other charismatic groups carry regular reports of pastors and laymen who claim to have experienced the baptism in the Holy Spirit.

Leaders of the charismatic renewal are greatly encouraged by the fact that the movement has also made inroads into certain intellectual centers in America. Neo-Pentecostals frequently publicize the fact that Yale University experienced a Pentecostal revival in October 1961 when nineteen students and one faculty member received the baptism in the Holy Spirit. From Yale the movement then spread to Dartmouth, Princeton, and other university campuses across the nation.

Although the charismatic movement began to enter The Lutheran Church — Missouri Synod some twenty years ago, the main thrust began in the middle sixties. By April 1968, when the first gathering of Missouri Synod charismatic pastors was held at Crystal City, Missouri, there were 44 pastors across the Synod claiming to have received the baptism of the Holy Spirit. When a conference of Lutheran pastors in the charismatic movement was held at Concordia Seminary, St. Louis, in May 1971, it was estimated that there were over 200 pastors in the Synod claiming to have received the baptism in the Holy Spirit.

Lutheran charismatics, like their counterparts in other denominations, explain that their goal is not to separate from the organized church but to assist in revitalizing the church by bearing testimony to the remarkable work the Lord is doing in their own lives through the power of the Spirit. It is their hope that the mainline churches will regard the movement with an open mind and incorporate it into the mainstream of the church's life.

Various attempts have been made to account for the apparent success of the charismatic movement. Dennis Bennett explains its phenomenal growth in these words:

"The church is in a mess, organized Christianity a failure. Why? Because the Holy Spirit has not had a fair chance to work experientially in the church. . . . It is time to stop relying on intellectual analyses and to start relying on spiritual experience. After all Christianity is not an intellectual matter at all. It is a purely personal and spiritual matter."[2]

Frederick Dale Bruner expresses the view that Protestant as well as Roman Catholic churches since the Second Vatican Council have exercised vigorous criticism of their own churches, especially with respect to their irrelevancy, institutionalism, and spiritual deadness.

Appealing to harried Protestant pastors and to spiritually malnourished Protestant and Catholic laity, neo-Pentecostal Christians claim that the power for spiritual life in the individual and in the church is to be found in the long-neglected but now discovered and experienced baptism in the Holy Spirit with its charismatic manifestations.[3]

A Lutheran pastor, recently won over to the movement, states: "It was obvious to me that my own ministry lacked the supernatural power of the Holy Spirit. Certainly souls had been saved through the preaching and teaching of the Gospel. But what about the other works that Jesus did?"[4]

B. Sociological and Psychological Dimensions

Psychologists too have sought an explanation for the spectacular growth experienced by the charismatic movement. Luther P. Gerlach and Virginia H. Hine, members of the Department of Anthropology at the University of Minnesota, have produced a study in which they discount the popular view that economic deprivation, social disorganization, and psychological maladjustment have been primary causes in the development of this movement. It is their opinion that the success of the charismatic revival is to be sought rather in the dynamics of the movement itself. They point to five factors that in particular have been instrumental in the rapid growth of neo-Pentecostalism:

1. The network of friendship, kinship, and other social ties that unites ministers, leaders, evangelists, and people in a "reticulate acephalous organizational structure" that enables them to reach all strata of society.

2. "Face-to-face recruitment along lines of pre-existing significant social relationships." Gerlach and Hine found that relatives accounted for the recruitment of 52 percent of their total sample, and close friends for another 29 percent. "Other recruiting relationships were those between neighbors, business associates, fellow students, employer-employee, or teacher-student, in which previous significant interaction had occurred."

3. A strong sense of commitment that grew out of a transforming act such as the practice of glossolalia, "which set the believer apart in some way from the larger social context, cut him off from past patterns of behavior and sometimes from past associations, identified him with other participants in the movement, and provided high motivation for changed behavior."

4. Encouragement to demonstrate a boldness of spirit for promoting the Lord's work.

5. A psychology of persecution. Among neo-Pentecostals it was found that ridicule, nonacceptance, or painful ejections from mainline denominational churches often resulted in increased growth; on the other hand, in cases where local officialdom posed little or no opposition, recruitment was more difficult.[5]

In recent years psychologists have also conducted controlled and comprehensive studies to ascertain whether participants in the charismatic revival are maladjusted individuals, emotionally unstable, or intellectually deprived. While older psychological opinion tended to relate glossolalia to schizophrenia, hysteria, group hypnosis, unadaptive anxiety reactions, or a higher degree of susceptibility to suggestion, more recent studies have claimed that such conclusions are no longer acceptable in the light of recent sociocultural and psychological data. Gerlach and Hine have reported that in seven studies conducted by psychologists or psychiatrists, Pentecostal glossolalia could not be related to mental illness. Speaking in tongues was not considered an indicator of neurosis or psychosis. Data indicate that although disturbed individuals may be attracted to the movement, there is no evidence that they exist in greater proportion within this movement than within the organized church. It is quite possible that the disturbed may be attracted because of their great need of help, and they may even do or say bizarre things as a manifestation of their illness, but it is not the result of the dynamics of the movement.[6]

Somewhat different conclusions were reached in a psychological and linguistic examination of glossolalia conducted recently by the Lutheran Medical Center in Brooklyn under the direction of John P. Kildahl, Ph.D., and Paul A. Qualben, M.D., and financed by the National Institute of Mental Health. According to their report, they compared the personalities of certain individuals who spoke in tongues with those who did not. Their purpose was "to determine the relationship between certain personality variables and the practice of speaking in tongues" (p. 5). In their study they employed a sampling of 39 individuals, 26 of whom were glossolalists and 13 nonglossolalists. All the participants were volunteers and were equated for age, sex, marital status, and education. All were considered "very religious." An important part of the study was a structured interview and four psychological tests. Among the significant findings in their "Final Progress Report" were the following:

1. As far as emotional and mental health is concerned, the two groups were found to be very similar. Neither group was mentally more healthy than the other. However, it was discovered that an individual's level of maturity did affect the way in which he used glossolalia. The more disturbed use it in a more "bizarre" way, while the maturer person employed it in a more careful manner and made more modest claims concerning its value and effectiveness. (Pp. 25–26)

2. Tongue-speakers are more dependent on authority figures than are nonglossolalists. They have a strong need for guidance "from some external authority" and a strong tendency to lean on "someone more powerful." Having such authority figures "often brings with it great feelings of peace and relaxation." (P. 27)

3. Glossolalists invariably initiate their speech in the presence of a benevolent authority figure, in reality or fantasy (p. 15). "They are able to develop a deeply trusting and submissive relationship to the authority figure who introduces them to the practice of glossolalia. Without completely turning oneself over to the leader, one cannot begin to speak in tongues. In psychotherapy this is called a "dependent transference" (pp. 26f.). This ability to submit oneself to a mentor "is not a function of either mental health or illness"; rather, it is "the same general trait that is called hypnotizability." (P. 28)

4. The influence of a leader is also apparent in the style and type of glossolalia that is employed by a group. The Kildahl report states: "Where certain prominent tongue speakers had visited, whole groups of glossolalists would speak in his style of speech." (P. 27)

5. While speaking in tongues, the individual "does not lose contact with his environment and his senses continue to operate during the experience. But there is an apparent lessening of conscious control" (p. 6). Some believe that the movement of their tongues is directly controlled by God. This experience apparently brings with it a feeling of peace, joy, and inner harmony, and in certain cases gives the charismatic a "tremendous feeling of worth and power." (Pp. 7, 29)

6. Speaking in tongues "is not gibberish. The sounds appear to a non-linguist to have the rhythm and qualities of language." However, glossolalia as it is practiced today lacks the ordinary features that are characteristic of human speech and is not

therefore to be classified among natural languages, either living or dead. (Pp. 5, 16, 25)[7]

Lutheran charismatics feel that the Kildahl report is unsatisfactory. They point out, in the first place, that the Kildahl-Qualben conclusions are based on too small a sample to be truly scientific and conclusive. Lutheran charismatics also deny that the Holy Spirit takes control of the person's mouth and tongue while speaking in tongues. They explain that those who speak in tongues have control over when and where they exercise the gift (just as St. Paul indicates in 1 Cor 14:27-28). While speaking in tongues may be accompanied by a feeling of joy or closeness to God, it does not occur in a semihypnotic state, nor does it involve the speaker in a loss of consciousness or awareness of all that is going on about him. Lutheran charismatics admit that many people are taught the mechanics of speaking in tongues, but they emphasize that others have received the gift simply in response to prayer and without receiving any instruction or hearing anyone speak in tongues. Finally, Lutheran charismatics deny that speaking in tongues means that they are specially chosen by God; they emphasize that speaking in tongues is purely a gift of God's grace.[8]

While the congregations and pastors of The Lutheran Church — Missouri Synod may find various psychological studies of neo-Pentecostalism to be interesting and helpful, such studies appear to be largely inconclusive at the present time. Furthermore, our concern as Christians should center especially on the theological aspects of this movement.

C. Theological Views of Lutheran Charismatics

In spite of the fact that many books, pamphlets, and articles relating personal experiences and views have been produced by Lutheran charismatics in the past decade, it must be understood that no single voice speaks for the entire movement. Moreover, no single authoritative theological interpretation has emerged that is commonly accepted by all charismatics (or even by all *Lutheran* charismatics). There are, however, several basic theological viewpoints that appear with some frequency in the writings of Lutheran charismatics.[9] Among them are the following:

1. In the early church those who came to faith in Jesus Christ were baptized with water. But then as a second or succeeding step they expected also to be baptized in the Holy Spirit. The

normal (although not the only) sequence of events was repentance, faith, water baptism, and baptism in the Holy Spirit.

2. Ordinarily this baptism in the Spirit was an experience that happened at a definite moment in time and was readily recognizable to all who were present since it was accompanied by manifestations of the Spirit, usually speaking in tongues. (Acts 2:1-4; 8:12-17; 10:44-48; 19:1-6)

3. The various gifts of the Holy Spirit mentioned in Scripture are being given to God's people also today and may be sought according to the sovereign will of God. These gifts include extraordinary faith, power to witness to Jesus Christ, miraculous healing, speaking in tongues, the interpretation of tongues, prophecy, exorcism, and others. (1 Cor 12:4-11, 27-31; 1 Cor 14:1-5, 37-40; 1 Thess 5:19, 20; Acts 2:17-18; Mark 16:15-20; Luke 11:13; Acts 1:8; 1 Cor 13:8-12)

4. God's Word alone should determine the nature, purpose and exercise of these spiritual gifts.

5. Baptism in the Holy Spirit and the gifts of the Holy Spirit are founded on the Word and guided by the Word. In addition to the study of the Word and the reception of the sacraments, they are to empower and equip the church for her ministry of proclaiming the Gospel of Jesus Christ to herself and to the world.

6. Baptism in the Holy Spirit is not to be identified with emotionalism, nor does it occur as a result of one's wrestling or because one has reached a certain stage of holiness or spirituality. The baptism in the Spirit is a gift offered by grace to both the strong and the weak in faith. It is to be claimed and received as one claims and receives any promise in the Word. When one becomes a child of God, the Lord gives him the Spirit as a gift; he is then "born of the Spirit" (John 3:5-6). But the Christian may also be "filled" or "baptized with the Holy Spirit" (Acts 1:5-8). With this "filling," the Spirit is allowed to express Himself more fully in and through the Christian's life. There are, however, various opinions among Lutheran charismatics with respect to the manner in which baptism in the Spirit is to be received. Some have listed specific steps that are to be followed in the attainment of this gift; for example, the desire for baptism in the Spirit, an earnest effort to yield one's will to Jesus in all areas of life, fervent prayer for the gift, receiving the gift by faith, thanking God for granting baptism in the Spirit, and releasing the Spirit by praising the Lord in an unknown tongue.

7. Speaking in tongues, which in apostolic times was one of the

manifestations of the Spirit, is an act of spiritual devotion (1 Cor 14:2). As one worships God in tongues, his mind is at rest and his spirit prays, unhindered by the limitations of human understanding (1 Cor 14:14). Though the worshiper does not understand with the mind what he is saying, he does have a clear sense of communion with God.

8. Praying in tongues is a power that the exalted Christ gives members of His church to express the inexpressible and praise God in new speech. It is a gift that should neither be disparaged nor discouraged in the church. To despise or even take lightly a gift of the Spirit is to put oneself in spiritual danger. (1 Thess 5:19, 20; 1 Cor 12:31; 14:1-39)

9. Speaking in tongues is not divisive. The cause of divisions in the church is always to be found in the ignorance and sinfulness of man, coupled with the agitation and devices of Satan.

10. The gift of healing, according to Mark 16:17-18, is one of the "sign gifts" by which God manifests His power to the world in a particularly striking manner. It is one of God's ways of confirming the truth of the Christian message.

11. Miraculous healing, which was very evident in the ministry of Jesus as well as in the apostolic church, is a gift of the Spirit that is still available to the Christian church today. However, it does not find ready acceptance in our day partially because even Christians have been affected to some extent by a naturalistic, materialistic philosophy — particularly popular in the Western world — which rules out any direct supernatural or divine intervention in the course of human events.

12. Prophecies exist in the church today even as in apostolic times. God still speaks directly to His children, communicating to them information to guide and direct them in a given situation in temporal matters. Some charismatics assert that this "word from God comes, not in connection with the sacraments nor with hearing the written or spoken Word, but at times of prayer or even in dreams" or in "prophecy, tongues, and interpretation." It is said that this view does not conflict with those statements of the Lutheran Confessions that are directed against enthusiasm, since Lutheran charismatics uphold the principle that conversion occurs solely through the Gospel.[10]

13. No member of a congregation should be pressured into seeking spiritual gifts or the baptism in the Holy Spirit nor be made to feel inferior because he does not possess or desire such gifts and experiences, but those members who claim the baptism

in the Holy Spirit should be accepted as Lutheran Christians and be given proper instruction from God's Word as to how they should live with their gifts and experiences in a harmonious, edifying manner in the local congregation.

14. The pastor and elders of the church should prayerfully, carefully, and evangelically govern the use and correct any abuse of all spiritual gifts in the life of the church according to the Word of God.

15. A person is saved solely by faith in Jesus Christ as his personal Savior from sin and not because of any special measure or experience of the Holy Spirit or because of the presence or absence of any spiritual gift.

16. The Lord will bless any congregation that gives Christ and His Word its highest allegiance and allows God's Spirit the freedom to move in the lives of its members as He wills. Conversely, the Lord will withhold His full blessing from any congregation that places the traditions and interpretations of men above His Word or on a par with His Word or limits the activity of the Holy Spirit according to past patterns and human definitions.

II. BIBLICAL ANALYSIS

Lutheran charismatics claim that their theological views supplement rather than contradict traditional Lutheran doctrine. That claim can be properly evaluated only on the basis of what the Scriptures teach. We shall first examine the Biblical teaching on the baptism of the Holy Spirit. We will then summarize what the Scriptures teach concerning the Holy Spirit and His spiritual gifts in general before giving particular attention to St. Paul's treatment of spiritual gifts in 1 Corinthians 12-14. Finally, we will discuss whether the Scriptures promise extraordinary charismatic gifts to the church of every age.

A. Baptism of the Holy Spirit

The distinctive doctrine and major emphasis of the neo-Pentecostal or charismatic movement is the baptism of the Holy Spirit. It is therefore crucial to understand what the Scriptures say about this teaching.

1. Baptism with the Holy Spirit is an expression that occurs in a slightly different form in six passages of the New Testament. It appears first in Matthew 3:11 where John the Baptist, speaking to the multitudes concerning Jesus, said: "I baptize you with water

for repentance, but He who is coming after me is mightier than I. . . . He will baptize you with the Holy Spirit and with fire." (See also the parallel passages: Mark 1:8, Luke 3:16, John 1:33.)

Jesus employed the same terminology shortly before His ascension into heaven. In Acts 1:5 it is reported that on the day of His departure into heaven, Jesus told His disciples: "For John baptized with water, but before many days you shall be baptized with the Holy Spirit."

Act 11:16 relates the reactions of Simon Peter when the Holy Spirit "fell on" Cornelius and his household. The apostle exclaims: "And I remembered the word of the Lord, how He said, 'John baptized with water, but you shall be baptized with the Holy Spirit.'"

While these are the only passages that employ the specific terminology, "baptize with the Holy Spirit," there are other parts of Scripture that describe the same concept in different words; for example, "they were all filled with the Holy Spirit" (Acts 2:4; 7:55; 9:17), or "the Holy Spirit fell on all who heard the Word" (Acts 10:44-46), or "the gift of the Holy Spirit had been poured out even on the Gentiles" (Acts 10:45), or "the Holy Spirit came on them" (Acts 19:6). In each of these instances the context indicates an experience similar to baptism with the Holy Spirit.

2. Scripture is also very clear regarding the meaning of Spirit baptism in the apostolic church. The promise Jesus had given His disciples, "but before many days you shall be baptized with the Holy Spirit" (Acts 1:5), was fulfilled on Pentecost when God poured out His Spirit on 120 followers of the ascended Lord, giving them power to be witnesses in Jerusalem, Judea, Samaria, and the uttermost parts of the earth. A similar experience occurred among the Samaritans when Philip preached the Gospel to them (Acts 8:14-15), and in the case of Cornelius and his family to whom Peter brought the Gospel (Acts 10:44-48). It was also experienced by the disciples at Ephesus when Paul baptized them in the name of Jesus (Acts 19:1-6). In each of these instances believers in Jesus were endowed with special supernatural gifts (Acts 2:43; 3:6-7; 5:12; 6:8; 7:55; 8:13; 9:40; etc.). Significantly, nowhere in Acts is the gift of the Spirit given to individuals in isolation from the community of Christians.

3. It will be noted, furthermore, that in each of these instances baptism with the Spirit occurred after conversion. The apostles were Christians before Pentecost. The Samaritans had given heed to the preaching of Philip before Peter was sent to them and

prayed that they might receive the Holy Spirit (Acts 8:6, 14-15). Likewise in the case of Cornelius, he was "a devout man who feared God with all his household" and prayed constantly to Him even before Peter entered into his house and preached to him with the result that the Spirit fell on all who heard the Word. (Acts 10:2, 44-48)

4. There is nothing in these narratives to indicate that Luke is intent on giving the church a formula for receiving the baptism of the Spirit. The apostle Peter had already proclaimed to his conscience-stricken hearers on Pentecost: "Repent, and be baptized every one of you in the name of Jesus Christ for the forgiveness of your sins; and *you shall receive the gift of the Holy Spirit.* For the promise is to you and to your children and to all that are far off, every one whom the Lord our God calls to Him" (Acts 2:38-39). This promise is given not only to Christians in the apostolic age but to all future generations as well. It should be noted that there is no suggestion of a time interval between baptism in the name of Jesus and receiving the gift of the Spirit. Nor is there any indication in this important promise that the believer, after coming to faith, must then actively seek the gift of the Spirit before receiving it.

Lutheran theologians are generally agreed that Luke's purpose in recording the events in Acts 8 and 10 is to relate how God in a marvelous way demonstrated before the eyes of Peter and other representatives of the congregation at Jerusalem that the Gentiles also were to be received into the church even as the Jews. It has, therefore, been suggested by some Lutheran exegetes that the lapse in time between conversion and baptism with the Spirit, in the case of the Samaritans and of Cornelius, was for the purpose of bringing Peter and others to the scene and making them eyewitnesses as God poured out His Spirit on the Gentiles as He had done on the Jews at Pentecost. (Acts 11:13-18)

5. According to the Book of Acts, Christians in the apostolic church always received the baptism of the Holy Spirit solely as a gift, never as a blessing achieved on the basis of human effort. While charismatics sometimes emphasize that the Spirit must be earnestly sought after and prayed for, the major passages in Acts constantly refer to Him as the result of a promise from the Father (Acts 1:4-5; 2:33; 2:38-39; 8:20; 10:45), bestowed on the believer when he comes to faith.

When one looks specifically at the promise Jesus gave His

disciples prior to Pentecost, it is evident that there were no conditions stated and no requirements made of them before they would receive the baptism of the Spirit. No mention is made of the need to pray for the gift of the Holy Spirit, nor that they should empty themselves of sin, surrender their wills to God, and make special preparations in other ways. Luke simply relates that Jesus charged His disciples "not to depart from Jerusalem, but to wait for the promise of the Father, which, He said, 'you heard from Me, for John baptized with water, but before many days you shall be baptized with the Holy Spirit.'" (Acts 1:4-5)

There is no indication here that only those would receive the baptism who met certain conditions. Instead Jesus addressed Himself to all His disciples and made the general promise, "you shall be baptized with the Holy Spirit." When the evangelist records the fulfillment of the promise on Pentecost, he states very specifically that "they were all filled with the Holy Spirit" (Acts 2:4). It is significant that throughout the Book of Acts when the Spirit descended on a group of believers, it is always stated or strongly implied that all were filled with the Spirit. There is no indication that one or more persons were ever denied the full gift of the Spirit due to insufficient preparation. Nor is there any suggestion of a partial filling by the Spirit as if to imply that He first enters the believer's heart and life to bring conversion and sanctification and then only later comes in His fullness and power when the justified person is ready, having sought baptism of the Spirit by earnest prayer.

Luther writes very forcefully on this point in his commentary on the Epistle to the Galatians. In Gal 3:5, the apostle Paul asks: "Does he who supplies the Spirit to you and works miracles among you do so by works of the law, or by hearing with faith?" Commenting on this verse, Luther writes that the entire Book of Acts "treats nothing else than that the Holy Spirit is not given through the law (men's deeds) but is given through the hearing of the Gospel. For when Peter preached, the Holy Spirit immediately fell on all those who heard the Word. On one day 3000 who heard Peter's proclamation believed and received the gift of the Holy Spirit (Acts 2:41). Thus Cornelius received the Holy Spirit, though not on the basis of the alms he gave, but when Peter opened his mouth and was still speaking, the Holy Spirit fell on all those who were listening to the Word with Cornelius (Acts 10:44) . . . Thus Cornelius and his friends whom he called to his house do not do anything, nor do they look to any preceding works, and yet as many as are present receive the Holy Spirit."[11]

Luther understood that the gift of the Holy Spirit, which was promised to the church on Pentecost, is given to all believers solely by the grace of God, not because of any effort or deed on the part of the recipient.

To be sure, Scripture frequently urges us to pray for the gift of the Spirit (Luke 11:13; Acts 4:31; 5:29-32). But these exhortations are not intended to imply that God will withhold His Spirit from those who do not earnestly seek Him. God grants His Spirit to all who believe. Nevertheless the Lord also wants us, His children, to pray for this gift and thereby indicate our earnest desire to be His temple and our humble dependence on all His gifts. Christians frequently pray for those blessings they already possess.

6. It is highly important also that the church today understands what the Scripture means when it exhorts the Christian to be filled with the Spirit and when it speaks of men full of the Spirit. Pentecostals and many neo-Pentecostals equate these terms with the possession of charismatic gifts. They assert that when Scripture urges the believer to be filled with the Spirit (Eph 5:18), it is encouraging him to seek and pray for the baptism of the Holy Spirit, which will bestow on him such spiritual gifts as prophecy, divine healing, miracles, or speaking in tongues. (1 Cor 12:8-10)

However, a study of pertinent passages in the Scripture indicates rather clearly that these expressions may have various meanings. On Pentecost the disciples, filled with the Spirit, spoke in tongues, proclaiming the wondrous works of God (Acts 2:11). The deacons in Acts 6:3 were to be men full of the Spirit and of wisdom in order that they might distribute food and clothing to the needy in a fair and equitable manner. Stephen, full of the Spirit, disputed with the members of the Jewish Sanhedrin and put them to silence (Acts 6:10). Paul was filled with the Spirit at his baptism and so was equipped to be a missionary to the Gentiles (Acts 9:15-18). In Ephesians 5:18 the apostle exhorts all Christians to be filled with the Spirit, obviously meaning that they should employ the powers given them by the Spirit to live Christian lives, for the entire fifth chapter of the epistle deals with sanctification.

Thus the expression "filled with the Holy Spirit," as it is used in Scripture, very frequently has no apparent relationship to charismatic gifts. Consequently, it is often used in conjunction with such terms as "wisdom" or "faith" (Acts 6:3). Men full of the Spirit are children of God whom the Spirit has endowed with the gift of faith in Jesus Christ as Lord (1 Cor 12:3), as well as gifts and talents that enable them to serve Christ and their fellowmen in the church.

B. *The Holy Spirit and His Gifts*

The baptism of the Holy Spirit must be studied in the larger Biblical context of the Holy Spirit and His spiritual gifts. One of the themes that appears prominently in both Testaments represents the Holy Spirit as the Spirit of Power who gives special gifts to the people of God in order to enable them to serve Him according to His will. In Old Testament times it was the Spirit who gave the rulers and military leaders the ability to govern in times of emergency. (1 Sam 10:1-7; 16:13)

He gave the judges of Israel physical strength, courage, and wisdom to wage war against the enemies of God's people (Judg 3:7-10; 6:33ff.). He endowed the artisans with craftsmanship in building the tabernacle (Ex 31:2-4). In a very special sense of the word, He equipped His "prophets" to serve as mouthpieces of God in order to reveal His will to the people. (2 Sam 23:2; Neh 9:20, 30; Ezek 11:5; Hos 9:7; Zech 7:12)

Throughout the New Testament, the Spirit is presented as the mark of the new age that began with the resurrection of Jesus and Pentecost. The Holy Spirit in whose name we are baptized is the Spirit who was promised in the Old Testament (cf. Ezek 36:25-38; Jer 31:31-34; Ps 51:10-12). But He is associated with God's new covenant and the passing away of the old covenant (cf. 2 Cor 3). To confess Jesus as Lord by the Holy Spirit (1 Cor 12:3) is to confess that we stand in the new testament in distinction from the old, for the Spirit is the "down payment" or "firstfruits" of the new age (cf. Rom 8:23; 2 Cor 5:5; 1:22). The church, created by the Holy Spirit through Baptism and the Word, is the *new* Israel of God.

In the New Testament the Spirit's work was intensified. This became evident even before the events of Pentecost. Early in his ministry John the Baptist proclaimed the good news that Jesus would "baptize" His people with the Holy Spirit. This indicated that with the coming of the Kingdom Jesus would pour out His Spirit on them in a very special measure.

Prior to His suffering and death on the cross, Jesus gave His disciples the promise of the Spirit. The Spirit would be their *parakleetos*, their Comforter and Counselor (John 14:26). He would guide them into all truth; He would teach them all things and again remind them of all that Jesus had told them while He was with them. (John 14:17, 26; 16:13)

Shortly before His ascension into heaven, the Savior told the disciples to remain in Jerusalem until they had received the baptism of the Holy Spirit (Acts 1:5); then they should employ this power to bear witness to Christ in all the world. (Acts 1:8)

In the Book of Acts it is evident that these promises concerning the Holy Spirit were fulfilled. The coming of Pentecost brought with it the baptism of the Holy Spirit. Jesus equipped His followers with such spiritual gifts as were needed to carry out the task of evangelizing the world. Some of these gifts were miraculous. The disciples on Pentecost were heard speaking of the wonderful works of God in languages they had not learned (Acts 2:6-12). Some time later in the history of the early church, this experience was repeated with other believers in Christ. (Acts 10:46; 19:6)

Filled with the Holy Spirit, the disciples of Jesus performed many signs and wonders (Acts 5:12; 6:8); they healed the lame (Acts 3:6), the sick and those afflicted with unclean spirits (Acts 5:16; 8:6-8), and those who were paralyzed (Acts 9:34); on occasions they even raised the dead. (Acts 9:40; see also Acts 13:9-11; 14:8-11; 16:18; 19:11-12; 20:7-12.)

Of special importance, however, were the less spectacular spiritual gifts that were directly related to the proclamation of the Gospel. After Pentecost the disciples possessed an intense desire to preach the Gospel of Jesus Christ. They employed every opportunity to witness to the crucifixion, death, and resurrection of their Lord. They proclaimed Christ with new courage and boldness, and it is very evident that they understood better than before Pentecost the purpose and significance of Christ's death and resurrection. (Acts 2:14-40; 3:12-26; 4:1-22; 5:29-32; 7:1-60; 8:32-35)

After Pentecost the Holy Spirit took a very active part in directing the early church into an intensive program of carrying the Gospel into all the world. It was the Spirit who led Philip to the chariot of the Ethiopian and gave him the opportunity to speak to him of the Savior (Acts 8:29). It was the Spirit who directed Simon Peter to the house of the Gentile Cornelius to proclaim to him the Gospel (Acts 10). Again it was the Spirit who chose Paul and Barnabas to be missionaries to the Gentile world (Acts 13:1-3) and then directed them through Asia Minor into Macedonia. (Acts 16:6-10)

The Bible also provides a number of lists that enumerate specific spiritual gifts with which God has endowed His church. One of the more familiar listings is recorded in 1 Corinthians 12 where the spiritual gifts mentioned are wisdom, knowledge, faith, gifts of healing, working of miracles, prophecy, the ability to distinguish between spirits, various kinds of tongues, and the interpretation of tongues. It should be carefully noted that while the apostle clearly indicates that miraculous gifts of the Spirit were possessed by some individuals in the Corinthian congregation, he does not deal with the subject extensively in his letters to other churches. When Paul in other epistles presents to his readers lists of spiritual gifts, or when he discusses the duties and functions of the church, or even when he catalogs the qualifications of pastors and other church leaders, he mentions only the less spectacular gifts, and his emphasis is on communicating the Gospel (Eph 4:4-11; Rom 12:6-8; 1 Tim 3:1-13; Titus 1:7-9). Some have interpreted this silence to mean that the miraculous gifts that were originally given to the followers of Christ soon disappeared from the early church after they had served their special purpose. Others, however, feel that such an argument from silence is inconclusive because there may have been no problem in these churches with regard to the proper use of these gifts.

In the fifth chapter of Galatians the apostle discusses the fruits of the Spirit which are love, joy, peace, patience, kindness, goodness, faithfulness, gentleness, and self-control (vv. 22-23). Here it should be noted that St. Paul lists the less spectacular gifts of the Spirit, namely, the more common attitudes and spiritual qualities of the Christian that result from his regeneration.

To be considered also is that Holy Scripture indicates with remarkable consistency that the Spirit imparts His gifts in response to the needs of His kingdom (Gen 41:38; Num 11:16-17, 24-26, 29; 27:18-23; 1 Sam 16:13; Judg 6:1-6, 33-34; 13:1-3, 24-25; Acts 2:1-43; 4:1-22; 6:1-11; 8:26-40). He bestows His special gifts on God's people in a historical context. In the New Testament the primary emphasis is that the Spirit equips the church to meet the world's need for the Gospel (Acts 8:5-8; 8:14-17; 11:1-18; 13:1-3;

16:6-10). For this reason the apostle strongly emphasized the importance of proclaiming Christ in a clear, intelligible manner. (1 Cor 14:1-12)

In short, the Spirit is the Spirit of Jesus Christ our Lord and no other. Jesus promises not only that the Spirit "will convince the world of sin and of righteousness and of judgment" but that He will glorify Jesus Christ, "for He will take what is Mine and declare it to you" (John 16:8, 14). He is quite willing to be anonymous as long as Christ is proclaimed and exalted (John 16:13-14). The Spirit does not provide a second foundation for faith but bears witness to Jesus Christ as the church's one Foundation. Through Him we confess Jesus as Lord (1 Cor 12:3) and call God our Father (Gal 4:6). It is through the Spirit that we serve God and one another and overcome the temptations that arise in our lives. The Spirit transforms and empowers the whole life and outlook of those who receive Him, gives birth to the community of the church, and enables that church to proclaim the Word with boldness.

C. The Nature and Purpose of Spiritual Gifts in 1 Corinthians 12-14
One of the most instructive sections in Holy Scriptures on the nature and purpose of spiritual gifts is 1 Corinthians 12-14. We shall not attempt to reconstruct the total problem that troubled the church at Corinth with respect to charismatic gifts, nor shall we seek to review the questions that may have been asked by the congregation. Instead we shall note some of the basic instructions that Paul gives in these chapters regarding spiritual gifts. Among the points made by St. Paul that are particularly relevant to our discussion are the following:

1. Already in the preface to his letter the apostle calls the attention of the Corinthians to the many blessings they possess in Christ. In Him they have every spiritual gift (1:7); they have sanctification (1:2), the grace of God (1:4), enrichment in speech and knowledge (1:5). Because they are in Christ, they lack no spiritual gift. They also wait for the "revealing of the Lord Jesus Christ." Only the return of the Savior would bring complete victory for them. Apparently the Corinthian Christians thought of themselves as already existing in the realm of glory, engaging in the work of the Spirit, which they conceived of as being beyond Christ. Therefore, the apostle reminds them again and again that the spiritual gifts they now possess are theirs *in the crucified and*

resurrected Christ. And at His return they will be complete.

But while possessing all spiritual blessings, they were not using them as they should, and in chapters 12 to 14 Paul proceeds to give them instructions on the nature, purpose, and proper use of these great gifts.

2. The fact that an individual is in an ecstatic state does not in itself indicate that he is spiritual. Ecstasy is not limited to Christians. The Corinthians knew this from past experience. Before they were children of God, the very essence of their religious experience was their feeling of being carried away by spiritual forces. But then they were led away to dumb idols. Now the Corinthians are being led by the Spirit. They can recognize this from the fact that they are able to call Jesus their Lord. This confession of Christ is the characteristic mark of those possessed by the Spirit of God, says Paul.

3. But if the central work of the Spirit is leading men to honor Christ by confessing faith in Him as Lord, the Holy Spirit also manifests Himself through a variety of gifts and services with which He endows the Christian church. In 1 Cor 12:8-10, 28-30, the apostle provides lists of the spiritual gifts he had in mind. They include the utterance of wisdom, the utterance of knowledge, faith, healing, miracles, prophecy, the ability to discern spirits, various kinds of tongues, and the interpretation of tongues. Prominent at the head of the lists are gifts of intelligent and thoughtful utterance. Prominent at the end are gifts of tongues and their interpretation.

Among the spiritual gifts referred to in 1 Corinthians 12 are a number of terms that require some explanation. In verse 8 "the utterance of wisdom" and "the utterance of knowledge" may refer to an exceptionally thorough knowledge of the great truths of divine revelation, particularly the mysteries of the Gospel, and the ability to expound them in a clear and convincing manner as well as to apply them to individual cases in life. "Faith," in this context, can hardly refer to saving or justifying faith but must point to a heroic, unwavering trust and confidence in the power of God to reveal Himself in extraordinary deeds that may seem impossible to men. The expression "gifts of healing" no doubt refers to those remarkable deeds performed in the early Christian church by certain believers who were enabled by the power of God to heal the sick without medication, cast out unclean spirits, cure the lame, and even on occasions raise the dead. "The working of miracles" is a broader term including the many wondrous deeds performed by the early Christians through the almighty power of Christ.

"Prophecy" is a rather difficult term to understand, since it is used in various ways in Scripture. It does not refer primarily to the gift of declaring coming events in advance, although this did occur in the apostolic church (Acts 11:27: Agabus). It includes also the God-given ability to interpret Scripture correctly and to apply its message of Law and Gospel to the needs of men. It is the gift of expressing what the will of God was in a given situation. The ability to "distinguish between spirits" refers to a God-given power by which certain individuals in the early church were able to test the prophets to determine whether they were false or true and to judge whether a doctrine was of God or not.

"Various kinds of tongues," in the case of the Corinthians, apparently had reference to a "language," unintelligible to others as well as to the speaker, by which a Christian praised God. (Paul discusses this gift at great length in 1 Corinthians 14.) "The interpretation of tongues" evidently was the ability to transmit the content and message of such "language" for the benefit and edification of the speaker and other members of the body of Christ.

4. These spiritual gifts are not reserved for the select few in the church, who are consequently in a privileged class above the rest; instead, Paul states that all Christians have been endowed by the Spirit with gifts of one kind or another. (v. 7)

5. All Christians have been baptized into the body of Christ, and all are made to drink of the one Spirit (v. 13). Therefore the spiritual gifts that each possesses are for the benefit of the entire church; they are given "for the common good" (v. 7). The Christian is to use his gifts in the service of Christ's body, the church, and not merely to serve himself. Any use of the Spirit's gifts that does not edify the church is contrary to the Spirit's intention.

6. In 1 Corinthians 13 Paul discusses the basic attitude with which the Christian is to use the spiritual gifts God has given him. In the previous chapter he has indicated that they are *charismata*, gifts of grace. Now the apostle admonishes the Corinthians to employ them in a spirit of love.

7. It appears that in the congregation at Corinth the possession of certain spiritual gifts had led to senseless pride and chaotic confusion. Paul, therefore, admonished them in a most forceful

manner that love must permeate and motivate their use of spiritual gifts or they become meaningless and useless. Even though a person may possess the very loftiest kind of tongue-speaking and though he may be able to speak not only in an unknown human language but with the tongues of angels, unless this gift is exercised in a spirit of love, it becomes nothing more than an unintelligible, meaningless set of sounds. Neither speaking in tongues nor prophetic insights nor heroic faith that can move mountains nor superhuman sacrifice can be useful and meaningful unless they are exercised in a spirit of Christian love. Thus it is not the miraculous nature of a gift nor the spectacular character of one's willingness to sacrifice that makes spiritual gifts unambiguous marks of the Spirit's presence and power; it is only the spirit of Christian love in which the gifts are exercised.

8. St. Paul then proceeds to describe very carefully the nature of this love about which he is speaking. It is not primarily something emotional or ecstatic, passionate or fiery; instead, it tends to tame those emotions that are so apt to lead to the abuse of spiritual gifts. Love is patient, long-suffering, and kind. More specifically, it is not jealous or boastful, arrogant or rude, irritable or resentful. It does not insist on having its own way. It does not rejoice in wrongdoing but rejoices in what is right.

9. Christian love also has the remarkable characteristic that it will continue on into the unending future, always relevant. Other gifts of the Spirit such as prophecies, tongues, and knowledge are imperfect and incomplete in this life and shall therefore pass away when they have served their purpose, but Christian love will remain intact even in the state of perfection. (13:9-13)

10. In the context of this magnificent discussion of Christian love, the apostle then exhorts the Corinthian congregation: "Make love your aim, and earnestly desire the spiritual gifts, especially that you may prophesy" (14:1). Immediately thereafter, he addresses himself to certain problems that had arisen in Corinth with regard to speaking in tongues.

11. St. Paul, who himself possessed the gift of tongues (1 Cor 14:18), believed that it could be an authentic gift of the Spirit. He did not forbid its use for self-edification or, when interpreted, for the edification of others (1 Cor 14:5, 39). However, it should be carefully noted that the apostle in 1 Corinthians 12 to 14 is not discussing the gift of tongues for the purpose of encouraging or assisting the Corinthians in acquiring this gift. His purpose is rather to point out dangers and abuses that have resulted from its

misuse and to encourage the use of other spiritual gifts, especially prophecy.

12. St. Paul prefers prophecy to tongue-speaking for a number of reasons. One who speaks in tongues speaks not to men but to God, for no one understands him, and the result is that he edifies only himself (14:2). On the other hand, he who prophesies speaks to men for their upbuilding, encouragement, and consolation. Such a person edifies the church. Edification now becomes the theme of this chapter (vv. 3, 4, 5, 12, 17, 26). According to St. Paul's manner of thinking, the ultimate criterion for a spiritual gift is this: "Does it build the church?"

13. Tongue-speaking can be useful in the church only if it is supplemented with the gift of interpretation (v. 5), for only then will it edify the church. Without interpretation no one will know what is being said, and it will be as if one speaks into the air (v. 9). Therefore he who speaks in a tongue should pray for the power to interpret in order to edify (v. 13). Paul thanks God that he has spoken in tongues more than all of them (v. 18); nevertheless, he concludes: "I would rather speak five words with my mind, in order to instruct others, than ten thousand words in a tongue" (v. 19). In full accord with this expressed principle, we have no record of Paul ever speaking to his churches except in understandable language.

14. Accenting the gift of tongues out of proportion to other gifts is a sign of immaturity. In 1 Cor 14:20-25 the apostle therefore challenges the Corinthians to "grow up" in their thinking. They should consider the effect that speaking in tongues might have on the church's program of evangelism. At an assembly of the church the effect of speaking in tongues on "outsiders" and "unbelievers" may be adverse, for it may lead them to think Christians are mad (v. 23). In verse 21 the apostle inserts an Old Testament quotation (Is 28:11-12) into the discussion, emphasizing that the effect of tongues on an unbeliever will be to harden rather than soften his heart.[12] Thus the use of strange tongues in the Corinthian congregation might not serve to convert the sinner but instead could cause him to blaspheme.

On the other hand, when members of the Corinthian congregation prophesy, which involves a testimony of their faith, and an outsider is present, there is the possibility that the unbeliever will be made conscious of his sin and unbelief. The secret sins of his heart may be revealed, and the result might well be that such a one repents and worships God, openly recognizing God's presence in the congregation. Using the gift of prophecy in that way may result in winning people for Christ.

15. Each believer is to consider himself a vital and responsible participant in the life of the congregation. In a church service everything should be done in an orderly fashion. Although Paul does not forbid speaking in tongues in their worship services (v. 39) he makes three important stipulations: (a) not more than three should speak in tongues in any one service; (b) these three should take turns and not speak all at once; (c) there should always be an interpreter present. Without an interpreter "let each of them keep silence in church and speak to himself and to God." (vv. 27-28)

The same rules of good order apply to those who prophesy. They should prophesy in turn while the rest exercise judgment on what is said. This sentence indicates that the assembly's right to criticize should not be suspended no matter what gift might be exercised. Since God is a God not of confusion but of peace, all gifts, even prophecy, should be used in an orderly fashion.

D. The Gifts of the Spirit Today

Of primary importance in the current discussion is the question whether the Lord has promised to give His Spirit to the Christian church today in the same manner that He gave the Spirit to the church of the first century, enabling believers to perform miracles, heal the sick, cast out demons, raise the dead, prophesy, or speak in tongues. Are the events recorded in Acts 2, 8, 10, and 19 to be interpreted solely as historical happenings that occurred in apostolic times, or should these passages be considered promises indicating what the Lord will do in behalf of His people also in future generations?

These narratives are presented by Luke as historical accounts and without any indication that they are to be considered promises also to future generations. Accordingly, Lutheran theologians in the past have usually interpreted them as experiences that occurred only in the apostolic church. Lutheran dogmaticians in earlier centuries carefully distinguished between baptism with the Holy Spirit and baptism in the name of Jesus. Only the latter was considered a sacrament to be performed in the church until the return of Christ. For these dogmaticians, baptism with the Holy Spirit, together with charismatic gifts, was limited to the apostolic age.

In more recent years, other Lutheran theologians identified the baptism of the Holy Spirit with the conversion of the sinner, which takes place through the Word and sacraments. Dr. Theodore Engelder, for example, writes:

"All Christians are 'baptized with the Holy Ghost,' Luke 3:16. This term describes the work of the Holy Ghost in saving, in regenerating and justifying the sinner, sanctifying and preserving the Christian, and bestowing upon him the gifts and power he needs in his Christian calling, Acts 2:17; Is 44:3; Zech 12:10; Titus 3:6; 1 Cor 12:3; Eph 5:18; 1 Cor 6:11; Gal 3:1; Luke 11:13. . . . The term is used in an unscriptural sense by the extreme enthusiasts, who define 'the baptism of the Holy Ghost' as the bestowal of sinless perfection . . . accompanied by miracle-working power, as the 'second blessing,' consequent upon the reconsecration of the soul to a higher and deeper life. . . . Some even go so far as to designate it the chief and greatest blessing, while according to Scripture justification by faith is the chief and supreme thing in the life of the Christian, the greatest blessing, the source of all blessings."[13]

While Lutheran theologians have at times differed in their understanding of the term "baptism with the Holy Spirit," they have rather consistently held that the extraordinary charismatic gifts mentioned in Acts and 1 Corinthians were no longer given after the close of the apostolic age.

Even passages such as Mark 16:17-18 and 1 Cor 13:8-10 do not clearly promise that God will endow His church throughout the centuries with the charismatic gifts that were given to the early Christians. Mark 16:17-18 does indeed state that "these signs will accompany those who believe: in My name they will cast out demons; they will speak in new tongues; they will pick up serpents, and if they drink any deadly thing, it will not hurt them; they will lay their hands on the sick, and they will recover." There is today almost unanimous agreement among scholars that verses 9 to 20 are not a part of the authentic text of the 16th chapter of the Gospel of Mark.[14] But even if these verses are authentic, they do not support the view of those who claim that in all ages of Christendom believers will be accompanied by a display of miracles. Understanding these verses in such an absolute sense would force one to conclude that these words of Jesus are unfulfilled, since such miracles have not always accompanied believers.

First Corinthians 13:8-10 has at times been quoted to prove that extraordinary charismatic gifts will remain in the church until the return of Christ, at which time that which is imperfect will pass away. However, if this passage is employed in this manner, one must conclude that not only tongues, prophecy, and knowledge will continue to exist in the church but also apostles and prophets, since they too are included among the spiritual or charismatic gifts listed in 1 Cor 12:28. On the other hand, 1 Cor 13:8-10 should not be used to prove the opposite. The apostle's statements that prophecies will pass away and tongues will cease are spoken in an eschatological context and do not prove that such gifts will end with the apostolic age. Moreover, his chief point in these verses is to stress the abiding character of love rather than the exact duration of extraordinary charismatic gifts.

It is noteworthy that the Scripture nowhere promises or encourages us to hope that extraordinary charismatic gifts will become the possession of the Christian church throughout the centuries. The pattern set in Scripture may actually indicate the opposite. While gifts of the Spirit are spoken of throughout the Bible, different gifts were given at different times in history depending on the needs of the Kingdom. The church can be sure that the Spirit will grant it those blessings that it will need to build the church, but it will remember that the Lord may have other gifts in mind for His people than those He granted the Christians in apostolic times. The church today must not reason in a manner that would lead us to conclude that because the Holy Spirit gave Samson the ability to fight lions or David the talent to govern, we can therefore expect Him to endow us similarly. The church must not conclude that because the Christian community in apostolic times had members who could speak in tongues, therefore the church today *must* possess similar gifts or it is somehow incomplete. It must not contend that because the church of the apostles had in its midst those with the ability to perform miracles of healing, therefore the church of the twentieth century *must* have members with similar gifts or it lacks an essential characteristic of the body of Christ. To be sure, the Lord *may* choose to give such gifts; but He gives to His church according to His good and gracious will and in keeping with His promises.

The Christian church today will accept with joy and gratitude any gift that the Spirit in His grace may choose to bestow on us for the purpose of edifying the body of Christ. It will recognize that the Lord does not forsake His church but promises the abiding presence of His Spirit. The church, therefore, will not reject out of hand the possibility that God may in His grace and wisdom endow some in Christendom with the same abilities and powers He gave His church in past centuries. It will take care lest it quench the Spirit by neither praying for nor expecting God's presence and power in building His church. But it will also take seriously the admonition of the apostle to "test the spirits to see whether they are of God, for many false prophets have gone out into the world." (1 John 4:1; 1 Cor 12:10).[15]

The church should seek the Holy Spirit and His gifts where God has promised them, in the Word and sacraments. The Scriptures make this point abundantly clear. In the house of Cornelius, for example, the preached word of Peter about Jesus Christ was the occasion for the gift of the Holy Spirit "on all who heard the word" (Acts 10:44). In Ephesus it was Paul's proclamation of Jesus that led to baptism in the name of Jesus and the coming of the Holy Spirit to the disciples of John (Acts 19:4-6). The Galatians, writes the apostle Paul, received the Spirit "by hearing with faith" (Gal 3:3, 5). Word and sacraments are the instruments of the Spirit of God through which God continues to give His gifts to the church in this and every age.[16]

III. CONCLUSIONS AND RECOMMENDATIONS

A. A Response to Issues Raised by the Charismatic Movement Within Lutheranism[17]

1. *Terminology*. The terminology "baptism in the Holy Spirit" is not frequently employed in Lutheran theological literature. However, it should be recognized that this language was used both by Jesus and by the apostolic church. Its use, therefore, should not be considered sectarian or contrary to sound doctrine.

Historically, however, this term has frequently been employed to describe concepts and doctrines that are not in accord with Scripture. Lutherans will exercise great care, therefore, to use this expression in such a way that it represents a truly Biblical concept.

2. *The Promise of the Spirit*. In accord with Jesus' promise (Acts 1:4, 5, 8), the followers of Christ were baptized with the Holy Spirit on the first Pentecost when the Spirit's presence and power were manifested in a most remarkable manner, and three thousand of those in attendance were converted to the Christian faith. Whether baptism in the Holy Spirit was a once-for-all event

that occurred solely on Pentecost or an experience that would be repeated in the Christian church throughout the centuries cannot be determined with certainty. But it is quite clear from Scripture that "the gift of the Holy Spirit" has been promised to all generations of Christians. (Acts 2:39)

While we Christians rejoice in this gracious promise, we should recognize that this gift of the Spirit does not necessarily include the promise of all extraordinary spiritual gifts that were once given to the apostolic church, such as speaking in tongues, miracles of healing, or prophecy. According to the pattern of Sacred Scripture, God does not necessarily give His church in all ages the same special gifts; instead, He bestows His blessings according to His good pleasure and the needs of the church.

Even in the apostolic church, where the gifts of tongues and healing were very evident, it is not clear that all Christians possessed these charismatic gifts. There is no indication that many important persons referred to in the Book of Acts as believers in Jesus, performing effective work in the Kingdom, were endowed with the gift of tongues or of healing. The Christian church must therefore be extremely careful not to place too much emphasis on any one of these gifts. For example, it is not in accord with the clear intent of Scripture when glossolalia is made the primary or indispensable sign of baptism in the Spirit.

3. *Christological Concerns.* In view of present world conditions, many Christians welcome the greater emphasis that has been placed on the work of the Holy Spirit in recent years. They yearn for a spiritual renewal in the church, for a greater amount of zeal and commitment and for less apathy in carrying on the Lord's work, and for power in proclaiming the Gospel of Jesus Christ to the nations. Christians in general are agreed that there is great need for a deeper appreciation of the work of the Spirit in the church today.

But in the light of recent developments in Christendom, the Lutheran Church is also deeply concerned lest the function of the Spirit be emphasized in a manner that would tend to make the saving work of Christ appear less important. This may be the unintentional result of teaching a Christian that it is necessary for him to experience two separate encounters: first, an encounter with Christ for conversion and forgiveness; and second, a further encounter with the Spirit to obtain power to serve effectively in Christ's kingdom. Lutherans believe that when they have Christ by faith, they also have the Holy Spirit and with Him all that is necessary for time and eternity as far as their spiritual life is concerned.

The work of Christ may also appear less important when baptism in the Holy Spirit is emphasized in such a way as to detract from the importance the Scripture places on baptizing with water or, as it is called in the Book of Acts, "baptism in the name of Jesus." History indicates rather clearly that those denominations that in the past have placed particular emphasis on Spirit baptism have also considered water baptism to be of less significance.

Lutheran Christians will also be careful to describe the life and work of Jesus in such a way that the inseparability of His divine and human natures is properly maintained and that His work of atonement receives the primary emphasis. Jesus was indeed richly endowed with the Holy Spirit. But when His work is portrayed as though He performed it merely or chiefly as a man filled with the Holy Spirit and not as the God-man, and when the Spirit-filled Jesus is proclaimed primarily as the pattern or example of what believers filled with the Holy Spirit can do today, then we have a Christology that has parted company with the Biblical, creedal, and confessional witness to Jesus Christ. Such emphases, when carried to their ultimate conclusion, would deprive the atonement of its divine redemptive power and treat Jesus more as man's pattern for life than his Redeemer from eternal death.

The Christian must exercise special caution as he defines the relationship between the Spirit and Jesus in the state of humiliation, lest he embrace a form of subordinationism. Scripture does indeed portray Jesus' ministry as having been conducted *in the power of the Spirit.* Both the Old and the New Testaments speak of Jesus being anointed with the Spirit (Is 11:2-9; 61:1ff.; Luke 4:18ff.). The Savior was led into the wilderness *by the Spirit* for the purpose of being tempted by Satan (Luke 4:1ff.). He returned and began His public ministry, preaching and teaching in Galilee *in the power of the Spirit* (Luke 4:14). It is even said that Jesus went through the land of Israel doing good, healing all who were overpowered by the devil, because God had anointed Him *with the Spirit and with power* (Acts 10:38f.). Moreover, Jesus' suffering and death are described in the Book of Hebrews as occurring through the Holy Spirit. (9:14)

However, especially in the Gospel of St. John, Jesus is

portrayed as the One who sends forth the Spirit to be a
parakleetos, a Counselor and Comforter who shall abide with His
church and equip it with the power needed to perform its task in
evangelizing the world. Moreover, the Scriptures also make it
clear that the Holy Spirit's work is not to exalt Himself above the
Father and the Son but to lead men to confess the Lordship of
Jesus Christ and to recognize His Father as their own. In
presenting this important doctrine, one must be extremely
careful, therefore, not to teach a subordinationism of either the
Son or the Spirit. Although the relationship between these two
Persons is presented in Scripture from both points of view, the
Bible clearly teaches that the three Persons in the Trinity are
coequal. A proper understanding of Spirit theology is dependent
on a correct view both of the Trinity and of the personal union of
the two natures in Christ.

4. *Conversion and Spirit Baptism.* In the contemporary theological
discussion there is considerable debate on the relation of
conversion to baptism in the Spirit. The question is asked: "Does
baptism in the Holy Spirit occur at the time of conversion, or is it
an experience distinct from and subsequent to one's coming to
faith?" Basing their conclusions on Acts 2:38-41, many exegetes
today favor the view that baptism in the Holy Spirit is bestowed
on *all* Christians when they receive Christian baptism and come to
faith in Christ. The view of the Lutheran Confessions that the
fullness of the Holy Spirit is bestowed on believers when they are
converted is in harmony with this interpretation. This view
recognizes, of course, that the Holy Spirit continues to give His
gifts and blessings to believers after their conversion. But it also is
opposed to the notion that "ordinary" believers somehow lack the
Holy Spirit.

Lutheran theologians are concerned, therefore, when baptism
in the Spirit is viewed as a second work of the Spirit in addition to
and beyond conversion and sanctification, and when the
Christian is required to fulfill certain preconditions before
receiving Spirit baptism, such as earnest wrestling with God,
heart purification, complete obedience, yielding, surrendering
oneself to God, and exercising "total faith," which is different
from ordinary trust in Christ. The frequent charismatic emphasis
that only those who are properly disposed to receive the baptism
of the Spirit through an attitude of expectancy, openness, and
searching will actually receive it, as well as attempts to train
people to receive such gifts of the Spirit as speaking in tongues,

may actually cultivate the notion that man's effort in some way is essential for the reception of God's free gifts. In his Epistle to the Galatians, St. Paul emphatically states that the Christians in Galatia had received the Spirit not by the works of the Law but by hearing with faith. (Gal 3:5)

5. *Means of Grace*. Lutherans are deeply concerned when the experience of baptism in the Holy Spirit is treated as the means by which God equips the church for her mission in the world, particularly when the baptism in the Spirit is regarded (in practice, if not in theory) as a supplement to the means of grace. Both the Scriptures and the Lutheran Confessions teach that the Word and the sacraments are the only means of grace and that the Holy Spirit always accompanies their use and through them bestows on the church *all* the blessings that are ours in Christ as well as every spiritual gift that is needed to carry out the mission of the church in a sinful world (cf. Matt 28:19; Rom 10:17; 1 Cor 11:26; Luke 16:29). Beyond the Word and sacraments nothing is needed to equip the church for its task, for through them the Spirit gives life, power, and growth to the church. Christians will therefore continue to seek power and renewal for the church in the Word and sacraments, not in special signs and miracles. [18]

Luther and the Lutheran Confessions describe as "enthusiasm" (*Schwärmerei*) the view that God reveals Himself and bestows His spiritual gifts apart from the objective and external Word and sacraments. Luther warns in the Smalcald Articles:

"In short, enthusiasm clings to Adam and his descendants from the beginning to the end of the world. It is a poison implanted and inoculated in man by the old dragon, and it is the source, strength, and power of all heresy, including that of the papacy and Mohammedanism. Accordingly, we should and must constantly maintain that God will not deal with us except through his external Word and sacrament. Whatever is attributed to the Spirit apart from such Word and sacrament is of the devil." [19]

In this connection it needs to be underscored that the Holy Spirit is given through the preaching of the work of Christ, that is, the Gospel — not through preaching about the Holy Spirit and His gifts (important as that is). The emphasis of our Lutheran heritage on the external Word as the instrument of the Holy Spirit helps prevent a subjectivism that seeks divine comfort and strength through an interior experience rather than in the objective word of the Gospel. To accent the former rather than the latter as the basis of Christian certainty can easily lead either to

The Charismatic Movement and Lutheran Theology

pride or despair instead of humble trust in the Gospel promises.

Moreover, when baptism with the Holy Spirit is considered to be a second experience beyond the sacrament of Holy Baptism and when it is said to grant powers and blessings that are not given through the Word and sacraments, the result is a view that fails to take into account the full benefits of Holy Baptism. Our Lutheran Confessions state that Baptism grants to the believer "the grace, Spirit, and power to suppress the old man so that the new may come forth and grow strong." [20]

6. *Unity of the Church.* When Scripture discusses the unity of the Christian church, it always involves the activity of the Holy Spirit. It is the Spirit who produces the fellowship of believers in the body of Christ. It is the Spirit who endows the members of the church with gifts by which they can serve one another in the kingdom of God. Christian unity must be unity in the Spirit. It is therefore unfortunate that the neo-Pentecostal distinction between Spirit-baptized Christians and other Christians easily fosters the incorrect and divisive notion that the former constitute a spiritually elite class of Christians. The faith that unites *all* believers to Christ and to one another also makes *all* members of His body equally acceptable to God (cf. Eph 4:3-6). In the body of Christ, the Spirit "apportions to each one individually as He wills" (1 Cor 12:11). Spiritual gifts are to be used in humble service and not as an occasion for anyone "to think of himself more highly than he ought to think." (Rom 12:3ff.)

7. *Unionism.* It is not in keeping with the Lutheran Confessions to maintain that when Christians are agreed on the theology of the Holy Spirit or share the experience of baptism in the Holy Spirit, there exists a sufficient basis for the exercise of Christian fellowship. Although Lutherans may feel a close affinity with other Christians who agree regarding the experience of baptism in the Spirit, they are reminded that The Lutheran Church — Missouri Synod seeks agreement in the doctrine of the Gospel, in *all* its articles, and in the right use of the holy sacraments as the Scriptural basis for the practice of fellowship.[21] *All* Biblical doctrine is taught by the Holy Spirit. Unionistic worship with those who deny doctrines of Holy Scripture dishonors the Holy Spirit and fails to give a proper Christian witness to the erring brother.

8. *Biblical Authority and Interpretation.* Charismatic Christians generally manifest a high regard for the authority of Holy Scripture and frequently display an impressive knowledge of its

contents. This can only be commended. However, caution needs to be observed by charismatic groups lest they in practice come to depend more on charismatic speech than on the Biblical word.[22] Moreover, many charismatic Christians give the impression that they read the Scriptures more from the perspective of Spirit baptism than from the Christ-centered, soteriological perspective that is central in Lutheran theology. While all Christians need to become more keenly aware of the rich Biblical testimony to the person and activity of the Holy Spirit, it should not be forgotten that the primary purpose of the Spirit's work, including the inspiration of Holy Scripture, is to make men wise unto salvation through faith in Jesus Christ.

9. *Miraculous Healing.* The charismatic movement has brought about an increased interest in miraculous healing. Today many testimonies are being given by Christian people to the effect that God has healed their ills and cured their sicknesses without the use of medical help, solely in answer to their prayers and by the laying on of hands.

As these instances multiply and these testimonies increase, the question is being raised: What shall the church say to the claim that healing miracles are being performed among God's people also today by the power of the Holy Spirit?

Christians will remember, of course, that the Scriptures record numerous examples of miraculous healings in both the Old and the New Testaments. It is clear from the gospels that healing the sick was an important and integral part of the ministry of Jesus; and when the Savior sent forth His twelve apostles into the cities of Galilee, He gave them specific instructions that they were "to preach the kingdom of God and to heal" (Luke 9:2). Soon thereafter, when He appointed seventy others and sent them ahead of Him, He told them also to "heal the sick . . . and say to them, 'The kingdom of God has come near to you'" (Luke 10:8-9). According to the Book of Acts the miracles of healing in the early church continued at least for a time even after the Savior's ascension into heaven.

It will also be granted that God can choose to perform mighty works in and through His church even today. Miracles of healing are not inherently impossible or absurd. The church must not deny the supernatural nor reject the possibility that God can intervene in the course of natural things as He did in apostolic times.

There are, however, a number of additional facts that must be taken into consideration as we explore the Scriptures in this regard.

a. As we noted earlier, the disciples performed miracles of healing in response to a specific command of Jesus that they should both preach and heal. When the Savior gave His final instructions prior to His ascension to the right hand of God, He said: "Go therefore and make disciples of all nations, baptizing them in the name of the Father and of the Son and of the Holy Spirit, teaching them to observe all that I have commanded you; and lo, I am with you always, to the close of the age." (Matt 28:19-20)

Neither this Great Commission nor our Lord's other instructions mention miraculous healing as part of the function of the church down through the ages until the return of Christ. To be sure, God may still give His gifts of healing to the church today. Moreover, the church will continue to engage in healing ministries as part of its effort to show love and compassion to all men. But the church's primary responsibility is to seek the salvation of the sinner through the Gospel of Jesus Christ. Even the healing miracles performed by the apostles after Pentecost were not the result of an explicit directive of Jesus. Their purpose was not only to gain a hearing for the Gospel at a time when the church was being established but to demonstrate that the new age had dawned in Jesus Christ. In the Book of Acts the pattern is that miraculous healings decreased in number as time passed, while the proclamation of the Gospel came more and more into the foreground of apostolic activity.

b. It needs to be remembered that God wants Christians to concern themselves with the physical needs of their fellowmen. The Bible gives many directives in that regard, and the church seeks to carry out the will of its Lord by praying fervently for healing in times of sickness and by using the earthly means that God in His goodness has provided for the healing of the physically and mentally distressed. It gratefully acknowledges as a blessing from God the healing ministry performed by doctors, nurses, and others who are skilled in the care and treatment of disease. The Christian will also seek personally to alleviate the sufferings and quiet the pains of his fellowmen to the extent that this is possible.

c. The child of God is grateful to his Lord when he is spared physical distress and affliction, but he also recognizes that illness and misfortune in general do not represent man's greatest evil, nor is physical health and prosperity man's greatest good. Many a believer has learned that there can be a victorious faith in Christ when there is no bodily healing and a glorious witness to the grace of God in the midst of suffering. Therefore, while the Christian prays for healing and earnestly hopes for recovery, he nevertheless submits patiently to the will of God since he knows that all things work together for good to them that love God.

d. The child of God is also aware that he is not yet in the realm of glory where sin and pain will disappear. Instead, he recognizes that according to the good and gracious will of God he is in a world where sin, sickness, and death are still very evident. He knows that the kingdom of God has been inaugurated, and in this he rejoices, but the final victory has not yet been consummated. Christ has atoned for sin, but its earthly consequences still remain. For the Christian these are chastenings, and he takes seriously the Biblical exhortation: "My son, do not regard lightly the discipline of the Lord, nor lose courage when you are punished by Him. For the Lord disciplines him whom He loves and chastises every son whom He receives" (Heb 12:5-6). We do not assume that it is the will of God that even in this life we must be free of all anguish and physical distress, for pain and suffering can also be a blessing from God. (Cf. Rom 8:28.)

e. The Christian does not expect to manipulate or control God, even with his prayers. He would hesitate to have in his own hands the power of life and death. With the psalmist he confesses: "Thou art my God. My times are in Thy hand" (Ps 31:14-15). In both joy and sorrow, the Christian knows that God does not abdicate. While He graciously invites us to seek His face in confident prayer, He and His will remain sovereign. The child of God prays confidently and persistently but with the provision "Lord, if it is Thy will."

B. The Primary Issues

As the church seeks to resolve the tensions that have arisen within its midst because of the charismatic movement, it is essential that the primary issues be clearly defined and understood. It should be noted that the basic question is not whether the Holy Spirit bestows marvelous gifts on His church also in the present day. Nor is there disagreement regarding the fact that the church should earnestly and fervently petition Almighty God to give us a full measure of His Spirit. What, then, are the issues? It cannot be denied that such questions as the following are very important, particularly for those involved in the charismatic movement, and that they merit our careful study:

a. Does Holy Scripture teach that baptism in the Holy Spirit is a second encounter with the Spirit, separate and distinct from conversion and baptism in the name of Jesus?

b. Is baptism in the Holy Spirit an experience that the Christian can have only if he meets certain preconditions, such as a conscientious desire for Spirit baptism, total surrender to Christ as Lord, a special degree of obedience, or fervent prayer for this gift?

c. Does Holy Scripture clearly and unmistakably designate speaking in tongues as the usual manifestation of baptism in the Spirit?

d. Does the Bible contain the specific promise that the same extraordinary charismatic gifts that were given to the apostolic church will be granted to God's people today?

Important as such questions are for the consideration of the charismatic movement, we believe that the primary issues from the perspective of Lutheran theology are the following:

1. *The Centrality of the Gospel.* Lutherans have always agreed that the central and most important teaching of Scripture is the Gospel, which brings the good news that the sinner is justified by grace, for Christ's sake, through faith. This is the doctrine by which the Christian church stands or falls. It is the article of faith in which all the sacred truths of Scripture converge. Neo-Pentecostal theology, with its special emphasis on baptism in the Holy Spirit as a second major experience in the Christian's life, sometimes tends to be more Spirit-centered than Christ-centered (in practice, if not in theory). This in turn lends itself to an understanding of the person and work of Christ that obscures His glory and benefits.

2. *The Power and Sufficiency of the Means of Grace.* Lutherans have always believed that through the Word and sacraments the Holy Spirit bestows on the believer *all* the blessings and spiritual gifts that are ours in Christ. The view that God gives His Holy Spirit apart from the "external word" is rejected by the Confessions as "enthusiasm." Neo-Pentecostal theology, with its emphasis on the baptism of the Holy Spirit as a new source of power and assurance for the Christian and with its claim that God communicates directly with believers through prophecy, visions, tongues, or other means, easily leads to a practical (if not theoretical) diminution of the significance of the means of grace.

3. *The Unity of the Church.* Lutherans confess that all who believe in Jesus Christ as Lord and Savior are one in Christ and one with each other. We therefore reject improper distinctions between members of the one holy Christian church (cf. Gal 3:28). Moreover, Christians are "eager to maintain the unity of the Spirit in the bond of peace" (Eph 4:3). Although the charismatic movement is sometimes described by its proponents as fostering the unity of the church through the baptism of the Spirit, the fact remains that neo-Pentecostal theology, with its distinction between Spirit-baptized Christians and other Christians, tends to create disharmony and disunity within the Christian church.

4. *The Nature of Spiritual Gifts.* Lutheran theology has stressed the importance of such fruits of the Spirit as love, joy, peace, patience, and kindness rather than extraordinary charismatic gifts. Moreover, it has emphasized that all fruits and gifts of the Spirit are given by grace alone. It has not understood the Scriptures to say that Christians are to expect extraordinary charismatic gifts in all ages of history, nor has it taught that speaking in tongues is the usual manifestation of the Holy Spirit. Neo-Pentecostal theology, with its claim that extraordinary charismatic gifts are the normal expectation of the church in every age, places greater importance on such gifts than the Scriptures do. Moreover, certain neo-Pentecostal accents sometimes give the erroneous impression that God's gifts are at least partially dependent on human efforts.

C. Recommendations

1. *Study the Scriptures.* In facing the issues raised by the charismatic movement within the Lutheran Church, we should earnestly seek the edification and spiritual welfare of the whole body of Christ. To that end, pastors and laymen should diligently and prayerfully study God's Word and its exposition in the Lutheran Confessions. Only by means of the Word and the Spirit will we be able to discern between what is true and what is false, what is God's will and what is man's. Subjective experience and human emotions are never safe guides in spiritual matters. Where God's Word speaks, Christians will submit in all humility and in the fear of God.

Our studies must deal not only with those passages in Mark, Acts, and First Corinthians that speak of the extraordinary gifts of the Spirit, but with those activities of the Holy Spirit that are described in other books of the New Testament such as the

Gospel of John and the epistles of Paul to the Romans, Galatians, Ephesians, and Colossians.

In our study, we must seek to gain a new appreciation of the nature of conversion and the effects this divine act produces in the hearts and lives of men. It must concentrate anew on the Gospel as a source of strength, peace, and joy in the life of the Christian. It must see again the rich benefits and blessings that God bestows through the Word and the sacraments of Baptism and the Lord's Supper.

Prayerful study needs to be given to those passages of Scripture that describe the church militant in its struggle against all the forces of evil in this world. It must be recognized anew that the kingdom of God has been inaugurated but not yet consummated. In this world of sin the church will continue to exist in a state of lowliness and at times even of persecution. God does not promise us miracles by which to escape the evils of the day, but He does assure us of His gracious presence to the end of time (Matt 28:19-20) and promises that the church will be preserved and will grow through Word and sacraments. It will live in the hope of an imperishable and unfading inheritance in heaven (1 Peter 1:3-9; Eph 1:1-14; Rom 8:14-39; 2 Tim 4:18). In this hope the Christian will find joy and peace as he endeavors to serve his Lord with the abilities and talents the Spirit gives. (1 Peter 1:6)

2. *Admonish and Encourage the Brethren.* As members of Christ's body who are sincerely interested in the spiritual well-being of our brethren, we should admonish and encourage one another with love and patience. When offense is given because of conduct or doctrine that is contrary to God's Word, care should be taken that proper brotherly procedures are followed and that the reasons for admonition or discipline are fully understood. Christian admonition and discipline are always evangelical and have as their goal the restoration of the brother.

3. *Test the Spirits.* Christians who are convinced that they have received a charismatic experience should earnestly seek to evaluate it and determine its validity not only on the basis of personal feelings and emotions but especially in the light of God's holy Word. Followers of the Lord Jesus must take seriously the warnings of Scripture to "test the spirits to see whether they are of God" (1 John 4:1), lest we be led astray into a path that is injurious to our Christian faith and hope. Scripture particularly urges Christians to test occurrences that give the appearance of being valid signs and wonders, with the reminder that in the last

days false prophets will arise who will seek to lead God's elect astray by such means. (Matt 24:24; Mark 13:19-23; 1 Cor 14:29)

Scripture suggests various ways in which Christians may test the spirits that have gone out into the world. (a) What do they say with regard to Christ? Do they steadfastly and clearly bear witness to His divine person and His work of salvation? Do they give greater attention to the cross and resurrection of our Lord than to various phenomenal experiences? (b) What fruits do they produce within the Christian congregation? Do they fulfill the simple service of Christian love among the people of God? Do they help edify the church, the body of Christ? (c) Do they accept what the Spirit of God teaches through His prophets and apostles in Holy Scripture? Do they accept what the apostle Paul has written "as a command of the Lord"? (cf. 1 Cor 14:37. Note that the apostle states in the next verse: "If anyone does not recognize this, he is not recognized.")

4. *Edify the Church.* The Christian will also exercise all spiritual gifts that God has given him in a spirit of love and humility, fully aware that spiritual pride or undisciplined enthusiasm may cause serious offense to the body of Christ. Recognizing that spiritual gifts may be abused, the child of God will employ the gifts that God has given him with tact and Christian love, always endeavoring to edify the body of Christ and to exalt the Lord.

5. *Know the Spirit.* The rapid and widespread growth of the charismatic movement in our day may indicate the church's need to devote much greater attention to the work of the Holy Spirit. Christians today will particularly benefit from a more detailed articulation of Christ's promises regarding the Holy Spirit as these are set forth in Holy Scripture. As the church in our age prays with new earnestness, "Come, Holy Ghost, God and Lord, Be all Thy graces now outpoured," it will also make every effort, particularly in its preaching and its various programs of instruction, to increase the church's awareness, understanding, and appreciation of the Holy Spirit and His gifts.

6. *Use the Word and Sacraments.* The Lutheran Church — Missouri Synod should be alert to the fact that the charismatic movement within our own as well as other church bodies did not arise out of a vacuum. In the opinion of many Christians, it has arisen to meet a pressing need within Christendom to use every resource available in the service of Christ and His church and to claim the power that God promises us through the Holy Spirit in Word and sacraments. As we face the questions raised by the

charismatic movement, we must earnestly endeavor to intensify and increase our use of Word and sacraments at every level of our existence so that the church may have a renewed sense of the joy, peace, and power God has promised.

1. In the preparation of this document, the commission consulted a number of books and articles. The following were found to be particularly helpful:
Bruner, Frederick Dale. *A Theology of the Holy Spirit.* Grand Rapids, Mich.: William B. Eerdmans Publishing Co., 1970.
Christenson, Larry. *Speaking in Tongues and Its Significance for the Church.* Minneapolis: Dimension Books, 1968.
Christian Faith and the Ministry of Healing. A statement prepared for the Church Council and approved for circulation to congregations of the American Lutheran Church (July 1965), pp. 12–15.
Hoekema, Anthony A. *What About Tongue-Speaking?* Grand Rapids: William B. Eerdmans Publishing Company, 1966.
Lensch, Rodney. *A Missouri Synod Lutheran Pastor Is Baptized in the Holy Spirit.* Selma, Calif.: Wilkins Printing and Publishing, 1969.
McDonnell, Kilian. "Catholic Problems in Evaluating Pentecostalism." *Dialog,* 9 (Winter 1970), 35–54.
Reports and Actions of the 2nd General Convention of the ALC, Columbus, Ohio, 1964, pp. 148–164.
Schweizer, Eduard, and others. "Spirit of God." *Bible Key Words,* Vol. III. Translated from Gerhard Kittel's *Theologisches Worterbuch Zum Neuen Testament.* New York and Evanston: Harper & Row, 1960.
Sherrill, John L. *They Speak with Other Tongues.* Westwood, N.J.: Revell, 1965.
Stagg, Frank, E. Glenn Hinson, and Wayne E. Oates. *Glossolalia.* Nashville and New York: Abingdon Press, 1967.
Williams, J. Rodman. *The Era of the Spirit.* Plainfield, N.J.: Logos International, 1971.
The Work of the Holy Spirit. Report of the Special Committee on the Work of the Holy Spirit to the 182nd General Assembly of the United Presbyterian Church in the United States of America, 1970.
Wunderlich, Lorenz. *The Half-Known God.* St. Louis: Concordia Publishing House, 1963.
2. *The New Pentecostal Charismatic Revival Seminar Report,* Full Gospel Business Men's Fellowship International, 1963, pp. 16–18.
3. Frederick Dale Bruner, *A Theology of the Holy Spirit* (Grand Rapids: William B. Eerdmans Publishing Co., 1970), p. 54.
4. Rodney Lensch, *A Missouri Synod Lutheran Pastor Is Baptized in the Holy Spirit* (Selma, Calif.: Wilkins Printing and Publishing, 1969), p. 14.
5. "Five Factors Crucial to the Growth and Spread of a Modern Religious Movement," in *Journal for the Scientific Study of Religion,* VII (Spring 1968), 30.
6. Ibid. See also *The Work of the Holy Spirit.* Report of the Special Committee on the Work of the Holy Spirit to the 182nd General Assembly of the United Presbyterian Church in the United States of America, 1970, p. 49.
7. "Final Progress Report, Glossolalia and Mental Health," a mimeographed report shared with the commission by its authors, Dr. John Kildahl and Dr. Paul Qualben. Page references in parentheses are to this report. The authors report that

their findings will be published in a forthcoming book entitled *Glossolalia: The Practice of Speaking in Tongues*.

8. The information in this paragraph was provided by a group of Lutheran Church — Missouri Synod pastors involved in the charismatic movement. They met with a committee of the CTCR in St. Louis on July 19, 1971, and provided additional information in writing.

9. The following statements were prepared on the basis of such Lutheran sources as booklets, position papers, essays, tape recordings, and personal interviews. It needs to be understood that the formulations are our own and that not all Lutheran charismatics necessarily hold all these positions. Among the Lutheran sources used in preparing this section are the following:

Christenson, Larry, *Speaking in Tongues and Its Significance for the Church* (Minneapolis: Bethany Fellowship, Inc., 1970), especially pp. 81, 87, 115, 134.

——, "Come, Holy Spirit," *Loaves and Fishes* (June 1970).

Dorpat, D. M., "Prophecy, Preaching, and Enthusiasm: A Study of the Gifts of the Spirit in the Light of the Lutheran Confessions."

——, "Luthercostals. A Look at Some Issues in the Charismatic Renewal from a Lutheran Perspective."

Heil, Robert, *A Position and Guidelines for Immanuel Lutheran Church, Crystal City, Missouri, Concerning the Baptism of the Holy Spirit and Its Attendant Gifts*, pp. 1–2.

Kellogg, John P., "The Baptism with the Holy Spirit," a conference paper presented to the Midland Circuit of the Michigan District, April 1968, pp. 4–5.

Lensch, Rodney, *A Missouri Synod Lutheran Pastor Is Baptized in the Holy Spirit* (Selma, Calif.: Wilkins Printing and Publishing, 1969), pp. 26–28.

Tape-recorded essays from the Lutheran Charismatic Conference, May 18–21, 1971, Concordia Seminary, St. Louis, Missouri.

10. D. M. Dorpat, "Prophecy, Preaching, and Enthusiasm," a mimeographed essay distributed by the author, pp. 1, 10.

11. *Lectures on Galatians, 1535*, Chapters 1–4, Volume 26 of *Luther's Works*, translated and edited by Jaroslav Pelikan (St. Louis: Concordia Publishing House, 1963), pp. 204–206.

12. When the prophet Isaiah rebuked the drunkards of Ephraim, they mocked his repeated admonitions. Thereupon, Isaiah warned them that God would speak to them in a *foreign tongue* (the Assyrians — cf. Deut 28:49). When Israel would not listen when God spoke to them in their *own* language, God spoke to them "with stammering lips and in a foreign language" (Is 28:11). It is striking that, immediately after referring to the above words of Isaiah, St. Paul says, "Tongues are a sign, not for believers, but for unbelievers" (1 Cor 14:22). Coupled with the observation that tongues may give outsiders the impression of madness, Paul's use of Isaiah 28 appears to be a suggestion that the Corinthian church should be sufficiently mature (v. 20) to recognize that speaking in tongues (especially when overemphasized and accompanied by lovelessness and disorder) may be a sign of God's displeasure with Christians who have lost confidence in the power of the Word when proclaimed in ordinary human language and who feel that charismatic demonstrations are more effective media of the Spirit's presence and power.

13. Theodore Engelder, *Popular Symbolics* (St. Louis: Concordia Publishing House, 1934), pp. 69–70, note 3.

14. This opinion is based on the evidence in some of the most reliable manuscripts, as well as early Latin and Syriac versions, which do not include these verses. It is also supported by the Armenian, Ethiopian, and Georgian

versions, as well as by such early church fathers as Origen, Eusebius, and Jerome.

15. The concept and experience of a "spirit" is not uniquely Christian, nor is it necessarily a mark of the knowledge of the true God. In the Old Testament, it is sometimes associated with idolatry, wizardry, false prophecy, and the like (cf. Deut 18:9-22; 1 Sam 28:8; 1 Kings 22:21-24; Is 8:19-20; 28:7; Jer 23:23ff.). The false spirits against which St. Paul and Saint John contended were spirits that assumed the name of Christ but in reality made Him incidental by substituting various experiences for the event of the cross and resurrection as the way to the knowledge and wisdom of God. See 1 Cor 1–3 (especially 1:4-7, 2:2, and 3:11); 2 Cor 11:4, 13; 1 Cor 12:3; 1 John 4:1-3; and 5:6-12.

16. Luther's emphasis on the role of the means of grace as the instrument of the Spirit is well known. See, for example, his comments on Gal 3:5 (cited above in II, A, 5).

17. The commission is aware that many Lutheran charismatics share some of the concerns we express in the following paragraphs. We are discussing these matters not to imply that all Lutheran charismatics accept the points we criticize but because the widespread use of non-Lutheran literature by Lutheran charismatics, as well as unfortunate emphases by some Lutheran charismatics, strongly suggest that a word of caution is in order.

18. Dr. Francis Pieper states that God "builds up, maintains, and governs His church *exclusively* through His Word and the Sacraments, by which He creates and preserves faith in the Gospel through the Holy Ghost, and for the administration of which He gives His gifts to the church." In *Christian Dogmatics*, Vol. II (St. Louis: Concordia Publishing House, 1951), p. 388. Emphasis added.

19. Smalcald Articles, III, viii, 9–10, in *The Book of Concord*, ed. T. G. Tappert (Philadelphia: Fortress Press, 1959), p. 313.

20. Large Catechism, IV, 76, in *The Book of Concord*, pp. 445–446.

21. Cf. Formula of Concord, Epitome, X, 7, in *The Book of Concord*, p. 493.

22. It is not uncommon for charismatics to claim that God speaks directly and authoritatively through charismatic speech. J. Rodman Williams (in *The Era of the Spirit* [Plainfield, N.J.: Logos International, 1971]), for example, states that such speech goes "beyond the words of Scripture" and is not "simply some exposition of Scripture," for "the Spirit as the living God moves through and beyond the records of past witness, however valuable such records are as model for what happens today" (p. 16). He notes that those gifted by the Spirit not only "unfold mysteries about the ways of God" but may also provide "a word of guidance in economic, social or political affairs" (p. 22). He describes "prophecy" as "the very Word of God" with the same "Thus says the Lord" character as the words of Isaiah or Jeremiah (pages 28–29). He acknowledges that there must be a "weighing of things said" and states that such judgment is to be carried out by the "Spiritual community" (p. 22; cf. also note 8, pp. 29–30). Such statements are difficult to reconcile with the Lutheran position that the Holy Scriptures are the only rule and norm for Christian faith and life.

In this connection, it should be noted that the Scriptures provide no basis for the notion that the ongoing Christian community, because it has the Holy Spirit, is an "inspired" source of divine truth in addition to the prophetic and apostolic Scriptures. Such a view in fact reduces the authority of the Scriptures by exalting the authority of the church.

DECLARATION ON THE PENTECOSTAL MOVEMENT

The statement of the Puerto Rican bishops must be seen in the context of four factors. First, the bishops saw the charismatic renewal as an import from the United States. Second, the strong classical Pentecostal movement in Puerto Rico dictated a certain restraint. Third, the bishops saw the presence of a religious orientation which might suggest that if one had Jesus and the Bible one did not really need the church. Fourth, there was strong initial opposition to the charismatic renewal on the part of leaders of the Cursillo movement. The Cursillo is essentially a retreat technique though it shares with the charismatic renewal a number of characteristics: emphasis on personal commitment, witnessing, scriptural reading, a large role for lay leadership, and an overall experience orientation.

These factors account, to some extent, for the defensive attitude, concentrating for the most part on the abuses and the necessity of remaining fully Catholic. The bishops pointed to "pretended cures even resurrections," the unacceptable position that baptism in the Spirit confirms one in grace, and the religious indifferentism which asserts that "all religions are equally true even when religious denominations concerned have doctrines that are openly contradictory." Of special concern were the external manifestations of enthusiasm: "We must also condemn anything in the prayer meetings that has a flavor of hysteria, little seriousness, or even ridicule concerning the Catholic faith." On the other hand the bishops evaluated positively the knowledge of the presence of God, "somewhat experiential," which Catholic charismatics claim as the common inheritance of each Christian. While calling attention to the 1969 report of the Catholic bishops in the United States, the Puerto Rican bishops, because of the changed circumstances on that island, did not think that the American report "should be accepted in its totality." The bishops judged that their considerations did not lead them "as of now to reprove the movement," though they wanted to recall the notes of caution which Pope Paul VI had expressed in his general audience of June 23, 1971, when he commended prudence in the matters of personal religious experience.

The statement was published in El Imparcial *(June 15, 1972).*

INTEREST OF THE HIERARCHY

It must be remembered that this movement in Puerto Rico only began recently and was imported from the United States where it began in February, 1967. For this reason, it seems prudent to see how it develops in the United States as well as here.

This whole situation has been the object of study by the Conference of Bishops since their meeting on February 24 of this year. It was considered again at their following meeting on March 22, at which — upon their own initiative — the bishops heard a report given by Fr. Landelin Robling, O.S.B., a pastor from Humacao.

At a subsequent meeting on April 27, the bishops heard reports from the Auxiliary Bishop of Grand Rapids, in the United States, Msgr. Joseph C. McKinney, who is the episcopal moderator of the movement in the United States, and by Sister Susanne Hofweber, O.P, of the Interdiocesan Secretariat of Catholic Education in Puerto Rico.

And at the last meeting, on May 25, Father Jaime Capó, spiritual director of the Cursillos in Christianity in the Archdiocese of San Juan, was invited to attend. However, Father Capó was unable to be present at that meeting, due to previous commitments outside Puerto Rico. But the invitation to Father Capó remains open for a future meeting.

It is quite evident that the hierarchy has been concerned with the situation for over three months. And from the beginning, it has seriously considered the report from the Commission on Doctrine of the Conference of Catholic Bishops of the United States, presented on December 14, 1969, to the Conference by the president of that Commission, Msgr. Alexander Zaleski, bishop of Lansing.

THE NEED FOR MORE INFORMATION

Nevertheless, the investigation has not yet been concluded because the Conference of Catholic Bishops of Puerto Rico is seeking an opportunity to hear and weigh further testimony that is of interest.

As can be seen, such a position on the part of the Bishops cannot be criticised except by those who are lacking in the necessary elements of rightful judgment, because the proceedings of the conference have been characterized by diligence, seriousness, and a sense of responsibility.

It is a fact that the Pentecostal Movement in the Catholic Church, or — as others prefer to call it — the Movement for Charismatic Renewal, has been publicly denounced for alleged abuses. In this respect it must be assumed that all alleged or confirmed abuses should be reproved.

But at the same time, people should avoid the implication that, by condemning verified abuses, the entire Catholic Pentecostal Movement as such is being condemned.

We have pointed out that this Movement has been imported to Puerto Rico from the United States. The United States Bishops' Commission on Doctrine, presided by Msgr. Zaleski, indicates in the report referred to above that "the participants in the Catholic Pentecostal Movement hold that they receive certain charismatic gifts; and in all this there has been, without any doubt, abuses. But the remedy lies not in denying the existence of such gifts, but in the correct use of them."

The report adds, "Perhaps our most prudent way to judge the validity of the claims of the Pentecostal Movement is to observe the effects on those who participate in prayer meetings. And all seems to indicate that such participation leads to a better understanding of the role the Christian plays in the Church."

The report concludes that at this present moment the Movement "should not be inhibited, but allowed to develop. Yet certain precautions must be expressed."

We feel that this position on the part of the Bishops of the United States regarding the Catholic Pentecostal Movement is serious and prudent. This is not to say that the report quoted above should be accepted in its totality by the bishops of Puerto Rico. There is evidence that circumstances vary from there to here and vice-versa. However, we do not want to imply a pejorative judgment about anything or about anybody.

REPROVING VERIFIED ABUSES

We repeat that in Puerto Rico certain abuses have been publicly denounced, such as pretended cures and even resurrections.

Some people have attributed certain remarks to charismatics, including some priests, that are based on a poor knowledge of ecumenism and that assert that all religions are equally true even when religious denominations concerned have doctrines that are openly contradictory.

Moreover, many of the faithful have been alienated by the gift of tongues because they do not understand it. Likewise, they often have the impression that sacramental water baptism has diminished in value and that it is merely an external and empty act. Some people believe that they are assured salvation through confirmation in grace by the so-called baptism of the Spirit.

All these allegations can be refuted with precise explanation. Nevertheless, certain abuses have been pointed out which, upon their being verified, must also be condemned by the hierarchy because they are not upheld even by Catholic Pentecostals of good faith and sound spiritual formation.

We must also condemn anything in the prayer meetings that has a flavor of hysteria, little seriousness, or even ridicule concerning the Catholic faith.

INSISTENCE UPON THE GENUINE CATHOLIC POSITION

And to this respect, it is well fitting to recall here the wise counsel of Pope Paul VI, given in his speech of Wednesday, May 17. His Holiness observed: "There exists a rule, there is imposed a common demand upon whoever desires to 'tune in to' the spiritual waves of the Holy Spirit, and this is the inner self . . . The Christian, including the consecrated person . . . should not ever forget this fundamental plan in life, if the latter is to remain Christian and be enlivened by the Holy Spirit: the inner self . . . Interior silence is necessary in order to hear the Word of God, to experience his presence, to hear the calling of God . . ."

According to this serious admonition by the Pope, if the prayer meetings are to gather together in favorable conditions for experiencing the presence of God and for hearing his voice, such prayer meetings should be characterized by inner silence and meditation and not by bustle and disorderly noise.

However, at the same time we cannot in any way appear to be opposed to genuine Catholic doctrine concerning the indwelling and work of the Holy Spirit in the soul gifted with sanctifying grace, nor concerning the marvelous effects that the Holy Spirit can realize within a soul docile to his inspirations, which in the opinion of not a few masters of spirituality is to lead us to a knowledge, somewhat experiential, of the presence of God in the soul, of the presence of God as a reality to be grasped, and in which we can rejoice beginning now; the experience of the action of the Holy Spirit which brings the peace, the joy, the freedom and the power of Christ which is conferred upon us by means of his Spirit; the experience which the Catholic Pentecostals do not consider as a privilege of a particular mystic state, but as a common inheritance that each Christian can claim with a simple response of his faith to the promises of God.

We insist then that our consideration of the phenomenon of Catholic Pentecostalism in Puerto Rico does not lead us as of now to reprove the movement, except in regards to those things which have been verified to be abuses and which we have clearly pointed out above.

PRUDENCE AND PRECAUTION

It is for that reason that at this moment our position seeks to go along with the thought of Pope Paul VI, expressed in his speech at the general audience of Wednesday, June 23, 1971.

The Pope said: "Ought we perhaps to associate ourselves with the charismatics of our age, those who seek to reach their operative inspiration from some personal inner religious experience? We say: prudence. Here opens up one of the most difficult and complex chapters of the spiritual life, that of the 'discernment of spirits.'

Error is very easy in this field; illusion is no less. Many masters have spoken to us concerning it; we can content ourselves with reading once again Chapter 54, of Book III, of the always wise *Imitation of Christ*, and in this manner, we may humbly learn to discern the language of grace which speaks within us."

GUIDELINES

*The character of the Lutheran charismatic movement was not the same in
1973 as it had been in 1963 and 1964 when the first documents came out
from the American Lutheran Church. As further clarification was
thought necessary, in 1973 Walter Wietzke and Jack Hustad presented
"Guidelines" to the Council of Presidents of the American Lutheran
Church, which received the document and requested that it be made
available as resource material to the district presidents, though it does not
have the character of a new official policy statement for the American
Lutheran Church. Broadly theological rather than giving detailed
pastoral counsel, it acknowledged that the church is a charismatic
community, that the faith relationship is not exhausted by doctrinal
statements, that the church needs "to review and reconsider the whole
ministry of healing." Because there is only one baptism, one cannot
consider "baptism in the Spirit" as a "second or superior kind of
baptism." Faith, as trust and the response of the whole man to God,
should not become superstition. "It is not the irrational part of man that
connects him with God." Lutheran charismatics should not move the
peripheral (tongues) to the center, and those not involved in the
charismatic renewal should not make glossolalia the chief target of their
reactions. The temptation to exalt in a one-sided way either "pure
doctrine" or "true experience" should be avoided as occasions of pride.
Incumbent on the charismatics is the necessity of honoring the canonical
and noncanonical documents: Scriptures, Lutheran Confessions, and the
constitution of the American Lutheran Church.*

The "Guidelines" were published in Towards a Mutual
Understanding of Neo-Pentecostalism, *Walter Wietzke and Jack
Hustad, eds. (Minneapolis: Augsburg Publishing House, 1973), pp. 3–6.*

To our brothers in the faith: These guidelines do not presume
encyclical authority. They are, rather, some modest principles
subject to criticism, correction, and rebuttal. They are also
statements which attempt to deal constructively with tensions
within our church not always acknowledged or openly dealt with.

We present them, respectfully, to the President's Cabinet and
to the Council of Presidents who asked that we work on
guidelines for pastors and congregations of The American
Lutheran Church in dealing with the neo-Pentecostal
phenomenon.

Our concern is pastoral. It is with hope, joy, and high
expectation we submit them for the upbuilding of the church and
the perusal of each believer who, through the Holy Spirit, has
been called to faith in Christ.

I. Some things neo-Pentecostals emphasize that are important for
the American Lutheran Church:

A. *Charismata*, i.e., the gifts of the Spirit. To call attention to the
gracious gifts of God is no disfavor to the church. It is consistent
with biblical testimony and acknowledges that the church,
classically, has always been a charismatic community. "And his
gifts were that some should be apostles, some prophets, some
evangelists, some pastors and teachers, to equip the saints for the
work of ministry, for building up the body of Christ" (Ephesians
4:11-12).

B. *Freedom in worship.* The easy, uninhibited style of worship
observed in neo-Pentecostalism offers a constructive opportunity
to review both the content and method of staid liturgical forms. In
the Reformation tradition the style of worship has never been
canonized and we would both plead for toleration as men
worship more freely and ask that the Commission on Worship
make an earnest effort to see what facets might gainfully be used
in the development of new worship forms.

C. *The reality of God and the reality of the faith relationship.* That
we understand Christianity, not as our possession of religious
truths, but as the Lord's possession of us and that we stand
before him in a direct faith relationship is of ultimate importance.
We have not always been aware of the subtle shift in our attention
from God's person to the church's doctrine.

D. *Insistence on prayer.* A hallmark of neo-Pentecostals is a
rigorous life of prayer. Most surely this points to a neglected
portion of the church's life and calls us to a renewed exercise of
that which characterized the life of our Lord and the apostolic
church, viz., prayer.

E. *An emphasis on the ministry of healing.* While we should be
very cautious about trying to manipulate God for our purposes,
we should accept, in good grace, the challenge of neo-Pentecostal
friends to review and reconsider the whole ministry of healing.

Guidelines

II. Some things the American Lutheran Church emphasizes that are important for its neo-Pentecostals:

A. *A Reminder of the Historical Context*

No one concerned with the Spirit can ignore the relationship of Spirit to Word and Spirit and Word to church. What happened in Montanism or what happened to Luther in his struggle with Münzer is not unimportant, but it is even more important that we explore the meaning of the 19th and 20th century contexts in which the neo-Pentecostal phenomenon arises.[1]

B. *Theological Insights*

1. *The unity of God.* Christians have always struggled with the definition of God. Their describing efforts have sought to keep a creative tension between divinity and humanity, immanence and transcendence, mutability and immutability, wrath and love, but language is never totally adequate.

Our doctrine of the Trinity, e.g., has inherent in it the possibility of understanding God tritheistically. Men continue to deduce that Father, Son, and Holy Spirit are disjointed entities — three Gods. For this reason, the Athanasian Creed insists that we worship one God in Trinity and Trinity in unity . . . (insists that) there are not three Almighties, but one Almighty . . . not three Gods, but one God . . . not three Lords, but one Lord. . . . One altogether, not by confusion of substance, but by unity of person.

Nonetheless, some deal with God in tripartite or bipartite fashion. There is truth in the contention that "we sometimes divide Christ from God," that "Lutherans are dominated by a Second Article mentality."

It must also be recognized that we can be dominated by a First Article mentality or by a Third Article mentality. If, for example, we think of the Holy Spirit as a third entity, separate from Father and Son, we again distort the unity of God, and must be called back to that which the church has repeatedly affirmed, one God in Trinity, and Trinity in unity.

2. *Baptism.* St. Paul's great statement (Ephesians 4:4ff.) also points us to unity in other areas. One of vital importance is baptism. He says, "There is one body and one Spirit . . . one Lord, one faith, *one baptism*, one God and Father of us all, who is above all and through all and in all." Baptism is the sacramental act of God whereby a person is incorporated into the community

of faith. To be "baptized in the Spirit" or "with the Holy Spirit" (Luke 3:16) means, in rudimentary terms, to be brought into the life (*zoa*) of God — but that is not a second or superior kind of baptism.

To understand water baptism as having only symbolical significance, and spirit baptism as having actual (i.e., real, experiential) significance, is to revert to Manichean categories.[2] It is to deny the unity in baptism and the unity in God who gives it.

3. *Church*. Another great concern, inspired by Christ and Paul, is the unity of the church. The word the apostle uses is *henotes*, meaning "oneness."

The church consists of those who know and believe "one hope . . . one Lord, one faith, one baptism, one God and Father of us all." At a time when men ponder the significance of denominations and live with the illusion that unity is an achievement of men, the New Testament reminds us that it is an act of God. Unity is something already created by God in Jesus Christ. We either witness to it or detract from it, but we cannot create it. It does not come by everyone being in the same ecclesiastical organization, by having the same conviction regarding every statement from the Bible (or the confessions of the church), or by having the same emotional experience and response.

Unity is realized when we know (*oidw*) the one Lord, faith, baptism, etc. But the unity of the church is a unity in it, not outside of it or against it. It would be the grossest of distortions to say, "There is Egypt and Israel. Israel is the 'spirit people,' Egypt is the church. We've got to get Israel out of Egypt." Such "spiritual" elitism is foreign to the New Testament.

4. *The acknowledgment of faith's intellectual, moral, and mystical content*. These components should neither be absolutized or eliminated. The challenge is to keep them in dynamic tension. Neo-Pentecostals should be dealt with no differently than those whose emphases incline toward the rational or moral. While the church must confess to the charge of "intellectual preoccupation," it must also insist that faith (i.e., trust, response of the whole man to God) not become superstition, and that it is not the irrational part of man that connects him with God.

C. Ecclesiastical Authority

Within our church, authority is not by episcopal right. Our synodical confraternity signifies that we freely enter into relationships with sister congregations and voluntarily give a portion of our freedom to the church at large. Our brother pastors, district presidents, and sister congregations are a support system. That doesn't mean giving approbation to everything; it does mean treatment as peers and allies, not inferiors and enemies.

III. Some things neo-Pentecostal Lutherans and traditional Lutherans should be conscious of in the pursuit of working relationships:

A. *Allowance for diversity.* There never was a time when the church was truly monolithic. Heterogeneity contributes to strength.

B. *The New Testament preeminence of love.* Passion for truth notwithstanding, the mark of the Master is love. "By this all men will know that you are my disciples, if you have love for one another" (John 13:35).

C. *Perspective on essentials.* The peripheral, e.g., speaking in tongues, should not be made essential by neo-Pentecostals as a sign of superior spirituality, nor should traditionalists make glossolalia the chief target of their reactions.

D. *Subtle temptations to pride.* Some may say, "We have the pure doctrine." Others may say, "We have the true experience." Both can become occasions of pride.

E. *The necessity of honoring canonical and noncanonical documents.* We are people rooted in the biblical tradition, people with an evangelical, confessional history. Therefore we must take seriously: (1) The holy Scriptures, (2) the Lutheran Confessions, (3) the constitution of the American Lutheran Church.

F. *Avoiding scandal to Christ* by unwarranted division and/or divorce within congregations and homes.

G. *Commonality of faith in the same Lord* under whom all spirits are tested.

H. *That growth comes through challenge.* We are in a circumstance where, together, we can existentially reflect anew on the relationship between Spirit, Word, and community.

1. Friedrich Schleiermacher, who stands at the fountainhead of this period, said:

"You reject the dogmas and propositions of religion. Very well. Reject them. They are not in any case the essence of religion itself. Religion does not need them. It is only a human reflection on the content of our religious feelings which requires anything of the kind. The religion to which I will lead you demands no blind faith, no negation of physics and psychology; it is wholly natural and yet again, as the immediate product of the universe, it is full of grace. . . . The nature of religion has been misapprehended. It is not science, it is not morality, its seat is not in reason, conscience or will. Since religion is the direct touch of the soul with the Divine, its home, its seat can be found nowhere but in feeling."

Addresses to the Cultured Despisers of Religion

In America, "religion as emotion" was popularized by Liebman, Peale, and Fosdick. Now, at a time in human history when outer absolutes have been eroded, men have sought certainty by "turning inward." Discerning pastors and congregations will explore all the ramifications of this.

2. Manicheism suggested two orders of reality: the material which is base and confining, and the spiritual which is above, apart from, and superior to that which belongs to earthly experience.

26 *Anglican Church, Australia, 1973*

BOTH SIDES TO THE QUESTION

A resolution was passed by the 1971 Session in Synod of the Anglican Church in Australia that a committee be appointed to study the charismatic renewal from a scholarly and pastoral point of view. In order to facilitate this mandate, the committee subdivided itself into study groups. In addition to consulting literary sources, the committee attended charismatic meetings and interviewed charismatic leaders. In the composition of the committee were found a wide range of viewpoints from enthusiastic support for the charismatic renewal to opposition. Though commissioned to study the renewal from a theological, linguistic, and psychological perspective, the report focused almost exclusively on the theological and exegetical aspects and paid only passing attention to the linguistic and psychological.

Instead of attempting to work out a consensus statement with varying differences of opinion clearly noted, the committee chose rather a confrontation approach which took the theological differences as the point of departure. Basically the differences are related to divergent ways religious experience is understood and divergent ways of approaching exegesis. Three issues were discussed with a pro and con presentation of each side. The three issues were: baptism in the Holy Spirit, the gifts of the Spirit, and healing. Very briefly some summary pastoral directions were given and the report closed with a bibliography.

What experience brings to exegesis divided the charismatics and non-charismatics. Charismatics readily admitted that after their experience of tongues and prophecy, their understanding of what Scripture was trying to say about them "changed considerably." Non-charismatics believe that what is not clearly taught in Scripture cannot be clarified by one's experience. The Scriptures illuminate one's experience, not vice-versa. Non-charismatics lay emphasis upon what God speaks from within the confines of a given historical setting. Charismatics pay less attention to this context and believe God speaks directly from his word.

Christian experience, according to the charismatics, is divided into two distinct elements: being born again and being baptized in the Holy Spirit. There is no chronological pause for the non-charismatics between entry into full relationship with Christ and entry into full relationship with the Holy Spirit. ". . . the total absence of reference to baptism in the Spirit in the epistles, as a work of grace subsequent to regeneration" significantly supports the position of the non-charismatics. While charismatics believe that the narrative, descriptive sections of the Bible – Acts, for instance – are normative for today, non-charismatics think they relate unique events which are strategic for the development of the early church and therefore they are not normative, not to be used for future guidance.

Not all charismatics see tongues as a necessary sign that one has received the baptism, but understand tongues as a sign. Granting that tongues has some value, the non-charismatics would warn against too readily accepting extravagant claims about the value of tongues. All agree that tongues cannot in itself be the basis or test for fellowship.

The most extensive considerations were reserved for the gift of healing, both charismatics and non-charismatics setting forth their views on the meaning of the healing ministry of Christ, of the disciples, and both treating of the traditional problem areas: Paul's thorn in the flesh, Trophimus, the will of God, and the value of redemptive suffering.

Charismatics recognized that there were a number of reasons why Christ healed. "It is plain He did not think of the Healing Ministry as unique to Himself. The same ministry is expressly committed to the twelve and the seventy." There is value in suffering "but we are not convinced that the New Testament description of suffering includes sickness."

The non-charismatics insisted that Christ's healings were instantaneous, unfailing, unlimited, but temporary (Lazarus eventually died). The use of healing in Acts functions as a bridge between the historic Christ and the church. They were signs of a transfer of authority from Christ to the apostles and an authentication of their message. If Jas 5:14-15 witnesses to the presence of healing gifts in apostolic times, "they should not rightly be regarded as ongoing." In fine, it is to misread the historical elements of the gospels and Acts if one understands them as a commission for spiritual healing today. As to the reported healings which take place, the miraculous cures "seem to occur in inverse ratio to the observer's medical knowledge." No Christian can deny that God can heal miraculously if he chooses. What the non-charismatic must explain is why there are cures. On the contrary, the charismatic must explain why there are so few.

The "Official Report of an Anglican Commission on the Neo-Pentecostal Movement" was received in October 1973 by the Synod of the Church of England, diocese of Sydney. Copyright by the Anglican Information Office, St. Andrew's House, Sydney Square, N.S.W. 2000, Australia.

CONTENTS

INTRODUCTION

At the 1971 Session of Synod a resolution was passed requesting the Standing Committee to appoint a Committee to consider the Charismatic Movement from a scholarly and pastoral standpoint with regard to: (i) the believer's personal life; (ii) the corporate life of the Church; (iii) the witness and evangelism of the Church.

The Committee to report its findings to the Synod in the light of: (a) a study from a theological, linguistic and psychological viewpoint on the question of tongues, the interpretation of tongues, and prophecy, (b) a study from a theological and medical standpoint on the subject of spiritual healing, (c) a study of kindred spiritual gifts and their place in the worship of a congregation, (d) a study of spiritual gifts and their place in the witness and evangelistic outreach of the Church.

The Committee appointed was: The Rev. A. M. Blanch (Secretary), The Rev. J. C. Chapman, The Rev. D. H. Crawford (resigned November 1972), The Rev. G. H. Feltham, The Rev. D. T. Foord, Canon A. J. Glennon, Canon D. B. Knox, The Rev. R. E. Lamb, Bishop J. R. Reid (Chairman), Dr. B. Hamilton, R. B. Hobart, Esq., Dr. D. T. Treloar.

Harvey Cox wrote in "The Secular City" as follows: "The real

Both Sides to the Question

ecumenical crisis today is not between Catholics and Protestants but between traditional and experimental forms of Church life". These experimental forms are seen in the Jesus people, and often in the charismatic movement. The modern Charismatic Movement is a novelty in the Church. It is wholly a twentieth century phenomenon. But it has antecedents of one kind or another. In 1900, at Bethel College, Kansas, a girl student, Agnes Osman, asked the Principal to lay hands on her head and she spoke in a strange language. It was from this source that American Pentecostalism was to spring and in 1906 a Church was opened in Agusa Street, Los Angeles.

Pentecostalism grew phenomenally in the first half of the twentieth century. In 1960 a new departure became evident when adherents of major Protestant denominations began to speak in tongues and in 1966 it was practised in the Roman Catholic Church. This movement, within the historic churches, is known generally as neo-Pentecostalism.

The Charismatic Movement is built theologically on the doctrine of "baptism in the Holy Spirit". It was enunciated at Finney's "Oberlin School of Theology" in New York in 1946. This doctrine teaches the necessity of a second "post conversion" work of grace in the Christian, to empower him for witness and service. This experience is usually authenticated by tongues. This doctrine of baptism in the Holy Spirit is related to John Wesley's doctrine of entire sanctification while Roman Catholic charismatics see it related to the piety of Francis Xavier and Thomas a Kempis.

The spiritual experience of many people has been radically altered through contact or participation in the Charismatic Movement. Both members of the clergy and laity have felt its impact. It is a movement which cannot be ignored and, throughout the Christian world, its message demands investigation and response.

The Committee divided into sub-committees and the report is the fruit of the work done in Committee. In addition, members attended charismatic meetings, interviewed charismatic leaders and in particular we were grateful to spend some hours with the Rev. Michael Harper of Fountain Trust, U.K. A remarkable "charismatic" centre, caring for the drug addicts and other socially deprived people, was visited and a psychiatrist who was a member of the Committee conducted a study with private interviews with 40 tongue speakers.

The members of the Committee represented different

viewpoints ranging from enthusiastic support for the Charismatic Movement to general opposition. These differences were not resolved and our report to Synod reflects our discussions. It makes no final judgement and it sets forth different points of view which will enable Synod members to make up their own minds. We have used the terms "neo-Pentecostal" and "non neo-Pentecostal" to describe the people who hold two different points of view. We acknowledge that the latter is a rather awkward term but it is clear in its meaning.

However we would wish to say that the difficult exercise which we undertook has brought us closer together and while we differ we have shared an unshakeable common work of the Spirit of God. Paul said, "No one can say 'Jesus is the Lord' except by the Holy Spirit" and in that joint experience of Jesus as our contemporary and Jesus as our Lord we have proved the value of staying together to think together and to pray together.

We present to the Synod our report and pray that the Holy Spirit will lead us all into more truth and a joyous experience of our faith.

John R. Reid, Chairman

DIFFERENT APPROACH — DIFFERENT CONCLUSION

1. Why We Do Not Agree

The Commission, as it investigated the neo-Pentecostal Movement, discovered that there were many areas where neo-Pentecostal and non neo-Pentecostal Anglicans agreed. We also discovered that there were fundamental areas in which there was strong and important disagreement. This report will aim to show both the areas of agreement and the areas of disagreement. We believe also that it is insufficient to highlight areas of disagreement without trying to trace these to the fundamental source of the differences.

The most important area of disagreement is in understanding the baptism in the Holy Spirit. Without the distinctive neo-Pentecostal view of this issue the Charismatic Movement would hardly exist.

Both neo-Pentecostal Anglicans and non neo-Pentecostal Anglicans believe the Bible to be the Word of God, inspired and authoritative, and therefore it is the arbiter in matters of doctrine. Why then do we arrive at different meanings to important issues like baptism in the Spirit, tongues, etc.?

Both Sides to the Question

The explanation lies in two directions: (a) the way religious experience is to be understood, and (b) the way the Bible is to be applied.

2. *Experience and Understanding the Bible*

The neo-Pentecostal and the non neo-Pentecostal differ in the importance they place on one's understanding of the Bible by experiences. Is the Bible to be understood by my experience of God and His workings with me, or is my experience to be understood in the light of what God says, or both?

The neo-Pentecostal in many areas is experience-centred in his approach to the Bible. This is especially true of baptism in the Spirit, tongues-speaking and prophecy. He readily admits that after experiencing these phenomena his understanding of what the Bible says concerning them changed considerably. To the non neo-Pentecostal, experiences can never make clear what is not clear in the scriptures.

The non neo-Pentecostal believes that what is not clearly taught in the scriptures cannot and will never be clarified by one's experience since the experience cannot be identified for certain because it is not clear in its definition. He does admit that what is clear may be given a greater extent of meaning by experience, but not clarity from ambiguity.

3. *How the Bible Is to Be Applied*

A. *Neo-Pentecostal Use.* In a Movement as diverse as the present neo-Pentecostal Movement in Australia it is not always possible to say that this is *the* view held by all neo-Pentecostals. However we have tried to say what seems to be true for most.

They believe the Bible is God's Word and He speaks *directly* to us from it. What God *says to us* may be obvious or it may be mystical, having little bearing on the true meaning of the words in their historical context. In the latter case, it is seen to be the miracle of the Word of God, that God says to their situation what the words may not have been saying to the historical situation.

Another feature of the neo-Pentecostal view of the scriptures is that experiences and promises and commands made to individuals in the Bible generally have a direct application to all God's children unless it is clearly otherwise. For example they reason: "There is a promise that Jesus will baptise with the Holy Spirit; there are several incidents in the New Testament where people were baptised in the Holy Spirit; because of the promise and because this happened to them, therefore it must be available to us today as it was to them then."

It should be pointed out, however, that many non neo-Pentecostal Anglicans have exactly the same view of the Bible as do neo-Pentecostals, but do not seem to have followed it into neo-Pentecostalism.

B. *Non Neo-Pentecostal Use.* Non neo-Pentecostals also are diverse in their use of the Bible. The non neo-Pentecostal believes that the Bible is the Word of God and that inasmuch as it gives accurate information about God and His world, man, and how man should live in that world, it has direct implications for us. He believes that God speaks to us from it *within the confines of its historical setting.* No one believes, on the basis of Matt 19:16-22, that "selling your goods and giving them to the poor" is a condition of salvation for all men. On any issue where there is an historical description of God working in a particular way with an individual the non neo-Pentecostal attitude generally is: "Since God acted like this in the past He *may* act again in this way now or in the future." In regard to promises and commands made to individuals, and to their experiences with God, the neo-Pentecostal assumes generality for all believers unless it is evidently otherwise; the non neo-Pentecostal assumes that these are specific unless it is stated otherwise.

4. *The Result Must Be Different*

Because of the difference in approach to the Bible opposing views are inevitable. The neo-Pentecostal, seeing the promise of baptism in the Spirit, believing baptism in the Spirit to be a post-conversion experience (different and distinctive from regeneration), and seeing several historical events showing this experience, concludes that it is for all God's people and consequently seeks it for himself and encourages others to do the same.

The non neo-Pentecostal, believing "baptism in the Spirit" to be a synonym for "becoming a Christian", sees the historical events of the baptism in the Spirit recorded in Acts to be unique in the development of the early church and consequently does not necessarily expect them to happen again, nor does he seek them.

These differences are also highlighted in the view of the gifts of the Holy Spirit. The neo-Pentecostal reads 1 Cor 12-14 and sees the lists of gifts given by God. He concludes that since God gave these gifts once He *will* give them all to us *now*. The Corinthians needed them; therefore, he assumes, we need them also.

The non neo-Pentecostal, reading the same passage, concludes that since God gave these gifts to the Corinthians He *may* give them again to us in this age. Since he believes the Spirit to be sovereign in this area he believes that the necessary gifts for the congregation's growth and maturity will be given.

Because of this the Committee is of the opinion that consideration must be given to the very important subject: "How can I know the Word of God for me today from the Word of God in history?" Or, to put it another way, "What is God saying to *me now* from what God said to *them then?*"

Also we call on all members of our congregations and especially clergymen, whose prime role it is to teach the Bible, not to lay on the consciences of men what is not *clearly* taught in scripture, nor to deprive them of that which is clearly taught, and to continue to treat those scriptures with reverence and to teach with care and accuracy.

5. *Experience Rightly Understood*

There can be no denying that many neo-Pentecostals have had an experience which is genuine in character. The question the non neo-Pentecostal wishes to ask is: "Has he rightly understood it?" Whether this new work which God has done is "baptism in the Spirit" or not, the experience cannot alter. However, the moment it is positively identified biblically as "baptism in the Spirit" then all must be encouraged to have this experience. The non neo-Pentecostal cannot identify the experience of the neo-Pentecostal as "baptism in the Spirit". He concludes that it is part of the sanctifying work of the Holy Spirit, whose work it is to transform His people into Christ-likeness of character from one degree of glory to another (2 Cor 3:18). It is to be expected that the Holy Spirit in His sovereign working may do this dramatically in one person and slowly and steadily in another.

6. *Are the Scriptures Clear Enough?*

Many non neo-Pentecostal Anglicans believe that in many areas in the present debate the scriptures are just not clear enough for us to be dogmatic. Is that which is happening at present the same as that which occurred in the first century church as recorded in Acts and 1 Cor 12-14?

Can we be certain that present-day "tongues", for example, can be positively identified with tongues in 1 Cor 12-14? There is so little information available that dogmatism seems impossible. Prophecy and miracles may well come into this category. We cannot really know for certain what the Corinthians did when they "spoke in tongues". Whether this matters, in working out how useful the present tongues-speaking is, remains another question. It may not in the long run matter whether it can be identified biblically or not. However, if we cannot be sure, we should not say we are sure, either positively or negatively.

It must be pointed out that if an experience cannot be positively identified biblically it must not be urged upon Christian people as helpful or desirable (2 Tim 3:16).

BAPTISM IN THE HOLY SPIRIT

The following is a brief statement of the different concepts which the neo-Pentecostal and the non neo-Pentecostal have concerning the biblical teaching related to being baptised in the Holy Spirit. For a fuller teaching of the various points of view it is recommended that the books listed in the Bibliography should be read.

Biblical Perspective

The Old Testament looked forward to the time when God would "pour out His Spirit upon the descendants of Jacob" (Isaiah 44:3); when He would "put a new spirit within His people" (Ezekiel 11:19; 36:27); when He would "pour out His Spirit upon all flesh" (Joel 2:28, 29). Godly men longed for an experience of the Spirit that all God's people would share (Numbers 11:29), that would bring them into a deeper, closer relationship with God.

John the Baptist, the last of the Old Testament prophets, gave clear and specific meaning to the fulfilment of this Old Testament promise concerning the Holy Spirit by revealing that this was to be the ministry of the Messiah to His people. "I baptise with water, for repentance; but He who comes after me is mightier than I, He will baptise you with the Holy Spirit and with fire" (Matt 3:11; Mark 1:8; Luke 3:16; John 1:26). Jesus Himself took this promise — and John the Baptist's phrase expressing this promise — and used it just before His ascension: "Wait for the promise of the Father which you heard from me, for John baptised with water, but before many days you shall be baptised with the Holy Spirit" (Acts 1:4, 5). Jesus had already taught extensively concerning the coming of the Holy Spirit and His ministry in the life of a Christian (John 14, 15, 16) and had indicated that this would be fulfilled when He departed from this earth (John 7:38, 39).

Thus, from the Old Testament, from the teaching of John the Baptist and from the ministry of Jesus the coming of the Holy Spirit was given primary significance. This coming of the Holy Spirit was referred to by John the Baptist (Matt 3:11, etc.), by Jesus (Acts 1:5) and by Peter (Acts 11:16) as being "baptised in the Holy Spirit".

Terminology

There are, however, a number of other terms which the Bible uses to describe the coming of the Holy Spirit into the life of a Christian. These are:

1. The Holy Spirit came upon you, e.g. Acts 1:8, 19:6.
2. Filled with the Holy Spirit, e.g. Acts 2:4, 9:17.
3. The Spirit poured out upon you, e.g. Acts 2:17, 2:33.
4. To receive the Holy Spirit, e.g. Acts 10:47, 8:15.
5. To be given the Holy Spirit, e.g. Acts 11:17, 8:18.
6. The Spirit falling upon you, e.g. Acts 10:44, 11:15.

While the phrase "baptism in the Holy Spirit" is nowhere found in the Bible we believe that it is not significantly different from the biblical phrase "baptised in the Holy Spirit", and to debate such terminology is to allow ourselves to be diverted from the real issues of neo-Pentecostalism which are the theological interpretations the neo-Pentecostal gives to the phrase.

Historical Interpretations of These Terms

Traditionally this concept of a baptism in the Holy Spirit has given rise to division of thought and understanding in the Church. Within more radical Protestantism it has led to the concept of a two-stage salvation experience: first, the experience of becoming a Christian; then, as a later and distinct event, a second experience of the Holy Spirit. For many Puritans the second experience was one of assurance. (J. I. Packer: *Wisdom of our Fathers* pp. 14–25.) For Wesley the first stage was justification and partial sanctification, the second the divine gift of entire sanctification or Christian perfection (J. Wesley: *A Plain Account of Christian Perfection*). "A direct line can be drawn from Puritan teaching on the Spirit through early Methodism to the nineteenth-century Holiness Movement with its 'Higher Life' message in which justification by faith (deliverance from the penalty of sin) was distinguished from the second Divine work of sanctification, also received by faith (deliverance from the power of sin). One of the Holiness Movement's most vigorous offspring, the Keswick Convention, used to be notable for its 'second blessing' teaching, and such metaphors as the one which characterised some Christians as living between Calvary and Pentecost still have currency at the Convention.

"Within this whole tradition the idea of Spirit-baptism has often been associated with the second stage. Thomas Goodwin equated the experience of assurance with the 'seal of the Spirit' in Ephesians 1:13 and with the Baptism with the Holy Spirit; he even called it a 'new conversion'. John Fletcher, the saintly Methodist, quite often used the phrase 'baptism in the Spirit' and understood it to describe the sudden receiving of entire sanctification. And among earlier 'Higher Life' teachers the second experience of sanctification was commonly called 'the baptism of the Holy Spirit'.

"However, towards the close of the nineteenth century, particularly in America, the emphasis in the use of the phrase gradually shifted from the idea of sanctification and holiness (a purifying baptism of fire cleansing from sin) to that of empowering for service, principally on the basis of Luke 24:49 and Acts 1:5, 8. At the same time in the United States there was a growing interest in spiritual gifts, and several prominent Holiness leaders taught that these could, and should, still be in operation within the Church." (James D. G. Dunn: *Baptism in the Holy Spirit* pp. 1–2.)

Thus, ever since Protestantism began, there has been a significant number within its ranks who have taught a second work of the Holy Spirit subsequent to Christian conversion. This experience has been periodically equated with Spirit-Baptism and was clearly enunciated as such by Jim Morgan in 1846 teaching at the Oberlin School of Theology. Present-day neo-Pentecostalism is of this tradition — though it has significant differences in its own particular teaching within this tradition.

Neo-Pentecostal Teaching of Baptism in the Holy Spirit
Simply, the neo-Pentecostal believes that the Christian experience involves *two* distinct elements:

(1) The first is that of being born again by the Holy Spirit. This is the experience referred to by Jesus in John 3 and results in

Both Sides to the Question

repentance and faith. The neo-Pentecostal believes that this is a conversion-work of the Holy Spirit (John 3:5) whereby a person is baptised into the Body of Christ and is established thereby in a full son-of-God relationship with God, Father, Son and Holy Spirit. He believes that the Christian receives the Holy Spirit in Jesus at regeneration, that he therefore has the Holy Spirit as a result of conversion (Rom 8:9) and that the Holy Spirit is operative in a Christian's life as a result of conversion to bring about the fruit of sanctification.

(2) The second Christian experience is that of being baptised in the Holy Spirit. This is essentially an experience of becoming related to the Holy Spirit in such a way that His power for witnessing to the authority of Christ in this world becomes operative in the Christian's life (Acts 1:8).

Thus he believes that conversion is the work of the Holy Spirit, whereby we are spiritually regenerated or born again, and united with Jesus Christ. The Holy Spirit abides in us, teaches us, and the fruit of His presence begins to develop in our character (John 3:5; 1 Cor 6:7; John 14, 15, 16; Rom 8:14; Gal 5:22, 23). But separately from all that, as something different, Jesus Christ to whom the Spirit brought us in regeneration, baptises the regenerate believer with the Holy Spirit, whereby we are freshly endued with spiritual power, and quickened in our experience of the spiritual gifts (Acts 1:8; 1 Cor 2:4-11). This is a further and distinct work of the Holy Spirit, it is not a fulfilment or appropriation of the original work of conversion.

Non Neo-Pentecostal Teaching of Baptism in the Holy Spirit
The historical fulfilment of the promise of baptism in the Holy Spirit took place on the day of Pentecost (compare Acts 1:4-5; 2:1-4). The prophecy of John the Baptist was that the baptising in the Spirit is the Messianic role. It cannot take place until Jesus is glorified (John 7) and it is experienced by all who repent and believe (Acts 2). Since Pentecost Spirit-baptism has been, and is now, an aspect of conversion in which the believer is sealed with the Spirit (Eph 1:13) and incorporated into the body of Christ (1 Cor 12:13). Every Christian upon believing the Gospel is justified, sealed with the Spirit and made a member of the body of Christ. There is no dichotomy between his encounter with, and experience of, Christ and the Spirit. Thus, he believes that a Christian enters into a full relationship with the Holy Spirit and possesses in fullness all that God offers him in Christ (Col 2:10).

This is his Christian standing. However, he may not live up to his possessions in Christ and he will, therefore, need to be exhorted to live out his fullness (Eph 5:18). A parallel is the Christian's experience of holiness. He is described as holy, once he is converted (Heb 10:14, 1 Pet 2:9). This is his standing. However he may need to be exhorted to live out that holiness (1 Pet 1:15, 16).

Therefore, the non neo-Pentecostal submits that:

(1) Every Christian is baptised in the Spirit when he repents and believes the Gospel. He also enters into a full and complete relationship with Christ and His Spirit (1 Cor 12:13; Titus 3:5-7).

(2) All Christians fail to live up to their standing in Christ and need to be exhorted (from time to time) to live up to their standing, i.e. be filled with the Spirit.

(3) Some Christians, realising that there has been a serious gap between their standing in Christ and the lives they have been living, may sometimes experience what appears to be a dramatic change or "second blessing", but this cannot rightly be termed "baptism in the Spirit".

Neo-Pentecostal Interpretation of the Bible

The neo-Pentecostal derives his understanding of what the Bible means by being baptised in the Holy Spirit by studying the Biblical descriptions of those who were baptised in the Holy Spirit in New Testament times. He takes these descriptions as being normative for today. There are six principal examples which he accepts from the New Testament as giving meaning to the baptism in the Holy Spirit.

1. *Jesus' Experience.* Jesus' human experience of and relationship with the Holy Spirit began at His conception and led to His identification with man's sin at Jordan. So He was baptised by John the Baptist in the Jordan to "fulfil all righteousness" (Matt 3:15). However, after having been baptised, the Holy Spirit descended on Him and God declared Him the beloved Son in whom He was well pleased (Luke 3:21, 22). Jesus is now described as "full of the Holy Spirit". The neo-Pentecostal believes that Jesus' baptism related to His fulfilling all righteousness and bearing the sin of man; His infilling with the Holy Spirit related to power for the ministry which lay before him (Acts 10:38).

2. *The Original Disciples.* Those original disciples in the upper room (Acts 2:1-4) were believers, many had left all to follow Jesus (Matt 19:27, 28), and their names were written in heaven (Luke

Both Sides to the Question

10:20). They had already, in a real sense, been enlightened, tasted the goodness of the Word of God and the powers of the age to come (Heb 6:4, 5), and been quickened in some way by the Holy Spirit in the upper room after Jesus' resurrection (John 20:22). They believed that Jesus was the Christ (Matt 16:17) which was an indication that they were born of God (1 John 5:1). Again Jesus claimed that His disciples were not of this world (John 17) which can only occur as a result of being born again (John 3:5). In the same prayer Jesus says that He had given His disciples the Word of God which had borne fruit in them (John 15:3); such fruit is the new birth through the power of that Word (1 Pet 1:23). However, on the day of Pentecost they were baptised in the Holy Spirit and began to speak in tongues by the power of that Spirit (Acts 2:4). Something new happened — their ministry was endued with an abiding supernatural, divine power; their preaching and witness was with divine effectiveness (Acts 2:37); many wonders and signs were done through the Apostles (2:43), and the Lord confirmed their words with the signs that followed (Mark 16:20).

3. *The Samaritans.* At Samaria, Philip proclaimed to them the Christ (Acts 8:5) and the power from on high came through his ministry in healing many who were paralysed and lame, and casting out evil spirits (8:7). The multitude heard, saw the signs he did, gave heed (v. 6) and believed him (v. 12) — they believed that Jesus Christ was really that power of God which is called Great; He was the Christ. Having believed, they were baptised. The neo-Pentecostal believes that this is clear proof that these men were converted; yet they did not receive at that time a baptism in the Holy Spirit. Peter and John came down from Jerusalem and prayed for this to happen (v. 15); they laid their hands on them, and they received the Holy Spirit in a very evident way (vv. 17, 18). They entered into a manifestly supernatural, divine experience.

4. *Saul.* Saul seems to have experienced a challenge from God well before his journey to Damascus, for he had been kicking against the convicting goads (Acts 26:14). The neo-Pentecostal believes that there is clear evidence that Paul was converted on the road to Damascus. He was confronted by Jesus Christ (Acts 9:1-19); he surrendered and called Jesus Lord (Acts 22:10) — he had seen the risen Lord, heard His voice, and he submitted to His command. This encounter — Paul maintains — justified his claim to be an apostle and a witness to the resurrection (1 Cor 9:1). Three days later, as a result of God commanding him to go to

Paul and pray for him to receive his sight, Ananias came to him and addressed him as brother and told him that he had been sent to pray for him to receive his sight AND to be filled with the Holy Spirit. The neo-Pentecostal believes that Paul's baptism was an act of faith and a sign of his conversion (Acts 9:18, 22:16, cf Acts 9:14), that his receiving of the Holy Spirit as a result of the laying on of Ananias' hands was for power in his future ministry.

5. *Cornelius*. Cornelius was evidently familiar with the ministry of Jesus Christ, at least by hear-say (Acts 10:36). He was a man who feared God, and who showed his devotion by liberal giving and in constant prayer for a clearer revelation of the way of salvation (10:2; 11:14). God responded by sending someone to him with a message by which he would be saved. While Peter was teaching him, and his household, the Holy Spirit fell on them in the same way as happened at Pentecost. As a consequence Peter accepted these men as truly converted and baptised them in water. Although it is not clear when these people were converted, the neo-Pentecostal believes that there still remains in this account a symbolic differentiation between conversion and the baptism in the Holy Spirit by water baptism being associated with the former and speaking in tongues and other signs being associated with the latter.

6. *The Ephesians*. A group of disciples (Acts 19:1) was found by Paul at Ephesus who had been converted under the ministry of Apollos, and had received John's baptism (Acts 19:3). Apollos was instructed in the way of the Lord and taught accurately the things concerning Jesus (Acts 18:25). Paul asked these disciples whether they had received the Holy Spirit when they believed. The neo-Pentecostal believes that Paul plainly assumed these people were Christians and that, therefore, Paul understood it to be possible for people to believe as Christians, but not "receive the Holy Spirit" in some sense. Furthermore, when he did point them to belief in Jesus, and baptised them in the name of the Lord Jesus (Acts 19:4, 5), he still was not satisfied that they had "received the Holy Spirit, having believed" — he laid hands on them with a separate intention (not to convert them, for they were converted and baptised), and when he did the Holy Spirit came on them in an evident way (v. 6), for they spoke in tongues and prophesied. These signs — which frequently occurred when people were baptised in the Holy Spirit — did not occur as a result of being baptised in water, they resulted from Paul laying

Both Sides to the Question

hands on these disciples and praying for them to receive the Holy
Spirit.

Non Neo-Pentecostal Interpretation of the Bible
1. *The Acts' Accounts.* It is generally agreed by non
neo-Pentecostals that there are "few problems so puzzling in New
Testament theology as that posed by Acts in its treatment of
conversion-initiation. The relation between the gift of the Spirit
and water-baptism is particularly confusing . . . The role and
significance of both John's baptism and the laying on of hands are
complicating factors." (Dunn, p. 90.) However, two general
comments are made concerning the events of Acts:
  a. They are unique and relate to representatives of special
groups of people, thus they are meant to be strategic within the
development of the early Church, and not to be normative.
  b. They are considered to be unusual instances of the baptism
in the Holy Spirit and that one of Luke's purposes in recording
them is to show that the one thing which makes a man a
Christian is the gift of the Spirit. "Men can have been for a long
time in Jesus' company, can have made profession of faith and
been baptised in the name of the Lord Jesus, can be wholly 'clean'
and acceptable to God, can even be 'disciples', and *yet not be
Christians*, because they lack [sic] and until they receive the Holy
Spirit. In the last analysis the only thing that matters in deciding
whether a man is a Christian or not is whether he has received
the Spirit or not." (Dunn, p. 93.)
  2. *The Original Disciples.* Undoubtedly, the day of Pentecost was
a subsequent experience of the Holy Spirit for the disciples of
Jesus. They were followers of Jesus; they had been ministered to
by the Holy Spirit already. However, the delay experienced by
these men was caused by their unique position in God's
timetable. They were both believers under the old covenant, and
they became believers under the New from Pentecost. Thus, it is
considered that this event was unique to those disciples (John
7:39; Acts 11:17).
  3. *Samaria.* Luke's understanding of this event seems to be that
something abnormal was happening. The Samaritans had
believed and had been baptised but the Spirit had not yet fallen.
Thus, it is considered that this abnormal incident (as suggested by
Luke's words "not yet fallen") cannot be made a basis for
imitation. Some non neo-Pentecostals believe that Philip's

evangelistic activity with the outcast Samaritans was so contrary to what many in Jerusalem believed ought to be done that an extraordinary sign was given, witnessed by apostles, to prove the authenticity of the conversions and their reception into the Christian congregation. Some believe that this delay may have been for the benefit of the apostles.

4. *Saul.* The non neo-Pentecostal at the same time would say that Paul's conversion experience included all those events beginning on the Damascus Road and until his water baptism.

5. *Cornelius.* Again, it is considered that Cornelius was converted when he received the Holy Spirit and that his experience therefore demonstrates no difference between conversion and the baptism in the Holy Spirit.

6. *Ephesus.* The Ephesian disciples (Acts 19:1-7) represented an unusual group. They had made a genuine response to the Word of God as it had come to them through John the Baptist. They were disciples of that prophet (compare Matthew 11:2). They were defective in the knowledge of the great acts of God in Jesus and the subsequent coming of the Holy Spirit. They did not know the gospel of grace. Their lack of knowledge was remedied and they entered into the same genuine experience of the Holy Spirit as was common to the apostles and to the members of their fellowship.

Significant Differences

(a) *Experience.* The neo-Pentecostal and non neo-Pentecostal differ significantly on the place of experience in Christian understanding. The neo-Pentecostal believes that experience is an essential ingredient of theological understanding (John 7:17) and that it is appropriate, therefore, that he search the scriptures to see that his experience of baptism in the Holy Spirit accords with that recorded of the early Church. He does not place his experience above the authority of the Bible, but he believes that his experience can give fuller meaning to his reading of the Bible.

b. *Doctrine from Narratives.* The non neo-Pentecostal states that it is wrong to use narrative passages from the Bible to establish doctrine. He states that "This is a common evangelical failing, and especially in relation to the book of Acts. We hear that the early Church did something and we assume that it is a command from God for us to do it — that is, we turn a description (an 'is') into a prescription (an 'ought') . . . some teachers seek to remove our liberty by turning narratives into commands . . . We may gather imperatives or doctrines from narratives where the author himself has given the details a theological significance known to us. This significance may be learned from his writings as a whole, or from the immediate context, or both." (Barnett & Jensen, pp. 14, 15.)

The neo-Pentecostal believes that since the Bible teaches that "all Scripture is inspired by God and is profitable for teaching, for reproof, for correction, and for training in righteousness . . ." (2 Tim 3:16) then the narrative passages of the Acts describing baptisms in the Holy Spirit are best described as doctrine of Spirit-baptism. He does not deduce the promise of a baptism in the Holy Spirit from these narratives; he has that promise from the teaching of John the Baptist and Jesus; the narratives give him a clear description of what Spirit-baptism means in the life and experience of a Christian.

c. The Acts' Accounts Unique. The non neo-Pentecostal believes that what happened at Jerusalem, Samaria, Caesarea and Ephesus was unique and is not, therefore, normative for a Christian today. It is considered that there was a progressive introduction of the New Covenant, and that each of these cases demonstrated that for the races and peoples whom they represented the full blessing of the New Covenant had arrived, according to the pattern outlined in Acts 1:8.

The neo-Pentecostal believes that such an explanation is an assumption, that there is no biblical statement to affirm that these accounts are unique. He states that if such an explanation is correct then the Holy Spirit has recorded in the Acts only examples of Spirit-baptisms which are *not* to be used for future guidance, and has not recorded an example which can give such guidance. The neo-Pentecostal, therefore, rejects this assumption and believes that the examples given of Spirit-baptisms in the Acts are given for the purpose of being normative, that is, for giving guidance to the Church today.

d. Baptism in the Spirit and Speaking in Tongues. Most neo-Pentecostals do not teach that a person must speak in tongues to be baptised in the Holy Spirit. He does, however, believe that the Bible shows a very significant relationship between speaking in tongues and Spirit-baptism because in three of the five Acts records of Spirit-baptisms the people spoke in tongues (Jerusalem, Cornelius, Ephesus). Most Bible commentators admit that there is every likelihood that they also spoke in tongues at Samaria, and we know that Paul spoke in tongues (1 Cor 14) though we do not know whether he did when Ananias prayed for him.

The non neo-Pentecostal recognises that speaking in tongues played a significant part in the Spirit-baptisms in the Acts but he believes that this was a special sign for the infant Church to indicate that the new Covenant had spread into the lives of all people who believe in Jesus — whether Jew or Gentile, bond or free. Such a sign, it is believed, is not necessary for today.

e. The Epistles. All Christians agree that the epistles teach doctrine. However neo-Pentecostals do not give to the epistles any primacy in this matter over other parts of Scripture. They urge that "All Scripture is profitable for . . . doctrine" and that it is quite as legitimate to deduce doctrine from any part of Scripture as it is from the epistles. Thus a doctrine of baptism in the Spirit may be validly established from the Acts of the Apostles alone, as long as it is not directly contradicted in the epistles. They deem the epistles to be either neutral on this question, or able themselves to be interpreted in a way which supports the doctrinal presuppositions coming from the Acts.

Non neo-Pentecostals regard the teaching of Jesus and the epistles as the apostolic exposition of that teaching, as the normative source of doctrine. The major doctrines of the faith are thus derived from these sources and they may well be illustrated elsewhere. Non neo-Pentecostals see the total absence of reference to baptism in the Spirit in the epistles, as a work of grace subsequent to regeneration, to be of significant importance to their position.

THE GIFTS OF THE SPIRIT

1. *The Terms*

A distinction should be drawn between the *gift* of the Holy Spirit and the *gifts* of the Holy Spirit. The former term, used for example in Acts 2:38, refers to the fact that all Christians receive God's Spirit at regeneration. The expression "the gifts of the Spirit" has become commonly accepted as a description of the lists of gifts mentioned in Romans 12:3ff, 1 Cor 1:5, 12:8ff, 12:28ff, Eph 4:7ff and 1 Peter 4:10, although the term also occurs elsewhere, e.g. Hebrews 2:4.

In fact, with the single exception of Romans 1:11 (where Paul himself is the donor) there are no expressions in the Greek New Testament which can be literally rendered "the gifts of the Spirit" or "spiritual gifts". These terms are paraphrases which have been used by the RSV, NEB and other modern translations or paraphrases of the New Testament. Certainly the gifts are closely associated with the Spirit who energises and distributes them (1 Cor 12:11) but St. Paul never says that the Spirit *gives* the gifts. They are given by God (e.g. 1 Cor 7:7) or by Christ (e.g. Eph 4:7).

Perhaps, by taking "of the Spirit" to imply a general relation, we are justified in speaking of these gifts as "gifts of the Spirit".

2. *The Categories*

The main categories of gifts are catalogued in the following lists:

Rom 12:3ff: prophecy, ministry, teaching, exhortation, giving money, giving aid, showing mercy.

1 Cor 1:5: every kind of speech, every kind of knowledge.

1 Cor 7:7: marriage, continence.

1 Cor 12:8ff: speaking wisdom, speaking knowledge, faith, healings, works of power, prophecy, distinguishing between spirits, tongues, interpretation of tongues.

1 Cor 12:28ff: apostles, prophets, teachers, works of powers, healers, helpers, administrators, tongues.

Eph 4:7ff: apostles, prophets, evangelists, pastors and teachers.

Non neo-Pentecostals are generally agreed that not all gifts are of equal importance. Some would say that the lists in 1 Cor 12 indicate a "hierarchy" of gifts (compare 1 Cor 12:28 "first . . . second . . . third . . . then") and it is significant that tongues, which is listed last in both lists, is therefore the least important. Others think that the reasons for this arrangement may be historical or structural. However, all non neo-Pentecostals agree that 1 Cor 14 clearly teaches the relative unimportance of tongues as compared especially with prophecy. Neo-Pentecostals claim that there is no such order-of-importance in God's gifts, and even if there were, tongues should be held in honour because of the idea expressed in 1 Cor 12:24 ". . . giving the greater honour to the inferior part". Non neo-Pentecostals would say that 1 Cor 12:24-26 refers not to the importance of gifts but to the value of every member of the congregation, with the emphasis on mutual care and sympathy.

The neo-Pentecostal expects to find all the gifts in every congregation whereas the non neo-Pentecostal believes that God will give to a congregation only those gifts which He deems necessary for its maturity in Christ. Therefore both neo-Pentecostals and non neo-Pentecostals *claim* to be *charismatic*.

3. *Are They Contemporary Gifts?*

Non neo-Pentecostals are divided as to whether the more supernatural of these gifts, viz., tongues, interpretation of tongues, healing miracles, are genuinely extant today. These particular gifts will be dealt with elsewhere in this Report, but some areas of difficulty are, first, that the non neo-Pentecostal believes there is not sufficient evidence available to us to be able to identify the current phenomena of tongues and their interpretation as being the same as those phenomena which are described in the New Testament; second, that there seems to be no evidence that miraculous healings are occurring today in the way described in the Bible. Neo-Pentecostals, on the other hand, believe that we are living in an age in which God is pouring out upon Christian churches all the gifts mentioned in the New Testament. They claim that many miraculous healings are occurring and maintain that it is possible for all Christians to speak in tongues.

4. *Are Gifts Natural or Supernatural?*

The issue here is whether Christians receive gifts from God as natural endowments before their conversion, or whether they are given at conversion or at a Spirit-baptism after conversion.

Some neo-Pentecostals believe that gifts of the Spirit are not dependent on baptism in the Spirit. Other neo-Pentecostals hold that a Christian can have no spiritual gift at all until and unless he has experienced baptism in the Spirit after conversion. Without that experience he is limited in his service for God to the use of natural endowments, with no real spiritual power and minimal effectiveness.

Still other neo-Pentecostals believe that while some of the gifts, e.g. contributing money, giving aid, doing acts of mercy, etc., relate to natural human abilities which are enhanced by baptism in the Spirit, other gifts such as tongues, interpretation, healings and prophecy are absolutely miraculous and supernatural. Such people would distinguish sharply between a healing by a miracle-worker and a healing by a physician. The non neo-Pentecostal, recognising that since God has made us and works through the natures He has made, observes that a

Christian who has the gift of administration, for example, usually had the gift before conversion. The realities of conversion and life in Christ give a new motivation and empowering for the employment of natural endowments. At the same time it is agreed that God may give additional gifts to His children at the time of their conversion or at any time thereafter. The experience of receiving a spiritual gift, or the awareness of having received a gift, which may come at some time after conversion, is not to be interpreted as an experience of being baptised in the Spirit.

The contrast between the non neo-Pentecostal and neo-Pentecostal views is well illustrated by their understanding of the gifts of a word of knowledge or a word of wisdom in a situation of pastoral counselling.

The non neo-Pentecostal believes that when the cause of difficulty has been explained to the counsellor, God will use the general and specific knowledge of God's Word which has been built up over the years, and will guide the gifted counsellor to explain passages of Scripture which are appropriate to the problem. Divine wisdom is given in the use of knowledge previously gained, enabling men "rightly handling the word of truth" (2 Tim 2:15).

The neo-Pentecostal believes this too and acts in the same way. He would go on and say that where something needs to be revealed to him, either to do with the problem or the answer, and does not lie within his previous experience, God will reveal it to him through the appropriate gift in response to faith.

5. *Prophecy*

Neo-Pentecostals and non neo-Pentecostals differ in parts of their understanding of prophecy. They would agree that the gift is given for the purpose of the clear and intelligible declaration of the will of God which includes the elements of upbuilding, encouragement, consolation and teaching (1 Cor 14:3, 31) and which can convict the unbeliever (1 Cor 14:24, 25).

The neo-Pentecostal takes the view that prophetic words come by an immediate revelation unrelated to the prophet's study of Scripture or preparation of his message. It is a supernatural activity, not an intellectual activity. The message usually comes as an inspired utterance which is fairly brief and given to the speaker in that moment. Further, the interpretation of a tongue is also classified as "prophecy". This is based on 1 Cor 14:5, and this thought is seen as nullifying the apparent inferiority of tongues, compared with prophecy, evident in 1 Cor 14:2, 3. Sometimes some neo-Pentecostals say that Christians should submit as obediently to the directions of prophecy and interpreted tongues as they should submit to the directions of the canonical Scriptures. The neo-Pentecostals on this Committee wholly reject this view. Other neo-Pentecostals are very much more cautious, emphasising the need to weigh and test everything carefully before obeying what is said (1 Cor 14:29, 1 John 4:1).

The non neo-Pentecostal believes that the import of 1 Cor 14 is that prophecy is far more important than tongues. Tongues are of no benefit unless accompanied by revelation, knowledge, prophecy or teaching; they are unintelligible whereas prophecy is intelligible; they affect the unbeliever adversely whereas prophecy has a good effect (1 Cor 14:6, 9, 23-25). While tongues-speaking is not to be forbidden, prophecy is to be earnestly desired (1 Cor 14:1-3, 5, 39). The manifestation of prophecy is closely associated with insight and exposition of the truth of Holy Scripture (this would fit the case of 1 Cor 14:3) and is therefore related to teaching and preaching. This allows the element of prediction in prophecy, but only within the limits of the written Word. All that is said must be weighed against that Word (cf. Deut 13:1-5). While some non neo-Pentecostals believe that under special circumstances God could still inspire specific contemporary predictive prophecy like that of Agabus (Acts 11:27, 38 and 21:10, 11), others believe that, especially since the closing of the Canon of Scripture, this no longer occurs. They believe that the prophet now expounds the truths of the Bible with an immediate relevance and application to the contemporary situation.

6. *The Purpose of Gifts*

Neo-Pentecostals and non neo-Pentecostals agree that the gifts of God which are apportioned by the Holy Spirit are given for building up the body of Christ to maturity (Eph 4:12). While 1 Cor 14:4 speaks of a tongue-speaker edifying himself, this is said rather in contrast with the major purpose of gifts which is to build up the congregation (1 Cor 12:4, 5, 6, 12, 17, 19).

All gifts are to be exercised with love, and indeed if they are not manifested with love they are worthless (1 Cor 13:1-3). There is no ground for boasting about spiritual gifts. In the Corinthian church some members had fallen into this error and were "puffed up in favour of one against another". This situation provoked St. Paul to write, "What have you that you did not receive? If then you received it, why do you boast as if it were not a gift?" (1 Cor 4:6, 7).

Also, all gifts are to be exercised with discipline and orderliness. Those who are gifted are able to control the exercise of their gifts, i.e. as the NEB puts it "it is for prophets to control prophetic inspiration" (1 Cor 14:32). Because "God is not a God of confusion but of peace", and because "all things should be done decently and in order" there is to be careful observance of strict guidelines and limitations in congregations (1 Cor 14:26:40).

The gifts and their message should be "judged" or examined by others who are like gifted. The Charismatic Movement takes these gifts seriously, which must also require that they bring them under the careful judgement of mature and spiritual people. Gifts must not be manifested selfishly and self-assertively, but "in honour we must prefer the other" in their use.

TONGUES

The practice of speaking in ecstatic speech is one of the distinctive marks of the Charismatic Movement. Although some may not regard it as a crucial issue as is the doctrine of the Baptism in the Spirit, nevertheless it is an important feature.

The Neo-Pentecostal View

The classic Pentecostal view taught that "tongues" was a necessary sign of baptism in the Holy Spirit. Some neo-Pentecostals do not endorse this. While insisting on a second work of the Holy Spirit distinct from conversion and called "the baptism in the Holy Spirit", neo-Pentecostals do not see tongues as a necessary sign, but as a sign. They see the gift to be either "the language of men or of angels", i.e. either a foreign language, though unknown by the speaker, or a "supernatural" language. It may be either spoken or sung. In the exercise of tongues the mind does not play an active role. This gift of tongues is to be valued as a vehicle of pure praise to God and of a supernatural way of prayer; as a source of edification in the life of the believer; as a sign of the supernatural presence of Christ; as a witness to unbelievers; and as a divine method of taming the unruly evil of the tongue. The Report of the Special Committee on the work of the Holy Spirit to the 182nd General Assembly of the United Presbyterian Church in the U.S.A concludes:

"The chief exegetical difficulty we found in the relevant

passages is to determine whether the 'tongues' were actual foreign languages or dialects not previously known by the speaker, or were a kind of rhapsody of sounds, unintelligible to others as well as to the speaker. Our conclusion, based on a study of the languages and analogies used by Paul, is that in 1 Corinthians he is speaking of a peculiar kind of utterance attained in prayer in which praise and adoration overflow in ways that transcend ordinary speech."

The neo-Pentecostal sees that the apostle Paul puts tongues on the same plane as other gifts like miracles, healings, faith, discerning of spirits, the utterances of knowledge and of wisdom (1 Cor 12:4-11). It was these gifts which Jesus said vindicated His claim to deity (Luke 11:20; John 14:11; John 7:46) and the gifts which marked Christ as divine also witnessed to His supernatural presence in the early Church (Acts 3:16; 4:13, 14). Thus tongues is a helpful and constructive activity in the congregation (1 Cor 14:26). Every gift is essential to the welfare of the spiritual body, and tongues must not be relegated to an inferior position, because God specifically established diversity through different gifts, and there is to be an equal concern for each member of the body and for his gift (1 Cor 12:25, 26).

Consequently, tongues are not to be forbidden in the congregation (1 Cor 14:39), and being offended at the exercise of tongues which is done decently and in order is a failure in love, or perhaps in understanding the gifts of the Spirit. The proper exercise of tongues is not divisive in the congregation; what causes the division is the attitude which makes them inferior, unnecessary, or denies them a place within the congregation at all. Further, tongues is not to be neglected in favour of prophecy. This preference for prophecy is to be held when tongues in the Church must always be accompanied by interpretation (1 Cor 14:28). If there is an interpreter there should be only two or three messages (1 Cor 14:27) just as there are only to be two or three prophecies (1 Cor 14:29). Such gifts as tongues-speaking and prophecy should be "judged" or examined by others who are like gifted (1 Cor 14:17), and a spiritual gift must never be manifested selfishly or assertively. Any discipline which the apostle Paul brings to the phenomena of tongues is to be seen on undisciplined use of tongues and not on tongues itself. While curbing its excesses, he was encouraging its proper use (1 Cor 14:5, 13, 26-33, 39, 40).

Testimony to the value of tongues-speaking differs amongst

neo-Pentecostals. Some do not find it helpful while others do. Some value it purely as a private spiritual exercise. Others exercise it in a congregation and expect that the gift of interpretation will be given.

The Non Neo-Pentecostal View

On the Committee there was not a cohesive view amongst non neo-Pentecostal members. Because of exegetical problems it is not easy to identify the current phenomena with the Corinthian practice. Consequently some would allow that it is a spiritual gift while others see it as a purely psychological device which fits into the contemporary "experience orientated" culture.

The non neo-Pentecostal notes that in the New Testament:

1. The tongues at Pentecost had nothing inherently unintelligible about them. All understood without the provision of an interpreter (Acts 2:7, 8).

2. Tongues occurred again at Caesarea and Ephesus. Luke sees these as repetitions of Pentecost. While he does not say that these were foreign languages, he also does not say that they were not understood. At Caesarea, Peter and his friends heard the Gentiles speaking in tongues and magnifying God (Acts 10:14); while at Ephesus their tongues-speaking was linked with prophecy.

Luke in Acts 2:14-21, by including Peter's long quotation from Joel, appears to regard tongues as prophesying. Thus, if tongues was an excited and emotional form of prophesying, it could well be mistaken for drunkenness.

3. 1 Cor 12, 13, 14 gives an account which is patently different from Acts. There, tongues is an activity in the congregation. These chapters are full of exegetical difficulties. Some of these difficulties arise out of our ignorance of the questions which were originally posed. Other difficulties arise out of Paul's method. For example, Dr. Henry Chadwick's article "All Things to All Men" in N. T. Studies May 1955, where he argues that in 1 Cor 6 where Paul deals with liberty and 1 Cor 7 with celibacy, the apostle identifies himself with the ascetic or libertine position only later to qualify that position. In respect to tongues he adopts the same method, i.e. he does not forbid it (14:39), but plays it down, insisting on the primacy of love (14:1) and the superiority of prophecy. As to his statement, "I want you all to speak in tongues" (14:5), the non neo-Pentecostal sees this as a relative and concessive statement. The most that can be construed from it is that Paul would genuinely like to see the Corinthians speaking

in tongues, but the real point of his remark is to be found in the words, "but RATHER to prophesy".

In 1 Cor 7:7 Paul used exactly the same phrase with regard to celibacy — "I wish that you were all celibate". But the context shows that he regards this as a good thing for all, but not a universal gift.

Thus Paul accepts the Corinthian practice, whatever it was, as a divine gift, but then relegates it to a place of inferiority.

4. Some see the 1 Corinthian chapters 12-14 referring to known languages. The exercise of tongues as known languages and their interpretation is still a common event on the mission field today where there are a number of linguistic groups.

There is in fact nothing in Paul's description of what happened at Corinth which forbids us assuming that those who spoke in tongues were using languages or dialects other than the Greek which was the common language in Corinth.

That is, it is argued that there is a consistency of use in the word "glossa" in Acts 2 and 1 Cor 12-14. So the unintelligibility of the tongue spoken in Corinth does not necessarily arise from its being glossolalia, but from either its being a foreign language which needed to be translated, as happens on the mission field regularly; or because of the manner of delivery and its spontaneity. Certainly Paul's quotation of Isaiah in 1 Cor 14:21 referring to strange tongues is dealing with the known language of the Assyrians and not some ecstatic speech.

5. If tongues is NOT understood as a foreign language known to the speaker but rather as a "supernatural" language, and if its purpose is for the therapy of the individual, that marks out this gift as completely inconsistent in character from all the others, which were given for the edification of the Church (1 Cor 12:7; 14:12). The neo-Pentecostal meets this objection by distinguishing between the gift of tongues, which edifies the Church when it is exercised in the congregation together with interpretation (14:5, 13); and in the private exercise of tongues which is for personal edification (14:4, 28).

It is reported in the book "They Speak with other Tongues" by John Sherrill that six linguists examined forty examples of tongue-speaking.

"1. No one heard a language they could identify, but added that with 2,800 known languages current at the present time, the odds against recognising a language are enormous.

Both Sides to the Question

"2. They frequently identified language patterns. They affirmed that the 'shape' of real language, with its variety of sound combinations, infrequency of repetition, etc., is virtually impossible to reproduce by deliberate effort.

"3. Two insertions of 'made-up gibberish' were immediately identified as 'not language, but noise'." (Pp. 112, 113.)

The non neo-Pentecostal recognises that the spiritual experiences of many people have been revolutionised by the Charismatic Movement and tongues has been an important feature of this renewal. Christian people must always rejoice when other Christians' obedience to God has been increased and strengthened.

On the other hand, tongues-speaking, like some other common religious practices, is not a distinctive Christian practice.

A practising psychiatrist has informed the Committee that similar speech has been observed by her — (a) in a baby's babbling speech; (b) during a patient's freaking out on lysergic acid; (c) from a patient suffering from an overdose of amphetamine drugs; (d) as a severe side-effect of major tranquillisers; (e) in the repressed speech of the acute psychotic; (f) in sleep talking.

Neo-Pentecostals would see such a "psychological" explanation as largely inappropriate to Christian tongues-speaking which, they say, is not a developed ability, but given by the Spirit.

6. The non neo-Pentecostal would urge that:

i. Tongues in Acts were evidential — an historical sign of the initial baptism of the Holy Spirit on the day of Pentecost and other key groupings who received the Gospel, viz. the Samaritans (?), Gentiles and the Ephesians "Baptists".

Tongues at Corinth were primarily edificatory (1 Cor 14:4-5) not evidential.

ii. Genuine tongues are given as the Spirit wills (12:1). Not all have them. The non neo-Pentecostal refuses, on the ground of lack of textual evidence, the distinction between a personal gift of tongues (which all Christians might have) and a gift for congregational use (which only some have).

iii. Though tongues has some value (cf. 1 Cor 14:4a, 5b) prophecy is a generally superior and more valuable gift (cf. 14:1, 4, 5, 6-12, 23-25, 39). Non neo-Pentecostals would advocate caution in too readily accepting extravagant claims about the value of tongues speaking.

iv. Tongues are "amoral" and "aspiritual" and cannot be regarded as a sign of special spiritual blessing or standing. Non neo-Pentecostals would certainly contest the claim that tongues is in any way the sign of baptism in the Holy Spirit today.

Non neo-Pentecostals generally regard the appearance of the miraculous gifts (including tongues) as occasional, extraordinary and special, belonging more to church founding and revival situations, rather than continuous, ordinary and normative for the whole Church age.

John Taylor in his Newsletter of June 1972 said: "No man, least of all Christian man, can live fully in that protracted paranoia which exalts and idealises his cerebral life and demotes his instinctual being"; and further on he warns of the ineffectiveness of a cerebral form of Christianity. "Bare intellectualism, doctrinal orthodoxy without a warm and living experience of God, can be very sterile and devoid of power to convince or attract."

The Charismatic Movement with its tongue speaking has introduced many Christian people into a Christianity which meets strong emotional needs. It is clear that some Christian people have needs which they cannot verbalise, and conflicts which they do not understand because they are repressed. We note the comments of Kildahl: "We believe anxiety is a prerequisite for developing the ability to speak in tongues."

This glossolalic experience does provide a definite release for them and that is why they "want you all to speak in tongues". (J. B. Kildahl, "The Psychology of Speaking in Tongues", page 58.) The fellowship groups associated with the Charismatic Movement meet the needs of some for acceptance, security and love which are basic needs of all men.

The American Presbyterian Report, already referred to, stated:

"From its investigation of the psychological character and dimensions of the Charismatic Movement the subcommittee has reached the conclusions that are similar to those of many other observers and scholars who have engaged in first hand evaluation. The conclusion affirms that Pentecostals generally, whether they are from the classic protestant denominations or the historic mainline protestant denominations, are essentially well-adjusted and productive members of the society . . . The data indicates that participants in the movement are emotionally and psychologically similar to the normal church population and to their occupational identity group."

Basis of Fellowship

Both the neo-Pentecostals and non neo-Pentecostals on this Committee agree that speaking in tongues cannot in itself be the basis or test for fellowship amongst Christians. Jesus Christ, filled with the Spirit, is never recorded as having spoken in tongues.

Christians are related to each other because of the grace of God. He has "made us alive together with Christ" (Eph 2:5). Our relationship together is a result of the work of God. The expression of that relationship is seen in our fellowship. The fellowship we enjoy is largely controlled by the agreement we possess in Christian understanding. This is illustrated in evangelism. Fellowship in the gospel usually presupposes general agreement on the nature and content of the gospel. Common doctrine and shared experience are essential to fellowship but it is to be noted that not all Christian doctrine can be experienced. The doctrines of the Second Coming, Judgement and the Final Rule of God are obviously such doctrines. Doctrine is first of all to be understood.

Thus the neo-Pentecostal and non neo-Pentecostal have shared real fellowship in this Committee because of this common agreement on so much of Christian doctrine. However, many neo-Pentecostals have crossed old doctrinal demarcations and experience fellowship with people who differ in their understanding of cardinal doctrines of the faith such as authority and salvation, but who have common agreement with them on Spirit-baptism and tongues. Our differences of attitude to this practice reflect our differences in understanding the importance of Spirit-baptism and tongue speaking. The Committee is agreed that tongues is not a necessary sign of the presence of the Holy Spirit. The Committee is divided as to whether tongues as ecstatic speech has a part in mature Christian discipleship.

HEALING

A. *Introduction: What is Healing*

To the average person, healing is "getting better". That is, it is something that usually happens to you when you are sick. Mostly it happens *by itself*, but sometimes it is aided by outside means. Today the commonest of these outside means is the practice of medicine. When healing occurs by either of the two above ways it is spoken of as being by "natural means". But today there is a growing awareness of another agent in the sphere of healing: healing in the name of Christ. Let us look at each of these in turn.

1. *Healing that just happens by itself:* This is usually attributed to the laws of nature. But this term is very ambiguous. A law to us is something that someone has made up, and then passed. But the "laws of nature" are nothing like this as far as a scientist is concerned. They are simply what things, under given circumstances, can be predicted to do. Newton didn't *make* the Law of Gravity, he *observed* and *deduced* it. But a scientist is of course limited to this process of observation and deduction. The Christian however has access to other means of information, i.e. to revelation. The Bible expressly attributes all things to the making and maintaining power of God. In Col 1:16, 17 Paul states "for in Him (Christ) all things were created, in heaven and on earth, visible and invisible . . . all things were created through him and for him. He is before all things and in him all things hold together."

Healing then is an inherent power in most tissues of the body to repair themselves when injured or to replace themselves when destroyed. This is a never-ending process in health and illness. This power varies tremendously from tissues to tissues and some do not heal at all.

2. *Healing that is helped by the doctor:* The key word here is "helped". There is no power inherent in or acquired by any doctor whereby he may cause tissues to heal. His help comes from a combination of numerous factors: the study of the structure and function of the body, the study of the various types of disease to enable diagnosis, and the study of the best possible means available whereby the disease process can be removed (cure), or alleviated (relief), or its symptoms lessened or removed (symptomatic relief). The whole time he is limited by the healing power of the patient's tissues and by the latter's will to live. The former is very largely out of his control and the latter is often so.

One of the Louis' of France is on record as having said "The king touches you. God heals you." Although the knowledge, means and skills of modern medicine are infinitely greater than that of the regal touch that was meant to cure sufferers of "The King's Evil", the king's words could still be said, with appropriate alterations, by any doctor in reference to his own skills. He is endeavouring to follow, for the best advantage of his patient, laws which he neither made nor maintains. The Christian doctor would acknowledge that God however did make them and still maintains them. He would do this on the basis of the biblical revelation that the maker and maintainer of these laws while on earth 2,000 years ago demonstrated His supremacy over them. Jesus Christ made water into wine without the intermediaries of grape vines, solar energy, wine presses or the lapse of time. Moreover He healed the sick, usually without the use of any physical means or even examination, in an instant by the word of His command. Such actions are classed as miraculous because the physical laws ("what things normally do") have been by-passed. However, Christ's miracles were never contradictions of natural laws but demonstrations to those who had eyes to see that among other things He, Jesus Christ, had made the laws.

All Christ's miracles were demonstrations of God's normal, continuing activity — healing, feeding, raising to life, etc.

3. *Faith Healing:* The neo-Pentecostal view is that healing is a gift of the Spirit (1 Cor 12:9) and a ministry of the Church. Furthermore to exercise it is a command of Christ (Mark 16:18; Luke 9:1, 2; 10:1-9). This is carried out after the fashion of the New Testament practice: by prayer, the exercise of faith and the laying on of hands.

Such questions arise as:

Does scripture authorise or command present-day Christians to exercise a Spirit-given ability to heal, apart from medical means?

What is the rightful expectancy of the Christian who is sick?

In what follows, there is unanimity in some points and divergence in others. The various views are set out and argued in the hope that, by seeing the issues more clearly, the reader will be helped not only to a better understanding but to a more satisfying acceptance of his duties, his rights and his expectancies in these vital personal matters.

B. *The Position Outlined: A Statement of Points of Agreement and Disagreement Between Neo-Pentecostals and Non Neo-Pentecostals*

As stated above, all healing is of God, as Colossians 1:15-17 shows that what we describe as a "natural law" is a law which God has brought into being and which He maintains. While the neo-Pentecostal recognises that healing resulting from medical practice is a consequence of the healing laws of God he also recognises that such healing is not often ascribed to God, either by the practitioner or the patient; indeed as medical practice is not generally performed in the name of the Lord Jesus, but rather as a consequence of man's scientific progress, its success is generally ascribed to that progress. Thus he believes that healing which results from the "prayer of faith" (James 5:15) and which is done in the name of the Lord Jesus Christ (e.g. Acts 3:16) is more likely to direct attention to God for His glory and to establish the reality and power of the name of Jesus Christ.

It is agreed that much medical practice neglects this concern for God's glory, and we would encourage Christian doctors, when appropriate, to testify to the working of God. It behoves all Christians to thank and praise God for all His benefits whether they come by prayer or by medical and scientific means.

It is also agreed that God is not honoured by inaccurate or exaggerated testimony. Therefore any person claiming healing through the prayer of faith should recognise that such a claim must be able to be substantiated over a period of time. In this respect care must be taken to recognise that the relief of symptoms may not indicate a cure of illness; likewise (in the neo-Pentecostal opinion), their continuation may not indicate a lack of healing. Symptoms are often so involved with the psychological state of a person as well as with the sickness that unless they are observed over time they may be unreliable indicators of either healing or the lack of it.

HEALING IN THE MINISTRY OF CHRIST

All are agreed on the eternal power and greatness of God and that the healings performed by Christ had the following purposes: to be (i) seals of His divinity; (ii) revelations of His nature (compassion, love, power); (iii) proofs that He was the Creator-God. The neo-Pentecostal would add (iv) revelations of the on-going will of God in terms of healing.

The neo-Pentecostal would maintain that Isaiah 53 makes certain propositions about the essential ministry of the Messiah, which will result from His atonement. Matthew 8:17 specifically defines a part of that atoning ministry to be healing. Matthew 8:17 is a stated exemplar of the Isaiah 53:4 promise, and part of the fulfilment of that promise.

The non neo-Pentecostal would maintain that Matthew 8:17 (cf. Isaiah 53:4) refers, both by its context and its etymology, to the compassionate healing ministry of Jesus the Messiah when He was on earth carrying illness by His identification with mankind in pain and suffering. Part of the atoning work of Christ is to take away all aspects of the Fall. The non neo-Pentecostal sees this as an eschatological reality, whereas the neo-Pentecostal sees it as a present reality.

Both Sides to the Question

HEALING IN NEW TESTAMENT TIMES

It is agreed that the healing ministry and all signs and wonders showed a transfer of the authority of Christ to the Church of New Testament times. John 14:12 expresses this and shows that the Father was doing His works, and in so doing was establishing Christ's authority. This is paralleled in John 14:10, 11. "Works" is by no means restricted to healings, but what "greater" means is ambiguous, i.e. (a) similar works but greater in degree, or (b) similar works but greater in extent, or (c) a different kind of work which is greater, e.g. John 11:25, 26, the proclamation of the gospel, etc. Healing authenticated the ministry of the apostles and showed a continuity with the ministry of Jesus. At the same time there were occasions (e.g. Paul, Timothy, Trophimus) when the gift of healing was either not invoked or was not successful. It is agreed that the following points can be demonstrated from the New Testament and are normative today: (i) There are times when God allows problems including sickness; (ii) God is able to remove all problems and all illness. Christians can pray with confidence in God's absolute power to alleviate all problems and sickness, but with a recognition that; (iii) God will work in a Christian's life through the existence of, and perhaps the continuance of, problems and illness to bring the fruit of spiritual grace and sanctity.

If these points are understood and explained they will do much to minimise and overcome possible pastoral problems associated with the apparent failure of prayer for healing. To these three points some would add: (iv) In the event that it was not God's will to heal, a Christian could expect this to be revealed by God the Holy Spirit. This thought is derived from 2 Corinthians 12.

HEALING TODAY

It is commonplace to find the instinct for survival expressed in prayer for recovery in the face of illness. It is a Christian duty to pray for the sick; this is consistent with Christ's command to love and to show compassion. The Scriptures exhort suffering Christians to pray and this includes prayer with a view to recovery from illness, e.g. 2 Corinthians 12, James 5.

There seem to be three lines of thought on the subject of a Christian's attitude towards, and expectation concerning, his illness. These are: (a) That every Christian has a right to healing, and if he is not healed it is because he has not fulfilled the conditions for healing. (b) That every Christian should approach God with a positive attitude and hope, and can expect that if God does not heal He will reveal His better will in the matter. (c) That every Christian should submit with fatalistic resignation rather like the Islamic "It is the will of Allah".

It is agreed that of these three the second, "b", is the most scriptural.

God may well use medical practice as an aid and means to healing. The neo-Pentecostal would not believe that medical practice fulfils completely either the 1 Cor 12:9, 28-30 and James 5:14, 15 promises for healing, although it may be a means of fulfilling them, since neither promise is subject to the intellectual development of men on which medical science depends. All Christian doctors would agree that by both prayer and medical help illness is fully treated, as man is a complex being and his spirit and emotions play a major part in his physical health or illness. The link between physical health and spiritual obedience is seen in James 5 where there is an intermingling and association of sin and sickness such as is found in the Old Testament.

The Christian who is ill should commit the matter to God in prayer, alone or in fellowship with others. At the same time he must recognise the existence of physical means which may alleviate or heal his illness and which are available for his use. Failure to use such means may be quite irresponsible, to say the least, because God may use such means to answer prayer for healing. However we also recognise that there is today an overdependence on drugs which afford symptomatic relief, and at the same time a neglect of coming to grips with the cause of problems.

There would be considerable division of opinion as to the effectiveness of "miraculous healing" today. Any approach to healing must be made in the light of the fact that sooner or later death claims all men, and through death Christians experience the victory of Christ (1 Cor 15).

This matter is of such major importance that there are included two papers which set forth in considerable detail two different approaches to healing.

C. *The Neo-Pentecostal View*

SYNOPSIS

1. Why Did Christ Heal?
2. The Healing Ministry of the Disciples
3. The Gift of Healings and James 5:14, 15

4. Three Common Objectives: (a) Paul's Thorn, etc., (b) The Will of God, (c) The Value of Suffering
5. The Prayer of Faith
6. Whose Responsibility is it to exercise Faith?
7. Progressive Healing
8. "Where there is no Vision . . ."
9. Summary

1. WHY DID CHRIST HEAL?

The Gospels record twenty-six cases of individual healings performed by Christ, and ten cases of multiple healings, ranging from "a few" to a "great multitude"! It was said of Him that He went about "healing all manner of sickness and all manner of disease among the people" (Matthew 4:23); and also that He healed "all that were oppressed of the devil" (Acts 10:38). There may be point in saying that this was intimately associated with doing the work of God.

Jesus came, not to do His own will, but the will of Him that sent Him (John 6:38). He declares that "My meat is to do the will of Him that sent Me, and to finish His work" (John 4:34). In the case of the healing of the man born blind, He specifies that: "I must work the works of Him that sent Me" (John 9:4). If we accept this witness of the Lord Himself, we cannot doubt that He regarded all His acts of healing as willed by God. They were also a sign of His compassion (Mark 1:41, etc.), for Jesus always took upon Himself the burden of those He came to save.

He often used those manifestations of power to draw attention to Himself and His work of redemption. This is illustrated in the account of the paralytic brought to Him by his friends (Mark 2:1-12). Before healing him He tells him his sins are forgiven. To the protests accusing Him of blasphemy, He replies that the healing miracle He is about to perform is the proof of His power to forgive sins, confirming that He is the Son of Man, the long-awaited Messiah.

There are occasions when He used sickness and healing to glorify God. Speaking of the man born blind, He declares that: "Neither hath this man sinned, nor his parents, but that the works of God should be made manifest in Him" (John 9:3). In the case of Lazarus He clearly says: "This sickness is not unto death, but for the glory of God, that the Son of God might be glorified thereby" (John 11:4).

It must also be noted that when people came to Christ for

healing, more often than not, He responds without any comment about spiritual things. Even when He emphasises the spiritual work of redemption, it is never with the object of minimising the importance of physical healing.

FAITH IN CHRIST FOR HEALING

A study of the healings show that a unifying theme is that He asked the sick to have faith that He would heal.

"Two blind men followed Jesus crying: Thou son of David, have mercy on us! And Jesus saith unto them: Believe ye that I am able to do this? They said unto Him: Yea, Lord. Then touched He their eyes, saying: According to your faith, be it unto you. And their eyes were opened" (Matthew 9:27-31).

Further examples are found in the case of the centurion of Capernaum (Matthew 8:5-13) when Jesus marvels at finding such faith, and in that of the resuscitation of Jairus' daughter (Matthew 9:18-26). These and many other cases show that one of the essential elements in the acts of healing performed by Christ was faith in Him to heal.

THE DYNAMIC OF HEALING

We have already seen that Christ healed to fulfil God's will. He healed because of compassion. He healed to demonstrate His power to forgive sins. He healed to confirm His Messiahship. He healed to give glory to God. He healed in response to faith.

More has to be said. The Gospels give plenty of evidence that for Jesus sickness is the work of Satan. This could be thought of as a "devil" and/or the work of Satan in what might be called a generic sense. ". . . the devil sinneth from the beginning. For this purpose the son of God was manifested, that He might destroy the works of the devil" (1 John 3:8). This could be as with the Gadarene demoniac (Luke 8:26-36) who "had devils a long time", or as with "one possessed with a devil, blind and dumb" (Matthew 12:22-30). Whether it was "devil possession sickness" or physical sickness in general, it was looked upon as being of Satan.

When the Pharisees accused Him of casting out devils ("one possessed with a devil, blind and dumb") by Beelzebub, the prince of the devils, He answered them by saying that it is impossible to cast out Satan by Satan; for then Satan would be divided against himself, and his kingdom would not stand.

Both Sides to the Question

Healing is therefore acting on behalf of God "that He might destroy the works of the devil".

The positive corollary of destroying the works of the devil, is the coming of the Kingdom of God. Healing the sick and the Kingdom of God are intimately and essentially related. Our Lord revealed that the Kingdom was both future and present. With regard to the former He said: "My Kingdom is not of this world" (John 18:36). The Kingdom is a heavenly or spiritual reality, and shall not be experienced in perfection until "the Kingdoms of this world are become the Kingdoms of our Lord and of His Christ" (Rev 11:15).

Jesus also affirmed that the Kingdom has already been established and was making progress during His earthly ministry and that it was destined to make progress, not by apocalyptic interference, but, as the grain grows — "first the blade then the ear, after that the full corn in the ear" (Mark 4:26-32). "Unto what is the Kingdom of God like?" He asked. "It is like a grain of mustard seed, which a man took, and cast into his garden; and it grew, and waxed a great tree" (Luke 13:18-21). The most remarkable of these statements is in Luke 17:20. "And being asked of the Pharisees, when the Kingdom of God cometh, He answered them and said, the Kingdom of God cometh not with observation; . . . the Kingdom of God is within you".

When it came to healing He said: "If I cast out devils by the Spirit of God, then the Kingdom of God is come unto you" (Matthew 12:28). This is the inner dynamic of what happened when Christ healed: the work of Satan was destroyed, the Kingdom of God came. Christ stressed the availability and dependability of the Kingdom by saying: "Fear not little flock, for it is your Father's good pleasure to give you the Kingdom" (Luke 12:32).

One thing is patent: the Kingdom did not have to be present in the way it will be at the end of the age, for Christ (and the disciples alike) to heal in a dependable and convincing way. Therefore it cannot be said that the Kingdom has to be present in that "future" sense for the same healing ministry to be exercised now. The Kingdom is here and growing, and we have every reason therefore to expect the signs of the Kingdom: the first-fruits of that which is to come. This does not preclude a future coming of the Kingdom with power at the time of the Second Advent, but it underlines the point that we do not have to wait for the final inauguration of the Kingdom. In that day healing will not be needed, for that which requires healing will have passed away.

A study of our Lord's healing ministry shows that, for Him, the needs of physical life and well being are worthy of His concern, as well as the spiritual needs of the soul.

A number of reasons are given as to why our Lord healed. They are all important and relevant. Together they make up the total reason. There is a repeated emphasis on the need for faith for healing, as there is on casting out Satan and the coming of the Kingdom of God.

2. THE HEALING MINISTRY OF THE DISCIPLES

Our Lord did not look upon His healing ministry as being unique to Himself. He committed the same ministry to His followers. The instruction and promise to Christ to this effect is found five times in the Gospels (Matthew 10:7-8; Mark 6:7; 16:17, 18; Luke 9:1, 2; 10:8, 9).

He gave the twelve "power against unclean spirits to cast them out and to heal all manner of sickness and all manner of disease" (Matthew 10:1). The same call and commission is given to the wider and more general circle of the seventy disciples. "Into whatsoever city ye enter, and they receive you . . . heal the sick that are therein, and say unto them, the Kingdom of God is come nigh unto you" (Luke 10:8, 9). A comparative study of the commission to the twelve and the commission to the seventy is valuable, because it shows them to be essentially the same: Matthew 10:1-16; Mark 6:7 — The Twelve; Luke 10:1-20 — The Seventy.

This means that all the disciples of the Lord are instructed to act in the same way, and in the same way as did the Lord Himself.

They knew that to heal the sick was something they had a personal responsibility to discharge. It was done by faith and in the Name of Christ. It was linked, as it was with Christ, with the commission to preach repentance and the advent of the Kingdom (Luke 9:1, 6). Evangelism and healing are to go hand in hand. Healing was to be as normal as the preaching of the Word. They were spoken of and practised together. He never sent His followers out to preach but that He also sent them out to heal.

In the Acts of the Apostles, cases of individual healing are mentioned nine times, and multiple healings are specifically referred to on four occasions, five probably, seven possibly. Acts 3:1-16; 9:10-19; 9:32-35; 9:36-42; 14:8-10; 16:16-18; 20:7-12; 28:3-6; 28:8. The multiple healings are recorded in Chapters 2:43; 5:12-16; 6:8; 8:5-8; 14:3; 19:8-12; 28:9.

Although the Deacons were not commissioned as such to preach and heal, Philip and Stephen had an extensive ministry in these areas, not less in its content and effect than the Apostles. It could be said from this that no specific commission to preach and heal was necessary in the early Church. Either that, or the commission to the general group of the seventy disciples was understood as a general commission to all disciples, or the commission in Mark 16:17, 18 was authentic and acted on.

It may be important to note that the Apostles disown the idea that this is something personal to them as Apostles. They act on behalf of Christ; they heal "in the Name of Jesus of Nazareth". After the healing of the paralytic at the Beautiful Gate, Peter declares that there is no reason why they should marvel at such a miracle "as though by our own power or holiness we had made this man to walk". He diverts all attention from himself as the instrument and directs it exclusively to Him who is the author of the manifestation. "It is through faith in His Name (Jesus Christ) that His Name hath made this man strong, whom ye see and know; . . ." Peter had said: "In the Name of Jesus of Nazareth, rise up and walk" (3:1-16). See also Paul at Lystra (14:8-18).

One can only marvel at the simple affirmation of Peter to Aeneas, the paralytic (9:32-35). "Aeneas, Jesus Christ maketh thee whole". If we are reliant on the Scriptures for the explanation we can but only refer to the command and commission of Christ, and the strength of the faith of the Apostles and Deacons that, as they stretched forth their hands in the Name of Christ to heal, God would raise up the sick man. They felt at liberty to affirm that healing would result from faith; either their faith or the faith of the one who was sick. (See 14:8-10 for the latter.)

This enumeration is sufficient to show that the infant Church practised the Healing Ministry in a wide and ongoing variety of circumstances. The problems that people today raise were no problem to them. Divine Healing was a living reality which was never in doubt. This is further confirmed by the concluding part of Mark's Gospel, which if not genuine, is very early, and demonstrates what was the understanding and practice in the early Church. Note how Mark 16:17, 18 echoes our Lord's ongoing commission to the seventy disciples (Luke 10:17-19).

3. THE GIFT OF HEALINGS
The only reasonable and logical way to interpret what is meant by the Gift of Healings in 1 Corinthians Chapter 12 is that they are what is otherwise and invariably understood by healing in the New Testament. That is, it is supernatural healing. Paul says the gifts are "the manifestation of the Spirit" (1 Corinthians 12:7).

JAMES 5:14, 15
The passage in James 5:14, 15 sets out in a Church-orientated way what has been previously set out in terms of an itinerant preacher/healer ministry. As such it furnishes special insights for the Church's ministry of healing. It is a valuable confirmation of what has been previously recorded in the New Testament, and plainly shows that the established and local church was expected to heal as well as preach.

"Is any among you sick, let him call the elders of the Church, and let them pray over him, anointing him with oil in the Name of the Lord; and the prayer of faith shall save the sick, and the Lord shall raise him up; and if he has committed sins, they shall be forgiven him".

In response to the sick person calling the elders of the Church, they are to anoint him and pray the prayer of faith. This prayer of faith will make operative three promises: the sick person shall be saved, the Lord shall raise him up, and he shall be forgiven his sins. It is plain that, while the presenting circumstances are to do with sickness, and there is the obvious need to do something effective about them, the provision and response of God covers the whole range of salvation. The sick person will be saved, healed and forgiven.

It shows how truly evangelistic the healing ministry of the Church is. It begins at the person's point of felt need and leads on to the deep and eternal things of the faith. Where this is acted out with that understanding, that is exactly what happens.

SUMMARY, SO FAR
The promise and provision of James 5:14, 15 is entirely consistent with all that has gone before. It is not in any way an isolated text.

It is difficult to see how much more consistent the revelation of divine healing could be. It is explained in much detail by the Lord Himself in the Gospels, and in a wholly consistent way. The commission to heal in the same way is given to the twelve and the seventy. The Deacons were not commissioned as such to preach and heal, but two of them have an outstanding ministry in these areas. This suggests there was a general commission, or a commission was not necessary. Paul states there is the gift of healings, and James sets it out in pastoral terms for the ongoing Church, linking it intimately with salvation.

4. THREE COMMON OBJECTIONS

A. PAUL'S THORN

This is often brought up to discount belief in the dependability of healing in response to faith. It is said that only one exception has to be found for a rule to be no longer a rule.

We do not accept this view. If there are exceptions to God's will, they *are* exceptions and the *rule* generally stands — to argue from the apparent exceptions to a *denial* of the rule is quite illogical and unfounded! In other disciplines, e.g. physics, "the exception *proves* (or illustrates) the rule". The exception does not invalidate the rule. We affirm that we could accept that Paul's thorn is an exception, and for that fact to not affect the general rule of healing at all. The rule is James 5:15 and the otherwise unanimous revelation in the New Testament.

From the content of 2 Corinthians 11:21 to 12:10, it cannot be said in a definitive way that Paul's thorn was a physical infirmity. If there is a lack of certainty that his thorn was a physical infirmity, then it cannot be affirmed with certainty that it is an exception. It can only be prejudice that enables someone to use an uncertain exception to set aside the otherwise unanimous testimony of the New Testament.

The circumstances which led Paul to be visited with this thorn have a uniqueness about them that makes it most difficult to apply them in a general way. It is implied that it was Paul who was caught up into the third heaven and heard unspeakable words. He went on: "Lest I should be exalted above measure through the abundance of the revelations, there was given to me a thorn in the flesh" (2 Cor 12:7). We might reasonably see a connection between "the abundance of the revelations" and the content of his letters. We do not remotely correspond to these circumstances.

It is true, of course, that we need to be made weak so that we are strong in dependence on God. But if the thorn was not a sickness, then it is irrelevant to the issue of healing. If it was a sickness, there is no New Testament authority for saying that that reason alone would prevent or qualify healing. (See Value of Suffering.)

When Paul's thorn is seen in its full perspective, we believe it cannot reasonably be used to weaken the rule of healing as revealed by Christ. It is an exception that is uncertain and has an application that is questionable — to use such an exception to deny the Dominical rule is, in our view, to take up an untenable position.

Having said this meaningfully, we would go on and say that we would accept that it is possible for a "messenger of Satan" in the form of sickness to be not removed by God, PROVIDED that that fact was revealed by God. And PROVIDED that up to that point, the prayer of faith was acted on in full expectancy of healing. As a general working rule, we believe it is His rule to heal. However, if there are exceptions to God's general will, they *are* exceptions and the *rule* generally stands.

EPAPHRODITUS, TROPHIMUS, TIMOTHY

That these three disciples were sick at the time of writing is urged as a reason for thinking that it may not be God's will to heal. If it were God's will to heal, surely Paul would have stretched forth his hands to heal.

As a possible explanation of the matter, we would refer to another occasion when the "disciples" (the twelve and the seventy) had actually attempted to heal someone and had failed, and the Lord had stated that it was their unbelief that was the hindrance (Matthew 17:14-21). When this was made good by His own perfect faith, the person concerned was immediately healed. He explained that this was a deeper problem which needed sacrificial prayer.

We are only concerned to show that these sick people cannot reasonably be used to make a deduction that healing is *not* available in response to faith. We do not have to prove from the incidents that healing *is* available.

When Paul's thorn and Epaphroditus, etc., are no longer urged in this way, there is nothing in the New Testament that qualifies the rule and practice of healing. In as far as it is still seriously

Both Sides to the Question

maintained that they are exceptions, we maintain, equally
seriously, the general rule is the otherwise unanimous testimony
of the New Testament.

It is frequently said that we do not know the will of God,
therefore we cannot pray with faith that does not doubt that God
will answer our prayer. We must conclude our prayer with the
proviso: "if it be Thy will".

That we have to pray according to God's will for our prayer to
be answered, we are agreed. That there are times when we do not
know God's will, again we are agreed. But there are many
matters in which we do know God's will, because it is revealed to
us in the Bible. His will for us is contained in the "great and
precious promises" (2 Peter 1:4). We search the Scriptures to
ascertain what are the promises He has chosen to make. Once
determined, we appropriate them by the prayer of faith.

One writer has recently said: "There are magnificent promises
in Scripture to do with prayer," and then refers to James 5:14, 15
as an illustration. He continues: "These are encouragements to
faith in God, for this is a necessity in prayer. But of course we
must realise that God does not give us the things which are
contrary to His will . . ."

The view that "there are magnificent promises in Scripture to
do with prayer", but that it may not be God's will for us to have
them in reality, is to our mind, a contradiction in terms. We are
"partakers of His promise in Christ by the Gospel" (Ephesians
3:6). "All the promises of God in Him are yea, and in Him,
Amen" (2 Cor 1:20). "Concerning the work of my hands,
command ye me" (Isaiah 45:11). If God's will and provision is
conveyed to us in one promise, it is conveyed in every promise. If
we are to appropriate one promise by faith, we are to appropriate
every promise by faith. We are not referring, of course, to
promises that expressly belong to the future, e.g. John 6:54.

We have already referred to James 5:14, 15 where there is a *very
clear promise of healing*, and shown that this is part of a wholly
consistent revelation by God in the New Testament on this
matter.

C. THE VALUE OF SUFFERING

It is rightly said that there is value in suffering. St. Paul expresses
his theology of suffering in 2 Corinthians 1:8, 9: "We would not,

brethren, have you ignorant of our trouble which came to us in Asia, that we were pressed out of measure, above strength, insomuch that we despaired even of life: but we had the sentence of death in ourselves, that we should not trust in ourselves, but in God which raiseth the dead."

Paul's difficulties brought him to "the end of his tether" (Phillips) so that he would be enabled thereby to trust not in his self-resourceful nature, but wholly in God, and what God does. In the context of his thorn, God said to him: "My strength is made perfect in weakness." Paul immediately sees the value of suffering and almost heaps it on himself, that he might have God's power. "Most gladly, therefore, will I rather glory in my infirmities, that the power of Christ may rest upon me. Therefore I take pleasure in infirmities, in reproaches, in necessities, in persecutions, in distresses for Christ's sake; for when I am weak, then I am strong" (2 Cor 12:9, 10).

It is significant that the "infirmities" he has been writing about in this passage are very different from "sickness". (The word "infirmities" in 2 Cor 12:9, 10 is the same word in the Greek which in James 5:14 is translated "sick". The word is translated in various ways, and the context has to be used to give the meaning. Context is always the final arbiter for meaning.) Suffering is more than sickness. Jesus suffered but He was not sick. We question whether "suffering" in the New Testament is ever used to mean "sickness" but rather "for being a Christian". Where in the New Testament is sickness shown to be suffering which is beneficial?

If anyone wishes to say that our experience shows that there is a value in sickness, our reply is that there was the same value in sickness to all who were ministered to in the Scripture narratives, and it was never so much as referred to. Nowhere did it limit the availability of healing.

There is a value in suffering and tribulation, and its importance cannot be overstressed. Nowhere does the New Testament speak about sickness in the same way.

Our view is that these objections are not sustained. They have been brought out for so long and so often that it has been assumed they are valid. We believe that our examination of them shows them to be weak and misleading. We adopt them with alacrity because they seem to be valid, and perhaps without realising it, because they excuse us from involvement in something that we don't want to face up to. If this is too strong, there is no offence intended.

Both Sides to the Question

5. THE PRAYER OF FAITH

It will be generally agreed that the Kingdom of God is a present and growing reality, and that healing is a demonstration of its reality. (See section — The Dynamic of Healing.) It is agreed that *not* all the benefits of the Kingdom are available now. The question is: is healing one of the benefits available to us at the present time? There would be agreement that it is consistent with God's character that He heals at the present time; there would be disagreement as to whether or not there is an unqualified promise for healing. (This is the question raised by Paul's thorn.) This is not a criticism of healing as such. It is a question of prayer method. How does one pray?

It says in James 5:15 that it is "the prayer of faith" that enables the Lord to "raise up" the sick person. Our Lord used His cursing of the fig tree to illustrate what He meant by faith in prayer. "Verily I say unto you, that whosoever shall say unto this mountain, Be thou removed, and be thou cast into the sea; and shall not doubt in his heart, but shall believe that those things which he saith shall come to pass; he shall have whatsoever he saith. Therefore I say unto you, what things soever ye desire, when ye pray, believe that ye receive them, and ye shall have them" (Mark 11:20-26).

For prayer to be answered, it is required by God that we believe we receive these things, so that we do not doubt in our heart. To conclude a prayer with a proviso — "if it be Thy will", expresses doubt straight away. Whatever reasons are advanced for concluding prayer in this way, they are wrongly applied if they invalidate faith as God requires it to be exercised.

Healing in the New Testament was always prayed for with complete assurance that it was going to eventuate, however serious was the sickness or incapacity. It was never associated with the proviso "if it be Thy will"! Our Lord's statement: "not my will, but Thine be done" is, with respect, irrelevant, as it concerns suffering, not sickness.

Those who say that doctrine is only deduced from the Epistles and not from narrative are flatly contradicted by the Epistle statement: "all scripture . . . (is) profitable for doctrine" (2 Tim 3:16). This cannot mean less than that narrative is doctrine in practice. On the above question, narrative explains the doctrine of how to pray for healing in a conclusive way.

The questions that arise from advancing age, the possibility of God permitting "a messenger of Satan" to remain, the fact of death, were just as real in the New Testament Church. But they did not affect the sureness with which they prayed. They did not try and make a synthesis between them. The negative did not compromise the positive. The Kingdom of God was the operative dimension.

It must be emphasised that when one prays in faith, discernment is given by the Spirit as to how to pray and minister appropriately. The difficulties that are seen in theory are usually not difficulties in practice. If one acts in faith, God guides and overrules.

6. WHOSE RESPONSIBILITY IS IT TO EXERCISE FAITH?

There is no general rule. Faith is to be exercised by those who can have faith. Scriptural illustrations show that it can be exercised by the sick person, by those acting on their behalf, or those ministering to them. There is good reason for requiring the sick person or those acting for them to have faith enough "to call" others to pray for them, for unbelief in those being ministered to can render impotent even perfect faith in those who pray from the outside. (See Matthew 13:58.) On the pastoral level, it is recognised that often pain and anxiety prevent the sick person from having faith, and it only makes the situation worse to ask them to do what they are unable to do. In such a situation, provided the sick person, or those acting on their behalf, want prayer for healing, those who pray for the sick are responsible for the exercise of faith.

When these scriptural principles are acted out, there are no pastoral problems in exercising a healing ministry. In practice it is found that the Spirit who quickens our mortal body, also quickens our spirit, so that irrespective of what happens on the physical level, the person concerned always draws upon a spiritual blessing that transforms circumstances and transcends this life.

7. PROGRESSIVE HEALING

Though healing may be immediate, the progressive nature of healing should also be noted. Healing is part of the greater reality called the Kingdom of God. "Heal the sick, and say, the Kingdom of God is come nigh unto you" (Luke 10:8, 9). "The Kingdom of God is like a grain of mustard seed, which, when it is sown in the earth, is less than all the seeds that be in the earth; but when it is sown, it groweth up and becometh greater than all herbs, and

Both Sides to the Question

shooteth out great branches . . ." (Luke 4:30-32). ". . . first the blade, then the ear, after that the full corn in the ear" (Mark 4:28). See also the blind man at Bethsaida (Mark 8:22-26).

Much healing that is drawn on today has this progressive character about it. It will be appreciated that this is often what makes it difficult to testify in a convincing way. Often the mountain is big and faith is small. Where the progressive aspect is understood, and "time is on our side", there is no limit to what can be accomplished. The progressive answer to prayer is understood and accepted in other areas of prayer, and it is accepted as being none the less answered prayer because of it. Compare conversion.

8. "WHERE THERE IS NO VISION . . ."

Much is made of the lack of experiential reality of healing in response to faith, or that what healing there is, is not in New Testament terms — immediate, complete, lasting. Because these things are not in common evidence, it means, it is said, as a probability, that God does not intend them for us.

One thing is sure; there is a lack of consistency in approach. The same brethren who will not allow experiential testimony in the area of "baptism in the Spirit", require it when it comes to "healing". In the first area we are told: it does not matter if it works, the question is: Is it true? In the latter area: if you can't demonstrate it, it is not for today.

Prejudice is not unknown in the "Queen of Sciences"!

Dr. Evelyn Frost, in her book "Christian Healing" p. 50, says that "the temperature of the spiritual life of the Church was the index of her power to heal. As far as the ante-Nicene Church is concerned, the history of her spiritual life is one of decline from the high peaks of the apostolic days to the lower spiritual level at which controversy, apostasy and heresy were formidable weakening factors in her life. Side by side with this growing weakness can be seen a decline in the power of healing."

Once other factors are introduced, it throws the matter open in a new way. The Gifts of the Spirit, including healing, are "manifestations of the Spirit". We are in the greatest need (as Bishop Howe said in his sermon at the opening service of General Synod) to know what are the factors that will enable the Holy Spirit to be stirred up or released in our contemporary situation. This is an historical study (see Frost) as well as a scriptural one.

That the supernatural Gifts of the Spirit, including healing, are not in *common* evidence, we agree. It is our conviction that the main single reason for the lack of these ministries today in New Testament reality is that the Body of Christ as a whole does not believe in them. Our teachers de-bunk them. If our teaching and practice about conversion were the same as it is for healing, there would be very few converted! As it is, there are few converted, and nothing like what we see described in the New Testament. But no one suggests that what little does happen is invalid because of that. We rejoice for what blessing there is, re-examine our position, and "move in for action".

6. SUMMARY

We have suggested that the reason why Christ healed was multifactored. Some factors were personal to Christ; other factors, such as the expression and demonstrations of the Kingdom, are common to all Christians. Apart from the factors that were personal to Him, it is plain that He did not think of the Healing Ministry as unique to Himself. The same ministry is expressly committed to the twelve and the seventy. There is no Scriptural statement that the ministry was unique to the twelve and the seventy. On the contrary, the ministry of Philip and Stephen shows that it was normal for any Christian to both preach and heal, and for that ministry to come not behind the Apostles in its effect. The Church-orientated statement of James shows that this ministry was intended to be exercised by the local church as well as by the individual Christian.

The only requirement was faith that Christ would heal. "Only believe," He said. When the Apostles failed to heal, He said it was because of "unbelief". He added that this particular sickness required deeper prayer, if healing were to be effected. At no time did Christ or the disciples say that it was not God's will to heal.

The objections to the dependability of healing that come from Paul's thorn are not well founded and cannot reasonably be urged when the otherwise unanimous testimony of the New Testament is taken into account.

There is value in suffering, but we are not convinced that the New Testament description of suffering includes sickness. If there is value in sickness, this could rightly have been urged upon the innumerable people who were ministered to in the Scripture narrative. But with no one did this limit the availability of healing in response to faith.

Faith is to be exercised by those who can have faith. Assuming

Both Sides to the Question

the sick person asks for prayer, it is then the responsibility of "the elders" to pray the prayer of faith.

The assumption that healing, etc., is not intended for today because it is not seen as it is described in the New Testament, cannot be urged in an exclusive way if there are other possible explanations. We have advanced Dr. Frost's claim as the true explanation.

In brief, we affirm that healing in response to faith is as available today as it was in the primitive Church. The Kingdom of God is available to us in the same way it was available to them. If there were no evidence of healing today (and this is certainly not the case) we believe this would not affect the issue. Failure is testimony, not that God has changed, but that we lack vision, unity and faith.

D. The Non Neo-Pentecostal Point of View

SYNOPSIS

1. The Old Testament
2. The Gospels
3. The Acts of the Apostles
4. The Epistles
5. Faith Healing Today: The Case for and against
6. Conclusion

1. THE OLD TESTAMENT

Texts such as Exodus 4:10, 11 place God as the creator of life, the curer of illness where it is His will and the creator of illness where it is His will. There is no Old Testament support for the popular thesis that "God doesn't want anyone to be sick." This is based on sentiment and the doctrine of divine "kindness" rather than "love". This teaching is not confined to the Old Testament as verses such as John 9:1-3 and Heb 12:5-11 carry it through the New.

One characteristic of Old Testament teaching is the interchangeability of the terms used between physical healing on the one hand and salvation from sins on the other. Psalm 41:3, 4 illustrates this. In verse 3 the words used are equally translated "thou HEALEST all his infirmities" (R.S.V.) and "thou CHANGEST all his bed" (R.S.V. Margin) and in verse 4 "HEAL me, for I have SINNED against thee". This ambiguity exists throughout the Old Testament and exists in the James' epistle reference to healing (5:14, 15).

One example of the latter is the translation of "astheneo" as "sick" in James 5:14, which the neo-Pentecostal uses as an unqualified promise of healing, while he refuses to translate it in 2 Cor 12:9 as though it were a physical sickness, but rather as a "weakness".

2. THE GOSPELS

The role of healing in the life and ministry of Christ was chiefly that of a seal upon the unique nature of His person (John 14:11). Matthew also stated this in Matt 8:17: This was to fulfil what was spoken by the prophet of Isaiah (53:4), "He took our infirmities and bore our diseases." The first word "this", refers to the miracles of healing which precede the passage and are taken traditionally as a reference to His life, which by His miracles, testified to His divinity and messianic office. To understand this one must look at the healing acts themselves.

It was said above that no doctor today has any power inherent or acquired whereby he may *cause* tissues to heal. The opposite must be said of Christ. By His command, cripples who had been confined to a stretcher for years and whose muscles would have undergone atrophy by disuse, quite apart from the disease itself, stood immediately, often leaping and carrying away the bed that had borne them in. Similarly the blind saw, the deaf heard and the dead arose. Lazarus was the supreme illustration of Christ's "healing" role. Having waited four days, during which Lazarus suffered and died, Jesus called upon a dead man to walk out of a tomb from which (as his sister Martha no doubt correctly predicted) there erupted the stench of death. This miracle carries a fourfold significance. Firstly, in Christ's view it is the final not the immediate state that matters most. This is amplified by His words to Martha in John 11:25, 26. Secondly, the glory of God is only achieved by the will and way of God. Thirdly, Christ's miracles were those of "creation" rather than "healing" and finally, God is seen to be a *loving God*, not a *kind God*. Lazarus' death is a clear-cut example of God's will intending death rather than healing, in a particular case, in order to introduce a blessing unforeseen by those who sought healing (John 11:25, 26).

Reference must be made to the neo-Pentecostal claim that by linking Matt 8:17 with 1 Peter 2:24 "He Himself bore our sins in His body on the tree", our sicknesses and infirmities were borne upon the cross and can henceforth be considered finished with, as can our sins. Matthew uses the word "bastaso" meaning to bear as a burden as in Romans 15:1. The word in 1 Peter is "anaphero" and is translated in the R.S.V. Margin: "He Himself *carried up our sins* in His body *to* the tree." The former signifies compassion and identification; the latter signifies the making of a sacrifice. The non neo-Pentecostal would not only separate the two functions of Christ expressed in these verses, and thus deny the neo-Pentecostal claim. He would further state that by making the claim, the neo-Pentecostal position changes the content of the gospel. (Cf. C. G. Scorer, "Contemporary Thought on Healing in the Light of the New Testament" pp. 10–12.)

If it is claimed that by faith in the crucified Christ we obtain forgiveness of our sins AND healing of our sicknesses and infirmities, how then can the penitent who remains sick be assured of forgiveness? What assurance can be given to him on his death bed?

The miracle of Mark 2:1-12 loses its significance if it is only seen as Jesus drawing attention to Himself, as Messiah. It is, as the scribes rightly observed in v. 7, a claim to be God. While other roles were played by His healing such as to reveal His nature of compassion, love and power, it pre-eminently served to prove that He was the Creator-God. Indeed the latter fact was so stamped upon the apostles that when two of them wrote of Christ later, both John and Paul spoke not of a Healer, nor of a Great Physician, but of a Creator-God. John 1 and Colossians 1 are relevant summaries of the apostolic view of Christ.

Neo-Pentecostals also claim that the same power as was shown by Christ in the New Testament records is available to us today on the basis of verses such as Heb 13:8, "Jesus Christ the same yesterday, today and forever." To this the non neo-Pentecostal replies that this verse refers to the nature of Christ, not to His activities or will. The theology of a "God who changes not" is held by all Christians, but to translate this to His activity in general or to His will in any particular case many would claim is to go beyond the limits of scripture. God has not contradicted Himself if the healing miracles of the Gospels have been discontinued today.

The characteristics of Christ's healings are seen as being INSTANT, UNFAILING, and UNLIMITED. But there is one characteristic of Christ's healing that He shared with that of the apostles' healing and with ours today, whether by orthodox medicine or by non-medical means. It was TEMPORARY. Lazarus is dead! We shall return to this, the doctrine of mortality and death, again.

3. THE ACTS OF THE APOSTLES

The need for authentication of the apostolic ministry after the ascension is easily overlooked. From this point of time we may fail to see that there was no obvious reason for the people accepting the apostolic ministry as a continuation of Christ's ministry unless there was a sign to authenticate it. Christ had died. True, His resurrection was widely acclaimed by His followers and been attested to by many in His post-resurrection appearances, but He had also ascended into heaven. Between this last event and the birth of the Church there was a great gulf fixed, a gulf that needed a bridge. When the Spirit descended at Pentecost on our side of that gulf, with visible and audible signs, two other signs immediately followed which were parallel to those of Christ's ministry: salvation and healing. (Cf. Isaiah 53; Mark 2:1-12.) These were Peter's sermon with its 3,000 converts (Acts 2:41) and the healing of the cripple by Peter and John (Acts 3 and 4). The fact that the latter event and its immediate consequences occupy two chapters in Luke's record of the apostles' actions is significant.

By these two signs the bridge was built and the link between Christ and His Church established. (See Acts 3:6; 4:10, 13.) The chief role of healing in the apostolic ministry therefore was that of transferring authority from Christ to the apostles and an authentication of their message as being from God. Both non neo-Pentecostal and neo-Pentecostal agree on this. But there are other facts about their healing that need to be noted. The healing miracles of the apostles bore marked similarity to those of Christ. They were INSTANT and apparently UNLIMITED in their extent (Acts 3:7, 8; 15:12; 2 Cor 12:12). But there were times in the apostles' ministry when their healing powers were either not invoked or not successful: Paul in 2 Cor 12:7-10; Timothy in 1 Tim 5:23; and Trophimus in 2 Tim 4:20. It would seem evident from this that it was not assumed to be the right of even apostles to be immune from sickness or always to be healed when sick. In regard to the thorn in Paul's flesh, it is stated by neo-Pentecostals that "the exception proves the rule". But, while the exception may in some cases illustrate the rule, it cannot *prove* it. However, even if it did, it cannot prove *this* rule if the rule is that God has declared His plan to heal *all who ask believing*, since Paul did just that.

4. THE EPISTLES

The further one progresses into the New Testament the exercise of this healing gift seems to diminish. Certainly the mention of it does. In his booklet "Contemporary Thought on Healing in the Light of the New Testament", Dr. Scorer has this to say (pp. 6, 7): "That remarkable miracles occurred at that time (i.e. the Acts) is obvious; but, if the reader notes carefully, he will see that they are mentioned only occasionally. They are always linked with the authority of the preacher and the authentication of his message. When we turn to the Epistles, any programme of healing or commission to heal is notably absent. Peter and John, those two pioneering leaders, are silent about it in their letters. In Paul's instructions to Timothy and Titus, leaders of a later date, who should have been well informed on such matters, there is no mention whatever of healing. In his letter to the Ephesians in which the Church's origin and status and function are so powerfully delineated there is no reference to healing."

There are two passages in the Epistles demanding special attention:

1. *1 Cor 12:9*. ". . . to another (is given) gifts of healing by the one Spirit." The inclusion of healing as one of the nine gifts of the Spirit listed in this passage is a chief point of division between the non neo-Pentecostal and the neo-Pentecostal views. The latter take them as *"The* Nine Gifts of the Spirit" and as ongoing to the present day. The non neo-Pentecostal takes the list as *"Nine* of the Gifts of the Spirit", used by Paul in his letter to illustrate the diversity of the gifts and the unity of both the giver and of the recipients (1 Cor 12:4, 7). Moreover, whereas the neo-Pentecostal view of the gift of healing is exclusively that of "faith" healing, the non neo-Pentecostal considers that the diversity of gifts of the Spirit will continue and change as time and societies change. For instance, in New Testament times orthodox medicine had little to offer, even if the sufferer were able to secure its help. The situation today is vastly different.

Whether a supernatural gift of healing is ever in evidence today is debatable. Some non neo-Pentecostals would say that any supernatural manifestation of this gift was limited to the apostolic church and that the gift of healing should be understood today as that being exercised by doctors who have ability to assist healing.

Others would not want to limit the supernatural appearance of this and other gifts to apostolic times and would say that these gifts may recur from time to time in the history of the Church. In this case a most careful assessment of healing claims today still needs to be made. Moreover, any exercise of "the gift of healing" today should be distinguished from Christ's miracles and the apostolic miracles of the New Testament.

Such neo-Pentecostal claims of healing are usually acceptable to those who accept that such miracles occur today, but some observers find such "proofs" unconvincing. Kathryn Kuhlmann's books would come into this category as they are badly documented. There is a great need for well documented and irrefutable evidence to be supplied by neo-Pentecostals to support their claims.

2. *James 5:14, 15.* It has been noted above that this Epistle is strongly Jewish in context and that it follows the Old Testament ambiguity when using the terms for healing, weakness and salvation. To refer to this passage as a "very clear promise of healing" is to read into an ambiguous passage a clarity which is not there. To go further, as has been done, and to include salvation as well as healing as a promise for the sick, when prayed for, is surely to exceed the authority of scripture. It should also be noted that due to its early writing this Epistle was extant in the apostolic era and if the healing gifts were apostolic gifts they should not rightly be regarded as ongoing. The crucial question arises in verse 15 with the words "the prayer of faith will save the sick man". Many neo-Pentecostals take this phrase to mean prayer in which we adamantly believe that healing is the only possible result. To believe that healing may not eventuate is to show lack of faith. In their book "The Holy Spirit and You" Rita and Dennis Bennett (Logos International) say (p. 114): "We have no scriptural warrant to end a healing prayer with the faith-destroying phrase, 'If it be Thy will'! God has made it perfectly clear in His Word that it is HIS will to heal the sick — period!"

The non neo-Pentecostal on the other hand rejects this definition of the prayer of faith on both theological and pastoral grounds. Faith expressed in prayer is a confident trust in God based upon the statement and promises of His Word which reveal His character and His purposes. Our knowledge of these things is restricted to this Word. All prayer must be based upon this revelation since faith is the child of knowledge and not the child of optimism.

The "prayer of faith" of James 5:15 is not a special kind of prayer, since prayer that does not express trust in God is not prayer at all.

There are times when, because His Word is crystal clear, we can be absolutely sure that God will grant things which are asked of Him, e.g. salvation to a penitent sinner. There are other cases and situations however in which we cannot be certain of His will. The non neo-Pentecostal cannot therefore agree with the neo-Pentecostal that because Jesus, Peter, Philip and others healed many people, and because a gift of healing is mentioned in 1 Corinthians and a prayer for healing in James 5, that therefore Christians can have a specific "faith-expectancy" with regard to healing which they cannot have in non-specific areas. The details of lives of individual people, their length of life, health, prosperity, etc., while known to God from eternity to eternity, are unknown to us.

Here faith cannot be placed in a scriptural promise in the same way that the sinner turns to the Lord and prays for forgiving acceptance. It can only be faith in the fact that God can provide perfect health, long life and prosperity for people but since He does not give these blessings to many it may not be His will to change the circumstances of a poor, sick or dying person. Whatever happens His will is "good and acceptable and perfect". The weakness of our faith and prayers, even failure to pray, does not hinder or interfere with the perfection of God's will and purpose (Eph 1:11). His power and wisdom are limitless and He does not make mistakes. Everything that happens advances His glory as He turns even the wrath of man to His praise (Ps 76:10).

Christ's words (Matt 17:20) that faith like a grain of mustard is sufficient to move mountains, further denies that it is the quantitative element of our faith that is the vital factor. Faith is the commitment of a person into the hands of a loving and omnipotent God.

James teaches us the uncertainty of life, both in its continuance and in all its circumstances, and tells us that we ought to say "if the Lord will" in regard to all things (James 4:13-16). Paul expressed both his own desire and hope, and his uncertainty about God's will, when he said to the Ephesians "I will return, again to you, if God wills" (Acts 18:21). When Jesus prayed in

Gethsemane He made His request for the cup to pass from Him in a prayer which contained hope and desire, but He surrendered His will to the wider will and perfect purpose of the Father, never doubting His power to take away the cup (Mark 14:36).

In the light of these facts it will be seen that to include the expression "if it be Your will" in our prayers is not to use an "escape clause", or lack of faith. Far from being a denial of faith it is a mark of quiet and humble trust in the loving powerful heavenly Father who *can* do what we ask but who *may* not because His glory and our well-being and spiritual maturity are better advanced by His not doing it.

The pastoral reasons for rejecting the neo-Pentecostal definition of the prayer of faith are that it places on a sick person who is often depressed and fearful, an additional burden. Should healing not occur they feel that their faithlessness is the cause and a vicious cycle is often commenced. To an emotionally stable person, this burden added to their already very great load, is a cruelty. To the psychotically depressed it can be catastrophic, and suicide is not unknown in such cases.

5. FAITH HEALING TODAY . . . THE CASE
   FOR AND AGAINST

The usual neo-Pentecostal arguments for the exercise of healing as a spiritual gift are as follows:

1. *"Healing is an essential part of the gospel. Jesus commanded it in Luke 9:1, 2; Mark 16:15-20; and Matt 10:8."* This is not in dispute, although the references in Luke and Matthew are specific commands, not ongoing commissions to the Church. Moreover the command to "raise the dead" in Matt 10:8 is usually omitted when it is quoted.

If healing in the Gospels and the Acts played the role of authenticating the person and ministry of Christ and of the Apostles, can it play the same role today?

If what has been said above on these topics is true, then it cannot do so. We cannot by our actions today *authenticate* what Christ was and did 2,000 years ago. We must accept the New Testament records both to reveal Him to us, and to validate His claims. Further healings will not add to this. Any authority for healing of this type today must rest on some basis other than the validation of the New Testament records. The Mark 16 text is subject to dispute as the oldest manuscripts end at verse 8. If the concluding part of Mark's gospel is not genuine, and it alone of all the gospels contains the commission to heal, then it is *not genuine*. To say that the passage is at least very early is irrelevant. If Christ did not so commission us, the date at which He is assumed to have done so is immaterial. But apart from this, the validity of this command by Christ to His disciples as an ongoing command and promise to us, rests on the one thing. Why was it given to the eleven? It has been argued above that it was to validate their ministry and thus to establish the Church. For miraculous healings then to cease is consistent: (a) with the establishing and availability of the scripture record which testifies of these things to subsequent generations, (b) with the scriptural practice of confining miracles to the establishment of some new thing that God is doing, (c) with the scriptural doctrine of mortality and death, and (d) with the doctrine of miracles itself.

To take the historical elements of the Gospels and of the Acts as mandates for an ongoing commission for spiritual healing today is unwarranted. The fact that the Apostles healed in the name of Christ and gave Him all the glory does not alter the fact that it was of God's choosing that they healed then as they did, and it is still God's choosing whether or not that gift is available in the same form today.

2. *"Healing is an evidence of the Kingdom of Christ on earth."* The non neo-Pentecostal argues that the Kingdom (Kingship) of Christ was established in scripture. To see the handiwork of God only in healings which are miraculous, is to create a "God-of-the-gaps" theology and this will diminish His glory. Furthermore it runs in conflict with the doctrine of miracles, which, in order to remain miraculous, must be the exception and never the rule which the neo-Pentecostal attitude would make them. If the manifestation of the Kingdom depended on faith healing today most impartial observers would not feel that it was enhanced thereby.

3. *"Healing is part of the atonement."* This has been answered above (vide — THE GOSPELS part 2). The non neo-Pentecostal looks upon his complete redemption both from sin and from sickness as an eschatological reality, not a present one.

He believes eschatologically that with Paul, we can confidently expect "a crown of righteousness" after death (2 Tim 4:8). Similarly, with regard to our mortal bodies, we have in store for us a spiritual body, immortal and imperishable, which will replace our present one which is physical, mortal and perishable. In this connection the reader is urged to study carefully 1 Cor 15 especially vv. 42-58, and 2 Cor 4:7 to 5:5. These passages define in unequivocal terms the scriptural doctrine of mortality and of death. If healing is the legal right of all Christians, why do we die? In this regard it must be asserted that "old age" is not a cause of death. What is meant by death by old age is death due to degenerative disease, which invariably accompanies old age. This group of diseases is the commonest in the world today. But their very commonness masks their nature. They are diseases or infirmities, which terms are synonymous.

The Bible states that mortality with its accompanying disease-states or wearing out processes (which is a euphemism) is our lot.

Furthermore, this will culminate in physical death. For the Christian the latter event although aweful is the ushering in of perfect life, immortal, eternal and full of glory (2 Cor 4:16-18; 1 Cor 15:53, 54; Phil 1:21-23; Rev 21:1-4). The neo-Pentecostal has the problem of explaining mortality and death without contradicting what he asserts to be biblical teaching on healing. It is interesting to note that at the end of Paul's exposition on the doctrine of mortality to the Corinthian Church (2 Cor 4:7–5:5) he ends the argument with the words: "He who has prepared us for this very thing (i.e. glory after death) is God, *who has given us the Spirit as a guarantee.*" This is one of the gifts of the Spirit which is often overlooked, i.e. He is our guarantee of glory after death.

6. CONCLUSION

In conclusion let us ask, and answer as far as one is able, what is the status of present day faith healing? The answer is difficult due to the paucity of thoroughly documented research, and to the difference in interpretation of events by different observers or participants. For instance, miraculous cures seem to occur in inverse ratio to the observer's medical knowledge. Equally important is the all too common practice of confusing "symptoms" with the "disease" itself. Most symptoms are capable of ready and quick relief by medication. What is not realised is the ease with which they can be relieved by emotional factors (which may also aggravate them), by hypnosis, by suggestion and by other methods used by many non-Christian faith healers. But relief of symptoms is not the same as cure or even relief of the disease. Similar problems arise with physical signs. Any arthritic CAN walk without crutches if sufficiently motivated. What he learns from experience is that the subsequent weight bearing on his inflamed or degenerative joints will cause a flare up of the disease and its symptoms. It is dishonouring to God and also cruel to the patient to declare an arthritic patient as healed because he is induced to discard his crutches. All illnesses must be assessed over a long period of time by people who are aware of and able to detect ALL the signs of the disease. Many such "cures" when followed up sufficiently are found only to be "remissions" of symptoms engendered by the high expectations and emotions of the moment.

All independent authorities who have investigated faith healing today agree on the following:

They are USUALLY UNSUCCESSFUL. Very few would assert that more than a few are healed although many may be helped in other ways. In many cases the "cure" rate is equal to the known spontaneous recovery rate for that disease. In addition they are USUALLY GRADUAL, USUALLY PARTIAL, USUALLY SYMPTOMATIC RELIEF rather than PHYSICAL CURE, and USUALLY CONFINED TO PSYCHOGENIC and PSYCHOSOMATIC types of illness. In all the above they are in stark contrast to healings in the Gospels and the Acts. The one common word is USUALLY. No Christian can deny that God *can* heal miraculously when and if He chooses. What seems apparent is that He does this very little, if at all. The miracle, to remain miraculous, must be the exception not the rule.

The term miraculous healing is preferred by many to the more common terms faith or divine healing. All healing is of divine origin, whatever the agency, and faith should not be confined to things that are supernatural. In the introduction it was stated that the laws of nature were what things can be predicted to do under given conditions, and that these laws are made and maintained by God (Col 1:17). How much then should we expect Him to intervene in their operation so that the unexpected and unpredictable happens? The non neo-Pentecostal makes bold to say that we should expect it very little and ask for it very cautiously for the following reasons:

a. All thought, reason, planning and communication to name just a few things depend on the predictability and reliability of natural laws. Without them chaos would reign. With them, God reigns.

b. Our Lord constantly forbade those whom He healed to tell others of what had happened (Matt 8:4; 9:30; Mark 7:36; Luke 8:56). The reasons for this are obvious. If miraculous healing were to become normative for Christians today, what would be its ultimate effect on the Church?

c. Having in mind the finiteness, fallibility and sinfulness of human mind and will, dare we omit to ask that our requests be over-ruled by the mind and will of God?

There are two problems posed by the relative ineffectiveness of faith healing today. The non neo-Pentecostal must explain why there are *any* cures. The neo-Pentecostal must explain why there are so *few*.

1. WHY ARE THERE ANY CURES?

It is not denied that God *may* heal miraculously. In case this appears to be assuming a "theological escape-chute", that will quickly slide its user out of difficult situations and on to safer ground, it should be said that a number of independent researchers who have examined the healing claims of many famous faith healers have failed to find any such miraculous healings. The following is given in support of this.

i. Dr. Louis Rose, "Faith Healing" (Penguin) p. 175, "I narrowed my quest to the search for a handful of cases — or perhaps only a single case — in which the intervention of a faith healer had led to an irrefutable cure. This must have been a cure, not in the vague sense of a patient's 'feeling better' or even that a progressive case had been limited, but in a sense that, as a result of a healer's work alone, a demonstrable pathological state had been entirely eliminated. To those who have read this book it will be clear in this search I have been unsuccessful. After nearly twenty years of work I have yet to find one 'miracle cure'."

See also

ii. The Archbishop of Canterbury's Commission of 1920, and

iii. The 1950 B.M.A. Commission Report: ("Faith Healing", Louis Rose, p. 176).

The "cures" that do occur are usually of psychological disorders, which find in healing ministries the necessary type of sympathetic concern and help which is often lacking in orthodox medical treatment. However sad the latter fact may be, medical failures do not constitute non-medical successes in the manner that healing was practised in the New Testament. It must be recorded, however, that charismatic groups are doing extremely valuable and effective work among people who are so often neglected by both the Church in general and by society. These are

Both Sides to the Question

the people who are drug and/or alcohol dependent. The reasons for their successes here are of great interest. They are dealing with people who often feel unwanted, who lack motivation and a sense of achievement. The atmosphere of outgoing genuine love, of less inhibited behaviour and especially the experience of baptism of the Spirit (whether it be scriptural or not is irrelevant in this particular situation), all give to these people the sense of identity, of belonging and of being loved, that medical and sociological workers are often unable to impart.

In other words they are healing these people by the methods of orthodox medicine, i.e. to seek out the cause of the disturbance and to treat it.

A similar situation exists with psychosomatic illnesses. Here the cause is psychological and often difficult to treat effectively. But if the patient can be faced with the reality of Christ and having accepted Him, experience relief of tensions and conflicts, then the subsequent remission of the physical manifestation of the illness is not the result of faith healing, in the sense of a supernatural effect directly on their diseased bodies, but rather it is healing by removal of the cause.

2. WHY ARE THERE SO FEW CURES?

There can be no unanimity on this question. From the opinion of the three authorities quoted above one can move through the whole spectrum of opinions to the point where claims of raising the dead are held. But there remains one question which is related to it, to which an answer must be found. If healing is God's will, and in His power to effect, and if He has promised it to believers in all ages, and if His Spirit is available to give it, why do we die? Is there a limit to God's power? Is His will capricious? Is it that when our faith fails, our healing fails? And, if the latter be true, what of our salvation? If the doctrine of death is accepted by the neo-Pentecostal but it is still claimed that we can be healed of all our diseases except the last and fatal one, we are left with a doctrine of "pie on the earth here and now". The non neo-Pentecostal states that there is no scripture to support this and much to contradict it (John 16:33; Acts 14:22; Rom 5:3). If it is claimed that spiritual healing, as practised in the New Testament times, is available today, and then to say that it occurs by "progressive healing" is a contradiction. The New Testament healing was instant. Any progressive healing today is indistinguishable from natural healing, and to ascribe this to a miraculous Divine intervention, rather than to the laws which God has set in motion and maintains, does not add to God's glory, but rather diminishes both it and the credibility of the Church with thinking people.

The following is a quotation from "The Problem of Pain" by C. S. Lewis pp. 21, 22: "That God can and does, on occasions, modify the behaviour of matter and produce what we call miracles, is a part of the Christian faith; but the very concept of a common, and therefore, stable world, demands that these occasions be extremely rare . . . so it is with the life of souls in a world: fixed laws, consequences unfolding by causal necessity, the whole natural order, are at once the limits within which their common life is confined and also the sole condition under which any such life is possible. Try to exclude the possibility of suffering which the order of nature and the existence of free wills involve, and you will find that you have excluded life itself."

PASTORAL ATTITUDES TO THE CHARISMATIC MOVEMENT

Pastoral attitudes must be determined in the light of the character of neo-Pentecostalism and the value judgements one makes of the theology and practice of the movement. Neo-Pentecostalism is as diverse as Anglicanism itself, and it is difficult to set down any uniform policy or guidelines for adoption by all the parishes. There are some people who regard neo-Pentecostalism as a Christian aberration and who therefore consistently reject its distinctive teaching.

The Position at an Earlier Time

At an earlier time it was customary for those who held neo-Pentecostal doctrines to leave their denomination and to join an assembly that specifically provided for those insights and practices.

The Present Position

A very different situation now exists. Almost invariably the neo-Pentecostal does not contemplate leaving his denomination. He may well want to see his congregation and his fellow churchmen changed (and he may well need guidance and correction so that he is mature in his attitudes and relationships) but he intends to remain in his own denomination.

This means that appropriate pastoral attitudes must be worked out for this new situation. Pastoral difficulties will probably arise if: (a) The neo-Pentecostals feel that they form a spiritual elite in their congregations. (b) The neo-Pentecostal becomes over-emotionally involved in his experience. (c) The neo-Pentecostal is sceptical of theology and sees it as a "barrier to blessing". (d) The non neo-Pentecostal minister over-reacts against the neo-Pentecostal or forbids him to meet with other neo-Pentecostals. (e) However, many non neo-Pentecostal ministers feel that the neo-Pentecostal understanding of the Christian faith and life is so erroneous that it is a danger to the congregation to be exposed to its teaching and testimony and that they must take steps to protect it.

Ministerial Attitudes

As things are at present only a few Anglican ministers identify themselves with this movement. Most ministers do not identify themselves with it, many of them because of theological convictions, some perhaps because they do not understand it sufficiently.

We would urge all ministers to study the Charismatic Movement, both theologically and pastorally, in order to arrive at informed viewpoints and attitudes.

In particular, the non neo-Pentecostal minister should —

1. Seek to understand each person in the congregation and his spiritual needs, and seek to maintain good relationships with him even when the minister cannot accept the way this person may express his faith.

2. Ensure, as far as he is able, that there is a satisfying ministry and fellowship within the congregation. He should keep the congregation within the stream of constant teaching on the whole counsel of God which obviously will include teaching about the Person and work of the Holy Spirit.

3. Correct error graciously but firmly, if he judges that there is error on the part of the neo-Pentecostal or anybody else, cf. 2 Tim 2:55 (a).

4. Encourage neo-Pentecostals in his congregation to co-operate generally in the parish life and witness.

A neo-Pentecostal minister should —

1. Remember that in the majority of cases he was called to his present parish before he became a neo-Pentecostal, and take into consideration the fact that the members of his present parish who are non neo-Pentecostal (almost always the great majority)

probably expect their worship and teaching patterns to continue in their accustomed ways.

2. Make any changes in statutory services with the necessary approval of the diocesan authorities as well as with the corporate approval of parish officers and church members as required by the Constitution.

3. Encourage any group with a neo-Pentecostal emphasis in the parish to exercise care and discretion in their activities and attitudes in an attempt to avoid unnecessary problems.

Necessary Disciplines for the Neo-Pentecostal

Neo-Pentecostals feel that it is important that they should be able to pursue the experiences associated with neo-Pentecostalism within the context of their own denomination. They feel the need to develop expressions of this movement which will harmonise with the ethos of their own denomination, yet at the same time not neutralise the understanding and experiences they have had. One of the reasons why this seems to be difficult today is that the movement has brought with it the ethos of the Pentecostal churches, which is not essential to the beliefs and experiences of the Charismatic Movement within the major denominations.

The most valid work of God must be subject to the discipline which will prevent it being marred and distorted by Satan. The neo-Pentecostal should learn to be subject to authority and respect the wisdom and guidance of God through other members of the Body of Christ.

He should express the disciplines of faithful and active service within his congregation and be ready to support its activities with sacrifice.

He should honour the gifts and abilities of others and not force an expression of his own gifts and beliefs on members of his own congregation who do not agree with him. He should learn to exercise the discipline of patience, trusting God in His wisdom to give him the opportunity to share his insights in an appropriate time and manner.

He should recognise that much of the teaching in the Bible concerning charismatic gifts is given in the context of the inter-dependence and Body-relatedness of Christians, and thus he should refrain at all times from being individualistic in his expression of these gifts, or in his pursuit of spiritual growth and maturity.

He should apply the biblical injunction to submit to his spiritual elders, whether they agree or not with his neo-Pentecostal beliefs (1 Thess 5:12; Heb 13:17; 1 Peter 5:5). Neo-Pentecostals would urge that this discipline can be a means of grace, which unrestrained individualism will never be.

Irreconcilable Differences?

It must be recognised that either a neo-Pentecostal or non neo-Pentecostal Christian, who is convinced of his position, will naturally want to see his point of view (which he regards as the truth) prevail and be acknowledged as such. He will want to be able to advocate it openly and will undergo a great conflict of conscience if he is unduly restrained.

Ultimately, the tensions between neo-Pentecostals and non neo-Pentecostals will depend on —

1. How importantly the neo-Pentecostal regards his doctrine of baptism in the Spirit. Is it a real essential to the faith? Is it the only way of getting power for ministry?

2. How strongly the non neo-Pentecostal minister feels about neo-Pentecostal influence and presence in the congregation.

We are reminded of the words, "in things essential — unity; in things indifferent — liberty; in all things — charity." Where the neo-Pentecostal distinctives are considered to be essentials, continued co-existence will be difficult.

If there are irreconcilable differences or tensions, two courses of action are possible. Some would advise such a person to submit himself to the local church tradition and turn his frustration into a greater dependence upon God and leave the outcome to Him. Others would advise that it would be best to leave that congregation and go elsewhere.

However, this should not be done quickly or lightly. Circumstances will vary from person to person, e.g. a man with a family will have to consider their welfare, while a mature, single person or couple may opt to remain and continue their ministries within a congregation with some emphasis not to their personal liking.

Fellowship Together

Truth and love must characterise all our actions (Eph 4:15). Truthfulness does not exclude love but is rather an expression of it, while love does not mean that error is overlooked. The neo-Pentecostal and the non neo-Pentecostal should not cause needless division in the congregation (cf. Rom 12:18).

The neo-Pentecostal and the non neo-Pentecostal are both "one in Christ". The possibility of their fellowship together in one congregation will flow from a mutual recognition of this fact and a readiness by all not to make neo-Pentecostal distinctives a test of fellowship.

The Archbishop of Canterbury said in the Cathedral of St. John The Divine, New York, on January 23, 1972, "At the present time the old Christian institutions are under the weather. While they have carried the Christian faith through the years they often present a Christianity which seems tired or conventional or formal. There are many today who are ready to follow Jesus, and then when they look at the institutional Churches they say 'Where is the radiant joy which Christianity ought to inspire? Where is the love and self-sacrifice which shocks and startles? Where is the authentic fellowship which the early Christians practised?' "

The neo-Pentecostal has sometimes tackled some of the extreme forms of social problems because he is convinced of the reality of the Spirit and the resources which He gives. This expectancy should likewise mark every Christian who confesses "I believe in the Holy Spirit". The non neo-Pentecostal too should be enthusiastic about the Holy Spirit's power.

Every Christian should ponder over these questions:

1. Does his experience of the Holy Spirit tally with his theology of the Holy Spirit?

2. Does he give his fellow believers the impression that they are accepted by him for what they are (Rom 14:1) and wanted by him and loved by him?

3. As a Spirit-born believer, is his life enriched by the Spirit's power, e.g. Eph 3:16?

BIBLIOGRAPHY

A. THE NEO-PENTECOSTAL VIEWPOINT

I. BAPTISM IN THE SPIRIT

Bennett, D. J., "Nine O'Clock in the Morning" (Charisma); Harper, M., "As at the Beginning" (Hodder & Stoughton); Schep, J. A., "Spirit Baptism and Tongues Speaking" (Abundant Life Publications); Williams, J. R., "The Era of the Spirit" (Logos).

II. GIFTS

Bittlinger, A., "Gifts and Graces" (Hodder & Stoughton); Bennett, D. & R., "The Holy Spirit and You" (Coverdale House).

III. TONGUES

Christenson, L., "Speaking in Tongues" (Dimension Books); Kelsey, M. T., "Speaking with Tongues" (Epworth Press); Schep, J. A., "Spirit Baptism and Tongues Speaking" (Abundant Life Publications); Sherrill, J., "They Speak with Other Tongues" (Hodder & Stoughton).

IV. HEALING

Ikin, A. G., "New Concepts of Healing" (Hodder & Stoughton); Kelsey, M. T., "Healing and Christianity" (Harper & Row); Martin, B., "Healing for You" (Lutterworth); Frost, Dr. Evelyn, "Christian Healing".

B. THE NON NEO-PENTECOSTAL VIEWPOINT

I. BAPTISM IN THE HOLY SPIRIT

Barnett, P., and Jensen P. F., "The Quest for Power" (ANZEA); Bruner, F. D., "A Theology of the Holy Spirit" (Hodder & Stoughton); Dunn, J.D.G., "Baptism in the Holy Spirit" (S.C.M.); Hoekema, A. A., "Holy Spirit Baptism" (Paternoster); Stott, J.R.W., "The Baptism and Fullness of the Holy Spirit" (I.V.F.).

II. GIFTS

Barnett, P., and Jensen, P. F., "The Quest for Power" (ANZEA); Bruner, F. D., "A Theology of the Holy Spirit" (Hodder & Stoughton).

III. TONGUES

Burdick, D. W., "Tongues — to Speak or not to Speak" (Moody Press); Hoekema, A. A., "What About Tongues Speaking?" (Paternoster); Kildahl, J. B., "The Psychology of Speaking in Tongues" (Hodder & Stoughton).

IV. HEALING

Lewis, C. S., "Miracles" (or) "Undeceptions" (Bles); Lewis, C. S., "The Problem of Pain" (Bles); Rose, L., "Faith Healing" (Penguin); Scorer, C. G., "Contemporary Thought on Healing in the Light of the New Testament" (Christian Medical Fellowship).

Note: A very extensive bibliography on literature on these subjects is included in "A Theology of the Holy Spirit" by F. D. Bruner.

THE WORK AND THE GIFTS
OF THE HOLY SPIRIT

*The Panel on Doctrine of the Church of Scotland set up what was called
"a Working Party" in 1972 to examine the doctrine of the Holy Spirit,
the gifts, and the contemporary charismatic movement. This brief interim
report stressed the ecclesial nature of the charisms: "The charismata are
given in the first instance to the whole Church and not necessarily to
each individual." A warning was issued against any theological
perspective which implies that the present period is "the age of the
Spirit." Recognized is the claim of the charismatic renewal to a legitimate
place within the church. This recognition does not imply an absolutizing
of its practices or of its exercise of the gifts so as to make them normative
for all.*

*The "Reports to the General Assembly" were published by the Church
of Scotland in 1973. See pp. 219–20.*

The Panel has set up a Working Party "to examine afresh the
Doctrine of the Holy Spirit, with particular reference to the gifts of
the Spirit and in the light of the contemporary charismatic or
Neo-Pentecostal movement . . ." (cf. remit, Assembly Reports
1972, coloured section, p. 18).

At this stage the Panel simply wishes to report progress and to
underline certain points which sooner or later will have to be
considered by the whole Church.

a. The Panel is not concerned with the origins and the history
of the Pentecostal Church or Churches but with the contemporary
charismatic movement which is found in all the traditional
Churches (including the Church of Rome) in many parts of the
world.

b. It is true that, in common with other Churches, the Church
of Scotland has far too often resisted the promptings of the Holy
Spirit by being too inflexible in outlook and structure. It is,
however, not true that the Church "has neglected" the Holy
Spirit in the sense of not giving Him His place in the doctrine and
worship of the Church. Reformed theology, in all its confessional
standards and pronouncements, has witnessed to the true God —
Father, Son and Holy Spirit. In doing so it has acknowledged and
affirmed that the primary work of God the Holy Spirit is to make
the Risen and Living Christ present and contemporaneous to His

Church and people. This is why the Church of Scotland together with the whole Reformed Church can, for instance, affirm "the real presence" of Christ in the Eucharist.

3. The Neo-Pentecostalists' concern with "the gifts of the Spirit", their reception and use, is legitimate. Indeed, the Church's rediscovery of the charismata is desirable and even necessary. Two points, however, must be borne in mind. Firstly, the charismata are given in the first instance to the whole Church and not necessarily to each believer. Secondly, the Church must be on guard against any idea or theory which implies that we are now living in "the age of the Spirit", an age somehow superior to what has gone before. Christ is the Lord of history — past, present and future.

d. Whatever else the Holy Spirit may be He is the Spirit of peace. Everything must therefore be done to prevent Neo-Pentecostalism leading to schism or disharmony. On the basis of the Biblical witness the Neo-Pentecostal movement has a legitimate place within the Church. Yet Neo-Pentecostalists must not expect or require the Church to make their practices or their use of the charismatic gifts they claim to possess normative for all.

At this point it should be mentioned that the Working Party, on which several schools of thought and theological outlook are represented, has worked in a spirit of mutual respect and understanding.

28 Methodist Church, Australia, 1973

THE REPORT ON THE CHARISMATIC MOVEMENT IN THE METHODIST CHURCH

Before the Methodist Church in South Australia became one of the members in the Uniting Church, the president of the state conference in South Australia in 1972 appointed a Committee of Enquiry into the Charismatic Movement, which made an interim report to the district synod in 1973.

The report is more descriptive than theological. Written accounts from forty persons and six in-depth interviews (three of these from Roman Catholics) formed the basis of the committee's judgment, two of whose members had "some experience of the movement."

Special attention was given to the subject of tongues, mostly because of the high interest in this aspect of the movement by uninvolved persons. The small sampling made it evident that tongues is rarely a highly emotional or ecstatic expression and that the speaker is always in control (anything uncontrollable is considered spurious and dangerous). Those who prayed in tongues witnessed to an increased liberty in prayer.

The classical contrast was posed between subjective religious experience on the one hand, and on the other concern for the social imperatives and "for the church's mission in its fullness." Here again the question of divisiveness was raised, but the causes were seen to be various. Giving too much importance to the subjective element (though the coming together of those who have had a common experience was evaluated positively) can be a real source of division. But divisions "can be caused by rigidity, or by ignorance or fear concerning unfamiliar experiences just as much as by fanaticism or undisciplined emotions." Two attitudes are alien to any appeal made to John Wesley and to the catholic Spirit (sic) which he advocated. No one should question the validity of anyone's experience if loyalty to Christ is visible in that person's life. Equally foreign to that Spirit (sic) is the insistence that every Christian's experience should be identical in every detail.

The conclusion of the Committee: ". . . the Church has nothing to fear from the charismatic movement, but rather has much to gain from it. . . ."

(An interim report from the Committee appointed by the President, following a resolution of the 1972 Conference)

While the Conference resolution does not call for this Committee to report to Synod, it was felt that an interim statement could be useful. It should be clearly understood that this report does not attempt a Biblical or theological analysis, but is concerned to describe what is going on, and to give some assessment from the pastoral point of view.

The Committee received and circulated among its members written submissions from some 40 people. It also spent two meetings interviewing six people at some depth. These were, a minister's wife, a minister of our Conference, a layman outside the movement who comes from a church where the movement has been active for several years, a Catholic priest, a nun, and a Catholic housewife. Two members of the Committee (a minister and a layman) have some experience of the movement. It is important to note that this report is mainly based on the information gained from these sources. It is not an assessment of

Pentecostalism, but of a movement among people who are Methodists (supplemented by valuable insights from the three Catholics).

The Committee has found that the *Charismatic Movement has a variety of expressions*, which can be placed broadly under TWO categories, which the Committee has called "PENTECOSTAL" and "CHARISMATIC". Those who lean towards the former tend to place *high emphasis on the gift of 'speaking in tongues'* and see it as having pre-eminent place in the life of the believer. Generally these people tend to appreciate services of worship which replicate those held in Pentecostal churches. For this reason in the past, they have tended to leave the Methodist church and join Pentecostal churches.

Those at the *"Charismatic" end* of the spectrum place an emphasis more on an understanding *of the whole doctrine of the Holy Spirit*, placing emphasis on His whole work in the life of the Christian. *They see the Spirit manifesting Himself in ALL the gifts* mentioned in Scripture, and do not give 'tongues' any *special* status. As well as this, they see the Holy Spirit working in all life and in all events. *This second grouping of people seek to find expression of their worship and service within their own church*. The Methodist Charismatic Fellowship, which has monthly rallies attended by some three hundred people, seeks to cater for such people within their own communion and to foster a deeper knowledge of the Spirit among us. (It is significant to note that 'charismatic' prayer and fellowship groups are meeting in some Catholic and Anglican churches, with the sanction of Archbishops Gleeson and Reed respectively).

The 'Charismatic' Experience. The committee found it difficult at times to distinguish this experience from that spiritual renewal which all active Christians may enjoy from time to time. However, there was a pattern common to all the testimonies heard and read:

A deeper love for God and for Our Lord Jesus Christ:
A deeper love for people and a longing to witness for Christ:
Joy, and a sense of new adequacy for the demands of life:
A zest for Bible study . . . the Bible really 'coming alive':
A greater desire and ability to pray, and with a great emphasis on praise and adoration:
The Catholics found a deeper significance in the worship and sacraments of their church . . . they were now better Catholics:

Most used the gift of tongues in private prayer. A few had used it in fellowship with other 'charismatics'.

Some had experienced physical and emotional healing.

These signs followed a definite rededication to Christ and a reception of the Spirit in a deeper way . . . most commonly called 'baptism in the Spirit' or being 'filled with the Spirit.'

GLOSSOLALIA OR THE GIFT OF TONGUES

The people interviewed *were unanimous that this is NOT the most important part of their new experience.* They did not deny the working of the Spirit in Christians who did not have this gift. The ministers concerned did not equate 'baptism in the Spirit' with speaking in tongues. One said he did not use 'tongues' until six months after his new experience began. Another said there was an interval of 37 years in his case. In one way, then, 'tongues' should not take up much space in this report.

However, *since glossolalia always arrests the attention of those outside the movement, and can cause division and misunderstanding unless care is taken, the committee has paid special attention to it.* The following were the emphases by those whom the committee questioned closely about this matter:

Tongues is a means of expressing in prayer those praises and petitions for which words are inadequate. It is a way of saying what cannot be said. (One committee member asked if this was not akin to that deep, wordless prayer which is sometimes experienced by many Christians. The tongue-speakers present readily assented).

Tongues is thus *primarily directed towards God*, and is most often used in *private prayer*. One or two had used it in fellowship. Others said they found it difficult if anyone else was present.

There was general agreement that *the experience is rarely emotional or ecstatic.* 'Almost matter-of-fact' was one description. (For most of the committee, this was an unexpected element in the testimonies). Unregulated tongue-speaking in groups could generate an emotional atmosphere, but St. Paul's wise warnings about public use of tongues should be heeded (1 Cor. 14:26–33).

There was unanimity that a *genuine experience is never overwhelming.* The speaker is always in control and can begin and end such prayer as he wills. It was said by the witnesses that anything uncontrollable is spurious and dangerous. "Discipline" after all, is one of the fruits of the Spirit!

All felt that tongues had been important to them, as it had increased their liberty to pray, and their awareness of the presence of God. But all agreed that the one *indispensable* sign of the Spirit at work is Christian love.

Conclusions. While our sample of tongue-speakers might be regarded as too small for any generalization, it did not appear that they were marked by any common emotional or intellectual characteristics. Three were university graduates, and all were critical of excesses which bring the charismatic experience into disrepute and cause disunity.

The committee unanimously agrees that, for the people concerned, *glossolalia is a meaningful element in a deeper experience of the Holy Spirit.*

WORDS OF CAUTION

There is danger that some 'charismatics' may attach too much importance to "tongues" . . . and indeed, to the whole subjective element in the Christian life. It must be stressed that it is a deeper knowledge of Christ rather than special 'experiences' which we must seek to have through the Spirit. In all experience-centred forms of Christianity, the results of concentrating on the gifts rather than on the Giver can be pernicious, especially for those who are unstable or have only a superficial knowledge of the Faith.

The committee fears that the *preoccupation of some with individual 'experiences' could weaken Christian concern for the social problems* of our time and *for the Church's mission* in its fulness. However, this is not necessarily consequent upon a 'charismatic' experience. Indeed, evidence to the contrary was noted. We are convinced that the concern for evangelism manifested by the 'charismatics' is something the whole church needs to share.

A word to 'charismatics'

Special care should be taken to avoid the creation of cliques in the local congregation. New-found zeal and love should be channelled into dedicated service and manifested in a loving acceptance of those who do not share their experience.

However, *it is recognized that those with a common experience may wish to meet for prayer and mutual edification.* But we urge that such gatherings should always be open to whoever wishes to attend. At this point tact and tolerance on BOTH sides will be needed if hurtful and divisive situations are to be avoided.

A word to the rest of the Church

Ministers and church people generally should recognize that *division can be caused by rigidity, or by ignorance or fear concerning unfamiliar experiences* just as much as by fanaticism or undisciplined emotions.

It is alien to the catholic Spirit advocated by John Wesley to question the validity of anyone's experience if loyalty to Christ is visible in the life. It is equally foreign to that Spirit to insist that every Christian's experience should be identical in all details.

EFFECTS OF THE 'MOVEMENT'

It is difficult to assess this in detail because of the limited evidence available to the committee. But we had reports from several ministers with an appreciable number of 'charismatics' in their congregations . . . the ministers themselves not having the 'tongues' experience themselves. From them we glean:

For the most part *these people are loyal and zealous*. As one minister puts it, 'The charismatics are where the action is'.

A few cases of unstable church loyalties are reported, but they were *a minority* (in the churches in question).

Where marked divisions have occurred, it seems that some charismatics have been unbalanced in their presentation and have over-emphasized their own experience. Some situations have been created too, by rigidity, fear and lack of acceptance on the part of some church people to whom 'charismatic' experience is unfamiliar.

CONCLUSIONS

The committee is unanimously of the opinion that the Church has nothing to fear from the charismatic movement, but rather has much to gain from it, provided that it is understood that (a) *Since we believe in a living God, we should not be surprised if the Spirit sometimes manifests Himself in new or unexpected ways* (The wind bloweth where it listeth . . .) (b) *It is not to be expected that each Christian will experience all the gifts of the Spirit.* A careful study of Chapter 12 of I Corinthians is recommended at this point. (c) WHATEVER THE GIFTS MAY BE, "WITHOUT LOVE WE ARE NOTHING".

We call all Methodists to study afresh the New Testament teaching about the Holy Spirit, and to give themselves to prayer that His working may be more manifest among us.

We especially recommend 'The Work of the Holy Spirit' . . . a report presented by a special committee to the 182nd General Assembly of the United Presbyterian Church in the U.S.A. Our Book Depot has been asked to secure more copies.

Grant Dunning, David Houston, Arnold Hunt, Arthur Jackson, David Pill, David Tulloch, Bob Vawser (Brian Phillips was not able to attend the crucial meetings of the committee, but assisted in the early stages of its investigation).

29 Methodist Church, Great Britain, 1973

THE CHARISMATIC MOVEMENT AND METHODISM

Historically the roots of classical Pentecostalism is in the Methodism of John Wesley. Wesley's theology is drawn from the British Anglo-Catholic tradition rather than from the continental Reformed Protestant tradition. It is perfectionist, evangelistic, experience oriented, based on justification by faith, conversion, witness of the Spirit, and scriptural holiness (sometimes called Entire Sanctification, which is not the same as sinless perfection). It was also Arminian (rejection of unconditional predestination, of limited atonement, and of irresistible grace and professing the universal salvation of all) as modified and interpreted in Wesley's sermons, his notes on the New Testament, and his Articles of Religion. Classical Pentecostals inherited this tradition from the nineteenth-century Holiness movement, which they in turn modified. The classical Pentecostal theological tradition is Arminian (in contrast to Calvinistic), perfectionistic, premillennial (the personal visible return of Christ will precede his reign for a thousand years on earth), and charismatic. F. D. Bruner's characterization is accurate: "Pentecostalism is Primitive Methodism's extended incarnation." [1]

The charismatic renewal in the historic churches too owes a theological debt to these Methodist sources, though they have not been taken over without change. When Methodists evaluate the contemporary charismatic renewal, they are touching their own deepest roots.

This booklet, written by two British Methodists, was published in 1973 by the Home Mission Division of the Methodist Church in Great Britain. A historical section is followed by chapters treating of various doctrinal issues, the structures of Methodist ministries, and the contribution of the charismatic renewal to Methodism.

Quite possibly Wesley was a dispensationalist when it came to the charisms of healing, tongues, and interpretation. An apology was given for the attention given in this book to tongues though this was justified "because of the attention so often wrongly focused upon it. . . . This whole movement is not a 'tongues movement,' a 'power movement,' or even a 'prayer movement.' It is a movement of the Spirit of the Lord Jesus Christ in His resurrection power."

All the charismatic gifts seem to be present in early Methodism, with the exception of interpretation, even though it is possible that the first generations of Methodists created a mental or spiritual block to their reception.

The work of Scriptural Holiness (which was an experience of Entire Sanctification preached by Wesley but never claimed) was subsequent to the conversion and was seen by Wesley as occurring either in a growth pattern, that is gradually, or, more desirably, instantaneously. In the nineteenth-century Holiness movement, out of which the Pentecostal movement emerged, this Wesleyan heritage of a second experience subsequent to conversion became the theological center of its doctrine of sanctification as perfect love. In classical Pentecostalism there developed either a two or three-stage doctrine of sanctification, the second or third stage being identified with the baptism in the Holy Spirit.

Authors disagree about the manner in which Methodist teaching can be accommodated to Pentecostal insights. Authors identify baptism in the Spirit variously with conversion, witness of the Spirit, and with scriptural holiness, though the authors of this document expressed a preference for identifying it with Assurance or Witness of the Spirit. An attempt to bring baptism in the Holy Spirit into harmony with sacramental life tentatively suggests that water-baptism represents faith in Jesus, confirmation reception of the Spirit, and ordination mission. Admittedly worship traditions which are more structured and disciplined (the Roman Catholic Eucharist and the Anglican Communion) have been more successful in making place for charismatic expressions within their services. It may be that "a fully charismatic happening must needs remain physically separate from normal worship. . . ."

The positive evaluation of charisms need not imply "an incessant use of extraordinary gifts." The authors warned against "building on manifestations." Many identify the renewal with enthusiastic elements ("tongues every service, prophecy at least once a month and hand-clapping through every hymn") forgetting a second strand of charismatic spirituality, the contemplative.

Attention was given to various community expressions of Methodist ministry such as the class/house meeting and how they differ from charismatic prayer meetings. It was recognized that a charismatic prayer group has something to contribute to this Methodist tradition. Like other denominational streams of the renewal, the dominant characteristic of Methodist prayer meetings is praise, so much so that many groups are giving themselves the title "Community of Praise."

The booklet entitled "The Charismatic Movement and Methodism" by William R. Davies and Ross Peart was published in 1973 by the Home Mission Division of the Methodist Church in Great Britain.

1. A Theology of the Holy Spirit *(London: Hodder and Stoughton, 1971), p. 37.*
2. *Vinson Synan,* The Holiness-Pentecostal Movement in the United States *(Grand Rapids: Eerdmans, 1971), p. 217.*

CONTENTS

Footnote: The Introduction is the work of both authors; the first two Chapters the work of W. R. Davies; the remaining Chapters the work of R. Peart.

PREFACE

One of the important tasks of Home Mission is to listen to what the Spirit is saying to the Churches, which sometimes means keeping one's ear to the ground. And on the ground, in places all over Britain and indeed all over the world, exciting things are happening. Without doubt one thrilling aspect has been the rediscovery by many men and women of the doctrine of the Holy Spirit, as a vital fact of experience rather than a chapter in some dusty volume of theology. This fact has been seen and documented by scholars of all denominations, most massively and comprehensively in Walter Hollenweger's volume on the Pentecostal Movement.

In British Methodism our own late General Secretary, Leslie Davison, was highly esteemed by many in connection with the Charismatic Movement. His interest and foresight led to the formation of a small working party of British Methodists supported by the Home Mission Department, and he was guide, friend and counsellor to many ministers, deaconesses and laymen who had come into a new experience of the Holy Spirit. Because of his untimely death several fragments of writing which may in time, through Dr. Davison's highly individual method of working, have grown into books will never see the light of day.

We are therefore happy, both in tribute to Leslie Davison, and in its own right, to commend this Occasional Paper to the people called Methodists. Bill Davies and Ross Peart collaborated to write this paper from their own double concern for the Charismatic Movement and for the Methodist Church. We share with them the hope that their Occasional Paper will both help Methodists to understand the Charismatic Movement and those who have this new experience to understand Methodism. In our common task of mission we need this full understanding.

George W. Sails, Jeffrey W. Harris, Alan J. Davies

June 1973

INTRODUCTION

This paper is about the Charismatic movement which is the term given to a world-wide movement of the Spirit within the historic Churches of Christendom in which the Spiritual Gifts of Romans 12 and 1 Corinthians 12 are manifested. People belonging to this movement are sometimes referred to as Neo-Pentecostals because of certain similarities with the worship, teaching and practice of Classical Pentecostals. Whereas the Neo-Pentecostals or the Charismatic movement belongs to the post second World War era, the Classical Pentecostals find their origin in the early part of this century and amongst these are the Elim and Apostolic Churches and the Assemblies of God.

The word charismatic comes from the Greek word 'charisma' meaning 'gift of grace' or 'spiritual gift', such gifts being manifested in the life of believers subsequent to a spiritual experience often termed 'Baptism in the Holy Spirit', but also called 'being filled with the Holy Spirit' or 'receiving the Holy Spirit.'

A stumbling-block for some is the Gift of Tongues but it need not be so when understood as a medium of praise and prayer valuable to those who have experienced it and when it is recognized that this is but one of the many endowments which God has to give. Some Christians whose spiritual lives have been deeply enriched by an infilling do not speak in tongues, yet it is recognized that one must be open to all God has to give. Space does not permit a detailed treatment of individual gifts in this paper but the particular gift of tongues is mentioned here because of the attention so often wrongly focussed upon it.

Throughout Christian history God worked amongst His people through the power of His Spirit in different ways and with different emphases at different times. In times past, apart from the New Testament era and the Early Apostolic era and subsequent, occasional, limited manifestations of charismatic activity there has never been in Western Christendom the kind of outpouring of the Spirit in this distinctive way as it is seen today. (Perhaps however this is not so true of the Eastern Orthodox Churches.) What is happening now is a rediscovery of the secret of power experienced by the early Church and this is adding a new dimension to the traditional types of spirituality of the historic Churches.

In recent years a growing number of Methodists have entered into this new dimension and an ever increasing number have been showing a deep desire to understand and appropriate all that it has to offer. With this in mind this paper has been prepared in the hope that some Methodists may be helped in relating their experience to traditional Methodism and others may have before them sufficient material to arouse their interest.

William R. Davies, Ross Peart

HISTORICAL BACKGROUND

When it is remembered that in Acts 1:8 Jesus stated the purpose of the gift of the Holy Spirit to be that of giving His disciples power to be His witnesses, there can be no doubt that a mighty baptism of power took place amongst the early Methodists, with revival as its fruit. In this study it is with Wesley and his preachers that the historical outline begins.

1. Spiritual Experiences

John Wesley never used the phrase 'baptism in the Spirit' to describe any of his personal religious experiences. Others have made their own interpretations. Leslie Davison suggests that something happened in November, 1725, which could be regarded as his conversion experience, whereas his Aldersgate Street experience of May, 1738, was a direct confirmation of what Paul calls 'the witness of the Spirit', a filling with righteousness, peace, joy and love. (L. Davison. Pathway to Power, Pgs. 57–58.) Charles Clarke, on the other hand, refers not to May, 1738, but to January 1st, 1739 as Wesley's baptism in the Spirit, for on that morning during a love-feast at Fetter Lane, Wesley records "the power of God came mightily upon us insomuch that many cried out for exceeding joy, and many fell to the ground . . . we broke out with one voice, We praise Thee, O God, we acknowledge Thee to be the Lord". (C. Clarke. Pioneers of Revival. Pgs. 20–21. Wesley's Journal. Vol. 2. Pgs. 121–125.)

Although caution needs to be adopted in interpreting Wesley's experiences and the danger should be noted of trying to label them and force them into a system, it would be a brave man who would doubt that Wesley was a Spirit-filled believer. The same could be said of Charles Wesley, John Fletcher, and early Methodist preachers like Richard Whatcoat, Thomas Rankin, George Storey and John Nelson, to name but a few.

2. The Charismata

In 1744, Wesley preached a sermon on Scriptural Christianity in which he questioned whether the extraordinary gifts like healing, speaking in tongues and interpretation of tongues were designed to remain in the church throughout all ages and expressed the conviction that in Acts 4:31, the filling with the Holy Spirit was for the more excellent purpose of being given the mind that was in Christ and those ordinary fruits of the Spirit like love, joy, peace, longsuffering, gentleness and goodness. (Wesley's Fifty Three Sermons. Pgs. 41–42.) Later, in 1750, Wesley expressed the view that the reason why the miraculous gifts were so soon withdrawn was not only that faith and holiness were well nigh lost, but that dry, formal, orthodox men began even then to ridicule whatever gifts they had not themselves, and to decry them all as either madness or imposture. (Wesley's Journal, Vol. 3. Pg. 490.)

Fletcher of Madeley used the term 'baptism of the Spirit', believing such baptism necessary for believers to be sanctified and united in love and specially necessary for ministers in order that they should preach the word with power, bear up under troubles and persecutions, be directed into all truth and testify of Jesus but "not to work miracles and speak with tongues". (Fletcher's Works. Vol. 7. Pgs. 464–5.) Nevertheless, Fletcher, whilst contending only for "ordinary manifestations of Christ" was "far from supposing that all extraordinary or mixed manifestations have ceased". (Fletcher's Works. Vol. 8. Pg. 25.)

But did the early Methodists exercise spiritual gifts? According to Leslie Davison, "It could well be that because the first Methodists did not expect to receive the charismata, and indeed did not particularly want them, that they created a mental or spiritual block to their reception". (Pathway to Power. Pg. 73.) In answer to this, it may be argued that a careful study of Wesley's Works and particularly of the lives of the early Methodist preachers reveals evidence that all the spiritual gifts listed in 1 Cor 12:8-10 were exercised, with the one exception of the interpretation of tongues. Admittedly, the evidence has to be looked for in scattered references, but it is there. No doubt when early Methodists exercised the gifts, because there was no specific teaching on the charismata, they were not consciously aware of manifesting them as such. Thomas Walsh, for example, in 1751 does not say that he spoke in tongues, but that "the Lord gave me a language I knew not of". (Lives of Early Methodist Preachers. Vol. 3. Pg. 211.) William Black did not speak of the miracle of exorcism or deliverance but when confronted with one in need of deliverance, "was peculiarly helped to wrestle with the Lord that he would either bind or cast out the evil one". (Ibid. Vol. 5. Pgs. 272–3.) John Nelson did not speak of the word of wisdom, but when confronted with a clergyman who called talk of the Spirit all delusion, Nelson, with such a word replied, "How could you affirm before God and the congregation that you were inwardly moved by the Holy Spirit to take upon you the office of a deacon, and now testify there is no such thing as being moved by the Spirit?". (Ibid. Vol. 1. Pg. 114.)

Neither would any deny that John Wesley exercised some of the charismatic ministries mentioned in 1 Cor 12:28 and Ephesians 4:11. E. W. Thompson attempts to justify Wesley's ordinations on the ground that he was a truly apostolic man. (E. W. Thompson. Wesley Apostolic Man.) Reading Wesley's Works, who can deny the spiritual quality of his teaching ministry? In acknowledging the genius of Wesley in the developing organization of the Methodist Societies, who can deny his administrative talent? When one reads his Sermons, Journal and Letters who can deny his effectiveness either as evangelist or pastor? He was truly a 'charismatic man'.

3. Bridging the Gap

Emmanuel Sullivan regarded the revivalist, Charles G. Finney (1792–1875) as "A bridge-builder between primitive Wesleyanism and modern Pentecostalism". (E. Sullivan. Can the Pentecostal Movement Renew the Churches? Pg. 3.) Having experienced several enduements of the Spirit's power, Finney taught that following conversion there were further outpourings of the Spirit which he called "baptism in the Spirit", their purpose being that of holiness. Wesley, earlier, had taught the doctrine of Scriptural Holiness or Christian Perfection as a further work of the Holy Spirit subsequent to the New Birth which could be perhaps "gradually wrought" but more desirably "done instantaneously". (J. Wesley. Fifty Three Sermons. Pg. 621.) F. D. Bruner has argued that the nineteenth century holiness movement was derived from a Wesleyan heritage and that its theological centre was a second experience, the nature of which was sanctification or perfect love. This "subsequent experience" was later to assume importance in Pentecostalism. (F. D. Bruner. A Theology of the Holy Spirit. Pg. 42.)

Leslie Davison points out that the major holiness groups taught that sanctification and the baptism in the Spirit were one and the same experience, but at the turn of the nineteenth century "there were many earnest seekers, of all denominations, vaguely discontented even with the experience of holiness, who were looking for something more in accordance with the triumphant life of the Apostolic Church depicted in the pages of the New Testament". (Pathway to Power. Pg. 89.) Bruner regards the Welsh Revival as the last 'gap' across which the sparks of holiness enthusiasm leapt to ignite the Pentecostal Movement. (A Theology of the Holy Spirit. Pg. 46.)

Evan Roberts, the Welsh Revival leader, was converted through the preaching of Seth Joshua, a Methodist minister. In 1904,

Roberts experienced baptism in the Spirit, which he distinguished sharply from conversion. (W. Hollenweger. The Pentecostals. Pgs. 179–180.) Roberts' ministry during the Welsh Revival has been described as "a ministry of gifts rather than a ministry of the Word", although because of its "susceptibility to abuse" Roberts discouraged the use of tongues until Christians were more acquainted with the counterfeiting methods of the spirits of evil. (E. Evans. The Welsh Revival of 1904. Pgs. 163, 195.)

4. Classical Pentecostals

Mention should be made of Edward Irving, who in some ways was a forerunner of the Classical Pentecostals. Whilst minister of the Scots National Church in Regent Square, London, he came to the conclusion that the Second Coming of Christ was imminent and that the spiritual gifts bestowed on the Apostolic Church of the first century were not exceptional, but only absent since that time through a lack of faith. In November, 1831, he reported the gift of tongues and prophecy in his own congregation and these manifestations continued in worship for three months. He was deposed from the ministry of the Church of Scotland in 1833, having been found guilty of holding heretical views about the Incarnation. Irving became one of the founders of the Catholic Apostolic Church in which the spiritual gifts were exercised but his leadership was usurped by others and he died in 1834.

The real roots of Classical Pentecostalism are found at the beginning of the twentieth century. In 1900, Charles Parham, an American Methodist minister in search of deeper spirituality, began a Bible School in Topeka, Kansas. His students discovered whilst searching through the Acts of the Apostles, that in Acts the gift of tongues usually accompanied the outpouring of the Spirit. Agnes Ozman, one of the students, asked Parham to lay hands on her and pray for the gift. After some hesitation he complied and she began to speak in a strange tongue. Later, in 1905, Parham started another Bible School in Houston, Texas, and one of his students was W. J. Seymour, a young negro minister, who in 1906, took over a property in Azusa Street, Los Angeles, a stable which had once been used as a Methodist chapel. Here began a pentecostal revival which lasted for three years.

Thomas Ball Barratt, a Methodist minister in Oslo, went to America in 1905 to raise money for his church. He never visited Azusa Street but corresponded with the people there. Following a communion service in New York in 1906, he experienced baptism in the Spirit and on his return home began a powerful and fruitful ministry.

One who had visited Evan Roberts in the Welsh Revival centres was Alexander Boddy, Vicar of All Saints' Parish Church, Monkwearmouth, Sunderland. He invited Barratt to minister in his parish. Barratt came over in August, 1907, and as a result of his visit, All Saints' became the 'Azusa Street' of England. Smith Wigglesworth was amongst those baptized in the Spirit in the Sunderland revival. He became a prominent figure in Pentecostal circles and exercised a notable healing ministry.

From a Methodist viewpoint it is interesting to note that one Methodist minister, Charles Parham, was involved in the origins of the twentieth century pentecostal movement and another, T. B. Barratt, played a large part in carrying the work into Europe.

In England, arising from the revivals in Wales and Sunderland, there is a number of Pentecostal Churches. Perhaps the best known are the Apostolic Church, the Elim Church and the Assemblies of God. Daniel P. Williams and W. Jones Williams of Penygroes, founders of the Apostolic Church, were converted in the Welsh Revival of 1904. The Elim Church finds its origin in the work of George and Stephen Jeffreys of Maesteg in Wales. The Assemblies of God arose with the decline of the Pentecostal Missionary Union in which Alexander Boddy and Cecil Polhill (a former missionary in Tibet) had worked, Donald Gee becoming a leading figure amongst the Assemblies.

Both Boddy and Polhill urged people who had been baptized in the Spirit during this period to remain within the established churches. It seems, however, that "new wine" could not be contained in "old skins". Undoubtedly there were faults on both sides, but the sad fact remains that some who had entered into this new experience felt ostracized and obliged to come apart. The hopeful aspect of Neo-Pentecostalism is that it is developing within the historic churches of Christendom and it is desirable that there it should remain as a renewing force.

5. Neo-Pentecostals

In 1936, David du Plessis, then General Secretary of the Apostolic Faith Mission in South Africa, received a prophecy through Smith Wigglesworth. He was told that through him God would work to revive the churches in the last days and through the churches, God would turn the world upside down. Years later, he made contact with the World Council of Churches, whilst working in America. Dr. Visser 't Hooft, in 1954, invited du Plessis to attend the World Council of Churches at Evanston as a staff member and in 1956 he was able to speak to twenty four ecumenical leaders. His subsequent work in the historic churches of Christendom, including his visit as an observer to the Second Vatican Council, is of real importance in the developing Charismatic or Neo-Pentecostal Movement.

The Charismatic Movement took root in the Episcopal Church of America through the ministry of men like Dennis Bennett, whose charismatic ministry began first in 1959 at St. Mark's Church, Van Nuys, and continued at St. Luke's Church, Seattle. A similar work of the Spirit began in the American Roman Catholic Church at the Duquesne University, Pittsburgh, and at Notre Dame University, South Bend, Indiana, in the 1960's. Since then a pentecostal revival has swept through the North American Roman Catholic Church which received guarded approval from the American Roman Catholic bishops in 1969. Many Roman Catholics see this movement of the Spirit as God's answer to the prayer of Pope John XXIII for God to renew the Church, in which the Pope used the phrase "a new pentecost". Not only Episcopalians and Roman Catholics have been involved, but also Lutherans, Presbyterians, Baptists and Methodists, and what happened in America in these churches also began to happen in Europe.

In the early 1960's a number of speakers involved in the Charismatic Movement visited Britain from America including the Pentecostal minister David du Plessis, the Episcopalian priest Frank Maguire and the Lutheran pastor and theologian Larry Christenson. By 1964 the gentle wind of the Spirit was being experienced in England and in that year David du Plessis spoke to many meetings and attended the General Assembly of the Church of Scotland in Edinburgh. Michael Harper was amongst the first of the Anglican clergy to experience the pentecostal blessing. It resulted in 1964 in his founding the Fountain Trust which has as its aim, "the renewal of the spiritual life of the Christian Church" and seeks "to enable Christians to receive the power of the Holy Spirit and the full benefits of charismatic renewal whilst at the same time safeguarding these blessings from dangers such as fanaticism, schism and doctrinal error". It was the Fountain Trust which sponsored the first International Conference on the Holy Spirit, ecumenical in nature, at the University of Surrey, Guildford, in 1971.

6. Methodist Pentecostals

Amongst the first English Methodists to experience baptism in the Holy Spirit was Charles J. Clarke, now a supernumerary minister. His experience took place in February, 1963, and gradually he discovered others who had been similarly blessed. To keep contact with Methodists interested in charismatic renewal, Charles and Mary Clarke began to issue, in September, 1968, a quarterly newsletter.

By 1969, it was evident that Dr. Leslie Davison, then General Secretary of the Home Mission Department, was acutely aware of the need for spiritual awakening as his article in the Home Mission Report for that year showed. He pointed to the Holy Spirit as the power for such an awakening, giving the New Testament teaching about the Spirit together with an account of the modern pentecostal movement. Dr. Davison received a large number of appreciative letters from Methodists for the lead he had given. In subsequent work, his sympathetic involvement in the Charismatic Movement continued right up to his death in 1972.

Beginning in February, 1970, Leslie Davison met with a group of Methodist ministers in his London office once a quarter for four hours of fellowship, study and prayer concerning charismatic renewal in Methodism, and in July, 1970, he called a number of interested colleagues together at the Luton Industrial College. Dr. Davison was a speaker at the above mentioned International Conference at Surrey University, in July, 1971. There, he testified to his experience of the work of the Holy Spirit in his own life and his lectures have been published in the book, 'Pathway to Power'. Lord Rank, a leading Methodist layman, and Treasurer of the Home Mission Department was equally sympathetically involved in the work of the Charismatic Movement until his death, and was a source of encouragement to Dr. Davison.

The quarterly magazine for Methodists entitled 'Dunamis' was first published by the authors of this paper in September, 1972, its purpose being to share charismatic teaching and testimony. Since then, this magazine has been merged with the afore-mentioned quarterly newsletter. The circulation of 'Dunamis' at the time of writing is 3,500, indicating something of the interest being shown amongst Methodists. There exists, too, amongst Methodists, a nationwide network of fellowships interested in charismatic renewal meeting mid-week, some of which are ecumenical in character.

Sponsored by the Home Mission Department, a conference took place in October, 1972, at the Cliff College Conference Centre involving some seventy people including ministers, deaconesses and missionaries. Since then several day Charismatic Conferences have been held throughout the country and the meeting of ministers begun by Dr. Davison continues as a Working Party encouraged by the Home Mission Department.

The evidence to hand is of an increasing interest amongst the Methodist people in this work of God's Spirit in the twentieth century. The publication of this paper is yet another milestone along the way, leading, not a few believe, to a renewal of spiritual power within the Methodist Church.

DOCTRINAL ISSUES

The Charismatic Movement, like Methodism, has an experiential emphasis in its theology. In recent times, religious experience has been subjected to the scrutiny of scientific analysis and as a result, some have been suspicious of claims made to religious experiences. Psychologists and sociologists have described the processes involved in such experiences in terms of inner conflicts, tensions, group pressures and the resolving of conflicts, etc. Such descriptions may well be accurate. For the Christian it is the faith factor that makes all the difference, for the Christian believes that the processes so described, often in very technical terms, are either the way God's Spirit has worked or the means God has used to bring a person into the wonder of a personal experience of God. The possibility of a genuine Christian experience need not be doubted, nor need there be any reason to abandon an experience-centred theology.

Much of what follows will be concerned with experience. The subject is a difficult one and questions will be posed rather than answered, though with some pointers given towards possible solutions to the problems raised. Certainly, as Leslie Davison has said, "great theological issues must be clarified if the perils of exaggeration and error are to be avoided", and "much sifting has yet to be done". (Pathway to Power. Pg. 11.)

1. Baptism in the Spirit

This is the term commonly used in the Charismatic Movement to describe the experience common to most of those involved in it. Strictly, the term is unscriptural, because in scripture it is the verbal form that is found. The Baptist says of Jesus, "He shall baptize you with the Holy Spirit" (St. Matthew 3:11) and Jesus promises His disciples, "you shall be baptized with the Holy Spirit". (Acts 1:5)

Other scriptural phrases used to describe the experience include "filled with the Holy Spirit" (Acts 2:4) and "received the Holy Spirit" (Acts 8:17; 10:47). In Acts 19:6, after Paul had laid hands on the Ephesian disciples, the experience is described in this way: "the Holy Spirit came upon them". The experience is spoken of as a gift in St. Luke 11:13 where Jesus says that God will "give the Holy Spirit to those who ask Him".

Care should be taken not to confuse baptism in the Spirit with the manifestations that follow. Such manifestations, whether tongues or prophecy, whether love, joy, or peace are confirming signs which in point of time may well accompany baptism in the Spirit, but should not be confused with it. Although signs more often than not accompany baptism in the Spirit, it is possible for one to experience it without signs following immediately, as, for example, was the case with Oswald Chambers, who only received confirmation of the reality of his experience two days later. (M. James. I believe in the Holy Ghost. Pg. 151.) Nevertheless, it is baptism in the Spirit which has been for many the entrance into a new spiritual dimension in which the charismata have become manifest in personal experience and used as tools of ministry for the Body of Christ.

What, then, is baptism in the Spirit? Definitions are really inadequate. E. Sullivan has described it as "an encounter with God which makes a person a more effective witness of Christ". (Can the Pentecostal Movement Renew the Churches? Pg. 6.) Others have talked in terms of "an implosion of God's Spirit" or "the release of God's Spirit" or "a filling of the life of God in the soul of man" or "the fulness of Christ indwelling the human personality". The definition given by John Horner at the Eastbrook Hall Conference in February 1973 may be of help: "The Baptism in the Holy Spirit is the name given to a gift of God in the Holy Spirit in which a believer is made conscious of the indwelling presence of Christ and is empowered to make an effective witness to Christ in word and deed".

2. Classical Pentecostal Teaching

There are differences between the various branches of Classical
Pentecostals on matters of belief and practice but it would be true
to say that a doctrine in which most are unified is that of two
major Christian experiences, of a first and second blessing. Such
doctrine teaches that one becomes a Christian in a "new birth"
experience and is baptized in the Holy Spirit in a second
experience. In stating this doctrine, George Jeffreys wrote "that at
conversion the person is made a new creature in Christ, that he is
cleansed from all sin by the blood of Christ, and that he receives
the subsequent gift of the Holy Spirit to empower him for
service". (G. Jeffreys. Pentecostal Rays. Pg. 33.) Jeffreys strongly
contested the traditional Methodist teaching and that of the
Holiness Movement on sanctification as being the purpose of a
further work of the Spirit following conversion, by arguing, "The
Holy Spirit convicts of sin but is the Blood that cleanses".
(Pentecostal Rays. Pg. 33.)

On the question of confirming signs following the experience of
baptism in the Spirit, Jeffreys wrote, ". . . there are three main
schools of thought. The first teaches that every person who
receives the gift of the Holy Spirit will have the sign of speaking
in tongues; the second, that everyone who receives should have
some definite supernatural manifestation of the Spirit in the
mortal body, not necessarily the sign of speaking in tongues;
while the third stands for the reception of the Spirit by faith
without an outward sign. The second view is the Scriptural
one. . . ." (Pentecostal Rays. Pg. 34.)

Jeffreys was here expressing his own viewpoint and,
incidentally, that of the Elim Church, where speaking in tongues
is seen as a frequent sign of baptism in the Spirit but not the only
initial evidence, whereas other Pentecostal Churches, for
example, the Assemblies of God, would regard speaking in
tongues as *the* initial evidence of baptism in the Spirit.

Many people in the Neo-Pentecostal or Charismatic Movement
share the Classical Pentecostal teaching of a two-stage experience.
Michael Harper, for instance, says that baptism in the Spirit in the
New Testament is treated as distinct from the new birth and that
many Christians experience it some time after the new birth,
although he qualifies this by saying that ideally, both should be
experienced at the outset of the Christian life. (M. Harper. Life in
the Holy Spirit. Pgs. 4–5.) Similar differences of belief exist
amongst Neo-Pentecostals as amongst Classical Pentecostals on

the question of whether or not speaking in tongues is the initial evidence of baptism in the Spirit.

How far this kind of teaching can be related to Methodist doctrine is a question for careful consideration, but first, a reminder about particular Methodist emphases will not be out of place.

3. Methodist Doctrinal Emphases

Whilst accepting all the doctrines of the Nicene Creed, Methodist emphasis has been on the evangelical doctrines of Justification by Faith, the New Birth, the Witness of the Spirit and Scriptural Holiness.

JUSTIFICATION BY FAITH

Wesley described "the plain scriptural notion of justification" as being "pardon and forgiveness of sins". It is an act of God who forgives the penitent sinner "for the sake of the propitiation made by the blood of his Son". Faith in Jesus is "the only necessary condition" of justification, for faith is the only way "of obtaining a share in his merit". Such faith is "a sure trust and confidence that Christ died for my sins, that he loved me and gave himself for me". (J. Wesley. Fifty Three Sermons or Sermons on Several Occasions. Pgs. 63–67.)

CONVERSION OR NEW BIRTH

Conversion or the New Birth is defined by Wesley as "that great change which God works in the soul when he brings it to life; when he raises it from the death of sin to the life of righteousness . . . the change wrought in the soul by the almighty Spirit of God when it is 'created anew in Christ Jesus' . . . in a word, it is that change whereby the earthly, sensual, devilish mind is turned into the mind that was in Christ Jesus". (Fifty Three Sermons. Pg. 641.) The new birth is the work of the Holy Spirit. Colin W. Williams points out that "Wesley makes a logical, not a temporal distinction between justification and the new birth". In other words justification and the new birth happen together. The "logical distinction" is that justification is seen as reliance upon the "objective" work of Christ; sanctification, which begins with the new birth, is seen as reliance upon the "subjective" work of the Spirit. In other words, justification is what Christ does for us whereas the new birth and sanctification are what the Holy Spirit does within us. (C. W. Williams. John Wesley's Theology Today. Pgs. 99–100.)

The doctrine of Assurance or the Witness of the Spirit, Wesley based on Romans 8:16, "The Spirit itself beareth witness with our Spirit, that we are the children of God." It was the doctrine of an assurance of personal salvation. Wesley experienced such assurance at Aldersgate Street in May 1738, for after writing that he felt his heart strangely warmed and that he did trust in Christ alone for salvation, he continued, "and an assurance was given me that He had taken away my sins, even mine, and saved me from the law of sin and death" (Wesley's Journal. Vol. 1. Pgs. 475–6.)

C. W. Williams makes the point that for Wesley, assurance was not merely a matter of emotional feeling, but rather "a divine conviction God works in the soul, or more accurately, the spirit". (John Wesley's Theology Today. Pg. 105.)

Wesley described what he called "the testimony of God's Spirit" in this way: "The testimony of the Spirit is an inward impression on the soul, whereby the Spirit of God directly witnesses to my spirit, that I am a child of God; that Jesus Christ hath loved me, and given himself for me; and that all my sins are blotted out, and I, even I, am reconciled to God." In modern terms this has been described as an awareness "of being grasped by God's Spirit". (John Wesley's Theology Today. Pg. 110.)

It would be easy to mistake feelings for true assurance and of this Wesley was not unaware, so he outlined several scriptural tests to apply to distinguish a genuine experience from "the presumption of a natural mind". These were: "repentance or conviction of sin"; an awareness of being born of God in which "a vast and mighty change" has taken place, "from darkness to light" and "from death unto life"; "lowliness" together with meekness, patience, gentleness and longsuffering; loving God and keeping His commandments. All these comprise "the answer of a good conscience toward God" or the testimony of one's own Spirit. (Fifty Three Sermons. Pgs. 127–135.)

Scriptural Holiness is sometimes called Christian Perfection, sometimes Perfect Love, sometimes Full Salvation and sometimes Entire Sanctification. Wesley believed that God had raised up the Methodist people to propagate this doctrine. (Wesley's Letters.

Vol. 8. Pg. 238.) Perfect love was an experience Wesley preached but never claimed.

Wesley did not teach an absolute perfection. Christians could not be "so perfect in this life as to be free from ignorance". They could not be free from mistake or infirmities, by which he meant "all those inward or outward imperfections which are not of a moral nature" such as incoherence of thought, slowness of understanding, slowness of speech and impropriety of language, and they could not be free from temptation. (Fifty Three Sermons. Pgs. 564–568.)

In various places Wesley defines Christian Perfection. He describes it as "that love of God and our neighbour which implies deliverance from all sin"; it is "loving God with all our heart, soul, mind and strength" which implies "no wrong temper" and by which all thoughts, words and actions are governed by pure love. (J. Wesley. A Plain Account of Christian Perfection. Pgs. 41. 42. 51.) His sermon on the subject says that "a Christian is so far perfect as not to commit sin" and is freed from evil thoughts and evil tempers, being purified from pride, self-will, and anger. (Fifty Three Sermons. Pgs. 579–582.)

Wesley declared this work of the Holy Spirit to be an experience which was received by faith and given instantaneously, although he qualified what he meant by instantaneously, in writing of the experience, "there is a gradual work, both before and after that moment, so that one may affirm the work is gradual, another it is instantaneous, without any manner of contradiction". (A Plain Account of Christian Perfection. Pgs. 41, 81.)

The implication of a gradual work following the gift of perfect love is that those who receive it still fall short of God's perfect law and need the constant illumination of God to reveal their continuing imperfections. (John Wesley's Theology Today. Pg. 185.) Wesley would never use the term "sinless perfection" for he saw that "involuntary transgressions" consequent upon ignorance and mistakes were inevitable. (A Plain Account of Christian Perfection. Pg. 45.) When he referred to perfect Christians not committing sin, he excluded from such sin "involuntary transgressions". His doctrine was really one of relative Christian Perfection.

4. The Question of Correlation

How far and in what way, if at all, does the Pentecostal teaching about baptism in the Spirit accord with Methodist doctrine? There are several possibilities.

IDENTIFICATION WITH CONVERSION

Some would take the view that baptism in the Spirit is to be associated with conversion, indeed that it is part of the event or process of becoming a Christian, and that only those who have been baptized in the Spirit can properly be called Christians. It is not something subsequent to conversion but an integral part of it. J. D. G. Dunn concludes, "It is, in the last analysis, that which makes a man a Christian". (J. D. G. Dunn. Baptism in the Holy Spirit. Pg. 226.) In support of this view it is sometimes argued that in certain cases in Acts, (Acts 8:17; Acts 19:6) where there appears to have been a 'second blessing' of receiving the Spirit, it is because there has been a defect in experience which has to be put right and it is the decisive gift of the Spirit which makes a man properly a Christian. John's teaching that a man must be born of the Spirit (St. John 3:3-5) is equated with Spirit-baptism. Paul's teaching, that anyone who does not have the Spirit of Christ does not belong to Him (Romans 8:9) is also used in support of this argument.

IDENTIFICATION WITH WITNESS OF THE SPIRIT

Others would identify baptism in the Spirit with the Witness of the Spirit of Assurance.

Leslie Davison alludes to Wesley's description of the Witness of the Spirit in his second discourse on the subject (Fifty Three Sermons. Pg. 138) where Wesley writes "the Spirit of God . . . so works upon the soul by his immediate influence and by a strong though inexplicable operation, that the stormy wind and troubled waves subside, and there is a sweet calm; the heart resting as in the arms of Jesus, and the sinner being clearly satisfied that God is reconciled, that all his iniquities are forgiven and his sins covered". On this Davison comments, "It would be difficult to find a better description of the experience now called the baptism in the Spirit". (Pathway to Power. Pg. 60.)

Michael Harper would seem also to support this view. Having shown that Jesus, after His anointing with the power of the Holy Spirit at the river Jordan received a fresh assurance of His Father's love, His satisfaction with His life and His divine Sonship, he goes on to say, "A similar experience often comes when we have been filled with the Spirit. We may hear no voice from heaven but we do receive a deeper assurance of God's love for us and of our status as His children". (M. Harper. Walk in the Spirit. Pg. 25.)

Probably the reason why in Methodist teaching this Witness of the Spirit or Assurance is not referred to as a second experience or blessing is that it points back to the earlier conversion experience for the purpose of confirming it, and in this way is bound up with that earlier experience. Whilst for some assurance has come after conversion, nevertheless for others conversion and assurance have occurred concurrently.

IDENTIFICATION WITH SCRIPTURAL HOLINESS

Like the Pentecostals, Methodists believe in a work of the Spirit subsequent to conversion, but in Methodist doctrine this refers to the experience of Scriptural Holiness or Christian Perfection. Wesley himself used the term "second blessing" for this experience. (Wesley's Letters. Vol. 5. Pg. 333.) Methodists who testified to this experience clearly regarded it as the power of God's Spirit working within them. Robert Wilkinson says that some months following his conversion, in July 1767, a preacher "earnestly exhorted all present to look for the second blessing" and he describes his response: ". . . the power of God seized me. I found I could not resist . . . I found such an emptying and then such a heaven of love springing up in my soul as I had never felt before with an application of these blessed words, — He that believeth on me, as the Scripture hath said, out of his belly shall flow rivers of living water," which was a clear reference to the indwelling Holy Spirit. (Lives of Early Methodist Preachers, Vol. 6. Pg. 217.) Many others, like John Fletcher, Matthias Joyce, John Furz, William Hunter, John Pawson and James Rogers testified to a similar experience.

Such a "second blessing", some Methodists would associate with baptism in the Spirit, but would extend the purpose of the baptism beyond that of entire sanctification, to include also spiritual gifts and the power to witness.

This view was expressed by Samuel Chadwick in an earlier decade this century. Chadwick taught that "Baptism of the Holy Spirit" was an experience definite and distinct from that of regeneration, which brought "a gift of power" to equip believers for service and witness, but he also describes this as "an experience of Sanctification and the abiding fullness of the Spirit". He sums it up in these words: "Deliverance from sin, efficiency in service and effectiveness in witnessing are given with the fullness of Pentecostal blessing". (S. Chadwick. The Way to Pentecost. Pgs. 37–38.) Both spiritual fruit and spiritual gifts were important for Chadwick. Gifts were enduements of power for service, whereas fruit was for character and quality of life; both were of the Spirit. To eliminate any possible confusion, Chadwick wrote, "The Blessing is known by many names and it is often confused with other experiences of Grace. It is known as the Pentecostal Gift of the Spirit, as Entire Sanctification, Christian Perfection and Perfect Love". (The Way to Pentecost. Pgs. 108, 124.)

A POSSIBLE SOLUTION TO THE PROBLEM

If the experience of baptism in the Spirit has any place at all in the Methodist theological framework, perhaps it is best identified with Assurance or the Witness of the Spirit for the following reasons:

a. Many who experience the gifts of the Spirit subsequent to baptism in the Spirit make no claim to Entire Sanctification. Thomas Walsh, for example, spoke in tongues in 1751, but was still seeking Entire Sanctification in 1758. (Lives of Early Methodist Preachers. Vol. 3. Pg. 257.) Moreover, much of the point of 1 Corinthians was to remind the Corinthian Church of the need for love in using the spiritual gifts. One cannot therefore identify the experience of baptism in the Spirit with Entire Sanctification.

b. At conversion, the Holy Spirit brings the believer into Christ and begins His work of sanctification, but the new-born Christian will be less inclined to witness without the personal assurance of the reality of his experience. Baptism in the Spirit is that which brings the power to witness boldly and effectively to Christ in word and deed.

c. It is with the Witness of the Spirit that real assurance comes. The conversion experience of the believer is confirmed by this "divine conviction" which the Holy Spirit gives and as a result the believer is confident to declare what he knows to be true. Not only has the Holy Spirit brought assurance, but also the power of effective witness. It was after Wesley's experience of the Witness of the Spirit that his revolutionary ministry really began.

d. The reason why the extraordinary spiritual gifts have not been manifested in the experience of many who claim the Witness of the Spirit is simply one of ignorance, or, possibly, unbelief. To manifest spiritual gifts, man's cooperation with God is necessary. If one is ignorant of the possibility of manifesting spiritual gifts, or does not believe it is possible for them to be used, then clearly the gifts will lie dormant.

Needless to say, other conclusions can be drawn and other solutions offered, but this merely indicates the complexity of the problem and the need for further study.

5. Other Doctrinal Problems

Questions such as those concerned with the relationship of baptism in the Spirit to water-baptism, confirmation and ordination are ones that have to be faced, but these are not specifically Methodist problems. There are differences between the historic churches about the sacrament of water-baptism, some churches do not have confirmation and there are also differences in belief about what happens in the ordination of the ministry. The scene is complex even before the question of baptism in the Spirit in relation to these things is considered. It may well be that the Charismatic Movement is pointing forward to a situation in which water-baptism, confirmation and ordination become re-charged with meaning.

Two thoughts from J. Rodman Williams may be of help. He says that ". . . the dynamic movement of the Spirit does not fit very well into traditional theological categories" but later adds, "The turn we need to make . . . is towards an action of the Holy Spirit which fits no category, but one that does make much of our traditional theology operational". (J. Rodman Williams. The Era of the Spirit. Pgs. 39, 41.)

One possible way forward is tentatively suggested here. If a sacrament may be defined as an "outward and visible sign of an inward and spiritual grace", then water-baptism would express the believer's faith in Jesus Christ, that is, his conversion, as well as the fact that the Church receives him as a member of her Body. Confirmation would be a following ordinance, in which there would take place the laying on of hands with prayer for baptism in the Spirit. Ordination of the ministry would be by the laying on of hands with prayer for the necessary "ministry-gifts" of the Spirit, (1 Corinthians 12:28; Ephesians 4:11) to be conferred upon those separated to ministerial office in the church of Christ.

Admittedly, this way forward begs the question of existing

The Charismatic Movement

differences, but perhaps theologians of different traditions who are "one in the Spirit" may be led to examine these together in order to try and find a way through.

6. A Faith Experience

An examination of the passages in Acts where people were baptized in the Spirit (Acts 2; 8; 10; 19) reveals that different people experience Spirit-baptism in different ways and this concurs with contemporary experience. Some were already Christians, whereas others, like Cornelius, were not. Cornelius and his household became Christians and were baptized in the Spirit in one glorious experience. For others, like the Samaritan Christians and the Ephesian disciples, there was a "second blessing". There was the laying on of hands with prayer prior to Spirit-baptism for some, but not for others. Some were baptized in water, which presupposes repentance, before their Spirit-baptism; others experienced water-baptism following baptism in the Spirit. Speaking in tongues accompanied Spirit-baptism in three out of the four instances and in one of these there was prophecy also. In one instance there was no speaking in tongues, although it is clear that there was some distinctive evidence of Spirit-baptism.

The one common factor in all these instances was that of faith in Christ, and presumably together with that faith, a desire for all that Christ had to give. The New Testament makes it plain that Jesus is the one who baptizes in the Holy Spirit, so faith in Jesus is the one clear essential. How people arrive at that faith and in what precise set of circumstances Jesus will baptize in the Holy Spirit can be neither specified nor anticipated. The dynamism of the Spirit requires a diversity of pattern which must be allowed for in any theology of the Spirit. Even if it were agreed that water-baptism and confirmation related to conversion and Spirit-baptism respectively and Christians were properly required by the church to be baptized in water and confirmed, it would have to be understood that the operation of the Holy Spirit could not be limited to such ordinances, because neither scripture nor experience would validate such a position. In the end, God is sovereign.

Essentially then, baptism in the Spirit is a faith-in-Christ experience in that it is when one genuinely desirous of being baptized in the Spirit trusts Christ to do this for him, that Spirit-baptism occurs. At that moment, there may be gifts accompanying or there may be none, but sooner or later, clearly discernible confirmation is given. This may be the gift of tongues or some other gift; it may be a sense of love, peace or joy, but withal a deep "divine conviction" or assurance, through faith, that Christ has surely acted. Wesley wrote that faith was "the only instrument of salvation" (Fifty Three Sermons. Pg. 67.) Faith in Christ the Baptizer is the only instrument of baptism in the Spirit.

THE BODY MINISTRY OF THE METHODIST SOCIETY

The Church as the Body of Christ is the ideal — a corporate whole working beautifully and harmoniously in unbroken fellowship with all parts in co-ordinated activity. Methodism has ever been rich in this Body Ministry. Its ecclesiastical machinery has had both the Ministry and the laity complementing one another in the Lord's work.

1. Class/House Meeting

In the spiritual economy of Methodism the class meeting was "the germ cell out of which the whole economy develops" and from that "primitive life-tissue" all else evolved. Beginning as an "Enquiry meeting" for confession it later developed into an "Experience meeting". In either case it was a *sharing together* in Christ.

The decline of the class lay in its becoming a "formula" for salvation rather than a bringer and nourisher of salvation. Its leadership became in the nineteenth century the illiterate, and the middle class merchant would not be so ruled. By the early twentieth century, it has died its death in its original form as a sharing in Christ.

The fellowship-gap needed to be filled and the house group and the small Church fellowship have sought to perpetuate the tradition of the class meeting. These, in most cases, have had a limited success. They have been at the level of the study group — the mind exercised and fed but the spirit still largely cold. A "Class Leaders Treasury" of 1880 had warned that the cry was becoming "Give us intellect". Although this was a gift from God there was "little cry for heart-fire, and life-energy". Some Methodist people are tiring of the house group being offered as the salvation of the Church — to them it manifestly has not been such!

The Charismatic Movement

Whilst offering an informal situation there has been lack of complete freedom to share fully due to a measure of structured formality still being present. There has still been a tendency for these to cling to ministerial and local preacher domination and in their absence the outgoing personality of the group has felt obliged to stimulate the discussion.

Real freedom to share at depth has been difficult.

The present movement of God's Spirit centres round the small group meeting often in the home. Here many are experiencing an amazing freedom to share of themselves and their personal experiences and difficulties without any inhibition and embarrassment. What we for some thirty years have been trying to simulate, the Spirit is making a reality.

What then, is the real, essential difference between the traditional class/house group and the charismatic Bible study-prayer group?

The differences are many and varied.

a. *There is no preparation* apart from the daily individual devotions of the participants. They bring the fruits of their spiritual lives ready to give and in so doing all receive. Revelation in the Spirit of Jesus day by day is the subconscious preparation.

b. *There is consequently no set agenda,* no study outline, and no questionnaire is needed. The Spirit sets the programme and He sees to its implementation. It is true that the Spirit works through the mind to set the programme. New attention is drawn to Bible passages, new questions are asked of the faith and new difficulties and joys examined in the light of the Spirit.

c. *There is no leader* (ministerial or lay). The Spirit leads and moves each one as He wills. "Each one contributes a hymn, a psalm, a spiritual song." There are very few who do not contribute. Embarrassed silences are not the order of the day whilst pregnant, Spirit-filled ones are experienced. People *want to share* their inner lives to build and edify the Body. They (even the most shy and reserved of them) do it without effort or strain. This freedom of the Spirit seems to be directly experienced as a result of the release of the Spirit which comes with being baptized in Holy Spirit. Newcomers are amazed at the way in which the loving atmosphere convicts them of their lack of freedom of Spirit and also allows them the environment in which to become free.

d. *Ingredients of Bible study, gifts — ministry, prayer, devotional singing, discussion and counselling are all mixed in a remarkable way.* Most charismatic groups would have all of these elements in almost every meeting. In this sense it is not easy to announce the meeting. One cannot say "Come to our prayer meeting", "Come to our Bible study", "Come to our fellowship". One must just say "Come and share with us in the deep things of Christ as the Spirit leads". The meeting may turn out to be a joyful session of Worship in the Spirit or it may prove to be an evening of deep theological searching about the faith. Incidentally, one cannot say whether or not the extraordinary gifts of the Spirit (1 Cor 12:8-10) will be in operation in any one meeting — that decision rests with God and not with us. People who claim this deeper experience of Christ have only been termed 'charismatic' in that this expresses the new dimension of spiritual gifts (it may be a peculiar emphasis to some) into which they have been led in terms of their spirituality. They are evangelical and missionary and are only following the leading of the Spirit. It is precisely this Spirit who makes the meeting of these people seem so untidy. The way the Spirit works is not untidy — it is only so in terms of the way our minds work! Here is an unpredictability and a mixture of various elements rarely encountered in a traditional house group.

e. *The topic of conversation in house groups is widely varied. In groups of Spirit-filled Christians the talk is of basic and essential Christianity.* Jesus and the Word are always given the centre. With the baptism in the Holy Spirit goes a deep and new desire for fresh personal revelations of the Truth as it is revealed in the Bible. Questions about God, Jesus, the Holy Spirit, Salvation, etc. come with unrehearsed spontaneity. Problems of Church growth and organization, current affairs and world politics are in the background and the spirituality is turned upon Jesus as Lord and Saviour. The inner life of the believer and the desire for the Methodist people to share in that life is a deep concern for many.

f. *House groups tend to be of one age group and in the main denominational. Charismatic fellowships bring together folk of all ages,* from teenagers to pensioners of many years standing *and join in the Spirit people across the denominational barriers.* The true 'Ecumenism of Spirit' encountered in such groups is one of the greatest joys of the present movement.

g. It would be foolish to suppose that the new-found freedom of those interested in charismatic renewal needs to lead to licence. *There should be within charismatic groups a longing for growth in discipleship and holiness,* (the appropriation of the fruits of the Spirit). *There is a return to discipline of Spirit.* Two well known charismatic authors make this point very clear.

Merlin Caruthers in "Power in Praise" (p. 39) says: "The

baptism in the Holy Spirit is a cleansing, purging, stripping experience; it is total exposure to the searchlight of God's Truth into every corner of our lives. The baptism is designed to flush out and empty us of our self-reliance, our pride, our little shady areas of deception, and the excuses we've been holding on to — all the things that block our faith and the inflow of God's power and presence in our lives." Stephen B. Clark in "Baptized in the Spirit" (p. 36–7) tells us: "The gift of the Spirit is given to us to make spiritual growth much easier, and it does. People who are baptized in the Spirit can grow much more quickly than people who are not. I spent a number of years in Christian work before seeing charismatic renewal and I have spent a number of years since then. Both times I was working with the same kind of people — college students. Since we have been praying with them to be baptized in the Spirit, their spiritual growth has been much more rapid. The Spirit of God is producing a much deeper holiness in them. . . . It is not that they are trying harder, but that they are experiencing more. The Spirit of God is doing more of it in them".

Charismatic activity in its mainstream conventional elements (it does have its frauds and fanatics of course) is a holiness movement as well as a movement of power of Spirit. In charismatic groups they seek to *be*, (through the fruits) and *act* (through the gifts) like Jesus the Lord. This 'double-dimensional' Christian spirituality offers a balance to the life of the believer which may not be found in traditional fellowships and house groups.

We are aware that comparisons are odious but have engaged in this exercise to highlight the features which are dominant in groups attended in the main by people who are seeking baptism with the Holy Spirit. We are not at all calling into question the value of the small house fellowship — we are merely focussing attention on the deeper fullness and richness it can assume when fed, led and controlled by the Spirit of Christ.

Many would say that charismatic groups are simulated class meetings, that they are a reversion to type. In this sense this movement is an old-fashioned movement. This is not so. The Spirit does a new thing for every age and what he is doing in this age is to add to our Methodist inheritance a fuller and freer use of the gifts of the Spirit so that we may by way of sharing in fellowship become holier. But we are not copying the traditional class meeting. There is no inquisition (as there was until the mid-nineteenth century), there is no compunction in the running of or attendance at the charismatic meeting. Freedom is the keynote rather than structure and this in itself makes the class meeting and the charismatic fellowship very different. They have a similarity of purpose — discipleship and sharing — but their whole feel, outlook and modes of operation are different.

2. Prayer Meeting

This meeting, usually after the Sunday evening service, was part of the life of Methodism in the nineteenth century. Whilst it was predominantly a rural and Primitive Methodist feature, it nevertheless existed happily in even the highest of Wesleyan circles. T. B. Stephenson was "never afraid of a good roaring prayer meeting of the old-fashioned sort", and another Wesleyan, H. J. Pope, said with approval that the meetings "which followed the public services were frequently scenes of intense excitement and holy expectation". After the turn of the century by and large this meeting had become extinct and few were held.

The meeting itself was strange in that many left after the normal service before it began (as some now do with communion). It consisted of a basic diet of hymns juxtaposed with prayers many of which were long and frequently by the same people in the same wordings. Especially in rural and Primitive Methodist circles the participants were illiterate men with limited vocabulary. This is not to call in question their holiness or sincerity. Often the preacher or minister who had conducted the service would lead the meeting.

What can the charismatic prayer meeting add to this tradition of Methodism?

a. Quite obviously *it can add the realm of the vocal gifts of the Spirit.* Prophecy which Paul covets above all gifts can build, edify and exhort the gathered community. A 'Word' from the Lord can be the most spiritually uplifting experience in the life of the Christian. Tongues when used in accord with the principles laid down in 1 Cor 14 can be spiritually uplifting, pointing to Jesus. In any prayer meeting, the mind is on the day and its problems, myself and my needs. When tongues are divinely exercised the whole mind of the community is fixed on nothing else but Jesus. It is a 'trigger' which calls Christ into the midst. Interpretation (which can be either praise or a prophetic mechanism word) can speak to any or all. Very often this is verified immediately by another present bursting into prayer in thankfulness for the new

The Charismatic Movement

direction and guidance offered through the interpretation. Someone in tune with the infinite has been used to build up the Body without even being conscious of the fact. These gifts are love-service gifts. They are meant to be given away. We must use them in community or else they are as clanging gongs.

b. The tongue-tied prayer is not one who shares the filling of the Spirit. It is not only in glossolalia that fluency is expressed — in fact not more than one or two tongues are used in the balanced group in any one meeting. *It is the increased prayer vocabulary in the mother tongue which is the joy to so many.* What was an effort to seek for correct wording in prayer becomes a well of living water which just flows through the Spirit's inspiration. The mind-conscious prayer is to many the first deep enriching experience of the new infilling of the Spirit. In this way *all* may pray and not just the few; and none need worry about their natural command of the English language.

c. In general prayers are shorter. The A.B.C. of charismatic praying stresses B as brief. You are not leading, you are sharing, and everyone will want to do that. Here we enter what is for many a new concept — that of SHARED PRAYER. When we meet together we should bring the fruit of private devotion with us and give it in faith to the BODY. We share in an attitude of thankfulness what God has been doing for us. Others share in return and we become one in the Spirit. How beautiful and distinct is the prayer of every man and woman! If one holds back a prayer then the Body is impoverished. In the early Church "each one" had something to contribute. So it is with those deeply in the Spirit.

d. *Bible readings and the reading aloud of devotional verses from the hymn book or any other sources are often used.* This allows everyone the ability to offer of themselves even if not in their own words. These small, yet Christ-centred additions can often set the tone of the whole meeting. In one group recently people were just encouraged to say any scriptural adjective or phrase to describe Jesus that presented itself to their minds. He was Lord to one, King to another, Saviour to another, The Way to another and to another Lamb of God. Each person added a new facet of Jesus and He alone in this simple way was glorified.

e. The keynote of traditional prayer groups is often intercession and this is the staple diet of the group. Here charismatically inspired prayer differs greatly. *Praise flowing from full, thankful hearts is always the starting point of prayer.* "We praise and bless" is an oft found beginning and invocation of prayer. Many charismatic prayer groups are now giving themselves the title "Community of Praise". Praise is a basic element of prayer and its rediscovery is vitally needed in a doubting, frustrated Church. It is from this Jesus centrality that need-prayers for healing, guidance and others in trouble flow. Praise Jesus and your heart is bound to be naturally led to the needs of others. In the midst of this praise and the centring on others our own personal prayer requests are often forgotten and yet they seem to be answered or resolved simply by having been so mightily in the presence of the Lord Jesus. When self is forgotten one seems to have been given first place by virtue of one being prepared to give Jesus and others first place. The last seems to have become gloriously first in one's appropriation of the blessing of the Spirit.

   f. *The enthusiasm which can often be engendered in charismatic groups may very well need a 'brake' to stop healthy enthusiasm becoming fanatical excess. Here the charismatic group has a tool of invaluable proportions. The gift of the discerning of Spirits can be and ought to be exercised continually in the group.* If one is in the wrong (evil) Spirit or the spirit of self (natural enthusiasm) then one ought to be told. Indeed it would be very unloving not to correct this missing of the 'providential way'. If Christians care for one another in Christ then they should be 'watchmen' for one another that the whole Body might be blameless before Christ (Ezekiel 3:7, 33:6-7). This gift just allows one to test the spirits to see if they be of God. The faculty exercised in this case is supernatural. It is not natural discernment! This gift is not necessarily an oral pronouncement. A brother in Christ may have to be taken on one side after the meeting and led into all the truth. If the offence is such that it demands radical attention then one is in duty bound to apply the test and bring into the light that which is troubling the whole group. Even charismatic prayer groups can feel a sense of 'being bound' or 'burdened' and this extra gift of discerning of spirits (not, note, natural discernment which would lead further astray) is needed to uncover the cause of the heavy load.

   Christians are all used to being "together in one place" (Acts 2), but need to learn how to raise their voices "as one man" (Acts 2:24) as they call upon God. Christians all feel the necessity of "the whole body of believers" being "united in heart and soul". (Acts 4:32) And don't they want to do that which is "acceptable to the whole body"? (Acts 6:5). Charismatic people feel they are

The Charismatic Movement

finding one way in which God in His love is allowing them to become just this. An unbiased reporter from the 'National Catholic' magazine had this to say about a Pentecostal Roman community he was investigating:

"While tongues is said to be a common occurrence in the Pentecostal community at Notre Dame, it is considered only as an aid to the fruits of the Holy Spirit. These are catalogued as love, joy, peace, patience, kindness, and generosity. And, in all fairness, it must be said that these virtues are more pronounced in the pentecostal community than is the ability to speak in tongues". (Cited in Catholic Pentecostals. Pg. 157.)

Love for Christ brings to the Spirit-filled love for one another and love for the Church and the world to which they belong. The Wesleys as prophets of love would have joined happily with the new move of the Spirit whose emphasis and seal in prayer is LOVE and PRAISE. When on Jan. 1st. 1739 they broke out at three in the morning "We praise Thee O God, we acknowledge Thee to be the Lord" under the influence of the Spirit's descending upon them they were entering upon one limb of the present charismatic movement. They were experiencing a foretaste of the glory which God in his salvation history was to pour upon their children and grandchildren in the Lord.

Priesthood of All Believers

The origin of this theological term is interesting. It is not Biblical, is not found in any Reformation document, but is first used by the Free Church Council in 1917 and appears for the first time in Methodism in paragraph 30 of our Deed of Union of 1930. (Constitutional Practice and Discipline, 5th ed. p. 289.) Whilst the term is recent the concept is old and dear to Methodism. It was the backbone of our ecclesiastical economy

A recent charismatic conference may be used to illustrate how the movement builds firmly upon this doctrine. During a worship session at the conference many came forward for ministry. Some six or seven ordained clergy ministered by prayer and the laying on of hands whilst the rest of the people (some 800 or 900) prayed and sang devotionally. Whilst the ordained ministers were at work in the Lord, the whole body of believers was simultaneously at work. Neither in this instance could have been effective without the mutual support of the other. Mutual ministry was a reality!

Mutual refreshing in the Spirit is needed vitally for us all. A minister in a charismatic prayer group can if he so wants become a LEANER rather than a LEADER. If, for some special reason he is worn out (and this frequently occurs, doesn't it?), then the rest of the group can feed and minister to him in prayer. This is a joy to many ministers who are often in spiritual deserts. One Methodist minister has been quoted as referring to a charismatic group to which he was invited as a 'spiritual oasis'.

The term we are discussing is of ALL believers. Not all can be Priests and Ministers. They say they have not the gifts and graces. But they can have the Spirit in all its fullness and so be set free for ministry. This happens to many quiet reserved teenagers and others who find it even hard to pray. They open up in prayer and even at that level they enter a ministry which previously was denied them.

Some deeply committed Christians have been led into new ministries for the Lord since their being baptized in the Holy Spirit. One lady has been used deeply for prayerful divine healings and the subsequent testifying to them through unsought for invitations to speak of them at ladies' meetings. One person healed and Spirit-filled feels that she may be called to preach (both pulpitwise and by pen) of what the Lord can do for an incurable.

Charismatic fellowships are notorious for their after meeting talk. This *spiritual conversation* (see Paul in Acts 20:7-12)) is one of the greatest areas of ministry in fellowship. The most unlikely characters are drawn together by the Lord and they share their problems, doubts and difficulties. They are resolved as they share! Charles Wesley was aiming in this direction when he wrote:

"He bids us build each other up; And gathered into one,

To our high calling's glorious hope, We hand in hand go on". (M.H.B. 745)

It is also not without significance that in this context charismatic groups and rallies often contain a joining together of hands as a gesture of their being brothers and sisters together in Christ. Is this not an extension of the recently reintroduced 'Peace' in the Communion Service?

Charismatic renewal highlights with great force the Methodist doctrine of the Priesthood of all Believers without which the Body would be incomplete.

4. Spiritual Experience Expressed in Song

Every revival produces its own music expressing the core of its Spirit. That this was true of Methodism in particular is seen in the first phrase of the preface to the Methodist Hymn Book: "Methodism was born in song". Song is the sign that a heart has been lightened and in the charismatic movement song features very largely. One does not know whether the song comes from the experience of Christ or whether one can sing oneself into a deeper spiritual experience.

With the advent of Methodist 'Hymns and Songs', a musical distinction of some importance was made. (See Preface, especially paragraph 2.) *The charismatic movement is producing songs rather than hymns and they are mainly scripturally inspired songs which can be sung with deep devotion.* In charismatic meetings the songs are mostly spontaneously, unaccompanied and sung whilst actually in an attitude of prayer. They are part of the prayer-expression of those who have found Christ in a new and deeper way. In many fellowships a chorus will be sung over and over again as the Spirit leads. "O how I love Jesus" is one such example. It is here that the charge of over emotionalism may be levelled but this is manifestly not the case in the majority of fellowships. The tone of the meetings is one of quiet devotion rather than one of enthusiastic hand clapping with the use of tambourines. Most songs are sung within the context of prayer and this in itself is a sobering influence upon any wayward element.

Inner joy is one of the first fruits of being filled with the Spirit of Jesus and *many testify to themselves singing inwardly for hours* and even days as a result of their experience. One Methodist minister having received the blessing of the Spirit had two punctures in the dark on the way home from the meeting and through it all he could not possibly stop this inner joy of song. It would seem that the springs of living water which Jesus promised us are flowing through the charismatic movement in exuberant song.

Special mention must be made here of the phenomenon often called 'Singing in tongues' but which is more aptly named *'singing in the Spirit'*. In this occurrence people liken what happens to their having taken part in a 'heavenly choir'. This arises always in prayer time and it simply begins by making a joyful noise to the Lord in syllables which are not known to the human mind. It is rather like humming a tune because you are happy. It flows from the sheer inner joy. Others then join and soon a beautiful melody is resounding in praise to the Lord. It normally builds to a crescendo and then dies away so perfectly that no one person hangs on after the rest have ceased to praise the Lord. The pregnant silence following is one of the most divinely beautiful experiences of the spiritual life. This can occur in a small fellowship with only six to ten persons or in a large gathering of some hundreds. Often one is completely unaware of the one who starts it and yet because of the presence of the Lord you are literally compelled to join in. This new dimension of 'song-prayer-praise' (for want of a better term!) is one of the most dramatic spiritual innovations that the charismatic movement is bringing and it is remarkable in that it is one of the most spiritually rewarding in terms of the inner man being drawn to Christ.

If Methodism prides itself on its spiritual past being reflected in song it has nothing but good to gain from the present movement of the Holy Spirit.

F. D. Bruner in "A Theology of the Holy Spirit" (p. 37) shows great discernment when he claims, "Pentecostalism is Primitive Methodism's extended incarnation". This would be abundantly true in terms of song!

THE CONTRIBUTION OF THE CHARISMATIC MOVEMENT TO METHODISM

1. Renewal of the Ministry

In the previous chapter the place of the laymen was fully explored in terms of charismatic renewal. What of the Ministry? 'Devaluation' is an in word. There is talk of the devaluation of the pound and the laity but never of the devaluation of the Ministry. There has been talk about 'God's Frozen People' but left on one side have been God's frozen parsons.

The cause of this low ebb of the Ministry has gone under various guises. 'Loss of call' has been singled out amongst many and others see the 'Sectors' as a way out for some who have become despondent with 'Circuit work'. There has been much talk of the 'role' of the minister, some wondering whether he has any at all! There has been the argument of the 'community man' versus the 'church based man' and all this has led to an often confused leadership. The blind seem to have been leading the blind!

During past revivals the time came when the pulpit was

The Charismatic Movement

wonderfully blessed of God. Presumably God will renew his called servants for pulpit leadership if they seek His Spirit in their times of doubt and uncertainty. One minister testified to seeking baptism with the Holy Spirit because he knew he was drying up in the pulpit. The ministry must be renewed in the Spirit if they are to be true spiritual leaders. Where a man receives this deeper experience of Jesus, fruits are often seen in terms of the power and effectiveness of preaching. Some do away with notes which have tied them for years whilst others so led by the Spirit change a whole text and sermon during the actual course of the service. As long ago as 1936 Rev. Samuel Chadwick could say "From the first day of my Pentecost I became a winner and seeker of souls". (The Way to Pentecost, 1966 edition. Pg. 33.) Others and their hearers tell of the same thing today. *Power in preaching is often one of the most direct fruits for the Ministry after having been baptized in the Spirit.*

A careful note must be made that preaching in itself is not a gift of the Spirit, although many called to preach are naturally gifted as preachers and empowered by the anointing of the Spirit. Many adduce Romans 12:6 in support of preaching being a gift of the Spirit. The Word used here is the same root as that in 1 Corinthians 12:10 and it is only modern translations which have changed the prophecy into preaching. Many fine scholars maintain prophecy is the right word in Romans 12:6. Preaching can be prophetic but it only becomes so as the preacher is anointed with the Holy Spirit and utters words which he would not possibly have conceived in his normal preparations. Only this limited area of preaching is prophetic and as such a gift of the Spirit.

The relevance of preaching has been called into question under the radical influences of the 60's but it is certainly not so when seen through the eyes of charismatic renewal. Our ministry has a great responsibility in this matter and it must not evade that unto which it has been ordained.

2. Integration of Charismatic Activity Within Local Societies
What is it we are trying to integrate? Many feel it will mean tongues every service, prophecy at least once a month and hand-clapping through every hymn. This is folly. What the baptism in Holy Spirit does first and foremost is to intensify and highlight the generally accepted gifts and fruits of the Spirit. *Many are ignorant of the existence of a second strand in distinctive charismatic spirituality* — this is the vital strand of the CONTEMPLATIVE. It is a new,

deeper, spiritual dimension that needs to be incorporated and not a formulated list of extraordinary gifts which must be used if the service is to be valid. (This is however not to deny that they may be used if the Spirit so directs.) Some charismatic groups despair because the extraordinary gifts are not always in use. To be charismatic means only one thing, that we are open to all the gifts that God can give in spiritual worship and service. This cannot be measured in an incessant use of extraordinary gifts. It is a fact that where this is the case a counterfeit is sometimes at work and a lack of love is shown to those who are not so spiritually gifted and articulate. It is thus that a pamphleteer writes the following as a warning to some of his 'friends' who are engaged in the charismatic movement. He expresses the concern of many who are hesitant about the movement. They "feel the leaders of the movement are majoring in a minor aspect of the Holy Spirit's activity by New Testament standards". (Leith Samuel, Speaking in Tongues, Pg. 1.) This is precisely it! A new dimension is being offered through Christ and it must be grafted on to the whole balanced work of the Spirit in convicting of sin and convincing of salvation and truth. (See John 16:7–13.)

Again the ministry of the Church bears deep responsibility in this field. Every minister should be mentally informed (edified, educated) about what the Spirit is doing; every minister ought to be experientially informed (even if this simply means attending a charismatic fellowship or meeting) and every minister needs to be spiritually open to all that God has to give in this age if he is to make any judgement upon the things before us. Many are making rash and hasty value-judgements from completely outside the camp and this can only lead to error and mistrust. The lay person is bound to come and ask the minister what he feels about these topical spiritual affairs and it is the minister's job to be armed for the reply with mental, first-hand experiential and spiritual knowledge which befits his calling. In this way integration can begin. Without it break-aways are inevitable.

Emmanuel Sullivan shows great discernment when he argues: "The proper pastoral attitude toward charismatic people, or Jesus people, cannot be cultivated in an atmosphere of arrogance, mistrust or anxiety. It must be *positive* and *integrating* — positive through adequate study and information for the purpose of spiritual direction; integrating by the full inclusion of such charismatic Christians in the life of the local Church". (Introduction. Paper, British Council of Churches D M U/17/1972.)

The precise place of integration within the economy of the Church is an open question. It may prove to be the wisest counsel not to encourage full-blooded charismatic activity within the setting of Sunday worship. Indeed this might be cruelly devastating to those who are uninitiated in terms of the new teaching and practice. Might it not be that the meeting for prayer, praise and exultation in Christ which we give the title 'charismatic' can no more be fully incorporated within the Sunday service than could the early class meeting.

Having said this, there is every encouragement that the spirit of the charismatic group should overflow into the regular ordinances of the Church. Leslie Davison told, before his death, how he had done this in the simple act of singing a hymn. He had entered a service which he considered 'dead'. He determined that in the next hymn he would let the Spirit within him be released and at that point the whole tone of the service changed. The minister afterwards remarked that he had felt the change and it had prompted him to completely change his sermon. He had entered the pulpit feeling downhearted and 'empty' but through the singing of one person 'in the Spirit' the reality of spiritual worship had been achieved. Minister and people had been blessed. It is true that one man and Christ is a majority!

The blessing and depth received during a midweek meeting for praise ought to be felt in the service on a Sunday. No person who claims a new deeper experience of Jesus need opt-out of the Church, nor should he feel obliged to move out, neither should he be made to feel that he need be thrown out. All that Christ has to give must be grasped by His Church and contained within it.

Methodist worship has always prided itself on being 'free' in style. It is difficult to see how one can become more free without the danger of a losing of dignity and order. It is interesting to note that those church systems which are more structured and disciplined than the Methodist service (Roman Catholic Mass, Anglican Communion) seem able to make way for charismatic activity more readily. Within the Mass or the Eucharist a place is often made for free prayer and praise. This must be terminated for there is a liturgical pattern laid down and this must be followed in order that total 'celebration' is complete. One practical way in which Methodists could introduce such a practice is in the intercession section of the new Sunday service. Another way in which this could be operated is within the context of a healing and ministry service to those sick or in mental and spiritual need.

It states in the Conference Declaration on Healing (1952 Minutes, Pgs. 55–6) that "The gift of healing is best exercised within the local Christian community and under her control". With the increased interest and evidence of healing in the charismatic movement a way forward could be the holding of healing services within the local society based church under the supervision of a minister and directed by a suitably approved and theologically sound healing service. Our Church has not yet seen fit to provide us with such a document but various services do exist. Often in these services either during the laying on of hands or in the times of devotional preparation other gifts of the Spirit are used. Tongues, interpretation, prophecy, wisdom and knowledge might well be helpful to those who have offered themselves as candidates for healing and counselling, and indeed may well be desirable. Also, if within the structure of a Catholic liturgy a place can be found for charismatic worship should this not be even more possible within the so-called 'free' worship of nonconformist churches at a suitably designated place.

Apart from these areas outlined above, it may be that a fully charismatic happening must needs remain physically separate from normal worship whilst seeking to offer its spiritual insights to the whole gathered community on a Sunday. The Spirit can and will, however, do as He wills and if silent prayer, or general thanksgiving (in which congregational participation is invited) presents the setting in which the Spirit can work then work He will. As a guide to those unsure of when the Spirit is asking them to exercise a gift of the Spirit it is better not to do so until one is literally compelled. This is not to 'quench' the Spirit, it is simply to wait upon the Lord until a divine certainty is apparent in the soul.

With regard to the gift of tongues, this is a gift which, whilst an oral gift can be exercised silently or quietly 'under the breath', this gift can be introduced in either way actually in a service of worship or a prayer fellowship. In this way, the gift is being exercised devotionally and not publicly and as such it may build the Body of Christ by uplifting the spirit of the individual who so exercises the gift.

Much is spoken about *'spiritual warfare'* in charismatic circles. That Occult and Satanic powers are greatly at work in this age is beyond question. With the new authority and certainty many find in Christ after having been baptized in the Holy Spirit they seem divinely led into ministries of deliverance. People are freed from the power of Satan and won for Christ. This *confrontation with the*

The Charismatic Movement

wicked one is accelerated in the life of one claiming to be filled with the Spirit. That this battle can become an obsession and persons become 'demon mad' is true. *This aspect of the movement must be contained and channelled within our Church where it rightly belongs if gross fanaticisms are not to ensue.*

That our church has not been unaware of this need in the past and that it has discerned a connection between evil possession and illness is seen in these words from the most recent Conference Statement on Healing (Minutes 1963, Pgs. 245–6) "Throughout the New Testament the power of God in Christ is seen to be defeating evil. . . . Meanwhile the Church confesses that Jesus is Lord, and demonstrates the truth by the power to heal sufferers, the defeat of demonic powers and the conquest of death". The statement continues; "many realise that evil is a powerful force infecting all life". The Church should thank God that He is providing her, through the Charismatic Movement, with an increased armoury for this fight. This is the job of the Church. Methodists have left this battle too long to the 'Gospel Hall' and 'fringe group'. The fight should be taken up with the increased measure of the Spirit being poured upon the Church. More of the "sword of the Spirit" is needed as also is learning how to "Pray at all times in the Spirit" (Ephesians 6:17-18) if the sound advice of Paul on these matters is to be followed to "Put on the whole armour". The fullness of the Spirit would seem an indispensable tool for the mission of the Church in this vital and topical area of its ministry. *For specific cases of deliverance incorporation may well have to be within the context of healing services or in a smaller gathering of the brethren* after services of midweek devotional meetings. *In every case it is advisable to have a clergyman present.*

3. Reaction/Division — What to Do?

The present movement of God's Spirit is unlike any other in history in that it is uniting (even across denominational barriers) rather than dividing. Considering the large number of people involved in charismatic activity the number of splinter groups has been very small.

Due to the newness of much that is being offered one would expect reaction. This questioning before acceptance is healthy and ought to be welcomed. It will make those involved within the movement become more theologically precise and it will make all face new questions in the Church. Nothing but good can come from such reaction.

It is Christ who unites and the devil who divides. That there are counterfeits in this movement we have already allowed. *How can the validity of any experience or happening claiming to be charismatic be measured and what tests can be applied?*

a. Satan had ever been the 'Father of Lies' and one meaning of 'occult' is 'hidden'. The antidote for that ailment is to *bring everything into the light. Scripture gives very clear guidance* on a dispute between brothers and sisters in Christ. Matthew 18:15-17 gives clear guidance. First there is to be discussion between the offended parties, then in front of other Christian witnesses and then finally in front of the leaders of the Church. In any point of disagreement, this must be discussed openly *with the Leaders Meeting* and the Minister of the Church from the outset. Ministers themselves have the brotherhood of the ministry, through the staff-meeting or other media for checking their own feelings and decisions on any matter. The Superintendent has a valuable role to play in this brotherhood.

b. Still in the territory of scriptural injunction Paul in 1 *Corinthians 14 gives very clear and concise teaching on the proper use of the gifts of the Spirit.* If gifts are being used in any fellowship other than the Word allows then this matter should immediately be pointed out and if a Church based group, the events reported to the relevant ecclesiastical authority.

Lewi Pethrus, a pioneer of the Pentecostal movement in The Wind Bloweth Where It Listeth says:

"It is my conviction that the great spiritual awakening we have experienced and the wonderful results achieved have been due to the fact that the revived people have moved forward according to the Word, and abided in its clear and faithful teachings. If this way be set aside it is very evident that we will then build upon feelings, emotions, and manifestations, there will be times of crisis and breaking up of the work of God".

The best test of the Spirit is the "sword of the Spirit which is the Word of God". (Ephesians 6:17)

c. *The tradition of the Church* to which we belong is a plumb-line to keep the Church upright. The Revealed Truth in the Doctrines of the Church is that which Christ has entrusted to her. There is also the truth as seen in the Church Catholic. This is not to say that if John Wesley did not speak in tongues later Methodists must not do so! *This tradition must have room for growth* as the treasures of God's riches are more abundantly showered upon it.

Fidelity to Wesley is not the ultimate test of the correctness of any issue but it is a pointer which one needs to consider.

d. The authority of the Church has already been touched upon in (1) above but this needs further exposition. Scripture sets Jesus as the example of the man of obedience. Churches are to be like Him. "Be subject to every ordinance of man for the Lord's sake . . . Honour all men. Love the brotherhood." (1 Peter 2:13-17) (See also Ephesians 5:21, 1 Peter 5:5, for further New Testament teaching on submission.) A minister at his ordination in the Methodist Church submits himself to those whom the church shall put in authority over him. Although the Methodist Church does not have a rigid hierarchical system of government it has always been proud of 'our discipline'. From the early inquisitorial of the class-meeting to the present day this has been a safeguard to that which is right and proper. Methodists are 'sons of the Gospel' and should respect the decisions of those the church appoints to be the guardians of their souls. *In any consultation about a charismatic difficulty the Chairman of the District must be brought fully into the discussion.* He is not emotionally involved and is also not too remote from the situation to be thought of as an outsider or an intruder. After all he is the 'Bishop' and with wide experience and knowledge of difficult situations could be the one to calm the troubled waters. A Chairman of District has described himself as one who "shows care for the people of God from within the people of God". It is the Methodist people who put their trust in their episcopos by election right and at point of need, in cases of discipline, they must allow this trust to be exercised amongst them. "Let every soul be subject to the higher powers". (Romans 13:1.)

e. *The world of what is reasonable, what is sound common sense has something to offer in this matter.* Wesley was not opposed to having 'right reason' as a test (that is after Scripture and Tradition) and Luther said that reason 'is a natural light' kindled from a 'divine light' and above all other things in life was 'excellent and divine'. Samuel Taylor Coleridge said that reason was 'the eye of the spirit whereby spiritual reality is discerned'. Although reason can never take the place of the Spirit of God as a teacher of Truth, it can, when acting in the capacity of 'sanctified common sense', be an excellent aid to sorting out involved arguments which are in danger of becoming too theological.

f. *Love is the essence of the Gospel of Jesus Christ and it is an*

altogether worthy test as to validity of any gift or religious experience. In
1 Corinthians 14:1, where Paul talks about the gifts of the Spirit
he encourages their being sought after but he urges "Follow after
love". That is his number one priority and that comes before any
gifts of the Spirit. John Horner in a recent address "What does
Scripture say about the power of the Holy Spirit in relation to
individual Christian experience" claims that the baptism in the
Holy Spirit does three things in terms of love: (a) it greatly
increases love of Christ, (b) it greatly increases love of others,
(c) it greatly increases the desire and ability to witness to others of
this love of Christ.

A charism is a gift of grace; it is a love-gift to give away to
others and if there is no love emanating from one claiming
charismatic abilities then that one is none of Christ's. *Make love a
test.* There are many groups meeting whom one would describe as
'cold' and 'hard'. Such groups are in themselves in need of
spiritual renewal whatever their claims.

g. This whole movement is not a 'tongues movement', a
'power movement' or even a 'prayer movement'. It is a movement
of the Spirit of the Lord Jesus Christ in His resurrection power. It
is a Jesus Movement (but not 'The Jesus Movement'). If Jesus is
not raised and glorified then the enemy is at work as a
counterfeit. *It is more important for Jesus to be uplifted than the gifts to
be used. Jesus must be the beginning and the end of all true charismatic
activities.* David Wilkerson of Cross and the Switchblade fame
writes, "I now travel the nation warning about the phonies in the
Jesus Movement. The Bible warns of an entire group who will
appear in the last days crying "Jesus, Jesus", but who would be
phoney, false and unconverted. They would preach Jesus, cast
out devils, go about doing good, but still go on sinning. Every
person must walk as Jesus walked. There can be no other way".
(Jesus Person Maturity Manual, cited by W.T.H. Richards The
Charismatic Movement in the Historic Churches. Pg. 15.) Do
people raise and glorify Jesus because they act like Jesus? Then
they must be sound. If there is 'charismatic individualism',
'charismatic extrovertism' and 'exhibitionism' then they are false
and unsound. *The gifts of the Spirit help Christians to be like Jesus as
well as act like Him.*

4. Theological Conclusion — Evangelical and Missionary Contribution

There never can be any readily identifiable 'theology' of the charismatic movement which will be acceptable to all. There are no statutes, canons or declarations of intent. This is because the people who would claim an experience of having been baptized in the Spirit are not and would not wish to belong to a party.

As well as not being a party (indeed the movement includes people from all points of the theological spectrum) many would even resist the term movement in its nominative form. *There is no organized movement* but there is a deep moving of the Spirit of God amongst His people and that is the sum total of the matter. Rev. Michael Harper, Anglican and Director of Fountain Trust, said in the opening editorial of the October 'Renewal' magazine, "The charismatic renewal is already too large for anyone to organize, thank God!". Even within Methodism in Britain alone 'Dunamis', a magazine on the work of the Holy Spirit, has within nine months gone from 300 to 3,500 in circulation. Roman Catholics, along with Anglicans and Methodists, have expressed concern over this same matter. Father Peter Hocken in a talk "Prayer Groups, Christian Community and World Transformation" report in the March, 1973, edition of the English Roman Catholic 'Day of Renewal' newsletter says in an appropriate sub-section:

"*Apostles of Jesus, not of a movement.*

"Our job is not to spread a movement. Since the movement is basically the work of the Spirit, it spreads when we talk about God, whenever we pray. We must not be apostles of charismatic renewal, but only apostles of Christ".

This *moving* of the Spirit is now far too immense to be party-minded or movement-directed.

Yet the term 'Charismatic' as well as 'movement' is here to stay. The Church has always been charismatic and always will be. Every revival is charismatic, since it begins with God's giving of a gift. *To call the Wesley movement a 'revival' and the 20th century movement 'charismatic' is extreme. Both were and are charismatic and evangelical.*

The missionary and evangelical nature of the present renewal is seen in the case of prayer groups. Many of these have a regular but small clientele. One particular group has never more than 40 and never less than 6 at its weekly meetings and yet very regularly it has visitors, some for a once only session, others for a few weekly visits. This group has now had some 100 people who have passed through its doors in little over a year. Many of these have gone away and begun their own groups. They have given to the mother group a missionary adventure and a widening of horizons beyond the locality whilst they themselves have been given new missionary impetus and ability by the Spirit. Other groups have had similar experiences both in large city church groups and in smaller house groups.

The nominal form of that experience held dear by charismatic people, namely 'Baptism in the Holy Spirit' is, to use the words of Rev. John Horner, *"fast becoming a bone of theological contention"*. The verbal form is used in scripture (see Mt. 3:11, Acts 1:4-5) and it is upon this that any building and discussion which is creative must take place. The words "being filled with Holy Spirit" or "receiving the Holy Spirit" are other scriptural alternatives. That people today all over the world are having an experience similar to the early disciples is indisputable. That similar visitations and manifestations are accompanying these experiences is also beyond doubt. People are expecting the miraculous to happen and many of these are ordinary Church folk who have had little hope of revival for the whole of their sometimes long Church careers. They do not necessarily want to become theologically articulate; their experience may be enough. Yet, others need depth study.

F. D. Maurice was a philosopher and theologian of the 19th century. When asked what it meant to be a theologian he replied, "I am a digger. . . . Therefore my business because I am a Theologian is not to build but to dig". *The present move of the Spirit in the mainstream denominational churches is only about fifteen years old. Charismatic people are still yet babes. There remains to be done a lot of theological digging* to discover the truths of what is happening in the light of scripture and then the application of these to Church systems and daily life.

For example attention should be paid to these questions: How is Baptism in the Spirit related to Infant Baptism?, How does it relate to traditional views of Conversion?, How does it stand in relation to Confirmation?, Is it the same as Wesley's "Second Blessing"?, How will it help inter-church relations? These and many others all need time and attention given to them.

Meanwhile, the work of the Holy Spirit must not be hindered by 'quenching', 'resisting' or 'grieving' the Spirit. Jesus must be glorified through the present manifestation of the Spirit which is permitted the title Charismatic renewal. Methodists must in faith (although articulate rather than blind faith) appropriate all that God is giving by his Spirit and must gather it into the storehouse of the Church. They must do no other than "praise Him for all that is past, And trust Him for all that's to come". (Methodist Hymn Book 69.)

BIBLIOGRAPHY

A. HISTORICAL AND THEOLOGICAL

Bruner, F. D. A Theology of the Holy Spirit. Hodder and Stoughton, London, 1971.

Davison, L. Pathway to Power. Fountain Trust. London, 1971.

Dunn, J. G. D. Baptism in the Holy Spirit. S.C.M. 1970.

Evans, E. The Welsh Revival of 1904. Evangelical Press. London, 1969.

Hollenweger, W. J. The Pentecostals. S.C.M. 1972.

Jackson, T. (Ed.) The Lives of the Early Methodist Preachers. 4th edition, London, 1873–6.

Sullivan, E. Can the Pentecostal Movement Renew the Churches? Item SE/35 in Study Encounter, Vol. III, No. 4, W.C.C. 1972.

The Journal of John Wesley. Standard Ed. Epworth Press. London, 1938.

The Letters of John Wesley. Standard Ed. Epworth Press. London, 1931.

The Works of John Fletcher. London, 1844 edition.

Thompson, E. W. Wesley, Apostolic Man. Epworth Press. London, 1957.

Tugwell, S. Did You Receive the Spirit? Darton, Longman and Todd. London, 1972.

Wesley, J. A Plain Account of Christian Perfection. Epworth Press. London, 1952.

Wesley, J. Fifty Three Sermons or Sermons on Several Occasions. London, (Undated).

Williams, C. W. John Wesley's Theology Today. Epworth Press. London, 1960.

Williams, J. Rodman. The Era of the Spirit. Logos. New Jersey, 1971.

B. DEVOTIONAL

Bennett, D. Nine O'Clock in the Morning. Coverdale House Publishers, Eastbourne, 1971.

Bennett, D. and R. The Holy Spirit and You. Coverdale House Publishers, Eastbourne, 1971.

Caruthers, Merlin. R. Power in Praise. Logos International, New Jersey, 1972.

Chadwick, S. The Way to Pentecost. Hodder and Stoughton. London, 1932.

Clarke, C. Pioneers of Revival. Fountain Trust. London, 1961.

Foulkes, Ronald. W. The Flame Shall Not Be Quenched. Methodist Charismatic Fellowship. Tasmania, (Undated).

Gasson, R. The Challenging Counterfeit. Logos. New Jersey, 1966.

Harper, M. Life in the Holy Spirit. Fountain Trust. London, 1966.

Harper, M. Spiritual Warfare. Hodder and Stoughton. London, 1970.

Harper, M. Walk in the Spirit. Hodder and Stoughton. London, 1971.

Harper, M. None Can Guess. Hodder and Stoughton. London, 1971.

Hession, R. Be Filled Now. Christian Literature Crusade. London, 1967.

James, M. I Believe in the Holy Ghost. Oliphants. London, 1969.

Jeffreys, G. Pentecostal Rays. Second edition. London, 1954.

Schlink, B. Ruled by the Spirit. Lakeland, 1970.

Sherrill, J. They Speak with Other Tongues. Hodder and Stoughton. London, 1965.

Ranaghan, K. and D. Catholic Pentecostals. Paulist Press Deus Books. New York, 1969.

Richards, W. T. H. Pentecost is Dynamite. Lakeland, 1972.

Richards, W. T. H. The Charismatic Movement in the Historic Churches. Ambassador Productions (distributed Marshall, Morgan, Scott). London, 1972.

Wallace, A. Pray in the Spirit. Victory Press. London, 1970.

30 *Presbyterian Church, New Zealand, 1973*

THE CHURCH AND PENTECOSTALISM

Both the Doctrine Committee and the Life and Work Committee of the Presbyterian Church in New Zealand studied the charismatic renewal and made separate reports in 1973, each with the special methods traditionally proper to the doctrinal and to the more broadly theological-cultural evaluations.

The growth of the charismatic renewal in Presbyterianism in New Zealand had developed to the point where Christchurch and Leeston emerged by 1968 as charismatic centers. Though the numbers of Presbyterians personally involved were not large, they were sufficient to prompt the two above named committees to make their reports to the 1973 General Assembly.

The Life and Work report took the form of a letter to the church. After an appeal to honor the body function of each person's gift and therefore to live in mutuality and harmony, the latter described its procedure, glanced briefly at some biblical and historical evidence of "charismatic and ecstatic experience," recorded what seems to be the positive results of this experience, made a few passing theological reflections, noted the psychological and sociological dimensions, reproduced four personal testimonies (two ministers, a certified public accountant, and a woman teacher), and closed with a pastoral appeal that each member respect the others' gifts and experience.

The Life and Work Committee asked charismatics not to over-spiritualize the gifts of the Spirit. Social workers, doctors, nurses, musicians, therapists, and ploughmen can all be exercising their proper gift of the Spirit. Over and above that gift, which may be the key to participation in the life of the church, "there is one gift which is timeless and full in its virtue and meaning: the grace of love."

494   *The Church and Pentecostalism*

Both in the Old and New Testaments there is recorded charismatic and ecstatic experience. "Subsequently in the Church there has been a fairly continuous tradition of such experience, often disregarded by the 'main body' of Christendom, but insistently claiming a place." In detailing what typifies the charismatic and his or her experience, it seemed to the committee that such a person will almost invariably already have been a Christian who felt some dissatisfaction with the depth of Christian life heretofore attained. The charismatic experience "comes into this state of searching with tremendous significance, great satisfaction, peace of mind, and a sense of great energy finding outlet, great enrichment, relief of tension, conquest of doubt, and deepened faith." Also typical is a new interest in evangelism and mission, more precisely "bringing to the Church the message of the availability of such gifts," some being persuaded "that such experiences are essential to the whole Church."

To explain the rise of classical Pentecostalism at the beginning of the century, to which the charismatic renewal is historically indebted, the committee turned to theories of social and economic deprivation, namely the poor, who have few social advantages and possibilities, turn to emotional experience-oriented religions to relieve their miseries. The committee recognized that scientific studies seem to indicate that charismatic experience often serves "a useful psychological purpose in giving a source of orientation and stability to people who are under stress."

All of the four testimonies recorded strongly beneficial results. The ministers defined charismatic renewal in terms of spiritual power, a dominant charismatic category. It is "receiving power to serve God and be open to God's leading in the most effective way." In reading the Book of Acts, the accountant was struck with the unfairness of God to empower the early church "and yet leave us . . . to simply grit our teeth and believe like mad and hope that God was still around someplace." The baptism in the Holy Spirit seemed to take care of this discrepancy. A minister recalled the changes which he had seen in the lives of people during his eight years of involvement in the renewal, while another was impressed with the loving care found in the charismatic fellowship.

One of the pastoral problems faced by the committee was the alienation from the life of the church which some persons in the renewal felt, consequent on their becoming objects of suspicion, sometimes of hostility and fear. On occasion this was a prelude to withdrawal from the church. Rather than be isolated, such persons, the committee recommended, "should be made to feel very much at home in the family of the Church."

Those involved in the renewal should understand and expect that those who do not share their experience to be taken by surprise. Those not involved will recall those moments when a particular experience seemed to be a doorway into new areas of awareness and assurance. This should move them to tolerance, patience, and gentleness when persons in the renewal think they have had such an experience and are excited about it.

The Life and Work Committee came back to the issue of charismatic renewal in its 1974 report urging that the church move beyond defensiveness. Especially to be deplored was any attempt to discredit or ridicule another's experience. One way of bringing another's experience into disrepute is to explain it away. "'It is only . . .' or 'it's really . . .' or 'it's a phase they are going through.'" In effect this is a way of dismissing the value of the experience.

In a tangential way the committee returned to charismatic renewal in its 1976 report when discussing new forms of Christian communities. Here only the 1973 report is reproduced.

"The Report of the Life and Work Committee to the 1973 General Assembly" was published in The White Book, Presbyterian Church of New Zealand *(Wellington, 1973), pp. 86–96.*

A LETTER TO THE CHURCH

Brethren, as you know, the Spirit is the bearer of grace.

All of us, all through life, experience enthusiasms which sharpen us up; and set us off on new experiences and adventures of living. Often the talents used at such times have been natural to us, but sometimes our service may have been as a result of influences coming upon us from outside ourselves to inspire us to express talents quite new to our experience. Following such a train of thought, we know that if anyone ever denies Christ it can only be because they are subject to some influence that is opposed to Christ; but if anyone ever claims earnestly and evidently that Jesus is the master of their life and the motive of their service, then God must be given the glory, and we must acknowledge that here the Spirit is at work.

When the Spirit thus comes into the life of the Church, He does all sorts of things. He develops talents we already have in Christian service, and He brings new talents to birth in us. He calls some men and women to the task of ministry; He persuades some people to teach in Sunday Schools, Youth groups, State Schools. He convinces some people that they must go to the ends of the earth to bind up wounds, to bear witness to Christ, to survey roads, to teach in schools, to teach men to plough. Some men and women are enabled to use their gifts of speech in new and lifegiving ways as the Spirit inspires their proclamation of Christ. At other times we may be aware of great resources of healing power, sometimes at work quietly within the fellowship of the Church, sometimes in awesome events, at other instances dispersing into the world through the skills and devotion of trained nurses, doctors, social workers, therapists, and many others. To some people the Spirit comes with the calling to give music to which others may sing as they worship.

All of these people (and many others) in their different ways and with their different talents go together to enrich the life of the Church, and to confirm it, in its unity, as the body of Christ. Have you ever thought of what it would be like if the organist insisted on playing right through the sermon? Have you ever thought of what it would be like if the congregation engaged in a wide range of discussion activities every time the organist played? In effect they would be saying to each other, "I have no need of you; I can function without your help; go away, and take your Spirit with you." But of course this would be absolutely foolish, because the whole rich life of the Church (on which each of us depends) is built through the co-operation and co-ordination of all these divers parts of the Christian body.

We must honour each other as brethren; as members of Christ's body we must respect the function each serves, and recognise the gift each bears. It is well for us all to give serious and devout thought to the way in which the contribution of each can best be integrated into the whole and full life of the community of faith; of how we can most caringly and profitably accept the talents and service of others as brought to fruit by the Spirit.

We must remember that over and above the simple gift that may be the key to our own participation in the life of the Church, there is one gift which is timeless and full in its virtue and meaning: the grace of love. Only as we learn love, only as we subordinate and carefully employ the other talents the Spirit may give and enrich in us, in love, only then do we truly honour and serve the Spirit who gives and empowers, and the Christ who calls and saves and commissions.

> Love is glad when you are glad
> Is sad when you are sad
> Is hurt when you are.
> Love is never so wrapped in itself

He can't listen to you,
And hear you.
Love accepts you exactly as you are —
Is happy for your strengths
Is sorry for you in your weakness,
(However unacceptable it may appear)
Stands beside you in your struggle.
Love knows no time
And is always available.
Love may criticise what you do
But never you,
And looks with you
For the right path, for you.
Love makes no judgements
And has a deep respect for you:
Love shares his all with you
His time, his possessions, his talents.
Love grows by sharing himself;
Love drives out fear;
Love is eternal and never dies;
Love cares.

("Sometimes I Weep"; Ken Walsh; scm 1973)

INTRODUCTION

The 1972 report of this committee said, inter alia, ". . . our
concern (with Pentecostalism) is . . . to make contact with, to
learn from, those with a dimension to their religious experience
which appears never to have been emphasised (or even
recognised) by a large majority of the members of our Church.

"The committee would welcome contact and suggestions on
. . . Pentecostalism, which will be a major study area in 1973".

We are grateful to the many Sessions and individuals who have
responded to this invitation, and have described to us their
experiences and convictions (and sometimes their uncertainties)
as pentecostal-type experiences have come to bear on them and
their Church.

We have studied a large amount of the literature that is
concerned with pentecostal experience, and we have tried to
become as aware as is possible to us of the full dimensions of all
that is summed up under the term 'Neopentecostalism'. We have
met with some people of other Churches who tell of pentecostal

experience, but we have felt the main necessity of meeting and sharing with people of our own Church, who by their faithfulness and commitment bear witness to what they believe are promising possibilities of co-operation and sharing.

A consulting and sharing event was arranged in Rotorua in mid-June, between members of the Life and Work, Doctrine, and New Life Committees, and a number of laymen and ministers who have had some personal experience of that order often known as 'Spirit baptism'. The sharing and dialogue of that consultation was most profitable for all concerned; in particular it opened up a clear way of reconciliation and advance for some who had logical and theological difficulties in regard to the general concepts involved in pentecostal experience; the consultation also opened up a joyful avenue of acceptance and reconciliation for some who had felt pressures of ostracism because of their particular experience and emphasis.

Although this report is written very much in the 'light' of that consultation, we hope it is fully and truly informed from all relevant sources. Yet we do not consider that this report can be anywhere near a final word for the Church, even in the immediate situation; rather we offer this report to the Church in the hope that it may open up useful areas and patterns of discussion for the whole Church; a discussion in which this Committee hopes to have a continuing part; a discussion which will enable every member of the Church to find profit in what the Spirit is saying to the Church.

A TENTATIVE EXPLORATION OF THE TERM 'NEOPENTECOSTALISM'

Neopentecostalism, as we refer to it, is concerned with the experience of those people in the Church who have a particular conviction about the Spirit's presence and His gifts in the Church, centring primarily on a conviction that there is now being repeated in the Church, and particularly in their own experience, the manifestations of the Spirit recorded on Pentecost in the Acts of the Apostles.

Charismatic and ecstatic experience is recorded in the Old Testament (Numbers 11, 1 Samuel 10) and in the New Testament (Acts 2, 8, 10, 19, 1 Corinthians 12-14). Subsequently in the Church there has been a fairly continuous tradition of such experience, often disregarded by the 'main body' of Christendom, but insistently claiming a place. Historians of the Church record the significance of a far broader stream with the Montanists, Anabaptists, Luther's "Schwärmer", Quakers, Pietists, Irvingites and Revivalists. At the turn of the century in the United States particularly, but in other countries as well, there was a widespread hungering for revival in the Church, and renewal of Missionary enterprise. At that time some people had a type of ecstatic experience which seemed to them to be verified in what they read of Pentecost. The experience, and the movement which developed, quickly came to be known as Pentecostal. This Pentecostalism appeared and flourished in an area of the Church which had a particular and restless concern for conversion, Christian experience, and obedience expressed in witness. Many of the people and groups devoted to such concerns at that time were rather estranged from the general pattern of Church life, and so it may be understandable that Pentecostalism came to be regarded with suspicion by traditional Churches; Pentecostalism became firmly fixed outside the mainstream of Christendom.

For a long time Pentecostalism remained 'separated', even though it has come to such strength as to be recognised as 'the third force' of the world Church. But over recent years many people in 'orthodox', or 'historic, mainstream Churches', have come to have this same pentecostal type of experience. In this context we use the term 'Neopentecostal'. Typically, almost invariably, the person who has this experience will already have been a Christian. There will probably have been some sense of dissatisfaction with their prior Christian status, and some encouragement to find further fulfilment through a definite openness to the Spirit's manifestation in a particular way. The pentecostal experience comes into this state of searching with tremendous significance, great satisfaction, peace of mind, and a sense of great energy finding outlet, great enrichment, relief of tension, conquest of doubt, and deepened faith. The person who has such experience will be quite certain that it is far broader and richer than simply 'speaking in tongues', even though this is typically of special significance as a sign; exclusively so in some sectarian attitudes. The person will be quite certain that the other 'gifts of the Spirit' as they are variously described and set out in the New Testament statements are either within their experience or within their reach. Particular emphasis may be placed on 'tongues' with their 'interpretation', 'prophecy' and 'healing'.

The person who has pentecostal experience will most likely be

The Church and Pentecostalism

inspired to the practice of evangelism, and the mission of what we may call 'charismatising': bringing to the Church the message of the availability of such gifts. Some may be so impressed by what they have experienced that they will be persuaded to suggest that such experiences are essential for the whole Church.

With such a simple account, we leave to others the task of making full description and analysis of such terms as: pentecost, charismatic, baptism of the Spirit, filling by the Spirit, spiritual gifts, tongues, and so on.

THEOLOGICAL PERSPECTIVE

Pentecostalism can be discussed in positive or in negative terms.

Positively, in Pentecostal Churches, and from such experience, a great body of literature has been built up: a literature that is emphatically biblically based. It is a literature which holds together the experience of the Pentecostals and the New Testament, especially the Acts of the Apostles.

Correspondingly, there is elsewhere in the Church a large quantity of literature and a large body of thought which questions the validity of Pentecostalist interpretations and uses of the scriptures. Sometimes this is aimed at the simple fundamentalism which is often bound up with Pentecostal sects.

There is also a philosophic criticism which questions the validity of the search for second experience, and questions the emphasis and interest which is attached to the phenomenon of 'speaking in tongues' as a simple or primary evidence of having received spiritual gifts.

We should be on our guard against extreme and polarised positions around the issues raised in Pentecostalism. Michael Harper, Editor of 'Renewal' magazine, warns his brethren in the charismatic movement of dangers which haunt them: "Anti-intellectualism and unthinking fundamentalism . . . ; pietism . . . ; elitism . . .". Those whose stance is rather that of being 'over against' Pentecostalism face equivalent dangers. At either hand the Church is placed at schismatic risk for questionable advantage.

In between extreme or arrogant claims either for or against the beliefs and experiences involved in Pentecostalism, we believe that the primary call is for a broad tolerance; certainly the call must be made for an avoidance of closed minds or bigotry.

The simple form of theological statement that is contained in

the report 'The Work of the Holy Spirit' of the United
Presbyterian Church in the United States of America seems to us
to be quite adequate.

PSYCHOLOGY, SOCIOLOGY, AND PENTECOSTALISM

We think that there is no begging the question that in its origins
in the United States of America at the turn of the century,
Pentecostalism was closely tied up with particular awareness of
social conditions. The interest of the American Negro people, the
effect of this movement on people in areas of deprived and
depressed living conditions in many parts of the world, are
matters of historical fact. The idea must be at least entertained
that, in many instances, the greatest gift of Pentecostalism to
these people was a release from the severity of their bondage, and
the tension and frustration and indignity of life as they knew it.
Some sociologists are concerned to show that still today, not only
in our own culture, and not only in Christianity, but in a very
broad survey of the world scene, ecstatic experience is a
significant way of release, a solution to social conscience, and a
compensatory source of status to many who face serious loss of
human dignity. Similarly, modern study indicates that
Pentecostalism, ecstatic and charismatic experience, often serve a
useful psychological purpose in giving a source of orientation and
stability to people who are under stress.

However, all we have said here only parallels what is normal in
every other area of religious and social experience; there are
dimensions of psychological and social usefulness which
specialists may analyse without necessarily reflecting disfavour
on, or emptying of significance, the primary convictions and
feelings.

Some may feel that there are unanswered questions about the
relationship between the rise of this experience today to the much
broader questions of modern, technologically conditioned, man's
search for freedom, self-assurance, and experiences which
emphasise and give recognition and credibility to the human and
the non-rational rather than the mechanical and the
mathematical.

In all our study of the theme of pentecostal experience, we find
nothing to lead us to either reject the experience or to ridicule
those who have it.

Within the Committee we have come to a far more fruitful and brotherly understanding of Neopentecostalism than many of us would have imagined possible at the beginning of our work. We are now firmly agreed that those of our Church who have had some form of pentecostal experience need to be recognised as contributing members of the Body. So we consider it necessary not only to report to the Church on our understanding of the 'movement', but also to become involved in the process of dialogue in the Church. We therefore present within our report these statements from some of the brethren, fully realising that these do not represent the whole spectrum of opinion of those in the Church who are part of the charismatic movement.

'A' Is a Minister of the Church

"I spend a good lump of my time with the unchurched and with people at the end of their tether and they couldn't care less what your theology is. What they want to know is, can you help them or not? I think my pentecostal awareness has made me better able to help them.

"It is over eight years since I discovered there were people called pentecostals. About that same time I attended a retreat with a number of other ministers from mainline Churches. It was all very low key. I had no special experience there, but I returned to my parish with a new faith in the power and goodwill of God towards His creatures. I was determined to claim and to exercise the authority inherent in my ordination and to pray for the gifts of the Holy Spirit.

"About this time I was greatly encouraged by an article in Forum written by the Very Rev. J. S. Murray (May 1966) in which he said:

'One of the most distinctive things about the Holy Spirit is that He manifests Himself in the realm of human experience. He is indeed God entering our personal lives in such a way that man becomes aware of Him and of what His coming means, as really as any other factors that enter our conscious experience. His coming is something that is felt, as certainly as other things — like the results of an injection, or the effect of good news, or the lifting of a worry from our lives'.

"It seemed to me that I was becoming personally acquainted with the Holy Spirit. I spoke in tongues (at least that is what I assumed it was) in my own devotions and this was important to me. When I read the Bible what I was experiencing seemed to be a commentary on so many passages that had formerly been a mystery, and in turn, the scriptures were searched for guidelines for daily living. Prayer became a real option for practical issues in the Church and in one's personal life.

"I shared in the leadership of a small group where it was possible to be honest, where faith was in the air, where there was genuine caring for one another and where reports of miraculous intervention of the Holy Spirit were frequent. I observed that whenever wonders and signs were reported they invariably led the focus back to God. There was gratitude for the particular manifestation, but it was always a door through which to come to God the Father, Son and Holy Spirit.

"I have come to see a lot of people changed in these eight years. I rejoice that this gospel we preach is true and that the salvation of God is for the whole man, body, mind and spirit.

"I have attended the occasional Assembly of God service and sat on one committee which sponsored a pentecostal evangelist from overseas. I was able to enter into these events with enthusiasm at the time but I suffer something of a cultural shock now if I attend such gatherings. Yet I meet numerous people who are helped there. I am glad to be a Presbyterian. I am grateful for our theological education, Church government and the breadth of opinion which is allowed in our Church.

"I have come to meet the living God through the witness of those who have said, I have seen him do this; this is what he has done for me. So I know I must be faithful to my knowledge of him".

'B' Is a Chartered Accountant

"Paul, in his letter to the Romans, said in Chapter 5, 'God's love has been poured into our hearts through the Holy Spirit which has been given to us'. That verse in essence sums up any testimony my wife and I would give as a result of having been released in the Spirit by the Lord Jesus.

"I have been an elder in the Church for 10 years but six years ago as I was reading through the Book of Acts it struck me as quite unfair that God would empower the early Church to do their work as witnesses unto Him and yet leave us in this day and age to simply grit our teeth and believe like mad and hope that God was still around some place. My frustrations grew as I

The Church and Pentecostalism

realised my ineffectiveness as an elder and my lack of power and desire to communicate my faith. About that time I came to hear about what is called the Baptism in the Holy Spirit and I began to wonder 'is this what is missing in the Church — is this what gave the early Church that dynamic which turned the world upside down?' And through a series of events which I will not relate here, I came to know this experience as a reality in my life and my wife and family followed. Much has been said and written about the 'Baptism in the Holy Spirit' but to us the greatest release was to be set free to love. We have grown more in love with Jesus, more in love with each other as a family, more in love with the Church where God has placed us, more in love with people whoever they may be.

"We would have thought that our brothers and sisters in the Church we attend would have been pleased to share our joy and to respond to the new-found love and yet strange to us, we found a coolness, not a little hostility, and yet as I reflect, faults have occurred on both sides, which, with more sharing and caring, need not have occurred.

"Our family life has completely changed and we never know from one minute to the next how many extra will be living with us or who will be calling for prayer or counsel and the office has indeed become the same. I am a Chartered Accountant with a growing practice, but it is not unusual for me to spend time counselling or praying for the sick in between business appointments.

"God has been very gracious to us as a family by enriching our lives with this experience. How anyone could not want to share in the life of God this way I will never understand".

'C' Is a Minister of the Church

"My own reactions to being baptised in the Holy Spirit were pretty quiet. No great waves of emotion. In fact, speaking in tongues was a pretty arid and arduous happening! But things began to happen. I wanted to praise God for being God. Study for devotions became more insistent and the desire for evangelism grew. A healing ministry started to grow as confidence in God's ability to still work 'miracles' grew. Above all a sense of joy and assuredness in calling was established.

"I am right where God put me, therefore something vital must happen for I am surrendering in obedience to him and not imposing patterns on God. There hasn't really been any black area here in spite of what could be depressing conditions, neither is there any sense of 'struggling for survival'.

"What is Pentecostalism? After being baptised in the Spirit for nearly two years, Pentecostalism is receiving the power to serve God and be open to God's leading in the most effective way.

"What Pentecostalism is not: it is not speaking in tongues, nor healing, etc. These are ministries arising from the baptism. It is not a way of finding God — it is only for Christians who know God in Christ already. It is not something which makes us adequate — our adequacy is found only in Christ who is in us. It is not a shortcut to holiness or a system where Christianity is made easy — it is the reverse! The baptism gives us a holy joy whereby we see the need to open up to God, to learn of him, to trust in him, to die to oneself as we wish to be used more and more. I am not saying that it does not impart spiritual strength. It does. But not of itself. The Spirit glorifies Jesus and imparts his strength and joy and frees us to live more and more, trustfully and confidently, in Jesus, and to invite others to share his resurrection life.

"In respect to my own parish, Pentecostalism or the charismatic movement has not made any overt impact as far as most of my few flock know. Yet the whole of my ministry draws on assurance and strength, and a growing one to one evangelistic ministry owes its power to this. I am not ready as yet to engage in direct teaching but could well do later this year. I feel that a little more maturing reflection won't be out of place. Also, because the baptism gave me a thirst to know God better and to know the Bible better as a spiritual resource, I deliberately took on the educational discipline drawn up by 'Navigators'. This has enriched me wonderfully, and has placed an educational tool in my hands which enables me to effectively meet with and teach others. My experience of the discipline needed to run such a course is one reason why I say the baptism is no shortcut — the Spirit needs material to build on! The personal 'glow' that one gets from walking with God in a closer and more spiritual way, enables me to catch the attention of others and show them just how practical God's answer in Christ is".

'D' Is a Woman School Teacher
"It is difficult to describe my experience of the baptism in the Holy Spirit without conveying some impression that the merit

might be my own. And yet I am not in any way worthy of this beautiful and continuing act of his grace.

"I can only remember a few years of my life when I didn't believe in the reality of a personal experience with God. As a child the awareness of his presence was very real — a place of refuge and a source of comfort whenever it was needed. The first few years of High School brought in other influences and doubts until I joined the Church and gave myself back to God again.

"My new peace with God was beautiful but there were some things about my faith (or lack of it) that disturbed me. One of these was that I was usually ashamed of my faith in front of my friends who described Christianity as a prop for the weak and insecure; another was that because of this shame I often did things about which, before God, I would later feel ashamed; yet another was that although I read the Bible dutifully I usually found it rather dull, and Bible study and prayer were heavy chores.

"Now, however, since being baptised in the Holy Spirit, an experience in which he not only indwelt, but also flooded and filled my whole being, I feel an enabling to live in a slightly more Christ-like fashion, which I believe is more satisfying to myself and to him.

"Jesus himself is real to me so that it is not usually difficult to talk about him, and whenever I do I find a new ability to speak the right words to the right people. I am not ashamed of my faith, for how can anyone be shamed of someone so real and dear to them? This is a miracle to me. As soon as I was blessed by this experience the Bible became far more relevant to me. It is now a source of spiritual strength, wisdom and comfort, in which I marvel at the wonder of our God and the 'mystery' of our faith.

"Prayer (when I discipline myself to draw aside) has become a beautiful place of rest, and of victorious battle against evil, where I know the Lord is hearing my prayers in Jesus' name and for his sake.

"This rich experience of the Lord and his grace has enhanced my love for the Church, his people and his creation, and increased my zeal and abilities in his service".

PASTORAL STATEMENT

We have become aware that many people of our Church, who have had some form of pentecostal experience, have, as a result of this, felt themselves to be somewhat estranged from the life of their Church; very often separated from other people who have any personal insight into this particular type of experience, they have come to feel very lonely. Often, if they have made their experiences and feelings known, thy have become the object of suspicion, sometimes of hostility and fear. Many such people have felt a strong pressure to withdraw from the Church where they had perhaps first found faith. There a very sad thing has come into the life of Christ's Church. It is our experience, as well as our conviction, that the person whose life has been enriched and warmed through pentecostal type experience is certainly no less a child of God, and a needed member of Christ's Church. They should be accepted and listened to attentively as they give their witness to this further confirmation of their faith, this enrichment of their experience, and to their greater confidence in the faith than they had felt themselves to have prior to this experience. With such conviction and warmth of testimony, such persons should be held dear, and should be made to feel very much at home in the family of the Church.

What we are saying can be broken down under two broad headings:

First we address ourselves to those who have had what they feel to have been a pentecostal experience. To such persons we say, "Understand, and even expect, that those who have not shared your particular experience should be taken by surprise.

"Be prepared to find that their surprise may cause them to react in ways which you may feel to be even unfavourable. We ask you, for the sake of your Lord and his Church, to be sympathetic to the shock and surprise which these your brethren experience in their relationship with you. This means be neither arrogant nor demanding; do not aggravate their feelings. This means, be gentle in your insistence (if insist you must) on the reality of your experience. This means treating your brethren gently, allowing them to come to terms in their own time with the new person you feel yourself to be, and which they find you to be".

Then we address ourselves to those people in the Church who (as it were) look on as observers to this new thing in the experience of their fellows. You may recall times in your own life when a particular experience has been a doorway into new areas of awareness and assurance. You may recall times when you have been comforted, or encouraged, or inspired and motivated in a special way by what you have been convinced was a Christian experience or understanding. By recalling such times in our own experience, you will surely set the stage for a sensitive and helpful understanding of the experience of your fellow Christian. Then, if your brother seems to be so excited as to be almost troublesome because of his experience, you will discover the merit of tolerance, with the virtue of gentleness and the grace of patience, and you will recall that love binds together people who otherwise might be driven far apart from each other.

We have confidence in proposing to you all that you should respect each other's gifts and experiences, that you should be tolerant of each other's weaknesses, and thankful for their enthusiasms; that you should not insist on others conforming to your own experiences and awarenesses, nor spend too much endeavour on being envious of what others have, which you feel yourself to lack.

The Church is one. The Church is Christ's. The Church is that community where in the name and the fellowship of Christ, we gather for mutual enrichment, for common worship, and for the strengthening of the witness and service that is given individually and corporately to the world of God's love and Christ's mission.

> The dove descending breaks the air,
> With flame of incandescent terror
> Of which the tongues declare
> The one discharge from sin and error.
> The only hope, or else despair
> Lies in the choice of pyre or pyre —
> To be redeemed from fire by fire.

T. S. Eliot, "Four Quartets", 'Little Gidding' iv

THE HOLY SPIRIT AND THE CHARISMATIC RENEWAL OF THE CHURCH

In 1973 the Doctrine Committee made a report to the General Assembly of the Presbyterian Church in New Zealand drawn up by S.J.D. McCay. An introduction noting the variety of stances taken by persons in the renewal and the positive attitudes the church should take to its witness was followed by a synopsis of biblical teaching on the baptism in the Holy Spirit. A glossary of terms was presented indicating their biblical roots and their typical use in the charismatic renewal with a judgment on the appropriateness of such usage.

The report recorded the usual diverse reactions of persons in the charismatic renewal: leaving the church to join sects, remaining in the church and defending it against all criticism, remaining in the church in an attempt to correct shortcomings from within.

The biblical evidence would indicate that the specific work of the Holy Spirit is the bestowal upon persons of all the benefits of God which come in Jesus Christ. Since all Christians have received the Holy Spirit, "It is impossible to speak of a transition within Christian existence from the state of the Spirit's being with to being in." Biblically baptism in the Holy Spirit has to do with initiation rather than a later stage of Christian life. Therefore the post baptismal or post conversion experience should not be called a baptism. "At least the New Testament never uses this term for it." A more appropriate term would be "filling." Any Christian is, in the theological sense, a charismatic. The baptism in the Spirit is truly descriptive of "a further radical experience of the Spirit" but confusion would be avoided if other terms were found.

The report called for an open mind regarding those who claim that experience. "If this experience signifies in some sense a deepening of faith and awareness of God's presence and power, we may be thankful." This openness should extend to the exercise of such charisms as tongues and prophecy. "The Spirit usually manifests Himself in other ways. However, that such manifestations may occur is quite in accord with the witness of the New Testament."

The charismatic experience does not signify "a higher level of spirituality nor ought it to suggest that some Christians have more of the Spirit than others." An experience of the Spirit cannot be validated as regards its theological significance by the norms of the precise sciences. "Regardless of the scientific conclusions which may be reached, the question of the theological significance of these phenomena will remain,

and it may be answered only within the context of the Christian faith."
The unusual character of an experience is no guarantee of its
authenticity. Divisiveness, harsh judgment and spiritual boasting are
indications that the Spirit of God is not present or at work.

Also in 1973 the Life and Work Committee made a report, drawn up by
R. H. Lane, which was more descriptive than analytic. It contained,
among other items, four witnesses of persons who had come into contact
with the renewal.

The above report, as well as that which follows here, was published in
the committee's The White Book, Presbyterian Church of New
Zealand *(Wellington, 1973), pp. 36–41 and 86–96.*

INTRODUCTION:

For years we have talked about the Church's need for Renewal.
Some have gone to other denominations or sects, where the grass
is greener. Other have gone out of the Church on their own.
Many who remain with deep loyalty maintain that God speaks to
them within the Church and have resisted all criticism of it; yet
others acknowledge many shortcomings in the Church and
attempt to correct these by liturgical, linguistic, and other
techniques.

Renewal is being experienced in some parishes and some
Churches overseas. Our Church is careful and does not want to
be swept off its feet by a short-lived fad, but many people with
fewer reservations are enjoying abundantly their new-found faith.
It would be a tragedy if we, like the elder brother of Christ's
parable, were in danger of missing out because of a dour
self-righteousness and judgmental attitude toward those whose
return to Christ is buoyant.

No responsible office-bearer can throw caution and pastoral
care to the wind. Renewal has to be biblical to be genuine and
doctrinally sound to be lasting and significant. Courageous
participation and deeply caring love are essential. The Doctrine
Committee would therefore encourage the Church eagerly to
search the Bible anew and find again the resources of true
renewal in God. God can give us new Life in the Spirit and He is
willing to give it abundantly to those who seek him in open faith
(Matthew 13:51-52).

God the Father Who gave us life acted in giving us Christ Jesus.
After we had crucified Him, God gave Him again to us, raising
Him from the dead and pouring His Spirit upon men who repent

and believe in His grace. This releases a great new power of love to those who believe and a real sense of belonging to the Body of Christ in fellowship with all believers in peace and joy. This is the true mainspring of genuine evangelism.

SUMMARISED EXTRACT *from the Report of the Permanent Theological Committee of the United Presbyterian Church of the U.S.A.* adopted by their 1971 General Assembly. It was further agreed by that Assembly "That the General Assembly commend this paper to the churches for study, and authorise the Office of the General Assembly to publish it in booklet form, distribute copies to all ministers and clerks of session and make copies available to the Church at large".

An evaluation of contemporary events involving a "baptism of the Holy Spirit" must begin with the guidance given by Scripture. Likewise, it is imperative that we should seek to understand what is deeply involved and at stake for those who claim to have had such a "baptism". It is likewise imperative that we observe the New Testament's close identification of the Spirit with Jesus Christ.

A.

1. All our speech about the Spirit is speech about God.

2. There is no understanding of the Spirit apart from faith (Calvin's Institutes III:4). In speaking of the Holy Spirit we speak from faith to faith.

3. We must "test the spirits to see whether they are of God" by the measure of their confession of Jesus Christ (1 John 4:1-3). Nothing that contradicts what we see in Christ can rightly be regarded as the activity of the Spirit. On the other hand, whatever bears witness to Christ exhibits the incontrovertible evidence of the Spirit's presence.

B.

1. The greatest emphasis in the Bible is to be found in the work of the Spirit in bestowing upon man all the benefits of God which come to him in Jesus Christ.

2. The Holy Spirit accordingly dwells in all who believe. It is impossible to speak of a transition within Christian existence from the state of the Spirit's being with to being in.

3. "Baptism with the Holy Spirit" is a phrase which refers most often to the empowering of those who believe to share in the mission of Jesus Christ. The significance of "baptism with the Spirit" is also represented in terms such as "outpouring", "falling upon", "filling" and "receiving" being for the most part attempts

The Holy Spirit and Renewal of the Church

to depict that action of God whereby believers are enabled to give expression to the gospel through extraordinary praise, powerful witness, and boldness of action. Since "baptism with the Spirit" may not be at the same time as baptism with water and/or conversion, we need to be open-minded toward those who claim an intervening period of time. If this experience signifies in some sense a deepening of faith and awareness of God's presence and power, we may be thankful.

4. We are called upon to recognise a work of the Holy Spirit which involves the application of special gifts and benefits to the members of Christ's church. "The Holy Spirit . . . qualifies all other officers in the church for their special work and imparts various gifts and graces to its members" (Westminster Confession IX, 4). Both a fresh confrontation with the biblical record and contemporary spiritual experience are bringing us into a fuller understanding of the work of the Holy Spirit.

5. The "baptism of the Holy Spirit" may be signified by certain phenomena such as speaking in tongues and prophecy (Acts 2:4, 10:46, 19:6). In the Old Testament the Holy Spirit is frequently associated with ecstatic prophecy though this was limited to certain persons. With the New Testament dispensation the Spirit is now available to all who believe in Jesus Christ. Hence such signs as ecstatic language and prophecy could occur with anyone who has experienced this visitation, though it would be a mistake to say that all upon whom the Spirit comes *must* manifest these phenomena. The Spirit usually manifests Himself in other ways. However, that such manifestations *may* occur is quite in accord with the witness of the New Testament.

6. "Baptism with the Spirit" signifies the initial outpouring of God's Spirit wherein the community and/or person is filled with the presence and power of God. But also there may be later bestowal in such fashion as to signify implementation of the original event, whether or not accompanied by pneumatic (spiritual) phenomena (cf. Acts 2:4 with 4:31). This renewed activity of the Spirit ought not to be designated "baptism" (at least, the New Testament never uses this term for it), but as "filling" wherein the empowering Spirit moves to renew the believer and believing community.

7. The bestowal of the Spirit, or of the gifts of the Spirit, does not signify a higher level of spirituality nor ought it to suggest that some Christians have more of the Holy Spirit than others. The Spirit is active in all believers and they may be "filled" with

the Spirit in various ways for the mission of the church. (The Spirit fosters Christian growth in grace and power to witness. Generally those in whom the Spirit works most strongly are least likely to make claims concerning the Spirit's filling.)

8. The charismata (gifts of the Spirit) are the benefits of God's free grace and may not be considered "possession" of the believer. He does not own them, nor can he presume that they are, or will be, at all times (or at any given time) available. There should be no jeopardising of the peace, unity and fellowship of the church because of special experiences of the Holy Spirit, but a rejoicing together in all those ways whereby God leads His people into fuller apprehension of the riches of His grace.

9. An experience of the Spirit can neither be validated as such, nor evaluated with respect to its theological significance, by any scientific (i.e., psychological, sociological, etc.) means. Regardless of the scientific conclusions which may be reached, the question of the theological significance of these phenomena will remain, and it may be answered only within the context of the Christian faith. Neither psychology nor any other science can answer the question as to whether the Spirit is active in speaking in tongues. The extraordinary or unusual nature of an experience (and the same would apply to gifts) is no criterion by which to judge its significance for faith.

10. It is clear that there is Biblical and Reformed witness concerning baptism of the Holy Spirit and special endowments of the Holy Spirit in the believing community. But where there is divisiveness, judgment (expressed or implied) on the lives of others, an attitude of pride or boasting, etc., the Spirit of God is not at work. However, where such an experience gives evidence of an empowering and renewing work of Christ in the life of the individual and the church, it may be acknowledged with gratitude. This means above all that Christ should be glorified, His own Spirit made manifest in human lives, and the Church edified. For such evidence of the Holy Spirit, the Church may rejoice.

GLOSSARY:

I. Baptised in the Spirit

i. Biblical — This phrase is used seven times in the New Testament: Matt 3:11; Mark 1:8; Luke 3:16; John 1:33; Acts 1:5; 11:16; 1 Cor 12:13. In these seven instances its use is confined to three events.

a. The pouring out of the Holy Spirit at Pentecost (the first five refs. above). This event is recognised as the "birthday" of the church and like the Cross and Resurrection is a unique event.

b. The conversion of Cornelius (Acts 11:16). It would seem from the relevant passages in Acts that while Cornelius was undoubtedly a religious person, a God fearer, yet he was not a Christian until after he was baptised in the Spirit. See Acts 10:1-2; 11:17-18; 15:8-9.

c. A general term for conversion or regeneration (1 Cor 12:13). What makes us Christians is our being baptised into the Spirit which is being baptised into the Body of Christ: two ways of saying the same thing.

ii. *General* — This phrase is commonly used in the charismatic movement to describe a second experience of the Holy Spirit after conversion. While strictly this is not the biblical sense, it is nevertheless a descriptive phrase for those who do undergo a further radical experience of the Holy Spirit. To avoid confusion, however, it would be better for other terms to be used.

II. Charismatic

i. *Biblical.* Charismatic comes from the Greek word charismata which is the plural form of the word charisma meaning gift. It is derived from the word charis which means grace; so it is a gift or gifts freely given. Charisma is used to describe all sorts of gifts, e.g., rescue from danger (2 Cor 1:11); redemption (Rom 5:15); eternal life (Rom 6:23); given to everyone (1 Cor 7:7). In particular, it is used of the list of gifts in Rom 12:1-6 and 1 Cor 12.

So in its biblical sense any Christian may be described as charismatic in that all have received at least one charisma from God.

ii. *General.* Within the charismatic movement it has commonly come to mean those who have had a second crisis experience of the Holy Spirit, and who have experience of certain gifts such as tongues, interpretations, healing, prophecy. But as we see from its biblical usage, it has a very much wider usage and may legitimately be used of any Christian. It is an inclusive rather than an exclusive term. Used in a non biblical way it becomes divisive.

III. "Filled with the Holy Spirit" and "Full of the Holy Spirit"

i. *Biblical.* "Filled with the Holy Spirit" occurs nine times in the New Testament, all but one in Luke's two books: Luke and Acts:

They are Luke 1:15; 1:41; 1:67; Acts 2:4; 4:8; 4:31; 9:17; 13:9; and Eph 5:18. "Full of the Holy Spirit" occurs five times: Luke 4:1; Acts 6:3; 6:5; 7:5; 11:24.

1. The phrases appear to have a two-fold use in scripture.

a. A special visitation of the Spirit for some particular task, e.g., Paul rebuking Elymas (Acts 13:9); Peter facing the Jewish rulers (Acts 4:8); Elizabeth and Zechariah when they prophesied (Luke 1:41; 1:67). "Filled" is used of special occasions.

b. A general state to which all should aspire. So Barnabas (Acts 11:24), John the Baptist (Luke 1:15) the deacons (Acts 6:3). "Full" is used of the general state.

2. The phrase is only once identified with the baptism of the Holy Spirit (Acts 2:4).

3. It normally describes an experience after conversion either in the particular or general sense mentioned.

4. All are exhorted to experience it and to maintain it (Eph 5:18).

5. The disciples themselves experienced more than one filling but only one baptism (Acts 2:4; 4:31; 9:17; 13:9).

6. The *method* of experiencing the filling is never defined.

ii. Common Use. It is used by persons involved in the charismatic movement as an identifiable term with the phrase "baptism in the Holy Spirit", i.e., as a second spiritual crisis after regeneration. The two terms describe the same experience. Certain persons are frequently referred to as "Spirit filled". This is biblically legitimate so long as it is not confined to those who are in the charismatic movement and who have had a deep experience of the Holy Spirit and so long as it is recognised that a person may be Spirit filled one moment and fall from such a state the next. Otherwise the terms become divisive.

IV. Other Biblical Phrases Which Should Be Noted in Connection with the Action of the Holy Spirit

These terms are often interchangeable and denote different aspects of the same action of the Holy Spirit. They are intimately associated or identifiable with being baptised in the Holy Spirit.

i. *fall upon* Acts 8:16; 10:44; 11:15.

ii. *poured* Acts 2:17, 18; 10:45.

iii. *received* John 20:22; Acts 1:8; 2:33; 2:38; 8:15, 17, 19, 10:47; 19:2; Rom 8:15; 1 Cor 2:11, 12.

SUGGESTED READING

Bill Bright: "Revolution Now" and other L.I.F.E. material; F. D. Bruner; "A Theology of the Holy Spirit"; H. Berkhoff: "The Doctrine of the Holy Spirit"; J. D. G. Dunn: "Baptism in the Holy Spirit" (scm); A. J. Gordon: "The Ministry of the Spirit" (Bethany Fellowship); A. A. Hoekema: "Holy Spirit Baptism" (Paternoster Press); A. A. Hoekema: "What About Tongues Speaking" (Paternoster Press); M. C. Harper: "Power for the Body of Christ" (Fountain Trust); R. Hession: "Be Filled Now" (Christian Literature Crusade); J. W. R. Stott: "The Baptism and Fullness of the Holy Spirit" (ivp); U.P.C., U.S.A. "The Work of the Holy Spirit" (report).

32 Baptist General Conference, USA, 1974

BIBLICAL CHARISMA AND THE CONTEMPORARY NEW TESTAMENT CHURCH

The Baptist General Conference of the United States proposed an extended resolution to the district conferences which in content is similar to that of the Baptist Union of New Zealand (1970). "Historically and experientially the church was baptized in the Holy Spirit at Pentecost," an event which, like Christ's death on the cross, is once for all, never to be repeated. Each believer shares in that baptism through personal experience at the moment of the new birth. It is not an experience subsequent to conversion. This means that the church and every believer is by necessity charismatic. For this reason "no single group within the universal church has the right to be called charismatic to the exclusion of others." The gifts of the Spirit, including prophecy, tongues, healing, and exorcism are manifested in the church as she needs them, though "they may or may not be evident at any given time." The exercise of charismatic gifts by a believer is not proof of spiritual maturity, which is rather to be found in "living and extending agape love."

The resolution was reprinted in the "Baptist General Conference: 1974 Annual" (Statistics for 1973–74), published by the Board of Trustees, Baptist General Conference, pp. 58–59.

Whereas in our day there is so great an emphasis on the present ministry of the Holy Spirit; and whereas there is so much confusion and differences of definitions among groups of those who call themselves Christian; and whereas there is frequent spiritual and/or organic schism occurring as a result of inadequate understanding of biblical teachings concerning both the historical and contemporary ministry of the Holy Spirit . . .

We, as the constituent members of the Baptist General Conference, accept as a standard of faith the following statements in relationship to the ministries of the Holy Spirit and the New Testament charismatic church.

1. NEW TESTAMENT DOCTRINE

a. *The Word of God.* We affirm our belief that the Bible is the Word of God, given under the inspiration of the third member of the Trinity, who is the executor of the Godhead in this church age.

b. *The Church Age.* We believe that historically and experientially the church was baptized in the Holy Spirit at Pentecost. This event, like Christ's death on Calvary, was once for all, never to be repeated. We believe that every believer receives the Holy Spirit as a gift and partakes through personal experience in that baptism of the Holy Spirit at the moment of the new birth. It is not a separate experience subsequent to the new birth.

c. *The Executor of the Church.* We believe that the Holy Spirit invests Himself in the local church to guide its ministry for the praise and glory of God. As the Executor of the Trinity He uses talents and sovereignly gives spiritual gifts to all believers "to prepare God's people for works of service, so that the body of Christ may be built up."

d. *Conclusion.* We believe that every church experiencing this ministry of the Holy Spirit of God is truly a charismatic church. It follows that the New Testament concept of the working of the Holy Spirit which was established on the day of Pentecost will continue until the Lord Jesus Christ reappears at His second advent.

2. APPLICATIONS FOR TODAY

Therefore, we need to proclaim from our pulpits, teach in our Christian education programs and Bible study fellowships that:

a. No single group or movement within the universal church has the right to be called charismatic to the exclusion of others, since the church by its very nature is charismatic.

b. The Holy Spirit is sovereign and gives gifts (*charismata*) to whomever He chooses, no one of these being required for every believer.

c. As the church has need, in order to fulfill its ministry, gifts are Spirit-given for that ministry — whether they be the abilities (*charisma*) of teaching, prophecy, helps, administrations, hospitality, tongues, liberality in giving, physical healing, exorcising of demons, discernment of spirits, or others; and they may or may not be evident at any given time.

d. Spiritual maturity in a believer is not necessarily proven by his exercising charismatic gifts, nor are such gifts a guarantee of having been baptized in the Holy Spirit.

e. Charismatic gifts are justification for humility, rather than pride, since they are Spirit-given, and always glorify Christ rather than the one who exercises the gifts.

f. Living and extending agape love, rather than possession of gifts, is one sure indicator of growth toward spiritual maturity, and is the norm for every believer.

1975 RESOLUTIONS COMMITTEE
Mrs. Paul Berggren, Vincent Cyphers, Frank Doten, George
Dvirnak, Arthur Freedburg

33 Church of Scotland (Presbyterian), 1974

THE CHARISMATIC MOVEMENT WITHIN THE CHURCH OF SCOTLAND

The final report of the Panel on Doctrine of the Church of Scotland was greatly influenced by reports which had issued from the two major Presbyterian bodies in the United States. Like the American Commissions, the Scottish Panel on Doctrine included in its working group ministers who identified with the renewal.

The report of the United Presbyterian Church in the United States had a sizable section on the results of psychological surveys and concluded that those in the charismatic renewal "are essentially well-adjusted and productive members of society" and that there is "no justification for making a sweeping generalization that participants in the movement are maladjusted individuals, emotionally unstable, or emotionally deprived." On the basis of corroborative evidence, the Scottish panel supported this conclusion and made no attempt to elaborate on it further.

The report recounted the history and teaching of classical Pentecostalism, gave a critical assessment of its doctrine, related briefly the history and teaching of the charismatic renewal (neo-Pentecostalism) and subjected that doctrine to a critique, examined the biblical evidence, commented on certain aspects of the renewal (water-baptism and Spirit-baptism, the influence of cultural environment, prophecy, the role of the supernatural and the miraculous), and concluded by giving some provisional guidelines.

The Panel expressed some concern that the Holy Spirit was being isolated from the trinitarian context and was given an independent status. The tension which exists between the Holy Spirit constituting the church and bringing the church under judgment should be maintained. The theology of subsequence (there is a second blessing posterior to conversion) may be the basis for elaborating a doctrine of the baptism in the Holy Spirit which creates two kinds or levels of Christians, those converted and those who in addition to a conversion experience have received the baptism in the Holy Spirit. What is called into question here is not the reality of the spiritual experience but how it is interpreted, with special care being shown lest it be the basis for a "Church within the Church."

In attempting to relate water-baptism to Spirit-baptism, the panel recognized the problems of temporal sequence: "Spirit-baptism may precede, coincide with or follow water-baptism," but "these two elements of the one unity should not be allowed to drift apart." There is only one baptism. The grace given at baptism or conversion "comes variously and successively into the consciousness of the believer, through faith." Baptism in the Spirit should therefore not be interpreted as a second blessing "but as a release of what was already there, as a growth in grace."

The promise of the gifts was seen as "valid for all times, and to the end of time." Also evaluated positively was Edward Irving's teaching that some of the gifts had ceased to be operative in the church "simply because of lack of faith." The charismatic renewal challenges the church to accept by faith that which has already been granted by grace. "The gifts of the Spirit are to be expected."

Yet the nature of the gifts the Spirit gives to the church may have changed, "so that the gifts he gave to the Church of the first century are not necessarily the gifts he is offering the Church today." Given the changed cultural environment, should not charismata be expected which are directed to the achievement of political and industrial reconciliation, "gifts which appear all too rare today?" The panel indicated that prophecy can be turned in upon itself "for the internal edification of the

Church, or outwards towards the world at large," the latter being more typical of the great prophets of the Old Testament.

Caution was expressed concerning the unqualified use of the word "ecstatic" in regard to charismatic phenomena. To many the word connotes frenzied, uncontrolled behavior, which may or may not be present. The root meaning of ecstatic is one of spiritual exaltation, which can appear strange, even bizarre to the uninitiated, but which at the same time can still remain decent and in good order.

A tendency of those in the charismatic renewal to speak of spiritual gifts and to mean such gifts as tongues, interpretation, and healing was remarked. No objection can be taken to this as long as this title is not denied to more ordinary ways of service. While commenting on the exaggerated supernaturalism found in some circles within the renewal, the panel pointed out that the gifts of justification and sanctification are just as supernatural as the extraordinary charismata: "Speaking in tongues is miraculous, but so is the gift of reconciliation between God and man."

In speaking of the relation of charisms to natural abilities, the reception of a gift of the Spirit, the panel concluded, does not exclude the possibility that the believer "would then be able to do something he was unable to do before." But preference was given to the view that in a charism "an inborn ability is heightened, or the believer discovers a new way of fulfilling an old task – the way of love." Those members of the panel personally involved in the charismatic renewal expressed the conviction that "a natural gift is not a charism."

Reprint copies of "The Charismatic Movement Within the Church of Scotland" can be obtained from the Secretary of the Panel on Doctrine, Rev. Roderick Pettigrew, Burnside Manse, Dalbeattie, Kirkcudbrightshire, Scotland DG5 4JS.

A. INTRODUCTION

In May 1972, the General Assembly instructed the Panel on Doctrine "to examine afresh the doctrine of the Holy Spirit, with particular reference to the gifts of the Spirit and in the light of the contemporary charismatic or neo-Pentecostal movement"; in May 1973, the Panel made an interim report and now seeks to discharge this remit.

In doing so, the Panel wishes to express its very sincere gratitude both to certain New Testament scholars in the faculties and to certain ministers of the Church identified with the charismatic movement who, as members of the Panel's working party, have given most freely of their time and talents and have very greatly assisted the Panel in completing the work which lies behind this report.

The Panel had also the advantage of being able to take note of two extensive reports made in recent years to the General Assemblies of the United Presbyterian Church in the U.S.A. and of the Presbyterian Church in the United States, entitled respectively *The Work of the Holy Spirit* and *The Person and Work of the Holy Spirit*. In particular, the Panel noted that the former of these reports, which was able to take cognisance of large scale psychological surveys, came to the conclusion that "Pentecostals generally . . . are essentially well-adjusted and productive members of society" (p. 11) and that there is "no justification for making a sweeping generalisation that participants in the movement are maladjusted individuals, emotionally unstable, or emotionally deprived" (p. 12).

In the light of this conclusion, of the careful research on which it was based and of such further corroborative evidence as came to the Panel's own notice, the Panel is of the opinion that it cannot usefully add to this aspect of the matter.

The facts which have given rise to these two reports as well as to the present study by the Panel on Doctrine have received widespread and increasing attention over the last ten years or so, and they have been conveniently summarised by the report which has already been quoted. "It is now fairly well-known," it says (p. 4), "that clergy and laymen within the Roman Catholic Church and all of the main protestant denominations have claimed to have received a 'baptism in the Spirit' with attendant manifestations, such as speaking in tongues, powers of healing, exorcism, and other practices not normally associated with our style of congregational life. 'Neo-Pentecostalism' is thus a movement *within* the established churches, and its exponents would regard it as a legitimate instrument of revival with strong scriptural justification."

In seeking to assess this movement of neo-Pentecostalism, the Panel has come to the conclusion that there are certain truths of a doctrinal nature which the Church of Scotland, standing as it does within the Reformed tradition, is bound to bear in mind.

1. In our theological thinking, the Holy Spirit ought not to be assigned a status independent of the other two persons of the Godhead so that the Spirit is no longer manifestly the Spirit of the God and Father of our Lord Jesus Christ, and we in turn fall into the danger of committing the error of tri-theism. Rather we are to

"try the spirits" and there is no criterion above or alongside Jesus Christ.

2. While there have been times and movements for which the Holy Spirit has been regarded as the Spirit of the Church, it is important to reject any such facile identification. The Holy Spirit is closely identified with the Church. He indeed creates the Church; but he also brings the Church under judgement and renews the Church, so that the grace by which the Church exists is a living thing which the Church can never wholly domesticate.

3. One of the phrases most frequently used to describe certain of the experiences characteristic of neo-Pentecostalism is "baptism in (or of, or with) the Holy Spirit". While the Panel is prepared to accept the reality of these experiences, it does question the use of this phrase to describe them. It is not difficult to understand how this expression came to be used, but it may well be that it is more misleading than suggestive. In particular, since baptism has properly the character of being once-for-all and since it clearly refers to entrance into the Church, the Panel considers that in the context of neo-Pentecostalism it cannot but suggest the idea of a Church within the Church and that accordingly it is in this connection wholly indefensible.

4. Not uncommonly some of the experience characteristic of neo-Pentecostalism are interpreted as gifts of the Spirit which betoken a special empowering for ministry; but once again the Panel is of the opinion that if it is important strictly to avoid any suggestion of a Church within the Church it is no less important to avoid as strictly any suggestion of a ministry within the ministry. The Panel believes that the Church's thinking in this area ought to fall within a triangle defined by three points; the diversity of gifts, the many members, and the one body which is the body of Jesus Christ our Lord.

B. PENTECOSTALISM

1. Introduction

The Panel recognises that the charismatic movement within the traditional Churches is not to be identified with classical Pentecostalism. However, it has come to the conclusion that a survey of classical Pentecostalism is required to enable a more accurate assessment to be made, which would distinguish the neo-Pentecostal movement within the Church of Scotland, from the Pentecostal Churches on the one hand, and the Reformed Tradition on the other.

2. The History of Pentecostalism

Throughout the history of the Christian Church, there have been movements akin to Pentecostalism; for instance, Montanism, the Mediaeval Spiritualists, the Anabaptists, the Revivalism of the seventeenth and eighteenth centuries, and the Holiness Movement in the United States. Revival meetings at which speaking with tongues occurred, for example at Azusa Street, Los Angeles (1906) have come to be regarded as the beginning of the Pentecostal Churches.[1] Pentecostalism was soon established in Europe. Revivals had already prepared the way in England and Wales, from where it spread to Scotland (Kilsyth) by 1908.

Today, Pentecostal Churches are to be found in practically every part of the world. Pentecostals are said to number at least ten million, and claim to be the most rapidly growing denominations in the world, being increasingly regarded as the third force in Christendom.[2]

3. Theological Ancestry

The characteristic teaching of Pentecostalism is a development of doctrines taken over from two main sources: Methodism, and the American Holiness Movement.

A. METHODISM

One of the marks of John Wesley's thinking was his teaching on "Christian perfection".[3] While he believed in gradual sanctification, a "growing in grace, a daily advance in the knowledge and love of God",[4] he also taught that it was possible to achieve "entire sanctification" during one's earthly life. Wesley himself surrounded this doctrine with careful qualifications, but it can be understood how his doctrine of "entire sanctification" can lead to the idea of a second work of grace, subsequent to conversion. As believers we are justified and subsequently we (or some of us) are entirely sanctified.

B. THE HOLINESS MOVEMENT

A further coarsening of Wesley's doctrine of Christian perfection is to be found in the teaching of the American Holiness Movement, which emphasised the necessity of a second work of

The Charismatic Movement

grace, a "second blessing", subsequent to conversion, leading to Holiness. Frederick Dale Bruner introduced the phrase "theology of subsequence" to describe this approach.

We note that this implies the rejection of the Reformed rediscovery of the biblical truth of *simul justus et peccator* (righteous and sinner at the same time).

From the Holiness Movement, Pentecostalism adopted this theology of subsequence: Conversion is, and must be, followed by a subsequent blessing, commonly called "baptism in the Holy Spirit". A theology of subsequence implies two or more classes of believers, a distinction being made between the converted and those who have been subsequently baptised in the Holy Spirit.

4. The Teaching of Pentecostalism

Pentecostals believe that what distinguishes them from other Evangelical Christians is their claim to be baptised in the Holy Spirit, which they see as a decisive event wherein the Holy Spirit takes hold of them, transforms their lives, empowering them for service, and imparts to them the gifts of the Spirit, such as speaking in tongues.[5]

A. THE PENTECOSTAL RULE OF FAITH

Although a verbally inspired bible is regarded as the infallible rule of faith and life, Pentecostals are somewhat selective in their choice of proof texts or passages. Their distinctive doctrines are almost exclusively based upon the Lucan parts of the New Testament, especially the Acts of the Apostles (*e.g.*, Acts 2:1–4; 2:38; 8:4–25; 9:1–19; 10; 11; 19:1–7). The remainder of the New Testament is interpreted in the light of such passages.

B. THE PENTECOSTAL CRISIS EXPERIENCE

For Pentecostals, the essential experience is to be filled with the Holy Spirit in exactly the same way as happened at the first Pentecost;[6] but before this can happen there are certain definite conditions to be met, normally considered to be regeneration, obedience, prayer and faith.[7]

Baptism in the Holy Spirit is an additional gift which has to be actively sought as a result of receiving Christ.[8] This raises the Christian, who is already regenerate and who has a clean heart, to an even higher level of existence. "As sinners we accept Christ, as saints we accept the Holy Spirit."[9]

It is not sufficient to believe or claim that one has been baptised in the Holy Spirit. There must be an external criterion, which, for most Pentecostals, is "speaking with tongues" (*glossolalia*). This, however, is regarded as the initial but not the only, or even the most important, evidence of the indwelling Spirit. It is the external, verifiable and assuring evidence that, having been baptised in the Holy Spirit, the spirit of man is dominated by the Spirit of God.

D. THE CONSEQUENCE OF BAPTISM IN THE HOLY SPIRIT

The Holy Spirit, given and received once and for all, makes the believer eligible for the reception of his gifts (1 Cor 12–14). These gifts have the effect of "empowering" or "enabling" the believer for service, because they provide "a spiritual capability far mightier than the finest natural capabilities could ever supply".[10]

5. Critical Assessment of Classical Pentecostal Teaching from a Reformed Point of View

A. THE TRINITY

While Pentecostal teaching on the Trinity appears to be orthodox, further examination gives rise to grave doubt. Reformed theology has always affirmed that the primary work of the Holy Spirit is to reveal the risen and living Christ, the only Lord and Saviour, to his Church and people. For Pentecostals, on the other hand, the Holy Spirit, while not exactly replacing Christ, is acting independently of, and in addition to, what Christ has done, and is doing. He comes "in his own person", as the "third Person of the Trinity, in addition to the coming of Christ, which takes place at conversion".[11]

Thus, Pentecostals emphasise, not the one-ness of God, but his three-ness. The Holy Spirit has an existence of his own, and it is the encounter with the Holy Spirit, apart from and beyond the encounter with Christ, which makes the Christian's life complete.[12]

B. FAITH

For Pentecostals, the fullness of the Holy Spirit is a "second blessing" and is not to be "appropriated simply by faith".[13] Thus the great Reformed doctrines of *sola fide* (by faith alone) and *sola gratia* (by grace alone), both grounded in *solus Christus* (Christ alone) are rejected. Pentecostals emphasise what man has to do, "to yield at every point", "to go all the way with Christ" [14] and "to make the yieldedness complete".[15] This work of total surrender thus becomes man's achievement. Faith is then only a good work, though often devotional language disguises this fact.

C. JUSTIFICATION AND SANCTIFICATION

The Reformers rediscovered the biblical truth that justification and sanctification are two aspects of one and the same reality. Any suggestion that justification is the work of Christ, and sanctification that of the Holy Spirit is firmly rejected. Both are equally the work of Christ, through the Holy Spirit. Pentecostals are right in asserting that salvation depends on the final overcoming of sin, but they overlook the fact that Christ is fully victorious over sin in his death and resurrection. In their view, man must rid himself totally of sin, and so acquire a clean heart to work out his own salvation. As a result, "the doctrine of justification is emptied of meaning and reduced to a preliminary stage for beginners in Christianity".[16]

If this were true, there would be no real assurance for the Christian. According to Calvin, our conscience would "never be pacified, for we are very far from being perfectly renewed".[17] The Christian has assurance, because God "does not justify in part, but liberally" and believers "may appear in heaven as if endowed with the purity of Christ".[18]

D. BAPTISM IN THE HOLY SPIRIT

Pentecostals regard "baptism in or with the Holy Spirit" as an additional working of the Holy Spirit which goes beyond the initiation of the Christian life (justification) and also beyond its progress (sanctification). From the Reformed point of view, to insist on baptism in the Holy Spirit as an experience subsequent to conversion is to deny the all-sufficiency of Christ. Although there are passages in Acts which suggest a theology of subsequence when interpreted literally, there are others which are not in harmony with this; and if the New Testament witness is taken as a whole, it is seen that faith in Christ and the reception of the Holy Spirit cannot be separated. How can faith in Christ, the sole Lord and Saviour of men, the only King and Head of the Church, be a half-way house where the believer receives life, but not sufficient power to witness and to serve?

C. NEO-PENTECOSTALISM

1. Introduction

Neo-Pentecostals are believers who hold to some of the insights of classical Pentecostalism, but who choose to remain within the fellowship of the more traditional Churches, believing that if the traditional Churches really practised what they profess to believe regarding the Holy Spirit, the charismatic movement would be welcomed by them. From the side of the traditional Churches, neo-Pentecostals are to be commended for their loyalty and devotion. Originally, classical Pentecostalism was a movement of renewal within the Churches, but doctrinal and other tensions led to separation, and eventually to division among the Pentecostal Churches themselves. To prevent this happening again, our aim should be to hold the charismatic movement and witness within the traditional Churches, and in particular within the Church of Scotland.

2. History of Neo-Pentecostalism

Some trace the origin of the present neo-Pentecostal movement to events within a congregation of the Episcopal Diocese of Los Angeles, California. From there the movement spread rapidly throughout the world and penetrated the historic denominations. Neo-Pentecostals understand their movement to have grown, not so much because of the direct influence of classical Pentecostalism, but rather as a reaction to a certain feeling of dryness and inadequacy within the traditional Churches. The Roman Catholic Church, though apparently not in Scotland, has proved to be receptive to neo-Pentecostal ideas, because of its readiness to accept the supernatural within the terms of its faith and life. The movement is also proving to be influential in many countries amongst the younger generation.

In Scotland today, neo-Pentecostals claim with considerable justification to be growing rapidly, particularly within the Church of Scotland.

3. Doctrinal Position

To what extent are neo-Pentecostals in doctrinal agreement with classical Pentecostalism on the one hand, and the Reformed position on the other?

No definite answer can be given to this question, because strictly speaking there is no unified system of neo-Pentecostal doctrine. Most neo-Pentecostals are primarily concerned with what is to them the all-important experience of the gift of the Holy Spirit, rather than with its doctrinal interpretation.

Neo-Pentecostals face a challenge to their identity by the very fact that they owe allegiance both to their charismatic insights, and to the Church of their fathers. From a logical point of view, neo-Pentecostals would tend either towards accepting the classical Pentecostal interpretation of their experiences, and so attempt to change the Reformed position from within, or towards accepting the orthodox Reformed teaching and so attempt to re-interpret their charismatic experience in that light.

In the course of its study of the subject, the Panel discovered that there are neo-Pentecostals within the Church of Scotland who choose the latter alternative; others may not have realised that the alternatives exist. The charismatic movement within the Church of Scotland is not then bound to a theology of subsequence. Consequently its members are free to recognise that commitment to Christ and the reception of the Holy Spirit are correlative. In other words, the believer is baptised in the Holy Spirit when he receives Christ, yet the Spirit will reveal himself successively and variously in the consciousness of each believer. All Christians without exception can, however, quench (cf. 1 Thes 5:19) or grieve (cf. Eph. 4:30) the Holy Spirit.

On the other hand, the Panel would agree that neo-Pentecostals may have legitimate criticisms against certain aspects of Reformed teaching, and that in making these criticisms, they have an ancestor in the person of Edward Irving.

4. *Criticism of the Reformed Position*
   from a Neo-Pentecostal Point of View

Charismatics have criticised the Churches of the Reformed tradition for not giving sufficient attention to the development of the doctrine of the Holy Spirit. Yet both the Panel and the neo-Pentecostal members of its working party found themselves in general agreement as to the basic doctrine of the Holy Spirit. It was agreed that more attention would have to be given to the sphere of the activity or the manifestations of the Holy Spirit, not just as the third person of the Trinity, but as the Spirit of the Lord Jesus Christ, so that the life of the Church as a whole might be enriched.

In one important respect, however, the Reformed position is criticised and rejected by members of the charismatic movement, even by those who essentially share Reformed insights against those of classical Pentecostalism. What is involved is this very question of the continued manifestation of the Holy Spirit in and through his various gifts made available to the Church, as the body of Christ. The criticism is that Calvin and the other Reformers rejected for all practical purposes the possibility of the Holy Spirit continuing to operate through his gifts, such as speaking in tongues, healing and prophecy. The Reformers and their successors confined, quite arbitrarily, it is alleged, extraordinary gifts and ministries to the apostles and the apostolic age.

For example, Calvin, in his commentary on Mark 16:17,* "And these signs (*e.g.*, speaking in tongues, exorcism and healing) shall follow them that believe", explains that although Christ does not expressly state whether such gifts were to be temporary or perpetual, it is the more likely that they were appointed for one specific purpose, "that nothing which was necessary for proving the doctrine of the Gospel should be wanting at its commencement".[19]

In assessing this criticism, the Panel acknowledges that since God has finally spoken in Christ, what have undoubtedly ceased are new revelations.[20] What has not ceased according to scripture is the promise of gifts. The promise in Mark was made "to them that believe", and this is a promise valid for all times, and to the end of time. There is no warrant in scripture for confining it to the "commencement" of the gospel. Here again, we seem to be faced with a case of the Reformers over-reacting against the Roman Catholic doctrine and practice of their day, including, for instance, the raising of "tradition" to the same level as scripture, and the popular ascribing of miraculous powers to relics. In defence of the Reformers, however, it must be recognised that they did not reject everything miraculous. The Second Helvetic Confession, for instance, proclaimed the miracle of preaching: the preaching of the Word of God is the Word of God. The on-going life of the Church is the true miracle.

5. The Insights of Edward Irving (1792–1834)
The situation in Scotland is now being influenced by the life and teaching of Edward Irving. We do not need here to assess his

---

*The Panel is aware that the authenticity of Mark 16:9-20 is disputed by some scholars.

The Charismatic Movement

theology in detail, which would lead us into the discussion of aspects outside the scope of this remit, such as his Christology. What is immediately relevant is the fact that he made the first authentic attempt known to the Panel to interpret charismatic phenomena in terms of Reformed theology.

In this connection, Irving discovered a discrepancy between the Reformers' principle of *sola scriptura* (by scripture alone) and its application in the case of spiritual gifts. The Reformers recognised the signs which "follow them that believe", but refused to extend the validity of this promise to believers in all ages. Irving, however, despite a thorough search, could find no scriptural warrant that would justify belief in the cessation of spiritual gifts.[21]

Irving made a further point of particular interest in our present attempt to produce a synthesis between Pentecostal and Reformed insights. He refused to accept the Reformed viewpoint that the outward gift of power had ceased while the inward gift of sanctification and fruitfulness had not. Apparently for him the reception of miraculous gifts and ministries did not depend on the theology of subsequence with which Pentecostal thinking has become associated. Irving taught that the outward gifts of the Spirit had generally ceased not because they were intended to be temporary, as the Reformers had taught, or because believing Christians had not received a second blessing in the gift of the Holy Spirit, as most Pentecostals were to teach, but simply because of a lack of faith, over the centuries.[22] According to him, miraculous gifts and ministries would be received both by the Church and individual members, if only there was faith.

This is the challenge of the neo-Pentecostal movement to the Church, to accept by faith that which has already been granted by grace.

6. The Gifts of the Holy Spirit: Exegesis of 1 Cor 12-14

One of the phrases most frequently used by the charismatic movement is "gifts of the Spirit". The Greek word for gift is *charisma*, in the plural *charismata*. This plural form is frequently used in English to refer to the gifts of the Spirit, and from it is derived the adjective *charismatic*. The purpose of the Spirit in giving these gifts is the upbuilding or edification of the Church.[23]

How these charismata affect the Church may be studied in 1 Cor 12-14. The Church at Corinth seems to have asked Paul's advice on how to control unseemly behaviour during public worship, where certain practices including charismatic activities were proving to be divisive. In his reply, Paul gives a list of gifts, but it would appear that the contents of this list are not exhaustive, nor can too much meaning be placed upon the particular order in which they are listed. Paul's point is that the Holy Spirit gives many gifts, not for the glory of the individual, but for the common good.

The list in 1 Cor 12 should be compared with that in Rom 12. Because of the different backgrounds of the two Churches, and the different contexts within which the two letters were written, the lists, though similar, are not identical. In particular, speaking in tongues is not mentioned in Rom 12. Neither individually nor together do these lists mention all the charismata that do or could exist, nor is it necessary that all that are mentioned should appear in every situation. The variety exists to build up the internal life of the community and to develop missionary enterprise.

As the faithful engaged in their normal daily activities, in governing the Church, teaching, administering charity and pastoral care, and seeking to understand the secrets of God's purposes, they believed that they were not acting wholly by themselves, but that the Spirit was at work in and through them. Some of his gifts are continuing, and have continued without break to this day, such as the utterance of knowledge and wisdom (cf. 1 Cor 12:8), or administration, teaching, exhortation, generosity, leadership, helpfulness to others (Rom 12:6ff., N.E.B.), and without these there could be no Church. In this sense, they may be called the "ordinary" gifts of the Spirit to the Church.

Others are "extraordinary". It is to such gifts that the use of the term charismatic has now come to be normally limited, although it strictly refers to spiritual gifts in general. For the purpose of this study, two of these extraordinary gifts are of special importance.

A. PROPHECY

Prophecy is not to be identified with inspiring preaching. It is a charismatic utterance in intelligible language. On occasion, the prophet can foretell the future (*e.g.*, Agabus, Acts 11:28) but primarily it is the gift of interpreting the will of God for the present, disclosing the very secrets of God's purpose, for the upbuilding of the Church.

The Charismatic Movement

The New Testament evidence can be interpreted to suggest that speaking in tongues can be either ecstatic, unintelligible speech, or the miraculous ability to speak foreign languages.[24] Neo-Pentecostals believe that both phenomena are to be found today. Paul implies that speaking in tongues is basically directed towards God, and not to man. However, when the gift of interpretation is also present, it harnesses the God-directed activity for the common good.

The Panel wishes to issue a warning about the unqualified use of the word "ecstatic" in regard to the charismatic phenomena currently under review. To many, this carries overtones of frenzied, uncontrolled behaviour. This might have been the case at Corinth. It may also be the case in modern times, but this is not necessarily so. The basic meaning of "ecstatic" is one of spiritual exaltation, which can appear strange, even bizarre to the uninitiated onlooker, but which at the same time can still remain "decent and in good order" (1 Cor 14:40).

C. THE RELATIONSHIP BETWEEN PROPHECY AND SPEAKING IN TONGUES

In 1 Cor 14, Paul discusses the relative value of prophecy and speaking in tongues. His argument is not clear to us, because we cannot be sure of the exact situation to which he was speaking. His apparent confusions and contradictions can be untangled in different ways, depending on our own presuppositions. A possible interpretation from a Reformed point of view is as follows.

Paul is faced at Corinth with two sets of phenomena, the first, prophecy, being the more regular, ethical and the more obviously useful for the upbuilding of the Church, and the second, speaking in tongues, being the more strange and bizarre. Paul is careful not to condemn speaking in tongues, which is a gift he himself possesses, or to forbid them, lest he appear to be stifling the Holy Spirit. At the same time he stresses the spiritual gift (charisma) of being able to "discern the spirits" and inclines to prefer the use in worship of the more useful types of spiritual manifestation. He does allow speaking in tongues, provided it is accompanied by interpretation, but in doing so he is showing the same preference for the intelligible. He appears to be moving away from an initial unqualified acceptance of the gifts of the Spirit to a preference for those gifts more generally applicable to the upbuilding of the Church.

7. *Alternative Exegeses of 1 Cor 12-14, from Charismatic Points of View*

Some neo-Pentecostal members of the working party, while agreeing in general with the above exegesis, have put forward alternative explanations. As they see it, Paul is dealing with one specific problem, which has shown itself in Corinth, that of undisciplined speaking in tongues in public worship.

While these members are not themselves of one mind, they agree that the passage does not show that Paul is moving away from the practice of speaking in tongues to a more general preference for gifts which are more relevant to the upbuilding of the community. He does show a preference, but it is either for the use of tongues in private, rather than in public worship, or for discipline and good order in public worship.

Some neo-Pentecostals hold that, although from the point of view of the outsider prophecy is to be preferred to speaking in tongues, the latter cannot be forbidden in public worship, because one cannot by legislation control the activities of the Spirit. It is not to be positively encouraged, and if it does take place it should be done "decently and in order", and should be accompanied by interpretation (1 Cor 14:27). Speaking in tongues may, however, be used in private devotions, which is claimed to be Paul's own personal practice (1 Cor 14:18), or in specially convened charismatic prayer groups. Its use in such circumstances is to be encouraged today.

Other neo-Pentecostals stress that the real point of Paul's advice is the control of the use of tongues in public worship. Paul does not object to speaking in tongues as such, but values it. In the particular case of the Church at Corinth, where some believers appeared to regard speaking in tongues as the essential element of Christian experience, and to despise those who did not have this gift, a "noise of many tongues" had become a threat to the good ordering of public worship and to the unity of Christian fellowship, resulting in the loss of other valuable manifestations of the Spirit. Paul, however, stresses the variety of gifts in a positive way, so as to persuade the Corinthians to broaden their view-point, and to accept other abilities and ministries as the actual evidence of the work of the Spirit.

It is further maintained, and here we find the chief neo-Pentecostal argument for charismatic worship, that within the context of this Spirit-filled worship, not merely do the faithful worshippers minister to the Spirit, but the way is laid open for the Spirit to minister to them in a new and wonderful way. Accordingly, the whole Church should re-examine its expectations from worship. Speaking in tongues, followed by interpretation, can, it is said, lift the corporate life of the Church to a higher level, or direct the attention of the worshippers to some hitherto neglected aspect of God in His glory. From this point of view, prophecy, healing and the discernment of spirits are as proper to worship as they are to pastoral care. There will be in any congregation honoured ministries, men and women gifted with lasting charismata, but in addition to such ministries there will be evidence of the Spirit bestowing his gifts by means of whomsoever he wills, for the good of the people of God.

As the Panel has to give some practical guidance to the Church, it must assess these varying views. It finds that they vary, not so much in denying each other's positive insights, as in the comparative stress they place upon the interpretations they hold in common. The Panel has come to the conclusion that Paul's basic preference is for charismata more obviously relevant to the upbuilding of the Church, both for its own edification, and, what is sometimes overlooked in the charismatic debate, for the fulfilment of its outward-looking mission to the world. Because of this basic preference the other preferences follow. For the upbuilding of the Church, he prefers those more relevant to the community to the more personal and God-directed, which he feels are more suitable for use in private. He prefers the intelligible to the unintelligible, and he stresses the need for good order in all things, both for the spiritual welfare of the believer and for the uninitiated onlooker.

8. The Fruit of the Spirit

In whatever way we interpret Paul's underlying motives, we note that it was in the midst of this controversy that Paul's great "Hymn to Love" (1 Cor 13) was set. If the gifts of the Spirit disrupt the Christian bond of love, something is surely wrong.

Paul is again stating a preference, on the one hand for love over and against all charismatic phenomena, and on the other against the qualities of the Christian character, such as faith and hope.

Paul places love first in a list of the "fruit* of the Spirit", which he gives in Gal 5:22f.

From a charismatic point of view, it has been maintained that the fruit of the Spirit, the first of which is love, is made available to all believers on baptism or conversion, but the gifts of the Spirit, and in particular the extraordinary charismata, are given only to some. Both the more traditional and the neo-Pentecostal members of the working party would agree that this particular distinction is not tenable. It is not possible to draw such a hard and fast distinction between two lists, one in Galatians, the other in Corinthians, for there is no clear logical or historical relationship between them. They were both drawn up in response to particular problems. In Galatia, it was the Christian way of life that required exposition, in Corinth it was the use of tongues in worship that had to be put in its proper place.

In Gal 5, the "fruit" of the Spirit is contrasted with the "works" of the flesh, that is, qualities like love, joy and peace are opposed to a list of sins, such as immorality and impurity. In 1 Cor 13, the presence of love is put forth as the pre-condition without which the exercise of the gifts of the Spirit is valueless. Love, joy and peace can only be exercised in a Christian way. They are contrasted with a list of sins. In the case of the gifts of the Holy Spirit the contrast lies in how they are exercised. If they are exercised in a Christian way, they manifest love, joy and peace, but if sinfully, they cause the opposite, division and strife.

From the Reformed point of view, both the fruit of the Spirit, as it shows itself through the Christian character, and the gifts of the Spirit are made available to the believer through faith. While the individual believer receives the fruit of the Spirit, he does not necessarily manifest all the varieties of the fruit to the same degree. Similarly with the gifts of the Spirit. Therefore the believer should expect to manifest the fruit of the Spirit in his daily life, and to show the evidence of at least one of the gifts, but not necessarily one in the list in 1 Cor 12.

Whatever other gift or gifts the believer may display, he must have love, which expresses itself in the growth of the Christian character, and flourishes in a diversity of spiritual gifts. Thus the

---

*Paul does not talk of the "fruits" of the Spirit, but of "fruit" in the singular, so emphasising their unity, arising as they do from the same Spirit. Yet their most significant characteristic is their diversity, which is such that they are mentioned, not in the plural, but in a list, which like other similar lists, is open-ended, rather than exhaustive in nature.

The Charismatic Movement

fruit and gifts of the Spirit are not directly contrasted. If there is any difference, it is that all Christians should cultivate the whole fruit of Christian character, but be prepared to differ on the gifts which they share.

9. Panel's Critique of Certain Charismatic Points of View
The Panel now turns to particular points raised by the current charismatic debate.

A. WATER-BAPTISM AND SPIRIT-BAPTISM
The phrase frequently used by charismatics "baptism in the Holy Spirit" implies that there is a distinction between what have been called "water-baptism" and "Spirit-baptism". The continuing use of this phrase within the framework of the Church raises a particularly acute problem. The implication is that those who have received "Spirit-baptism" become a "Church within the Church".

In the Reformed tradition, baptism is "once and for all", because it is essentially connected with the prevenient grace of God, and the unique saving events of Christ's life, death and resurrection. In baptism, God sets us within the body of Christ, the fellowship of the Holy Spirit, which is the Church.[25] In the New Testament, the phrase "to be baptised in the Holy Spirit" is "never directly associated with the promise of power, but is always associated with entry into the Messianic Age or the Body of Christ".[26] There is therefore a necessary coincidence between water-baptism and Spirit-baptism. Although it must be recognised that the New Testament evidence is that Spirit-baptism may precede, coincide with or follow water-baptism, these two elements of the one unity should not be allowed to drift apart. Rather Spirit-baptism should be understood as the inner substance, and water-baptism as the outward shell.[27]

In the context of a theology of subsequence, the phrase "baptism in the Holy Spirit" implies a "first, partial and initiatory experience of the Spirit" (Christ for us), and a second "full reception of the Holy Spirit" (Christ in us).[28] Further, there is a thread of logic that connects these two baptisms, running from water-baptism through conversion, obedience, prayer and faith to Spirit-baptism.[29] This is in effect the denial of that prevenient grace which belongs to the essence of baptism and the gospel.

Within the context of neo-Pentecostalism, therefore, it is important that if the phrase "baptism in the Holy Spirit" is to continue in use to describe the essential charismatic experience, it must not be allowed to sever its necessary connection with water-baptism. If it does it will inevitably suggest entrance into a "Church within the Church", so disrupting the fellowship of the Holy Spirit, which is the inner reality of the Church, and destroying the love, joy and peace which are unambiguously the fruit of the Spirit.

B. THE INFLUENCE OF THE CULTURAL ENVIRONMENT

There is a living connection between the faith of the Church and the surrounding cultural environment. Religious phenomena cannot be understood by themselves, but only by taking psychological and sociological factors into account. In particular, charismata are part of a total theological and cultural system from which they cannot be isolated. How we understand this system, consciously or unconsciously, will affect our understanding of charismata.

Cultural factors encouraged the development of charismatic phenomena in biblical times, when prophecy, speaking in tongues and faith healing were all known in the pagan world. In modern times, certain psychological and sociological factors have influenced the re-emergence of superstition in a materialistic world. Interest in the paranormal is a mark of our times, ranging from faith-healing, through the bending of forks to extra-sensory perception. Entertainers stage demonstrations of mind-reading and thought-control. Whether these are genuinely paranormal, mere stage trickery or false is beside the point, for this is an age when people are interested in these things, and want to believe in them. The existence of these phenomena outside the Church is a fact, and so it would not be surprising if a simultaneous interest in similar paranormal phenomena developed within the Church.

Our situation today may have superficial similarities to that of biblical times. We have the same rapidly changing religious situation, with traditional patterns disappearing, strange sects appearing, and magic, astrology and witchcraft flourishing. Yet our situation is in fact quite different from that of the Corinth which Paul knew, for our basic presuppositions are different, following the collapse of the generally accepted classical world-view, and the emergence of new and conflicting sets of imagery.

This means that the nature of the gifts the Spirit gives to the Church may have changed, so that the gifts he gave to the

The Charismatic Movement

Church of the first century are not necessarily the gifts he is offering to the Church today. Some gifts could be less relevant than they formerly were. For example, it could be held that faith-healing is less important in the context of modern medicine than it was before our present knowledge evolved. More important, perhaps, gifts are to be expected which are especially related to the problems of modern times. Should we not expect charismata directed to the achievement of political and industrial reconciliation, gifts which appear to be only too rare today?

It is in the light of such expectations, and the peace and joy which is certainly possessed by individual charismatics, that we must assess speaking in tongues. The Panel therefore raises the question of whether the current emphasis upon the more exciting spiritual gifts, such as speaking in tongues, does not hinder the development of those less exciting but possibly more relevant to our modern situation, and above all delay the emergence of gifts of the Spirit specifically geared to the needs of the Church in a modern age.

C. FURTHER NOTES ON CHARISMATA

I. THE AUTHENTICITY OF THE CHARISMATIC EXPERIENCE

Pentecostals look upon speaking in tongues as the initial evidence of the gift of the Holy Spirit. Discussion with the neo-Pentecostal members of the working party, however, showed that they do not understand speaking in tongues to provide definite proof of the presence of the Holy Spirit. Examples were quoted where, even within the context of charismatic prayer groups, speaking in tongues appeared to be "demonic" in nature, although no conclusion was reached on whether these "demonic forces" were personal or not. Such a situation gives rise to further charismata, such as the ability to discern between spirits, and exorcism. One result of the Reformers' discouragement of the supernatural was to close effectively the area of the demonic and exorcism from the thinking of their followers. Whether the re-opening of this area will be advantageous the Panel cannot yet determine.

Ecstatic states attributable to influences other than the Holy Spirit are thus a distinct possibility. Speaking in tongues in the context of charismatic worship should therefore be regarded only as *prima facie* evidence of the Holy Spirit, and should be put to the proof in Christian love, by interpretation or discernment between the spirits. "Not the manner but the content of ecstatic speech determines its authenticity." [30]

II. NATURE OF CHARISMATA

It is not correct to talk of individual believers possessing the gifts of the Spirit. It is the Spirit who "possesses" the believer. His gifts are given to the Church, the body of Christ, and are imparted to individuals only in so far as they are members of that body. These gifts are not to be sought, which is a work, but rather to be expected, as a matter of faith in the fulfilment of God's promises. The more we submit to God, the more the supernatural is likely to happen.

Although the Panel has adopted the Reformed position of the gifts of the Holy Spirit coming variously and successively into the consciousness of the believer, it does not exclude the possibility that the believer would then be able to do something he was unable to do before. What is more normal is that an inborn ability is heightened, or the believer discovers a new way of fulfilling an old task — the way of love.

III. EFFECT ON THE BELIEVER

Neo-Pentecostals believe that the gifts of the Spirit are creative and therapeutic phenomena, leading to the integration of the personality. The believer who speaks in tongues, though he may not understand what he is saying, feels that there is something of importance in what he is saying, and that he is talking sense. Through his experience he receives release of mind and spirit, is filled with a deep sense of abiding joy and peace, and is empowered for service.

Some members of the working party questioned this stress on power, which they felt was the result of the theology of subsequence. They would agree that Pentecostals have a real and lasting religious experience which gives them a new feeling of life, but this should be interpreted, not as a second blessing, but as a release of what was already there, and as a growth in grace.

IV. PROPHECY

The charisma of prophecy can be turned either in upon itself for the internal edification of the Church, or out towards the world at large. Classical Pentecostalism, developing as it did out of the sectarian background of the Holiness Movement, tended to look upon the Christian faith in individual and personal terms, and to see prophecy in an inward-looking way. Pentecostals have believed in the work of the prophet within the Church, but not in the ministry of the prophet as it was understood by the great

The Charismatic Movement

prophets of the Old Testament. Classical Pentecostals tended to look upon themselves as a small minority in an alien state. Within the Reformed tradition, on the other hand, a meaningful relationship between Church and state has been established, and a sensitive balance created.

As we now seek a fruitful marriage between the Reformed and Pentecostal traditions, the challenge is presented to the Church as a whole, to grow in an outward-looking way, and bring back the voice of the true prophet, whose ministry is related to the world, where God is already working.

V. THE HOLY SPIRIT AND THE WORLD

Charismata are normally considered in relation to the Church, but very similar phenomena appear in the secular world. The question arises of how these are to be interpreted. Are they the signs of the Holy Spirit working in the world? Or are they demonic, or natural and so neutral happenings? Does the Holy Spirit operate outside the Church, as modern secular theologians maintain, or does he limit himself to working through the Church? If he operates outside the Church, in what ways does he show himself? The development of neo-Pentecostalism has made the resolution of these live issues particularly relevant.

D. THE SUPERNATURAL AND THE MIRACULOUS

A gift of the Spirit has been defined as a "gratuitous manifestation of the Holy Spirit, working in and through, but going beyond the believer's natural ability for the common good of the people of God".[31] Some members of the working party are concerned at certain interpretations of this definition, particularly at the stress laid upon the supernatural over and against the natural by some neo-Pentecostals, who appear to "stress the extraordinary gifts of the Spirit more than some of the historic Pentecostal churches".[32] These members are concerned at what they feel is an overstressing of the miraculous and of the distinction between the ordinary and the extraordinary, which leads to the suggestion that the extraordinary is in some way more spiritual than the ordinary.

They ask if a distinction can in fact be made between "natural" gifts on the one hand, and charismatic gifts on the other? From the Pentecostal side, it is suggested that a natural gift is not a charisma. The charisma lies in being given an extra sensitivity beyond the normal. Against this, it is asked if a genuine gift for, say, teaching or pastoral care, is not also in a sense supernatural, even if the person so gifted does not recognise it as such. These members of the working party also point out that Paul (Rom 12:6ff.) recognises such "ordinary" gifts as charismata, and suggest that the gifts of justification and sanctification are just as supernatural as the extraordinary charismata. Speaking in tongues is miraculous, but so is the gift of reconciliation between God and man.

The Panel concluded that certain extraordinary phenomena do occur, such as speaking in tongues and divine healing. These are unusual in the sense that the former is not a normal means of human communication, nor is the latter the normal medically and scientifically recognised way of curing bodily ailments. As such, these phenomena are often called "paranormal". They cannot be explained by any known law of nature, or by any known psychological abnormality. They have to be accepted as facts. To the man of faith, who comes steeped in the atmosphere of the Gospels and the book of Acts, or to the charismatic who finds in his own experience that such events are of frequent occurrence, they are no longer unusual, in the sense of going beyond the normal sequence of events, but they remain unusual in the sense of being hard to account for in rational or natural terms.

This does not mean, however, that these extraordinary phenomena are more "divine" than the parallel more usual and scientifically accountable occurrences, nor can it be said, for example, that a man who habitually speaks in tongues is consistently nearer to God than one who does not. To say that these extraordinary charismata are "gifts of the Spirit", but to deny this title to more ordinary ways of service, is to suggest that they are more divine, and it is exactly this against which we must guard.

What binds the theologian and the scientist together is the sense of wonder, but to wonder only at the abnormal and the unusual is to fail to recognise the working of the Holy Spirit in the normal and the usual. The man who can demonstrate no unusual talents or gifts may be just as much a spiritually gifted person as the man who speaks with tongues or who heals by the laying on of hands. Miracles do happen, but the miraculous is not necessarily more important than the non-miraculous. Indeed the miraculous may be a sign pointing beyond itself to a greater reality.

It can be a disrupting experience for a congregation and for an individual to be faced with unusual happenings in worship or practice. Admittedly, the effect can be enhancing and enlivening, but it can also be disastrous. It should be clearly understood that a congregation or group of worshipping people can be alive and inspired by the Holy Spirit, without necessarily experiencing or exhibiting anything that is paranormal.

10. Guidelines

From the earliest days there has been a dynamic and fruitful tension within the Church between the institutional and the charismatic. Where the Church is alive, it is not possible by legislation to attempt to control the activity of the Holy Spirit. However, in the light of its Report, the Panel feels that it should offer not rules but guidelines for the better ordering of the Church. The aim of these is to safeguard the peace and fellowship both within the congregation and between congregations.

The guidelines can only be provisional at this stage and must be open to revision, but the Panel now makes the following suggestions:

1. Charismatic worship in public should neither be forbidden nor encouraged. However, such practices should not normally be expected during the main diet of public worship on the Lord's Day.

2. There may be special occasions where a certain experimentation can be carried out in public worship, provided it is not likely to be divisive, and not during the main diet of worship. Such experimentation may take place, subject to the guidance and approval of the courts of the Church, but this should be regarded as an exceptional rather than a normal practice.

3. The practice of speaking in tongues should not be unduly emphasised, or made normative for Christian experience.

4. Speaking in tongues may be practised in private, or in small groups.

5. Prayer meetings (or study groups) where charismatic phenomena are likely to occur should be held under the jurisdiction of the Kirk Session. They could be intimated as "charismatic prayer meetings", and should be open to all.

6. Such charismatic prayer and study groups should not be stressed rather than any other group within the congregation's spiritual life. Above all, they must resist any temptation to become a Church within the Church.

7. Whenever speaking in tongues occurs in public, and this

includes such groups, it should be accompanied by interpretation.

8. In particular, when any charismatic phenomena occur in the presence of those who are not familiar with them, a careful explanation should be given in order that they might understand what is happening.

9. Ministers and others who lead worship should make themselves familiar with the charismatic movement, in order to give such an explanation.

10. Instruction in the gifts of the Spirit should be given a full but not disproportionate place in a congregation's Christian Education programme.

11. A minister who has had charismatic experience should exercise his gifts with caution, remembering that he is pastor to the whole congregation and is called to preach the gospel in its fullness. A charismatic group can function only with the consent of the minister and Kirk Session.

12. It should be realised by all concerned that there is a real danger of divisiveness where charismatic phenomena occur in a congregation, therefore relationships should be those of mutual respect, tolerance and love.

13. Everything should be done decently and in good order, for the common good of the people of God.

11. The Way Ahead

If the charismatic movement is to find a legitimate place within the Reformed tradition, the Church will have to make an attempt to combine two great biblical truths:

a. "For it is by his grace you are saved, through trusting him; it is not your own doing. It is God's gift, not a reward for work done." (Eph 2:8-9, N.E.B.)

Salvation, which includes the reception of the Holy Spirit, is by grace through faith, the gift of God.

b. ". . . when God gives you the Spirit and works miracles among you, why is this? Is it because you keep the law, or is it because you have faith in the gospel message?" (Gal 3:5, N.E.B.)

This faith is however not merely the intellectual assent to certain verities but also the outward power which enables the body of Christ as a whole and its members as individuals to accomplish today the mighty acts of faith witnessed to in Heb 11:33ff. Spiritual gifts received by faith will renew the Church, but more than that, such gifts will take the Church right out into the world.

The Charismatic Movement

12. *Brief Summary of Conclusions*

1. There is a legitimate place for neo-Pentecostals within the Church of Scotland, as long as they exercise their gifts for the benefit and spiritual enrichment of the whole Church.

2. The Panel does not deny the reality of an experience which can transform the faith of a believer or give new life to a jaded ministry, but it does question how this experience is to be interpreted. There is only one baptism, once and for all, whereby we are made members of the body of Christ and empowered for his service.

3. The Panel questions the theology of subsequence in terms of which the gifts of the Holy Spirit are given to the believer as a second blessing, empowering him for service. In place of that theology, the Panel understands these gifts in terms of the Reformed doctrine of justification in which the Spirit given by grace at baptism or conversion comes variously and successively into the consciousness of the believer, through faith.

4. The Panel questions emphases made by certain neo-Pentecostals, on:

a. the more exciting gifts, such as speaking in tongues, at the expense of the less exciting gifts, which in the long run may be the more valuable, and

b. the extraordinary gifts at the expense of the more ordinary gifts, which are essential for the on-going life of the Church.

5. The Panel questions the continuing use of the phrase "baptism in the Holy Spirit".

6. The gifts of the Spirit are to be expected. Where there is expectation, the Church may well be endowed with a larger and more evident measure of these gifts than a Church which has long believed that these gifts have ceased may hope for.

7. Neo-Pentecostals are interested in new kinds of ministry. The Church should look again at the traditional connection between charisma and office.

8. Some believers are equipped with charismata of a startling or even conspicuous character. They should not feel superior, nor should those not so endowed feel inferior. All members of the body of Christ have their own proper gift of the Spirit.

APPENDIX I

REFERENCES

1. Walter J. Hollenweger, *The Pentecostals*, S.C.M., London, 1972, pp. 22–24.
2. Henry Pitney van Dusen, article in *Life Magazine*, 6th June 1958.

3. John Wesley, *A Plain Account of Christian Perfection*, London, 1952.

4. John Wesley, *Minutes of Several Conversations*, VIII, 329.

5. cf. T. B. Barratt, *Urkristendom*, Oslo, 1934, p. 14.

6. Ernest Williams, Your Question, *Pentecostal Revival*, 49, 15th June 1961.

7. cf. Charles W. Conn, *Pillars of Pentecost*, Cleveland, Tenn., 1956, p. 96.

8. cf. Frederick Dale Bruner, *A Theology of the Holy Spirit*, Eerdmans, London, 1970, p. 88.

9. Myer Pearlman, *Knowing the Doctrines of the Bible*, Springfield, Mo., 1937.

10. Donald Gee, *Concerning Spiritual Gifts*, A Series of Bible Studies, Assemblies of God, London, 1967, p. 15.

11. cf. Ralph M. Riggs, *The Spirit Himself*, Springfield, Mo., 1949, pp. 79–80.

12. F. D. Bruner, *A Theology of the Holy Spirit*, p. 71.

13. cf. David du Plessis, *The Spirit Bade Me Go*, Dallas, 1961, p. 62.

14. cf. T. B. Barratt, *In the Days of the Latter Rain*, London, 1909, pp. 214–215.

15. cf. Lewi Pethrus, *Thoughts and Experiences Concerning the Baptism in the Holy Spirit*, 2nd ed., Chicago, 1945, p. 61.

16. W. J. Hollenweger, *The Pentecostals*, p. 329.

17. John Calvin, *Commentary on the Book of the Prophet Isaiah*, Vol. 4, Edinburgh, 1853, p. 269.

18. John Calvin, *Institutes*, II, 11, 11.

19. John Calvin, *Commentary on a Harmony of the Evangelists*, Vol. III, Edinburgh, 1846, p. 389.

20. cf. *Westminster Confession of Faith*, I.

21. cf. Edward Irving, Second Sermon on Baptism, *Collected Writings*, Vol. II, Ed. G. Carlyle, Strahan, 1864, p. 276.

22. cf. Edward Irving, Facts Connected with Recent Manifestations of Spiritual Gifts, *Frasers Magazine*, Jan. 1832.

23. cf. 1 Cor 3:9; 2 Cor 5:1; Eph. 2:21; Eph 4:12, 16, 29.

24. Robert Gundry, Ecstatic Utterance, *Journal of Theological Studies*, New Series, vol. XVII, pp. 299ff.

25. cf. Oscar Cullman, *Baptism in the New Testament*, S.C.M., London, 1950, p. 31.

26. James D. G. Dunn, *Baptism in the Holy Spirit*, S.C.M. London, 1970, p. 228.

27. cf. F. F. Bruce, *New Century Bible Commentary*, on 1 Cor 12:13.

28. cf. F. D. Bruner, *A Theology of the Holy Spirit*, p. 62.

29. cf. ibid., p. 114.

30. C. K. Barrett, *Black's New Testament Commentary*, 1 Cor 12:3.

31. *Vatican-Pentecostal Theological Commission Meeting*, 1972.

32. *The Work of the Holy Spirit*, United Presbyterian Church in the U.S.A., p. 4.

APPENDIX II

BOOKS FOR FURTHER READING

Nils Bloch-Hoell, *The Pentecostal Movement, Its Origin, Development and Distinctive Character*, Allan & Unwin, 1964.

Frederick Dale Bruner, *A Theology of the Holy Spirit, The Pentecostal Experience and the New Testament Witness*, Eerdmans, 1970.

James D. G. Dunn, *Baptism in the Holy Spirit, a Re-examination of the New Testament Teaching on the Gift of the Spirit in Relation to Pentecostalism Today*, S.C.M., 1970.

John Gunstone, *Greater Things than These*, Faith Press, Leighton Buzzard, 1974.

Walter J. Hollenweger, *The Pentecostals*, S.C.M., 1972.

J. P. Kildahl, *The Psychology of Speaking in Tongues*, Hodder & Stoughton, 1972.

I. H. Lewis, *Ecstatic Religion*, Penguin Books, 1971.

W. J. Samarin, *Tongues of Men and Angels, The Religious Language of Pentecostalism*, New York, Macmillan Co., 1972.

John L. Sherrill, *They Speak with other Tongues*, Hodder & Stoughton, 1965.

F. Stagg, E. Glen Hinson, Wayne E. Oates, *Glossolalia, Tongue Speaking in Biblical, Historical and Psychological Perspective*, Nashville, Abingdon Press, 1967.

C. Gordon Strachan, *The Pentecostal Theology of Edward Irving*, Darton, Longman & Todd, 1973.

John V. Taylor, *The Go-Between God*, S.C.M., London, 1972, pp. 198–222.

In the name of the Panel, RUDOLF J. EHRLICH, *Convener*; R. STUART LOUDEN, *Vice-Convener*; RODERICK PETTIGREW, *Hon. Secretary*

34 Lutheran Church in America, USA, 1974

THE CHARISMATIC MOVEMENT IN THE LUTHERAN CHURCH IN AMERICA: A PASTORAL PERSPECTIVE

At the biennial convention in 1972 of the Lutheran Church in America, the Indiana-Kentucky Synod requested guidance regarding the rise of the charismatic renewal in the parishes, especially because of the "divisiveness and confusion" which it seemed to cause.[1] A document was drawn up by the Division for Parish Services, with Dr. Eugene Brand as the responsible staff person. After discussion of various drafts with other members of the staff and with the College of Synod Presidents, the statement was approved by the Management Committee of the Division for Parish Services, thus making it an official document of the division provided to parishes and church agencies as a guidance tool.

The definition of terms was followed by a description of its goals and character, a discussion of baptism in the Holy Spirit, glossolalia, prophecy, healing, worship in prayer groups, their relation to parish life, and the involvement or non-involvement of charismatics in the church's mission to the world. The document ends with a set of guidelines.

The document recognized that however one wishes to label the phenomenon, "the life in the Spirit is being experienced in a new and different way" and lives have been "manifestly changed" by the experience. Many of the characteristics found in the Lutheran renewal are not unlike those found in earlier evangelistic forms of pietism and perhaps in earlier types of mysticism.

As a whole the charismatic movements are unique in being overwhelmingly lay, though in Lutheran churches the leadership has tended to remain with the clergy. The document recognized a growth and maturing in the renewal as it takes seriously the task of bringing itself theologically and exegetically into harmony with Lutheran tradition. Because of this development "one ought not to judge the present movement by earlier expressions of it."

Without opting for any of the current theological explanations of baptism in the Holy Spirit, the document recalled the theological plurality existing in this area and warned against a classical Pentecostal view which would separate water and Spirit. In fact the presentation of charismatic experience to the Lutheran Church in categories taken from classical Pentecostalism constitutes one of the major obstacles to its acceptance. "A narrow concept of the activity of the Holy Spirit is unacceptable and open to all Luther's criticism of Enthusiasts. . . . God works through means: the Word and sacraments." In relating the Spirit to the Word and sacraments, one should not be locked into a time sequence. "In an experiential sequence the Spirit and the means of grace may seem disconnected." The statement that God works through the Word and sacraments is a theological assertion and not a description of a given person's experience.

Lutheran zeal to preserve sacramental objectivity has produced a mistrust of the experiential dimension. "The charismatic emphasis on the power of the Spirit in the whole of the Christian life can challenge what has often become a severely minimalistic view of baptism among Lutherans." To this extent the charismatic emphasis has contact with Luther's teaching on the baptismal character of the whole Christian life.

Glossolalia was viewed as a "super-rational prayer." The presence of similar phenomena in non-Christian religions "does not make them inauthentic for Christians." John Kildahl's conclusion was mentioned, namely that glossolalists tend to be submissive to authority figures and that persons who can be hypnotized can speak in tongues.[2] However Kildahl's work does not represent a consensus of psychological studies.

Only slight emphasis on prophecy was found in much of the charismatic literature. Nonetheless the document warned against the naive view of prophecy which has "an almost magical belief that one's life in every detail is infallibly guided by the Holy Spirit."

Healing services have for some years been held in Lutheran churches by persons not identified with the charismatic renewal. The interest of charismatics in healing is rooted in the conviction that salvation is for the whole man. There is always the tendency to make those who were not healed to feel guilty because they did not have enough faith. This was *seen as a borrowing from classical Pentecostal theology which "is always in danger of transforming faith into the greatest of human works, seeing it as a prerequisite for God's action."*

When faced with the possibility of entering into programs of social action, some charismatics say that the community must be certain that the Spirit is leading them to deal with a specific situation. "The social posture of the charismatics, then, tends to be selective," a selectivity which may turn into an excuse for non-involvement. If those in the renewal need help in sharpening their social vision, the charismatics can spread some of their cheerful trust in God among those "who may have become tired or cynical in their efforts at social reform."

Where no integration of the charismatics into parish life takes place, they often live at the periphery and they become, for all practical purposes, classical Pentecostals. "There is no cause for Lutheran pastors or people to suggest either explicitly or implicitly that one cannot be charismatic and remain a Lutheran in good standing." On the contrary, Lutheran charismatics have much to offer in the sense of expectancy and joy with which they participate in liturgical worship. Seminaries and programs of continuing education should assist pastors in developing skills for pastoring those in the renewal.

The document is available as a pamphlet from the Lutheran Church in America, 231 Madison Ave., New York City, 10016. The text with more extensive notes, bibliography, and resource list is available in "Minutes, Seventh Biennial Convention of the Lutheran Church in America, 1974," pp. 600–13.

1. *"Minutes, Sixth Biennial Convention of the Lutheran Church in America, 1972," pp. 52–53, 746.*
2. The Psychology of Speaking in Tongues *(New York: Harper and Row, 1972). For a critique of Kildahl's research,* see *Kilian McDonnell,* Charismatic Renewal and the Churches *(New York: Seabury Press., Inc., 1976), pp. 130–40.*

In the decade past, increasing numbers of people in the Lutheran church have had religious experiences of the kind formerly associated with Pentecostalist groups. It has happened among Lutherans in Europe as well as in North America. It has happened in the Episcopal church, the Presbyterian churches, and the Roman Catholic church. However the phenomenon is labeled, the life in the Spirit is being experienced by many in a new and different way; their lives have been manifestly changed by their experience.

These phenomena in the so-called mainline Western churches come at a time when Pentecostalism is sweeping Asia, Africa, and

South America. Walter Hollenweger, a prominent researcher of the Pentecostal movement, predicts that the day is not far off when Christians with a Pentecostalist orientation will outnumber those of the historic churches of the West.

It is not the purpose of this paper to comment upon the spread of Pentecostalism in other continents nor is it to study the Pentecostal churches. We shall be focusing on "Pentecostal manifestations" in the Lutheran Church in America and, to some extent, in other mainline churches. In so doing, we hope to offer a pastoral perspective which will be useful both to church leaders and to those involved in the growing movement. Much work remains to be done; this statement is only a first step.

PENTECOSTAL OR CHARISMATIC?

The name one calls this movement is significant. Those American groups called Pentecostalist trace their origins to a revival in 1906 held in the Azusa Street Mission, Los Angeles. Prominent among the many groups are the Assemblies of God, the Churches of God, the Pentecostal Holiness church and the Full Gospel Business Men's Fellowship International. The Full Gospel Business Men have often bridged the gap between the Pentecostalist groups and the mainline churches. The label *Pentecostal* emphasizes what for many outside the movement is the typical characteristic of the adherents: the gift of tongues. Most Pentecostalist groups teach a two-stage way of salvation. The first step is conversion or regeneration; the second and distinct step is baptism in the Holy Spirit evidenced by speaking in tongues. This teaching allows Pentecostalists to distinguish between two groups of Christians: those who have received the baptism in the Holy Spirit and those who have not.

Recently it has become common to distinguish between the Pentecostalist groups themselves and the later neo-pentecostals — those who share the experience called baptism in the Holy Spirit but are members of the mainline churches. It is this latter group which is our major concern. Roman Catholics have preferred the designation *charismatic* rather than neo-pentecostal for the movement among them. Lutherans also prefer that designation because neo-pentecostal suggests a closer tie with the theology of the Pentecostalist groups and with certain Pentecostalist stereotypes than they wish to have. For this reason we shall refer to the charismatic movement among Lutherans.

The charismatic movement in the mainline churches is usually traced back to the emergence in 1960 of speaking in tongues at St. Mark's Episcopal Church, Van Nuys, California. It should not, however, be seen as without precedent in the Lutheran church. It has points of contact with earlier evangelistic forms of pietism and, perhaps, with an even earlier type of mysticism.

Some have objected to the designation *charismatic* claiming that, on the grounds of Lutheran theology, all Christians are charismatics (*charismatic* derives from the Greek word *charisma* which is used in the New Testament for the gifts [graces] of the Holy Spirit). While that is true, one may still agree to a somewhat arbitrary use of the term for the sake of convenience. A better term than neo-pentecostal is needed; charismatic is in common use. *To avoid misunderstanding what follows, it is important to distinguish between Pentecostalists and charismatics.*

RENEWAL

Charismatics understand themselves as a power for renewal. Their purpose is to revitalize Christian community and thus to revitalize the mission of the church. That goal is similar to goals of other renewal enterprises — the ecumenical and liturgical movements for example. Since it has implications both for Christian fellowship across denominational lines and, at least potentially, for the quality of congregational worship, the charismatic movement could become an ally of the ecumenical and liturgical movements.

Among the various thrusts for renewal, however, the charismatic movement is unique in being overwhelmingly a lay movement.* Therefore, its proponents have often had little or no professional training in biblical or systematic theology and may not articulate their experience in language harmonious with the confessional stance of the church.

It is important to distinguish between the experience itself and the verbalization of it. It is one thing to question the validity of the description; it is quite another to question the validity of the experience. The most important contribution for pastors and theologians is helping charismatics understand their experience in harmony with the Scriptures and the confessional position of the Lutheran church. Not enough has been done in this area.

The charismatic movement among Lutherans has grown and

---

*This is true of the charismatic movement as a whole. In the Lutheran churches, interestingly, the leadership has tended to rest with the clergy.

matured since its earliest manifestations. Its leaders have begun to take seriously the task of bringing it theologically and exegetically into harmony with Lutheran tradition. This work has the potential of giving the charismatics a new solidarity and the Lutheran church new zeal. Because of it, one ought not judge the present movement by earlier expressions of it.

BAPTISM IN THE HOLY SPIRIT

No Christian is without gifts of the Holy Spirit — that we have affirmed. The Lutheran church teaches unequivocally that one receives the Holy Spirit in one's baptism (Augsburg Confession 2; Apology 2; *Large Catechism*, Part 4). That is why Lutheran theologians have problems with the usual answer to "Who is a charismatic?" which is "A charismatic is one who has received the baptism in the Holy Spirit." Such an answer seems to imply that baptism in the Holy Spirit is something separate from baptism with water and that those baptized with water have not yet received the Holy Spirit.

The Pentecostalist two-baptism concept corresponds to the two-stage way of salvation taught by most groups. It is the source of the condescending attitude Christians sometimes experience from their "Spirit baptized" colleagues. Pentecostalist theology implies that persons who have not received the baptism in the Holy Spirit are less fortunate members of the Christian community.

The Pentecostalist teaching of a separate baptism in the Holy Spirit has a long and complex history. It has points of contact with such New Testament passages as Luke 3:16 (and parallels) and Acts 10:44-48. Given the lineage of the Pentecostalist groups and their general lack of theological and biblical scholarship, it is not surprising that they should use *baptism in the Holy Spirit* to describe their experience.

Since Lutheran charismatics have often had their initial experience in company with Pentecostalists, and since the Lutheran church has not given them much guidance, it is not surprising if they have accepted the Pentecostal explanation. The charismatic movement among Lutherans has been marked from the beginning by little theological engagement. Charismatics have therefore often taken a theological stance in conflict with the teaching of the Lutheran church. On the one hand, they cannot deny their experience, but on the other they are caught between irreconcilable theologies, each claiming biblical support.

Because of this conflict, other expressions have been suggested for baptism in the Holy Spirit. Larry Christenson, a Lutheran charismatic leader, points out that St. Peter used four terms in Acts 10 and 11: "receive the Holy Spirit, the Holy Spirit fell on them, baptized with the Holy Spirit, the same gift."[1] To these should be added "filled with" (Acts 2:4, 7:55, 9:17), "poured out" (Acts 10:45), and "came on" (Acts 19:6). Kilian McDonnell, a Roman Catholic researcher of the movement, lists extra-biblical alternatives: "release of the Spirit, renewal of the sacraments of initiation, a release of the power to witness to the faith, actualization of gifts already received in potency, manifestation of baptism whereby the hidden grace given in baptism breaks through into conscious experience, revivescence of the sacraments of initiation."[2]

What is this charismatic experience usually called the baptism in the Holy Spirit? It is indicated in the alternative terms listed above; it is described below:

". . . The Holy Spirit comes to him in a way that he can know it. As a result of this coming of the Holy Spirit he experiences a new contact with God . . . the Holy Spirit not only comes to that person in a new way, but he also makes a change in him. His life is different because his relationship with God has been changed. . . . Being baptized in the Spirit is an introduction to the life of the Spirit.[3]

"The essence of a charismatic experience is the experience of encountering Jesus Christ as the Head of His Body, which is the church.[4]

". . . The most commonly accepted interpretation [among Roman Catholics] of that ambiguous phrase "baptism in the Holy Spirit" is that it represents a saying yes, with expanded expectations, to what was received in Christian initiation.[5]

"The baptism in the Holy Spirit . . . is simply the full reception of the Holy Spirit."[6]

In the Pentecostalist tradition, baptism in the Holy Spirit, then, is an experience marking the threshold into a life of heightened awareness of God's Spirit in one's life and a consequent joy and zeal not present before. It may be dramatic and intense; more often it is a growing awareness. (Lutherans should note the similarity between this description of awareness of the presence of the Holy Spirit in one's life with that which would be offered by a Lutheran pietist in answer to questions about conversion.)

The best New Testament scholarship and the mainline

traditions of theology insist that such an experience of the Holy Spirit is always to be understood in relationship with the sacrament of Holy Baptism. Scholars insist that passages such as Luke 3:16 and Acts 10:44-48 be taken in the context of the whole New Testament witness.

The Lutheran zeal to preserve sacramental objectivity (baptism is God's act) may have led to an undue focusing on the rite itself with a corresponding neglect of the paradigmatic function of baptism (a pattern for the Christian life). ". . . The old Adam . . . should be drowned by *daily* sorrow and repentance and be put to death, and that the new man should come forth *daily* and rise up . . ." (*Small Catechism*, Part IV, 4.) It has certainly produced a mistrust of emotional or highly experiential manifestations of the life in the Spirit. Where this truncation of the vitality and scope of Luther's own teaching on baptism is encountered, the proper remedy is not a Pentecostalist separation of water and Spirit. It is rather to restore the fulness and reality of a total New Testament theology and practice of baptism (see Guideline 7 below).

For baptism to accomplish its function in God's economy there must be a response of will and style of life. This response is a lifelong task; it is not a mechanical reaction. God's act (traditionally called justification) and the life it initiates (traditionally called sanctification) must be separated for purposes of theological clarity, but they are not so neatly separable in a person's life. The Lutheran emphasis on the doctrine of justification can lead to a neglect of the doctrine of sanctification. The charismatic emphasis on the power of the Holy Spirit in the whole Christian life can challenge what has often become a severely minimalistic view of baptism among Lutherans.

Lutheran theologians are encouraged to study this area carefully to provide help for charismatics in understanding their experience in consonance with a full Lutheran concept of baptism. We must neither cast doubt on the authenticity of "baptism in the Holy Spirit" nor accept a Pentecostalist explanation of it.

GLOSSOLALIA

Glossolalia is the biblical term for speaking in/with tongues. Most classical Pentecostalists insist that one must speak in tongues as a validation of having received the baptism in the Holy Spirit. Outsiders are prone to spotlight this activity seeing it as the center of the charismatic movement; insiders tend to have a more balanced, less exotic view. LCA pastors who are intimately associated with the charismatic movement state that glossolalia should not be overemphasized. A balanced view is reflected in this statement:

"Many outside of the renewal attribute a centrality to tongues which is not reflected in most sectors of the renewal. On the other hand, persons involved in the renewal rightly point out that the charism was quite common in the New Testament communities. Those who stand outside the renewal and attempt to evaluate the charism of tongues will fail if it is not understood in the framework of prayer. It is essentially a prayer gift enabling many using it to pray at a deeper level." [7]

Glossolalia has a prominent place in the account of Pentecost (Acts 2:4). It is one of the charismata or gifts of the Spirit (1 Corinthians 12:10). It results from Peter's preaching in the household of Cornelius where it follows the falling-upon-them of the Holy Spirit and precedes baptism (Acts 10:46), and, in Ephesus, from the laying-on-of-hands and the coming of the Holy Spirit following baptism (Acts 19:6). It is part of the problem in Corinth (1 Corinthians 12:30; 14).

Debate among scholars on how the speaking in tongues by the apostles on Pentecost is to be understood and how that relates to glossolalia as reported elsewhere in Acts and 1 Corinthians is of little immediate concern here, because in the charismatic movement, glossolalia is primarily used in personal prayer and in prayer group meetings. It seldom, if ever, becomes part of the liturgical worship of the entire congregation. If it does, St. Paul's words about interpretation should apply (1 Corinthians 14:26-28).

Praying in tongues is supra-rational prayer (1 Corinthians 14:14), prayer which is expressive of depths of being words cannot express (Romans 8:26). "It seems as though every gift and every blessing I have already experienced in the Lord is refreshed and revitalized." [8] Once the gift of tongues has been received, a person can exercise it at will as one can engage in other forms of prayer at will. Glossolalia is not confined to speaking; there is also singing in tongues (1 Corinthians 14:15).

To the Christian conditioned by the piety of mainline churches, glossolalia may seem threatening because it is supra-rational and may be emotional. He may, therefore, try to discredit it by noting St. Paul's evaluation of it in Corinth or even by linking it with psychological instability. St. Paul does put glossolalia at the end of the list (1 Corinthians 12:26), but he still encourages its use (1

Corinthians 14:5). The temptation to generalize on the basis of the Corinthian situation must be resisted; St. Paul is speaking against the abuse of the gift. The remedy, as Larry Christenson reminds us, "is not disuse but proper use."[9] As for psychological instability:

"The glossolalists represented a cross-section of all the usual personality types; they employed the full range of personality mechanisms and character defenses. This came to us as a surprise."[10]

There is nothing specifically Christian or even religious about speaking in tongues. It is a phenomenon which has been characteristic of various kinds of behavior. John Kildahl, a Lutheran psychotherapist, maintains that it is learned either directly or indirectly, and that glossolalists tend to be submissive to authority figures (their models for glossolalia). He states that if one can be hypnotized, under proper conditions one is able to speak in tongues — the two phenomena root in similar relationships between subject and authority figure. He notes that a situation of personal stress or crisis generally precipitates the charismatic experience. This latter is testified to by Lutheran respondents.

(Kildahl's work is cited because it is known among Lutherans. It does not, however, represent a consensus of psychological studies. Vivier, for example, found that Pentecostalists scored *lower* in suggestibility [the issue in the hypnosis comparison] than the non-Pentecostalist control group.[11] Vivier appears in Kildahl's bibliography, though his work is not mentioned within the book.)

Whether or not one agrees with each of these psychological observations is, for our purposes, beside the point. All religious behavior is open to psychological analysis, and such studies should be pursued. But their proper function should be kept clear. For example, to demonstrate that certain types of people are attracted to the ordained ministry does not preclude the theological concept of divine call. Or, the fact that most of the liturgical acts which shape Christian worship can be found in other religions as well does not make them inauthentic for Christians.

The crucial question is how glossolalia is used, in what spirit and to what end. Addressing the situation in Corinth, St. Paul saw the possibility of the wrong use of tongues. This possibility puts a burden upon the church to guide and evaluate the use of the gift.

The Charismatic Movement: A Pastoral Perspective

If one's use of glossolalia enriches and deepens prayer, if it leads to greater joy and service, if it strengthens one's sense of fellowship with God and the Christian community — if it is an expression of *agape* (love, charity), it is beneficial and should not be condemned. If one's use of glossolalia is divisive, if it leads to arrogance, if it makes one judgmental of fellow Christians, if it results in histrionic display — if it lacks agape, it is detrimental and should be condemned. Kilian McDonnell has observed:

"A certain healthy skepticism with regard to religious experience is very much in place . . . but a deep fear of religious experience, with the consequent complete rejection of all religious experience as hysteria can lead to another kind of religious superficiality." [12]

"The tree is known by its fruit," said Jesus. St. Paul gave us the standard: "If I speak in the tongues of men and of angels, but have not love, I am a noisy gong or a clanging cymbal" (1 Corinthians 13:1).

It is important to emphasize that the evaluation of the gifts must also exhibit love and a true understanding of the Christian fellowship. Where glossolalia has polarized congregations, the fault does not necessarily lie only with the charismatics. Kildahl observes:

"Since many of the churchgoers we interviewed thought of their institution as a private club, new opinion and new practice was looked upon with suspicion." [13]

Christian love requires an openness to the Spirit's leading and, on all sides, a climate of mutuality.

This section began with the statement that glossolalia should not be overemphasized. Yet more space is given it than any of the other gifts. That seemed necessary since so much debate has centered upon it.

PROPHECY

Just as the concept of priest is expanded from the Old Testament to the New, so the concept of prophet is broadened from the few to the many. St. Paul writes to Corinth, ". . . Earnestly desire the spiritual gifts, especially that you may prophecy" (1 Corinthians 14:1). St. Paul makes a sharper distinction between glossolalia and prophecy (*prophecy* is speaking rationally to others; *glossolalia* is speaking supra-rationally to God) than does Luke-Acts (compare Acts 2:4 and 17). In both writings, however, *prophecy* is obviously understood as speaking to other people.

Scholars are concerned with the difference just cited and also with the difference between St. Paul and St. John the Divine where the element of ecstacy is more prominent. As it is reflected in the New Testament generally, prophecy is authoritative proclamation of the will and purposes of God with appropriate exhortation to action on the part of the Christian community. (It is prophecy in this sense that is implied when speaking of the great prophetic tradition of the Bible.) It is authoritative because it is a gift of the Spirit; in terms of edification, St. Paul says it is the most important gift. The prophet is not generally a seer but a recipient and preacher of the Word. He is not possessed by God in such a way that he has no control and therefore becomes a mere mouthpiece; he is full of self-awareness. There is also, however, the picture of the prophet as ecstatic seer.

Formerly, among Pentecostalist groups prophecy in the sense of foretelling the future played an important role. It was seen as more than inspired utterance; it was the actual voice of the Spirit himself. Prophecy was *the speaking Spirit*. Where Pentecostalism has become more structured, spontaneous prophecy which is more than edification seems to retreat into the background. One finds only slight emphasis on prophecy in much of the literature in the charismatic movement.

Prophecy is obviously hazardous and the church always has the duty to test it against the clear testimony of the Scriptures. Gullible acceptance can lead to great difficulty. In St. Paul's congregations, just as the glossolalist had an interpreter, so the prophet had his examiners who assessed what he said (1 Corinthians 14:29). Prophecy requires the checks and norms operative within the Christian community. Special pastoral vigilance is required vis-à-vis a naïve view of prophecy which has an almost magical belief that one's life in every detail is infallibly guided by the Holy Spirit. It is on this level that mischief or sometimes even tragedy most frequently occurs.

HEALING

Charismatics believe that divine miracles still occur, and testify to miraculous healings in answer to prayer. Other Christians in the mainline churches are often either skeptical about miracles or deny them altogether. As one becomes aware of the "psychosomatic" dimensions of illness, however, one becomes at least more tolerant of accounts of spiritual healing. There are numerous accounts of healings at places such as Lourdes or by such charismatics as Oral Roberts. A combination of the personal magnetism of healers and the suggestive atmosphere of the gathered congregation can be explained psychologically, but they can also be seen as God's gift. That a phenomenon has a psychological explanation does not prevent it from being a gift of the Spirit. As with other charismata, everything depends upon how the gift of healing is used.

But prayer for healing can also be much less dramatic and not centered in the personality of a healer. Prayer for healing also need not be set against medical procedures. Healing services have been held in Lutheran churches for some time by people who have not identified with the charismatic movement at all. In recent decades pastors have given high priority to their ministry to those disabled by illness.

Healing as an emphasis of the charismatic movement is rooted in the conviction that salvation is for the whole man, and is related to the expectancy with which prayer is offered. When charismatics pray, they expect something to happen, also when the prayer is for healing. Surely that attitude can only be affirmed. Lutheran respondents testify to healings in response to their prayers.

What happens, however, when healing does not follow? Many Pentecostalists would say that the patient himself is the problem, that he hasn't enough faith. Many Lutheran charismatics as well as Lutherans in general reject such a view not only because of the untold despair it can foster, but also because of the concept of faith which is operative. Pentecostalist theology is always in danger of transforming faith into the greatest of human works, seeing it as a prerequisite for God's action. When prayers for healing result in no healing, the Christian can neither regard it as God's will that the person should not recover nor as the fault of a weak faith in the patient. The Christian can only bow in humility before a mystery not revealed and continue to pray and offer comfort. Jesus did not promise his followers a life free from suffering — quite the contrary!

Good pastoral care requires that people be shielded from the cruelty which can result when, having been led to think that a miracle will surely occur, nothing happens. Prayer of the community rather than the impassioned prayer of a healer is less of a problem along these lines. Pastoral concern requires that an emphasis on healing be free of any anti-medical bias. The capacity to heal medically must also be regarded as part of God's preserving care.

The characteristic form of the charismatic movement is the prayer meeting. Even where clergy are involved, the leader of the meeting can be a lay person. The content and form of these sessions varies and will likely reflect the backgrounds of most of the people. Usually, however, they consist of reading from the Bible, much prayer, perhaps singing in tongues, perhaps speaking in tongues, perhaps prophecy, perhaps healing. If someone is present who desires the "baptism in the Holy Spirit," people will pray over him and lay hands upon him in the expectation that the Spirit will respond. Where a number of charismatics are present in a congregation, the prayer meeting may consist only of people from one denomination. More often, however, the group contains a mixture of Pentecostalists and charismatics from mainline churches. One finds in this mixture an indication of the ecumenical thrust of the movement.

The prayer meeting can be divisive or it can enrich a congregation's life. Where the meetings exist harmoniously within the congregation, it is usually because of the involvement and guidance of the pastor who may or may not be a charismatic. A few LCA prayer groups have succeeded in blending charismatics and non-charismatics together. Lutherans influenced by the pietistic tradition should find groups for prayer and Bible study unremarkable.

Where there has been no effort to integrate the charismatics into parish life, they often exist on its edges — having, for all practical purposes, become Pentecostalists. But a few Lutheran situations indicate and the Catholic charismatic movement demonstrates dramatically that this need not happen.

Rather than turning their backs upon the traditional worship and the forms of Lutheran congregational life, charismatics often find new depth and significance in them. They testify that the liturgy and the celebration of the Lord's Supper have more meaning for them than ever before. Charismatics have much to offer the rest of the congregation in the sense of expectancy and joy with which they participate in liturgical worship. Our historic liturgy does not have to be used with the stiff formalism and lack of joy and humanity it often is. The spirit of celebration is in the words waiting to be released. Clothed in a ceremonial of color and movement and involvement, the liturgy can be exciting; allowed to be naturally flexible rather than narrowly rubricistic, it can accommodate spontaneity within its structure.

Adherents of the charismatic movement are often accused of having no social vision, of being concerned only with the quality of individual piety. Whether this is true of Pentecostalists is not for us to say, but a few observations are in order about charismatics in mainline churches.

The charismatic experience can be so overwhelming and so filled with joy that the period immediately following it may be compared with a honeymoon. One must have time to come to terms with the new experience and may be excused an overenthusiastic buttonholing of everyone in sight to share it. Charismatics must be helped to a more mature understanding of their experience which recognizes the implications of the life in the Spirit for serving others. The Holy Spirit is not given only for our enjoyment, but to make us more effective servants of those who need us. The church must hold that truth before the charismatics. The charismatics, on the other hand, by demonstrating the joy of the Spirit-life are a sign to the church to keep this power-for-others view from becoming a grim duty ethic.

Charismatics have reacted against what they have seen to be a concept of social action which had little time for prayer, worship, or biblical preaching. Their emphasis upon these basics is at the root of their call for renewal, and can be a witness within the church toward keeping its priorities in proper balance.

The orientation of charismatics to Christianity and the Scriptures prompts them to interpret responsibility toward others in individualistic terms. The social posture of mainline churches, however, is that because of the complexities of modern society Christians must go beyond person to person service to affect the social structures themselves. This stance has developed out of an ethical viewpoint informed by the clear thrust of biblical theology, though it cannot merely be proof-passaged from the New Testament.

Some charismatics reject this position outright. More often, however, they are sympathetic to it, questioning only whether Christians should respond to a social need just because it is there. Rather, they say, the community must be certain that the Spirit is leading them to deal with a specific situation. That leading will be related to the community's having the necessary gifts to be of service. The social posture of the charismatics, then, tends to be selective. While it is true that without the needed capability one can hardly serve, it is also true that the selective posture could easily become an excuse for non-involvement. At this point too the ultimate test is what love requires.

The Christian community is to be a servant within the larger human community. That means that the Christian life is lived for others, not for one's own pleasure or gain. The gifts of the Spirit are given the *community* to enable its mission both by building up the Christian fellowship and by making its service more effective. All gifts used in this way, not just tongues and healing, are gifts of the Spirit. The church needs the "non-remarkable" as well as the "remarkable" gifts. It has been pointed out that a gift is "not a *what* but a *how*." [14] The lists of charismata in the New Testament are not inclusive lists. In fact, it is probable that gifts are needed by today's church which were unknown in bible times or were irrelevant to the mission of the primitive church. Keeping the understanding of gifts related to the community context and the church's mission is an antidote for an undue emphasis upon one's own spirituality. It should also illumine the social implications of the church's mission.

Just as it must help the charismatics to deal with their experience on a level deeper than that of Pentecostalist exegesis and theology, so the Lutheran church must help to sharpen and deepen their vision of social concern. In return, the charismatics can spread some of their cheerful trust in God among Christians who may have become tired or cynical in their efforts at social reform.

GUIDELINES

On the basis of what has been discussed, some guidelines are offered the Lutheran Church in America for its relationship to the charismatic movement within its congregations:

1. Where it is authentic — that is, where it bears good fruit — the charismatic experience must be understood *within* the scope of the church's life. There is no cause for Lutheran pastors or people to suggest either explicitly or implicitly that one cannot be charismatic and remain a Lutheran in good standing.

2. The church on all levels should make every effort to help those who are charismatics understand the "baptism in the Holy Spirit" in a manner consonant with the Scriptures and traditional Lutheran theology (including the legitimacy of baptizing infants born within the Christian fellowship). Where this effort has not been made, many Lutherans and a few Lutheran congregations have, to all intents and purposes, become Pentecostalist.

3. As a renewal movement, the charismatic movement should be welcomed as a judgment against mechanical worship, non-biblical preaching, preoccupation with church structure and congregational success, lukewarm faith which expects nothing, compromise with the life-style of the world, etc., wherever these exist. Willingness to benefit from the movement does not require uncritical acceptance of its answers and remedies. Other groups and movements are also dealing with renewal; the charismatic movement does not have the only answer.

4. Congregations and pastors should endeavor to deal with the charismatic movement naturally and objectively, divesting themselves of stereotypes built through hearsay or experience with the more radical forms of Pentecostalism. The image of Pentecostalists which many mainline church people have is one of the greatest barriers to acceptance of the movement. Lutheran people need help to put such issues as "baptism in the Holy Spirit" in the context of the whole biblical witness so they can deal effectively with the questions of proof-passage quoting Pentecostalists. They need to become informed through study and mutual discussion with charismatics.

5. While the church should recognize the validity of charismatic piety, adherents of the charismatic movement must be helped to see that the form or style of their piety is one of several within the Christian community:

"The difference between a devout Christian who is not particularly drawn to the Charismatic spirituality on the one hand and a charismatic Christian on the other is a matter of focus. The charismatic Christian's focus is on fulness of life in the Spirit, the exercise of the gifts of the Spirit directed toward the proclamation that Jesus is Lord to the glory of the Father. The devout Christian who is not drawn to the charismatic spirituality in no way excludes those elements of the charismatic spirituality, but they are not where he focuses his spiritual attention. Further, his own personal sanctity may far exceed that of his charismatic brother." [15]

6. A distinction must be made between the renewal aspect of the charismatic movement *within* the church and the evangelistic outreach which charismatics share with all others in the church. Zeal for charismatic experience must not lead charismatics to regard fellow church members as proper objects of evangelization. Charismatics share the responsibility to proclaim the gospel to those outside the people of God.

7. Lutheran charismatics should resist any understanding of the Spirit's indwelling which deemphasizes or renders superfluous the proclamation of the Word, the sacraments, or the Christian fellowship. A narrow concept of the activity of the Holy Spirit is unacceptable and open to all Luther's criticism of the Enthusiasts. An individual's experience of the Holy Spirit is not immediate; the Spirit's work cannot be separated from the mission of Jesus of Nazareth. God works through means: the Word and sacraments.* To deny that is eventually to fly in the face of the incarnate Word, for the Holy Spirit is the Spirit of the incarnate Son. The teaching of the Spirit's sovereignty must not be separated from the teaching of the means of grace (see the Augsburg Confession 5 and 18). God, of course, cannot be bound to our perceptions of him, but *we* are bound to his self-revelation in Jesus Christ, the incarnate Word.

8. As persons who have pledged to minister to the whole congregation, pastors should involve themselves in counseling with charismatics in their parishes and with prayer groups. Pastors should not accept all manifestations of what seem to be the Spirit's gifts uncritically, but neither should they be intolerant or judgmental vis-à-vis a form of piety they do not share. If pastors feel unable to deal adequately with the situation, especially at first, they should seek the counsel and help of a fellow pastor who is involved in the movement or who has had experience with it.

9. Pastors who are themselves part of the charismatic movement should not use their office to pressure their members into the movement, nor should they give preferential pastoral care to those members who are adherents. They are pastors of the whole congregation and must also respect the integrity of other styles of piety.

10. Since it is normal for charismatics to attend a prayer group, such groups could be established in Lutheran congregations, especially those with several charismatics. Prayer groups need not be exclusively for charismatics; they should be open to all members. A Lutheran prayer group better enables the pastor to offer guidance and support to charismatic members, and it allows natural interaction among charismatics and other members. In

---

*It must be understood that this is a theological assertion, not a description of a given person's experience. In an experiential sequence the Spirit and the means of grace may seem disconnected; the theological statement should not be understood as implying an immediate cause-immediate effect sequence.

some instances several Lutheran congregations together might establish prayer groups.

11. The Lutheran Church in America should, through its synod presidents and district deans, give assistance to congregations and pastors caught in the tensions which usually arise when the charismatic movement first appears. It should be a network through which experience and information may be shared and counsel given.

12. The Lutheran Church in America should, through its various divisions and agencies, recognize the charismatic movement as a part of its life and provide educational materials and opportunities both for pastors and lay people to increase understanding of the movement and to help adherents toward a deeper and more authentic understanding of their experience.

13. Seminaries and programs of continuing education should assist pastors in gaining knowledge about the charismatic movement and developing skills in ministering to Lutherans who are adherents.

14. Theologians should be encouraged to undertake a sympathetic but critical study of the charismatic movement in general and many particular issues which cannot be covered in this kind of paper. In addition to the problem of interpreting the "baptism in the Holy Spirit," issues such as these should be addressed: the relationship between the periodic emergence of the charismatic phenomena and the cultural and/or ecclesial context; justification and sanctification in the light of the charismatic experience; baptism and the Holy Spirit; and so on.

AFTERWARD

Church history is punctuated with accounts of individuals and groups who have testified to uncommon religious experiences. It also records that such people generally left the parish churches to become hermits or monastics, or to form sects. In their initial resistance to organizational structures, this has also been true of Pentecostalist groups from the turn of the century until now. What is different about the charismatic movement, as the noted historian Jaroslav Pelikan has pointed out, is the disposition of its adherents to remain in the established churches. It remains to be seen, he said, whether the attempt to blend charismatic piety with sacraments and ecclesial structures will be successful.

Certainly one element in that possible success is the attitude in which charismatics and others within the Lutheran Church in

America deal with each other, and the climate created by pastors and church officials for that interaction. The charismatic movement has a contribution to make to the quality of the life of the LCA. The LCA has a rich tradition of knowledge and experience to contribute to the charismatic movement. Neither group has cause to be arrogant or exclusivist toward the other. As St. Paul taught the Corinthians, the hallmark of all authentic Christian behavior is the kind of love which is not arrogant, rude, imperious, irritable, resentful or gloating, but rather which is patient, kind, affirming — a love which bears all things, believes all things, hopes all things, endures all things.

1. Larry Christenson, *A Message to the Charismatic Movement* (Minneapolis: Dimension Books, 1972), p. 66.

2. Kilian McDonnell, "Statement of the Theological Basis of the Catholic Charismatic Renewal," *Worship* 47 (1973), p. 617.

3. Stephen B. Clark, *Baptized in the Spirit* (Pecos, New Mexico: Dove, 1970), pp. 15–16.

4. Arnold Bittlinger, "Baptized in Water and in Spirit," *The Baptism in the Holy Spirit as an Ecumenical Problem* (Notre Dame: Charismatic Renewal Services, n.d.), p. 14.

5. McDonnell, "Statement," p. 610.

6. Frederick Dale Bruner, *A Theology of the Holy Spirit* (Grand Rapids: Eerdmans, 1970), p. 60.

7. McDonnell, "Statement," p. 616. On the commonness of tongues in New Testament times, see Krister Stendahl, "Glossolalia in the New Testament," *The Charismatic Movement, Confusion or Blessing*, ed. Michael Hamilton (Grand Rapids: Eerdmans, 1974).

8. Larry Christenson, *The Gift of Tongues* (Minneapolis: Bethany Fellowship, 1963), p. 16.

9. Ibid., p. 11.

10. John P. Kildahl, *The Psychology of Speaking in Tongues* (New York: Harper & Row, 1972), p. 49.

11. *Glossolalia* (Microfilm, American Theological Library Association, 1963).

12. Kilian McDonnell, *Catholic Pentecostalism: Problems in Evaluation* (Pecos, New Mexico: Dove, 1970), p. 8.

13. Kildahl, p. 68.

14. Kilian McDonnell, *Baptism in the Holy Spirit as an Ecumenical Problem* (Notre Dame: Charismatic Renewal Services, n.d.), p. 50.

15. Ibid., p. 48.

FOR FURTHER STUDY

MATERIALS OF THE LUTHERAN CHURCH IN AMERICA

Gifford, Hartland H., ed. *The Charismatic Movement*. A Special Study for Adults and Youth. Philadelphia: Lutheran Church Press, 1973; Johnson, Benjamin. *The Church in the New Testament, A Conversation with the Book of Acts*. Philadelphia: Lutheran Church Press, 1973; Immedia Series. "The Jesus People." Philadelphia:

Fortress Press, 1973, (Tape cassette of interviews with Jesus People, plus other materials); Kerr, John Stevens. *The Fire Flares Anew*. Philadelphia: Fortress Press, 1974.

OTHER SOURCES OF INFORMATION

Bittlinger, Arnold. *Gifts and Graces*. Michigan: Eerdmans Publishing Company, 1967/68; Hendry, George S. *The Holy Spirit in Christian Theology*. Philadelphia: Westminster Press, 1956; Hollenweger, Walter. *The Pentecostals*. Minneapolis: Augsburg Publishing House, 1972; Jones, James W. *Filled With New Wine, The Charismatic Renewal of the Church*. New York: Harper & Row, Publishers, 1974; Prenter, Regin. *Spiritus Creator*. Philadelphia: Muhlenberg Press, 1953; Schlink, Edmund. *The Doctrine of Baptism*. St. Louis: Concordia Publishing House, 1972; Sherrill, John L. *They Speak With Other Tongues*. Old Tappan, New Jersey: Revell Company, 1964.

35 Methodist Church, Great Britain, 1974

REPORT ON THE CHARISMATIC MOVEMENT BY THE FAITH AND ORDER COMMITTEE OF THE METHODIST CONFERENCE

This brief report recognized the difficulties inherent in analyzing an experience which has the character of a pilgrimage rather than that of a static reality. When Methodists theologize about the baptism in the Holy Spirit, they do so in a pluralistic way. Some theological descriptions go in the direction of second blessings (an experience subsequent to conversion), while others move closer to assurance (a conviction of personal salvation). Though the charismatic renewal has Arminian influences, it is not typified by "a grim striving to achieve" but by "a patient acceptance of the Spirit's influence." The renewal represents a Jesus movement rather than a Spirit movement. The attention in the renewal given to the Spirit is not based on an abstract desire to give symmetry to a theological system whereby the Spirit is used as the God of the theological gaps to fill in the voids and bring a system to balanced wholeness. Rather the attention given to the Spirit rises from below, "out of necessity to formulate a theological framework adequate to the experienced reality. . . ."

The charismatic renewal has restored the gifts of the Spirit to the realm of the ordinary, where they belong to the everyday functioning of the normal Christian community. No fixed order of priority is given to the gifts, no unalterable hierarchy of worth is established. In considering the gifts there is a double view, on the one side the actual giving of the gifts and on the other the Spirit releasing and directing gifts already possessed but virtually unused. The single foundation of the renewal is "the primacy of intimate personal experience of the Lord, with evidences," an experience which is seen as central to the Holy Spirit's work.

Reservations were expressed. There is some doubt as to the appropriateness of the phrase "baptism in the Holy Spirit," especially in view of the New Testament texts used, texts which normally refer to Christian initiation, not to a later experience. An expression like "fulness of the Spirit" might be more accurate so long as there is "a proper balance between the context of an event in Acts, and a process in Pauline teaching about the Spirit in the believer." No attempt should force a completely unified New Testament teaching on the Spirit. Within the Scripture there exists various interpretations of the work of the Spirit which exist alongside of each other, unharmonized. Further, there should be no attempt to absolutize any one pattern as to how the Spirit is experienced. Claims are not to be magnified. "This one Christian experience is not the clue to the solution of all problems in the Christian life."

The report was reprinted in "Agenda for the Annual Methodist Conference" (Bristol, 1974), pp. 267–71. See also "Minutes and Year Book of the Methodist Conference, 1974" (London: Methodist Conference Office), p. 36.

1. TERMS OF REFERENCE

"In view of the great interest throughout the Church in the Charismatic Movement, Conference asks the Faith and Order Committee for guidance regarding the experiences and insights involved, in the light of the doctrine of the Holy Spirit" (Conference 1973 "Daily Record" pp. 32, 68).

2. LIMITATIONS

The task set by Conference is a difficult one. The Charismatic Movement itself spreads across all the major Christian denominations, though with variations in each. It is not classical Pentecostalism and yet it has much in common with it. Those who claim the "charismatic experience" do not as a result abandon more generally held traditional beliefs about the Holy Spirit, nor do they seek a different church structure or denominational allegiance. They readily admit that the experience itself has the character of a pilgrimage and is therefore not easily definable in a static way. In any case the attempt to discover the boundaries and the exact nature of a personal experience is in itself a difficult task.

Two further difficulties must be noted at this point. The first is that a full scale examination of the biblical bases of the "charismatic experience" would require much more time and a much fuller report than is possible here. The Committee has therefore limited itself to a few of the more obvious topics in this connection. The other difficulty is that the charismatic experience and teaching exist alongside the more usual Christian experience and teaching, but also draw into their orbit certain aspects of the latter which the "charismatic experience" highlights — differently for different people. Thus some descriptions are close to "second blessing" teaching, others to "assurance" and so on. Discovering with exactness what is the precise differentia of the Charismatic Movement is perhaps the most difficult task of all because of this.

In facing this task the Committee has been greatly assisted by leaders of the Charismatic Movement in Methodism, whose co-operativeness, frankness and concern to avoid divisiveness were most helpful.

3. POSITIVE CONTRIBUTIONS

a. One striking characteristic of this Movement is the way in which genuine Christian qualities are sought and enjoyed — qualities such as joyful engagement in living, inner peacefulness of personality, a sense of being empowered to obey God's will. And such experience is characterised not as "a grim striving to achieve", but "a patient acceptance of the Spirit's influence". Arising from this is the significant factor that the Movement focusses attention on the doctrine of the Holy Spirit, not in order to complete a specific theological system, but out of necessity to formulate a theological framework adequate to the experienced reality of Christian faith.

b. Closely linked to this is the concept of rediscovering the extraordinary gifts of the Spirit — such as speaking with tongues, interpretation and prophecy — and learning to treat them as ordinary, or at least normal, within the Christian community. At best this is more than "gift seeking" for it enlarges one's vision to see that all of life is gift. We were glad to have charismatic leaders affirming that their list of gifts did not have any fixed order of priority, and that gifts like ministry, celibacy, martyrdom were also included. The stress upon what are viewed as extraordinary gifts is attributed to their previous neglect by the church at large.

c. In particular the Movement is leading to renewed interest, and encouraging a new confidence, in the areas of healing and personal devotional life. Against a cultural background that includes excessive rationalism, secularism and scepticism the charismatic emphasis has enabled many to discover hope and liberation in these elements of Christian living.

d. The nature of the Spirit's giving of gifts includes a double view within the Movement. On the one side the actual *giving* of gifts is envisaged, the receipt by the believer of abilities hitherto not possessed. But on the other side there is concentrated upon the Spirit *releasing* and directing gifts already possessed but virtually unused. Here again there is a welcome emphasis upon the potential of the whole of one's life under the Spirit's control.

e. Nor is this a purely individualistic experience. There is a strong sense which finds expression in group fellowship and in worship. In the former there is emphasis upon the ministry exercised within the group to its members. In the latter there is the interdependence of those with various gifts; the speaker in tongues and the interpreter for example, or the prophet and the group testing the prophecy. There is also a freedom and spontaneity which enables full congregational participation; the involvement of the whole man; the evolution of spontaneous group preaching and the removal of unhealthy rigidity in distinguishing between laity and ordained ministry. And there is a new experience in ecumenism afforded by this Movement, a joyous unity in the Spirit and in shared experience.

f. A positive attitude to those outside the Church is also observable. Many in the Charismatic Movement testify to a new-found freedom to speak about their faith, partly because their love and concern for others has been deepened by their spiritual experience.And there is evidence of a broader concept of responsibility to the world as the gifts of the Spirit for service outside the Church are increasingly recognised and exercised.

g. Perhaps the most striking of all is the repeated emphasis upon the Movement as essentially a "Jesus" movement. Although there is stress upon the work of the Spirit, in both the individual and the group, His supreme role is seen as "glorifying Jesus". A greater love for and obedience to Christ figures constantly in charismatic testimonies. The primacy of intimate personal experience of the Lord, with evidences, is seen as central

Faith and Order Report

to the Holy Spirit's work in the believer, and much of the liberation and growth experienced within the Movement is based upon this single foundation.

4. CAUSES FOR CONCERN

We were (mercifully) not called upon to pass judgment upon the Movement. It seems right, however, that part of the "guidance" called for by Conference should include some comment about aspects of the Movement which required further clarification or safeguards against abuse.

a. It is doubtful whether "Baptism in the Spirit" is the most appropriate phrase to describe the charismatic experience. In its favour there is the impression of a decisive and powerful happening, which is what the charismatic wishes to communicate by the phrase. Also, in the true verbal form "baptize in the Holy Spirit", it occurs in the New Testament. The debate, however, revolves around the exact application of these New Testament passages, which have normally been taken to refer to the initial entry into Christianity. The use of the phrase "Baptism in the Spirit" to describe a later Christian experience thus causes confusion in many minds about its relationship to the liturgical act of water-baptism and the psychological experiences of conversion. An expression like "the fulness of the Spirit" might be more accurate, so long as there was a proper balance between the context of *an event* in Acts, and *a process* in Pauline teaching about the Spirit in the believer. Here we note that various forms of theological interpretation of the work of the Holy Spirit are present alongside each other in the New Testament.

b. There is constant danger that a movement emphasising the more exhilarating gifts of the Spirit might unintentionally create a devaluation of more ordinary gifts, such as "administration", or lay too much stress upon any particular gift, such as "tongues". In fairness, it must be noted that the leaders interviewed were aware of both dangers and sought to guard against them. Ministers who filled in a recent questionnaire also showed great balance in this matter. Nevertheless, the danger is inherent in this kind of emphasis and ought at least to be noted. In particular we would stress the importance of the use of the gift, rather than the emotional experience of receiving it.

c. There is need of further study of the sociological and psychological factors involved in the experience, factors which operate in other "charismatic" experiences both Christian and non-Christian; so that the precise differentia of the Movement, and the distinctiveness claimed for the "baptism in the Spirit", may be more clearly identified.

d. Where a person feels that a gift, previously exercised, has been lost, we advise caution about teaching or pastoral care which suggests that God has removed it.

e. It should be made clear that this one Christian experience is not the clue to the solution of all problems in the Christian life. Some Christians face difficulties with psychological and sociological roots, requiring more than a spiritual experience for their resolving. It should also be emphasised that some Christians find other routes to an equally mature, satisfying and spiritual Christian experience, manifesting gifts of the Spirit without being able to testify to the particular pattern outlined within the Movement. Again, leaders were quick to take these points. Our plea is for the spread of such teaching throughout the Movement.

f. While it is true — and the Charismatic Movement has underlined the fact — that Christianity is greatly impoverished when the rational element is stressed at the expense of the emotional and the volitional, it is equally important to guard against any danger of irrationality, with the consequent devaluing of the mind in Christian experience, since for many Christians reason is the supreme tool for discerning the Spirit. Such safeguards are particularly necessary in a Movement in which the extraordinary and the unusual receive emphasis.

At times, it must be repeated, some of those deeply involved in the Movement — including those we interviewed — have expressed their concern about some of these matters. They are listed here as part of the attempt to establish a balanced view of the total phenomenon and to show proper care for those who benefit from the "charismatic experience".

5. GUIDANCE

a. We recommend that this Movement be allowed the freedom to be itself within the life of our Church, and to continue to share its insights with those who wish to receive them. We offer the comments above as guidelines to be noted, not rules to be obeyed.

b. We welcome the renewed emphasis upon the individual and corporate experience of the Holy Spirit, including those aspects of the experience high-lighted by the Charismatic Movement, so long as they are not held to be universally obligatory, exclusive or superior to other Christian insights.

c. We wish to encourage those involved in the Charismatic Movement as they continue to explore the theological and biblical — as well as the psychological and sociological — bases of their experience and teaching. We would presume to advise, however, that they avoid the snare of stultifying the joyful experience they know in the interests of a watertight apologia for their position.

d. We urge that all Methodists, whatever their experience of the Holy Spirit, show tolerance in seeking to understand the claims and experiences of others. In particular we would hope to avoid the splitting of societies over this issue, or the creating of a "second-class Christian" outlook *in either direction.*

The Spirit blows where He wills. We express the hope that none of us will oppose His doing so, and equally that none will claim a monopoly of His presence.

36 *Presbyterian Church, Canada,* 1974

REPORT OF THE COMMITTEE TO STUDY THE CHARISMATIC MOVEMENT

In 1973 the General Assembly of the Presbyterian Church in Canada appointed a Special Committee to study and report on the charismatic renewal. The committee had expected to give a full report at the 1974 General Assembly but found the subject matter too large to complete in one year, and therefore it made an interim report which was not a systematic presentation but rather a response to a series of questions which had been raised by young people. An important dimension of this report is the definition of charismatic experience, a definition which was modified by an amendment from the floor of the assembly. "The 'Charismatic' experience is the experience of the presence of Jesus Christ through the Holy Spirit in a gathering of Christians or in an individual's personal life, and of a response of enthusiasm and exaltation. This is documented in Holy Scriptures and, therefore, has a legitimate place in the life of the Body of Christ, the Church."[1]

The use of the category of presence is important for understanding not only the general character of all charismatic experience but also the baptism in the Holy Spirit which is seen as "a new breakthrough in

Christian experience. . . ." Rather than sequestering the experience of the Spirit as the property of a few elect, the committee held that "every Christian should have the experience of the presence of the Holy Spirit," though "the manifestation of that presence need not be in the same form for everyone." The committee rejected dispensationalism and declared that the gifts of the Spirit, tongues included, are for today. Gifts of healing are operative in the contemporary church. "Incidents of healing are so numerous, and well-documented that there can be no doubt of the validity of Christ's healing ministry today." The character of the report is obviously determined by the preoccupations of certain segments of the youth, such as the demonic.

The report was published in The Acts and Proceedings of the One Hundredth General Assembly of the Presbyterian Church in Canada, *Kitchener, Ontario, June 2–7, 1974, pp. 385–88.*

1. *The original had read ". . . or in an individual's personal life, and of an enthusiastic or ecstatic response thereto. This is documented in Holy Scriptures and. . . ." Those in the charismatic renewal prefer to avoid the word "ecstatic" which connotes uncontrolled behavior or altered states of consciousness (trances). Though light trances are not unknown, they are in no necessary way related to charismatic experience.*

To the Venerable the 100th General Assembly:

The Special Committee, appointed by the ninety-ninth General Assembly to study and report on the Charismatic Revival, respectfully submits the following report.

It was our purpose in the beginning to make a full study of the subject and report to this One-Hundredth Assembly. However we found the subject and the task much too large for us to accomplish our purpose in that length of time.

Therefore we decided to deal first with questions, which had been raised by young people, and submitted to the Committee. It is our hope that the questions and the answers which we have given may serve as a study paper for the church, and that submissions will be made to the Committee concerning the answers.

It is also our hope that the work of the Committee may continue for another year, in order that we can present a full statement to the next General Assembly on the Charismatic Movement.

"The 'Charismatic' experience is the experience of the presence of Jesus Christ through the Holy Spirit in a gathering of Christians or in an individual's personal life, and of an enthusiastic or ecstatic response thereto. This is documented in

Holy Scriptures and, therefore, has a legitimate place in the life of the Body of Christ, the Church".

What is the Baptism of the Holy Spirit?

"The Baptism of (in) the Holy Spirit" is the expression most frequently employed by the "Charismatic movement" to designate the experience of the Holy Spirit that stands at the centre of the movement. What is indicated is a new breakthrough in Christian experience which results in a deepened and joyful sense of the presence of God, not infrequently accompanied by "speaking in tongues".

What does the Bible say about the Baptism in the Holy Spirit?

In the New Testament the term "Baptism in the Holy Spirit" is never used but a corresponding verb does appear (Matthew 3:11; Mark 1:8; Luke 3:16; John 1:33; Acts 1:5; 11:16). The contexts in which this term appears would prompt three observations:

1. The primary reference is to the day of Pentecost (Acts 2:1ff cf. "the promise of the Father" Luke 24:49; Acts 2:33). "The Baptism of the Holy Spirit" has taken place. Pentecost is unrepeatable, and in this sense "the Baptism of the Holy Spirit" is also unrepeatable.

2. It would, however, also refer to the entrance into the Christian life, for it is associated with the "gift of the Spirit" (Acts 11:16, 17; cf. 10:45; 2:38) and Baptism (10:48). We may infer from the Book of Acts that it is "the gift of the Holy Spirit" that marks entrance into Christ's Body.

3. The basic reality to which it refers is that of being placed in the realm of the Holy Spirit. Here God is present in a very real way, and here the possibility of the Christian life and all gifts and powers for Christian service are present.

Should every Christian have this experience?

Every Christian should have the experience of the presence of the Holy Spirit, but it should be kept in mind that the manifestation of that presence need not be in the same form for everyone.

What is "Speaking in Tongues"?

Basically it is talking to God in a language that He gives to us by His Spirit ("the language of ecstasy". 1 Corinthians 14:2 NEB).

It appears in different forms:

a. as a response to receiving the Holy Spirit — Acts 2:4 (at Pentecost), Acts 10:44-48 (in the house of Cornelius), Acts 19:1-7 (in Ephesus);

b. as a means of communication where the words are understood by the hearers but not by the speakers;

c. as self-edifying conversation with God in prayer. 1 Corinthians 14:2-4, 14;

d. There is also a "gift of tongues" (1 Corinthians 12) in which God publicly communicates to His people through someone who receives this gift of unknown language. But this must always be used according to Scripture in conjunction with the gift of interpretation or it is not edifying to the congregation.

Paul states that we should not forbid speaking in tongues, but we should not seek after it as an end in itself, nor allow it to stand alone in a public worship service. (Read 1 Corinthians 14.) "Do not quench the Spirit . . . , but test everything; hold fast to what is good . . ." (1 Thes 5:19, 21).

The important thing is to be open to, and filled with, the love of God the Father, Son and Holy Spirit.

Do you have to speak in tongues to be a Christian?

No. To be a Christian you have to have faith in Jesus Christ. Many outstanding and deeply devoted followers and servants of Christ never did speak in tongues.

Do you have to speak in tongues to have the Spirit within you?

No. The indwelling of the Holy Spirit may manifest itself in many different ways, which are not meant to demonstrate or prove His indwelling, but to equip the Christian for service and witness, and for "building up the body of Christ" (see Ephesians 4:11-12 and 1 Corinthians 12:7). Neither is the absence of one particular gift of the Spirit a reason to conclude that, therefore, the Holy Spirit is absent from one's life. The touchstone and evidence of the indwelling of the Holy Spirit is the fruit of the Spirit (see Galatians 5:22-23).

Did these things only happen in the Bible or do they still happen today?

They still happen today.

When a person is speaking in tongues, does he know what he is saying?

Yes and No. Yes, in the sense that such a person is aware be it only in his emotional realm, that he is praising God, adoring Him and thanking Him. No, in the sense that the word-for-word content of his speaking does not consciously register in his mind or memory.

Can anyone have this experience? How? What must I do?

Many different people from different walks of life have received

Report on the Charismatic Movement

the gift of tongues. Yet one ought not to seek out one or another of the gifts of the Spirit as though that would somehow make him better as a Christian. Paul tells us (Romans 3:24) that all are justified by God's free grace alone. He also says (1 Corinthians 12:7) that in each of us the Spirit is manifested in particular ways for some useful purpose. Gifts are not signs of divine favouritism; rather, they are the avenues, given to us by God, through which we may better serve him.

What is a Faith Healer?

"Faith Healer" is a name given to those who claim to have, or who have demonstrated the power to heal. The term is used of non-Christians as well as Christians.

This term, faith healer, is however seldom used of those who have received the gift of healing in Christ, because it conveys the mistaken idea that the healing is done by the healer; whereas the person who has been used in healing by Christ knows that this gift is from God.

Are Faith Healers Special People?

In the context of the Christian faith those who have the gift of healing, are special in that they have received a precious gift of the Holy Spirit. They have exercised the gift of healing in ministry in the name of Jesus Christ, as a member of His body, to the Glory of God. It is well to remember that the gifts are always to be used to glorify God.

Is Faith Healing something that happened in the Bible times only, or does it happen today?

The gift of healing, which was manifested in Bible times, is also manifested today, as are other gifts of the Spirit. Incidents of healing are so numerous, and well documented that there can be no doubt of the validity of Christ's healing ministry today. It is also a very common experience for people who have sought physical healing to receive healing in soul and spirit.

Do you have to have someone pray for you before you can be healed?

Prayer is not laid down as a condition of spiritual healing, but prayer is normally a part of the healing ministry, either in the person who needs healing, or by the person who performs the ministry. Prayer is usually offered by others as well, who are burdened by the need of the person who is sick. There are indications in James 5:15 that prayer for the sick should be offered.

Why doesn't everyone get healed?

Only God knows the answer to that question.

We must remember that God's purpose for us is greater than for the healing of our bodies. Whether or not one's body is healed of sickness, the promise of God stands. Romans 8:28.

"All things work together for good to them that love God, who are called according to his purpose".

Paul's thorn in the flesh was not removed even though he prayed earnestly three times. The answer he received from God was: 2 Corinthians 12:9.

"My Grace is sufficient for you, for power is perfected in weakness".

Can a Christian be possessed or oppressed by a demon?

Possession means ownership. If someone has yielded his life to Jesus Christ, he is His own. See Romans 14:8; Isaiah 43:1; 1 Corinthians 6:20 and John 10:28.

To be oppressed by a demon may be a Christian's experience in some area of his life, from which he has barred Jesus Christ as Lord, or at such a point at which he has consciously opened up his life to the influence and sway of demonic powers. Where the rule of Christ is held at arm's length, a Christian may well find himself powerless, and driven helplessly by fierce passions or obsessions. Where a person's life has given access to forces of evil, these forces may mount a frightening attack on him, even after he has committed himself to Christ, and they may try to drive him to destruction. But the Christian's way is always open to turn to Christ for the victory, especially when he is surrounded by prayer.

Therefore, demon *possession* is something the Christian need not fear.

Oppression by a demon holds no ultimate threat for the Christian. His victory is assured him in Jesus Christ. See Romans 8:35-39; Galatians 2:20; Psalms 125:2; Psalms 34:7; Colossians 3:3.

How do I know it is the Lord and not me, or the devil tricking me?

There are many references in the Bible to false prophets and teachers exerting their influence. John tells us (1 John 4:1) to test those who come to us to see whether they are from God. Only those who acknowledge that Jesus Christ is the Word made flesh are of God. Christ reminds us (Matthew 7:16) that we will recognize people of God by the fruits they bear. The fruit of the

Report on the Charismatic Movement

spirit is love, joy, peace, patience, kindness, goodness, fidelity, gentleness, and self-control. (Galatians 5:22).

Is it right to show so much emotion in church?

The "rightness" or "wrongness" of emotion in church is not a debatable question. Some people express themselves emotionally and others do not. The question is, do emotional displays or outbursts contribute to the act of corporate worship i.e., do they serve to praise God and build up the church? (cf. 1 Corinthians 14:26.) Paul reminds us that worship ought to be done decently and in order. This does not rule out emotional expression, because people are emotional creatures. People ought to worship in the manner which is natural and reasonable to them, remembering that their purpose is to glorify God, not to make a show of their religion.

How do I know whether I am just being overwhelmed by the atmosphere or whether it is the Lord?

It is a common occurrence for Christians to be influenced by the "atmosphere" of a worship service. And this is healthy provided that our attention remains focused on Jesus Christ and is not diverted to something or someone else. James tells us (James 1:22) to be sure that we act on the message and do not merely listen. The true sign that God has spoken to us lies in our response *after* the worship service. If we feel somehow changed, encouraged, or inspired to go out and act on what we've heard . . . to extend God's love, to ease suffering, to rejoice with others in their happiness . . . God is with us.

What are the gifts, fruits and offices of the Holy Spirit and what are the differences between them?

The gifts of the Holy Spirit are the bestowal of supernatural abilities for worship, witness and ministry. 1 Corinthians 12.

The fruits of the Spirit are the evident result of the life of Jesus Christ in the believer. cf. Galatians 5:22f; Colossians 3:11f.

The fruit of the Spirit which enriches is the product of the Gifts of the Spirit which empower.

The offices of the Holy Spirit refer to God's appointment and equipping of members of the body of Christ for specific ministries all of which enjoy the enrichment of the fruit and the empowering and enabling of the Gifts of the Holy Spirit.

MESSAGE OF THE BISHOPS OF THE WESTERN PROVINCE OF QUEBEC ON THE CATHOLIC CHARISMATIC RENEWAL

The western ecclesiastical province of Quebec is one of four divisions in Quebec, six dioceses which meet together to plan a common strategy. In this document the bishops wrote of the formation of charismatic groups in their dioceses, the relation of the Spirit to the church and to individual ministries, the responsibility of pastors, and discernment.

Recalling the teaching of Vatican II, the bishops taught that the Spirit is the principle of life in the church, guides her into the fulness of truth and unity, and expresses himself in a plurality of ministries. Though "exceedingly suitable and useful for the needs of the church," the gifts are not to be rashly sought after nor are the fruits of the apostolate to be presumptuously expected from them. To the bishop of the diocese belongs the competence of discerning the gifts, but he should exercise this function in such a way that he elicits and facilitates the charism which is given to each of the faithful.

Of paramount importance is a solid biblical and theological formation, and to that end the bishop in each diocese should appoint competent persons who will promote these training programs. Without wishing to smother initiatives at the level of the parish, the bishops cautioned against anyone assuming the role of teacher.

The encouraging signs in the renewal were "more desire for personal and community prayer, a greater thirst for the word of God, a greater openness to the call of the Spirit, a more marked concern to carry the Good News to all, deeper fraternal bonds, and above all, service to those who are the poorest. . . ." At the same time the bishops wanted to point out the dangers of "sensationalism, a false ecumenism, a false prophetism, fundamentalism . . . sectarian tendencies, divisions of all sorts, psychological abnormalities, illuminism, and the want of spiritual discernment." The bishops questioned whether there was not some uncritical acceptance of the authenticity of the more exceptional gifts, such as tongues, prophecy, deliverance, and healing, and urged the primacy of charity.

There is a wide divergence between the tone and content of this 1974 document from the bishops of the western province of Quebec and that of the 1975 message of the whole Canadian hierarchy to all Canadian Catholics.

The French text is found in Orientations Pastorales *6, no. 140 (November 1, 1974), 1–4.*

The Catholic charismatic renewal touches our six dioceses in various degrees. We feel ourselves called upon to make some remarks on the renewal and on the various phenomena which accompany it. Also, we wish to search the faith in order to comprehend the signs through which God manifests his presence and his goodness; and we wish also to say to you what our pastoral discernment is and to tell you of our care for the unity in the liberty of Christ which the actual situation inspires in us. We desire, therefore, to continue a dialogue already begun but which would be good to intensify and to deepen.

I. THE SPIRIT AND THE CHARISMS

According to the promise made to the prophets (Joel 3:1) and realized at Pentecost (Acts 2:17), the Spirit dwells in the church and in the faithful.

"In them he prays and bears witness to the fact that they are adopted sons (cf. Gal 4:6; Rom 8:15-16, 26). The Spirit guides the church into the fulness of truth (cf. John 16:13), and gives her a unity of fellowship and service. He furnishes and directs her with various gifts, both practical and charismatic, and adorns her with the fruits of his grace" (Constitution on the Church of Vatican Council II, par. 4).

"There is only one Spirit who, according to his own richness and the needs of the ministries, distributes his different gifts for the welfare of the church." (Constitution on the Church, par. 7). This Spirit is the source of mission, of service, of ministries and of charisms.

"These charismatic gifts, whether they be the most outstanding, or the more simple and widely diffused, are to be received with thanksgiving and consolation, for they are exceedingly suitable and useful for the needs of the church. They ought to be accepted with gratitude and spiritual joy. However, extraordinary gifts are not to be rashly sought after nor are the fruits of apostolic labor to be presumptuously expected from them" (Constitution on the Church, p. 12).

We recognize with admiration and thanksgiving this loving presence of the Spirit in the long history of the church and again today. And we know that such manifestations of the power of God are accompanied by fruits which are criteria of their authenticity: "charity, joy, peace, patience, kindness, goodness, confidence in others, gentleness, self-control" (Gal 5:22-23).

II. RESPONSIBILITY AS PASTORS

We recall also that "judgment as to their genuineness and proper use belongs to those who preside over the church and to whose special competence it belongs not indeed to extinguish the Spirit, but to test all things and to hold fast to that which is good (cf. 1 Thess 5:19-21)" (Constitution on the Church, p. 12). We wish to exercise this spiritual discernment which belongs to our responsibility, having in mind the grave warning of the Second Vatican Council: "The pastors . . . know that they themselves were not meant by Christ to shoulder alone the entire saving mission of the church toward the world, but that they have the sublime duty of so shepherding the faithful that all cooperate in their proper measure and with one heart in the common work" (Constitution on the Church, p. 30). This message which we address to you wishes then to deepen our communion and our unity in the same Spirit in such a way that "each one according to the grace received," might be "good servants of God's varied grace" (1 Peter 4:10), in view of the edification of the entire Body in charity and peace.

We ought to discern this renewal in the actual state that it exists among us. We will willingly continue our pilgrimage, with the collaboration of all, in order that what the Spirit wishes to say to the churches might always be better understood.

III. SOME REMARKS ON DISCERNMENT

First of all, we insist on the urgent necessity of giving doctrinal instruction to all those who are engaged in this renewal. Not only the facilitators but all the participants ought to receive this biblical and theological formation. For it is impossible to understand that which is happening without correctly situating the Holy Spirit in relationship to the Trinity, to Christ, to the Body of Christ and its structure, to the magisterium of the church.

To this end we insist, above all, that our priests and other pastoral leaders attain a knowledge of some depth in the doctrine and the cult of the Holy Spirit, as Pope Paul VI has recently requested (Audience of June 6, 1973, reproduced in *La Documentation Catholique* 70 (1973), p. 601). We recommend to charismatic prayer groups that they obtain the aid of priests and other competent pastoral leaders in order to assure good doctrine and also to maintain and even intensify their collaboration with the local church. We have the intention, at the level of each of our dioceses, to designate one or a number of counselors, particularly charged with promoting this adequate formation and also with assuring that the different groups of the diocese meet together.

It would be dangerous if one, without training, took upon oneself to play the role of "teacher" in order to give the teaching of which we have just spoken. This task belongs to those to whom it has been assigned in the diocese, who will see that they are surrounded with competent persons and with persons of sure judgment in order to give this formation and teaching. It is not a question of smothering the initiatives at the grass roots but of seeing that the person or persons whom the bishop has called to collaborate with him in this ministry of discernment and of teaching authenticate such initiatives.

We believe that it is also opportune to recall that "each one receives the gift of manifesting the Spirit in view of the common good" (1 Cor 12:7). Further, the one and same Spirit distributes "his gifts to each one as he pleases" (1 Cor 12:11). Finally, all the gifts have their sense and their value in charity and they ought to contribute to unity and to the peace: "God is not a God of disorder but a God of peace" (1 Cor 14:33). Therefore, it is necessary to know how to judge the tree from its fruits. Also, we rejoice when we see more desire for personal and community prayer, a greater thirst for the word of God, a greater openness to the call of the Spirit, a more marked concern to carry the Good News to all, deeper fraternal bonds, and above all, service to those who are the poorest, a real preoccupation to grow in unity and mutual respect and to use one's gift in the service of the Christian community and of the world.

We are aware, besides, that this renewal is not a shelter for every error or strange doctrine. We wish to point out the dangers such as sensationalism, a false ecumenism, a false prophetism, "fundamentalism," or a too exclusively literal interpretation of the Holy Scripture, sectarian tendencies, divisions of all sorts, psychological abnormalities, illuminism, and the want of spiritual discernment. We intend to correct these deviations wherever they exist, with charity and with a sense of our responsibility.

Sometimes also, we ask ourselves, along with many of the faithful, concerning the authenticity of certain more exceptional gifts, such as the gift of tongues, of prophecy, of deliverance, and of healing. We want to recall that they do not have value in themselves, but for the glory of God and the service of the community. It is necessary in this matter to guard particularly against the exaggerated desire for the spectacular or the extraordinary. It is also good to recall frequently how St. Paul urges discretion and recommends that love which "is patient and kind; is not jealous or boastful; is not arrogant or rude, does not insist on its own way; is not irritable or resentful; does not rejoice at wrong, but rejoices in the right, bearing all things, believing all things, hoping all things, and enduring all things" (1 Cor 13:4-7).

CONCLUSION

We want to exercise our charism of discernment because we joyfully hope to see flourish under the action of the Holy Spirit a harvest of vocations to all these ministries and to the services of which our churches have such need in order to always be better signs which tell persons of the infinite love of God for them. Through this common quest and through our hope and our love, may we be able to come "all together to the unity of the faith and knowledge of the Son of God, to mature manhood, to the measure of the stature of the fulness of Christ" (Eph 4:13).

Gaston Hains, Bishop of Amos; Jean-Guy Hamelin, Bishop of Rouyn-Noranda; Jules Leguerrier, Bishop of Moosonee; André Ouellette, Bishop of Mont-Laurier; Adolphe Proulx, Bishop of Hull; J. R. Windle, Bishop of Pembroke

The Feast of All Saints, 1 November 1974

ACKNOWLEDGMENTS

"A Report on Glossolalia," "A Statement with Regard to Speaking in Tongues," and "Guidelines," is reprinted from *Towards a Mutual Understanding of Neo-Pentecostalism*, © 1973, by permission of Augsburg Publishing House.

The Work of the Holy Spirit, © 1970, is reprinted by permission of the General Assembly of the United Presbyterian Church in the United States of America.

Both Sides to the Question, © 1973, is reprinted by permission of the Anglican Information Office, Sydney, Australia.

The Charismatic Movement and Methodism, © 1973, is reprinted by permission of the Home Mission Division of the Methodist Church in Great Britain.

The Charismatic Movement in the Lutheran Church in America: A Pastoral Perspective, © 1974, is reprinted by permission of the Board of Publication, Lutheran Church in America.

INDEXES

SUMMARY LIST OF DOCUMENTS

GENERAL INDEX

The entries below concern only this volume. A similar index follows volume 2 and volume 3.

Baptism in [with] the Holy
Spirit (cont.)

at beginning of century, 5
biblical,
context of, 214–216, 332–333,
382–383, 553, 563, 575
synonyms for, 516
concomitant with conversion,
383–386
conditions for, 269–270, 321, 335,
351, 357, 525
confirmed by signs, 388–389
confirming in grace, 367
consequences of, 526
and contemporary experience,
289
and danger in preoccupation
with, 144–145
defined, 462–463, 506–507, 525
devalues baptism, confirmation,
and the Eucharist, 100
different from,
conversion, 385, 457
regeneration, 380
do not doubt authenticity of, 554
effects of, 278, 505, 507
and empowerment, 304, 314
experience not doubted but
interpretation questioned,
523
extra-biblical alternatives, 553
fosters growth, 475
fulfillment of promise, 303
as gateway, 93
in the Holiness movement, 220
how received, 330
and human cooperation, 334
identified with rebirth, 202
as the inner substance, 537
and laying on of hands, 462
and means of grace, 352
more than an entrance into faith,
290
and neo-Pentecostalism, 384–385

in New Testament, 300, 302–303,
514
no proof of sanctity, 315
non neo-Pentecostal teaching in,
385–386
normative, 391
not to be separated from
water-baptism, 222, 270, 538
not to be used for non-
sacramental experience, 102
not a panacea, 139, 144–145
not same as baptism with water,
303
not a sectarian term, 348
re-baptism. See Re-baptism
other expressions of, 383
outpouring of gifts and power,
161
part of his sanctifying work, 381
and personal transformation, 142
plurality of views, 548
power for witnessing, 385
preparation for, 335
and regeneration, 215
results of, 143
at Samaria, an abnormal event,
389
same as becoming a Christian,
380
and sanctification, 455
as second blessing, 346, 351, 353,
357
a sectarian over-interpretation,
229
separation from water-baptism
and conversion, 513
Should every Christian have?,
575
six biblical examples of, 386–389
source of,
disputes, 492
spiritual renewal, 325–326
unity, 310
and speaking in tongues,
391–392

and prophecy, 315
Spirit-centered, 357
and spiritual manifestations,
304–305, 453
subsequent to faith, 300–301
suggestibility, 87
symbols of, 304
synonyms for, 512–513
and teachings of Charles Finney,
199
three views of, 463
at Topeka, Kansas, 201
and two classes of Christians,
353
use of phrase questioned, 545
various outpourings of, 315
and witness, 450
and water-baptism, 76, 163, 289,
310, 314, 317, 371–372, 388,
470, 520, 537, 548, 552, 554
Baptize, meaning in New
Testament, 270
Barnett, P., and Jensen, P. F.,
390–391
Barratt, Thomas, 201, 457–458
Barth, Karl, 231
Behavior, socially unacceptable
nature of tongues, 209
Behavioral sciences,
and experience, 571–572
limits of, 222
and the renewal, 573
Belgum, David, 27–28
Believers, two categories of, 179,
199, 200
Bennett, Dennis, 1, 70, 324, 325, 459
and Bennett, Rita, 428
Berkhof, Hendrikus, 231
Berlin, Declaration of, 202
Bernhard, Leopold W., 28–31
Bible,
authority of, 353–354
and charisms, 330
and Christology, 353
comes alive, 507

direct word to us, 379
and discernment, 360
infallible rule of, 525
neo-Pentecostal interpretation
of, 379, 386–389
no consistent doctrine of the
Spirit, 312
and non-canonical passages,
78–79
non neo-Pentecostal use, 380
as norm of Jesus' life, 159
as normative, 156, 291
only rule of faith, 363
and overloading proof texts, 181
reading of, as a means of grace,
91
speaks from within its too trivial
setting, 380
study of, 70, 358–359, 473–474
and tradition, 47
unclear areas, 382
as validating three types of
tongues, 89–90
where silent one cannot prohibit
certain practices, 221
Biblical,
criticism, necessary to
acknowledge in the renewal,
93–94
holiness,
emphasis, 465–466
identified with baptism in the
Holy Spirit, 468
scholarship, acceptance of, 90–91
Bishop(s),
pastoral responsibility to the
renewal, 210
safeguarding peace and unity, 97
Bittlinger, Arnold, 104
Black, William, 455
Bloy, Francis, 1, 70
Boddy, Alexander, 458
Boisen, Anton, 240, 275
Book of Confessions, silence on
certain practices, 224

Brand, Eugene, 547
Bresee, Phineas, 220
Bronsveld, Peter, 203
Bruner, F. D., 449, 456, 482, 525
Brunner, Emil, 231–232
Burrill, Gerald, 10, 75

Calvin, John, 272, 312, 527, 530
    and infant baptism, 313–314
Care of souls, defined, 105
Caruthers, Merlin, 475
Catholic and Apostolic Church, of
    Edward Irving, 5
Celibacy, a gift, defined, 106
Certitude,
    as reason for attractiveness of
        Pentecostalism, 154
    and re-baptism, 192
Chadwick, Samuel, 468–469, 483
Change as a result of
    involvement, 504
Charism(s) of the Holy Spirit,
    216–217, 261, 337–340
    absence of, 457
    abuse of, 342–343
    all available to one baptized in
        the Holy Spirit, 184
    ambiguity of, 316
    ceased because of lack of faith,
        531
    and a Christological focus, 67,
        171
    and the church, 216, 298, 370
    for the common good, 18, 138,
        173, 342
    contemporary or not?, 394
    continuation of the gospel, 175
    at conversion or at
        Spirit-baptism, 394
    counterfeited, 138
    defended by Christian and
        Missionary Alliance, 65
    definition of, 170–171, 263–264,
        280, 562
    difficult to identify
        unequivocally, 138

as directed to mission, 337
as divisive, 291, 536
and edification, 307
and enduements of power, 469
even necessary, 443
exercise of in the church, 19
existence of, 454–456
extraordinary, 315
    not to be rashly sought, 581
    stress on, 541, 545
    uncritically accepted, 583–584
of faith, hope, and love, 18
given,
    to all, 518
    in first century not necessarily
        those given today, 539
    according to needs, 339–340
    and released by the Spirit, 570
and glory after death, 432
and graces, 311
greater and lesser, 307
and growth, 162
hierarchy of, 190
highest are those directed to
    community, 191
intelligible preferred to
    unintelligible, 535
judged by fruits, 366
lists of, 170–171, 217, 226, 262,
    290, 393
    compared, 263, 532
    not exhaustive, 532
    and St. Paul, 18, 341, 532
may or may not accompany
    Spirit-baptism, 471–472, 513
means mistaken for ends, 173
messages of, 397
misuse of, 242
more exciting hinder less
    exciting, 539
more than natural abilities, 540
and the Mystical Body, 396, 438
nature and purpose, 340
new ones can be expected, 107
in New Testament, 339, 532

no command to seek a particular
gift, 216–217
no one required of every
believer, 519
no single one sign of Spirit's
presence, 172–173
not all,
Christians possess, 349
included in promise of the
Spirit, 349
not to be,
over-spiritualized, 494
sought, 540
used incessantly, 484
not norm for all, 402, 443
not possessions, 514
of believers, 315–316, 540
not recognized out of ignorance
or unbelief, 469–470
not related to filled with the
Spirit, 336–337
not a sign of,
favoritism, 577
Spirit-baptism, 395
number and order, 3
and office, 177
one new birth, 286
order of priority, 532
ordinary,
devaluated, 571
and extraordinary, 174–175,
532, 562, 569–570
overemphasized, 139, 358
as paranormal, 542
and St. Paul, 19–20, 170
plurality of, 330
private use of, 535
proper use of, 488
purpose of, 173–174, 396, 450,
453–454, 531
restricted to apostolic age, 346
result of Spirit's continual action,
305
a return to immaturity, 176

same as those of New Testament
or not?, 394
as service, 285
silence in post-biblical sources,
230
and social and behavioral
sciences, 237
social and political necessity of,
539
for special work, 314
spectacular not to be forced, 191
as the Spirit coming to visibility,
107
and spiritual blockage, 455
terminology of, 393
for today, 345
and triumphalism, 340
under control, 397
valid distinction between gift
and gifts, 392
variety of, 171–173, 534
when to be exercised, 486
for the whole church, 443
worth of, 396
Charismatic,
defined, 453, 515, 550, 552
leaders, and the Spirit, 293–294,
315
renewal. See Renewal,
charismatic
Charity,
and the charisms, 18–19
as sign of the Spirit, 447
Christenson, Larry, 459, 553,
555–556
Christian(s)
invitation, and baptism in the
Holy Spirit, 553
name without a gift, 552
as a sinner justified by faith, 128
two classes of, 353
Christology,
centrality of, 162
concerns of, 349
and discernment, 18, 313, 360
lack of a full, 100

Christology (cont.)
  as a norm of,
    experience, 496
    renewal, 490
    verification, 110
  obscuring works of Jesus, 357
  and the reading of Scripture, 353
  renewal is Jesus oriented,
    570–571
  and the Spirit, 137
  subordinationism, 350
  and tongues, 83
  two-nature doctrine
Church (*see also* Community,
  Parish),
  baptism in the Holy Spirit,
    legitimate place in, 574–575
  as a body, 172
  Can structure and charism be
    blended?, 565
  cannot exist without ordinary
    gifts, 532
  a charismatic community, 370,
    491, 518
  charismatic experience not
    recognized in, 498
  charisms exercised in, 18
  classical Pentecostalism directed
    to revival in all churches,
    205
  confronted by Jesus, 62–63
  as constituted and judged by the
    Spirit, 523
  continuous tradition of
    experience, 499–500
  defined, 57
  departure from, 511
  development from spontaneous
    to institutional gifts, 179
  and discernment, 13, 183
  early, and healing in, 119,
    123–124
  edification of, 360
  and elitism, 372
  exists for communication of
    grace, 6

  and the extraordinary as a norm
    of vitality, 168
  failures of, 157
  and the gifts, 531–532, 540
    and service to the world, 544
  healing as a gift continuously
    present in, 185
  inadequacy of as reason why the
    renewal was accepted, 528
  legitimate place for renewal, 545
  love of as effect of baptism in the
    Holy Spirit, 507
  may neglect part of revelation,
    11
  membership not automatic, 165
  movements,
    should remain in full history
      of, 21
    stress one aspect of, 20
  moves by reason, law, and
    authority, 13
  mutuality of the gifts, 172, 178
  as the new Israel, 337
  and newness of the gifts, 108
  no intention of founding a new,
    200
  not the context for experience,
    153
  not identified with any existing
    organization, 320
  openness to new movements,
    97, 157
  operation of the Spirit outside,
    541
  and ordinary gifts, 562
  over-officing of, 180–181
  and the paranormal, 538
  and pastoral responsibility, 11
  after Pentecost, 338–339
  Pentecostalism as an indictment
    of, 156
  and pluralism, 373
  and prayer for gift of prophecy,
    183–184
  reexamination of her life, 157
  relation of prayer groups to, 212

and the renewal, 62, 528
  found more in disciplined
    structures, 485–486
  in mutuality, 561
  remains within, 568–569, 572
  rightful place for those in, 508
  room for new movements in, 99
 and self-examination, 168
 and the Spirit, 98, 177, 231, 298,
   308, 371, 581
 a supernatural fellowship, 229
 swings from enthusiasm to
  secularism, 233
 and tongues, 81
 undervalued, 177
 uniformity is demonic, 203–204
 unity of, 353, 358, 372
 within a church, 523
  and prayer groups, 543
  and separation of water and
   Spirit-baptism, 538
 where integration takes place,
  485
Clark, Stephen, 475
Clarke, Charles, 454
 and Clarke, Mary, 460
Clergy,
 not distinct from laity, 179
 not to participate in worship
  where tongues are spoken,
  101
 not to promote charismatic
  movement, 102
 reacting with suspicion to
  Pentecostal movement, 95
Coleridge, Samuel, 489
Common sense, as a norm, 489
Communication, and tongues, 576
Communion of saints, against
  individualistic pietism,
  167–168
Community,
 action of the Spirit in, 159–160,
  178
 care for the total person, 46

and the gifts, 107, 170, 174, 562
 extraordinary as normal,
  569–570
 judged by usefulness for,
  583–584
and healing, 46, 47, 53
and maturity, 175–177
order and common good, 15
place where the kingdom is
  manifested, 40–41
plurality in, 171–172
primary locus of the Spirit, 46
receiving the Spirit, 83
as tool of evangelism, 142
work of the Spirit in, 159
Compassion, and healing, 119–120,
  124
Confessional meetings, as norms,
  369, 373
Confessions, as normative, 291
Confirmation,
 and baptism in the Holy Spirit,
  91, 93, 470
 and living faith, 93
 no speaking in tongues by
  clergy, 102
Confusion, and loss of control, 110
Congar, Yves, 6–7
Consciousness,
 and control, 110
 and tongues, 329
Consequence, doctrine of, 154,
  330, 346, 349–350, 369
Constitution on the Church,
  581–582
Contemplation, as second strand,
  483–484
Control, and tongues, 110, 329
Conversation, spiritual, 479
Conversion,
 action of the Spirit, 309, 311
 baptism in the Holy Spirit, 199,
  211, 351, 390, 466, 515
 and Ephesians, 390
 and further outpourings, 456
 and growth, 166

Conversion (cont.)
and infant baptism, 195, 198
as a Methodist emphasis, 464
nature of, 359
necessity of experience, 469
occurs solely through the gospel, 331
and reception of the Spirit, 301–302
and sanctification, 385
Corinth, charisms at, 340
Corinthians,
neo-Pentecostal way of interpreting, 533
reformed way of interpreting, 533
Cornelius, and the Pentecost of the Gentiles, 17, 214, 301, 388, 390, 471, 515, 555
Covenant, and infant baptism, 193–194, 198
Cox, Harvey, 376–377
Creation,
and healing, 121
and the Spirit, 296
Creed, Athanasian, 371
Crisis experience, and the Spirit, 301, 330
Cultural environment, and the gifts, 538–539
Cutten, George, 239–240, 274

Davies, William R., 452
Davison, Leslie, 452–454, 455, 460, 467, 485
Deaconship, defined, 105
Death, believers still subject to, 187
Decision, and baptism, 197
Deliverance,
abuses of, 487
and/or exorcism, 455
Demonic,
and the Berlin Declaration, 202
and infant baptism, 194
and Jesus, 243–244
and loss of control, 108

oppression, 578
possession, 578
excuse for personal responsibility, 244–245
and sickness, 189
in this age, 486–487
and tongues, 4, 8, 18–19, 181, 539
Dependency, and fulness of the Spirit, 110, 271–272
Discernment, 8–9, 183, 214, 286–287, 313, 512, 564, 578, 582–584
and bishops, 580
Christology and Scripture, 359–360
within commonality of faith, 373
and community, 176
at Corinth, 533
defined, 106, 342
and fruits of the Spirit, 169
of a genuine renewal, 319–320
and objective norms, 18
and Pope Paul VI, 368
tongues, and the demonic, 8
willingness to submit to the church, 13
Disciples, empowered for ministry, 386–387
Discipline,
of the church, 206
in exercise of the gifts, 497
and fruit of the Spirit, 446
and holiness, 474
Disillusionment, and the spectacular, 156
Dispensationalism, 1, 272, 321, 345–347, 357, 358
of John Calvin rejected, 530
modified, 519
of Reformed tradition criticized, 530
rejected, 230, 531
Division,
causes of, 444, 448
and the demonic, 487–488

Divisiveness,
in the church, 322, 517–518
and the gifts, 514
not always fault of the renewal,
557
and prayer meetings, 560
and the renewal, 544, 547
Doctrine,
displaces God's person, 370
does not exhaust faith
relationship, 369
and ecumenism, 353
and experience, 369
full agreement as basis of
fellowship, 322
Lutheran, not contradicted by
charismatic insight, 332
and narrative, 390
as norm, 318, 320
not to be opposed to experience,
373
purification of, 318
Double allegiance, of
neo-Pentecostals, 529
Drugs, overdependence on, 408
Dunamis, 460–461, 491
Dunn, J.D.G., 384, 388, 467
du Plessis, David, 458–459

Economic deprivation, as theory to
explain growth of
Pentecostalism, 502
Ecstasy,
and the charisms, 108, 341
defined, 227
not to disrupt structure, 232
not sign of the Spirit, 181
and prophecy, 295, 557–558
safeguard against, 204
states of, and the demonic, 539
and tongues, 16, 181, 274, 305,
400
Ecstatic, caution in use of the term,
533
Ecumenism (*see also* Unionism),

and basis of fellowship, 322
breaking barriers, 223
as defined by Assemblies of
God, 320
and man-made mergers, 318–319
and prayer meetings, 560
renewal as ally of, 551
and shared experience, 570
and the Spirit, 353
and two kinds of Christians, 358
unequalled in history, 487
Edification,
norm for,
authentication, 15
the gifts, 360
and St. Paul's preferred gifts,
533–534
and worship, 95
Eliot, T. S., 509
Elitism (*see also* Superiority),
in ecclesiology, 372
and experience, 138
and the gifts, 286, 342
Emotionalism,
and baptism in the Holy Spirit,
330
as a danger, 13, 15
and the ecstatic, 533
and the gifts, 214
of prayer groups, 208
and the renewal, 235
as unhealthy, 91
Emotions
and assurance, 465
and the gifts, 341
and tongues, 17, 555
at worship, 579
Empowerment, 384 (*see also*
Power),
and baptism in the Holy Spirit,
526
Enthusiasm, 352, 357
and discernment, 478
and healing, 30
in Methodist prayer meetings,
476

Enthusiasts,
  Martin Luther's objection to,
    548, 564
  and the Spirit, 231
Eschatology,
  and healing, 122, 130
  and victory over evil, 130
Eternal life, as a gift, defined, 106
Eucharist, and church formation,
  205
Evangelization,
  of church members, 563
  and experience, 570
Evans, E., 457
Evil,
  primal in the unconscious, 10
  spirits, and tongues, 457
Exaltation, and the ecstatic, 533
Excommunication,
  grounds for, 218
  and re-baptism, 192
Exorcism, 188, 243–245
  doubts about, 101
  grave dangers of, 244
  only with authorization of
    bishop, 102
Expectancy,
  and faith, 46
  false, 48
  and the gifts, 540, 545
  and healing, 42, 559
  and the Spirit, 165
  what renewal has to offer, 560
Experience,
  authenticity of, 539
    not doubted but interpretation
      questioned, 545
  of baptism in the Holy Spirit
    differs, 471
  cannot be denied, 552
  Christian, two elements of,
    384–385
  confirmatory, 162
  compensation for loss of dignity,
    502
  contribution of Lutheran Church

  in America to the renewal,
    566
  crisis, 525
  danger of out-of-hand
    condemnation, 92
  defined, 573, 574
  of a different kind, 549
  and doctrine, 369
  and elitism, 138
  essential to,
    understanding, 390
    whole church, 501
  exaggerated, 145
  fact is clear, nature unclear, 136
  and faith, 321
  fear of, 209, 236, 273
  guidelines for, 246–247
  how to relate to others, 508–509
  immune to proof, 137
  in itself and its verbalization, 551
  as leading to fuller insight,
    314–315
  necessity of,
    passing beyond, 146
    peak, 162
  no *a priori* validity, 135
  as the norm, 139, 143, 181
  normed by love, 490
  not to be opposed to true
    doctrine, 373
  not to be rejected, 502
  not continuous, 285
  not a cure-all, 572
  not doubted, 523, 547
  not individualistic, 570
  not a safe guide, 358
  in Old and New Testaments,
    143–144, 499
  pluriformity of, 135
  as proof that one has fulness of
    Christ, 162–163
  as psychologically beneficial, 502
  and re-baptism, 192–193
  results of, 142
  and retreat from social
    involvement, 561

General Index

and scriptural holiness, 466
as second blessing and
assurance, 569
significant differences, 390
of the Spirit, contemporary,
289–291
substituted for doctrine, 210
suspicions of, 461
theological, assertions not
descriptions of, 548
today as in New Testament
times, 492
and traditional forms, 377
two elements in a Christian, 375
and understanding the Bible, 379
understood within church's life,
562
unhealthy subjectivism, 70
validation of, 288
by Scripture, 359
value of, 374–375
Externalism, of Episcopalian
Church, 91
Extraordinary,
as antidote to ills of the church,
168
and charisms, 541, 545, 581,
583–584
defined, 542
way of the Spirit, 165

Faith,
bond with baptism, 197
common to all theologies of
baptism in the Holy Spirit,
471
context for validity of
experience, 288
defined, 106, 263, 341
a direct relationship, 370
and the failure of healing, 559
and filled with the Holy Spirit,
301, 337, 512
formalized in Episcopalian
churches, 85

God's initiative in infant
baptism, 196
as a good work, 527, 559
and healing, 26, 40, 42, 43,
114–116, 122, 405, 410, 413,
429, 430–432
and infant baptism, 194–195
intellectual, moral, and mystical
content, 372
makes gifts and fruits available,
533
must be permitted to remain
faith, 129
no understanding of Spirit apart
from, 312–313
and reception of the Spirit, 336,
527–528
salvation through, 310, 332
separated from reception of the
Spirit, 300
should not become superstition,
372
Spirit received by, 351–352
and superstition, 369
Faith healer, defined, 24, 48–49,
527
Feelings, confused with God's
presence, 91
Fellowship,
basis of, 403, 439–440
Methodist, 461
as sign of the kingdom, 121–122
in small groups, 46
and tongues, 218
Ferrer, St. Vincent, and tongues, 4
Filled with the Holy Spirit,
and charisms, 336
defined biblically, 515–516
not identified with baptism in
the Holy Spirit, 216
occurs repeatedly, 216
term preferred to baptism in the
Holy Spirit, 513
various meanings, 336
Finney, Charles Grandison, 199,
201, 456

Fletcher, John, 384, 454–455, 468
Forgiveness,
    and the Lord's Supper, 46
    of sin, 304
Formation, theological and biblical,
    582
Frank, Jerome, 278
Freedom,
    in charismatic fellowship, 476
    of the Spirit, in prayer, 473
    and tongues, 90
Frost, Evelyn, 421
Fruits of the Holy Spirit, 358, 535
    as authentication of the gifts, 8,
        581
    and baptism in the Holy Spirit,
        553
    different from the gifts and
        offices, 579
    do not necessarily accompany
        the gifts, 58
    how to discern, 169
    list of, 339, 536
    love is primary, 111
    not always present, 145
    not directly contrasted with the
        gifts, 536–537
    not manifested to some degree,
        536
    power in preaching, 483
    preferred to the gifts, 108–109
    take precedence over the gifts,
        202
Fruits of the presence of God,
    367–368
Full Gospel Businessmen's
    Fellowship, 204, 206, 550
    and healing, 112–113
Fundamentalism,
    biblical, 70
    in classical Pentecostalism, 501
    doctrinal, 318
    among Episcopalians, 84
    among laity, 78, 90–91
    not necessary to the renewal, 78

Gee, Donald, 112, 458
Gerlach, Luther, and Hine,
    Virginia, studies of, 234,
        273–276, 278–279, 325–327
Gerrard, Nathan, 240–241, 277–278
Gifts,
    of grace, in New Testament,
        defined, 105–106
    of the Holy Spirit. See Charism(s)
        of the Holy Spirit
Glossolalia. See Tongues
God,
    bipartite, 371
    inadequacy of our concepts of,
        371
    not to be manipulated, 356
    reality of, 370
    tripartite, 371
    unity of, 371
Goodwin, Thomas, 384
Gospels,
    centrality of, 357
    healing as preparation for, 355
    Synoptics, doctrine of the Spirit
        in, 255–256
Grace,
    and baptism in the Holy Spirit,
        352
    cheap, 198
    prevenient, denied by doctrine
        of subsequence, 537–538
    and the Spirit, 363
    sufficiency of, 357
Groningen, General Synod of
    (1963), 206–207
Growth,
    and community, 373
    in the Spirit, 306
Guidelines, and religious
    experience, 246–247

Harper, Michael, 459, 463, 467–468,
    491, 501
Healer, faith,
    condemned, 27

defined, 24, 48–49, 527
Healing,
abuses of, 49, 112, 185, 272
and criticism, 22
recognized, 23
an accompaniment, 120
and Acts of the Apostles,
426–427
and anointing, 37, 52, 414
and atonement, 214, 431
as an attempt to live by law and
not the gospel, 45
authority for, 430, 433
call for a reevaluation of, 370
causes of decline, 112
characteristics of Christ's,
425–426
and chemical dependency,
434–435
and Christian,
attitude toward, 32, 408
physician, 26
and the church,
failure to focus power of the
gospel on the world,
47–48
ministry of, 127
should provide more
opportunities for, 48
command of Christ, 405
and community, 46–47, 53, 113
the total person, 46, 48
and compassion, 120
as concern for the whole human
need, 37
as a controversial issue, 29
as a cross-disciplinary process,
44
and dangers of enthusiasm and
magic, 30
and death, 186–187
decline of power of, 421
defined, 36, 106, 115, 341–342,
403

and definition of a person, 39
and deliverance, 487
as demonstration of personal
power, 49
as destructive, 45
as a devaluation of the gospel,
190
and dialogue between faith and
science, 29
different approaches to, 408
disappearance of in early church,
37
and discernment, 32
and the "divine man," 22
Does it happen today?, 577
and doubt, 419
dynamics of, 410
in early church, not performed
as command of Christ, 42
effected by God alone, 121
and efficacy of prayer, 429
and enabling groups, 53
enters main-line Protestant
churches, 21–22
and the epistles, 427–430
and eschatology, 41, 122, 130
and evangelism, 412
everyone is not healed, 578
excluded from church's ministry,
38
and expectancy, 42, 53
false, 48
integral to faith in Christ, 31,
38
and experience, 421
and faith, 26, 40, 42, 43, 114–116,
405, 410, 413, 429–432
of the unhealed, 129
failure of, 416
to distinguish ultimates from
penultimates, 50
to give it sufficient attention,
50
false claims of, 130
and forgiveness, 425

Healing (cont.)
and formal liturgical worship, 53
fulfillment of promise, 406
and general ministry, 113
a gift of the Spirit, 36–37, 405,
414, 427
given for salvation of ministry,
431
glorification of God, 409
God as sovereign and free, 129
and the gospels, 425
not to be perverted to other
ends, 4
priorities of, 32
happens by itself, 404
how to pray for, 419
if it becomes central, then all is
lost, 48
important but not central, 45
as instrument of opening historic
churches, 147
and Jesus,
in his name, 413–414
and his ministry, 118–119,
122–123, 354, 406, 409–414
not commanded by, 41, 113,
123, 355
as physician, 26
purpose of, 406, 422
his redemptive work, 409
sign of his victory, 32
testimony to his divinity, 424
and intercessory prayer, 52–53
and kingdom of God, 122
and lack of faith, 49
and laws of nature, 404
and laying on of hands, 52, 242,
405
and Lazarus, 424
and the leader, 559
linked to authority of message,
427
a living reality, 413–414
and the local church, 28, 486
and the Lord's Supper, 37
and magic, 30, 37, 45, 129

and mass meetings, 49, 202
and medicine, 27–28, 123, 404
ministry of, 242–243, 405
in Acts of the Apostles, 413–414
and the American Lutheran
Church, 24, 51–55
and the disciples, 412–414
to the whole community, 125
as miraculous event, 331,
354–356, 405, 433, 558
and the misuse of the gospel, 45
and mortality, 431–432
must not displace centrality of
the gospel, 124
Must someone pray for you?,
577
and mystery, 32
necessity of faith, 422
need not be everywhere present,
184
a neglected penultimate, 48
neo-Pentecostal view of, 408–423
a new confidence, 570
in New Testament times, 407
no explicit command for today,
23
non neo-Pentecostal view of,
423–436
normative points, 407
not an end in itself, 122
not limited, 418
not manipulating God, 356
not signs for unbelievers, 43–44
not substitute for medicine, 242
not of ultimate significance, 127
in Old Testament, 116, 423
opposition of classical
Pentecostal denominations,
112
outside,
face-to-face Christian
fellowship, 24
on-going life of congregation,
127
the renewal, 559
pastoral context of, 559

and St. Paul's thorn, 415–416, 426
as a penultimate, 23, 45
and a person's responsibility for health, 26
physician as co-worker with pastor, 25, 54
possibility not in question, 190
prayer of faith, 405–406, 414, 428–430
and preaching the gospel, 113
preferred to medicine, 176
and the present, 423, 432
presumptuous suggestion that God wills, 53
progressive nature of, 420–421, 435–436
and the prophets, 117
and psychological disorder, 434
and psychosomatic,
    dimensions, 558
    illnesses, 435
reasons for caution, 433
and the recognition of divine and demonic conflict, 38
and the renewal of faith, 29–30
and salvation, 42, 423–424
and science, 37–38, 44, 405–406
secondary concern of the early church, 37
services of, part of on-going life of congregation, 128
should be within fellowship with right priorities, 50
as a sign of the kingdom, 41, 189, 413–414, 431
and sin, 39
and special people, 577
as spiritual,
    blessing, 420
    gift, 430
study by pastor and people, 28
substantiation of, 406
and suffering, 407
supernatural gift, 427

and symptoms, 406, 432–433
as team effort, 27
theology of, 119
and total person, 50
three scriptural objections, 415
as a true experience, 126
and unbelief today, 421–422
and unhealthy publicity, 128
unwarranted today, 431
use and misuse, 46
usually unsuccessful, 433
verification of, 130
and the victory of faith, 43
viewed differently, 375
what is available in Christian church, 27
and the whole person, 27
and wholeness, 36, 39
Why any cures?, 434–435
Why so few cures?, 435–436
and will of God, 417, 429–430
work of God, 410–411
Health,
    defined, 115
    and sin, 43
Heresy, in embryo, 100
Hermeneutics, didactic over historical, 230
Hine, Virginia, and Gerlach, Luther, studies of, 234, 273–276, 278–279, 325–327
Historicism, and the gifts, 179
Hocken, Peter, 491
Hoekendijk, Karel, 148, 204–205
Holiness movement, 199, 219, 456, 525
Hollenweger, Walter, 452, 457
Horner, John, 490, 492
Hypnosis,
    and authority figures, 328
    and healing, 49
    and tongues, 556
Hysteria,
    and prayer meetings, 367
    safeguard against, 204
    and tongues, 71, 86, 234, 276, 329

Knox, Ronald, and tongues, 4
Kuhlmann, Kathryn, 428
Kuyper, Abraham, 147

Labadie, Jean de, 199
Laity,
  gifts remain unused, 180
  with neo-Pentecostal experience,
    268–269
Lancaster, Conference of, 285
Lane, R. H., 511
Language, need for a relevant,
  137–138
Lapsley, J. N., and Simpson, J. M.,
  239, 278
Larger Catechism, 310, 311, 552
Law and the gospel, penultimates
  and ultimates, 45
Laying on of hands, 290
  and healing, 52
  only in accordance with accepted
    usage, 102
  and tongues, 100
Leaders, charismatic, ends with
  Daniel, 294
Leadership, defined, 105
Lester, Andrew D., 239
Lewis, C. S., 436
Lindsay, Gordon, 112
Liturgical movement, renewal as
  ally of, 551
Liturgy,
  charismatic elements in Catholic,
    486
  and free prayer, 485
  separated from charismatic
    events, 486
  and spontaneity, 560
Lord's Supper,
  and forgiveness, 46
  and healing, 37
  new meaning of, 560
Love,
  as effect of baptism in the Holy
    Spirit, 505

as matrix,
  of gifts, 173, 190–191, 218–219,
    343, 494, 497–498
  of tongues, 557
  and maturity, 519
  nature of, 343
  never passes away, 343
  as norm, 489–490
  preeminence of, 373
  understood even by animals,
    110
Lucan ethos, of classical
  Pentecostalism, 525
Lumen Gentium. See Constitution
  on the Church
Luther, Martin, 130, 352, 489, 554,
  564
  and receiving the Spirit, 335
Lutheran Confessions, normative
  value of, 373
Lutherans,
  and the renewal,
    do not accept all
      neo-Pentecostal doctrines,
      323
    guidelines for (LCA), 562–565
  take over classical Pentecostal
    theology uncritically, 22–23,
    552

McCay, S.J.P., 510
McDonnell, Kilian, 235–237,
  239–241, 272–273, 276, 278,
  553, 557
McKinney, Joseph, 365
Magic,
  and healing, 30, 37, 45, 129
  and prophecy, 558
  and use of oil, 52
Maguire, Frank, 459
Manicheanism, 372
Mark 16:17-18, not authentic,
  81–82, 346
Marriage, defined as a gift, 106
Martyrdom, defined as a gift, 106
Massbach, John, 185, 205

Maturity,
  and balance, 320
  and community, 175–177
  of faith, 158
  and the gifts, 307, 519
  in the renewal, 548
  and tongues, 8–9, 56, 58, 328
Maurice, F. D., 492
Medicine,
  and compassion, 125
  distrust of, 189
  and healing, 123
  and providential care, 242–243
  and wholeness of the person,
    241
Meetings,
  house,
    and charismatic renewal,
      differences, 473
    in Methodism, 472
    leaderless, 473
    Spirit-led, 473
Mental health,
  and the renewal, 234
  and the Spirit, 238–239
Mental illness, and tongues,
    274–275
Messianic king, and the Spirit, 294,
    297
Methodism,
  and Body Ministry, 472
  doctrinal emphases of, 464–466
  as forerunner of classical
    Pentecostalism, 199, 524
  and house meetings, 472
  influence of, 200
Meyer, Emil, 201
Ministers (see also Pastors,
    Priests),
  learning about the renewal,
    482–483, 544
  with neo-Pentecostal
    experiences, 247
  void of, 247–248
  not to pressure parishioners into
    the renewal, 564

Ministry,
  the gospel as central to, 124
  and healing today, 123
  not to be limited to those who
    speak in tongues, 58
  role of, 482
  within-a-ministry to be avoided,
    523
Minnesota Multi-Phasic
    Personality
    Inventory, and snake
    handling, 277–278
Miracles,
  defined, 341
  Jesus' promise of, 155
  and a living faith, 190
  not inherently absurd, 126
  overreaction of Reformers to,
    530
  possibility of, 188
  prevalence of, 155
  as a sign, 346
  and the supernatural, 541–542
  and tongues, 533
Mission to the world, and the gifts,
    535
Missionary situation, and infant
    baptism, 197
Montgomery, G. H., 112
Moody, Dwight Lyman, 199
Morals, as norm, 318, 320
Morgan, Jim, 384
Movements,
  divisiveness and abuses, 99
  enrich the church, 20
  openness to in the church, 99
Mühlheim Theses (1963), intent of,
    104
Music, and experience, 481–482
Mystery religions, and tongues, 88

Natural abilities, and the gifts,
    176–177, 496–497, 540–542
Navigators, and educational
    discipline, 506
Nelson, John, 455

General Index

Neo-Pentecostalism,
  beginnings of, 377
  defined, 226, 499–501, 550
  differs from classical
    Pentecostalism, 528
  doctrinal position of, 528–529
  double allegiance, 529
  factors of growth, 326
  and non neo-Pentecostal, 378
Nes, William, 11
Neurotics,
  drawn to dramatic religious
    movements, 238–239
  and the renewal, 235, 239
New age, and the Spirit, 297
New birth,
  identified with baptism in the
    Holy Spirit, 286, 456, 518
  as a Methodist emphasis, 464
New creation, and the Spirit, 164
New Testament experience, not
    same as today, 135
Nonrational,
  in Christian life, 14
  and the Spirit, 232
Nouwen, Henri, 278

Oberlin School of Theology, 377,
    384
Objectivity, and the renewal,
    obstacles to a fair hearing,
    272–273
Occultism, sign of spiritual
    vacuum, 245
O'Connor, Edward, 235
Office(s),
  as all-embracing reality, 177
  without baptism in the Holy
    Spirit, 177
  and charisms, 171, 178, 180, 545
  gift and fluidity of relationship,
    178
  opposed to institutional concept,
    177
Oil, as a sacrament, 52
Order, in worship, 15

Ordinances, and the Spirit, 308
Ordinary,
  becomes special, 176
  defined, 542
Ordination, and baptism in the
    Holy Spirit, 470
Osborn, T. L., 147, 150, 185, 203
Ozman, Agnes, 457

Packer, J. I., 383
Pagans,
  acquainted with tongues,
    prophecy, and healing, 538
  and the gifts, 541
Paranormal, interest in, 538
Parham, Charles, 457, 458
Parish,
  effects of Pentecostalism on, 506
  and prayer,
    groups, 485
    meetings, 560
Pastors (see also Ministers, Priests),
  Missouri Synod, and the
    renewal, 325
  and responsibility, 582
Pattison, Mansell, 240, 275,
    279–280
Paul, Jonathan, 200
Paul VI, Pope,
  address of,
    June 23, 1971, 364, 368
    June 6, 1973, 582
  and discernment, 368
Paul, St.,
  and charisms, 340–345
  and conversion, 390
  dangers mentioned have
    materialized, 99–100
  as one who spoke in tongues,
    343
  preferred prophecy to tongues,
    534
  and spiritual,
    gifts, 340–345
    speaking, 14–15
  and his thorn, 415–416, 426

Peart, Ross, 452–453
Pelagianism,
  and Christian life, 133
  and classical Pentecostalism,
    526–527
  and the gifts, 358
Pelikan, Jaroslav, 565
Pentecost,
  and abnormal manifestations,
    1–2, 8
  attempt to repeat, 179
  basis of the renewal, 209
  and the Cornelius event, 17, 214,
    301, 388, 390, 471, 515
  and enthusiastic movements, 4
  an era of the Spirit, 109
  exegesis of the event, 228–229
  fulfillment of Jesus' promise,
    299–300
  healing after, 355
  and the new age, 337
  normative, 525
  promise of the Spirit, 334–336
  receiving the Spirit, 214–215
  as a reversal of Babel, 19
  and tongues, 17, 136, 181, 555
  as unitive event, 82
  unrepeatable, 575
  and the works of God, 338
Pentecostal(s),
  rejected as a name, 209
  as well-adjusted members of
    society, 522
Pentecostalism, classical
  beginnings of, 377, 500, 524
    in United States in twentieth
      century, 5, 201, 524
  categories borrowed from, 100
  conversions to, 318
  a critical assessment, 526
  defined, 225–226, 550
  in dialogue with historic
    churches, 147
  distinguished from Catholic
    renewal, 208
  in Germany, 201–202

  growth of, 141
  history of, 199–206, 524
  in Holland, 203
  as inter-church movement, 528
  interdenominational character
    of, 318
  lack of theological and biblical
    scholarship, 552
  a major movement, 225–226
  moves up social ladder, 21
  not included in Catholic
    document, 209
  provides theological categories,
    90
  teachings of, 463–464
  tendency toward the individual
    and the personal, 540
  three "brands" of, defined, 140
  and tongues, 64
  uncritical borrowings from, 548
  as an unpaid bill, 156
  why its power of attraction?, 152
Penultimates and ultimates, as
    distinction between law and
    the gospel, 45
Perfectionism,
  in John Wesley, 199
  in Jonathan Paul, 200–201
Personal element as reason for
    attractiveness of
    Pentecostalism, 153
Personality,
  integration of, and the gifts, 540
  types of, and participation in the
    renewal, 145
  pathological influence on
    certain, 13
Pethrus, Lewi, 488
Physician,
  as co-worker with pastor, 54
  as part of healing ministry of the
    church, 54–55
Pietism, and conversion, 553
Pike, James, 20, 70
  pastoral letter of May 2, 1963,
    96–104

Plog, Stanley, 275
Plurality, in the church, 373
Pneumatika, as distinct from
 charismata, 19
Polhill, Cecil, 458
Polman, Gerrit, 203
Pope, H. J., 476
Possession, by the unconscious,
 87–88
Post-apostolic times, disinterest in
 tongues, 136
Power (*see also* Empowerment),
 and baptism in the Holy Spirit,
 314–315, 387–388, 512–514,
 526
 defined as a gift, 106
 as definition of Pentecostalism,
 506
 in early church but not today,
 504–505
 and the gifts, 469
 not the issue, 490
 and reception of the Spirit, 304,
 337, 544
 and the Spirit in the Old
 Testament, 294
 and tongues, 540
Praise, role of, 477–478
Prayer,
 always answered, 429
 as effect of baptism in the Holy
 Spirit, 507
 insistence on, 370
 intercessory, and healing, 241
 in a known tongue, 134
 not the issue, 490
 and repetitive incantation, 100
 shared, 477
 short, 477
 and tongues, 555, 575–576
 unity in, 478
Prayer group(s) (*see also*
 Community),
 Catholic,
 need priests' involvement,
 582–583

 and unstable people, 209–210
 in Lutheran parishes, 564–565
 open to all, 543
 and the parish church, 73–74
Prayer meeting(s),
 as most characteristic expression
 of renewal, 560
 not to be disorderly, 367
 regulated by the bishop, 94
Preaching,
 as a gift, 483
 of the gospel, and imparting of
 the Spirit, 352
 with signs accompanying, 175
Presbyteries, guidelines for the
 renewal, 250–251
Presence,
 and baptism in the Holy Spirit,
 513
 experience of, 289, 575
 and the Spirit, 2, 296
 and tongues, 17
Priesthood of all believers, 479
Prince, Derek, 113
Promise,
 and narratives, 391
 of the Spirit, meaning for today,
 348–349
Prophecy,
 and the clear will of God, 395
 conditions for use, 345
 defined, 105, 183, 226–227, 263,
 342
 equated with word of God, 363
 and excesses, 183
 as extraordinary gift, 532
 false, 183, 363
 gift of, 183–184
 God speaks directly, 363
 and immediate revelation, 395
 and interpretation, 395–396
 not emphasized in the renewal,
 558
 Old Testament world not
 realized, 541
 and prediction, 396

Prophecy (cont.)
    preferred to tongues, 18,
        270–271, 344, 534
    teaching and preaching, 396
    termed inward or outward, 540
    and tongues, 18, 61, 270–271,
        344, 396, 399–402, 533–534,
        557
    and unbelievers, 344–345
Prophet(s), approached as
    clairvoyant, 69
Psychological,
    evaluation, and religious
        experience, 288
    normality, and tongues, 71
    norms of, not criteria to judge
        experience, 237
    works of the Spirit reduced to,
        232
Psychology,
    abnormal manifestations on
        Pentecost, 8
    and experience, 461
    and incursion of irrational forces,
        13

Qualben, Paul A., 327–328

Ranaghan, Kevin, 236–237
Rank, Lord, 460
Readings in fellowship meetings,
    477
Re-baptism, 161
    as cause of dissension, 191
    discipline of the church, 206
    not permitted, 163
    not sufficient reason for
        disfellowship, 192
    reasons given for, 192
    and the Re-reformed Church,
        150–151
Receiving the Spirit, and
    community, 83
Re-creation, and the Spirit,
    169–170
Recruitment, 331–332

Reformed witness to baptism in
    the Holy Spirit, 514
Reformers,
    and the demonic, 539
    and dispensationalism, 529–530
Reid, John R., 377–378
Religion, dogmas and feelings, 374
Renewal, charismatic,
    abuses of, publicly
        denounced, 366
    church has much to gain, 448
    and common assumptions,
        329–332
    and contribution to Methodism,
        482–493
    and dangers, 583
    defined, 445, 490, 499–501
        no definition acceptable to all,
            491
    and divisiveness, 212, 213, 223,
        291, 448, 573
    and ecumenism, 318–319
    effects of, 68, 208–209, 210, 213,
        283–284, 569–571, 583
    emerged in historic churches
        when the healing revival
        faltered, 112
    evaluation of, 448
        from outside, 555
    experience of, 445–446
    growth of, 223, 279, 322–325
        among Lutherans, 551–552
        Pentecostal charismatic types
            will outnumber other
            Christians, 549–550
    guidelines for, 543–544
    history of, 324, 371, 550–551
    imported from United States,
        365
    irreconcilable differences, 439
    as a Jesus movement, 570–571
    lay character of, 548, 551
    in Lutheran churches, ministerial
        character of, 555
    marks of a genuine, 319
    ministerial attitudes to, 437–438

Samaria, and Philip's witness, 387
Samaritans, and reception of the
Spirit, 301
Samuel, Leith, 484
Sanctification,
entire, 351, 384, 466, 469
and conversion, 450
as on-going Christian life, 554
second work of grace, 220
two-level doctrine, 290–291, 321,
463–464, 515, 516, 524–525,
529, 550, 552
creates two kinds of
Christians, 520, 524
and divisiveness, 573
questioned, 501, 529
Sanctity, not to be sought by
dubious means, 14
Sankey, Ira D., 199
Sargent, William, 278–279
Satan, father of lies, 488
Scandal, and divisiveness, 373
Schizophrenia, and tongues, 71,
98, 234
Science, a validation of experience,
514
Second blessing,
not baptism in the Holy Spirit,
386
doctrine of, 154
Second experience, and
sanctification, 456
Second Helvetic Confession, 530
Sectarianism, to be displaced, 13
Secular vocation, and the gifts, 180
Self-righteousness,
and the church, 92
and new movements, 20
as problem among charismatics, 59
Separation,
of baptism and conversion from
reception of the Spirit,
302, 317
of baptism with water from
baptism in the Holy Spirit,
311

of conversion and baptism from
reception of the Spirit, 308
of faith, baptism, and reception
of the Spirit, 300–302
of justification from
sanctification, 554
of water and the Spirit, 554
Sessions, and the renewal,
guidelines for, 251–252
Seymour, W. J., 457
Sharing, defined, 105
Sherrill, John, 400–401
Shorter Catechism, 311, 554
Sick,
ministry to, 355
not all will be cured, 184, 186
Sickness (see also Healing),
as a continuing reality in
Christian life, 129
and the demonic, 188
and guilt, 31–32
no problem of freedom from,
128
not caused or willed by God, 39,
53, 186
as punishment for sin, 187
as redemptive suffering, 40
and sin, 39–40, 43
work of Satan, 410
Silence, necessary to hear word of
God, 367
Simpson, A. B., 63–66
Simpson, J. M., and Lapsley,
J. N., 239, 278
Simul justus et peccator, and
sanctification, 525
Sin,
and entire sanctification, 466
and healing, 39, 43
and sickness, 39–40, 187–189
as a sign of evil, 43
Smalcald Articles, 352
Snake handlers, 277–278
Social,
action, conditions for the
renewal, 561

concern, and lack of among
charismatics, 561–562
sciences, and the renewal, 573
Societies, and the renewal, 483–487
Sola scriptura,
allowed to Lutheran
charismatics, 23
and the gifts, 531
Song,
as a gift, defined, 106
as prayer, 481
Spectacular,
emphasis upon in Pentecostal
movement, 155
no interest in, 290
St. Paul warns against, 175
as reason for attractiveness of
Pentecostalism, 155
Spirit, as defined in Old
Testament, 291, 296
Spirit of God,
and Judges, 294
and prophecy, 295
sign of fulfillment of covenant
promise, 295
Spirit, Holy,
activity of, 307–308, 313
in Acts of the Apostles, 259–261,
299
assistance in need, 294
bestowal after baptism, 311
bond of unity, 298
builder of community, 160–161
cannot be controlled by
legislation, 534
and his charisms. *See* (Charism(s)
of the Holy Spirit
and the church, 231, 298, 308,
371
and creation, 296
and crisis experience, 301
degrees of reception of, 537
difference between fruits of and
offices of, 579
and discernment, 286–287
disposition for, 292, 302

doctrine of, not given sufficient
attention, 529
dwells in every believer, 512
evidence of presence is fruit
of, 576
exaggerated role of, 321–322
as experienced, 503–504
not validated by science, 316
fruits of. *See* Fruits of the Holy
Spirit
fullness of, 271–272, 306–307
both event and process, 571
and dependence, 108
defined biblically, 516
not to be confused with
tongues, 110
as God's action in his people,
312
and healing, 36–37
inductive method of
understanding, 312
indwelling of, 100, 313
infilling of, 289
and Israel's leaders, 293–294
and Jesus, 297, 350–351
acts independently from, 526
identification with, 312
lordship of, 137
ministry of, 337–338
promise of, 360
as Spirit of, 340
testifies to, 316
unites us to, 159
in St. John's writings, 256–259
leads mankind, 164, 166
manipulation of, 137
marks of the moving of, 319–320
means of grace, 161
nature of his work, 163–164
and new age, 297, 337
and new life, 290
in New Testament, 227, 253–255,
296–307, 315
unique place in, 296
no second encounter, 321
opposed to other spirits, 307

Technology, and faith, 158
Tellegan, Auke, 277
Theological evaluation, lacking in
   the renewal, 90
Theology,
   experience oriented, 461
   lack of in Lutheran renewal, 552
   necessity of depth, 492
   Reformed,
      criticized by neo-Pentecostals,
         529
      Edward Irving's attempt to
         interpret charismatic
         phenomena within, 531
      synthesized with the
         Pentecostal, 531
Therapy, and the gifts, 540
Third blessing, 220
Thompson, E. W., 456
Tillich, Paul, 232
Tolerance,
   call for, 501–502
   of gifts and weaknesses, 509
   in understanding experiences of
      others, 573
Tongues, 181–182, 264–265, 305,
      400–401, 453 (see also
      Spiritual speaking),
   in Acts of the Apostles, 19, 81,
      82, 215, 264, 266–268, 271,
      288, 400–401
   and anxiety, 402
   and authority, 328
   and baptism in the Holy Spirit,
      391–392, 446
   as belonging to spiritual infancy,
      8–9
   Catholic, Anglican, Orthodox
      point of view toward, 6
   as a classical Pentecostal
      movement, 64
   and commitment, 326–327
   conditions for use, 345
   contradictory nature of evidence,
      136
   and control, 78, 86, 328

   danger when viewed in
      isolation, 10
   defined, 106, 226, 342, 575
   and the demonic, 8, 18, 19, 539
   difficult to integrate into the life
      of a congregation, 57
   directed to God, 446
   as distinct from the Spirit, 16
   as distinguished from spiritual
      speaking, 11
   as divisive, 59, 69, 557
      and Christian and Missionary
         Alliance, 64
   and early Methodists, 455
   and ecstasy, 16, 181, 274, 305,
      400
   edificatory, 401
   emotional form of prophesying,
      399
   and enthusiasm, 7
   and emotions, 17, 555
   as an escape, 137
   evaluation of, 7–8
   as an extraordinary gift, 533
   and freedom, 90
   fruits of, claimed, 76, 97
   healthy or unhealthy, 87
   helpful and constructive, 398
   heresy or abuse, 132
   hermeneutical practice, 61
   in historic churches, 65, 73
   in history of the church, 4–5
   and hypnosis, 329, 556
   and hysteria, 71, 86, 234, 276,
      329
   induced, 102, 317
   as initial evidence, 5–6, 63–64,
      110, 181, 221, 269, 271, 357,
      463, 526, 539, 554
   rejected, 67, 68, 349
   and initiatory process, 84
   and instability, 555
   and intelligence, 274
   and interpretation, 81
   and the irrational, 70–71
   as irrelevant, 8

Tongues (cont.)
  and Jesus, 271, 403
  and languages,
    of the irrational, 88–89
    known, 400
    supernatural, 400
    true?, 5–6, 78, 144, 228, 329,
      397–398
  leading persons to, 16, 60
  as learned behavior, 556
  least of the gifts, 144
  a lesser gift, 110
  on level with healing, faith, etc.,
    398
  mark of charismatic movement,
    397
  and St. Mark's Gospel, 82, 268
  and mature discipleship, 403
  and means of prayer, 446
  and mental illness, 274–275
  and Methodist fellowship,
    476–477
  and miracles, 533, 542
  and missionary activity, 66
    tool of, 1, 2, 7
  and mystery religions, 88
  neither despised nor normative,
    230
  neither essential nor chief target,
    369, 373, 490
  no sign of special spirituality,
    402
  in normal assembly, 67
  and normality, in psychological
    terms, 1
  normative source of doctrine,
    392
  not for all, 138
  not basis of fellowship, 403
  not to be
    exaggerated, 555
    introduced, 62
    promoted, 109
    rejected, 94
    sought, 576

  not the definition of the renewal,
    500
  not divisive, 331, 398
  not a gateway, 55
  not gibberish, 55
  not a must for today, 347
  not necessarily,
    religious, 71
    wholesome, 71
  not necessary to be a Christian,
    576
  not a necessary sign, 375, 397
  not normative, 58, 70, 93, 95, 543
  not part of on-going life of a
    Christian, 83
  not per se Christian or religious,
    85, 401, 556
  not a psychological device, 399
  not self-authenticating, 19
  not a sign of the Spirit, 215, 403
  not un-Lutheran, 56
  not an unmitigated blessing, 111
  and 1 Corinthians, 19, 81, 83, 88,
    204, 264–265, 267, 270–271,
    340–345, 476, 533–534,
    555–557
  and overemphasis, 344, 447
  as part of normal Christian life, 6
  St. Paul's,
    low evaluation for public use,
      62, 229
    regulations for, 270
  and Pentecost, 3–4
    same then as today, 2
  personal or congregational gift,
    401
  as a phase, 5
  phonetic structure of, 77
  and possession, 4
  as praise, 80, 331
  as prayer without the mind, 77
  and presence of the Spirit, 2, 17,
    76
  private use of, 101, 181, 218, 272,
    398–399, 486

promotion of, 60
proper use of, 398
and prophecy, 61, 396, 399–402,
    533, 557
and psychological,
    aspects of, 85–86, 101
    explanation of, 401
    findings in speakers of,
        239–241
    normality, 71
    phenomenon, 98, 236
    predisposition to, 87
    pressure extended on persons,
        56
    release, 402
as psychologically good, 85–86
public use of, 8
    and private use of, 84
question of right use of, 556
rarely an emotional experience,
    443–444, 446
relationship between certain
    personality variables,
    327–329
relative importance of, 393
and revival, 68
and Romans 8:26, 83
same dynamic as in other
    groups, 86
and schizophrenia, 71, 86, 234
as sign, 79, 288, 317, 331
    and gift, 76
    of the Spirit, 289, 305
    of Spirit-baptism, 397
    for unbelievers, 362
    of universalism, 3
and "spirit possession," 78, 87
and spiritual,
    maturity, 1–2
    speaking, 10–11
studies inconclusive, 329
subordinate role of, 271
and suggestibility, 87
and the suprarational, 555

and surrender, 85, 90
and tensions in parishes, 58
three,
    approaches to, 1
    types of, 89
at Topeka, Kansas, 201
and unbelievers, 344
uniquely Christian, 16
as un-Lutheran, 59
users always in control, 446
valid for today, 131–132, 135
value of, 446
as vehicle of messages, 77
and the whole counsel of God,
    60
wholesome effects of, 279
Topeka, Kansas, and
    Pentecostalism, 5, 201
Torrey, R. A., 200
Total person, and the community,
    46, 48
Tradition,
    appealed to against the Lutheran
        renewal, 23
    in the church, 157
    as remembered history, 47
    room for growth, 488
    understanding of charismatic
        reality within Lutheran
        concepts, 554
Trance, and conversion, 278
Transformation of Christian lives,
    142
Transitory possession of the Spirit,
    294
Trinity,
    imbalance in doctrine of, 145
    isolation of the Spirit from,
        522–523, 526
    and tritheism, 371
Tritheism, 371
    of classical Pentecostalism, 526
    danger of, 572–573

Unionism (*see also* Ecumenism),